Mac OS X Snow Leopard
THE MISSING MANUAL

*The book that
should have been
in the box*®

Mac OS X Snow Leopard

David Pogue

POGUE PRESS™
O'REILLY®

Beijing · Cambridge · Farnham · Köln · Sebastopol · Taipei · Tokyo

Mac OS X Snow Leopard: The Missing Manual
by David Pogue

Published by O'Reilly Media, Inc.,
1005 Gravenstein Highway North, Sebastopol, CA 95472.

O'Reilly Media books may be purchased for educational, business, or sales promotional use. Online editions are also available for most titles: *safari@oreilly. com.* For more information, contact our corporate/institutional sales department: 800-998-9938 or *corporate@oreilly.com.*

October 2009:   First Edition.

ISBN-13: 978-0-596-15328-1

Table of Contents

Part Four: The Technologies of Mac OS X

The Missing Credits

About the Author

 **David Pogue** (author) is the weekly tech columnist for *The New York Times,* an Emmy-winning correspondent for *CBS News Sunday Morning,* a weekly CNBC contributor, and the creator of the Missing Manual series. He's the author or coauthor of 50 books, including 25 in this series, six in the "For Dummies" line (including *Macs, Magic, Opera,* and *Classical Music*), two novels, and *The World According to Twitter.* In his other life, David is a former Broadway show conductor, a piano player, and a magician. He lives in Connecticut with his wife and three awesome children.

Links to his columns and weekly videos await at *www.davidpogue.com.* He welcomes feedback about his books by email at *david@pogueman.com.*

About the Creative Team

Julie Van Keuren (copy editor) is a freelance editor, writer, and desktop publisher who runs her "little media empire" from her home in Billings, Montana. In her spare time she enjoys swimming, biking, running, and (hey, why not?) triathlons. She and her husband, M.H., have two sons, Dexter and Michael. Email: *little_media@yahoo.com.*

Phil Simpson (design and layout) works out of his office in Southbury, Connecticut, where he has had his graphic design business since 1982. He is experienced in many facets of graphic design, including corporate identity/branding, publication design, and corporate and medical communications. Email: *pmsimpson@earthlink.net.*

Brian Jepson (technical consultant) is a Senior Editor for O'Reilly Media. He co-wrote *Mac OS X for Unix Geeks,* and has written or edited a number of other tech books. He's also the co-founder of Providence Geeks, and serves as an all-around geek for AS220, a non-profit, unjuried, and uncensored arts center in Providence, RI. Email: *bjepson@oreilly.com.*

Chris Stone (author of Chapter 16) is a senior systems administrator at O'Reilly Media and coauthor of *Mac OS X Tiger in a Nutshell*, published by O'Reilly. A San Francisco native, he got his English degree from Humboldt State University and spent 10 years hidden away in the Japanese countryside before returning to the North Bay area, where he lives with his wife, Miho, and sons, Andrew and Jonathan.

Rich Koster (beta reader) bought his first Mac, a 17-inch MacBook Pro, in 2009, and has never looked back toward the Dark Side (PCs). Rich served as the tech editor of David Pogue's *iPhone: The Missing Manual, 3rd Edition*. He's a husband, a father, and creator of the Disney Echo at *DisneyEcho.emuck.com*, which he has fun tending daily with his MacBook Pro!

Acknowledgments

Man was this book a lot of work. Apple just could not leave well enough alone. For an OS update that supposedly "put a pause on new features," Apple sure put a lot of effort into rejiggering, rewording, or shuffling around what was already there!

Over the years, many friends and colleagues have contributed enthusiasm, expertise, and even prose to this book's editions. They include Zachary Brass, teenage screenshot machine; Dan Pourhadi, Mac writer extraordinaire, who updated Chapter 7 for the previous edition; J.D. Biersdorfer, *New York Times* computer Q&A columnist, who updated Chapters 18, 20, and 21 for the previous edition; and Lesa Snider, my assistant for several years, who was the graphics goddess and co-indexer on previous editions.

In addition to the dream team members identified above, I owe debts of thanks to O'Reilly's Missing Manuals editor-in-chief, Peter Meyers; Teresa Noelle Roberts, copy editor for previous editions; Apple's Monica Sarker and Bill Evans for helping me get answers to baffling tech questions; piano/indexing virtuoso Jim Jacoby; and to my crack team of eleventh-hour proofreaders, Kellee Katagi, Diana D'Abruzzo, and Julie Van Keuren. I also wish I could send out an "I Made the Book Better!" T-shirt to every reader who ever took the time to write with corrections, suggestions, tips, and tricks. And thanks, as always, to David Rogelberg for believing in the idea.

Above all, this book owes its existence to the patience and affection of Jennifer, Kelly, Tia, and Jeffrey. They make these books—and everything else—possible.

—David Pogue

The Missing Manual Series

Missing Manuals are witty, superbly written guides to computer products that don't come with printed manuals (which is just about all of them). Each book features a handcrafted index; cross-references to specific page numbers (not just "see Chapter 14"); and an ironclad promise never to put an apostrophe in the possessive pronoun *its*.

Here's a list of current and upcoming titles:

- *iPhone: The Missing Manual,* 3rd Edition by David Pogue
- *iPod: The Missing Manual,* 8th Edition by J.D. Biersdorfer
- *David Pogue's Digital Photography: The Missing Manual* by David Pogue
- *Photoshop CS4: The Missing Manual* by Lesa Snider King
- *JavaScript: The Missing Manual* by David Sawyer McFarland
- *CSS: The Missing Manual,* 2nd Edition, by David Sawyer McFarland
- *Creating a Web Site: The Missing Manual* by Matthew MacDonald
- *The Internet: The Missing Manual* by David Pogue and J.D. Biersdorfer
- *Dreamweaver 8: The Missing Manual* by David Sawyer McFarland
- *Flash CS4: The Missing Manual* by E. A. Vander Veer and Chris Grover

- *eBay: The Missing Manual* by Nancy Conner
- *Wikipedia: The Missing Manual* by John Broughton
- *Google: The Missing Manual* by Sarah Milstein and Rael Dornfest
- *Google Apps: The Missing Manual* by Nancy Conner
- *Google Sketchup: The Missing Manual* by Chris Grover
- *Palm Pre: The Missing Manual* by Ed Baig
- *Netbooks: The Missing Manual* by J.D. Biersdorfer
- *Home Networking: The Missing Manual* by Scott Lowe
- *Your Brain: The Missing Manual* by Matthew MacDonald
- *Your Body: The Missing Manual* by Matthew MacDonald
- *Living Green: The Missing Manual* by Nancy Conner
- *Facebook: The Missing Manual* by E.A. Vander Veer
- *Wikipedia: The Missing Manual* by John Broughton

For Macintosh:
- *Photoshop Elements for Mac: The Missing Manual* by Barbara Brundage
- *iMovie '09 & iDVD: The Missing Manual* by David Pogue and Aaron Miller
- *iPhoto '09: The Missing Manual* by David Pogue and J.D. Biersdorfer
- *Switching to the Mac: The Missing Manual*, Snow Leopard Edition by David Pogue
- *iWork '09: The Missing Manual* by Josh Clark
- *AppleScript: The Missing Manual* by Adam Goldstein
- *iPod: The Missing Manual,* 7th Edition by J.D. Biersdorfer
- *Office 2008 for Macintosh: The Missing Manual* by Jim Elferdink et al.
- *FileMaker Pro 10: The Missing Manual* by Geoff Coffey and Susan Prosser

For Windows:
- *Windows 7: The Missing Manual* by David Pogue
- *Windows Vista: The Missing Manual* by David Pogue
- *FrontPage 2003: The Missing Manual* by Jessica Mantaro
- *Office 2007: The Missing Manual* by Chris Grover, Matthew MacDonald, and E. A. Vander Veer
- *Word 2007: The Missing Manual* by Chris Grover
- *Excel 2007: The Missing Manual* by Matthew MacDonald
- *PowerPoint 2007: The Missing Manual* by Emily A. Vander Veer

- *Access 2007: The Missing Manual* by Matthew MacDonald
- *Microsoft Project 2007: The Missing Manual* by Bonnie Biafore
- *PCs: The Missing Manual* by Andy Rathbone
- *Photoshop Elements 8: The Missing Manual* by Barbara Brundage
- *Quicken 2009: The Missing Manual* by Bonnie Biafore
- *QuickBooks 2010: The Missing Manual* by Bonnie Biafore
- *QuickBase: The Missing Manual* by Nancy Conner
- *Windows XP Home Edition: The Missing Manual,* 2nd Edition by David Pogue
- *Windows XP Pro: The Missing Manual,* 2nd Edition by David Pogue, Craig Zacker, and L.J. Zacker
- *Windows XP Power Hound* by Preston Gralla

Introduction

Introduction

Mac OS X is an impressive technical achievement; many experts call it the best personal-computer operating system on earth. But beware its name.

The X is meant to be a Roman numeral, pronounced "10." Don't say "oh ess ex." You'll get funny looks in public.

In any case, Mac OS X Snow Leopard is the seventh major version of Apple's Unix-based operating system. It's got very little in common with the original Mac operating system, the one that saw Apple through the 1980s and 1990s. Apple dumped that in 2001, when CEO Steve Jobs decided it was time for a change. Apple had just spent too many years piling new features onto a software foundation originally poured in 1984. Programmers and customers complained of the "spaghetti code" the Mac OS had become.

On the other hand, underneath Mac OS X's classy translucent desktop is Unix, the industrial-strength, rock-solid OS that drives many a Web site and university. It's not new by any means; in fact, it's decades old and has been polished by generations of programmers.

The Snow Leopard Anomaly

Mac OS X 10.6, affectionately known as Snow Leopard, is a strange beast, for a couple of reasons.

The first has to do with the Law of Software Upgrades, which has been in place since the dawn of personal computing. And that law says: "If you don't add new features every year, nobody will upgrade, and you won't make money."

And so, to keep you upgrading, the world's software companies pile on more features with every new version of their wares. Unfortunately, this can't continue forever. Sooner or later, you wind up with a bloated, complex, incoherent mess of a program.

The shocker of Snow Leopard, though, is that upping the feature count wasn't the point. In fact, Steve Jobs said, "We're hitting Pause on new features."

Instead, the point of Snow Leopard was *refinement* of the perfectly good operating system that Apple already had in the previous version, Mac OS X Leopard (10.5).

Refinement meant fixing hundreds of little annoyances, like the baffling error message that sometimes won't let you eject a disk or a flash drive because it's "busy." Refinement meant making the whole thing faster, replacing substantial chunks of its plumbing—including rewriting the Finder from scratch—to be more modern and streamlined. Refinement also meant making Snow Leopard *smaller*—if you can believe it, half the size of the previous Mac OS X, saving you at least 6 gigabytes of hard drive space right off the bat.

As though to hammer home the point, Apple priced Snow Leopard at $30, about $100 less than its usual new-version Mac OS X price.

So wait. Apple's not adding any new features? It's spending all its time on polish, optimization, and *making things work better*? Has Steve Jobs gone completely nuts?

If so, be grateful. Snow Leopard builds beautifully on the successes of previous Mac OS X versions. You still don't have to worry about viruses, spyware, or service pack releases that take up a Saturday afternoon to install and fine-tune. And you still enjoy stability that would make the you of 1999 positively drool.

But as it turns out, not all of Apple's programmers got the "no new features" memo. As you'll see in this book, there are *hundreds* of tiny new features and options. Maybe

---

FREQUENTLY ASKED QUESTION

All About "Snow Leopard"

What's this business about big cats?

Most software companies develop their wares in secret, using code names for new products to throw outsiders off the scent. Apple's code names for Mac OS X and its descendants have been named after big cats: Mac OS X was Cheetah, 10.1 was Puma, 10.2 was Jaguar, 10.3 was Panther, 10.4 was Tiger, and 10.5 was Leopard. Since 10.6 is considered "only" a refinement of the existing Leopard version, it's called Snow Leopard.

(The real snow leopard is an endangered species, native to Central Asia. It has no larynx and so it can't roar. It can kill animals three times its size. Insert your own operating-system metaphor here.)

Usually, the code name is dropped as soon as the product is complete, whereupon the marketing department gives it a new name. In Mac OS X's case, though, Apple thinks its cat names are cool enough to retain for the finished product.

You do have to wonder what Apple plans to call future versions. Apple increases only the decimal point with each major upgrade, which means it has four big cats to go before it hits Mac OS XI.

Let's see: Bobcat, Cougar, Lion…um…Ocelot?

---

there's a blurry line between "new feature" and "refinement of an existing feature," but whatever; there are *tons* of enhancements.

A few of the big-ticket items:

- **It's faster.** Not everything is faster, but wherever Apple put effort into speeding things up, you feel it.

  As noted above, the Finder—the desktop, where you manage your files, folders, and disks—was rewritten from scratch in Mac OS X's native language; you'll feel the zippiness right away. Startup and shutdown are faster. Mail and Safari open faster. Time Machine backups are faster. And installation is faster (and many steps simpler).

- **It's better organized.** Features like Exposé and stacks (pop-up Dock folders) have been redesigned to make more sense and reduce scrolling.

- **It talks to Exchange corporate computers.** Just by entering your name and password for your company's network, you make your Mac part of a Microsoft Exchange system. That is, your corporate email shows up in Mac OS X's Mail program, the corporate directory shows up in Address Book, and your company calendar shows up in iCal—right alongside your own personal mail, addresses, and appointments.

- **It's better for laptops.** The Mac now adjusts its own clock when you travel, just like a cellphone. The menu of nearby wireless hot spots now shows the signal strength for each. Three- and four-finger trackpad "gestures" now work on even the oldest multitouch Mac laptops.

- **QuickTime Player is new.** The Mac's built-in movie player is brand new. It features a very cool frameless "screen," plus a Trim command and one-click uploading to YouTube, MobileMe, or iTunes (for loading onto an iPod or iPhone). The new Player can even make audio recordings, video recordings, and—a first for a mainstream operating system—even *screen* recordings, so you can create how-to videos for your less-gifted relatives and friends.

- **It has major new text-editing features.** Mac OS X's system-wide spelling and grammar checker is joined this time around by a typing-expansion feature. You can create your own abbreviations that, when typed, expand to a word, phrase, or even a blurb of canned text many paragraphs long. It's great for autofixing typos, of course, but also great for answering the same questions by email over and over.

- **Services are reborn.** *Services,* a strange little menu of miscellaneous commands, has been in the Application menus for years now, baffling almost everyone. In Snow Leopard, they've been completely reborn. They now appear only when they'll actually do something. Better yet, creating your own system-wide Services commands is a piece of cake, as Chapter 7 makes clear. You can also assign any keystroke you like to them. So for the first time in Macintosh history, you have a built-in means of opening favorite programs from the keyboard: Control-S for Safari, Control-W for Word, and so on.

• **Improved navigation for blind people.** One feature turns your laptop's trackpad into a touchable map of the screen; the Mac speaks each onscreen element as you touch it. In general, VoiceOver (as the talking-screen feature is called) has been given an enormous expansion/overhaul.

About This Book

By way of a printed guide to Mac OS X, Apple provides only a flimsy "getting started" booklet. To find your way around, you're expected to use Apple's online help system. And as you'll quickly discover, these help pages are tersely written, offer very little

---

POWER USERS' CLINIC

Power Tools for Software Companies

A couple of the biggest-deal features in Snow Leopard are under-the-hood overhauls that you won't see, but you may someday feel. They're tools for software companies to exploit. And when they do, substantial speed and security gains may result.

64-bit rewrites. First, most of Mac OS X and its flotilla of accompanying software programs have been rewritten in 64-bit code. You can read more about this geeky term on page 194; for now, it means (a) you can theoretically install *16 terabytes* of memory in a Mac (if Apple ever sells one with that many RAM slots, that is); (b) in programs that have been rewritten as 64-bit apps—like Safari—there can be noticeable speed payoffs; and (c) since more numbers can be crunched simultaneously, programs can be even better protected against nasties like viruses and hacker attacks.

(If you're scoring at home, all but four of Snow Leopard's included software programs have been recast in 64-bit. The holdouts: DVD Player, Front Row, Grapher, and iTunes.)

Grand Central Dispatch. You may have noticed that the days of the megahertz marketing are over. Processors are no longer advertised with speed numbers like "3 gigahertz! 4 gigahertz! 5 gigahertz!" They pretty much topped out at 3 gigahertz; they're just getting too hot to run any faster. Anything much higher, and your processor would melt a hole through your desk.

Instead, the focus these days is for Intel and other chip makers to put *multiple* chips on a single processor—or multiple cores. All current Macs have multicore processors (two, four

or even eight cores), which can operate in parallel to get computing tasks done faster.

Unfortunately, unless a software program is rewritten to take advantage of the additional cores, it doesn't run any faster than before. The additional cores just sit there, wasted. And doing that rewrite—managing *threads* of a program—is an expensive, time-consuming hassle for software companies.

So Apple did the work for them. Grand Central Dispatch technology lets the *operating system* do the threading, making it far easier for software companies to exploit modern Macs' horsepower.

OpenCL. The main processor in a modern computer isn't the only important chip; your Mac also has a *graphics* processor. This chip is traditionally dedicated to graphics and images. And every year, as the demand for realistic movies and 3-D games grows, these graphics chips have been getting more powerful.

But what about when you're not running a graphics-intensive program? Well, then your expensive, very fancy graphics chip just sits there, idle.

The idea behind OpenCL, then, is: "Use this high-horsepower chip for regular computing tasks when it's free!" When software companies rewrite their apps to take advantage of OpenCL, then intensive computing tasks—financial, scientific, number-crunchy stuff—will be able to go much faster. They'll exploit your graphics processor for what it really is: a very powerful computer chip.

---

technical depth, lack useful examples, and provide no tutorials whatsoever. You can't even mark your place, underline, or read it in the bathroom.

The purpose of this book, then, is to serve as the manual that should have accompanied Mac OS X—version 10.6 in particular.

Mac OS X Snow Leopard: The Missing Manual is designed to accommodate readers at every technical level. The primary discussions are written for advanced-beginner or intermediate Mac fans. But if you're a Mac first-timer, miniature sidebar articles called Up To Speed provide the introductory information you need to understand the topic at hand. If you're a Mac veteran, on the other hand, keep your eye out for similar shaded boxes called Power Users' Clinic. They offer more technical tips, tricks, and shortcuts.

When you write a book like this, you do a lot of soul-searching about how much stuff to cover. Of course, a thinner book, or at least a thinner-looking one, is always preferable; plenty of readers are intimidated by a book that dwarfs the Tokyo White Pages.

On the other hand, Apple keeps adding features and rarely takes them away. So if this book is to remain true to its goal—serving as the best possible source of information about every aspect of Mac OS X—it isn't going to get any thinner.

Even so, some chapters come with free downloadable appendixes—PDF documents, available on this book's "Missing CD" page at *www.missingmanuals.com*—that go into further detail on some of the tweakiest features. (You'll see references to them sprinkled throughout the book.)

Maybe this idea will save a few trees—and a few back muscles when you try to pick this book up.

Snow Leopard Spots

When your job is to write a new edition of a computer book, and you hear about a "no new features" mantra, you can't help but be delighted. That should make the job easy, right? But in this case—*wow,* would you be wrong.

There may be very few big-ticket changes, but the number of *tiny* changes runs into the hundreds! Undocumented, tweaky little changes. For example:

The menu bar can now show the date, not just the day of the week. When you're running Windows on your Mac, you can now open the files on the Macintosh "side" without having to restart. Icons can now be 512 pixels square—that's *huge*—turning any desktop window into a light table for photos. There's now a Put Back command in the Trash, which flings a discarded item right back into the folder it came from, even weeks later. You can page through a PDF document or watch a movie right on a file's icon. Buggy plug-ins (Flash and so on) no longer crash the Safari Web browser; you just get an empty rectangle where they would have appeared. Video chats in iChat have much smaller connection-speed requirements. And on and on and on.

Not all of changes will thrill everyone, though. Snow Leopard runs only on Macs with Intel processors, meaning that pre-2006 Macs aren't invited to the party. Here and there, long-standing features have disappeared, especially in QuickTime Player. Plenty of little non-Apple utility programs no longer work in Snow Leopard, especially browser plug-ins and shortcut menu add-ons. And some ancient file-management features, like invisible Type and Creator codes, are gone.

In any case, it'd be pointless to try to draw up a single, tidy list of every change in Snow Leopard. Instead, throughout this book, within the relevant discussions, you'll be alerted to all those little changes in little blurbs labeled like this:

Snow Leopard Spots: Little items like this one point out subtle changes from the previous version(s) of Mac OS X—a good change, a bad change, or just a change.

About the Outline

Mac OS X Snow Leopard: The Missing Manual is divided into six parts, each containing several chapters:

- **Part One, The Mac OS X Desktop,** covers everything you see on the screen when you turn on a Mac OS X computer: the Dock, the Sidebar, Spotlight, Dashboard, Spaces, Exposé, Time Machine, icons, windows, menus, scroll bars, the Trash, aliases, the menu, and so on.

- **Part Two, Programs in Mac OS X,** is dedicated to the proposition that an operating system is little more than a launchpad for *programs*—the actual applications you use in your everyday work, such as email programs, Web browsers, word processors, graphics suites, and so on. These chapters describe how to work with applications in Mac OS X: how to launch them, switch among them, swap data between them, use them to create and open files, and control them using the AppleScript and Automator automation tools.

- **Part Three, The Components of Mac OS X,** is an item-by-item discussion of the individual software nuggets that make up this operating system—the 27 panels of System Preferences, and the 50 programs in your Applications and Utilities folders.

- **Part Four, The Technologies of Mac OS X,** treads in more advanced territory. Networking, file sharing, and screen sharing, are, of course, tasks Mac OS X was born to do. These chapters cover all of the above, plus the prodigious visual talents of Mac OS X (fonts, printing, graphics, handwriting recognition), its multimedia gifts (sound, speech, movies), and the Unix that lies beneath.

- **Part Five, Mac OS X Online,** covers all the Internet features of Mac OS X, including the Mail email program and the Safari Web browser/RSS reader; iChat for instant messaging and audio or video chats; Web sharing; Internet sharing; and Apple's online MobileMe services (which include email accounts, secure file-backup features, Web hosting, and more). If you're feeling particularly advanced, you'll also find instructions on using Mac OS X's Unix underpinnings for connecting to, and controlling, your Mac from across the wires—FTP, SSH, VPN, and so on.

- **Part Six: Appendixes.** This book's appendixes include a Windows-to-Mac dictionary (to help Windows refugees find the new locations of familiar features in Mac

OS X); guidance in installing this operating system; a troubleshooting handbook; a list of resources for further study; and an extremely thorough master list of all the keyboard shortcuts in Mac OS X Snow Leopard.

About→These→Arrows

Throughout this book, and throughout the Missing Manual series, you'll find sentences like this one: "Open the System folder→Libraries→Fonts folder." That's shorthand for a much longer instruction that directs you to open three nested folders in sequence, like this: "On your hard drive, you'll find a folder called System. Open that. Inside the System folder window is a folder called Libraries; double-click it to open it. Inside that folder is yet another one called Fonts. Double-click to open it, too."

Similarly, this kind of arrow shorthand helps to simplify the business of choosing commands in menus, such as →Dock→Position on Left.

About MissingManuals.com

To get the most out of this book, visit *www.missingmanuals.com*. Click the "Missing CD-ROM" link—and then this book's title—to reveal a neat, organized, chapter-by-chapter list of the shareware and freeware mentioned in this book.

The Web site also offers corrections and updates to the book. (To see them, click the book's title, and then click View/Submit Errata.) In fact, please submit such corrections and updates yourself! In an effort to keep the book as up to date and accurate as possible, each time O'Reilly prints more copies of this book, I'll make any confirmed corrections you've suggested. I'll also note such changes on the Web site so that you can mark important corrections into your own copy of the book, if you like. And I'll keep the book current as Apple releases more Mac OS X 10.6 updates.

VERSION ALERT

Version 10.6.1 and Beyond

Only two weeks after the debut of Mac OS X 10.6, Apple rolled out a free update to 10.6.1, and thus began its traditional flood of system updates. These installers patch holes, fix bugs, improve compatibility with external gadgets, and make everything work more smoothly.

Version 10.6.1, for example, delivered a long list of bug fixes in compatibility with cellular modems, DVD playback, printer compatibility, automatic login bugs, glitches in Mail, and so on.

This book covers 10.6.1, but it's only a matter of time before 10.6.2 comes out, then 10.6.3, and so on.

You don't have to go out of your way to get these updates:

One day you'll be online with your Mac, and a Software Update dialog box will appear before you, offering you the chance to download and install the patch.

As for the differences between the "first decimal point" versions of Mac OS X: You'll find this book useful no matter which version you have, but it describes and illustrates version 10.6 and later.

If you're still working with 10.1 through 10.5, you'll probably feel most comfortable if you seek out the first, second, third, fourth, or fifth edition of this book.

Or, better yet, upgrade to Snow Leopard.

The Very Basics

To use this book, and indeed to use a Macintosh computer, you need to know a few basics. This book assumes you're familiar with a few terms and concepts:

- **Clicking.** This book gives you three kinds of instructions that require you to use the Mac's mouse. To *click* means to point the arrow cursor at something on the screen and then—without moving the cursor—press and release the clicker button on the mouse (or your laptop trackpad). To *double-click,* of course, means to click twice in rapid succession, again without moving the cursor at all. And to *drag* means to move the cursor while holding down the button.

  When you're told to ⌘-click something, you click while pressing the ⌘ key (which is next to the space bar). Shift-clicking, Option-clicking, and Control-clicking work the same way—just click while pressing the corresponding key.

  (There's also *right-clicking.* But that important topic is described in depth on page 224.)

- **Menus.** The menus are the words at the top of your screen: , File, Edit, and so on. Click one to make a list of commands appear.

  Some people click and release to open a menu and then, after reading the choices, click again on the one they want. Other people like to press the mouse button continuously after the initial click on the menu title, drag down the list to the desired command, and only then release the mouse button. Either method works fine.

- **Keyboard shortcuts.** If you're typing along in a burst of creative energy, it's disruptive to have to grab the mouse to use a menu. That's why many Mac fans prefer to trigger menu commands by pressing certain combinations on the keyboard. For example, in word processors, you can press ⌘-B to produce a boldface word. When you read an instruction like "press ⌘-B," start by pressing the ⌘ key, then, while it's down, type the letter B, and finally release both keys.

Tip: You know what's really nice? The keystroke to open the Preferences dialog box in every Apple program—Mail, Safari, iMovie, iPhoto, TextEdit, Preview, and on and on—is always the same: ⌘-comma. Better yet, that standard is catching on with other software companies, too; Word, Excel, Entourage, and PowerPoint use the same keystroke, for example.

- **Icons.** The colorful inch-tall pictures that appear in your various desktop folders are the graphic symbols that represent each program, disk, and document on your computer. If you click an icon one time, it darkens, indicating that you've just *highlighted* or *selected* it. Now you're ready to manipulate it by using, for example, a menu command.

- **Checkboxes, radio buttons, tabs.** See Figure I-1 for a quick visual reference to the onscreen controls you're most often asked to use.

A few more tips on mastering the Macintosh keyboard appear on page 220. Otherwise, if you've mastered this much information, you have all the technical background you need to enjoy *Mac OS X Snow Leopard: The Missing Manual.*

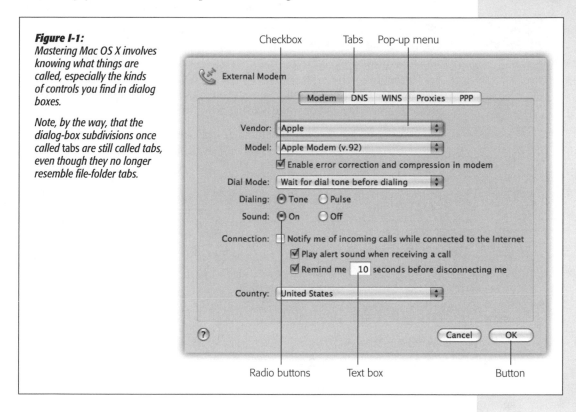

Figure I-1:
Mastering Mac OS X involves knowing what things are called, especially the kinds of controls you find in dialog boxes.

Note, by the way, that the dialog-box subdivisions once called tabs *are still called tabs, even though they no longer resemble file-folder tabs.*

Checkbox   Tabs   Pop-up menu

External Modem

Modem | DNS | WINS | Proxies | PPP

Vendor: Apple

Model: Apple Modem (v.92)

☑ Enable error correction and compression in modem

Dial Mode: Wait for dial tone before dialing

Dialing: ⦿ Tone ◯ Pulse

Sound: ⦿ On   ◯ Off

Connection: ☐ Notify me of incoming calls while connected to the Internet

☑ Play alert sound when receiving a call

☑ Remind me 10 seconds before disconnecting me

Country: United States

Cancel   OK

Radio buttons   Text box   Button

Part One:
The Mac OS X Desktop

1

Folders & Windows

Getting into Mac OS X

When you first turn on a Mac running OS X 10.6, an Apple logo greets you, soon followed by an animated, rotating "Please wait" gear cursor—and then you're in. No progress bar, no red tape.

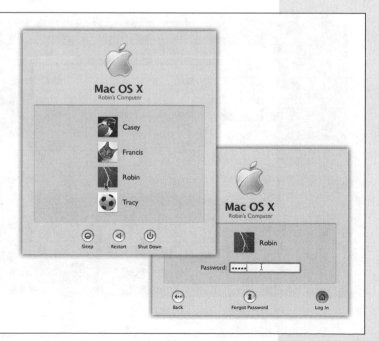

Figure 1-1:
Left: On Macs configured to accommodate different people at different times, this is one of the first things you see upon turning on the computer. Click your name. (If the list is long, you may have to scroll to find your name—or just type the first few letters of it.)

Right: At this point, you're asked to type in your password. Type it, and then click Log In (or press Return or Enter; pressing these keys usually "clicks" any blue, pulsing button in a dialog box). If you've typed the wrong password, the entire dialog box vibrates, in effect shaking its little dialog-box head, suggesting that you guess again. (See Chapter 12.)

Logging In

What happens next depends on whether you're the Mac's sole proprietor or you have to share it with other people in an office, school, or household.

- **If it's your own Mac,** and you've already been through the Mac OS X setup process described in Appendix A, no big deal. You arrive at the Mac OS X desktop.

- **If it's a shared Mac,** you may encounter the Login dialog box, shown in Figure 1-1. Click your name in the list (or type it, if there's no list).

  If the Mac asks for your password, type it and then click Log In (or press Return). You arrive at the desktop. Chapter 12 offers much more on this business of user accounts and logging in.

The Elements of the Mac OS X Desktop

The *desktop* is the shimmering, three-dimensional Mac OS X landscape shown in Figure 1-2; technically, you're in a program called the *Finder*. On a new Mac, it's covered by a starry galaxy photo that belongs to Snow Leopard's overall outer-space graphic theme. (If you upgraded from an earlier version of Mac OS X, you keep whatever desktop picture you had before. In fact, at first glance, you probably won't spot anything different about Snow Leopard at all.)

If you've ever used a computer before, most of the objects on your screen are nothing more than updated versions of familiar elements. Here's a quick tour.

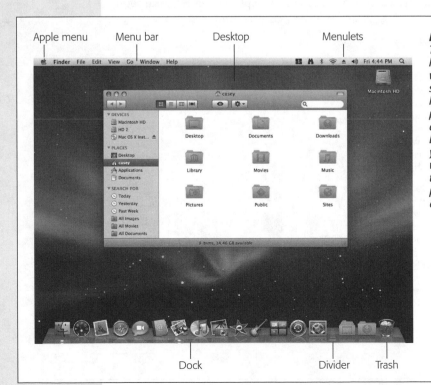

Apple menu   Menu bar   Desktop   Menulets

Dock   Divider   Trash

Figure 1-2:
The Mac OS X landscape looks like a more futuristic version of the operating systems you know and love. This is just a starting point, however. You can dress it up with a different background picture, adjust your windows in a million ways, and, of course, fill the Dock with only the programs, disks, folders, and files you need.

Note: If your desktop looks even barer than this—no menus, no icons, almost nothing on the Dock—then somebody in charge of your Mac has turned on Simple Finder mode for you. Details on page 472.

Disk icons

For years, Apple has encouraged its flock to keep a clean desktop, to get rid of all the icons that many of us leave strewn around. Especially the hard drive icon, which has appeared in the upper-right corner of the screen since the original 1984 Mac.

In Snow Leopard, the Macintosh HD icon no longer appears on the screen (unless it was there before you upgraded). "Look, if you want access to your files and folders, just open them directly—from the Dock or from your Home folder (page 63)," Apple seems to be saying. "Most of the stuff on the hard drive is system files of no interest to you, so let's just hide that icon, shall we?"

Note: If you'd prefer that the disk icons return to your desktop where they used to be, then Snow Leopard can accommodate you. Choose Finder→Preferences, click General, and turn on the checkboxes of the disks whose icons you want on the desktop: hard disks, external disks, CDs, and so on.

The Dock

This row of translucent, almost photographic icons is a launcher for the programs, files, folders, and disks you use often—and an indicator to let you know which programs are already open. In Snow Leopard, they appear to rest on a sheet of transparent smoked glass.

In principle, the Dock is very simple:

- **Programs go on the left side.** Everything else goes on the right, including documents, folders, and disks. (Figure 1-2 shows the dividing line.)

- **You can add a new icon to the Dock by dragging it there.** Rearrange Dock icons by dragging them. Remove a Dock icon by dragging it away from the Dock, and enjoy the animated puff of smoke that appears when you release the mouse button. (You can't remove the icon of a program that's currently open, however.)

- **Click something once to open it.** When you click a program's icon, a tiny, bright, micro-spotlight dot appears under its icon to let you know it's open.

   When you click a folder's icon, you get a pop-up arc of icons, or a grid or list of them, that indicates what's inside. See page 122 for details.

- **Each Dock icon sprouts a pop-up menu.** To see the menu, Control-click it or right-click it. A shortcut menu of useful commands pops right out.

- **Hold the mouse button down** on a program's Dock icon to see mini versions of all that program's open windows. This feature, new in Snow Leopard, is an extension of the *Exposé* feature described on page 155. (Click the window, or the Dock icon, to close Exposé.)

Because the Dock is such a critical component of Mac OS X, Apple has decked it out with enough customization controls to keep you busy experimenting for months. You can change its size, move it to the sides of your screen, hide it entirely, and so on. Chapter 4 contains complete instructions for using and understanding the Dock.

The menu

The menu houses important Mac-wide commands like Sleep, Restart, and Shut Down. They're always available, no matter which program you're using.

The menu bar

Every popular operating system saves space by concealing its most important commands in *menus* that drop down. Mac OS X's menus are especially refined:

- **They stay down.** Mac OS X is *multithreaded,* which means it's perfectly capable of carrying on with its background activities while you study its open, translucent menus. Therefore, Mac OS X menus stay open until you click the mouse button, trigger a command from the keyboard, or buy a new computer, whichever comes first.

Tip: Actually, menus are even smarter than that. If you give the menu name a quick click, the menu opens and stays open. If you click the menu name and hold the mouse button down for a moment, the menu opens, but closes again when you release the button. Apple figures that, in that case, you're just exploring, reading, or hunting for a certain command.

- **They're translucent.** Unless you've turned off this option in System Preferences →Desktop & Screen Saver, you can faintly see the background through the menu bar.

- **They're logically arranged.** The first menu in every program, which appears in bold lettering, tells you at a glance what program you're in. The commands in this *Application menu* include About (which indicates which version of the program you're using), Preferences, Quit, and commands like Hide Others and Show All (which help control window clutter).

In short, all the Application menu's commands actually pertain to the application you're using.

The File and Edit menus come next. As in the past, the File menu contains commands for opening, saving, and closing *files.* (See the logic?) The Edit menu contains the Cut, Copy, and Paste commands.

The last menu is almost always Help. It opens a miniature Web browser that lets you search the online Mac help files for explanatory text (page 60).

- **You can operate them from the keyboard.** Once you've clicked open a menu, you can highlight any command in it just by typing the first letter (*g* for Get Info, for example). (It's especially great for "Your country" pop-up menus on Web sites, where "United States" is about 200 countries down in the list. Now you can type *united s* to jump right to it.)

You can also press Tab to open the next menu, Shift-Tab to open the previous one, and Return or Enter to "click" the highlighted command.

All that's left is figuring out a way to open the menu itself from the keyboard to start the process (details on page 178).

Otherwise, the menu bar looks and works much as it has in operating systems past.

Windows and How to Work Them

In designing Mac OS X, one of Apple's goals was to address the window-proliferation problem. As you create more files, stash them in more folders, and launch more programs, it's easy to wind up paralyzed before a screen awash with overlapping rectangles.

That's the problem admirably addressed by Exposé and Spaces. They're described in detail in Chapter 5.

But some handy clutter and navigation controls are built into the windows themselves, too. For example:

The Sidebar

The Sidebar is the pane at the left side of every Finder window, unless you've hidden it (and by the way, it's also at the left side of every Open dialog box and every full-sized Save dialog box).

The Sidebar has as many as four different sections, each preceded by a collapsible heading:

- **Devices.** This section lists every storage device connected to, or installed inside, your Mac: hard drives, CDs, DVDs, iPods, memory cards, USB flash drives, and so on. The removable ones (like CDs, DVDs, and iPods) bear a little gray ⏏ logo, which you can click to eject that disk.

- **Shared.** It took 20 years for an operating system to list all the other computers on the home or small-office network, right there in every window, without any digging, connecting, button-clicking, or window-opening. But here it is: a complete list of the other computers on your network whose owners have turned on File Sharing, ready for access. See Chapter 13 for details.

- **Places.** This primary section of the Sidebar lists *places* (in this case, folders) where you might look for files and folders. Into this list, you can stick the icons of anything at all—files, programs, folders, anything but disks—for easy access.

  Each icon is a shortcut. For example, click the Applications icon to view the contents of your Applications folder in the main part of the window (Figure 1-3). And if you click the icon of a file or program, it opens.

- **Search For.** The "folders" in this Sidebar section are actually canned searches that execute instantly when you click one. If you click Today, for example, the main window fills with all the files and folders on your computer that you've changed today. Yesterday and Past Week work the same way.

The All Images, All Movies, and All Documents searches round up everything in those file-type categories, no matter what folders they're actually sitting in.

These instasearches are very useful all by themselves, but what's even better is how easy it is to make your *own* search folders to put here. Page 117 has the details.

Snow Leopard Spots: If you drag away everything listed under the Devices, Places, or Search For headings, the heading itself disappears to save space. The heading reappears the next time you put something in its category back into the Sidebar.

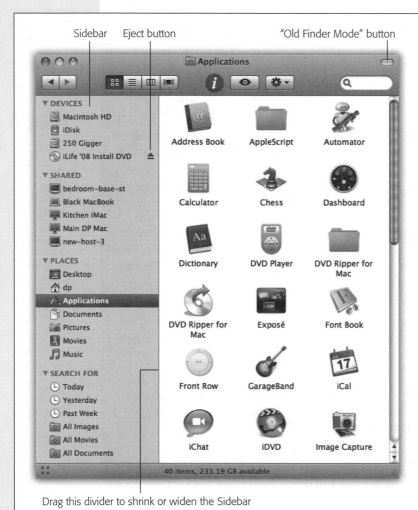

Sidebar   Eject button   "Old Finder Mode" button

Drag this divider to shrink or widen the Sidebar

Figure 1-3:
The Sidebar makes navigation very quick, because you can jump back and forth between distant corners of your Mac with a single click. In column view, the Sidebar is especially handy because it eliminates all the columns to the left of the one you want, all the way back to your hard-drive level. You've just folded up your desktop!

Good things to put here: favorite programs, disks on a network you often connect to, a document you're working on every day, and so on. Folder and disk icons here work just like normal ones. You can drag a document onto a folder icon to file it there, drag a downloaded .sit file onto the StuffIt Expander icon, and so on. In fact, the disks and folders here are even spring-loaded (page 77).

Fine-tuning the Sidebar

The beauty of this parking lot for containers is that it's so easy to set up with *your* favorite places. For example:

- **Remove** an icon by dragging it out of the Sidebar entirely. It vanishes with a puff of smoke (and even a little *whoof* sound effect). You haven't actually removed anything from your Mac; you've just unhitched its alias from the Sidebar.

Tip: You can't drag items out of the Shared list. Also, if you drag a Devices item out of the list, you'll have to choose Finder→Preferences→Sidebar (and turn on the appropriate checkbox) to put it back in.

- **Rearrange** the icons by dragging them up or down in the list. (You're not allowed to rearrange the computers listed in the Shared section, though.)

- **Install a new icon** by dragging it off your desktop (or out of a window) into any spot in the Places list of the Sidebar. Unlike previous versions of Mac OS X, you can't drag icons into any old section of the Sidebar—just the Places place.

Tip: You can also highlight an icon in any window, and then choose File→Add to Sidebar, or just press ⌘-T.

- **Adjust the width** of the Sidebar by dragging its *right edge*—either the skinny divider line or the extreme right edge of the vertical scroll bar, if there is one. You "feel" a snap at the point when the line covers up about half of each icon's name. Any covered-up names sprout ellipses (…) to let you know (as in "Secret Salaries Spreadsh…").

TROUBLESHOOTING MOMENT

Fixing the Sidebar

In the pre-Leopard days, dragging stuff out of the Sidebar to get rid of it sometimes created a small quandary: Once you dragged the Macintosh HD, Home, or iDisk icons out of the Sidebar, you couldn't drag them back in. Suddenly you were stuck with the orphaned horizontal divider, with nothing to divide. The top half of your list was empty.

Nowadays, mercifully, anything you drag out of the Sidebar can be dragged back in again, including the big-ticket items like Home and Macintosh HD.

(Furthermore, entire *headings* now appear and disappear as needed.)

Even so, there's a quicker way to restore the Sidebar to its factory settings.

If you choose Finder→Preferences and then click the Sidebar button, you discover the checkboxes shown here. They let you put back the Apple-installed icons that you may have removed in haste. Just turn on a checkbox to restore its icon to your Sidebar. So if something you expect to see in your Sidebar isn't there, check back here.

On the other hand, you might as well streamline your computing life by turning *off* the checkboxes of icons that you *never* want to see filling your Sidebar.

CHAPTER 1: FOLDERS & WINDOWS

- **Hide the Sidebar** by pressing ⌘-Option-S, which is the shortcut for the new View→Hide Sidebar command. Bring it back into view by pressing the same key combination (or using the Show Sidebar command).

Note: The Sidebar also hides itself when you click the Old Finder Mode button, described on page 29.

Then again, why would you ever *want* to hide the Sidebar? It's one of the handiest navigation aids since the invention of the steering wheel. For example:

- **It takes a lot of pressure off the Dock.** Instead of filling up your Dock with folder icons (all of which are frustratingly alike and unlabeled anyway), use the Sidebar to store them. You leave the Dock that much more room for programs and documents.

- **It's better than the Dock.** In some ways, the Sidebar is a lot *like* the Dock, in that you can stash favorite icons of any sort there. But the Sidebar reveals the *names* of these icons, and the Dock doesn't until you use the mouse to point there.

- **It makes disk-ejecting easy.** Just click the ⏏ button next to any removable disk to make it pop out. After 20 years, Mac has finally beaten the "It's illogical to eject a disk by dragging it to the Trash!" problem. (Other ways to eject disks are described in Chapter 11.)

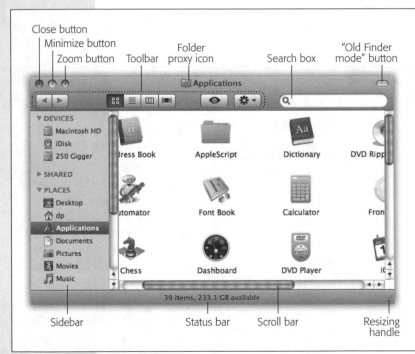

Figure 1-4:
When Steve Jobs unveiled Mac OS X at a Macworld Expo in 1999, he said that his goal was to oversee the creation of an interface so attractive, "you just want to lick it." Desktop windows, with their juicy, fruit-flavored controls, are a good starting point.

Close button
Minimize button
Zoom button
Toolbar
Folder proxy icon
Search box
"Old Finder mode" button

Sidebar
Status bar
Scroll bar
Resizing handle

- **It makes disc-burning easy.** When you've inserted a blank CD or DVD and loaded it up with stuff you want to copy, click the ☢ button next to its name to begin burning that disc. (Details on burning discs are in Chapter 11.)

- **You can drag onto its folders and disks.** That is, you can drag icons onto Sidebar icons, as though they were the real disks, folders, and programs they represent.

- **It simplifies connecting to networked disks.** Park your other computers' hard drive icons here, as described in Chapter 13, and you shave several steps off the usual connecting-via-network ritual.

Title Bar

The title bar (Figure 1-4) has several functions. First, when several windows are open, the darkened title bar, window name, mini-icon, and colored left-corner buttons tell you which window is *active* (in front); in background windows, these elements appear dimmed and colorless. Second, the title bar acts as a *handle* that lets you move the window around on the screen.

Of course, you can also move Mac OS X windows by dragging *any* "shiny gray" edge; see Figure 1-5.

Tip: Here's a nifty keyboard shortcut: You can cycle through the different open windows in one program without using the mouse. Just press ⌘-~ (that is, the tilde key, to the left of the number 1 key on U.S. keyboards). With each press, you bring a different window forward within the current program. It works both in the Finder and in your everyday programs, and it beats the pants off using the mouse to choose a name from the Window menu. (Note the difference from ⌘-Tab, which cycles through different open programs.)

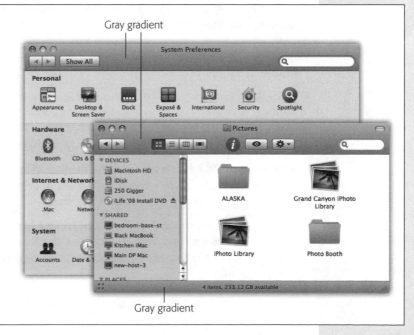

Figure 1-5:
Mac OS X is no longer made of simulated brushed aluminum, as in years past. Now it's accented with strips of gradient gray (that is, light-to-dark shading). All these gradient gray strips are fair game as handles to drag the window.

Gray gradient

Gray gradient

After you've opened one folder that's inside another, the title bar's secret *folder hierarchy menu* is an efficient way to backtrack—to return to the enclosing window. Get in the habit of right-clicking (or Control-clicking, or ⌘-clicking) the name of the window to access the menu shown in Figure 1-6. (You can release the Control or ⌘ key immediately after clicking.)

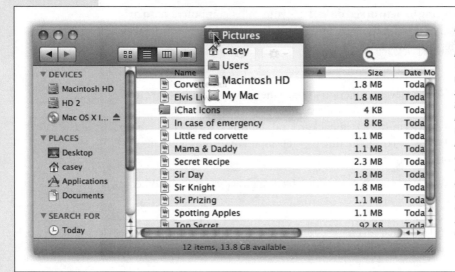

Figure 1-6:
Control-click (or right-click, or ⌘-click) a Finder window's title bar to summon the hidden folder hierarchy menu. This trick also works in most other Mac OS X programs. For example, you can ⌘-click a document window's title to find out where the document is actually saved on your hard drive.

By choosing the name of a folder from this menu, you open the corresponding window. When browsing the contents of the Users folder, for example, you can return to the main hard drive window by Control-clicking the folder name Users and then choosing Macintosh HD from the menu.

Tip: Keyboard lovers, take note. Instead of using this title bar menu, you can also jump to the enclosing window by pressing ⌘-↑ (up arrow), which is the shortcut for the Go→Enclosing Folder command.

Pressing ⌘-↓ (down arrow) takes you back into the folder you started in, assuming that it's still highlighted. (This makes more sense when you try it than when you read it.)

Once you've mastered dragging, you're ready for these three terrific title bar tips:

- **Pressing the ⌘ key** lets you drag the title bar of an *inactive* window—one that's partly covered by a window in front—without bringing it to the front. (Drag any empty part of the title bar—not the title itself.)

  By the way, you can close, minimize, or zoom a background window *without* the help of the ⌘ key. Just click one of those three corresponding title-bar buttons normally. Mac OS X does its thing without taking you out of your current window or program.

- **By double-clicking the title bar,** you *minimize* the window, making it collapse into the Dock exactly as though you had clicked the Minimize button (assuming you haven't turned off this feature in System Preferences, of course).

The Go to Folder Command

Sometimes a Unix tentacle pokes through the friendly Mac OS X interface. Every now and then, you find a place where you can use Unix shortcuts instead of the mouse.

One classic example is the Go→Go to Folder command (Shift-⌘-G). It brings up a box like the one shown here.

The purpose of this box is to let you jump directly to a certain folder on your Mac by typing its Unix *folder path*. Depending on your point of view, this special box is either a shortcut or a detour.

For example, if you want to see what's in the Documents folder of your Home folder, you could choose Go→Go to Folder and type this:

/Users/chris/Documents

Then click Go or press Return. (In this example, of course, *chris* is your short account name.)

In other words, you're telling the Mac to open the Users folder in your main hard drive window, then your Home folder inside that, and then the Documents folder inside that. Each slash means "and then open." (You can leave off the name of your hard drive; that's implied by the opening slash.) When you press Return, the folder you specified pops open immediately.

Of course, if you really wanted to jump to your Documents folder, you'd be wasting your time by typing all that. Unix (and therefore Mac OS X) offers a handy shortcut that means "home folder." It's the tilde character (~) at the upper-left corner of the U.S. keyboard.

To see what's in your Home folder, then, you could type just that ~ symbol into the Go to Folder box and then press

Return. Or you could add some slashes to it to specify a folder inside your Home folder, like this:

~/Documents

You can even jump to someone *else's* Home folder by typing a name after the symbol, like this:

~chris

If you get into this sort of thing, here's another shortcut worth noting: If you type nothing but a slash (/) and then press Return, you jump immediately to the Computer window, which provides an overview of all your disks.

Note, too, that you don't have to type out the full path—only the part that drills down from the *window you're in*. If your Home folder window is already open, for example, then you can open the Pictures folder just by typing *Pictures*.

But the Go to Folder trick really turns into a high-octane timesaver if you use *autocompletion*. Here's how it works: After each slash, you can type only enough letters of a folder's name to give Mac OS X the idea—*de* instead of *desktop*, for example—and then wait a fraction of a second (or, if you're late for a plane, press the Tab key). Mac OS X instantly and automatically fills in the rest of the folder's name. It even auto-capitalizes the folder names for you. (In Unix, capitalization matters.)

For example, instead of typing */Applications/Microsoft Office/clipart/standard,* you could type nothing more than */ap/mi/cl/st,* remembering to press Tab after each pair of letters. Now *that's* a way to feel like a Unix programmer.

• **The Option key** means "Apply this action to all windows in the current program." For example, Option-double-clicking any title bar minimizes *all* desktop windows, sending them flying to the Dock.

Close Button

As the tip of your cursor crosses the three buttons at the upper-left corner of a window, tiny symbols appear inside them: ✕, ─, and ✚. Ignore the gossip that these symbols were added to help color-blind people who can't distinguish the colors red, yellow, and green. Color-blind people are perfectly capable of distinguishing the buttons by their positions, just as they do with traffic lights.

But for people who aren't paying attention to button position, these cues appear to distinguish the buttons when all three are identical shades of *gray,* as they are when you use Graphite mode (page 314). They also signal you when it's time to click. For example, as described in the previous section, you can use these three buttons even when the window is not at the front. You know the buttons are ripe for the clicking when you see the little symbols appear under your cursor.

The most important window gadget is the Close button, the red, droplet-like button in the upper-left corner (Figure 1-7). Clicking it closes the window, which collapses back into the icon from which it came.

Tip: If, while working on a document, you see a tiny dot in the center of the Close button, Mac OS X is trying to tell you that you haven't yet saved your work. The dot goes away when you save the document.

The universal keyboard equivalent of the Close button is ⌘-W (for *window*)—a keystroke well worth memorizing. If you get into the habit of dismissing windows with that deft flex of your left hand, you'll find it far easier to close several windows in a row, because you won't have to aim for successive Close buttons.

In many programs, something special happens if you're pressing the Option key when using the Close button or its ⌘-W equivalent: You close *all* open windows. This trick is especially useful in the Finder, where a quest for a particular document may have left your screen plastered with open windows for which you have no further use. Option-clicking the Close button of any *one* window (or pressing Option-⌘-W) closes all of them.

On the other hand, the Option-key trick doesn't close all windows in every program—only those in the current program. Option-closing a Pages document closes all *Pages* windows, but your Finder windows remain open.

Moreover, Option-closing works only in enlightened applications. (In this department, Microsoft is not yet enlightened.)

Minimize Button

Click this yellow drop of gel to *minimize* any Mac window, sending it shrinking, with a genie-like animated effect, into the right end of the Dock, where it then appears as an icon. The window isn't gone, and it hasn't even closed. It's just out of your way for the moment, as though you've set it on a shelf. To bring it back, click the newly created Dock icon; see Figure 1-7. Chapter 4 has more on the Dock.

Minimizing a window in this way is a great window-management tool. In the Finder, minimizing a window lets you see whatever icons were hiding behind it. In a Web browser, it lets you hide a window that has to remain open (because you're waiting for some task to finish) so you can read something else in the meantime.

Figure 1-7:
Clicking the Minimize button sends a window scurrying down to the Dock, collapsing in on itself as though being forced through a tiny, invisible funnel. A little icon appears on the lower-right corner of its minimized image to identify the program it's running in.

And now, some Minimize button micro-goodies:

- If you enjoy the ability to roll up your windows in this way, remember that you actually have a bigger target than the Minimize button. The *entire title bar* becomes a giant Minimize button when you double-click anywhere on it. (That's an option in the Appearance panel of System Preferences, described in Chapter 9.)

  Better yet, you can also minimize the frontmost window of almost any program (including the Finder) from the keyboard by pressing ⌘-M. That's a keystroke worth memorizing on Day One.

- The Minimize button harbors a very entertaining hidden feature. If you Option-click it, *all* windows in the current program shrink away simultaneously—great when you've got several Web browser windows open, for example, or an abundance of word processor documents.

- You might expect that Option-clicking one minimized window on the Dock would un-minimize *all* of a program's windows—and indeed, that's true for Cocoa programs (page 188). But if it's a Carbon program, like Word or Photoshop, then you have to click the windows one at a time on the Dock to bring them back.

Tip: Mac OS X can change menu commands as you press modifier keys. For example, open a couple of Finder windows and then click the Window menu. Focus your eyes on the Minimize Window command. Now press Option and watch both the wording and the listed keyboard equivalent change instantly to Minimize All (Option-⌘-M).

The Option key works wonders on the File menu, too.

• In the bad old days (up to late 2009), minimizing a bunch of documents could get really messy. Each one flew onto the Dock, creating a new icon there, creating a tighter and tighter squeeze, shrinking the Dock's icons until they were the size of Tic Tacs.

In Snow Leopard, you can have your document windows minimize themselves into their *program's* Dock icon, rather than creating *new* Dock icons for themselves. That way, your Dock doesn't get any more crowded, and the icons on it don't keep shrinking away to atoms.

To turn on this feature, choose ⌘→System Preferences→Dock. Turn on "Minimize windows into application icon."

So how do you get those windows back *out* of the Dock icon? You use Dock Exposé, which is described on page 158.

POWER USERS' CLINIC

Adjusting the Genie Speed

Apple has a name for the animation you see when you minimize, open, or close a window: the *genie effect*, because it so closely resembles the way Barbara Eden, Robin Williams, and other TV and movie genies entered and exited their magic lamps and bottles.

But you don't have to watch the "genie" animation in precisely the same way, day in and day out. You can slow it down or speed it up, like this:

Slow it down. When Steve Jobs first demo'ed Mac OS X, one of his favorite bits was slowing down the animation so we could see it in graceful, slow motion. How did he do that?

If you Shift-click a window's Minimize button, it collapses into the Dock at about one-fifth its usual speed—an effect sure to produce gasps from onlookers. The Shift key also slows the un-minimizing animation, the one you see when you click a window icon in the Dock to restore it to full size.

(Shift-clicking a button to slow down its animation is a running theme in Mac OS X. You'll find it mentioned in several spots in this book.)

Speed it up. There's no keystroke for making the animation go faster. You can, however, substitute a faster *style* of minimizing animation.

To do so, choose ⌘→Dock→Dock Preferences. From the "Minimize windows using" pop-up menu, choose Scale Effect, and then close the window. Now, instead of collapsing through an invisible funnel, minimized windows simply shrink as they fly down to the Dock, remaining rectangular. The time you save isn't exactly going to get you home an hour earlier each day, but at least you have the illusion of greater speed.

(Actually, there's a third animation style, too, but there's a trick to unleashing it; see page 657.)

Zoom Button

A click on this green geltab (see Figure 1-7) makes a desktop window just large enough to reveal all the icons inside it (or, in application programs, large enough to reveal all the text, graphics, or music). If your monitor isn't big enough to show all the icons in a window, then Zoom resizes the window to show as many as possible.

In either case, a second click on the Zoom button restores the window to its previous size. (The Window→Zoom command does the same thing.)

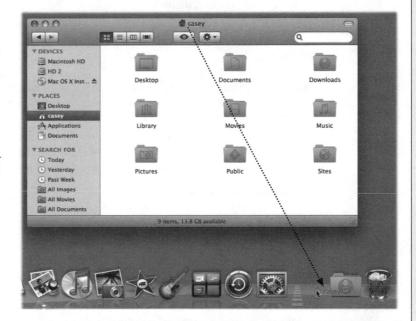

Figure 1-8:
When you find yourself confronting a Finder window that contains useful stuff, consider dragging its proxy icon to the Dock. You wind up installing its folder or disk icon there for future use. That's not the same as minimizing the window, which puts the window icon into the Dock, and only temporarily at that. (Note: Most document windows also offer a proxy-icon feature but produce only an alias when you drag the proxy to a different folder or disk.)

The Folder Proxy Icon

In the Finder, there's a tiny icon next to the window's name (Figure 1-8). It's a stand-in—a *proxy*—for that window's folder itself.

By dragging this tiny icon, you can move or copy the folder into a different folder or disk, into the Sidebar, into the Trash, or into the Dock without having to first close the window.

Tip: You have to hold down the mouse button on the folder proxy icon until the icon darkens before dragging. (It darkens in a fraction of a second.)

When you drag this proxy icon to a different place on the same disk, the usual folder-dragging rules apply: Hold down the Option key if you want to *copy* the original disk or folder; ignore the Option key to *move* the original folder. (You'll find details on moving and copying icons in the next chapter.)

Many programs, including Microsoft Word, Preview, QuickTime Player, and others, offer the same mini-icon in open *document* windows. Once again, you can use it as a handle to drag a document into a new folder or onto a new disk. Sometimes, doing that really does move the document—but more often, you just get an alias of it in the new location.

The Finder Toolbar

Chapter 4 describes this fascinating desktop-window element in great detail.

Two Clicks, One Window

In Mac OS X, double-clicking a folder in a window doesn't leave you with *two* open windows. Instead, double-clicking a folder makes the original window disappear (Figure 1-9).

Tip: If you Option-double-click a folder, you don't simply replace the contents of a fixed window that remains onscreen; you actually switch windows, as evidenced by their changing sizes and shapes.

So what if you've now opened inner folder B, and you want to backtrack to outer folder A? In that case, just click the tiny ◄ button—the Back button—in the upper-left corner of the window (shown in Figure 1-9), or use one of these alternatives:

- Choose Go→Back.

- Press ⌘-[(left bracket).

- Press ⌘-↑ (up arrow).

- Choose Go→Enclosing Folder.

None of that helps you, however, if you want to move a file from one folder into another, or compare the contents of two windows. In that case, you probably want to see both windows open at the same time.

You can open a second window using any of these techniques:

- Choose File→New Finder Window (⌘-N).

- ⌘-double-click a disk or folder icon.

- Double-click a folder or disk icon on your desktop.

Tip: What folder contents fill the "new" window that appears when you use this command? Usually, it's your Home folder, the folder that contains your entire universe of files, folders, and settings.

But you can choose any window you want. To make the change, choose Finder→Preferences. Click the General icon. Change the "New Finder windows open" pop-up menu to whatever folder you'd like to use as the starting point for your computing life. Your Home folder is a good choice, but you're also free to choose your Documents folder, your iDisk, or any folder at all. Now every new Finder window shows you that specified folder, which is a much more useful arrangement.

- Press ⌘ as you make a selection from a window's title-bar menu (page 22).

- Choose Finder→Preferences and turn on "Always open folders in a new window." Now when double-clicked, *all* folders open into new windows. (This is the option for veteran Mac fans who don't care for the new behavior.)

- Switch to Old Finder Mode, described next.

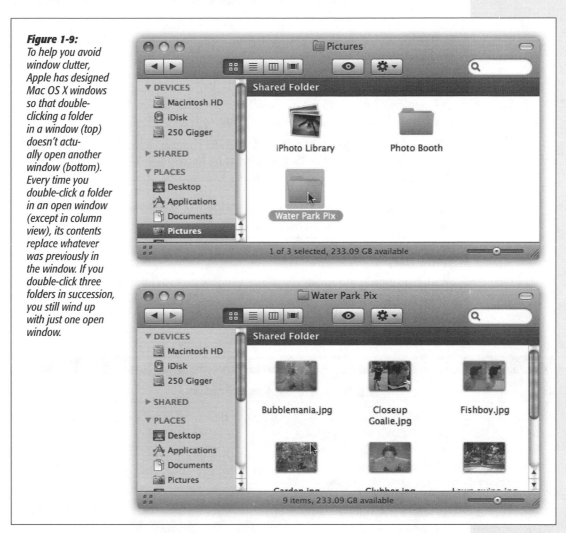

Figure 1-9:
To help you avoid window clutter, Apple has designed Mac OS X windows so that double-clicking a folder in a window (top) doesn't actually open another window (bottom). Every time you double-click a folder in an open window (except in column view), its contents replace whatever was previously in the window. If you double-click three folders in succession, you still wind up with just one open window.

Old Finder Mode: The Toolbar Disclosure Button

The upper-right corner of every Finder window contains a little button that looks like a half-inch squirt of Crest toothpaste. When you click it, you enter Old Finder Mode.

Tip: You can also turn Old Finder Mode on or off by pressing Option-⌘-T, the equivalent for the View→Hide Toolbar command.

"Old Finder Mode," of course, isn't the technical Apple term, but it should be. It was designed for people who come to Mac OS X from an earlier version of the Mac OS, like Mac OS 9, and lose half their hair when they discover how different things are in Mac OS X.

In this mode, two of the biggest behavioral differences between Mac OS X and its predecessor disappear:

- The Sidebar and the toolbar blink out of sight.

- Double-clicking a folder now works like it did back in 2000. Every time you double-click a folder, you open a new corresponding window.

When you've had enough of Old Finder Mode, you can return to regular Mac OS X mode either by clicking the Toolbar Disclosure button again, or by pressing Option-⌘-T again (that is, View→Show Toolbar).

Note: You'll find a little white toolbar-control nubbin in a number of toolbar-endowed programs, including Mail, Preview, and others. Clicking it always makes the toolbar go away.

Scroll Bars

Scroll bars appear automatically in any window that isn't big enough to show all its contents. Without scroll bars in word processors, for example, you'd never be able to write a letter that's taller than your screen. You can manipulate a scroll bar in three ways, as shown in Figure 1-10.

GEM IN THE ROUGH

Multiple Views, Same Folder

If you've read this section carefully, you may have discovered a peculiar quirk of the Mac OS X Finder: By choosing File→New Finder Window (or ⌘-double-clicking a disk or folder icon), you open a second, completely independent Finder window. If you stop to think about it, therefore, there's nothing to stop you from opening a third, fourth, or fifth copy of *the same folder window.* Once they're open, you can even switch them into different views.

Try this, for example: Choose Go→Applications. Choose File→New Finder Window (⌘-N), and then choose Go→Applications *again.* Using the View menu or the con-trols in the toolbar, put one of these windows into list view and the other into icon view.

This ability has its advantages. For example, you might decide to open the same window twice while doing some hard-drive housekeeping. By keeping a list view open, you can check the Size column as you move your files into different folders (so you can make sure the folders fit onto a blank CD, for example). By keeping a *column* view open, on the other hand, you gain quicker navigational access to the stuff on your drive.

Ordinarily, when you click in the scroll bar track above or below the gelatinous handle, the window scrolls by one screenful. But another option awaits when you choose ★→System Preferences→Appearance and turn on "Scroll to here." Now when you click in the scroll bar track, the Mac considers the entire scroll bar a proportional map of the document and jumps precisely to the spot you clicked. That is, if you click at the very bottom of the scroll bar track, you see the very last page.

Tip: No matter which scrolling option you choose in the Appearance panel, you can always override your decision on a case-by-case basis by Option-clicking in the scroll bar track. In other words, if you've selected the "Scroll to here" option, you can produce a "Jump to the next page" scroll by Option-clicking in the scroll bar track.

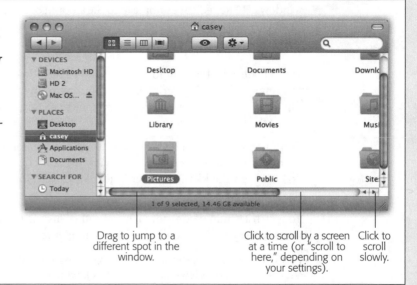

Figure 1-10:
Three ways to control a scroll. The scroll bar arrows (lower right) appear nestled together when you first install Mac OS X, as shown here. And what if you, an old-time Windows or Mac OS 9 fan, prefer these arrows to appear on opposite ends of the scroll bar? Visit the Appearance panel of System Preferences and, under "Place scroll arrows," choose "At top and bottom."

Tip: On a laptop, you can even scroll diagonally—by dragging with two fingers on the trackpad.

Drag to jump to a different spot in the window.

Click to scroll by a screen at a time (or "scroll to here," depending on your settings).

Click to scroll slowly.

It's worth noting, however, that the true speed expert eschews scroll bars altogether. Your Page Up and Page Down keys let you scroll up and down, one screen at a time, without having to take your hands off the keyboard to grab the mouse. The Home and End keys, meanwhile, are generally useful for jumping directly to the top or bottom of your document (or Finder window). And if you've bought a mouse that has a scroll wheel on the top, you can use it to scroll windows, too, without pressing any keys at all.

Resize Handle

The lower-right corner of every standard Mac OS X window is ribbed, a design that's meant to imply that you can grip it by dragging. Doing so lets you resize and reshape the window.

Path Bar

This little item appears when you choose View→Show Path Bar. It's a tiny map at the bottom of the window that shows where you are in the folder hierarchy. If it says Casey→Pictures→Picnic, well, then, by golly, you're looking at the contents of the Picnic folder, which is inside Pictures, which is inside your Home folder (assuming your name is Casey).

Tip: Each tiny folder icon in this display is fully operational. You can double-click it to open it, Control-click (right-click) it to open a shortcut menu, or even drag things into it.

Status Bar

The information strip at the bottom of a window tells you how many icons are in the window ("14 items," for example) and the amount of free space remaining on the disk.

The Four Window Views

You can view the files and folders in a desktop window in any of four ways: as icons; as a single, tidy list; in a series of neat columns; or in Cover Flow view, where you can flip through giant document icons like they're CDs in a music-store bin. Figure 1-11 shows the four different views.

Every window remembers its view settings independently. You might prefer to look over your Applications folder in list view (because it's crammed with files and folders) but view the Pictures folder in icon or Cover Flow view, where the larger icons serve as previews of the photos.

To switch a window from one view to another, just click one of the four corresponding icons in the window's toolbar, as shown in Figure 1-11.

You can also switch views by choosing View→as Icons (or View→as Columns, or View→as List, or View→as Cover Flow), which can be handy if you've hidden the toolbar. Or, for less mousing and more hard-bodied efficiency, press ⌘-1 for icon view, ⌘-2 for list view, ⌘-3 for column view, or ⌘-4 for Cover Flow view.

The following pages cover each of these views in greater detail.

GEM IN THE ROUGH

How Much Is That Doggie in the Window?

The status bar shows you disk-space information for the entire disk, but not how much disk space *this particular window's* contents occupy.

To find out *that* piece of information, make sure that no icon in the window is highlighted. Then choose File→Get Info (or press ⌘-I). The resulting Info window, which is described at the end of the next chapter, shows the size of the folder or disk whose window you're browsing, along with other useful statistics.

Note: One common thread in the following discussions is the availability of the View Options palette, which lets you set up the sorting, text size, icon size, and other features of each view, either one window at a time or for all windows.

Apple gives you a million different ways to open View Options. You can choose View→Show View Options, or press ⌘-J, or choose Show View Options from the ✿ menu at the top of every window.

Figure 1-11:
From the top: the same window in icon view, list view, column view, and Cover Flow view. Very full folders are best navigated in list or column views, but you may prefer to view emptier folders in icon or Cover Flow views, because larger icons are easier to preview and click. Remember that in any view (icon, list, column, or Cover Flow), you can highlight an icon by typing the first few letters of its name. In icon, list, or Cover Flow view, you can also press Tab to highlight the next icon (in alphabetical order), or Shift-Tab to highlight the previous one.

Icon View

In icon view, every file, folder, and disk is represented by a small picture—an *icon*. This humble image, a visual representation of electronic bits and bytes, is the cornerstone of the entire Macintosh religion. (Maybe that's why it's called an icon.)

Icon Size

Mac OS X draws those little icons using sophisticated graphics software. As a result, you can scale them to almost any size without losing any quality or clarity. And now, in Snow Leopard, doing so is almost pitifully easy.

That's because any icon-view window now sprouts a size slider, shown in Figure 1-12. Drag it to the right or left to make that window's icons larger or smaller. (For added fun, make little cartoon sounds with your mouth.)

Tip: Got a laptop? Then you can also make the icons larger or smaller by pinching or spreading two fingers on the trackpad, which may be quicker than fussing with the slider. Details on this feature (and the location of the on/off switch for it) are revealed on page 347.

Figure 1-12:
The new slider (bottom right) lets you choose an icon size to suit your personality. For picture folders, it can often be very handy to pick a jumbo size, in effect creating a slide-sorter "light table" effect. In Snow Leopard, icons can be four times as large as bdefore—an almost ridiculously large 512 pixels square.

Icon Previews

Snow Leopard expands the notion of "an icon is a representation of its contents" to an impressive extreme. As you can see in Figure 1-13, each icon actually looks like a miniature of the first page of the *real document*.

Because you can make icons so enormous, you can actually watch movies, or read PDF and text documents, *right on their icons*.

To check out this feature, make the icons at least about an inch tall (64 pixels square). A Play button (▶) appears on any movie or sound file; as shown in Figure 1-13, ◀ and ▶ page buttons appear on a multipage document (like PDF, Pages, or even presentation documents like PowerPoint and Keynote). You can actually page through one of these documents right there on its icon, without having to open the program!

Tip: If you Option-click the little ◀ and ▶ buttons on a PDF, PowerPoint, or Keynote icon preview, you jump to the first or last page or slide in the document.

Figure 1-13:
You can actually page through PDF and presentation icons, or play movies and sounds, right on their icons. During movie playback, you even get a circular progress bar around the play/stop button to let you know where you are in the movie.

THE HALF STEP.pdf

Kelly Balloons.mov

Icon View Options

Mac OS X offers a number of useful icon-view options, all of which are worth exploring. Start by opening any icon view window, and then choose View→Show View Options (⌘-J).

Always open in icon view

It's easy—almost scarily easy—to set up your preferred look for *all folder windows* on your entire system. With one click on the "Use as Defaults" button (described below), you can change the window view of 20,000 folders at once—to icon view, list view, or whatever you like.

The "Always open in icon view" option lets you *override* that master setting, just for *this* window.

For example, you might generally prefer a neat list view with large text. But for your Pictures folder, it probably makes more sense to set up icon view, so you can see a thumbnail of each photo without having to open it.

That's the idea here. Open Pictures, change it to icon view, and then turn on "Always open in icon view." Now every folder on your Mac is in list view *except* Pictures.

Note: The wording of this item in the View Options dialog box changes according to the view you're in at the moment. In a list-view window, for example, it says, "Always open in list view." In a Cover Flow–view window, it says, "Always open in Cover Flow." And so on. But the function is the same: to override the default (master) setting.

Icon size

As noted, Snow Leopard makes it super easy to make all your icons bigger or smaller; just drag the Icon size slider in the lower-right corner of the window.

But for the benefit of old-timers who expect to find that slider *here,* in the View Options window, well, there's an identical slider here.

Grid spacing

Listen up, you young whippersnappers! When I was your age, back when computers used Mac OS 9, you could control how closely spaced icons were in a window. Why, if I wanted to see a lot of them without making the window bigger, I could pack 'em in like sardines!

That feature disappeared—for seven years. But it finally returned to Mac OS X. Figure 1-14 shows all.

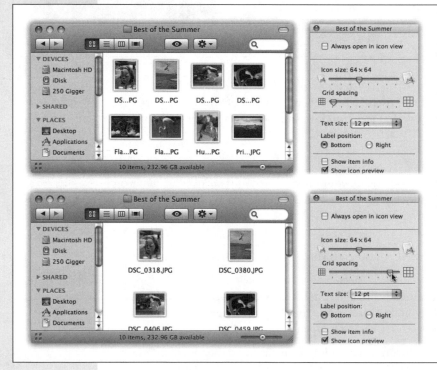

Figure 1-14:
Drag the "Grid spacing" slider to specify how tightly packed you want your icons to be. At the minimum setting (top), they're so crammed it's almost ridiculous; you can't even see their names. But sometimes, you don't really need to. At more spacious settings (bottom), you get a lot more "white space."

Text size

Your choices range only from 10 to 16 points, and you still can't choose a different font for your icons' names. But using this slider, you can adjust the type *size*. And for people with especially big or especially small screens—or for people with aging retinas—this feature is much better than nothing.

In fact, you can actually specify a different type size for *every window* on your machine. (Why would you want to adjust the point size independently in different windows? Well, because you might want smaller type to fit more into a crammed list view without scrolling, while you can afford larger type in less densely populated windows.)

Label position

Click either Bottom or Right to indicate where you want an icon's *name* to appear, relative to its *icon*. As shown in Figure 1-15, this option lets you create, in effect, a multiple-column list view in a single window.

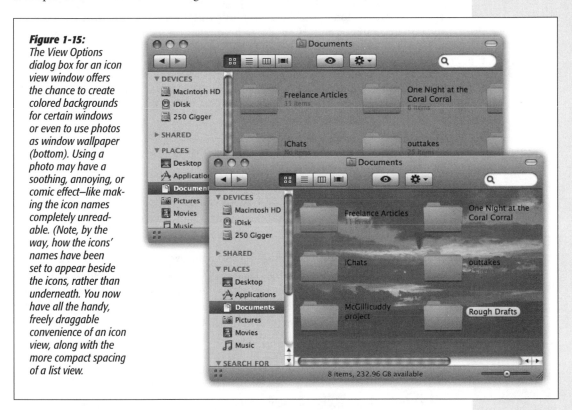

Figure 1-15:
The View Options dialog box for an icon view window offers the chance to create colored backgrounds for certain windows or even to use photos as window wallpaper (bottom). Using a photo may have a soothing, annoying, or comic effect—like making the icon names completely unreadable. (Note, by the way, how the icons' names have been set to appear beside the icons, rather than underneath. You now have all the handy, freely draggable convenience of an icon view, along with the more compact spacing of a list view.

Show item info

While you've got the View Options palette open, try turning on "Show item info." Suddenly you get a new line of information (in tiny blue type) for certain icons, saving you the effort of opening up the folder or file to find out what's in it. For example:

- **Folders.** The info line lets you know how many icons are inside each without having to open it up. Now you can spot empties at a glance.

- **Graphics files.** These display their dimensions in pixels.

- **Sounds and QuickTime movies.** The light-blue bonus line tells you how long the sound or movie takes to play. For example, an MP3 file might say "03:08"," which means 3 minutes, 8 seconds.

- **.zip files.** On compressed archives like .zip files, you get to see the archive's total size on disk (like "48.9 MB").

You can see some of these effects illustrated in Figure 1-12.

Show icon preview

This option is what makes icons display their contents, as shown in Figure 1-12 and 1-13. If you turn it off, then icons no longer look like miniature versions of their contents. Photos no longer look like tiny photos, PDF and Word documents no longer display their contents, and so on. Everything takes on identical, generic icons (one for all text documents, one for all JPEG photos, and so on).

You might prefer this arrangement when, for example, you want to be able to pick out all the PDF files in a window full of mixed document types. Thanks to the matching icons, it's easy now.

Arrange by

For a discussion of this pop-up menu, see the next section.

Background

Here's a luxury that other operating systems can only dream about: You can fill the background of any icon view window on your Mac with a certain color—or even a photo.

Color-coordinating or "wallpapering" certain windows is more than just a gimmick. In fact, it can serve as a timesaving visual cue. Once you've gotten used to the fact that your main Documents folder has a sky-blue background, you can pick it out like a sharpshooter from a screen filled with open windows. Color-coded Finder windows are also especially easy to distinguish at a glance when you've minimized them to the Dock.

Note: Background colors and pictures show up only in Icon view.

Once a window is open, choose View→View Options (⌘-J). The bottom of the resulting dialog box offers three choices, whose results are shown in Figure 1-15.

- **White.** This is the standard option.

- **Color.** When you click this button, you see a small rectangular button beside the word Color. Click it to open the Color Picker (page 199), which you can use to choose a new background color for the window. (Unless it's April Fool's Day, pick a light color. If you choose a dark one—like black—you won't be able to make out the lettering of the icons' names.)

- **Picture.** If you choose this option, a "Drag image here" square appears. Now find a graphics file—one of Apple's in the Desktop Pictures folder, or one of your own, whatever—and drag it into that "well." (Alternatively, double-click the empty square; an Open dialog box appears so you can navigate to a folder.)

When you click Select, you see that Mac OS X has superimposed the window's icons on the photo. As you can see in Figure 1-15, low-contrast or light-background photos work best for legibility.

Incidentally, the Mac has no idea what sizes and shapes your window may assume in its lifetime. Therefore, Mac OS X makes no attempt to scale down a selected photo to fit neatly into the window. If you have a high-res digital camera, therefore, you see only the upper-left corner of a photo in the window. For better results, use a graphics program to scale the picture down to something smaller than your screen resolution.

Use as Defaults

This harmless-looking button can actually wreak havoc on—or restore order to—your kingdom with a single click. It applies the changes you've just made in the View Options dialog box to *all* icon-view windows on your Mac (instead of only the *frontmost* window).

If you set up the frontmost window with a colored background, big icons, small text, and a tight grid, and then you click Use as Defaults, you'll see that look in *every* disk or folder window you open.

You've been warned.

Fortunately, there are two auxiliary controls that can give you a break from all the sameness.

First, you can set up individual windows to be weirdo exceptions to the rule; see "Always open in icon view" on page 35.

Second, you can *remove* any departures from the default window view—after a round of disappointing experimentation on a particular window, for example—using a secret button. To do so, choose View→Show View Options to open the View Options dialog box. Now hold down the Option key. The Use as Defaults button magically changes to say Restore to Defaults, which means "Abandon all the changes I've foolishly made to the look of this window."

Keeping Icons Neat and Sorted

In general, you can drag icons anywhere in a window. For example, some people like to keep current project icons at the top of the window and move older stuff to the bottom.

If you'd like Mac OS X to impose a little discipline on you, however, it's easy enough to request a visit from an electronic housekeeper who tidies up your icons by aligning them neatly to an invisible grid. You can even specify how tight or loose that grid is.

Grid alignment

Mac OS X offers an enormous number of variations on the "snap icons to the underlying rows-and-columns grid" theme:

- **Aligning individual icons to the grid.** Press the ⌘ key while dragging an icon or several highlighted icons. (Don't press the key until after you begin to drag.) When you release the mouse, the icons you've moved all jump into neatly aligned positions.

- **Aligning all icons to the grid.** Choose View→Clean Up (if nothing is selected) or View→Clean Up Selection (if some icons are highlighted). Now all icons in the window, or those you've selected, jump to the closest positions on the invisible underlying grid.

These same commands appear in the shortcut menu when you Control-click or right-click anywhere inside an icon-view window, which is handier if you have a huge monitor.

Tip: If you press Option, then the Mac swaps the wording of the command. Clean Up changes to read Clean Up Selection, and vice versa.

Note, by the way, that the grid alignment is only temporary. As soon as you drag icons around, or add more icons to the window, the newly moved icons wind up just as sloppily positioned as before you tidied up.

If you want the Mac to lock *all* icons to the closest spot on the grid *whenever* you move them, then choose View→Show View Options (⌘-J); from the "Arrange by" pop-up menu, choose Snap to Grid.

Even then, though, you'll soon discover that none of these grid-snapping techniques moves icons into the most compact possible arrangement. If one or two icons have wandered off from the herd to a far corner of the window, then they're merely nudged to the grid points closest to their current locations. They aren't moved all the way back to the group of icons elsewhere in the window.

To solve that problem, use one of the sorting options described next.

Tip: You can always override the grid setting by pressing the ⌘ key when you drag. In other words, when grid-snapping is turned off, ⌘ makes your icons snap into position; when grid-snapping is turned on, ⌘ lets you drag an icon freely.

Sorted alignment

If you'd rather have icons sorted and bunched together on the underlying grid—no strays allowed—then make a selection from the View menu:

- **Sorting all icons for the moment.** If you choose View→Arrange By→Name, all icons in the window snap to the invisible grid *and* sort themselves alphabetically. Use this method to place the icons as close as possible to one another within the window, rounding up any strays.

   The other subcommands in the View→Arrange By menu work similarly (Size, Date Modified, Label, and so on), but sort the icons according to different criteria. (Note that Snow Leopard offers keyboard shortcuts for these sorting commands.)

   As with the Clean Up command, View→Arrange By serves only to reorganize the icons in the window at this moment. If you move or add icons to the window, they won't be sorted properly. If you'd rather have all icons remain sorted *and* clustered, read on.

- **Sorting all icons permanently.** You can tell your Mac to maintain the sorting and alignment of all icons in the window, present *and* future. Now if you add more icons to the window, they jump into correct alphabetical position; if you remove icons, the remaining ones slide over to fill in the gaps. This setup is perfect for neat freaks.

   To make it happen, open the View menu, hold down the Option key, and choose from the Keep Arranged By submenu (choose Name, Date Modified, or whatever

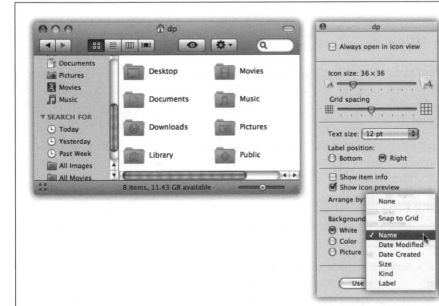

Figure 1-16:
Use either the View menu or the View Options window (right) to turn on permanent cleanliness mode. From now on, you're not allowed to drag these icons freely. You've told the Mac to keep them on the invisible grid, sorted the way you requested, so don't get frustrated when you try to drag an icon into a new position and then discover that it won't budge.

sorting criterion you like). As shown at left in Figure 1-16, your icons are now locked into sorted position, as compactly as the grid permits.

(This Option-key trick is a shortcut for choosing View→Show View Options and then, in the resulting dialog box, choosing from the "Arrange by" submenu.)

Tip: The Option key is up to its usual tricks here; as happens so often in the Finder, it means "reverse the usual logic."

For example, when you open the View menu, you see either Arrange By (which temporarily sorts the current batch of icons) or Keep Arranged By (which locks present and future icons into a sorted grid). The wording depends on whether or not you've already turned on permanent sorting.

But the point here is that pressing the Option key once the View menu is open changes the command—from Arrange By to Keep Arranged By, or vice versa.

Although it doesn't occur to most Mac fans, you can also apply any of the commands described in this section—Clean Up, Arrange, Keep Arranged—to icons lying loose on your *desktop*. Even though they don't seem to be in any window at all, you can specify small or large icons, automatic alphabetical arrangement, and so on. Just click the desktop before using the View menu or the View Options dialog box.

Note: There's only one View Options dialog box. Once it's open, you can adjust the icon sizes or arrangement options of other windows just by clicking them. Each time you click inside a window, the View Options dialog box remains in front, changing to reflect the settings of the window you just clicked.

Incidentally, you can get rid of the View Options box the same way you summoned it: by pressing ⌘-J.

List View

In windows that contain a lot of icons, the list view is a powerful weapon in the battle against chaos. It shows you a tidy table of your files' names, dates, sizes, and so on. Very faint alternating blue and white background stripes help you read across the columns.

You get to decide how wide your columns should be, which of them should appear, and in what order (except that Name is always the first column). Here's how to master these columns:

Sorting the List

Most of the world's list-view fans like their files listed alphabetically. It's occasionally useful, however, to view the newest files first, largest first, or whatever.

When a desktop window displays its icons in a list view, a convenient new strip of column headings appears (Figure 1-17). These column headings aren't just signposts; they're buttons, too. Click Name for alphabetical order, Date Modified to view the newest first, Size to view the largest files at the top, and so on.

It's especially important to note the tiny, dark-gray triangle that appears in the column you've most recently clicked. It shows you *which way* the list is being sorted.

When the triangle points upward, the oldest files, smallest files, or files beginning with numbers (or the letter A) appear at the top of the list, depending on which sorting criterion you have selected.

Tip: It may help you to remember that when the smallest portion of the triangle is at the top (▲), the smallest files are listed first when viewed in size order.

To reverse the sorting order, click the column heading a second time. Now the newest files, largest files, or files beginning with the letter Z appear at the top of the list. The tiny triangle turns upside-down.

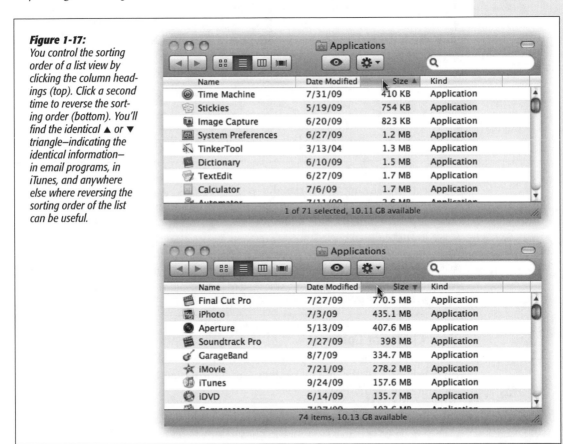

Figure 1-17:
You control the sorting order of a list view by clicking the column headings (top). Click a second time to reverse the sorting order (bottom). You'll find the identical ▲ or ▼ triangle—indicating the identical information—in email programs, in iTunes, and anywhere else where reversing the sorting order of the list can be useful.

Flippy Triangles

One of the Mac's most attractive features is the tiny triangle that appears to the left of a folder's name in a list view. In its official documents, Apple calls these buttons *disclosure triangles;* internally, the programmers call them *flippy triangles.*

When you click one, the list view turns into an outline, showing the contents of the folder in an indented list, as shown in Figure 1-18. Click the triangle again to collapse the folder listing. You're saved the trouble and clutter of opening a new window just to view the folder's contents.

Snow Leopard Spots: A subtle but nifty touch: When you've expanded a folder's flippy triangle, the tiny folder icon itself changes to look like an open folder. (Unless it's a "special" folder like Pictures, that is.)

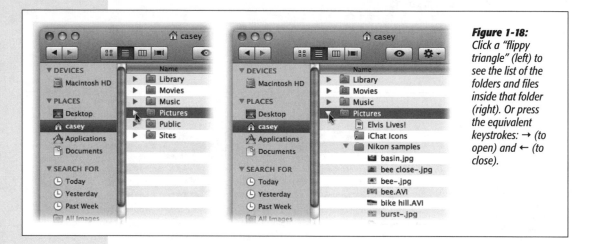

Figure 1-18:
Click a "flippy triangle" (left) to see the list of the folders and files inside that folder (right). Or press the equivalent keystrokes: → (to open) and ← (to close).

By selectively clicking flippy triangles, you can in effect peer inside two or more folders simultaneously, all within a single list view window. You can move files around by dragging them onto the tiny folder icons.

Tip: Once you've expanded a folder by clicking its flippy triangle, you can even drag a file icon out of its folder so that it's loose in the list view window. To do so, drag it directly upward onto the column headings area (where it says Name, for example). When you release the mouse, you see that the file is no longer inside the expanded folder.

Your Choice of Columns

Choose View→Show View Options. In the dialog box that appears, you're offered on/off checkboxes for the different columns of information Mac OS X can show you, as illustrated in Figure 1-19.

- **Date Modified.** This date-and-time stamp indicates when a document was last saved. Its accuracy, of course, depends on the accuracy of your Mac's built-in clock.

Note: Many an up-to-date file has been lost because someone spotted a very old date on a folder and assumed that the files inside were equally old. That's because the modification date shown for a folder doesn't reflect the age of its contents. Instead, the date on a folder indicates only when items were last moved into or out of that folder. The actual files inside may be much older, or much more recent.

- **Date Created.** This date-and-time stamp shows when a document was *first* saved.

- **Size.** With a glance, you can tell from this column how much disk space each of your files and folders is taking up in kilobytes, megabytes, or gigabytes—whichever the Mac thinks you'll find most helpful.

Figure 1-19:
The checkboxes you turn on in the View Options dialog box determine which columns of information appear in a list view window. Many people live full and satisfying lives with only the three default columns—Date Modified, Kind, and Size—turned on. But the other columns can be helpful in special circumstances; the trick is knowing what information appears there.

UP TO SPEED

Flippy Triangle Keystrokes

The keystrokes that let you open and close flippy triangles in a list view are worth committing to memory.

First, pressing the Option key when you click a flippy triangle lets you view a folder's contents *and* the contents of any folders inside it. The result, in other words, is a longer list that may involve several levels of indentation.

If you prefer to use the keyboard, then substitute → (to expand a selected folder's flippy triangle) or ← (to collapse the folder listing again). Here again, adding the Option key expands or collapses *all* levels of folders within the selected one.

Suppose, for example, that you want to find out how many files are in your Pictures folder. The trouble is, you've organized your graphics files within that folder in several category folders. And you realize that the "how many items" statistic in the status bar shows you how many icons are *visible* in

the window. In other words, you won't know your total photo count until you've expanded all the folders within the Pictures folder.

You could perform the entire routine from the keyboard like this: Get to your Home folder by pressing Shift-⌘-H. Select the Pictures folder by typing the letter P. Open it by pressing ⌘-O (the shortcut for File→Open) or ⌘-↑. Switch to list view, if necessary, with a quick ⌘-2. Highlight the entire contents by pressing ⌘-A (short for Edit→Select All).

Now that all folders are highlighted, press Option-→. You may have to wait a moment for the Mac to open every subfolder of every subfolder. But eventually, the massive list appears, complete with many levels of indentation. At last, the "items" statistic in the status bar gives you a complete, updated tally of how many files and folders, combined, are in the window.

Tip: For disks and folders, you see only a dash—at first. You can, however, instruct the Mac to reveal their sizes, as described on page 48.

- **Kind.** In this column, you can read what *kind* of file each icon represents. You may see, for example, Folder, JPEG Image, Application, and so on.

- **Version.** This column displays the version numbers of your programs. For folders and documents, you just see a dash.

- **Comments.** This rarely seen column can actually be among the most useful. Suppose you're a person who uses the Comments feature (highlight an icon, choose File→Get Info, type notes about that item into the Spotlight Comments box). The option to view the first line of comments about each icon can be very helpful, especially when tracking multiple versions of your documents, as shown in Figure 1-20.

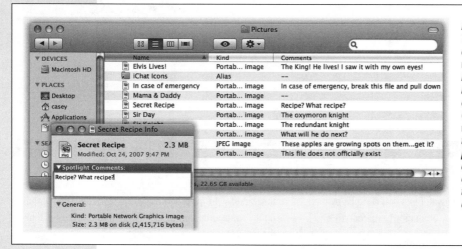

Figure 1-20:
The Comments column is often worth turning on. If your monitor is big enough, you can make the Comments column wide enough to show several paragraphs of text, all in a single line—enough to reveal the full life history of each icon.

- **Label.** Labels are colors and identifying phrases that you can slap onto icons, wherever they appear, to help you categorize and group them. For details, see page 82.

  Even with this column turned off, you can still see an icon's *color,* of course. But only by turning on this column do you get to see the *text phrase* you've associated with each label.

Other View Options

The View Options for a list view include several other useful settings; choose View→ Show View Options, or press ⌘-J.

- **Always open in list view.** Turn on this option to override your system-wide preference setting for all windows. See "Always open in icon view" on page 35 for details.

- **Icon size.** These two buttons offer you a choice of icon sizes for the current window: either standard or tiny. Unlike icon view, list view doesn't give you a size slider.

  Fortunately, even the tiny icons aren't so small that they show up blank. You still get a general idea of what they're supposed to look like.

- **Text size.** As described on page 37, you can change the type size for your icon labels, either globally or one window at a time.

- **Show columns.** Turn on the columns you'd like to appear in the current window's list view, as described in the previous section.

- **Use relative dates.** In a list view, the Date Modified and Date Created columns generally display information in a format like this: "Tuesday, March 9, 2010." (The Mac uses shorter date formats as the column gets narrower.) But when the "Use relative dates" option is turned on, the Mac substitutes the word "Yesterday" or "Today" where appropriate, making recent files easier to spot.

- **Calculate all sizes.** See the box on page 48.

- **Show icon preview.** Exactly as in icon view, this option turns the icons of graphics files into miniatures of the photos or images within.

- **Use as Defaults.** Click to make your changes in the View Options box apply to *all* windows on your Mac. (Option-click this button to restore a wayward window *back* to your defaults.)

Rearranging Columns

You're stuck with the Name column at the far left of a window. However, you can rearrange the other columns just by dragging their gray column headers horizontally. If the Mac thinks you intend to drop a column to, say, the left of the column it overlaps, you'll actually see an animated movement—indicating a column reshuffling—even before you release the mouse button.

Adjusting Column Widths

If you place your cursor carefully on the dividing line between two column headings, you'll find that you can drag the divider line horizontally. Doing so makes the column to the *left* of your cursor wider or narrower.

Best tip ever: If you double-click that little dividing line, the column to its left gets exactly wide enough to accommodate the longest bit of text within it. It's a quick way to make sure nothing gets truncated—while still keeping the column as narrow as possible.

What's delightful about this activity is watching Mac OS X scramble to rewrite its information to fit the space you give it. For example, as you make the Date Modified (or Created) column narrower, "Tuesday, March 9, 2010, 2:22 PM" shrinks first to "Tue, Mar 9, 2010, 2:22 PM," then to "3/9/10, 2:22 PM," and finally to a terse "3/9/10."

If you make a column too narrow, Mac OS X shortens the file names, dates, or whatever by removing text from the *middle*. An ellipsis (…) appears to show you where the missing text would have appeared. (Apple reasoned that truncating the *ends* of file names, as in some other operating systems, would hide useful information like the number at the end of "Letter to Marge 1," "Letter to Marge 2," and so on. It would also hide the three-letter *extensions*, such as Thesis.*doc*, that may appear on file names in Mac OS X.)

For example, suppose you've named a Word document "Ben Affleck—A Major Force for Humanization and Cure for Depression, Acne, and Migraine Headache." (Yes, file names can really be that long.) If the Name column is too narrow, you might see only "Ben Affleck—A Major…Migraine Headache."

Tip: You don't have to make the column mega-wide just to read the full text of a file whose name has been shortened. Just point to the icon's name without clicking. After a moment, a yellow, floating balloon appears—something like a tooltip in Microsoft programs—to identify the full name.

In fact, now you can move your mouse up or down a list over truncated file names; their tooltip balloons appear instantaneously. (This trick works in list, column, or Cover Flow views—and in Save and Open dialog boxes, for that matter.)

Calculate All Sizes

When I sort my list view by size, I see only dashes for folder sizes. What am I doing wrong?

Nothing at all; that's normal. When viewing a Finder window, you see a Size statistic for each file. For folders and disks, however, you're shown only an uninformative dash.

Most Mac fans study this anomaly only momentarily, scratch their chins, and then get back to their work. Former Windows people don't even scratch their chins; Windows PCs *never* show folder-size or disk-size information in list views.

Here's what's going on: It can take a computer a long time to add up the sizes of all files inside a folder. Your System→Library folder alone, for example, contains over 1,500 files. Instead of making you wait while the Mac does all the addition, Mac OS X simply shows you a dash in the folder's Size column.

On occasion, however, you really do want to see how big your folders are. In such cases, choose View→Show View Options and turn on "Calculate all sizes." You see the folder sizes slowly begin to pop onto the screen, from the top of the window down, as the Mac crunches the numbers on the files within.

In fact, you can even turn on the "Calculate all sizes" option *globally*—that is, for all windows. In the Mac operating systems of days gone by, this act would have caused a massive slowdown of the entire computer. But remember that Mac OS X is multithreaded; it has the opposite of a one-track mind. It's perfectly capable of devoting all its attention to calculating your folder sizes and all its attention to whatever work you're doing in the foreground.

Now consider this anomaly: Suppose you've opted to sort a particular window by folder size—in other words, you've clicked Size at the top of the column. Turning on "Calculate all sizes" bewilders the unprepared, as folders arbitrarily begin leaping out of order, forcing the list to rearrange itself a couple of times per second.

What's happening, of course, is that all folders begin at the bottom of the list, showing only dashes in the Size column. Then, as the Mac computes the size of your folders' contents, they jump into their correct sorted order at what may seem to be random intervals.

Column View

The goal of column view is simple: to let you burrow down through nested folders without leaving a trail of messy, overlapping windows in your wake.

The solution is shown in Figure 1-21. It's a list view that's divided into several vertical panes. The first pane (not counting the Sidebar) shows whatever disk or folder you first opened.

When you click a disk or folder in this list (once), the second pane shows a list of everything in it. Each time you click a folder in one pane, the pane to its right shows what's inside. The other panes slide to the left, sometimes out of view. (Use the horizontal scroll bar to bring them back.) You can keep clicking until you're actually looking at the file icons inside the most deeply nested folder.

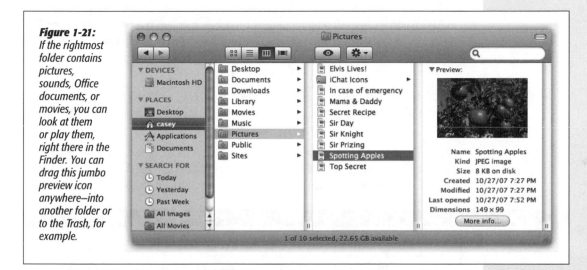

Figure 1-21:
If the rightmost folder contains pictures, sounds, Office documents, or movies, you can look at them or play them, right there in the Finder. You can drag this jumbo preview icon anywhere—into another folder or to the Trash, for example.

If you discover that your hunt for a particular file has taken you down a blind alley, it's not a big deal to backtrack, since the trail of folders you've followed to get here is still sitting before you on the screen. As soon as you click a different folder in one of the earlier panes, the panes to its right suddenly change, so that you can burrow down a different rabbit hole.

The beauty of column view is, first of all, that it keeps your screen tidy. It effectively shows you several simultaneous folder levels but contains them within a single window. With a quick ⌘-W, you can close the entire window, panes and all. Second, column view provides an excellent sense of where you are. Because your trail is visible at all times, it's much harder to get lost—wondering what folder you're in and how you got there—than in any other window view.

Snow Leopard Spots: You can change how Column view is sorted; it doesn't have to be alphabetical. Press ⌘-J to open the View Options dialog box, and then choose the sorting criterion you want from the "Arrange by" pop-up menu (like Size, Date Created, or Label).

Column View by Keyboard

Efficiency fans can operate this entire process by keyboard alone. For example:

- You can jump from one column to the next by pressing the ← or → keys. Each press highlights the first icon in the next or previous column.

- You can use any of the commands in the Go menu, or their keyboard equivalents, or the icons in the Sidebar, to fill your columns with the contents of the corresponding folder—Home, Applications, Pictures, and so on.

- The Back command (clicking the ◄ button on the toolbar, pressing ⌘-[, or choosing Go→Back) works as it does in a Web browser: It retraces your steps backward. You can repeat this command until you return to the column setup that first appeared when you switched to column view. Once you've gone back, in fact, you can then go forward again; choose Go→Forward, or press ⌘-].

- Within a highlighted column, press the ↑ or ↓ keys to highlight successive icons in the list. Or type the first couple of letters of an icon's name to jump directly to it.

- When you finally highlight the icon you've been looking for, press ⌘-O or ⌘-↓ to open it (or double-click it, of course). You can open anything in any column; you don't have to wait until you've reached the rightmost column.

POWER USERS' CLINIC

The Fine Points of the Column-View Triangle

This is really tweaky and geeky, but take a look: there's a tiny triangle (▸) to the right of every folder's name in column view. It can be either solid dark or hollow.

If you *click* a folder, that triangle is dark. But if you highlight a folder by typing a couple letters of its name, or by pressing the ↑ or ↓ keys, the triangle remains hollow. (At that point, pressing Tab makes it darken.)

Who cares? Well, it actually makes a difference here and there. When the triangle is dark,

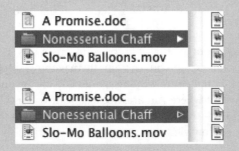

the Mac is trying to tell you that the *next column to the right* is actually selected. Pressing ⌘-A (Select All) at this point, for example, highlights all the icons in that *next* column. If you press the ↑ or ↓ keys, you walk up and down the list in that *next* column.

But when the triangle is hollow, you haven't left the *original* column. Pressing the arrow keys walks you up and down *this* list, and ⌘-A highlights everything in *this* list.

It's subtle. But cool.

Manipulating the Columns

The number of columns you can see without scrolling depends on the width of the window. In no other view are the zoom and resize controls so important.

That's not to say, however, that you're limited to four columns (or whatever fits on your monitor). You can make the columns wider or narrower—either individually or all at once—to suit the situation, according to this scheme:

- **To make a single column wider or narrower,** drag its right-side handle (circled in Figure 1-22).

Figure 1-22:
What you want to do most of the time is adjust one column. Adding the Option key as you drag the handle lets you adjust all columns at once.

- **To make *all* the columns wider or narrower simultaneously,** hold down the Option key as you drag that right-side handle.

- **To make a column precisely as wide as necessary** to reveal all the names of its contents, *double-click* a right-side handle.

- **To make *all* columns as wide as required**—when you absolutely, positively don't want any names truncated—*Option-double-click* a column's right-side handle.

View Options

Just as in icon and list view, you can choose View→Show View Options to open a dialog box—a Spartan one, in this case—offering additional control over your column views.

- **Always open in column view.** Once again, this option lets you override your system-wide preference setting for all windows. See "Always open in icon view" on page 35 for details.

- **Text size.** Whatever point size you choose here affects the type used for icons in *all* column views.

- **Show icons.** For maximum speed, turn off this option. Now you see only file names—not the tiny icons next to them—in all column views. Weird!

- **Show icon preview.** Turn off this option if you *don't* want the tiny icons in column view to display their actual contents—photos showing their images, Word and PDF documents showing their first pages, and so on. You get generic, identical icons for each file type (text, photo, or whatever).

- **Show preview column.** The far-right Preview column can be handy when you're browsing graphics, sounds, or movie files. Feel free to enlarge this final column when you want a better view of the picture or movie; you can make it *really* big.

  The rest of the time, though, the Preview column can get in the way, slightly slowing down the works and pushing other, more useful columns off to the left side of the window. If you turn off this checkbox, the Preview column doesn't appear.

Tip: No matter what view you're in, remember this if you ever start dragging an icon and then change your mind: Press the Esc key or ⌘-period, even while the mouse button is still down. The icon flies back to its precise starting place. (Too bad real life doesn't have a similar feature.)

Cover Flow View

Cover Flow is a visual display that Apple stole from its own iTunes software, where Cover Flow simulates the flipping "pages" of a jukebox, or the albums in a record-store bin (Figure 1-23). There, you can flip through your music collection, marveling as the CD covers flip over in 3-D space while you browse.

The idea is the same in Mac OS X, except that now it's not CD covers you're flipping; it's gigantic file and folder icons.

To fire up Cover Flow, open a window. Then click the Cover Flow button identified in Figure 1-23, choose View→as Cover Flow, or press ⌘-4.

NOSTALGIA CORNER

Everything Old Is New Again

To many observers, Mac OS X's column view was one of the most radical new features of the operating system. The truth, however, is that it's not new at all.

In fact, column view's most recent ancestor appeared in the NeXT operating system, which Apple bought (along with Steve Jobs, its CEO) in 1997. But column view is even older than that.

As you can see in this sketch from May 1980, the idea of a single-window, multiple-column view has been kicking around at Apple long before the Macintosh debuted.

In the end, this view was deemed too complex for the original Mac, which finally appeared (with only list and icon views) in 1984. It took 17 more years to find its way into the standard Mac OS.

Now the window splits. On the bottom: a traditional list view, complete with sortable columns, exactly as already described.

On the top: the gleaming, reflective, black Cover Flow display. Your primary interest here is the scroll bar. As you drag it left or right, you see your files and folders float by and flip in 3-D space. Fun for the whole family!

Figure 1-23:
The bottom half of a Cover Flow window is identical to list view. The top half, however, is an interactive, scrolling "CD bin" full of your own stuff. It's especially useful for photos, PDF files, Office documents, and text documents. And when a movie comes up in this virtual data jukebox, you can point to the little ▶ button and click it to play the video, right in place.

Cover Flow button

The effect is spectacular, sure. It's probably not something you'd want to set up for every folder, though, because browsing is a pretty inefficient way to find something. But in folders containing photos or movies (that aren't filled with hundreds of files), Cover Flow can be a handy and satisfying way to browse.

And now, notes on Cover Flow:

- **You can adjust the size of the Cover Flow display** (relative to the list-view half) by dragging up or down on the grip strip area just beneath the Cover Flow scroll bar.

- **Multipage documents, presentation files, movies, and sounds are special.** When you point to one, you get either the ▶ button (to play a movie or sound) or left/right arrow buttons (to flip through a PDF, Pages, PowerPoint, or Keynote document), exactly as you can with icons in Icon view (Figure 1-24).

- **You can navigate with the keyboard, too.** Any icon that's highlighted in the list view (bottom half of the window) is also front and center in the Cover Flow view. Therefore, you can use all the usual list-view shortcuts to navigate both at once. Use the ↑ and ↓ keys, type the first few letters of an icon's name, press Tab or Shift-Tab to highlight the next or previous icon alphabetically, and so on.

- **Cover Flow shows whatever the list view shows.** If you expand a flippy triangle to reveal an indented list of what's in a folder, then the contents of that folder become part of the Cover Flow.

- **The previews are actual icons.** When you're looking at a Cover Flow minidocument, you can drag it with your mouse—you've got the world's biggest target—anywhere you'd like to drag it: another folder, the Trash, whatever.

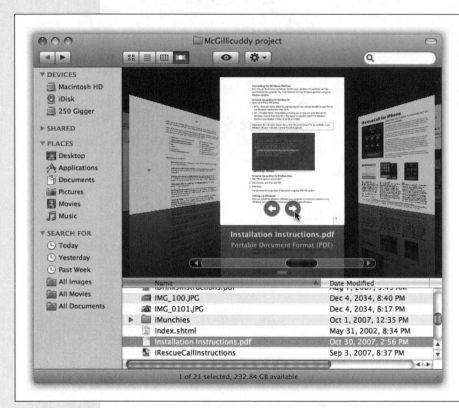

Figure 1-24:
When you point to a PDF file without clicking, you get special arrow buttons that let you turn pages.

Quick Look

As the preceding several thousand pages make clear, there are lots of ways to view and manage the seething mass of files and folders on a typical hard drive. Some of them actually let you see what's in a document without having to open it—the Preview column in column view, the giant icons in Cover Flow, and so on.

Quick Look takes this idea to another level. It lets you open and browse a document nearly at full size—without switching window views or opening any new programs. You highlight an icon (or several), and then do one of these things:

- **Press the space bar.** This is by far the best technique to learn. After all, unless you're editing a file's name, what's the space bar ever done for you in the Finder? Nothing. But in Mac OS X, you can highlight any icon and then tap the space bar for an instant preview.

- **Press ⌘-Y.** Another keystroke for the same function. The space bar is still better, though.

- Click the ◉ button at the top of the window. But who uses the mouse anymore?

- Choose File→Quick Look.

- Choose Quick Look from the Action menu (✿) at the top of every Finder window.

- Control-click (or right-click) an icon; from the shortcut menu, choose Quick Look.

You exit Quick Look in any one of these same ways.

Note: Whenever Quick Look appears in a menu or a shortcut menu, its wording changes to reflect the name of the icon. For example, it might say, "Quick Look 'Secret Diary.doc.' "

In any case, the Quick Look window now opens, showing a nearly full-size preview of the document (Figure 1-25). Rather nice, eh?

Figure 1-25:
Once the Quick Look window is open, you can play a file (movies and sounds), study it in more detail (most kinds of graphics files), or even read it (PDF, Word, and Excel documents). You can also click another icon, and another, and another, without ever closing the preview; the contents of the window simply change to reflect whatever you've just clicked.

Supertip: Quick Look even works on icons in the Trash, so you can figure out what something is before you nuke it forever.

Quick Look

Full Screen   Add to iPhoto

The idea here is that you can check out a document without having to wait for it to open in the traditional way—at full size. For example, you can read the fine text in a Word or PowerPoint document without actually having to *open* Word or PowerPoint, which saves you about 45 minutes.

What Quick Look Knows

You might wonder: How, exactly, is Quick Look able to display the contents of a document without opening it? Wouldn't it have to somehow understand the internal file format of that document type?

Exactly. And that's why Quick Look doesn't recognize *all* documents. If you try to preview, for example, a Final Cut Pro video project, a sheet-music file, a .zip archive, or a database file, all you'll see is a six-inch-tall version of its generic icon. You won't see what's inside.

Over time, people will write plug-ins for those nonrecognized programs. Already, plug-ins that let you see what's inside folders and .zip files await at *www.qlplugins.com*. In the meantime, here's what Quick Look recognizes right out of the box:

- **Graphics files and photos.** This is where Quick Look can really shine, because it's often useful to get a quick look at a photo without having to haul iPhoto or Photoshop out of bed. Quick Look recognizes all common graphics formats, including TIFF, JPEG, GIF, PNG, Raw, and Photoshop documents (except really huge Photoshop files).

- **PDF and text files.** Using the scroll bar, you can page through multipage documents, right there in the Quick Look window.

- **Audio and movie files.** These begin to play instantly when you open them into the Quick Look window. Most popular formats are recognized (MP3, AIFF, AAC, MPEG-4, H.264, and so on). A scroll bar appears so that you can jump around in the movie or song.

- **Pages, Numbers, Keynote, and ∂it documents.** Naturally, since these are Apple programs, Quick Look understands the document formats.

- **Saved Web pages from Safari.** That's a new one in Snow Leopard.

- **Microsoft Word, Excel, and PowerPoint documents.** Because these formats are so common, Mac OS X comes with a Quick Look plug-in to recognize them. Move through the pages using the vertical scroll bar; switch to a different Excel spreadsheet page using the Sheet tabs at the bottom.

- **Fonts.** Totally cool. When you open a font file in Quick Look, you get a crystal-clear, huge sampler that shows every letter of the alphabet in that typeface.

- **vCards.** A *vCard* is an address-book entry that people can send each other by email to save time in updating their Rolodexes. When you drag a name out of Apple's or Microsoft's address books and onto the desktop, for example, it turns into a vCard document. In Quick Look, the vCard opens up as a handsomely formatted index card that displays all the person's contact information.

- **HTML (Web pages).** If you've saved some Web pages to your hard drive, here's a great way to inspect them without firing up your Web browser.

Fun with Quick Look

Here are some stunts that make Quick Look even more interesting:

- **Zoom in or out.** Option-click the preview of a photo to magnify it; drag inside the zoomed-in image to scroll; Shift-Option-click to zoom back out. Or press Option as you turn your mouse's scroll wheel. (PDF documents have their own zoom in/ zoom out keystrokes: ⌘-plus and ⌘-minus.)

- **Full screen.** When you click the Full Screen arrows (identified in Figure 1-26), your screen goes black, and the Quick Look window expands to fill it. Keep this trick in mind when you're trying to read Word, Excel, or PDF documents, since the text is usually too small to read otherwise. (When you're finished with the closeup, click the Full Screen button again to restore the original Quick Look window, or the ⊗ button to exit Quick Look altogether.)

Tip: How's this for an undocumented shortcut?

If you Option-click the ◉ icon in any Finder window, or press Option-space bar, you go straight into Full Screen mode without having to open the smaller Quick Look window first. Kewl.

(OK, this is actually part of the slideshow feature described below, but it's also good for super-enlarging a single icon.)

- **Add to iPhoto.** This icon appears in the Quick Look windows of graphics files that you're examining. Click it to add the picture you're studying to your iPhoto photo collection.

- **Keep it going.** Once you've opened Quick Look for *one* icon, you don't have to close it before inspecting *another* icon. Just keep clicking different icons (or pressing the arrow keys to walk through them); the Quick Look window changes instantly with each click to reflect the new document.

The Quick Look Slideshow

Mac OS X is supposed to be all about graphics and other visual delights. No wonder, then, that it offers a built-in, full-screen slideshow feature.

It works like this: Highlight a *bunch* of icons, and then open Quick Look. The screen goes black, and the documents begin their slideshow. Each image appears on the screen for about 3 seconds before the next one appears. (Press the Esc key or ⌘-period to end the show.) It's like a slideshow, except that it plays *all* documents it recognizes, not just graphics.

Note: If you press the Option key as you start Quick Look—for example, as you hit the space bar, or as you click the Quick Look button—you get a full-screen version of that slideshow.

It's a useful feature when you've just downloaded or imported a bunch of photos or Office documents and want a quick look through them. Use the control bar shown in Figure 1-26 to manage the playback.

Note: This same slideshow mechanism is available for graphics in Preview and Mail; Preview even offers crossfades between pictures.

Figure 1-26:
Once the slideshow is underway, you can use this control bar. It lets you pause the slideshow, move forward or backward manually, enlarge the current "slide" to fill the screen, or end the show. (The iPhoto button appears only when displaying photos.) The Index view is especially handy. (You can press ⌘-Return to "click" the Index View button.) It displays an array of labeled miniatures, all at once—a sort of Exposé for Quick Look. Click a thumbnail to jump directly to the Quick Look document you want to inspect.

Previous Pause Next Index View Add to iPhoto Exit Full Screen Exit Quick Look

Logging Out, Shutting Down

If you're the only person who uses your Mac, finishing up a work session is simple. You can either turn off the machine or simply let it go to sleep, in any of several ways.

Sleep Mode

If you're still shutting down your Mac after each use, you may be doing a lot more waiting than necessary. Sleep mode consumes very little power, keeps everything you were doing open and available, and wakes up almost immediately when you press a key or click the mouse.

To make your machine sleep, do one of the following:

- **Close the lid.** (Hint: This tip works primarily on laptops.)

- **Choose** → **Sleep.** Or press Option-⌘-⏏.

- **Press Control-⏏** (or Control-F12, if you don't have a ⏏ key). In the dialog box shown in Figure 1-27, click Sleep (or type S).

- **Press the power button (⏻) on your machine.** On desktop models, doing so makes it sleep immediately; on laptops, you get the dialog box shown in Figure 1-27.

- **Hold down the Play/Pause button on your remote for 3 seconds.** Many Mac models come, or used to come, with Apple's tiny white remote control.

- **Just walk away,** confident that the Energy Saver setting described on page 334 will send the machine off to dreamland automatically at the specified time.

Restart

You shouldn't have to restart the Mac very often—only in times of severe trouble-shooting mystification, in fact. Here are a few ways to do it:

- **Choose →Restart.** A confirmation dialog box appears; click Restart (or press Return).

Tip: If you press Option as you release the mouse on the →Restart command, you won't be bothered by an "Are you sure?" confirmation box.

- **Press Control-⌘-⏏.** (If you don't have that key, substitute F12.)

- **Press Control-⏏** to summon the dialog box shown in Figure 1-27; click Restart (or type *R*).

Figure 1-27:
Once the Shut Down dialog box appears, you can press the S key instead of clicking Sleep, R for Restart, Esc for Cancel, or Return for Shut Down.

Are you sure you want to shut down your computer now?

Restart   Sleep   Cancel   Shut Down

Shut Down

To shut down your machine completely (when you don't plan to use it for more than a couple of days, when you plan to transport it, and so on), do one of the following:

- **Choose →Shut Down.** A simple confirmation dialog box appears; click Shut Down (or press Return).

Tip: Once again, if you press Option as you release the mouse, no confirmation box appears.

- **Press Control-Option-⌘-⏏.** (It's not as complex as it looks—the first three keys are all in a tidy row to the left of the space bar.)

- **Press Control-⏏ (or Control-F12)** to summon the dialog box shown in Figure 1-27. Click Shut Down (or press Return).

- **Wait.** If you've set up the Energy Saver preferences (page 334) to shut down the Mac automatically at a specified time, then you don't have to do anything.

Log Out

If you share your Mac, then you should *log out* when you're done. Doing so ensures that your stuff is safe from the evil and the clueless even when you're out of the room. To do it, choose →Log Out Chris (or whatever your name is). Or, if you're in a hurry, press Shift-⌘-Q.

When the confirmation dialog box appears, click Log Out (or press Return), or just wait for 2 minutes. The Mac hides your world from view and displays the Log In dialog box, ready for its next victim.

Tip: Last time: If you press Option as you release the mouse on the →Log Out command, you squelch the "Are you sure?" box.

Logging out is described in much more detail in Chapter 12.

Getting Help in Mac OS X

It's a good thing you've got a book about Mac OS X in your hands, because the only user manual you get with it is the Help menu. You get a Web browser–like program that reads a set of help files that reside in your System→Library folder.

You're expected to find the topic you want in one of these three ways:

- **Use the search box.** When you click the Help menu, a tiny search box appears just beneath your cursor (Figure 1-28). You can type a few words here to specify what you want help on: "setting up printer," "disk space," whatever.

Tip: You can also hit ⌘-Shift-/ (that is, ⌘-?) to open the help search box. And you can change that keystroke, if you like, in System Preferences→Keyboard.

After a moment or two, the menu becomes a list of Apple help topics pertaining to your search. Click one to open the Help browser described next; you've just saved some time and a couple of steps.

- **Drill down.** Alternatively, you can begin your quest for assistance the old-fashioned way: by opening the Help browser first. To do that, choose Help→Mac Help. (This works only in the Finder, and only when nothing is typed in the search box. To empty the search box, click the ⊗ button at the right end.)

After a moment, you arrive at the Help browser program shown in Figure 1-29. The starting screen offers several "quick click" topics that may interest you. If so, keep clicking text headings until you find a topic that you want to read.

You can backtrack by clicking the ◄ button at the top of the window. And you can always return to the starting screen by clicking the little Home icon at the top.

Tip: Annoyingly, the help window still insists on floating in front of all other windows; you can't send it to the back like any normal program. Therefore, consider making the window tall and skinny, so you can put it beside the program you're working in. Drag the ribbed lower-right corner to change the window's shape.

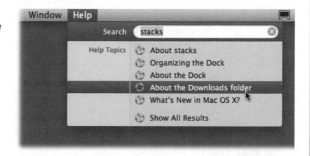

Figure 1-28:
You don't have to open the Help program to begin a search. No matter what program you're in, typing a search phrase into the box shown here produces an instantaneous list of help topics, ready to read.

GEM IN THE ROUGH

Menu Help in the Help Menu

Mac OS X contains a weird, wonderful little enhancement to its online help system. It helps you find menu commands you can't find.

You're floundering in some program. You're *sure* there's a page numbering command in those menus somewhere. But there are 11 menus and 143 submenus hiding in those menus, and you haven't got time for the pain.

That's when you should think of using the Help menu. When you type *page number* (or whatever) into its search box, the results menu lists, at the top, the names of any menu commands in that program that contain the words you typed. Better still, it actually *opens that menu* for you, and displays a big, blue, animated, floating arrow pointing to the command you wanted. You'd have to have your eyes closed to miss it.

Slide your cursor over, click the menu command, and get on with your life.

Supertip: This feature is especially helpful in Web browsers like Safari and Firefox, because it even finds entries in your Bookmarks and History menus!

In Safari, for example, you can pluck a recently visited site out of the hundreds in the daily History submenus, like the "Wednesday, January 9" submenu. You've just saved yourself a *lot* of poking around menus, trying to find the name of a site you know you've seen recently.

Ultratip: If you think about it, this feature also means that you have complete keyboard power over every menu in every program in the world. Hit ⌘-Shift-/ (⌘-?) to open the help search box, type a bit of the command's name, and then use the arrow keys to walk down the results. Hit Return to trigger the command you want.

• **Use the Search box.** Type the phrase you want, such as *printing* or *switching applications,* into the search box at the top of the window, and then press Return. The Mac responds by showing you a list of help-screen topics that may pertain to what you need; see Figure 1-29 for details.

This search box usually gives you a more complete list of results than you'd have gotten by using the search box in the Help *menu,* as described above.

Note: Actually, there's one more place where Help cropps up: in System Preferences dialog boxes. Click the blue, circled question-mark button in the lower-right corner of most System Preferences panels to open a help page that identifies each control.

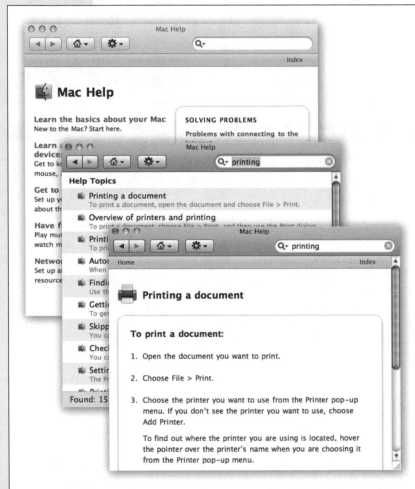

Figure 1-29:
The Mac OS X help system doesn't bunch together the help pages from every program on your Mac. When you're in the Finder, you get the general Macintosh help screens. When you're in iPhoto, you get only iPhoto help screens. And so on. But using the Home pop-up menu, you can switch to another program's help system even if that program isn't open.

Double-click a topic's name to open the help page. If it isn't as helpful as you hoped, click the ◀ button at the top to return to the list of relevant topics. Click the little Home button to return to the Help Center's welcome screen.

Organizing Your Stuff

The Mac OS X Folder Structure

For the first 20 years of the Mac's existence, you began your workday by double-clicking the Macintosh HD icon in the upper-right corner of the screen. That's where you kept your files.

These days, though, you'd be disappointed if you did that. All you'll find in the Macintosh HD window is a set of folders called Applications, Library, Users, and so on—folders *you* didn't put there.

Most of these folders aren't very useful to you, the Mac's human companion. They're there for Mac OS X's own use—which is why, in Snow Leopard, the Macintosh HD icon doesn't even appear on the screen. (At least not at first; you can choose Finder→Preferences and turn the "Hard disks" checkbox back on, if you really want to.) Think of your main hard drive window as storage for the operating system itself, which you'll access only for occasional administrative purposes.

Your Home Folder

So where is your nest of files, folders, and so on? All of it, everything of yours on this computer, lives in the *Home folder*. That's a folder bearing your name (or whatever name you typed in when you installed Mac OS X).

Mac OS X is rife with shortcuts for opening this all-important folder:

- Choose Go→Home, or press Shift-⌘-H.

- In the Sidebar (page 17), click the ⌂ icon.

• In the Dock, click the Home icon. (If you don't see one, consult page 133 for instructions on how to put one there.)

• Press ⌘-N, or choose File→New Finder Window. (If your Home folder doesn't open when you do that, see page 28.)

All these steps open your Home folder directly.

If you're the compulsive sort, you can also navigate to it the long way: Double-click the Users folder, and then double-click the folder inside it that bears your name and looks like a house (see Figure 2-1).

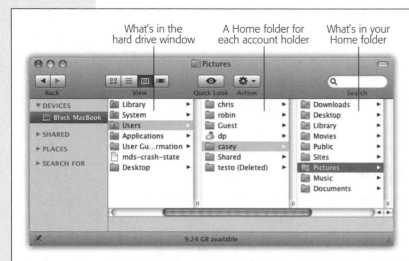

What's in the hard drive window

A Home folder for each account holder

What's in your Home folder

Figure 2-1:
This is it: the folder structure of Mac OS X. It's not so bad, really. For the most part, what you care about are the Applications folder in the main hard drive window and your own Home folder. You're welcome to save your documents and park your icons almost anywhere on your Mac (except inside the System folder or in other people's Home folders). But keeping your work in your Home folder makes backing up and file sharing easier.

So why has Apple demoted your files to a folder three levels deep? The answer may send you through the five stages of grief—Denial, Anger, Bargaining, Depression, and finally Acceptance—but if you're willing to go through it, much of the mystery surrounding Mac OS X will fade away.

Mac OS X has been designed from the ground up for *computer sharing*. It's ideal for any situation where different family members, students, or workers share the same Mac.

Each person who uses the computer will turn on the machine to find his own separate desktop picture, set of files, Web bookmarks, font collection, and preference settings. (You'll find much more about user accounts in Chapter 12.)

Like it or not, Mac OS X considers you one of these people. If you're the only one who uses this Mac, fine—simply ignore the sharing features. (You can also ignore all that business at the beginning of Chapter 1 about logging in.) But in its little software head, Mac OS X still considers you an account holder and stands ready to accommodate any others who should come along.

In any case, now you should see the importance of the Users folder in the main hard drive window. Inside are folders—the Home folders—named for the different people who use this Mac. In general, nobody is allowed to touch what's inside anybody else's folder.

If you're the sole proprietor of the machine, of course, there's only one Home folder in the Users folder—named for you. (The Shared folder doesn't count; it's described on page 488.)

This is only the first of many examples in which Mac OS X imposes a fairly rigid folder structure. Still, the approach has its advantages. By keeping such tight control over which files go where, Mac OS X keeps itself pure—and very, very stable. Other operating systems known for their stability, including Windows XP, Windows Vista, and Windows 7, work the same way.

Furthermore, keeping all your stuff in a single folder makes it very easy for you to back up your work. It also makes life easier when you try to connect to your machine from elsewhere in the office (over the network) or elsewhere in the world (over the Internet), as described in Chapter 22.

What's on Your Hard Drive

If you *did* want to explore the entirety of Mac OS X, to examine the contents of your hard drive (choose Go→Computer and double-click "Macintosh HD"), you'd find the following folders in the main hard drive window:

- **Applications.** The Applications folder, of course, contains the complete collection of Mac OS X programs on your Mac (not counting the invisible Unix ones). Even

---

UP TO SPEED

The Computer Window

In your explorations of the Finder's Go menu, you may have wondered about the command called Computer (Shift-⌘-C). ("Go to Computer? Jeez, I thought I was already *at* my computer!")

As in Microsoft Windows, the Computer window holds the icons for all the disks connected to your machine—the hard drive, a CD that you've inserted, an iPod, another external hard drive, and so on—as well as an icon called Network. (The Network icon appears even if you're not, in fact, on a network.) This is the topmost level of your Mac. This is the stuff that can't be put into any folder at all.

So what's it for? In some ways, the Computer window is redundant. After all, Mac OS X displays your disk icons on the desktop *and* in the Sidebar.

But some people, particularly Windows refugees, don't care for that icons-on-the-desktop feature. In the interest of creating a neater, cleaner desktop, they turn it off (by choosing Finder→Preferences and turning off the three checkboxes under "Show these items on the Desktop"). Furthermore, in the interest of creating neater, narrower windows, some people also *hide* the Sidebar.

In that case, the Computer window still provides access to all your disks.

Otherwise, the Computer window really doesn't serve much purpose except as a familiar landmark to Windows veterans and Mac fans who grew used to it in the era before the Sidebar came along.

CHAPTER 2: ORGANIZING YOUR STUFF

so, you'll rarely launch programs by opening this folder; the Dock is a far more efficient launcher, as described in Chapter 4.

- **Desktop.** This folder stores icons that appear on the Mac OS X desktop. The difference is that you don't control this one; Apple does. Anything in here also appears on your desktop. (This Apple-controlled one is usually empty.)

- **Library.** This folder bears more than a passing resemblance to the System Folder subfolders of Macs gone by, or the Windows folder on PCs. It stores components for the operating system and your programs (sounds, fonts, preferences, help files, printer drivers, modem scripts, and so on).

- **System.** This is Unix, baby. These are the actual files that turn on your Mac and control its operations. You'll rarely have any business messing with this folder, which is why Apple made almost all of its contents invisible.

- **User Guides And Information.** Here's a link to a folder that contains random Getting Started guides from Apple, including a Welcome to Snow Leopard booklet.

- **Users.** As noted earlier, this folder stores the Home folders for everyone who uses this machine.

- **Your old junk.** If you upgraded your Mac from an earlier Mac operating system, then your main hard drive window also lists whatever folders you kept there.

What's in Your Home Folder

Within the folder that bears your name, you'll find another set of standard Mac folders. (You can tell the Mac considers them holy because they have special logos on their folder icons.) Except as noted, you're free to rename or delete them; Mac OS X creates the following folders solely as a convenience:

UP TO SPEED

The Wacky Keystrokes of Snow Leopard

Mac OS X offers a glorious assortment of predefined keystrokes for jumping to the most important locations on your Mac: your Home folder, the Applications folder, the Utilities folder, the Computer window, your iDisk, the Network window, and so on.

Better yet, the keystrokes are incredibly simple to memorize: Just press Shift-⌘ and the first letter of the location you want. Shift-⌘-H opens your Home folder, Shift-⌘-A opens the Applications folder, and so on. You learn one, you've learned 'em all.

The point here is that Shift-⌘, in Snow Leopard, means *places*.

The other system-wide key combo, Option-⌘, means *functions*. For example, Option-⌘-D hides or shows the Dock, Option-⌘-H is the Hide Others command, Option-⌘-+ magnifies the screen (if you've turned on this feature), Option-⌘-Esc brings up the Force Quit dialog box, and so on. Consistency is always nice.

- **Desktop.** When you drag an icon out of a folder or disk window and onto your Mac OS X desktop, it may *appear* to show up on the desktop. But that's just an optical illusion, a visual convenience. In truth, nothing in Mac OS X is really on the desktop. It's actually in this Desktop folder, and mirrored on the desktop area.

The reason is simple enough: Everyone who shares your machine will, upon logging in, see his own stuff sitting on the desktop. Now you know how Mac OS X does it: There's a separate Desktop folder in every person's Home folder.

Tip: The fact that the desktop is actually a folder is handy, because it gives you a sneaky way to jump to your Home folder from anywhere. Simply click the desktop background and then press ⌘-↓ (which is the keystroke for Go→Enclosing Folder; pay no attention to the fact that the command is dimmed at the moment). Because that keystroke means "open whatever folder contains the one I'm examining," it instantly opens your Home folder. (Your Home folder is, of course, the "parent" of your Desktop folder.)

- **Documents.** Apple suggests that you keep your actual work files in this folder. Sure enough, whenever you save a new document (when you're working in Keynote or Word, for example), the Save As box proposes storing the new file in this folder, as described in Chapter 5.

  Your programs may also create folders of their own here. For example, you may find a Microsoft User Data folder for your Entourage email, a Windows folder for use with Parallels or VMWare Fusion (Chapter 8), and so on.

- **Library.** As noted earlier, the *main* Library folder (the one in your main hard drive window) contains folders for fonts, preferences, help files, and so on.

  You have your own Library folder, too, right there in your Home folder. It stores the same kinds of things—but they're *your* fonts, *your* preferences.

  Once again, this setup may seem redundant if you're the only person who uses your Mac. But it makes perfect sense in the context of families, schools, or offices where numerous people share a single machine. Because you have your own Library folder, you can have a font collection that's "installed" on the Mac only when *you're* using it. Each person's program preference files are stored independently, too (the files that determine where Photoshop's palettes appear, and so on). And each person, of course, sees his own email when launching Mac OS X's Mail program (Chapter 19)—because mail, too, is generally stored in the personal Library folder.

  Other Library folders store your Favorites, Web browser plug-ins and cached Web pages, keyboard layouts, sound files, and so on. (It's best not to move or rename Library folders.)

- **Movies, Music, Pictures.** The various Mac OS X programs that deal with movies, music, and pictures will propose these specialized folders as storage locations. For example, when you plug a digital camera into a Mac, the iPhoto program automatically begins to download the photos on it—and stores them in the Pictures folder. Similarly, iMovie is programmed to look for the Movies folder when saving its files, and iTunes stores its MP3 files in the Music folder.

- **Public.** If you're on a network, or if others use the same Mac when you're not around, this folder can be handy: It's the "Any of you guys can look at these files"

---

folder. Other people on your network, as well as other people who sit down at this machine, are allowed to see whatever you've put in here, even if they don't have your password. (If your Mac isn't on an office network and isn't shared, you can throw away this folder.) Details on sharing the Mac are in Chapter 12, and those on networking are in Chapter 13.

- **Sites.** Mac OS X has a built-in *Web server,* software that turns your Mac into a Web site that people on your network—or, via the Internet, all over the world—can connect to. This Mac OS X feature relies on a program called the Apache Web server, which is so highly regarded in the Unix community that programmers lower their voices when they mention it.

  Details of the Web server are in Chapter 22. For now, though, note that this is the folder where you will put the actual Web pages you want to make available to the Internet at large.

Icon Names

Every document, program, folder, and disk on your Mac is represented by an *icon:* a colorful little picture that you can move, copy, or double-click to open. In Mac OS X, icons look more like photos than cartoons, and you can scale them to practically any size.

A Mac OS X icon's name can have up to 255 letters and spaces. If you're accustomed to the 31-character or even eight-character limits of older computers, that's quite a luxurious ceiling.

If you're used to Windows, you may be delighted to discover that in Mac OS X, you can name your files using letters, numbers, punctuation—in fact, any symbol except the colon (:), which the Mac uses behind the scenes for its own folder-hierarchy designation purposes. And you can't use a period to *begin* a file's name.

FREQUENTLY ASKED QUESTION

Printing a Window—or a List of Files

In Mac OS 9, I could print a Finder window. I'd get a neat list of the files, which I could use as a label for a CD I was going to burn, or whatever. How do I print a Finder window in Mac OS X? (The File→Print command prints a selected document, not the list of files in a window.)

It's easy enough to make a list of files for printing. Once the window is open on your screen, choose Edit→Select All. Choose Edit→Copy. Now switch to a word processor and paste. (If you're using TextEdit, use Edit→Paste and Match Style instead.) You get a tidy list of all the files in that window, ready to format and print.

This simple file name list isn't the same as printing a window; you don't get the status bar showing how many items are on the disk and how full the disk is. For that purpose, you can always make a screenshot of the window (page 575) and print that. Of course, that technique's no good if the list of files is taller than the window itself.

Really, what you want is Print Window, a handy shareware program dedicated to printing out your Finder windows, without these workarounds and limitations. You can download it from this book's "Missing CD" page at *www. missingmanuals.com.*

To rename a file, click its name or icon (to highlight it) and then press Return. (Or, if you have time to kill, click once on the name, wait a moment, and then click a second time.)

In any case, a rectangle appears around the name (Figure 2-2). At this point, the existing name is highlighted; just begin typing to replace it. If you type a very long name, the rectangle grows vertically to accommodate new lines of text.

Tip: If you simply want to add letters to the beginning or end of the file's existing name, press the ← or → key immediately after pressing Return. The insertion point jumps to the beginning or end of the file name.

You can give more than one file or folder the same name, as long as they're not in the same folder. For example, you can have as many files named "Chocolate Cake Recipe"

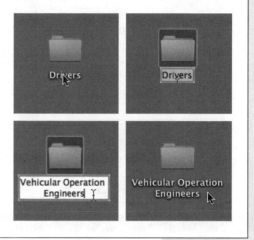

Figure 2-2:
Click an icon's name (top left) to produce the renaming rectangle (top right), in which you can edit the file's name. Snow Leopard is kind enough to highlight only the existing name, and not the suffix (like .jpg or .doc).

Now begin typing to replace the existing name (bottom left). When you're finished typing, press Return, Enter, or Tab to seal the deal, or just click somewhere else.

as you like, provided each is in a different folder. And, of course, files called Recipe. doc and Recipe.xls can coexist in a folder, too.

As you edit a file's name, remember that you can use the Cut, Copy, and Paste commands in the Edit menu to move selected bits of text around, just as though you were word processing. The Paste command can be useful when, for instance, you're renaming many icons in sequence (*Quarterly Estimate 1, Quarterly Estimate 2…*).

And now, a few tips about renaming icons:

- When the Finder sorts files, a space is considered alphabetically *before* the letter A. To force a particular file or folder to appear at the top of a list view window, insert a space (or an underscore) before its name.

- Older operating systems sort files so that 10 and 100 come before 2, the numbers 30 and 300 come before 4, and so on. You wind up with alphabetically sorted files like this: "1. Big Day," "10. Long Song," "2. Floppy Hat," "20. Dog Bone," "3. Weird

Sort," and so on. Generations of computer users have learned to put zeros in front of their single-digit numbers just to make the sorting look right.

In Mac OS X, though, you get exactly the numerical list you'd hope for: "1. Big Day," "2. Floppy Hat," "3. Weird Sort," "10. Long Song," and "20. Dog Bone."

- In addition to letters and numbers, Mac OS X also assigns punctuation marks an "alphabetical order," which is this: ` (the accent mark above the Tab key), ^, _, -, space, –, —, comma, semicolon, !, ?, ', ", (,), [,], {, }, @, *, /, &, #, %, +, <, =, ≠, >, |, ~, and $.

Numbers come after punctuation; letters come next; and bringing up the rear are these characters: μ (Option-M); π (Option-P); Ω (Option-Z), and (Shift-Option-K).

- When it comes time to rename files en masse, add-on shareware can help you. A Better Finder Rename, for example, lets you manipulate file names in a batch—numbering them, correcting a spelling in dozens of files at once, deleting a certain phrase from their names, and so on. You can download this shareware from this book's "Missing CD" page at *www.missingmanuals.com*.

Selecting Icons

To highlight a single icon in preparation for printing, opening, duplicating, or deleting, click the icon once. (In a list or column view, as described in Chapter 1, you can also click on any visible piece of information about that file—its size, kind, date modified, and so on.) Both the icon and the name darken in a uniquely Snow Leopardish way.

Long and Short File Names

Hey, what's the deal with long file names? I thought this was the big deal in Mac OS X! But I tried saving a Word 2004 document, and it didn't let me use more than 31 letters!

It's true that you can assign a very long name to a file in the Finder. But you may soon discover that some pre–Mac OS X programs, and even programs that have been rewritten (*Carbonized*) to run in Mac OS X, still limit you to 31 characters when naming a new document in the Save As dialog box.

Over time, software companies may get with the program and rejigger their software to overcome this glitch. For now, though, all is not lost.

Even though you can use only 31 characters when saving a new document from, say, AppleWorks or older versions of Word, you're welcome to rename the file in the Finder, using all 255 characters Mac OS X permits. When you reopen the document in the original program, you'll see an abbreviated name in the title bar. (A file that, on the desktop, is called *My Visit to Bill Gates's House and Why I'll Take the Apple Bumper Sticker Off My Car Next Time* opens into AppleWorks as something like *My Visit to Bill Gates's H…*)

The good news is that, behind the scenes, Mac OS X still remembers its long name. Even if you edit and resave the document, you'll still find its long file name intact when you view its icon on the desktop.

Tip: You can change the color of the oval highlighting that appears around the name of a selected icon. Choose ⬤→System Preferences, click Appearance, and use the Highlight Color pop-up menu.

That much may seem obvious. But most first-time Mac users have no idea how to manipulate *more* than one icon at a time—an essential survival skill in a graphic interface like the Mac's.

Figure 2-3:
You can highlight several icons simultaneously by dragging a box around them. To do so, drag from outside the target icons diagonally across them (right), creating a translucent gray rectangle as you go. Any icons or icon names touched by this rectangle are selected when you release the mouse. If you press the Shift or ⌘ key as you do this, then any previously highlighted icons remain selected.

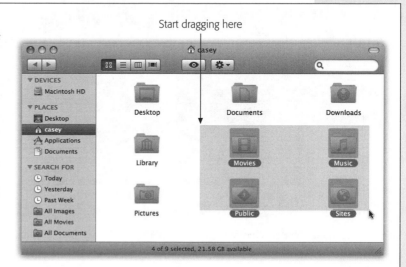

Start dragging here

Selecting by Clicking

To highlight multiple files in preparation for moving or copying, use one of these techniques:

- **To highlight all the icons.** To select all the icons in a window, press ⌘-A (the equivalent of the Edit→Select All command).

- **To highlight several icons by dragging.** You can drag diagonally to highlight a group of nearby icons, as shown in Figure 2-3. In a list view, in fact, you don't even have to drag over the icons themselves—your cursor can touch any part of any file's row, like its modification date or file size.

Tip: If you include a particular icon in your diagonally dragged group by mistake, ⌘-click it to remove it from the selected cluster.

- **To highlight consecutive icons in a list.** If you're looking at the contents of a window in list view or column view, you can drag vertically over the file and folder names to highlight a group of consecutive icons, as described above. (Begin the drag in a blank spot.)

There's a faster way to do the same thing: Click the first icon you want to highlight, and then Shift-click the last file. All the files in between are automatically selected, along with the two icons you clicked. Figure 2-4 illustrates the idea.

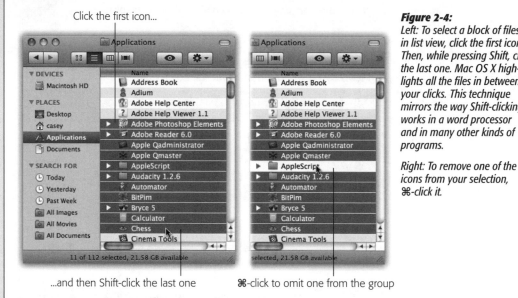

Click the first icon...

...and then Shift-click the last one   ⌘-click to omit one from the group

Figure 2-4:
Left: To select a block of files in list view, click the first icon. Then, while pressing Shift, click the last one. Mac OS X highlights all the files in between your clicks. This technique mirrors the way Shift-clicking works in a word processor and in many other kinds of programs.

Right: To remove one of the icons from your selection, ⌘-click it.

- **To highlight random icons.** If you want to highlight only the first, third, and seventh icons in a window, for example, start by clicking icon No. 1. Then ⌘-click each of the others (or ⌘-drag new rectangles around them). Each icon darkens to show that you've selected it.

If you're highlighting a long string of icons and click one by mistake, you don't have to start over. Instead, just ⌘-click it again so the dark highlighting disappears. (If you do want to start over, you can deselect all selected icons by clicking any empty part of the window—or by pressing the Esc key.) The ⌘ key trick is especially handy if you want to select almost all the icons in a window. Press ⌘-A to select everything in the folder, then ⌘-click any unwanted icons to deselect them.

Tip: In icon view, you can either Shift-click *or* ⌘-click to select multiple individual icons. But you may as well just learn to use the ⌘ key when selecting individual icons. That way you won't have to use a different key in each view.

Once you've highlighted multiple icons, you can manipulate them all at once. For example, you can drag them en masse to another folder or disk by dragging any *one* of the highlighted icons. All other highlighted icons go along for the ride. This technique is especially useful when you want to back up a bunch of files by dragging them onto a different disk, delete them all by dragging them to the Trash, and so on.

When multiple icons are selected, the commands in the File and Edit menus—like Duplicate, Open, and Make Alias—apply to all of them simultaneously.

Tip: Don't forget that you can instantly highlight all the files in a window (or on the desktop) by choosing Edit→Select All (⌘-A)—no icon-clicking required.

Selecting Icons from the Keyboard

For the speed fanatic, using the mouse to click an icon is a hopeless waste of time. Fortunately, you can also select an icon by typing the first few letters of its name.

When looking at your Home window, for example, you can type *M* to highlight the Movies folder. And if you actually intended to highlight the Music folder instead, then press the Tab key to highlight the next icon in the window alphabetically. Shift-Tab highlights the previous icon alphabetically. Or use the arrow keys to highlight a neighboring icon.

GEM IN THE ROUGH

Shortcut Menus, Action Menus

It's part of the Mac's user-friendly heritage: You can do practically everything using only the mouse. Everything is out front, unhidden, and clickable, whether it's an icon, button, or menu.

But as in rival operating systems, you can shave seconds and steps off your workload if you master *shortcut menus:* short menus that appear right on things you click and offer commands that the software thinks you might want to invoke at the moment, as shown here at top.

(They used to be called contextual menus, but Apple started calling them "shortcut menus" a few years ago, perhaps because that's what they're called in Windows and Unix.)

To summon one, just right-click or Control-click something—an icon, the desktop, a window, a link in Safari, text in a word processor, whatever. (If you have a laptop, see page 347 for additional options.) A menu drops down listing relevant com-

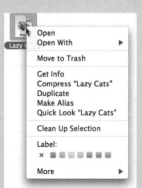

mands: Get Info, Move to Trash, Copy, and so on. You can either click the command you want or type the first couple of letters of it and then tap the space bar.

These menus become more useful the more you get to know them. The trouble is, millions of Mac fans never even knew they existed.

That's why there's a second way to access them. At the top of every Finder window, you'll find a ✿ pop-up menu that's technically called the *Action menu* (shown here at bottom).

It lists the same sorts of commands you'd find in the shortcut menus, but it offers two advantages. First, it's *visible,* so novices stand a better chance of stumbling onto it. Second, you don't need two hands to open it (one on the Control key, one on the mouse)—a distinct perk for anyone whose nondominant hand is already occupied with a refreshing beverage.

(The Tab-key trick works only in icon, list, and Cover Flow views—not column view, alas. You can always use the ← and → keys to highlight adjacent columns, however.)

After highlighting an icon this way, you can manipulate it using the commands in the File menu or their keyboard equivalents: Open (⌘-O), put it into the Trash (⌘-Delete), Get Info (⌘-I), Duplicate (⌘-D), or make an alias (⌘-L), as described later in this chapter. By turning on the special disability features described on page 351, you can even *move* the highlighted icon using only the keyboard.

If you're a first-time Mac user, you may find it excessively nerdy to memorize keystrokes for functions that the mouse performs perfectly well. If you make your living using the Mac, however, memorizing these keystrokes will reward you immeasurably with speed and efficiency.

Moving and Copying Icons

In Mac OS X, there are two ways to move or copy icons from one place to another: by dragging them and by using the Copy and Paste commands.

Copying by Dragging

You can drag icons from one folder to another, from one drive to another, from a drive to a folder on another drive, and so on. (When you've selected several icons, drag any *one* of them; the others tag along.) While the Mac is copying, you can tell that the process is under way even if the progress bar is hidden behind a window, because the icon of the copied material shows up *dimmed* in its new home, darkening only when the copying process is over. (You can also tell because Snow Leopard's progress box is a lot clearer and prettier than it used to be.) You can cancel the process by pressing either ⌘-period or the Esc key.

Tip: If you're copying files into a disk or folder that already contains items with the same names, Mac OS X asks you individually about each one. ("An older item named 'Fiddlesticks' with extension '.doc' already exists in this location.") Note that, thank heaven, Mac OS X tells you whether the version you're replacing is *older* or *newer* than the one you're moving.

Turn on "Apply to all" if all the incoming icons should (or should not) replace the old ones of the same names. Then click Replace or Don't Replace, as you see fit—or Stop to halt the whole copying business.

Understanding when the Mac *copies* a dragged icon and when it *moves* it bewilders many a beginner. However, the scheme is fairly simple (see Figure 2-5) when you consider the following:

• Dragging from one folder to another on the same disk *moves* the icon.

• Dragging from one disk (or disk partition) to another *copies* the folder or file. (You can drag icons either into an open window or directly onto a disk or folder icon.)

- If you press the Option key as you release an icon you've dragged, you *copy* the icon instead of moving it. Doing so within a single folder produces a duplicate of the file called "[Whatever its name was] copy."

- If you press the ⌘ key as you release an icon you've dragged from one disk to another, you *move* the file or folder, in the process deleting it from the original disk.

Tip: This business of pressing Option or ⌘ ***after*** you begin dragging is a tad awkward, but it has its charms. For example, it means you can change your mind about the purpose of your drag in mid-movement, without having to drag back and start over.

And if it turns out you just dragged something into the wrong window or folder, a quick ⌘-Z (the shortcut for Edit→Undo) puts it right back where it came from.

Copying by Using Copy and Paste

Dragging icons to copy or move them probably feels good because it's so direct: You actually see your arrow cursor pushing the icons into the new location.

But you pay a price for this satisfying illusion. You may have to spend a moment or two fiddling with your windows to create a clear "line of drag" between the icon to be moved and the destination folder. (A background window will courteously pop to the foreground to accept your drag. But if it wasn't even open to begin with, you're out of luck.)

There's a better way. Use the Copy and Paste commands to move icons from one window into another (just as you can in Windows, by the way—except that you can only copy, not cut, Mac icons). The routine goes like this:

1. **Highlight the icon or icons you want to move.**

   Use any of the techniques described starting on page 70.

2. **Choose Edit→Copy.**

   Or press the keyboard shortcut: ⌘-C.

FREQUENTLY ASKED QUESTION

Dragging to Copy a Disk

Help! I'm trying to copy a CD onto my hard drive. When I drag it onto the hard drive icon, I get only an alias—not a copy of the CD.

Sure enough, dragging a disk onto a disk creates an alias.

But producing a copy of the dragged icon is easy enough: Just press Option or ⌘ as you drag.

Honestly, though: Why are you trying to copy a CD this way? Using Disk Utility (page 414) saves space, lets you assign a password, and usually fools whatever software was on the CD into thinking that it's still *on* the original CD.

Tip: You can combine steps 1 and 2 by Control-clicking (or right-clicking) an icon and choosing the Copy command from the shortcut menu that appears—or by using the ✿ menu. If you've selected several icons, say five, then the command will say "Copy 5 items."

3. Open the window where you want to put the icons. Choose Edit→Paste.

Once again, you may prefer to use the keyboard equivalent: ⌘-V. And once again, you can also Control-click (right-click) inside the window and then choose Paste from the shortcut menu that appears, or you can use the ✿ menu.

A progress bar may appear as Mac OS X copies the files or folders; press Esc or ⌘-period to interrupt the process. When the progress bar goes away, it means you've successfully transferred the icons, which now appear in the new window.

Dragging from the Title Bar

You may remember from Chapter 1 that the title bar of every Finder window harbors a secret pop-up menu. When you ⌘-click it, you're shown a little folder ladder that delineates your current position in the folder hierarchy. You may also remember that the tiny icon just to the left of the window's name is actually a handle that you can drag to move a folder into a different window.

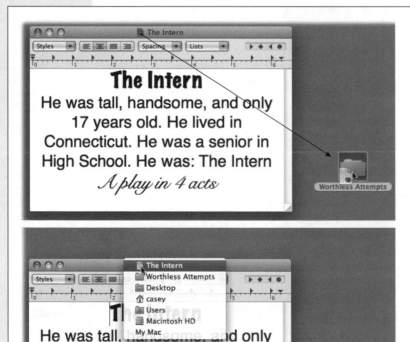

Figure 2-5:
Top: By dragging the document-window proxy icon, you can create an alias of your document on the desktop or anywhere else. (Make sure the icon has darkened before you begin to drag.)

Bottom: If you ⌘-click the name of the document in its title bar, you get to see exactly where this document sits on your hard drive. (Choosing the name of one of these folders opens that folder and switches you to the Finder.)

In many programs, you get the same features in *document* windows, as shown in Figure 2-5. For example, by dragging the tiny document icon next to the document's name, you can perform these two interesting stunts:

- **Create an alias on the desktop or the Dock.** By dragging this icon to the desktop or onto a folder or disk icon, you create an instant alias of the document you're working on. (If you drag into the right end of the Dock, you can park the document's icon there, too.) This is a useful feature when, for example, you're about to knock off for the night, and you want easy access to the file you've been working on when you return the next day.

- **Launch from a Dock icon.** By dragging this title-bar icon onto another program's Dock *icon,* you open your document in that other program. For example, if you're in TextEdit working on a memo and you decide that you'll need the full strength of Microsoft Word to dress it up, you can drag its title-bar icon directly onto the Word icon in the Dock. Word then launches and opens up the TextEdit document, ready for editing.

  Note to struggling writers: Unfortunately, you can't drag an open document directly into the Trash.

Spring-Loaded Folders: Dragging Icons into Closed Folders

Here's a common dilemma: You want to drag an icon not just into a folder, but into a folder nested *inside* that folder. This awkward challenge would ordinarily require you to open the folder, open the inner folder, drag the icon in, and then close both windows. As you can imagine, the process is even messier if you want to drag an icon into a sub-subfolder or a *sub*-sub-subfolder.

Instead of fiddling around with all those windows, you can instead use the *spring-loaded folders* feature (Figure 2-6).

It works like this: With a single drag, drag the icon onto the first folder—but keep your mouse button pressed. After a few seconds, the folder window opens automatically, centered on your cursor:

- In icon view, the new window instantly *replaces* the original.

- In column view, you get a new column that shows the target folder's contents.

- In list and Cover Flow views, a second window appears.

Still keeping the button down, drag onto the inner folder; its window opens, too. Now drag onto the *inner* inner folder—and so on. (If the inner folder you intend to open isn't visible in the window, you can scroll by dragging your cursor close to any edge of the window.)

Tip: You can even drag icons onto disks or folders whose icons appear in the Sidebar (Chapter 1). When you do so, the main part of the window flashes to reveal the contents of the disk or folder you've dragged onto. When you let go of the mouse, the main window changes back to reveal the contents of the disk or folder where you *started* dragging.

In short, Sidebar combined with spring-loaded folders makes a terrific drag-and-drop way to file a desktop icon from anywhere to anywhere—without having to open or close any windows at all.

Figure 2-6:
Top: To make spring-loaded folders work, start by dragging an icon onto a folder or disk icon. Don't release the mouse button. Wait for the window to open automatically around your cursor.

Bottom: Now you can either let go of the mouse button to release the file in its new window or drag it onto yet another, inner folder. It, too, will open. As long as you don't release the mouse button, you can continue until you've reached your folder-within-a-folder destination.

When you finally release the mouse, you're left facing the final window. All the previous windows closed along the way. You've neatly placed the icon into the depths of the nested folders.

Making Spring-Loaded Folders Work

That spring-loaded folder technique sounds good in theory, but it can be disconcerting in practice. For most people, the long wait before the first folder opens is almost enough wasted time to negate the value of the feature altogether. Furthermore, when the first window finally does open, you're often caught by surprise. Suddenly your cursor—mouse button still down—is inside a window, sometimes directly on top of another folder you never intended to open. But before you can react, its window, too, has opened, and you find yourself out of control.

Fortunately, you can regain control of spring-loaded folders using these tricks:

- Choose Finder→Preferences. On the General pane, adjust the "Spring-loaded folders and windows" delay slider to a setting that drives you less crazy. For example, if you find yourself waiting too long before the first folder opens, then drag the slider toward the Short setting.

- You can turn off this feature entirely by choosing Finder→Preferences and turning off the "Spring-loaded folders and windows" checkbox.

- Tap the space bar to make the folder spring open at your command. That is, even with the Finder→Preferences slider set to the Long delay setting, you can force each folder to spring open when *you* are ready by tapping the space bar as you hold down the mouse button. True, you need two hands to master this one, but the control you regain is immeasurable.

Tip: The space bar trick works even when the "Spring-loaded folders and windows" checkbox (in Finder→Preferences) is turned off. That's a handy arrangement, because it means folder windows never pop open accidentally.

Designing Your Own Icons

You don't have to be content with the icons provided by Microsoft, Apple, or whoever else wrote your software. You can paste new icons onto your file, disk, and folder icons to help you pick them out at a glance.

The easiest way to replace an icon is to copy it from another icon. To do so, highlight the icon you want to copy, hold down the Option key, and choose File→Show Inspector. In the resulting window, click the icon, and then choose Edit→Copy.

Next, click the icon to which you want to transfer the copied picture. Its icon now appears in the Info dialog box that's still open on the screen. Click the icon in the dialog box, and this time choose Edit→Paste.

If you'd rather introduce all-new icons, you're welcome to steal some of the beautifully designed ones waiting at *www. iconfactory.com* and the icon sites linked to it. Once you've

downloaded these special icon files, you can copy their images from the Get Info window as you would any icon.

To design a Mac OS X icon from scratch, use a graphics program like Photoshop or the shareware favorite Graphic-Converter.

Once you've saved your icon file, select it, and then copy and paste its icon using the Show Inspector method described above.

Note that you can't change certain folder icons that Mac OS X considers important, like Applications or System. You're also not allowed to change icons that belong to other people who share your Mac and sign in under a different name (Chapter 12).

You can, however, change the special Mac OS X folder icons in your Home folder—Pictures, Documents, and so on—and your hard drive icon.

• Whenever a folder springs open into a window, twitch your mouse up to the newly opened window's title bar or down to its information strip. Doing so ensures that your cursor won't wind up hovering on, and accidentally opening, an inner folder. With the cursor parked on the gradient gray, you can take your time to survey the newly opened window's contents, and plunge into an inner folder only after gaining your bearings.

Tip: Email programs like Entourage and Mail have spring-loaded folders, too. You can drag a message out of the list and into one of your filing folders, wait for the folder to spring open and reveal its subfolders, and then drag it directly into one of them.

Aliases: Icons in Two Places at Once

Highlighting an icon and then choosing File→Make Alias (or pressing ⌘-L) generates an *alias,* a specially branded duplicate of the original icon (Figure 2-7). It's not a duplicate of the *file*—just of the *icon;* therefore it requires negligible storage space. When you double-click the alias, the original file opens. (A Macintosh alias is essentially the same as a Windows *shortcut.*)

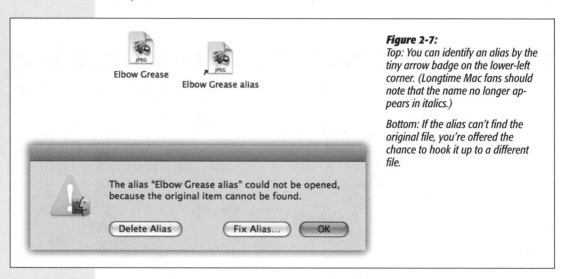

Figure 2-7:
Top: You can identify an alias by the tiny arrow badge on the lower-left corner. (Longtime Mac fans should note that the name no longer appears in italics.)

Bottom: If the alias can't find the original file, you're offered the chance to hook it up to a different file.

You can create as many aliases as you want of a single file; therefore, in effect, aliases let you stash that file in many different folder locations simultaneously. Double-click any one of them and you open the original file, wherever it may be on your system.

Tip: You can also create an alias of an icon by Option-⌘-dragging it out of its window. (Aliases you create this way lack the word *alias* on the file name—a distinct delight to those who find the suffix redundant and annoying.) You can also create an alias by Control-clicking (or right-clicking) a normal icon and choosing Make Alias from the shortcut menu that appears, or by highlighting an icon and then choosing Make Alias from the ✿ menu.

What's Good about Aliases

An alias takes up very little disk space, even if the original file is enormous. Aliases are smart, too: Even if you rename the alias, rename the original file, move the alias, and move the original around on the disk, double-clicking the alias still opens the original file.

And that's just the beginning of alias intelligence. Suppose you make an alias of a file that's on a removable disc, like a CD. When you double-click the alias on your hard drive, the Mac requests that particular disc by name. And if you double-click the alias of a file on a different machine on the network, your Mac attempts to connect to the appropriate machine, prompting you for a password (see Chapter 13)—even if the other machine is thousands of miles away and your Mac must go online to connect.

Here are a couple of ways you can put aliases to work:

- You may want to file a document you're working on in several different folders, or place a particular folder in several different locations.

- You can use the alias feature to save you some of the steps required to access another hard drive on the network. (Details on this trick are in Chapter 13.)

Tip: Mac OS X makes it easy to find the file an alias "points to" without actually having to open it. Just highlight the alias and then choose File→Show Original (⌘-R), or choose Show Original from the ✿ menu. Mac OS X immediately displays the actual, original file, sitting patiently in its folder, wherever that may be.

FREQUENTLY ASKED QUESTION

Favorites Reborn

Hey! Where the heck are my Favorites?

Skipped a few versions of Mac OS X, did you?

Several versions back, the File→Add to Favorites command placed the names of icons you've highlighted into a submenu of the Go→Favorites command. The Favorites scheme, in other words, was yet another mechanism of listing your favorite files, folders, programs, disks, and even network-accessible folders for quick access.

Trouble was, Mac OS X already had a number of different methods for stashing favorite icons for convenient access, like the Dock, the Finder toolbar, and the Sidebar. So Apple decided enough was enough; it hid the Add to Favorites command. It's now in your File menu only if you press the Shift key.

There is, however, still a Favorites *folder*. It's sitting right there in your Home→Library folder.

If you miss this feature—maybe you wandered away from the Mac for a few years—you'll find the new scheme to be much simpler.

First drag the Favorites folder into your Sidebar. From now on, whenever you want to designate an icon as a Favorite, drag it onto the Favorites folder icon in your Sidebar. (Or Option-⌘-drag it to create an alias, or use the hidden File→Add to Favorites command, or press Shift-⌘-T.)

Thereafter, to view your collection of faves, just click the Favorites icon.

This new system is both simpler and easier to understand than the previous mechanism. In fact, this feature may become one of your…favorites.

Broken Aliases

An alias doesn't contain any of the information you've typed or composed in the original file. Don't email an alias to the Tokyo office and then depart for the airport, hoping to give the presentation upon your arrival in Japan. When you double-click the alias, now separated from its original, you'll be shown the dialog box at the bottom of Figure 2-7.

If you find yourself 3,000 miles away from the hard drive on which the original file resides, click Delete Alias (to delete the orphan alias) or OK (to do nothing, leaving it where it is).

In certain circumstances, however, the third button—Fix Alias—is the most useful. Click it to summon the Fix Alias dialog box, which you can use to navigate the folders on your Mac. When you click a new icon and then click Choose, you associate the orphaned alias with a different file.

Such techniques become handy when, for example, you click your book manuscript's alias on the desktop, forgetting that you recently saved it under a new name and deleted the older draft. Instead of simply showing you an error message that says " 'Enron Corporate Ethics Handbook' can't be found," the Mac displays the box that contains the Fix Alias button. By reassociating the alias with the new document, you can save yourself the trouble of creating a new alias. From now on, double-clicking your manuscript's alias on the desktop opens the new draft.

Tip: You don't have to wait until the original file no longer exists before choosing a new original for an alias. You can perform alias reassignment surgery anytime you like. Just highlight the alias icon and then choose File→Get Info. In the Get Info dialog box, click Select New Original. In the resulting window, find and double-click the file you'd now like to open whenever you double-click the alias.

Color Labels

Snow Leopard includes a welcome blast from the Mac's distant past: icon labels. This feature lets you tag selected icons with one of seven different labels, each of which has both a text label and a color associated with it.

To do so, highlight the icons. Open the File menu (or the ✿ menu, or the shortcut menu that appears when you Control-click/right-click the icons). There, under the heading Color Label, you'll see seven colored dots, which represent the seven labels you can use. Figure 2-8 shows the routine.

What Labels Are Good For

After you've applied labels to icons, you can perform some unique file-management tasks—in some cases on all of them simultaneously, even if they're scattered across multiple hard drives. For example:

- **Round up files with Find.** Using the Find command described in Chapter 3, you can round up all the icons with a particular label. Thereafter, moving these icons at once is a piece of cake—choose Edit→Select All, and then drag any one of the highlighted icons out of the results window and into the target folder or disk.

Figure 2-8:
Use the File menu, ✿ menu, or shortcut menu to apply label tags to highlighted icons. You can even apply a label within an icon's Get Info dialog box (page 88).

Instantly, the icon's name takes on the selected shade. In a list or column view, the entire row takes on that shade, as shown in Figure 2-9. (If you choose the little X, you remove any labels you may have applied.)

Using labels in conjunction with Find like this is one of the most useful and inexpensive backup schemes ever devised: Whenever you finish working on a document that you'd like to back up, Control-click it and apply a label called, for example, Backup. At the end of each day, use the Find command to round up all the files with the Backup label—and then drag them as a group onto your backup disk.

- **Sort a list view by label.** No other Mac sorting method lets you create an arbitrary order for the icons in a window. When you sort by label, the Mac creates alphabetical clusters *within* each label grouping, as shown in Figure 2-9.

This technique might be useful when, for example, your job is to process several different folders of documents; for each folder, you're supposed to convert graphics files, throw out old files, or whatever. As soon as you finish working your way through one folder, flag it with a label called Done. The folder jumps to the top (or bottom) of the window, safely marked for your reference pleasure, leaving the next unprocessed folder at your fingertips, ready to go.

- **Track progress.** Use different-colored labels to track the status of files in a certain project. For example, the first drafts have no labels at all. Once they've been edited and approved, make them blue. Once they've been sent to the home office, make them purple. (Heck, you could have all kinds of fun with this: Money-losing projects get red tints; profitable ones get green; things that make you sad are blue. Or maybe not.)

Figure 2-9:
Sorting by label lets you create several different alphabetical groups within a single window. In Snow Leopard, in fact, you can sort by labels in any view using the View→Show View Options palette.

In a list view, the quickest way to sort by label is to first make the label column visible. Do so by choosing View→Show View Options and then turning on the Label checkbox.

Changing Labels

When you install Mac OS X, the seven labels in the File menu are named for the colors they show: Red, Orange, Yellow, and so on. Clearly, the label feature would be much more useful if you could rewrite these labels, tailoring them to your purposes.

Doing so is easy. Choose Finder→Preferences. Click Labels. Now you see the dialog box shown in Figure 2-10, where you can edit the text of each label.

The Trash

No single element of the Macintosh interface is as recognizable or famous as the Trash icon, which now appears at the end of the Dock.

You can discard almost any icon by dragging it into the Trash can (actually a wastebasket, not a can, but let's not quibble). When the tip of your arrow cursor touches the Trash icon, the little wastebasket turns black. When you release the mouse, you're well on your way to discarding whatever it was you dragged. As a convenience, Mac OS X even replaces the empty-wastebasket icon with a wastebasket-filled-with-crumpled-up-papers icon, to let you know there's something in there.

It's well worth learning the keyboard alternative to dragging something into the Trash: Highlight the icon, and then press ⌘-Delete (which corresponds to the File→Move to Trash command). This technique is not only far faster than dragging, but it also requires far less precision, especially if you have a large screen. Mac OS X does all the Trash-targeting for you.

Snow Leopard Spots: If a file is locked (page 88), a message appears to let you know; it offers you the chance to fling it into the Trash anyway. That's a better solution than before, when you'd be forced to unlock the file before you could trash it.

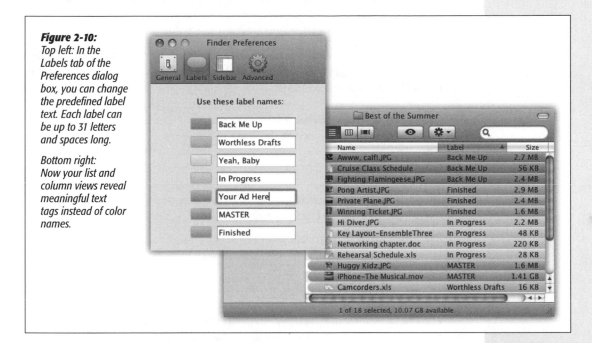

Figure 2-10:
Top left: In the Labels tab of the Preferences dialog box, you can change the predefined label text. Each label can be up to 31 letters and spaces long.

Bottom right: Now your list and column views reveal meaningful text tags instead of color names.

Rescuing Files and Folders from the Trash

File and folder icons sit in the Trash forever—or until you choose Finder→Empty Trash, whichever comes first.

If you haven't yet emptied the Trash, you can open its window by clicking the wastebasket icon once. Now you can review its contents: icons that you've placed on the waiting list for extinction. If you change your mind, you can rescue any of these items in any of these ways:

• **Use the new Put Back command.** This feature, new in Snow Leopard, flings the trashed item back into whatever folder it came from, even if that was weeks ago. (Well, *sort* of new—it's been in Windows for years, and was in Mac OS 9 before that.)

You'll find the Put Back command wherever fine shortcut menus are sold. For example, it appears when you Control-click the icon, right-click it, or click the icon and then open the ✿ menu.

Tip: The same keystroke you use to hurl something *into* the trash—⌘-Delete—also works to hurl it back *out* again. That is, you can highlight something in the Trash and press ⌘-Delete to put it back where it once belonged.

- **Hit Undo.** If dragging something to the Trash was the most recent thing you've done, you can press ⌘-Z—the keyboard shortcut for the Edit→Undo command. That keystroke not only removes it from the Trash, but also returns it to the folder from which it came. This trick works even if the Trash window isn't open.

- **Drag it manually.** Of course, you can also drag any icon out of the Trash with the mouse, which gives you the option of putting it somewhere new (as opposed to back in the folder it started from).

Emptying the Trash I: Quick and Easy

If you're confident that the items in the Trash window are worth deleting, use any of these three options:

- Choose Finder→Empty Trash.

- Press Shift-⌘-Delete. Or, if you'd just as soon not bother with the "Are you sure?" message, then throw the Option key in there, too.

- Control-click the wastebasket icon (or right-click it, or just click it and hold the mouse button down for a moment); choose Empty Trash from the shortcut menu.

Tip: This last method has two advantages. First, the Mac doesn't bother asking "Are you sure?" (If you're clicking right on the Trash and choosing Empty Trash from the pop-up menu, it's pretty darned obvious you *are* sure.) Second, this method nukes any locked files without making you unlock them first.

If you use either of the first two methods, the Macintosh asks you to confirm your decision. Click OK. (Figure 2-11 shows both this message and the secret for turning it off forever.)

Either way, Mac OS X now deletes those files from your hard drive.

Emptying the Trash II: Secure and Forever

When you empty the Trash as described above, each trashed icon sure looks like it disappears. The truth is, though, the data *in* each file is still on the hard drive. Yes, the space occupied by the dearly departed is now marked with an internal "This space available" message, and in time, new files may overwrite that spot. But in the meantime, some future eBay buyer of your Mac—or, more imminently, a savvy family member or office mate—could use a program like Norton Utilities to resurrect those deleted files.

(In more dire cases, companies like DriveSavers.com can use sophisticated clean-room techniques to recover crucial information—for several hundred dollars, of course.)

That notion doesn't sit well with certain groups, like government agencies, international spies, and the paranoid. As far as they're concerned, deleting a file should *really, really* delete it, irrevocably, irretrievably, and forever.

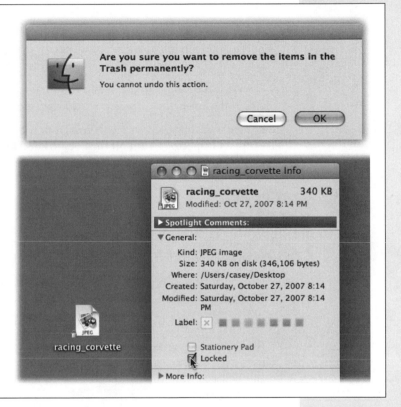

Figure 2-11:
Top: Your last warning. Mac OS X doesn't tell you how many items are in the Trash or how much disk space they take up.

If you'd rather not be interrupted for confirmation every time you empty the Trash, you can suppress this message permanently.

To do that, choose File→Preferences, click Advanced, and then turn off "Show warning before emptying the Trash."

Bottom: The Get Info window for a locked file. Locking a file in this way isn't military-level security by any stretch—any passing evildoer can unlock the file in the same way. But it does trigger an "operation cannot be completed" warning when you try to put it into the Trash—or indeed when you try to drag it into any other folder—providing at least one layer of protection against losing or deleting it.

Mac OS X's *Secure* Empty Trash command to the rescue! When you choose this command from the Finder menu, the Mac doesn't just obliterate the parking spaces around the dead file. It actually records *new* information over the old—random 0's and 1's. Pure static gibberish.

The process takes longer than the normal Empty Trash command, of course. But when it absolutely, positively has to be gone from this earth for good (and you're absolutely, positively sure you'll never need that file again), Secure Empty Trash is secure indeed.

Locked Files: The Next Generation

By highlighting a file or folder, choosing File→Get Info, and turning on the Locked checkbox, you protect that file or folder from accidental deletion (see Figure 2-11 at bottom). A little padlock icon appears on the corner of the full-size icon, also shown in Figure 2-11.

Locked files in Snow Leopard behave quite differently than they used to:

- Dragging the file into another folder makes a copy; the original stays put.

- Putting the icon into the Trash produces a warning message: "Item 'Shopping List' is locked. Do you want to move it to the Trash anyway?" If so, click Continue.

- Once a locked file is in the Trash, you don't get any more warnings. When you empty the Trash, that item gets erased right along with everything else.

You can unlock files easily enough. Press Option-⌘-I (or press Option as you choose File→Show Inspector). Turn off the Locked checkbox in the resulting Info window. (Yes, you can lock or unlock a mass of files at once.)

Get Info

By clicking an icon and then choosing File→Get Info, you open an important window like the one shown in Figure 2-12. It's a collapsible, multipanel screen that provides a wealth of information about a highlighted icon. For example:

- For a document icon, you see when it was created and modified, and what programs it "belongs" to.

- For an alias, you learn the location of the actual icon it refers to.

- For a program, you see whether or not it's been updated to run on Intel-based Macs. If so, the Get Info window says "Kind: Universal." If not, it says "Kind: PowerPC" and will probably run slower than you'd like because it must be translated by Rosetta (page 193).

GEM IN THE ROUGH

Opening Things in the Trash

Now and then, it's very useful to see what some document in the Trash *is* before committing it to oblivion—and the only way to do that is to open it.

Trouble is, you can't open it by double-clicking; you'll get nothing but an error message.

Or at least that's what Apple *wants* you to think.

First of all, you can use Quick Look (page 54) to inspect something in the Trash.

But if Quick Look can't open the file—or if you want to *edit* it instead of just reading it—drag the document onto the icon of a program that can open it. That is, if a file called Don't Read Me.txt is in the Trash, you can drag it onto, say, the Word or TextEdit icon in your Dock.

The document dutifully pops open on the screen. Inspect, close, and *then* empty the Trash (or rescue the document).

- For a disk icon, you get statistics about its capacity and how much of it is full.

- If you open the Get Info window when *nothing* is selected, you get information about the desktop itself (or the open window), including the amount of disk space consumed by everything sitting on or in it.

- If you highlight 11 icons or more simultaneously, the Get Info window shows you how many you highlighted, breaks it down by type ("23 documents, 3 folders," for example), and adds up the total of their file sizes. That's a great opportunity to change certain file characteristics on numerous files simultaneously, such as locking or unlocking them, hiding or showing their filename extensions (page 173), changing their ownership or permissions (page 517), and so on.

If you highlight fewer than 11 icons, Mac OS X opens up individual Get Info windows for each one.

Figure 2-12:
Top: The Get Info window can be as small as this, with all its information panes collapsed.

Bottom: Or, if you click each flippy triangle to open its corresponding panel of information, it can be as huge as this—shown here split in two because the book isn't tall enough to show the whole thing. The resulting dialog box can easily grow taller than your screen, which is a good argument for either (a) closing the panels you don't need at any given moment or (b) running out to buy a really gigantic monitor.

And as long as you're taking the trouble to read this caption, here's a tasty bonus: There's a secret command in Snow Leopard called Get Summary Info. Highlight a group of icons, press Control-⌘-I, and marvel at the special Get Info box that tallies up their sizes and other characteristics.

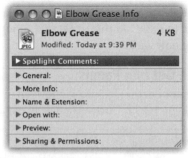

Uni-window vs. Multiwindow

In Mac OS X versions 10.0 and 10.1, a single Get Info window remained on the screen all the time as you clicked one icon after another. (Furthermore, the command was called Show Info instead of Get Info. Evidently "Show Info" sounded too much like it was the playbill for a Broadway musical.)

The single info window—officially called the Inspector—was great for reducing clutter, but it didn't let you compare the statistics for the Get Info windows of two or three folders side by side.

So beginning in 10.2, Apple returned to the old way of doing Get Info: A new dialog box appears each time you get info on an icon (unless you've highlighted 11 or more icons, as already described).

But the uni-window approach is still available for those occasions when you don't need side-by-side Get Info windows—if you know the secret. Highlight the icon and then press Option-⌘-I (or hold down Option and choose File→Show Inspector). The Get Info Inspector window that appears looks slightly different (it has a smaller title bar and a dimmed Minimize button), and it changes to reflect whatever icons you now click.

The Get Info Panels

Apple built the Get Info window out of a series of collapsed "flippy triangles," as shown in Figure 2-12. Click a triangle to expand a corresponding information panel.

Tip: The title-bar hierarchical menu described on page 22 works in the Get Info dialog box, too. That is, ⌘-click the Get Info window's title bar to reveal where this icon is in your folder hierarchy.

Depending on whether you clicked a document, program, disk, alias, or whatever, the various panels may include the following:

- **Spotlight Comments.** Here, you can type in comments for your own reference. Later, you can view these remarks in any list view if you display the Comments column (page 44)—and you can find them when you conduct Spotlight searches (Chapter 3).

- **General.** Here's where you can view the name of the icon, and also see its size, creation date, most recent change date, locked status, and so on.

  If you click a disk, this info window shows you its capacity and how full it is. If you click the Trash, you see how much stuff is in it. If you click an alias, this panel shows you a Select New Original button and reveals where the original file is. The General panel always opens the first time you summon the Get Info window.

- **More Info.** Just as the name implies, here you'll find more info, most often the dimensions and color format (graphics only) and when the icon was last opened. These morsels are also easily Spotlight-searchable.

- **Name & Extension.** On this panel, you can read and edit the name of the icon in question. The "Hide extension" checkbox refers to the suffix on Mac OS X file names (the last three letters of *Letter to Congress.doc,* for example).

  Many Mac OS X documents, behind the scenes, have filename extensions of this kind—but Mac OS X comes factory-set to hide them. By turning off this checkbox, you can make the suffix reappear for an individual file. (Conversely, if you've elected to have Mac OS X *show* all file name suffixes, then this checkbox lets you hide the extensions on individual icons.)

- **Open with.** This section is available for documents only. Use the controls on this screen to specify which program will open when you double-click this document, or any document of its type.

- **Preview.** When you're examining pictures, text files, PDF files, Microsoft Office files, sounds, clippings, and movies, you see a magnified thumbnail version of what's actually *in* that document. This preview is like a tiny version of Quick Look (page 54). A controller lets you play sounds and movies, where appropriate.

- **Sharing & Permissions.** This panel is available for all kinds of icons. If other people have access to your Mac (either from across the network or when logging in, in person), this panel lets you specify who is allowed to open or change this particular icon. See Chapter 12 for a complete discussion of this hairy topic.

Snow Leopard Spots: In Mac OS X 10.5, you sometimes saw other panels in the Get Info window. For example, iPhoto and iDVD each offered a Plug-ins panel that let you manage add-on software modules. In Snow Leopard, however, those panels are no longer available. Apple Tech Support probably received one too many call about a "broken" iPhoto that resulted from the customer's fiddling with the Plug-ins panel.

UP TO SPEED

Compressing, Zipping, and Archiving

Mac OS X comes with a built-in command that compresses a file or folder down to a single, smaller icon—an archive—suitable for storing or emailing. It creates .zip files, the same compression format used in Windows. That means you can now send .zip files back and forth to PC owners without worrying that they won't be able to open them.

To compress something, Control-click (or right-click) a file or folder, and choose "Compress [the icon's name]" from the shortcut menu. (Of course, you can use the File menu or ✿ menu instead.)

Mac OS X thoughtfully creates a .zip archive, but it leaves the original behind so you can continue working with it.

Opening a .zip file somebody sends you is equally easy: Just double-click it. Zip!—it opens.

On the other hand, Snow Leopard does not come with StuffIt Expander, the free unstuffing program that recognizes .zip files, .sit files, and many other forms of compressed files.

If you don't already have a copy of Expander from a previous Mac OS version, then you can download and install it yourself, which is worth doing. You can get it from, for example, this book's "Missing CD" page at *www.missing-manuals.com.*

Spotlight

Every computer offers a way to find files. And every system offers several different ways to open them. But Spotlight, a star feature of Mac OS X (and touched up in Snow Leopard), combines these two functions in a way that's so fast, so efficient, so spectacular, it reduces much of what you've read in the previous chapters to irrelevance.

That may sound like breathless hype, but wait till you try it. You'll see.

The Spotlight Menu

See the little magnifying-glass icon in your menu bar (⌕)? That's the mouse-driven way to open the Spotlight Search box.

The other way is to press ⌘-space bar. If you can memorize only one keystroke on your Mac, that's the one to learn. It works both at the desktop and in other programs.

In any case, the Spotlight text box appears just below your menu bar (Figure 3-1).

Begin typing to identify what you want to find and open. For example, if you're trying to find a file called *Pokémon Fantasy League.doc,* typing just *pok* or *leag* would probably suffice. (The Search box doesn't find text in the *middles* of words, though; it searches from the beginnings of words.)

A menu immediately appears below the Search box, listing everything Spotlight can find containing what you've typed so far. (This is a live, interactive search; that is, Spotlight modifies the menu of search results *as you type.)* The menu lists every file, folder, program, email message, Address Book entry, calendar appointment, picture, movie, PDF document, music file, Web bookmark, Microsoft Office (Word, Power-

Point, Excel, Entourage) document, System Preferences panel, To Do item, chat transcript, Web site in your History list, and even font that contains what you typed, regardless of its name or folder location.

Snow Leopard Spots: In fact, Spotlight in Snow Leopard recognizes a couple of new data types. It now finds photos according to who is in them (using iPhoto's Faces feature) or where they were taken (using iPhoto's Places feature). If you use iChat (Chapter 21), Spotlight also finds the lucky members of your Buddy lists.

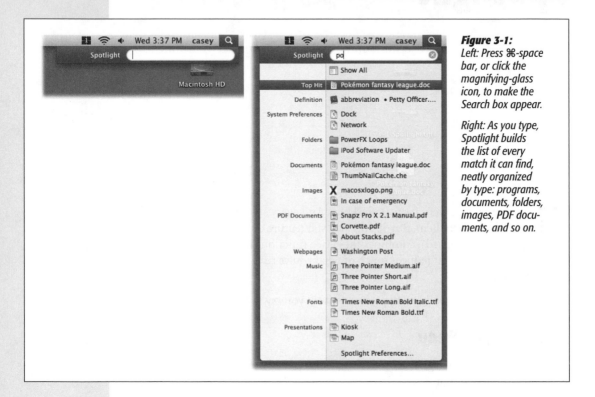

Figure 3-1:
Left: Press ⌘-space bar, or click the magnifying-glass icon, to make the Search box appear.

Right: As you type, Spotlight builds the list of every match it can find, neatly organized by type: programs, documents, folders, images, PDF documents, and so on.

If you see the icon you were hoping to dig up, just click it to open it. Or use the arrow keys to "walk down" the menu, and then press Return or Enter to open the one you want.

If you click an application, it pops onto the screen. If you select a System Preferences panel, System Preferences opens and presents that panel. If you choose an appointment, the iCal program opens, already set to the appropriate day and time. Selecting an email message opens that message in Mail or Entourage. And so on.

Spotlight is so fast, it eliminates a lot of the folders-in-folders business that's a side effect of modern computing. Why burrow around in folders when you can open any file or program with a couple of keystrokes?

Spotlight-Menu Tips

It should be no surprise that a feature as important as Spotlight comes loaded with options, tips, and tricks. Here it is—the official, unexpurgated Spotlight Tip-O-Rama:

- If the very first item—labeled Top Hit—is the icon you were looking for, just press Return or Enter to open it.

  This is a huge deal, because it means that in most cases, you can perform the entire operation without ever taking your hands off the keyboard.

  To open Safari in a hurry, for example, press ⌘-space bar (to open the Spotlight Search box), type *safa*, and hit Return, all in rapid-fire sequence, without even looking. Presto: Safari is before you.

  (The only wrinkle here is that the Spotlight menu may still be building itself. If you go too quickly, you may be surprised as another entry jumps into the top slot just as you're about to hit Return—and you wind up opening the wrong thing. Over time, you develop a feel for when the Top Hit is reliably the one you want.)

GEM IN THE ROUGH

Sweet Spotlight Serendipity: Equations and Definitions

Spotlight has two secret features that turn it into a different beast altogether.

First, it's a tiny pocket calculator, always at the ready. Click in the Search box (or press ⌘-space bar), type or paste *38*48.2-7+55,* and marvel at the first result in the Spotlight menu: *1879.6.* There's your answer—and you didn't even have to fire up the Calculator.

(For shorter equations—only a few characters long—the first result in the Spotlight menu shows the *entire* equation, like *.15*234=35.1.)*

And it's not just a four-function calculator, either. It works with square roots: Type *sqrt(25),* and you'll get the answer 5. It also works with powers: Type *pow(6,6)*—that is, 6 to the power of 6—and you'll get 46656. You can even type *pi* to represent, you know, pi.

For a complete list of math functions in Spotlight, open Terminal (see Chapter 16), type *man math,* and press Return.

Second, the Spotlight menu is now a full-blown English dictionary. Or, more specifically, it's wired directly into Mac OS X's *own* dictionary, which sits in your Applications folder.

So if you type, for example, *schadenfreude* into the Search box, you'll see, to your amazement, the beginning of the actual definition right there in the menu. Click it to open Dictionary and read the full-blown entry. (In this example, that would be: "noun: pleasure derived by someone from another person's misfortune.")

And what, exactly, is the Top Hit? Mac OS X chooses it based on its *relevance* (the importance of your search term inside that item) and timeliness (when you last opened it).

Tip: Spotlight makes a spectacular application launcher. That's because Job One for Spotlight is to display the names of matching programs in the results menu. Their names appear in the list nearly instantly—long before Spotlight has built the rest of the menu of search results.

If some program on your hard drive doesn't have a Dock icon, for example—or even if it does—there's no faster way to open it than to use Spotlight.

- To jump to a search result's Finder icon instead of opening it, ⌘-click its name.

- Spotlight's menu shows you only 20 of the most likely suspects, evenly divided among the categories (Documents, Applications, and so on). The downside: To see the complete list, you have to open the Spotlight *window* (page 104).

    The upside: It's fairly easy to open something in this menu from the keyboard. Just press ⌘-↓ (or ⌘-↑) to jump from category to category. Once you've highlighted the first result in a category, you can walk through the remaining four by pressing the arrow key by itself. Then, once you've highlighted what you want, press Return or Enter to open it.

    In other words, you can get to anything in the Spotlight menu with only a few keystrokes.

- The Esc key (top-left corner of your keyboard) offers a two-stage "back out of this" method. Tap it once to close the Spotlight menu and erase what you've typed, so that you're all ready to type in something different. Tap Esc a *second* time to close the Spotlight text box entirely, having given up on the whole idea of searching.

    (If you just want to cancel the whole thing in *one* step, press ⌘-space bar again, or ⌘-period, or ⌘-Esc.)

- Think of Spotlight as your little black book. When you need to look up a number in Address Book, don't bother opening Address Book; it's faster to use Spotlight. You can type somebody's name or even part of someone's phone number.

- Among a million other things, Spotlight tracks the keywords, descriptions, faces, and places you've applied to your pictures in iPhoto. As a result, you can find, open, or insert any iPhoto photo at any time, no matter what program you're using, just by using the Spotlight box at the top of every Open File dialog box (page 187)! This is a great way to insert a photo into an outgoing email message, a presentation, or a Web page you're designing. iPhoto doesn't even have to be running.

- Spotlight is also a quick way to adjust one of your Mac's preference settings. Instead of opening up the System Preferences program, type the first few letters of, say, *volume* or *network* or *clock* into Spotlight. The Spotlight menu lists the appropriate System Preferences panel, so you can jump directly to it.

- If you point to an item in the Spotlight menu without clicking, a little tooltip balloon appears. It tells you the item's actual name—which is useful if Spotlight listed something because of text that appears *inside* the file, not its name—and its folder path (that is, where it is on your hard drive).

- The Spotlight menu lists 20 found items. In the following pages, you'll learn about how to see the rest of the stuff. But for now, note that you can eliminate some of the categories that show up here (like PDF documents or Bookmarks), and even rearrange them, to permit more of the *other* kinds of things to enjoy those 20 seats of honor. Details on page 114.

UP TO SPEED

What Spotlight Knows

The beauty of Spotlight is that it doesn't just find files whose names match what you've typed. That would be *so* 2004!

No, Spotlight actually looks inside the files. It can actually read and search the contents of text files, RTF and PDF documents, documents from iWork, Keynote, Pages, Photoshop, Microsoft Office (Word, Excel, Entourage, and PowerPoint), and so on.

As time goes on, software companies will release bits of add-on software–plug-ins–that will make their documents searchable by Spotlight too. Check in periodically at, for example, *www.apple. com/downloads/ma- cosx/spotlight,* to look for Spotlight plug-ins relevant to the kind of work you do. Free Spotlight plug-ins are available for OmniGraffle, Om- niOutliner, TypeIt4Me, MacDraft, REALBasic, Painter, Wolfram Notebook, and many others.

But that's only the beginning. Spotlight searches files not only for the text inside them, but also for over 125 other bits of text–a staggering collection of information tidbits includ- ing the names of the layers in a Photoshop document, the tempo of an MP3 file, the shutter speed of a digital-camera photo, a movie's copyright holder, a document's page size, and on and on.

Technically, this sort of secondary information is called *metadata.* It's usually invisible, although a lot of it shows up in the Get Info dialog box described in Chapter 2.

You might think that typing something into the Spotlight Search box triggers a search. But to be technically correct, Spotlight has already done its searching. In the first 15 to 30 minutes after you install Mac OS X–or in the min- utes after you attach a new hard drive–Spotlight invisibly collects informa- tion about everything on your hard drive. Like a kid cramming for an exam, it reads, takes notes on, and memorizes the con- tents of all your files. (During this time, if you click the Spotlight icon on the menu bar, you'll be told that Spotlight is indexing the drives.) Once it has indexed your hard drive in this way, Spotlight can produce search results in seconds.

After that initial indexing process, Spotlight continues to mon- itor what's on your hard drive, indexing new and changed files in the background, in the microseconds between your keystrokes and clicks in other programs.

- Spotlight shows you only the matches from *your account* and the public areas of the Mac (like the System, Application, and Developer folders)—but not what's in anyone else's Home folder. If you were hoping to search your spouse's email for phrases like "meet you at midnight," forget it.

- If Spotlight finds a different version of something on each of two hard drives, it lets you know by displaying a faint gray hard drive name after each such item in the menu.

- Spotlight works by storing an *index*, a private, multimegabyte Dewey Decimal System, on each hard drive, disk partition, or USB flash (memory) drive. If you have some oddball type of disk, like a hard drive that's been formatted for Windows, Spotlight doesn't ordinarily index it—but you can turn on indexing by using the File→Get Info command on that drive's icon.

Tip: Spotlight can even find words inside files on other computers on your network—as long as they're also Macs running Leopard or Snow Leopard. If not, Spotlight can search only for the names of files on other networked computers.

- If you point to something in the results list without clicking, you can press ⌘-I to open the Get Info window for that item.

Advanced Menu Searches

Most people just type the words they're looking for into the Spotlight box. But if that's all you type, you're missing a lot of the fun.

Use quotes

If you type more than one word, Spotlight works just the way Google does. That is, it finds things that contain both words *somewhere* inside.

But if you're searching for a phrase where the words really belong together, put quotes around them. You'll save yourself from having to wade through hundreds of results where the words appear *separately*.

For example, searching for *military intelligence* rounds up documents that contain those two words, but not necessarily side by side. Searching for *"military intelligence"* finds documents that contain that exact phrase. (Insert your own political joke here.)

Limit by kind

You can confine your search to certain categories using a simple code. For example, to find all photos, type *kind:image*. If you're looking for a presentation document but you're not sure whether you used Keynote, iWork, or PowerPoint to create it, type *kind:presentation* into the box. And so on.

Here's the complete list of kinds. Remember to precede each keyword type with *kind* and a colon.

To find this:	Use one of these keywords:
A program	app, application, applications
Someone in your Address Book	contact, contacts
A folder or disk	folder, folders
A message in Mail	email, emails, mail message, mail messages
An iCal appointment	event, events
An iCal task	to do, to dos, todo, todos
A graphic	image, images
A movie	movie, movies
A music file	music
An audio file	audio
A PDF file	pdf, pdfs
A System Preferences control	preferences, system preferences
A Safari bookmark	bookmark, bookmarks
A font	font, fonts
A presentation (PowerPoint, iWork)	presentation, presentations

You can combine these codes with the text you're seeking, too. For example, if you're pretty sure you had a photo called "Naked Mole-Rat," you could cut directly to it by typing *mole kind:images* or *kind:images mole.* (The order doesn't matter.)

Limit by recent date

You can use a similar code to restrict the search by chronology. If you type *date:yesterday*, then Spotlight limits its hunt to items you last opened yesterday.

Here's the complete list of date keywords you can use: *this year, this month, this week, yesterday, today, tomorrow, next week, next month, next year.* (The last four items are useful only for finding upcoming iCal appointments. Even Spotlight can't show you files you haven't created yet.)

Limit by metadata

If your brain is already on the verge of exploding, now might be a good time to take a break.

In Mac OS X 10.4, Spotlight could search on either of the criteria described above: kind or date.

But these days, you can limit Spotlight searches by *any* of the 125 different info-morsels that might be stored as part of the files on your Mac: author, audio bit rate, city, composer, camera model, pixel width, and so on. Page 110 has a complete discussion of these so-called *metadata* types. (Metadata means "data about the data"—that is, descriptive info-bites about the files themselves.) Here are a few examples:

- *author:casey.* Finds all documents with "casey" in the Author field. (This presumes that you've actually *entered* the name Casey into the document's Author box. Microsoft Word, for example, has a place to store this information.)

- *width:800.* Finds all graphics that are 800 pixels wide.

- *flash:1.* Finds all photos that were taken with the camera's flash on. (To find photos with the flash *off*, you'd type *flash:0.* A number of the yes/no criteria work this way: Use 1 for yes, 0 for no.)

- *modified:3/7/10-3/10/10.* Finds all documents modified between March 7 and March 10, 2010.

You can also type *created:6/1/10* to find all the files you created on June 1, 2010. Type *modified:<=3/9/10* to find all documents you edited *on or before* March 9, 2010.

As you can see, three range-finding symbols are available for your queries: <, >, and -. The < means "before" or "less than"; the > means "after" or "greater than"; and the hyphen indicates a range (of dates, sizes, or whatever you're looking for).

Tip: Here again, you can string words together. To find all PDFs you opened today, use *date:today kind:PDF.* And if you're looking for a PDF document that you created on July 4, 2010, containing the word wombat, you can type *created:7/4/10 kind:pdf wombat*—although at this point, you're not saving all that much time.

Now, those examples are just a few representative searches out of the dozens that Mac OS X makes available.

It turns out that the search criteria codes that you can type into the Spotlight box (*author:casey, width:800,* and so on) correspond to the master list that appears when you choose Other in the Spotlight *window,* as described on page 103. In other words, there are *125 different* search criteria.

There's only one confusing part: In the Other list, lots of metadata types have spaces in their names. *Pixel width, musical genre, phone number,* and so on.

Yet you're allowed to use only *one* word before the colon when you type a search into the Spotlight box. For example, even though *pixel width* is a metadata type, you have to use *width:* or *pixelwidth:* in your search.

So it would probably be helpful to have a master list of the *one-word* codes that Spotlight recognizes—the shorthand versions of the criteria described on page 110.

Here it is, a Missing Manual exclusive, deep from within the bowels of Apple's Spotlight department: the master list of one-word codes. (Note that some search criteria have several alternate one-word names.)

Real Search Attribute	**One-Word Name(s)**
Keywords	keyword
Title	title
Subject	subject, title
Theme	theme
Authors	author, from, with, by
Editors	editor
Projects	project
Where from	wherefrom
Comment	comment
Copyright	copyright
Producer	producer
Used dates	used, date

Last opened	lastused, date
Content created	contentcreated, created, date
Content modified	contentmodified, modified, date
Duration	duration, time
Item creation	itemcreated, created, date
Contact keywords	contactkeyword, keyword
Version	version
Pixel height	pixelheight, height
Pixel width	pixelwidth, width
Page height	pageheight
Page width	pagewidth
Color space	colorspace
Bits per sample	bitspersample, bps
Flash	flash
Focal length	focallength
Alpha channel	alpha
Device make (camera brand)	make
Device model (camera model)	model
ISO speed	iso
Orientation	orientation
Layers	layer
White balance	whitebalance
Aperture	aperture, fstop
Profile name	profile
Resolution width	widthdpi, dpi
Resolution height	heightdpi, dpi
Exposure mode	exposuremode
Exposure time	exposuretime, time
EXIF version	exifversion
Codecs	codec
Media types	mediatype
Streamable	streamable
Total bit rate	totalbitrate, bitrate
Video bit rate	videobitrate, bitrate
Audio bit rate	audiobitrate, bitrate
Delivery type	delivery
Altitude	altitude
Latitude	latitude
Longitude	longitude
Text content	intext
Display name	displayname, name
Red eye	redeye
Metering mode	meteringmode
Max aperture	maxaperture
FNumber	fnumber, fstop
Exposure program	exposureprogram
Exposure time	exposuretime, time
Headline	headline, title
Instructions	instructions
City	city
State or province	state, province
Country	country
Album	album, title
Sample rate	audiosamplerate, samplerate
Channel count	channels
Tempo	tempo
Key signature	keysignature, key
Time signature	timesignature

Audio encoding application	audioencodingapplication
Composer	composer, author, by
Lyricist	lyricist, author, by
Track number	tracknumber
Recording date	recordingdate, date
Musical genre	musicalgenre, genre
General MIDI sequence	ismidi
Recipients	recipient, to, with
Year recorded	yearrecorded, year
Organizations	organization
Languages	language
Rights	rights
Publishers	publisher
Contributors	contributor, by, author, with
Coverage	coverage
Description	description, comment
Identifier	id
Audiences	audience, to
Pages	pages
Security method	securitymethod
Content Creator	creator
Due date	duedate, date
Encoding software	encodingapplication
Rating	starrating
Phone number	phonenumber
Email addresses	email
Instant message addresses	imname
Kind	kind
URL	url
Recipient email addresses	email
Email addresses	email
Filename	filename
File pathname	path
Size	size
Created	created
Modified	modified
Owner	owner
Group	group
Stationery	stationery
File invisible	invisible
File label	label
Spotlight comments	spotlightcomment, comment
Fonts	font
Instrument category	instrumentcategory
Instrument name	instrumentname

Boolean searches

What comp sci professors call *Boolean* searches are terms that round up results containing *either* of two search terms, *both* search terms, or one term but *not* another.

To go Boolean, you're supposed to incorporate terms like AND, OR, or NOT into your search queries.

For example, you can round up a list of files that match *two* terms by typing, say, *vacation AND kids*. (That's also how you'd find documents coauthored by two people—you and a pal, for example. You'd search for *author:Casey AND author:Chris.* Yes, you have to type Boolean terms in all capitals.)

Tip: *You can use parentheses instead of AND, if you like. That is, typing* (vacation kids) *finds documents that contain both words, not necessarily together. But the truth is, Spotlight runs an AND search whenever you type two terms, like* vacation kids*—neither parentheses nor AND is required.*

If you use OR, you can find items that match *either* of two search criteria. Typing *kind:jpeg OR kind:pdf* turns up photos and PDF files in a single list.

The minus sign (hyphen) works, too. If you did a search for *dolphins,* hoping to turn up sea-mammal documents, but instead find your results contaminated by football-team listings, by all means repeat the search with *dolphins -miami.* Mac OS X eliminates all documents containing "Miami."

Tip: *The word NOT works the same way. You could type* dolphins NOT miami *to achieve the same effect. But the hyphen is faster to type.*

The Spotlight Window

As you may have noticed, the Spotlight menu doesn't list *every* match on your hard drive. Unless you own one of those extremely rare 60-inch Apple Skyscraper Displays, there just isn't room.

Instead, Spotlight uses some fancy behind-the-scenes analysis to calculate and display the *20 most likely* matches for what you typed. But at the top of the menu, you usually see that there are many other possible matches; it says something like "Show All," meaning that there are other candidates. (Mac OS X no longer tells you how *many* other results there are.)

There is, however, a second, more powerful way into the Spotlight labyrinth. And that's to use the Spotlight *window,* shown in Figure 3-2.

Spotlight Window from Spotlight Menu

If the Spotlight menu—its Most Likely to Succeed list—doesn't include what you're looking for, then click Show All. You've just opened the Spotlight window.

Now you have access to the *complete* list of matches, neatly listed in what appears to be a standard Finder window.

Opening the Spotlight Window Directly

When you're in the Finder, you can also open the Spotlight window *directly,* without using the Spotlight menu as a trigger. Actually, there are three ways to get there (Figure 3-2):

- ⌘-F (for *Find,* get it?). When you choose File→Find (or press ⌘-F), you get an *empty* Spotlight window, ready to fill in for your search.

Snow Leopard Spots: When the Find window opens, what folder does it intend to search?

Until Snow Leopard came along, the answer was always: "Your whole Mac." Which was a pain. Most of the time, what you wanted to search was the folder you were in. So you had to take an extra second to click that folder's name at the top of the Find window.

In Snow Leopard, you're saved that step. Choose Finder→Preferences→Advanced. From the "When performing a search" pop-up menu, you can choose Search This Mac, Search the Current Folder (usually what you want), or Use the Previous Search Scope (that is, *either* "the whole Mac" or "the current folder," whichever you set up last time).

- **Option-⌘-space bar.** This keystroke opens the same window. But it always comes set to search everything on your Mac (except other people's Home folders, of course), regardless of the setting you made in Preferences (as described in the previous paragraphs).

- **Open any desktop window, and type something into the Search box at upper right.** Presto—the mild-mannered folder window turns into the Spotlight window, complete with search results.

Tip: You can change the Find keystrokes to just about anything you like. See page 179.

Figure 3-2:
The Spotlight window stands ready to search the currently open window—or your entire Mac, depending on the choice you've made in Finder Preferences.

The Basic Search

When the Searching window opens, you can start typing whatever you're looking for into the Search box at the upper right.

As you type, the window fills with a list of the files and folders whose names contain what you typed. It's just like the Spotlight menu, but without the 20-item results limit (Figure 3-2).

While the searching is going on, a sprocket icon whirls away in the lower-right corner. To cancel the search and clear the box (so you can try a different search), click the ⊗ button next to the phrase you typed. Or just hit the Esc key.

Power Searches

The real beauty of the Searching window, though, is that it can hunt down icons using extremely specific criteria; it's much more powerful (and complex) than the Spotlight menu. If you spent enough time setting up the search, you could use this feature to find a document whose name begins with the letters *Cro,* is over a megabyte in size, was created after 10/1/09 but before the end of the year, was changed within the past week, has the file name suffix *.doc,* and contains the phrase "attitude adjustment." (Of course, if you knew *that* much about a file, you'd probably know where it is without having to use the Searching window. But you get the picture.)

To use the Searching window, you need to feed it two pieces of information: *where* you want it to search, and *what* to look for. You can make these criteria as simple or as complex as you like.

Where to Look

The three phrases at the top of the window—This Mac, "Folder Name," and Shared—are buttons. Click one to tell Spotlight where to search:

- **This Mac** means your *entire* computer, including secondary disks attached to it (or installed inside)—minus other people's files, of course.

- **"Letters to Congress"** (or whatever the current window is) limits the search to whatever window was open. So if you want to search your Pictures folder, open it first and *then* hit ⌘-F. You'll see the "Pictures" button at the top of the window, and you can click it to restrict the search to that folder.

Tip: Remember: You can save yourself this click by visiting Finder→Preferences→Advanced and choosing "Search the Current Folder" from the pop-up menu.

- **Shared.** Click this button to expand the search to your *entire network* and all the computers on it. (This assumes, of course, that you've brought their icons to your screen as described in Chapter 13.)

  If the other computers are Macs running Leopard or Snow Leopard, Spotlight can search their files just the way it does on your own Mac—finding words inside the files, for example. If they're any other kind of computer, Spotlight can search for files only by name.

Tip: If the object of your quest doesn't show up, you can adjust the scope of the search with one quick click on another button at the top of the window, like This Mac or Shared. Spotlight updates the results list.

Search by Contents/Search by Name

The two other buttons at the top of the Spotlight window are also very powerful:

- **Contents.** This button, the factory setting, searches for the words *inside* your files, along with all the metadata attached to them.

- **File Name.** There's no denying that sometimes you already know a file's *name*—you just don't know where it is. In this case, it's far faster to search by name, just as people did before Spotlight came along. The list of results is far shorter, and you'll spot what you want much faster. That's why this button is so welcome.

Tip: If you press Shift as you open the File menu (or as you press ⌘-F), the Find command changes to Find by Name. It opens the Find window, preset to search for icons by name. What a shortcut!

Complex Searches

If all you want to do is search your entire computer for files containing certain text, you might as well use the Spotlight *menu* described at the beginning of this chapter.

The power of the Spotlight *window,* though, is that it lets you design much more specific searches, using over 125 different search criteria: date modified, file size, the "last opened" date, color label, copyright holder's name, shutter speed (of a digital

Figure 3-3:
By repeatedly clicking the + button, you can turn on as many criteria as you'd like; each additional row further narrows the search.

photo), tempo (of a music file), and so on. Figure 3-3 illustrates how detailed this kind of search can be.

To set up a complex search like this, use the second row of controls at the top of the window.

And third, and fourth, and fifth. Each time you click one of the **+** buttons at the right end of the window, a new criterion row appears; use its pop-up menus to specify *what* date, *what* file size, and so on. Figure 3-3 shows how you might build, for example, a search for all photo files that you've opened within the last week that contain a Photoshop layer named *Freckle Removal*.

To delete a row, click the **—** button at its right end.

Tip: If you press Option, the **+** button changes into a … button. When you click it, you get sub-rows of parameters for a single criterion. And a pop-up menu that says Any, All, or None appears at the top, so that you can build what are called exclusionary searches.

The idea here is that you can set up a search for documents created between November 1 and 7 or documents created November 10 through 14. Or files named Complaint that are also either Word or InDesign files.

The mind boggles.

Here's a rundown of the ways you can restrict your search, according to the options in the first pop-up menu of a row. Note that after you choose from that first pop-up menu (Last Opened, for example), you're supposed to use the additional pop-up menus to narrow the choice ("within last," "2," and "weeks," for example), as you'll read below.

Note: It may surprise you that choosing something from the Kind pop-up menu triggers the search instantly. As soon as you choose Applications, for example, the window fills with a list of every program on your hard drive. Want a quick list of every folder on your entire machine? Choose Folders. (Want to see which folders you've opened in the past couple of days? Add another row.)

If you also type something into the Search box at the very top of the window—before or after you've used one of these pop-up menus—the list pares itself down to items that match what you've typed.

Kind

When the first pop-up menu says Kind, you can use the second pop-up menu to indicate what kind of file you're looking for: Applications, Documents, Folders, Images, Movies, Music, PDF files, Presentations, Text files, or Other.

For example, when you're trying to free up some space on your drive, you could round up all your movie files, which tend to be huge. Choosing one of these file types makes the window begin to fill with matches automatically and instantly.

And what if the item you're looking for isn't among those nine canned choices? What if it's an alias, or a Photoshop plug-in, or some other type?

That's what the Other option is all about. Here, you can type in almost anything that specifies a kind of file: *Word, Excel, TIFF, JPEG, AAC, final cut, iMovie, alias, zip, html,* or whatever.

Last opened date/Last modified date/Created date

When you choose one of these options from the first pop-up menu, the second pop-up menu lets you isolate files, programs, and folders according to the last time you opened them, the last time you changed them, or when they were created.

- **Today, yesterday, this week, this month, this year.** This second pop-up menu offers quick, canned time-limiting options.

- **Within last, exactly, before, after.** These let you be more precise. If you choose before, after, or exactly, then your criterion row sprouts a month/day/year control that lets you round up items that you last opened or changed before, after, or on a specific day, like 5/27/10. If you choose "within last," then you can limit the search to things you've opened or changed within a specified number of days, weeks, months, or years.

  These are awesomely useful controls, because they let you specify a chronological window for whatever you're looking for.

Tip: You're allowed to add two Date rows—a great trick that lets you round up files that you created or edited between two dates. Set up the first Date row to say "is after," and the second one to say "is before."

In fact, if it doesn't hurt your brain to think about it, how about this? You can even have more than two Date rows. Use one pair to specify a range of dates for the file's creation date and two other rows to limit when it was modified.

Science!

Feeding the Barren Pop-up Menus

The first little pop-up menu in the Spotlight window lists those handy search starting points: Kind, Last opened date, Name, and so on.

But it's actually *less* fully stocked than it was in the Mac OS X of days gone by. Apple streamlined the options a bit.

For example, you used to be able to search by *label*. You could therefore easily round up all files pertaining to a certain project for backing up, deleting, or burning to a CD en masse. That's off the menu as you first see it.

Gone, too, is the Size criterion, which could be helpful when you're trying to make space on your overstuffed hard drive by ferreting out the huge, multigigabyte files and folders.

Fortunately, you can restore these options to the criterion pop-up menu easily enough. The trick is to use the Other option, as already described. In the dialog box shown in Figure 3-4, search for *label* or *size*. When you find the criterion you want, turn on the "In menu" checkbox and click OK.

Presto: You've got your menu back.

Name

Spotlight likes to find text *anywhere* in your files, no matter what their *names* are. But when you want to search for an icon by the text that's in only its *name,* this is your ticket. (Capitalization doesn't matter.)

Wouldn't it be faster just to click the File Name button at the top of the window? Yes—but using the Search window offers you far more control, thanks to the second pop-up menu that offers you these options:

- **Contains.** The position of the letters you type doesn't matter. If you type *then,* you find files with names like "Then and Now," "Authentic Cajun Recipes," and "Lovable Heathen."

- **Starts with.** The Find program finds only files beginning with the letters you type. If you type *then,* you find "Then and Now," but not "Authentic Cajun Recipes" or "Lovable Heathen."

- **Ends with.** If you type *then,* you find "Lovable Heathen," but not files called "Then and Now" or "Authentic Cajun Recipes."

- **Is.** This option finds only files named *precisely* what you type (except that capitalization still doesn't matter). Typing *then* won't find any of the file names in the previous examples. It would unearth only a file called simply "Then." In fact, a file with a file name suffix, like "Then.doc," doesn't even qualify.

  (If this happens to you, though, here's a workaround: From the first pop-up menu, choose Other; in the dialog box, pick Filename. The Filename criterion ignores extensions; it would find "Then.doc" even if you searched for "then.")

Contents

You can think of this option as the opposite of Name. It finds *only* the text that's inside your files, and completely ignores their icon names.

That's a handy function when, for example, a document's name doesn't match its contents. Maybe a marauding toddler pressed the keys while playing Kid Pix, renaming your doctoral thesis "xggrjpO#$5%////." Or maybe you just can't remember what you called something.

Other

If this were a math equation, it might look like this: *options × options = overwhelming.*

Choosing Other from the first pop-up menu opens a special dialog box containing at least 125 *other* criteria. Not just the big kahunas like Name, Size, and Kind, but far more targeted (and obscure) criteria like "Bits per sample" (so you can round up MP3 music files of a certain quality), "Device make" (so you can round up all digital photos taken with, say, a Canon Rebel camera), "Key signature" (so you can find all the GarageBand songs you wrote in the key of F sharp), "Pages" (so you can find all Word documents that are really long), and so on. As you can see in Figure 3-4, each one comes with a short description.

You may think Spotlight is offering you a staggering array of file-type criteria. In fact, though, big bunches of information categories (technically called *metadata*) are all hooks for a relatively small number of document types. For example:

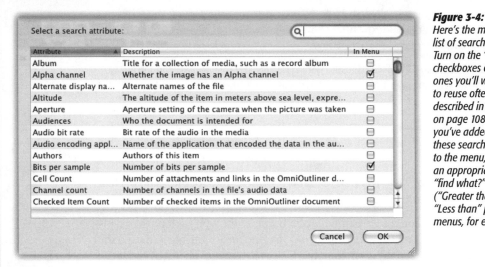

Figure 3-4:
Here's the master list of search criteria. Turn on the "In menu" checkboxes of the ones you'll want to reuse often, as described in the box on page 108. Once you've added some of these search criteria to the menu, you'll get an appropriate set of "find what?" controls ("Greater than" and "Less than" pop-up menus, for example).

- **Digital photos and other graphics files** account for the metadata types alpha channel, aperture, color space, device make, device model, EXIF version, exposure mode, exposure program, exposure time, flash, FNumber, focal length, ISO speed, max aperture, metering mode, orientation, pixel height, pixel width, redeye, resolution height, resolution width, and white balance.

- **Digital music files** have searchable metadata categories like album, audio bit rate, bits per sample, channel count, composer, duration, General MIDI sequence, key signature, lyricist, musical genre, recording date, sample rate, tempo, time signature, track number, and year recorded. There's even a special set of parameters for GarageBand and Soundtrack documents, including instrument category, instrument name, loop descriptors, loop file type, loop original key, and loop scale type.

- **Microsoft Office documents** can contain info bits like *authors, contributors, fonts, languages, pages, publishers,* and contact information (*name, phone number,* and so on).

This massive list also harbors a few criteria you may use more often, like Size, Label, and Visibility (which lets you see all the invisible files on your hard drive). See the box on page 108.

Now, you could argue that in the time it takes you to set up a search for such a specific kind of data, you could have just rooted through your files and found what you wanted manually. But hey—you never know. Someday, you may remember *nothing* about a photo you're looking for except that you used the flash and an f-stop of 1.8.

The Raw Power of the Raw Query

You may have just slogged through 20 pages of Spotlight details—but if you can believe it, this is only the beginning. It turns out that the Spotlight most people see is only a subset of the true power awaiting in Mac OS X.

For example, what if you wanted to see all the files you've opened in the past 24 hours *except* email messages and Address Book entries? Or what if you want to round up all PDF documents *and* PostScript files you've opened in the past week? Using the Spotlight tools that most people see, you wouldn't be able to set up searches or smart folders that are quite that smart.

Fortunately for the true Snow Leopard geek, Spotlight also understands a *query language*—a programming-like syntax that lets you establish far more specific and nuanced searches.

To read about the basics of the query language, start at *http://developer.apple. com/macosx/spotlight.html;* it will lead you to a number of Web pages that explain the full scope of Spotlight's internal lingo.

You may also get a kick out of studying how Spotlight uses the query language itself. To do that, create a smart folder, and then Get Info on it. On the General panel, inspect the string of query text that Spotlight generated behind the scenes (as shown here).

You'll learn that the basic search command always includes the command kMDItem. To search for something by its file type, your query should begin with *kMDItemContentType*; for when you last opened it, use *kMDItemLastUsedDate*.

For example, here's how to type a query that rounds up all files that contain the keyword "kumquat": *kMDItemKeywords == "*kumquat*"*. (The double equals symbol just means "equals." You can also use <, >, <=, and so on. The asterisks mean, "There may be other text here, or not; it's still a good

match.") To signify "and," use two ampersands, like this: &&. For "or," use two vertical bars, like this: ||.

Once you've read more about this query language, you can build much more complicated searches. This one, for example, finds all audio and video files whose author is either Kevin or Steve that were modified in the past week:

```
((kMDItemAuthors == "Kevin"wc ||
kMDItemAuthors == "Steve"wc) &&
(kMDItemContentType == "audio"wc ||
kMDItemContentType == "video"wc)) &&
        (kMDItemFSContentChange-
        Date == $time.this_week)
```

And here's how you'd find all PDF documents and PostScript files with a single search:

```
((kMDItemContentTypeTree
== 'com.adobe.pdf') ||
(kMDItemKind == 'Post-
Script document'))
```

(Most of this stuff actually stands for useful things: *MD* for metadata, *wc* for "word-based, case-insensitive," and so on.)

And where, you may ask, are you supposed to type all these queries? You have two options.

In the Finder, when you choose File→Find to produce the Spotlight window, choose Other from the Kind pop-up menu. In the list of six gazillion search parameters, choose Raw Query. You can type your elaborate search string into the text box that appears.

Second, you can open Terminal (Chapter 16) and use Spotlight's Unix equivalent. The main command you want to learn about is *mdfind*. For example, at the Terminal prompt, you could type *mdfind "kMDItemAcquisitionModel == 'Canon PowerShot S80'"* (and then press Return) to see a list of all photos you took with that particular camera model.

Spotlight: The Missing Manual? Hmm. Has a nice ring to it, doesn't it?

Tip: Don't miss the Search box in this dialog box. It makes it super-easy to pluck one useful criterion needle–Size, say–out of the haystack. Also don't forget about the "In menu" checkbox in the right column. It lets you add one of these criteria to the main pop-up menu, so you don't have to go burrowing into Other again the next time.

What to Do with Search Results

In Snow Leopard, more than ever, the results window is a regular old Finder window, with all the familiar views and controls (Figure 3-5).

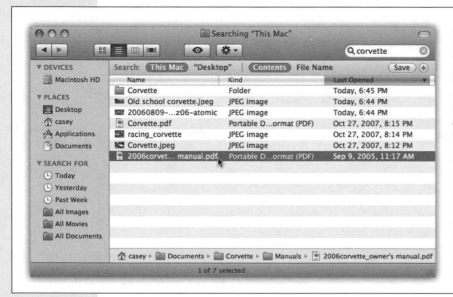

Figure 3-5:
Click a result once to see where it sits on your hard drive (bottom). If the window is too narrow to reveal the full folder path, run your cursor over the folders without clicking. As your mouse moves from one folder to another, Leopard briefly reveals its name, compressing other folders as necessary to make room. (Sub-tip: You can drag icons into these folders, too.)

You can work with anything in the results window exactly as though it's a regular Finder window: Drag something to the Trash, rename something, drag something to the desktop to move it there, drag something onto a Dock icon to open it with a certain program, Option-⌘-drag it to the desktop to create an alias, and so on.

You can move up or down the list by pressing the arrow keys, scroll a "page" at a time with the Page Up and Page Down keys, and so on. You can also highlight multiple icons simultaneously, the same way you would in a Finder list view: Highlight all of them by choosing Edit→Select All; highlight individual items by ⌘-clicking them; drag diagonally to enclose a cluster of found items; and so on.

Or you can proceed in any of these ways:

- **Change the view** by clicking one of the View icons or choosing from the View menu. You can switch among icon, list, or Cover Flow views (see Chapter 1). Actually, Cover Flow is a *great* view for search results; since this list is culled from folders all over the computer, you otherwise have very little sense of context as you examine the file names.

Note: Column view isn't available here, since the displayed search results are collected from all over your computer. They don't all reside in the same folder. Still, Apple's given you a consolation prize: the folder path display at the bottom of the window. It tells you where the selected item is hiding on your hard drive just as clearly as column view would have.

- **Sort the results** by clicking the column headings. It can be especially useful to sort by Kind, so that similar file types are clustered together (Documents, Images, Messages, and so on), or by Last Opened, so that the list is chronological.

Snow Leopard Spots: For the first time, you can sort the search results even in icon view. True, there are no column headings to click—but you can use the ✿ menu to choose "Keep Arranged by" [whatever criterion you like]. Snow Leopard will remember this sort order the next time you do an icon-view search.

- **Change the view options.** Press ⌘-J (or choose View→Show View Options) to open the View Options panel for the results window. Here, you can add a couple of additional columns (Date Modified, Date Created); change the icon size or text size; or turn on the "always" checkbox at the top, so that future results windows will have the look you've set up here.

- **Get a Quick Look at one result** by clicking it and then hitting the space bar. You get the big, bold, full-size Quick Look preview window.

- **Get more information** about a result by selecting it and then choosing File→Get Info (⌘-I). The normal Get Info window appears, complete with date, size, and location information.

- **Find out where it is.** It's nice to see all the search results in one list, but you're not actually seeing them in their native habitats: the Finder folder windows where they physically reside.

If you click once on an icon in the results, the bottom edge of the window becomes a folder map that shows you where that item is.

POWER USERS' CLINIC

All Roads Lead to Spotlight

As you know, you can open the Spotlight window using a keystroke or from the Spotlight menu after performing a search. But those methods are only the beginning.

Try this: Highlight a phrase in any program (except Microsoft ones and a few other weirdos). Control-click (or right-click) the highlighted phrase, and then choose Search in Spotlight from the shortcut menu. Boom: The Spotlight window opens, already stocked with the search results that match your highlighted phrase.

Remember, too, that Spotlight has its claws in all kinds of individual Mac OS X programs. You'll find a Spotlight Search box in System Preferences (so that you can pull up the correct panel), in Mail (to find a certain message), in Automator (to search for components for your software robots), and so on. As software companies get around to it, they're also welcome to incorporate pieces of the Spotlight technology into their own programs.

For example, in Figure 3-5, the notation in the Path strip means: "The 2006 corvette_owner's manual.pdf icon you found is in the Manuals folder, which is in the Corvette folder, which is in the Documents folder, which is in Casey's Home folder."

To get your hands on the actual icon, choose File→Open Enclosing Folder (⌘-R). Mac OS X highlights the icon in question, sitting there in its window wherever it happens to be on your hard drive.

- **Open the file (or open one of the folders it's in).** If one of the found files is the one you were looking for, double-click it to open it (or highlight it and press either ⌘-O or ⌘-↑). In many cases, you don't know or care where the file was—you just want to get into it.

Tip: You can also double-click to open any of the folders in the folder map at the bottom of the window. For example, in Figure 3-5, you could double-click the selected PDF icon to open it, or the Manuals folder to open it, and so on.

- **Move or delete the file.** You can drag an item directly out of the found-files list and into a different folder, window, or disk—or straight to the Dock or the Trash. If you click something else and then re-click the dragged item in the results list, the folder map at the bottom of the window updates itself to reflect the file's new location.

- **Start over.** If you'd like to repeat the search using a different search phrase, just edit the text in the Search box. (Press ⌘-F to empty the Search box and the Spotlight window.)

- **Give up.** If none of these avenues suits your fancy, you can close the window as you would any other (⌘-W).

Customizing Spotlight

You've just read about how Spotlight works fresh out of the box. But you can tailor its behavior, both for security reasons and to fit it to the kinds of work you do.

Here are three ways to open the Spotlight preferences center:

- **Choose Spotlight Preferences** at the bottom of the Spotlight menu just after you've performed a search.

- **Use Spotlight itself.** Hit ⌘-space bar, type *spotl,* and press Return.

- **Choose ⌘→System Preferences. Click Spotlight.**

In any case, you wind up face to face with the dialog box shown in Figure 3-6.

You can tweak Spotlight in three ways here, all very useful:

- **Turn off categories.** The list of checkboxes identifies what Spotlight tracks. If you find that Spotlight uses up valuable menu space listing, say, Web bookmarks or fonts—stuff you don't need to find very often—then turn off their checkboxes.

Now the Spotlight menu's 20 precious slots are allotted to icon types you care more about.

- **Prioritize the categories.** This dialog box also lets you change the *order* of the category results; just drag a list item up or down to change where it appears in the Spotlight menu.

  The factory setting is for Applications to appear first in the results. That makes a lot of sense if you use Spotlight as a quick program launcher (which is a great idea). But if you're a party planner, and you spend all day on the phone, and the most important Spotlight function for you is its ability to look up someone in your Address Book, then drag Contacts to the top of the list. You'll need fewer arrow-key presses once the results menu appears.

- **Change the keystroke.** Ordinarily, pressing ⌘-space bar highlights the Spotlight Search box in your menu bar, and Option-⌘-space bar opens the Spotlight window described above. If these keystrokes clash with some other key assignment in your software, though, you can reassign them to almost any other keystroke you like.

Figure 3-6:
Here's where you can specify what categories of icons you want Spotlight to search, which order you want them listed in the Spotlight menu, and what keystroke you want to use for highlighting the Spotlight Search box.

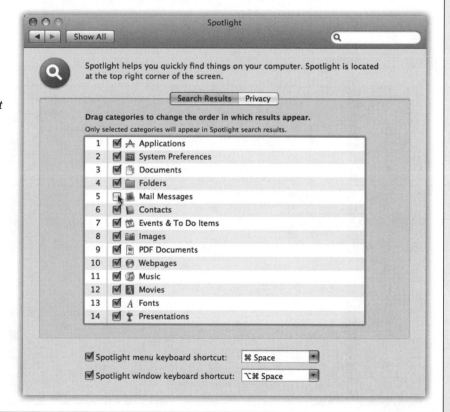

Most people notice only the pop-up menu that lets you select one of your F-keys (the function keys at the top of your keyboard). But you can also click inside the white box that lists the keystroke and then press *any* key combination—Control-S, for example—to choose something different.

Snow Leopard Spots: You can now choose any available keystroke. You're no longer required to include one of the F-keys (such as F4).

Apple assumes no responsibility for your choosing a keystroke that messes up some other function on your Mac. ⌘-S, for example, would not be a good choice.

On the other hand, if you choose a Spotlight keystroke that Mac OS X uses for some other function (like Shift-⌘-3), a little yellow alert icon appears in the Spotlight pane. This icon is actually a button; clicking it brings you to the Keyboard & Mouse pane, where you can see exactly which keystroke is in dispute and change it.

Privacy Settings

Ordinarily, Spotlight looks for matches wherever it can, except in other people's Home folders. (That is, you can't search through other people's stuff).

But even within your own Mac world, you can hide certain folders from Spotlight searches. Maybe you have privacy concerns—for example, you don't want your spouse

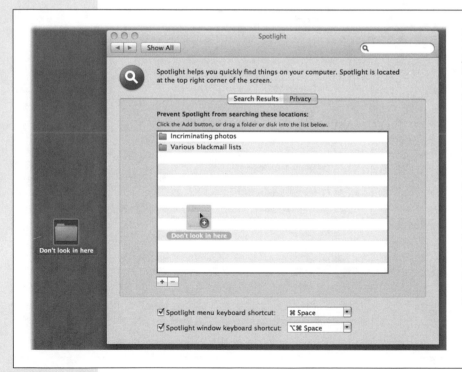

Figure 3-7:
You can add disks, partitions, or folders to the list of non-searchable items just by dragging them from the desktop into this window. Or, if the private items aren't visible at the moment, you can click the + button, navigate your hard drive, select the item, and click Choose. To remove something from this list, click it and then press the Delete key or click the − button.

Spotlighting your stuff while you're away from your desk. Maybe you just want to create more focused Spotlight searches, removing a lot of old, extraneous junk from its database.

Either way, the steps are simple. Open the Spotlight panel of System Preferences, as described previously. Click the Privacy tab. Figure 3-7 explains the remaining steps.

Tip: When you mark a disk or folder as non-searchable, Spotlight actually deletes its entire *index* (its invisible card-catalog filing system) from that disk. If Spotlight ever seems to be acting wackily, you can use this function to make it rebuild its own index file on the problem disk. Just drag the disk into the Privacy list and then remove it again. Spotlight deletes, and then rebuilds, the index for that disk.

(Don't forget the part about "remove it again," though. If you add a disk to the Privacy list, Spotlight is no longer able to find anything on it, even if you can see it right in front of you.)

Once you've built up the list of private disks and folders, close System Preferences. Spotlight now pretends the private items don't even exist.

Smart Folders

You may remember from Chapter 1 (or from staring at your own computer) that the Sidebar at the left side of every desktop window contains a set of little folders under the Searches heading. Each is actually a *smart folder*—a self-updating folder that, in essence, performs a continual, 24/7 search for the criteria you specify. (Smart folders are a lot like smart albums in iPhoto and iTunes, smart mailboxes in Mail, and so on.)

Note: In truth, the smart folder performs a search for the specified criteria at the moment you open it. But because it's so fast, it feels as though it's been quietly searching all along.

The ones installed there by Apple are meant as inspiration for you to create your *own* smart folders. The key, as it turns out, is the little Save button in the upper-right corner of the Spotlight window.

Here's a common example—one that you can't replicate in any other operating system. You choose File→Find. You set up the pop-up menus to say "last opened date" and "this week." You click Save. You name the smart folder something like Current Crises, and you turn on "Add to Sidebar" (Figure 3-8).

Tip: Behind the scenes, smart folders you create are actually special files that are stored in your Home→ Library→Saved Searches folder.

From now on, whenever you click that smart folder, it reveals all the files you've worked on in the past week or so. The great part is that these items' *real* locations may be all over the map, scattered in folders all over your Mac and your network. But through the magic of the smart folder, they appear as though they're all in one neat folder.

Tip: *If you decide your original search criteria need a little fine-tuning, click the smart folder. From the* ⚙ *menu, choose Show Search Criteria. You're back on the original setting-up-the-search window. Use the pop-up menus and other controls to tweak your search setup, and then click the Save button once again.*

To delete a smart folder, just drag its icon out of the Sidebar. (Or if it's anywhere else, like on your desktop, drag it to the Trash like any other folder.)

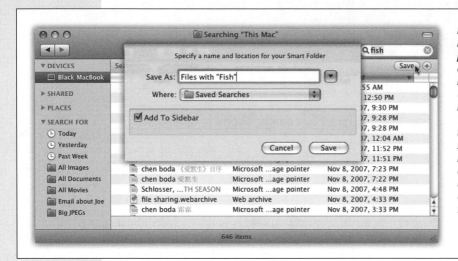

Figure 3-8:
Mac OS X can preserve your search as a smart folder listed in the Sidebar (lower left)—at least, it does as long as "Add To Sidebar" is turned on. You can stash a smart folder in your Dock, too, although it doesn't display a stack of its contents, as normal folders do.

Dock, Desktop, & Toolbars

Y ou can't help reacting, one way or another, to the futuristic, sleek looks of Mac OS X the first time you arrive at its desktop. There's the Dock, looking photo-realistic and shiny on its 3-D mirrored shelf. There are those Finder windows, slick and textureless with their gentle gradient-gray title bars. And then there's the shimmering, continually morphing backdrop of the desktop itself.

This chapter shows you how to use and control these most dramatic elements of Mac OS X.

The Dock

For years, most operating systems maintained two lists of programs. One listed *unopened* programs until you needed them, like the Start menu (Windows) or the Launcher (Mac OS 9). The other kept track of which programs were *open* at the moment for easy switching, like the taskbar (Windows) or the Application menu (Mac OS 9).

In Mac OS X, Apple combined both functions into a single strip of icons called the *Dock*.

Apple's thinking goes like this: Why must you know whether or not a program is already running? That's the computer's problem, not yours. In an ideal world, this distinction should be irrelevant. A program should appear when you click its icon, whether it's open or not.

"Which programs are open" already approaches unimportance in Mac OS X, where sophisticated memory-management features make it hard to run out of memory. You can have dozens of programs open at once in Mac OS X.

And *that's* why the Dock combines the launcher and status functions of a modern operating system. Only a tiny white reflective dot beneath a program's icon tells you that it's open.

Apple has made it as easy as possible to learn to like the Dock. You can customize the thing to within an inch of its life, use it to control and manipulate windows in elaborate ways, or even get rid of it completely. This section explains everything you need to know.

Setting Up the Dock

Apple starts the Dock off with a few icons it thinks you'll enjoy: Dashboard, Quick-Time Player, iTunes, iChat, Mail, the Safari Web browser, and so on. But using your Mac without putting your own favorite icons in the Dock is like buying an expensive suit and turning down the free alteration service. At the first opportunity, you should make the Dock your own.

The concept of the Dock is simple: Any icon you drag onto it (Figure 4-1) is installed there as a button. You can even drag an *open window* onto the Dock—a Microsoft Word document you're editing, say—using its proxy icon (page 27) as a handle.

A single click, not a double-click, opens the corresponding icon. In other words, the Dock is an ideal parking lot for the icons of disks, folders, documents, programs, and Internet bookmarks that you access frequently.

Tip: You can install batches of icons onto the Dock all at once—just drag them as a group. That's something you can't do with the other parking places for favorite icons, like the Sidebar and the Finder toolbar.

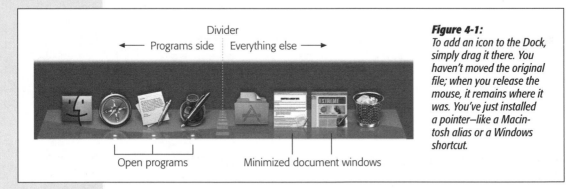

Divider

← Programs side   Everything else →

Open programs   Minimized document windows

Figure 4-1:
To add an icon to the Dock, simply drag it there. You haven't moved the original file; when you release the mouse, it remains where it was. You've just installed a pointer–like a Macintosh alias or a Windows shortcut.

Here are a few aspects of the Dock that may throw you at first:

- **It has two sides.** See the grayish dotted line running down the Dock? That's the divider (Figure 4-1). Everything on the left side is an *application*—a program. Everything else goes on the right side: files, documents, folders, disks, and minimized windows.

It's important to understand this division. If you try to drag an application to the right of the line, for example, Mac OS X teasingly refuses to accept it. (Even aliases observe that distinction. Aliases of applications can go only on the left side, and vice versa.)

- **Its icon names are hidden.** To see the name of a Dock icon, point to it without clicking. You'll see the name appear above the icon.

  When you're trying to find a certain icon in the Dock, run your cursor slowly across the icons without clicking; the icon labels appear as you go. You can often identify a document just by looking at its icon.

- **Folders and disks pop up to show what's inside.** If you click a folder or disk icon on the right side of the Dock, a list of its contents sprouts from the icon. It's like X-ray vision without the awkward moral consequences. Turn the page for details.

Tip: If you press Shift as you click, the stack opens in slow motion. Amaze your friends.

- **Programs appear there unsolicited.** Nobody but you (and Apple) can put icons on the right side of the Dock. But program icons appear on the left side of the Dock automatically whenever you open a program, even one that's not listed in the Dock. Its icon remains there for as long as it's running.

Tip: The Dock's translucent, reflective look is something to behold. Some people actually find it too translucent. But using TinkerTool, you can tone down the Dock's translucence—a great way to show off at user group meetings. See page 657 for details.

Living Icons

Mac OS X brings to life a terrific idea, a new concept in mainstream operating systems: icons that *tell* you something. If the Dock is big enough, you can often tell documents apart just by looking at their icons.

Some program icons even change over time. The Mail icon, for example (Chapter 19), bears a live counter that indicates how many new email messages are waiting for you. (After all, why should you switch into the Mail program if you'll only be disappointed?) The iChat icon lets you know how many chat responses are waiting. You can make

your Activity Monitor graph (page 408) show up right on its icon. Toast illustrates the progress of a disc you're burning. And if you minimize a QuickTime movie while it's playing, it shrinks down and continues playing right there in the Dock.

Think of the possibilities. One day the Safari icon could change to let you know when interesting new Web pages have appeared, the Quicken icon could display your current bank balance, and the Microsoft Word icon could change every time Microsoft posts a bug fix.

Organizing and Removing Dock Icons

You can move the tiles of the Dock around by dragging them horizontally. As you drag, the other icons scoot aside to make room. When you're satisfied with its new position, drop the icon you've just dragged.

To remove a Dock icon, just drag it away. (You can't remove the icons of the Finder, the Trash, or any minimized document window.) Once your cursor has cleared the Dock, release the mouse button. The icon disappears in a charming little puff of animated smoke. The other Dock icons slide together to close the gap.

Tip: You can replace the "puff of smoke" animation with one of your own, as described on page 661.

Something weird happens if you drag away a Dock program's icon while that program is running. You don't see any change immediately, because the program is still open. But when you quit the program, you see that its previously installed icon is no longer in the Dock.

Pop-up Dock Folders ("Stacks")

When you click a disk or folder icon on the Dock, you'll witness one of Snow Leopard's most enhanced features. The effect is shown in Figure 4-2.

In essence, Mac OS X is fanning out the folder's contents so you can see all of them. If it could talk, it would be saying, "Pick a card, any card."

Tip: You can change how the icons in a particular stack are sorted: alphabetically, chronologically, or whatever. Use the "Sort by" section of the shortcut menu (Figure 4-2, top left).

In principle, of course, pop-up folders are a great idea, because they save you time and clicking. Click a folder to see what's in it; click the icon you want inside; and you're off and running, without having had to open, manage, and close a window.

In practice, Apple has had a dickens of a time getting this feature to work. Over the generations of Mac OS X, this feature has changed, reverted, and changed again. (In the beginning, these pop-up balloons were called Stacks; nowadays, Apple reserves that name for a Dock folder whose icon changes to resemble what was last put into it, as described below.)

In Snow Leopard, pop-up folders are finally worth another look, thanks to two important tweaks:

- **Scroll bars.** If there are too many icons to fit in the pop-up contents list, you can scroll through them; you don't have to jump into their Finder window to do that.

- **Hierarchical folders.** Now you can click a folder in the contents display to see what's inside it, as shown in Figure 4-2.

Anyway, here's how to operate pop-up Dock folders.

Fan vs. grid vs. list

When you click a disk or folder icon on the Dock, you see its contents, arrayed in your choice of three displays:

Figure 4-2:
What happens when you click a folder in the Dock? You see its contents in one of three views. Top left: Here's how you choose which view you want: Fan, Grid, List, or Automatic. In List view, the folder contents appear as a menu; you can "drill down" into subfolders, and you open something by choosing its name.

Top right: In Fan view, click an icon to open it.

Bottom: In Grid view, many more icons appear than can fit in Fan view.

List view

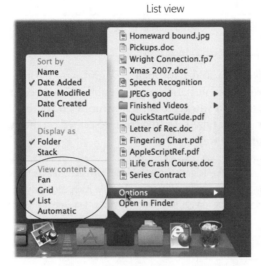

Fan view

Grid view

- **Fan.** The fan is a single, gently curved column of icons that pops out of the disk or folder icon. It's ideal for folders that contain very few icons, because there's room for only a handful of items in a fan (the exact number depends on your screen size). After the first few, you see only a "31 more in Finder" button, which you can click to see *everything* in that folder—but now you've *wasted* time, not saved it.

Note: When your Dock is positioned on a side of the screen instead of the bottom, the Fan option isn't available.

- **Grid.** If you've set a folder to open as a grid, you get to see the icons in a big rectangular window. File names often get abbreviated because there's not enough horizontal room, but you get to see many more icons this way. Actually, thanks to the scroll bar (or the type-selecting trick described on the facing page), you get to see *all* the icons this way.

Tip: A cool white-ghostly-highlighting effect is available, which makes it easier to see which icon you're pointing to as you move your mouse around in a grid or fan. To make it appear, click-and-hold a folder on the Dock—and then, without releasing the mouse, slide onto the grid or fan. The highlighting follows your cursor.

Alternatively, as soon as the grid or fan appears, press the arrow keys on your keyboard to move from icon to icon—complete with ghostly selection square.

- **List.** If you don't care about seeing the actual icons, you can also opt for a simple list of the folder's contents, like a pop-up menu. After all, if the folder contains nothing but a bunch of identical-looking audio or database icons, then seeing their icons isn't going to help you much—and a list appears much faster than a fan or a grid does.

   There's no scroll bar in a list balloon, but you can scroll the list nonetheless just by pointing to the top or bottom of it with your mouse. And, again, you can type-select as described below.

Tip: The List view also displays a little → to the right of each folder within the Dock folder. That is, it's a hierarchical list, meaning that you can burrow into folders within folders, all from the original Dock icon, all without opening a single new window. You can stick your entire Home folder, or even your whole hard drive icon, onto the Dock; now you have complete menu access to everything inside, right from the Dock.

- **Automatic.** There's a fourth option in the shortcut menu for a Dock folder, too: Automatic. If you turn this on, then Mac OS X chooses either Fan or Grid view, depending on how many icons are in the folder.

So how do you choose which display you want? Control-click (or right-click) the Dock folder's icon, and make a selection from the shortcut menu. Each disk or folder icon remembers its own fan/grid/list setting.

The Finer Points of Pop-up Dock Folders

Those were the basics of pop-up Dock folders. Here's the advanced course:

- **Ever-Changing Folder-Icon Syndrome (ECFIS).** When you add a folder or disk icon to the Dock, you might notice something wildly disorienting: Its icon keeps *changing* to resemble whatever you most recently put into it. For example, your Downloads folder might look like an Excel spreadsheet icon today, a PDF icon tonight, or a photo tomorrow—but never a folder. The annoying part is that you can't get to know a folder by its icon.

  Fortunately, this problem is easy to fix. Control-click (or right-click) the Dock folder. From the shortcut menu, in the "Display as" section, you can choose either Folder (which looks like a folder forever) or Stack (which changes to reflect its contents).

- **Ready-made pop-up folders.** When you install Mac OS X 10.6, you get a couple of starter Dock folders, just to get you psyched. One is Downloads; the other is Documents. (Both of these folders are physically inside your Home folder. But you may well do most of your interacting with them on the Dock.)

  The Downloads folder collects three kinds of Internet arrivals: files you download from the Web using Safari, files you receive in an iChat file-transfer session, and file attachments you get via email using Mail. Unless you intervene, they're sorted by the date you downloaded them.

  It's handy to know where to find your downloads, and nice not to have them all cluttering your desktop.

Tip: Once you've opened a stack's fan or grid, you can drag any of the icons right out of the fan or grid. Just drag your chosen icon onto the desktop or into any visible disk or folder. In other words, what lands in the Downloads folder doesn't have to stay there. (You can't drag out of a list, however.)

- **Hierarchical folders.** The fans and grids are hierarchical—that is, you can drill down from their folders into *their* folders. Figure 4-3 makes this concept clearer.

Tip: Figure 4-3 shows you how to open a folder in a grid or fan using the mouse—but you can do it all from the keyboard, too. Once a folder is selected, press Return, ⌘-O, or ⌘-↓ to see what's inside it; press ⌘-↑ to backtrack to the original display. When a folder is highlighted, you can press ⌘-Return to open it in a Finder window; add the Option key to open that Finder window without closing the grid or fan.

- **Type selecting.** Once a list, fan, or grid is on the screen, you can highlight any icon in it by typing the first few letters of its name. For example, once you've popped open your Applications folder, you can highlight Safari by typing *sa*. (Press Enter or Return to open the highlighted icon.)

Tip: Alternatively, you can "walk" through the fan, grid, or list by pressing the arrow keys. A highlighting effect makes it crystal clear which icon you're selecting. Once an icon is selected, press Return or Enter to open it.

Figure 4-3:
If you spot a folder inside a fan or grid (left), click it once. You're now looking at a fan or grid of its contents (right). You can also "back out" again by clicking the Back button in the upper-left corner, indicated here by the cursor.

- **Two ways to bypass the pop-up.** If you just want to see what's in a folder, without all the graphic overkill of the fan or the grid, then Control-click (right-click) the Dock folder's icon and choose "Open 'Applications' " (or whatever the folder's name is) from the shortcut menu. You go straight to the corresponding window.

  Actually, if you *really* value your time, you'll learn the shortcut: Option-⌘-click the Dock folder's icon. That accomplishes the same thing.

  (You jump immediately to the window that *contains* that folder's icon. That's not exactly the same thing as opening the Dock folder, but it's sometimes even more useful.)

Tip: Alternatively, you can ⌘-click a folder on the Dock—or, indeed, any icon on the Dock—to jump to the window that contains that folder's icon. (Bonus: This same trick—⌘-clicking—also works in the menu of Spotlight search results.)

Three Ways to Get the Dock Out of Your Hair

The bottom of the screen isn't necessarily the ideal location for the Dock. All Mac screens are wider than they are tall, so the Dock eats into your limited vertical screen space. You have three ways out: Hide the Dock, shrink it, or rotate it 90 degrees.

Auto-hiding the Dock

To turn on the Dock's auto-hiding feature, choose ⌘→Dock→Turn Hiding On (or press Option-⌘-D).

Tip: You also find this on/off switch when you choose ❖→Dock→Dock Preferences (Figure 4-4), or when you click the System Preferences icon in the Dock, and then the Dock icon. (Chapter 9 contains much more about the System Preferences program.)

When the Dock is hidden, it doesn't slide into view until you move the cursor to the Dock's edge of the screen. When you move the cursor back to the middle of the screen, the Dock slithers out of view once again. (Individual Dock icons may occasionally shoot upward into Desktop territory when a program needs your attention—cute, very cute—but otherwise, the Dock lies low until you call for it.)

On paper, an auto-hiding Dock is ideal; it's there only when you summon it. In practice, however, you may find that the extra half-second the Dock takes to appear and disappear makes this feature slightly less appealing.

Many Mac fans prefer to hide and show the Dock at will by pressing the hide/show keystroke, Option-⌘-D. This method makes the Dock pop on and off the screen without requiring you to move the cursor.

Shrinking and enlarging the Dock

Depending on your screen's size, you may prefer smaller or larger Dock buttons. The official way to resize them goes like this: Choose ❖→Dock→Dock Preferences. In the resulting dialog box, drag the Dock size slider, as shown in Figure 4-4.

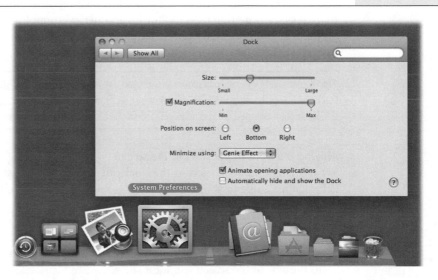

Figure 4-4:
To find a comfortable setting for the magnification slider, choose ❖→Dock →Dock Preferences. Leave the Dock Preferences window open on the screen, as shown here. After each adjustment of the Dock size slider, try out the Dock (which still works when the Dock Preferences window is open) to test your new settings.

There's a much faster way to resize the Dock, though: Just position your cursor carefully in the Dock's divider line so that it turns into a double-headed arrow (shown in Figure 4-5). Now drag up or down to shrink or enlarge the Dock.

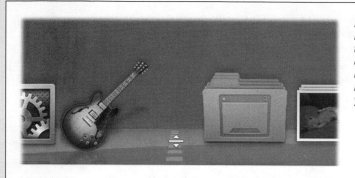

Figure 4-5:
Look closely—you can see the secret cursor that resizes the Dock. If you don't see any change in the Dock size as you drag upward, you've reached the size limit. The Dock's edges are already approaching your screen's sides.

As noted in Figure 4-5, you may not be able to *enlarge* the Dock, especially if it contains a lot of icons. But you can make it almost infinitely *smaller.* This may make you wonder: How can you distinguish among icons if they're the size of molecules?

The answer lies in the →Dock→Magnification checkbox. Turning it on triggers the swelling effect shown in Figure 4-4. Now your Dock icons balloon to a much larger size as your cursor passes over them. It's a weird, magnetic, rippling, animated effect that takes some getting used to. But it's another eye-popping demonstration of the graphics technology in Mac OS X, and it can actually come in handy when you find your icons shrinking away to nothing.

Tip: You can get Dock magnification à la carte, too. Pressing Shift-Control as your cursor approaches the Dock *reverses* your setting in the →Dock menu. So if magnification is turned off, you *do* get icon-swelling; if magnification is turned on, you *don't* get icon-swelling. (That makes sense, doesn't it?)

Moving the Dock to the sides of the screen

Yet another approach to getting the Dock out of your way is to rotate it so it sits vertically against a side of your screen. You can rotate it in either of two ways:

- **The menu way.** From the →Dock submenu, choose "Position on Left," "Position on Right," or "Position on Bottom," as you see fit.

- **The mouse way.** While pressing Shift, drag the Dock's divider line, like a handle, to the side of the screen you want.

You'll probably find that the right side of your screen works better than the left. Most Mac OS X programs put their document windows against the left edge of the screen, where the Dock and its labels might get in the way.

Note: When you position your Dock vertically, the "right" side of the Dock becomes the bottom of the vertical Dock. In other words, the Trash now appears at the bottom of the vertical Dock. So as you read references to the Dock in this book, mentally substitute the phrase "bottom part of the Dock" when you read references to the "right side of the Dock."

Using the Dock

Most of the time, you'll use the Dock as either a launcher (you click an icon once to open the corresponding program, file, folder, or disk) or as a status indicator (the tiny, shiny reflective spots identified in Figure 4-1 indicate which programs are running).

But the Dock has more tricks than that up its sleeve. You can use it, for example, to pull off any of the following stunts.

Switch Applications

The Dock isn't just a launcher; it's also a switcher. Here are some of the tricks it lets you do:

- **Jump among your open programs** by clicking their icons.

- **Drag a document** (such as a text file) onto a Dock application (such as the Microsoft Word icon) to open the former with the latter. (If the program balks at opening the document, yet you're sure the program *should* be able to open the document, then add the ⌘ and Option keys as you drag.)

TROUBLESHOOTING MOMENT

Recovering from a MicroDock

What is a MicroDock? It's what you get when you try to store 300 JPEG files by dragging them onto a folder in the Dock, but you miss the folder (thanks to its tendency to scoot aside). As a result, you drop all the graphics directly *onto*

The easiest way to return to a normal Dock is to delete the Dock preferences file from your Home→Library→Preferences folder. The file is named com.apple.dock.plist, and you can just drag it into the Trash. (If you're really obsessive

the Dock. They dutifully appear as shown here, at the size of subatomic particles.

Now you have a problem. How do you get the Dock back to normal? If you dragged the icons off the Dock one at a time, you'd spend two presidential administrations doing it.

about your Dock setup, you can create a backup of this file now, while everything is working properly. In the event of a MicroDock, you can replace the messed-up preferences file with the backup.)

When you log out and log back in again, you'll be back to the standard Apple Dock.

- **Hide all windows of the program you're in** by Option-clicking another Dock icon.
- **Hide all** *other* **programs' windows** by Option-⌘-clicking the Dock icon of the program you *do* want (even if it's already in front).

This is just a quick summary of the Dock's application-management functions; you'll find the full details in Chapter 5.

Operate the Dock by Keyboard Control

If you turn on *keyboard navigation,* you can operate the Dock entirely from the keyboard; see page 178.

Secret Menus

If you Control-click or right-click a Dock icon, you see its very useful shortcut menu (Figure 4-6).

Snow Leopard Spots: You can no longer produce the shortcut menu by click-and-holding on the Dock icon. Doing that turns on Dock Exposé (page 158).

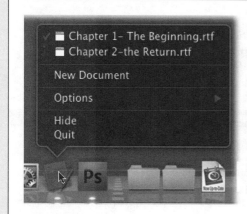

Figure 4-6:
Left: Control-click or right-click a Dock icon to open the secret menu.

Right: Control-click the divider bar to open a different hidden menu. This one lists a bunch of useful Dock commands, including the ones listed in the →Dock submenu.

If you've clicked a minimized window icon, this shortcut menu says only Open (unless it's a minimized Finder window, in which case it also says Close).

But if you've clicked any other kind of icon, you get some very useful hidden commands. For example:

- **[Window names.]** The secret Dock menu of a *running program* usually lists at least one tiny, neatly labeled window icon, like those shown in Figure 4-6. This useful feature means you can jump directly not only to a certain program, but also to a certain *open window* in that program.

For example, suppose you've been using Word to edit three different chapters. You can use Word's Dock icon as a Window menu to pull forward one particular chapter, or (if it's been minimized) to pull it up—even from within a different program. (The checkmark indicates the *frontmost* window, even if the entire program is in the background at the moment. A diamond symbol means the window is minimized and therefore not visible on the screen at the moment.)

Tip: The Finder tile that's always at the beginning of the Dock is, in effect, its own Window menu. Its shortcut menu lists all open desktop windows. The Window menu at the top of the Finder screen does the same thing, but the Dock is available no matter what program you're using.

- **Options.** This submenu contains a bunch of miscellaneous commands. Until Snow Leopard, they appeared as regular shortcut menu items; Apple evidently felt that people used them so rarely that they deserved to be swept away into a space-saving submenu. For example:

Options→Keep In Dock. Whenever you open a program, Mac OS X puts its icon in the Dock—marked with a shiny, white reflective spot—even if you don't normally keep its icon there. As soon as you quit the program, its icon disappears again from the Dock.

If you understand that much, then the Keep In Dock command makes a lot of sense. It means, "Hello, I'm this program's icon. I know you don't normally keep me in your Dock, but I *could* stay here even after you quit my program. Just say the word." If you find you've been using, for example, Terminal a lot more often than you thought you would, this command may be the ticket.

Tip: Actually, there's a faster way to tell a running application to remain in the Dock from now on. Just drag its icon off the Dock and then right back onto it–yes, while the program is running. You have to try it to believe it.

Options→Remove From Dock. On the other hand, what if a program's icon is always in the Dock (even when it's not running) and you *don't* want it there? This command gets the program's icon off the Dock, thereby returning the space it was using to other icons. (You can achieve the same result by dragging the icon away from the Dock.)

Use this command on programs you rarely use. When you *do* want to run those programs, you can always use Spotlight to fire them up.

Note: If the program is already running, using Remove From Dock does not immediately remove its icon from the Dock, which could be confusing. That's because a program always appears in the Dock when it's open. What you're doing here is saying, "Disappear from the Dock when you're not running"–and you'll see the proof as soon as you quit that program.

Options→Open at Login. This command lets you specify that you want this icon to open itself automatically each time you log in to your account. It's a great way to make sure your email Inbox, your calendar, or the Microsoft Word thesis you've been working on is fired up and waiting on the screen when you sit down to work.

To make this item *stop* auto-opening, choose this command again so that the checkmark no longer appears.

Options→Show In Finder. This command highlights the actual icon (in whatever folder window it happens to sit) of the application, alias, folder, or document you've clicked. You might want to do this when, for example, you're using a program that you can't quite figure out, and you want to jump to its desktop folder in hopes of finding a Read Me file there.

Tip: Once again, there's a much faster way to reveal a Dock icon in its enclosing window: ⌘-click its Dock icon.

- **Hide/Show.** This operating system is crawling with ways to hide or reveal a selected batch of windows. Here's a case in point: You can hide all traces of the program you're using by choosing Hide from its Dock icon.

   What's cool here is that (a) you can even hide the Finder and all *its* windows, and (b) if you press Option, the command changes to say Hide Others. This, in its way, is a much more powerful command. It tells all the programs you're *not* using—the ones in the background—to get out of your face. They hide themselves instantly.

Note: Once you've hidden a program's windows, this command changes to say Show, which is how you make them reappear.

- **Quit.** You can quit any program directly from its Dock shortcut menu. (Finder and Dashboard are exceptions.) The beauty of this feature is that you don't have to switch first into a program to get to its Quit command. (Troubleshooting moment: If you get nothing but a beep when you use this Quit command, it's because you've hidden the windows of that program, and one of them has unsaved changes. Click the program's icon, save your document, and then try to quit again.)

Tip: If you hold down the Option key—even after you've opened the pop-up menu—the Quit command changes to say Force Quit. That's your emergency hatch for jettisoning a locked-up program.

- **Miscellaneous.** You might find other commands in Dock shortcut menus; software companies are free to add specialty options to their own programs.

   For example, the Finder icon's shortcut menu offers direct access to commands like Find, Connect to Server, and New Finder Window. Microsoft Office programs (Word, Excel, and so on) come with an Open Recent command, with a list of documents you've opened recently. The Safari icon sprouts a New Window command. The System Preferences icon sprouts a complete list of the preference panes (Sound, Keyboard, Trackpad, and so on). You get the idea.

Tip: If you Control-⌘-click a program's Dock icon, you get only the Options, Hide, and Quit commands in the shortcut menu—not the usual list of windows. If all you want to do is quit a program or something, this abbreviated menu is faster and easier to comprehend.

Conduct Speed Tests

When you click an application icon in the Dock, its icon jumps up and down a few times as the program launches, as though with excitement at having been selected. The longer a program takes to start up, the more bounces you see. This has given birth to a hilarious phenomenon: counting these bounces as a casual speed benchmark for application-launching times. "InDesign took 12 bouncemarks to open in Mac OS X 10.5," you might read online, "but only three bouncemarks in 10.6."

Tip: If you find the icon bouncing a bit over the top, try this: Choose →Dock→Dock Preferences. In the Dock preference pane (shown in Figure 4-4), turn off "Animate opening applications." From now on, your icons won't actually bounce—instead, the little shiny spot underneath it will simply pulse as the application opens.

Drag and Drop

Dock icons are spring-loaded. That is, if you drag any icon onto a Dock icon and pause—or, if you're in a hurry, tap the space bar—the Dock icon *opens* to receive the dragged file.

Note: It opens, that is, if the spring-loaded folder feature is turned on in Finder→Preferences.

This technique is most useful in these situations:

- **Drag a document icon onto a Dock folder icon.** The folder's Finder window pops open so you can continue the drag into a subfolder.

- **Drag a document into an application.** The classic example is dragging a photo onto the iPhoto icon. When you tap the space bar, iPhoto opens automatically. Since your mouse button is still down, and you're technically still in mid-drag, you can now drop the photo directly into the appropriate iPhoto album or Event.

You can drag an MP3 file into iTunes or an attachment into Mail or Entourage in the same way.

Do Your Filing

Once you've tried stashing a few important folders on the right side of your Dock, there's no going back. You can mostly forget all the other navigation tricks you've learned in Mac OS X. The folders you care about are always there, ready for opening with a single click.

Better yet, they're easily accessible for *putting away* files; you can drag files directly into the Dock's folder icons as though they were regular folders.

In fact, you can even drag a file into a *subfolder* in a Dock folder. That's because, again, Dock folders are spring-loaded. When you drag an icon onto a Dock folder and pause, the folder's window appears around your cursor, so you can continue the drag into an inner folder (and even an *inner* inner folder, and so on). Page 77 has the details on spring-loaded folders.

Tip: When you try to drag something into a Dock folder icon, the Dock icons scoot out of the way; the Dock assumes you're trying to put that something onto the Dock. But if you press the ⌘ key as you drag an icon to the Dock, the existing Dock icons freeze in place. Without the ⌘ key, you wind up playing a frustrating game of chase-the-folder.

Great Things to Put in Your Dock

Now that you know what the Dock's about, it's time to set up shop. Install the programs, folders, and disks you'll be using most often.

They can be whatever you want, of course, but don't miss these opportunities:

- **Your Home folder.** Many people immediately drag their hard drive icons—or, perhaps more practically, their Home folders (see page 63)—onto the right side of the Dock. Now they have quick access to every file in every folder they ever use.

- **The Applications folder.** Here's a no-brainer: Stash the Applications folder here so you'll have quick pop-up menu access to any program on your machine.

- **Your Applications folder.** As an even more efficient corollary, create a new folder of your own. Fill it with the aliases of *just* the programs you use most often and park it in the Dock. Now you've got an even more useful Applications folder that opens as a stack.

- **The Shared folder.** If you're using the Mac's *accounts* feature (Chapter 12), this is your wormhole among all the accounts—the one place you can put files where everybody can access them (page 488).

Tip: Ordinarily, dragging an icon off the Dock takes it off the Dock. But if you press ⌘ as you drag, you drag the actual item represented by the Dock icon from wherever it happens to be on the hard drive! This trick is great when, for example, you want to email a document whose icon is in the Dock; just ⌘-drag it into your outgoing message. (Option-⌘-drag, meanwhile, creates an alias of the Dock item.)

The Finder Toolbar

At the top of every Finder window is a small set of function icons, all in a gradient-gray row (Figure 4-7). The first time you run Mac OS X 10.6, you'll find only these icons on the toolbar:

- **Back, Forward.** The Finder works something like a Web browser. Only a single window remains open as you navigate the various folders on your hard drive.

The Back button (◀) returns you to whichever folder you were just looking at. (Instead of clicking ◀, you can also press ⌘-[, or choose Go→Back—particularly handy if the toolbar is *hidden*, as described below.)

The Forward button (▶) springs to life only after you've used the Back button. Clicking it (or pressing ⌘-]) returns you to the window you just backed out of.

Figure 4-7:
If you ⌘-click the upper-right toolbar button repeatedly, you cycle through six combinations of large and small icons and text labels. (Three examples are shown here.)

Tip: This same ⌘-clicking business cycles through the same toolbar variations in Mail, Preview, and other programs that have toolbars.

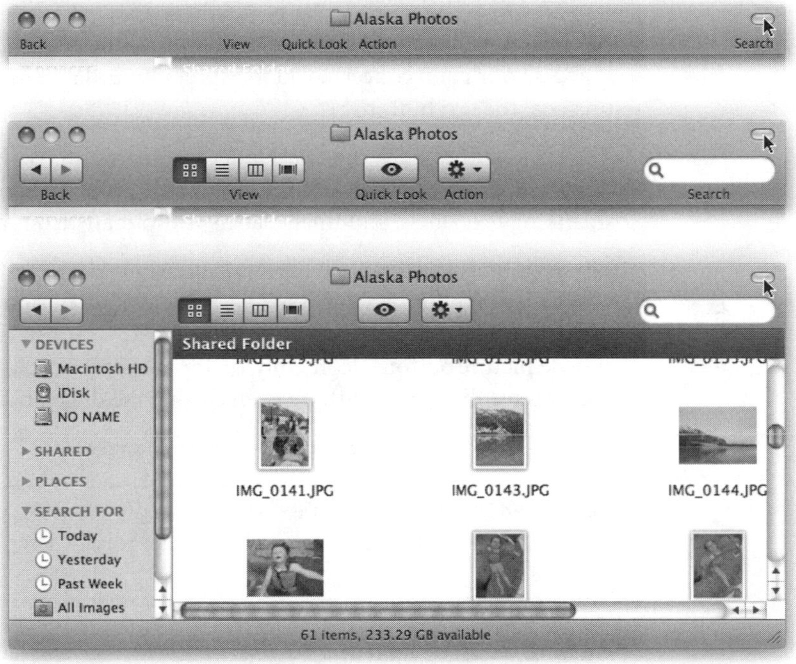

- **View controls.** The four tiny buttons next to the ◀ button switch the current window into icon, list, column, or Cover Flow view, respectively. And remember, if the toolbar is hidden, you can get by with the equivalent commands in the View menu at the top of the screen—or by pressing ⌘-1 for icon view, ⌘-2 for list view, ⌘-3 for column view, or ⌘-4 for Cover Flow view.

- **Quick Look.** The eyeball icon opens the Quick Look preview for a highlighted icon (or group of them); see page 54.

- **Action (✿).** You can read all about this context-sensitive pop-up menu on page 73.

- **Search box.** This little round-ended text box is yet another entry point for the Spotlight feature described in Chapter 3. It's a handy way to search your Mac for some file, folder, disk, or program.

Removing or Shrinking the Toolbar

Between the toolbar, the Dock, the Sidebar, and the large icons of Mac OS X, it almost seems like there's an Apple conspiracy to sell big screens.

Fortunately, the toolbar doesn't have to contribute to that impression. You can hide it with one click—on the white, oval "Old Finder Mode" button (page 29). You can also hide the toolbar by choosing View→Hide Toolbar or pressing Option-⌘-T. (The same keystroke, or choosing View→Show Toolbar, brings it back.)

But you don't have to do without the toolbar altogether. If its consumption of screen space is your main concern, you may prefer to collapse it—to delete the pictures but preserve the text buttons.

The trick is to ⌘-click the Old Finder Mode button. With each click, you make the toolbar take up less vertical space, cycling through six variations of shrinking icons, shrinking text labels, and finally labels without any icons at all (Figure 4-7).

There's a long way to adjust the icon and label sizes, too: Choose View→Customize Toolbar (or Option-⌘-click the Old Finder Mode button). As shown in Figure 4-8, the dialog box that appears offers a Show pop-up menu at the bottom. It lets you choose picture buttons, Icon Only, or, for the greatest space conservation, Text Only. You can see the results without even closing the dialog box.

Click Done or press Return to make your changes stick.

Note: In Text Only mode, the four View buttons are replaced by a little pop-up menu called View. Furthermore, the Search box turns into a one-word button called Search. Clicking it brings up the Spotlight window (page 103).

Adding Your Own Icons to the Toolbar

Mac OS X not only offers a collection of beautifully designed icons for alternate (or additional) toolbar buttons, but it also makes it easy to add *anything* to the toolbar, turning the toolbar into a supplementary Dock or Sidebar. This is great news for people who miss having their Home and Applications folder icons at the *top* of the window, as they were in early Mac OS X versions, or for anyone who's run out of space for stashing favorite icons in the Dock or the Sidebar. (Of course, if *that's* your problem, you need a bigger monitor.)

Apple's toolbar-icon collection

As noted above, the first step in tweaking the toolbar is choosing View→Customize Toolbar. The window shown in Figure 4-8 appears.

Tip: There's a great secret shortcut for opening the Customize Toolbar window: Option-⌘-click the Old Finder Mode button in the upper-right corner of every Finder window.

This is your chance to rearrange the existing toolbar icons or delete the ones you don't use. You can also add any of Apple's buttons to the toolbar by dragging them from the "gallery" onto the toolbar itself. The existing icons scoot out of your cursor's way, if necessary.

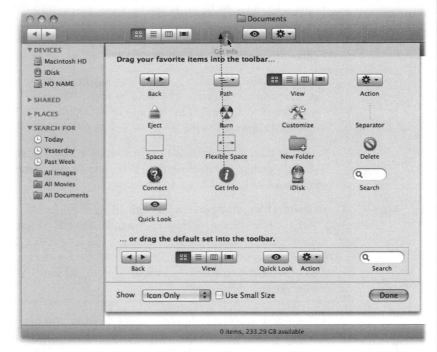

Figure 4-8:
While this window is open, you can add icons to the toolbar by dragging them into place from the gallery before you. You can also remove icons from the tool-bar by dragging them up or down off the toolbar. Rearrange the icons by dragging them horizontally.

Most of the options in the gallery duplicate the functions of menu commands. Here are a few that don't appear on the standard toolbar:

• **Path.** Most of the gallery elements are buttons, but this one creates a *pop-up menu* on the toolbar. When clicked, it reveals (and lets you navigate) the hierarchy—the *path*—of folders you open to reach whichever window is open. (*Equivalent:* ⌘-clicking a window's title, as described on page 22.)

• **Eject (⏏).** This button ejects whichever disk or disk image is currently highlighted. (*Equivalent:* The File→Eject command, or holding down the ⏏ key on your key-board.)

• **Burn.** This button burns a blank CD or DVD with the folders and files you've dragged onto it. (*Equivalent:* The File→Burn Disc command.)

• **Customize.** This option opens this customizing window you're already examining. (*Equivalent:* The View→Customize Toolbar command.)

- **Separator.** This gallery icon doesn't actually do anything when clicked. It's designed to set apart *groups* of toolbar icons. (For example, you might want to segregate your *folder* buttons, such as Documents and Applications, from your *function* buttons, such as Delete and Connect.) Drag this dotted line between two existing icons on the toolbar.

- **Space.** By dragging this mysterious-looking item into the toolbar, you add a gap between it and whatever icon is to its left. The gap is about as wide as one icon. (The fine, dark, rectangular outline that appears when you drag it doesn't actually show up once you click Done.)

- **Flexible Space.** This icon, too, creates a gap between the toolbar buttons. But this one expands as you make the window wider. Now you know how Apple got the Search box to appear off to the right of the standard toolbar, a long way from its clustered comrades to the left.

- **New Folder.** Clicking this button creates a new folder in whichever window you're viewing. (*Equivalent:* the File→New Folder command, or the Shift-⌘-N keystroke.)

- **Delete.** This option puts the highlighted file or folder icons into the Trash. (*Equivalent:* the File→Move to Trash command, or the ⌘-Delete keystroke.)

Tip: Weirdly enough, if you highlight an icon in the Trash and then click this Delete button, you trigger the Put Back function—flinging the icon back into the folder it came from. That is, clicking Delete in this case actually undeletes.

- **Connect.** If you're on a home or office network, this opens the Connect to Server dialog box so you can tap into another computer. (*Equivalent:* The Go→Connect to Server command, or ⌘-K.)

- **Get Info.** This button opens the Get Info window (page 88) for whatever's highlighted.

- **iDisk.** The iDisk is your own personal multigigabyte virtual hard drive on the Internet. It's your private backup disk, stashed at Apple, safe from whatever fire, flood, or locusts may destroy your office. Of course, you already know this, because you're paying $100 per year for a Mobile Me account (Chapter 18).

  In any case, you can bring your iDisk's icon onto the screen simply by clicking this toolbar icon.

- **Search.** This item represents the Spotlight Search box described in Chapter 3.

- **Drag the default set.** If you've made a mess of your toolbar, you can always reinstate its original Apple arrangement by dragging this rectangular strip directly upward onto your toolbar.

Note: If a window is too narrow to show all the icons on the toolbar, then the right end of the toolbar sprouts a **»** symbol. Click it for a pop-up menu that names whichever icons don't fit at the moment. (You'll find this toolbar behavior in many Mac OS X programs, not just the Finder: iPhoto, Safari, Mail, Address Book, and so on.)

Adding your own stuff

Millions of Mac fans will probably trudge forward through life using the toolbar to hold the suggested Apple function buttons, and the Sidebar to hold the icons of favorite folders, files, and programs. They may never realize that you can drag *any icons at all* onto the toolbar—files, folders, disks, programs, or whatever—to turn them into one-click buttons.

In short, you can think of the Finder toolbar as yet another Dock or Sidebar (Figure 4-9).

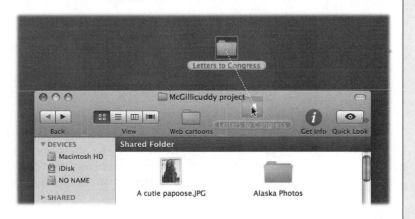

Figure 4-9:
You don't need to choose View→Customize Toolbar to add your own icons to the toolbar. Just drag them from the desktop or any folder window directly onto the toolbar, at any time. Pause with your cursor on the toolbar for a moment before releasing the icon.

Rearranging or Removing Toolbar Icons

You can drag toolbar icons around, rearranging them horizontally, by pressing ⌘ as you drag. Taking an icon off the toolbar is equally easy. While pressing the ⌘ key, just drag the icon clear away from the toolbar. It vanishes in a puff of cartoon smoke. (If the Customize Toolbar sheet is open, you can perform either step *without* the ⌘ key.)

You can also get rid of a toolbar icon by right-clicking it and choosing Remove Item from the shortcut menu.

Designing Your Desktop

In some ways, just buying a Macintosh was already a renegade act of self-expression. But that's only the beginning. Now it's time to fashion the computer screen itself according to your personal sense of design and fashion.

System Preferences

Cosmetically speaking, Mac OS X offers two dramatic full-screen features: desktop backgrounds and screen savers.

The command center for both of these functions is the System Preferences program (which longtime Mac and Windows fans may recognize as the former Control Panel). Open it by clicking the System Preferences icon in the Dock, if it's there, or by choosing its name from the menu.

When the System Preferences program opens, you can choose a desktop picture or screen saver by clicking the Desktop & Screen Saver button. For further details on these System Preferences panes, see Chapter 9.

Snow Leopard Spots: In Snow Leopard, there's a much faster way to turn a picture file into your desktop wallpaper background: Control-click (right-click) it. From the shortcut menu, choose Set Desktop Picture. Ta-da!

Graphic Designers' Corner: The Gray Look

One of the earliest objections to the lively, brightly colored look of Mac OS X came from Apple's core constituency: artists and graphic designers. Some complained that Mac OS X's bright blues (of scroll bar handles, progress bars, the menu, pulsing OK buttons, and highlighted menu names and commands), along with the red, green, and yellow window-corner buttons, threw off their color judgment.

These features have been greatly toned down since the original version of Mac OS X. The pulsing effects are subtler, the three-dimensional effects are less drastic, and the button colors are less intense. It's all part of Mac OS X's gradual de-colorization; in Snow Leopard, both the menu and the Spotlight menu have gone from colorful to black.

FREQUENTLY ASKED QUESTION

Desktop Fonts

How do I change the fonts used by the Mac OS X Finder?

In Mac OS versions gone by, you could choose any font you liked for your icon labels. You even had a choice of fonts for use in your menus.

Nowadays, that flexibility is gone. You get Lucida Grande in your menus and as icon labels—love it or leave it. You can change the type size in System Preferences, but not the font.

For now, Apple intends to remain conservative with the look of Mac OS X—both for "branding" reasons (to make Mac OS X instantly recognizable) and for technical ones (to make sure it doesn't open a Pandora's box of interface hacks that wind up destabilizing the machine).

But that's just Apple's intention. You can still fiddle with Mac OS X's look, as described in Chapter 17.

Tip: The Highlight Color pop-up menu lets you choose a different accent color for your Mac world. This is the background color of highlighted text, the colored oval that appears around highlighted icon names, and a window's "lining" as you drag an icon into it.

But in case they still bother artists, Apple created what it calls the Graphite look for Mac OS X, which turns all those interface elements gray instead of blue. To try out this look, choose ⌘→System Preferences; click Appearance; and then choose Graphite from the Appearance pop-up menu.

Desktop Sounds

Desktop *sounds* are the tiny sound effects that accompany certain mouse drags. And we're talking *tiny*—they're so subdued that you might not have noticed them. You hear a little *plink/crunch* when you drop an icon onto the Trash, a boingy *thud* when you drag something into a folder, a *whoof!* when you drag something off the Dock and into oblivion, and so on. The little thud you hear at the end of a file-copying job is actually useful, because it alerts you that the task is complete.

If all that racket is keeping you awake, however, it's easy enough to turn it off. Open System Preferences, click the Sound icon, and then turn off "Play user interface sound effects."

And if you decide to leave them turned on, please—use discretion when working in a library, church, or neurosurgical operating room.

Menulets: The Missing Manual

See the menu-bar icons in Figure 4-10? Apple calls them Menu Extras, but Mac fans on the Internet have named them *menulets*. Each is both an indicator and a menu that provides direct access to certain settings in System Preferences. One lets you adjust your Mac's speaker volume; another lets you change the screen resolution; yet another shows you the remaining power in your laptop battery; and so on.

Figure 4-10:
These little guys are the direct descendants of the controls once found on the Mac OS 9 Control Strip or the Windows system tray.

To make the various menulets appear, you generally visit a certain pane of System Preferences (Chapter 9) and turn on a checkbox called, for example, "Show volume in menu bar." Here's a rundown of the various Apple menulets you may encounter, complete with instructions on where to find the magic on/off checkbox for each.

Along the way, you'll discover that secondary, hidden features lurk in many of these menulets, if you happen to know the secret: *Press the Option key.*

Tip: The following descriptions indicate the official, authorized steps for installing a menulet. There is, however, a folder on your hard drive that contains 25 of them in a single window, so you can install one with a quick double-click. To find them, open your Macintosh HD→System→Library→CoreServices→Menu Extras folder.

- **AirPort** lets you turn your WiFi (wireless networking) circuitry on or off, join existing wireless networks, and create your own private ones. *To find the "Show" checkbox:* Open System Preferences→Network. Click AirPort.

Tip: Once you've installed this menulet, you can Option-click it to produce a secret menu full of details about the wireless network you're on right now. You see its channel number, password-security method (WEP, WPA, None, whatever), speed, and such geeky details as the MCS Index and RSSI.

- **Battery** shows how much power remains in your laptop's battery, how much time is left to charge it, whether it's plugged in, and more. Using the Show submenu, you can control whether the menulet appears as an hours-and-minutes-remaining display (2:13), a percentage-remaining readout (43%), or a simple battery-icon gauge that hollows out as the charge runs down.

  To find the "Show" checkbox: Open System Preferences→Energy Saver.

Snow Leopard Spots: You may see a new item at the top of the Battery menulet that conveys the battery's health. It might say, for example, "Service Battery," "Replace Soon," "Replace Now," or "Check Battery." Of course, we all know laptop batteries don't last forever; they begin to hold less of a charge as they approach 500 or 1,000 recharges, depending on the model.

Is Apple looking out for you, or just trying to goose the sale of replacement batteries? You decide.

- **Bluetooth** connects to Bluetooth devices, "pairs" your Mac with a cellphone, lets you send or receive files wirelessly (without the hassle of setting up a wireless network), and so on. *To find the "Show" checkbox:* Open System Preferences→Bluetooth.

Tip: You can Option-click this menulet to see two additional lines of nerdy details about your Bluetooth setup: the Bluetooth software version you're using and the name of your Mac (which is helpful when you're trying to make it show up on another Bluetooth gadget).

- **Clock** is the standard menu-bar clock that's been sitting at the upper-right corner of your screen from Day One. Click it to open a menu where you can check today's date, convert the menu-bar display to a tiny analog clock, and so on. *To find the*

"Show" checkbox: Open System Preferences→Date & Time. On the Clock tab, turn on "Show the date and time."

Snow Leopard Spots: For the first time, the Mac can now show you the date and the day of the week on the menu bar.

- **Displays** adjusts screen resolution. On Macs with a projector or second monitor attached, it lets you turn *screen mirroring* on or off—a tremendous convenience to anyone who gives PowerPoint or Keynote presentations. *To find the "Show" checkbox:* Open System Preferences→Displays→Display tab.

- ⏏ is the oddball: There's no checkbox in System Preferences to make this menulet appear. The fact that it even exists is something of a secret.

  To make it appear, open your System→Library→CoreServices→Menu Extras folder as described above, and double-click the Eject.menu icon. That's it! The ⏏ menulet appears.

  You'll discover that its wording changes: "Open Combo Drive," "Close DVD-ROM Drive," "Eject [Name of Disc]," or whatever, to reflect your particular drive type and what's in it at the moment.

- **ExpressCard** is useful only on laptops that have ExpressCard expansion slots. Its Eject command ejects a card that you've inserted. To make it appear, open your System→Library→CoreServices→Menu Extras folder, and then double-click the ExpressCard.menu icon.

- **Fax** reveals the current status of a fax you're sending or receiving, so you're not kept in suspense. (It's available only on Macs that have dial-up modems. Those are few and far between these days, although of course you can buy an external USB modem, like Apple's tiny white one, for this purpose.) *To find the "Show" checkbox:* Open System Preferences→Print & Fax, and then click Fax Modem.

- **HomeSync** is useful only if some friendly neighborhood network administrator has set up Mac OS X *Server* at your office.

  Thanks to a feature called *portable Home folders,* you can take your laptop on the road and do work—and then, on your return, have the changes synced automatically to your main machine at work over the network. Or *not* automatically; this menulet's Sync Home Now command performs this synchronization on demand.

- **iChat** is a quick way to let the world know, via iChat and the Internet (Chapter 21), that you're away from your keyboard, or available and ready to chat. Via the Buddy List command, it's also a quick way to open iChat itself. *To find the "Show" checkbox:* Open iChat; it's in your Applications folder. Choose iChat→Preferences→General.

- **Ink** turns the Write Anywhere feature on and off as you use your graphics tablet. (That may not mean much to you until you've read about the Ink feature, described on page 603.) *To find the "Show" checkbox:* Open the Ink panel of System Preferences. (Neither that panel nor the menulet appears unless a graphics tablet is attached.)

- **IrDA** is useful only to ancient PowerBooks that have infrared transmitters. That's something of a Catch-22, since none of them can run Snow Leopard!

- **Keychain.** This menulet isn't represented by an icon in the Menu Extras folder, but it's still useful if you use Mac OS X's Keychain feature (page 504). The menulet lets you do things like opening the Security pane of System Preferences and locking or unlocking a particular Keychain. *To find the "Show" checkbox:* Open your Applications→Utilities folder. Open the Keychain Access program, and then open the Keychain Access→Preferences→General tab.

- **PCCard** ejects a PC card that you've inserted into the slot in your laptop, if it has such a slot. To make it appear, open your System→Library→CoreServices→Menu Extras folder, and then double-click the PCCard.menu icon.

- **PPP** lets you connect or disconnect from the Internet if you've equipped your Mac with a dial-up modem. *To find the "Show" checkbox:* Open System Preferences→ Network. Click Internal Modem. Click the Modem tab button.

- **PPPoE** (PPP over Ethernet) lets you control certain kinds of DSL connections. *To find the "Show" checkbox:* Open System Preferences→Network. Click Built-in Ethernet. Click the PPPoE tab button.

- **Remote Desktop** is a program, sold separately, that lets teachers or system administrators tap into your Mac from across a network. In fact, they can actually see what's on your screen, move the cursor around, and so on. The menulet lets you do things like turning remote control on and off or sending a message to the administrator. *To find the "Show" checkbox:* Open System Preferences→Sharing, and then click Apple Remote Desktop.

- **Script menu** lists a variety of useful, ready-to-run Automator programs (see page 288). *To find the "Show" checkbox:* Open the AppleScript Editor program (in your Applications Utilities folder). Choose AppleScript Editor→Preferences→General.

- **Spaces** ties into Snow Leopard's virtual-screens feature (called Spaces and described in the next chapter). The menulet lets you choose which of your multiple virtual screens you want to see. *To find the "Show" checkbox:* Open System Preferences→ Spaces.

- **Sync** is useful only if you have a MobileMe account (Chapter 18)—but in that case, it's *very* handy. It lets you start and stop the synchronization of your Mac's Web bookmarks, Calendar, Address Book, Keychains, and email with your other Macs, Windows PCs, and iPhones across the Internet, and it always lets you know the date of your last sync. (Syncing is described in more detail in Chapter 19.) *To find the "Show" checkbox:* Open System Preferences→MobileMe, and then click Sync.

Tip: If you Option-click this menulet, you get a breakdown of data types—Calendar, Address Book, bookmarks, and so on—and a listing of when each was last synchronized with MobileMe.

- **TextInput** switches among different *text input modes.* For example, if your language uses a different alphabet, like Russian, or thousands of characters, like Chinese, this menulet summons and dismisses the alternative keyboards and input methods you need. Details on page 338. *To find the "Show" checkbox:* Open System Preferences→Language & Text→Input Sources.

Note: You also use this menulet when you're trying to figure out how to type a certain symbol like ¥ or § or ♥. You use the menulet to open the Character Palette and Keyboard Viewer—two great character-finding tools described in Chapter 9.

- **Time Machine** lets you start and stop Time Machine backups (see page 248). *To find the "Show" checkbox:* Open System Preferences→Time Machine.

- **UniversalAccess** offers simple on/off status indicators for features that are designed to help with visual, hearing, and muscle impairments. Chapter 9 has a rundown of what they do. *To find the "Show" checkbox:* Open System Preferences→Universal Access.

- **User** identifies the account holder (Chapter 12) who's logged in at the moment. To make this menulet appear (in bold, at the far-right end of the menu bar), turn on *fast user switching,* which is described on page 490.

- **Volume,** of course, adjusts your Mac's speaker or headphone volume. *To find the "Show" checkbox:* Open System Preferences→Sound.

- **VPN** stands for virtual private networking, which allows you to tap into a corporation's network so you can, for example, check your work email from home. You can use the menulet to connect and disconnect, for example. *To find the "Show" checkbox:* Open System Preferences→Network. Click the name of your VPN.

- **WWAN** is useful only if you've equipped your Mac with one of those glorious *cellular modems,* sold by Verizon, Sprint, AT&T, or T-Mobile. These little USB sticks get you onto the Internet wirelessly at near-cable-modem speeds (in big cities, anyway), no WiFi required—for $60 a month. And this menulet lets you start and stop that connection. *To find the "Show" checkbox:* Open System Preferences→Network. Click the name of your cellular modem.

To remove a menulet, ⌘-drag it off your menu bar, or turn off the corresponding checkbox in System Preferences. You can also rearrange them by ⌘-dragging them horizontally.

These little guys are useful, good-looking, and respectful of your screen space. The world could use more inventions like menulets.

Part Two:
Programs in Mac OS X

2

Documents, Programs, & Spaces

T he whole point of owning a computer, of course, is to run *programs*—or apps, as the iPhone crowd likes to call them. But if you're a software company, the history of apps on Mac OS X is a short and exasperating one.

When Apple rolled out Mac OS X in 2001, the world's software companies slapped their foreheads. This was a *completely new* operating system, and required *completely new* programs. It would require every single app to be rewritten: Photoshop, Quicken, Microsoft Office, and thousands of others.

It took several years, but finally they got there; all those old Mac OS 9 programs now ran on Mac OS X. They completed the rewrites just in time to hear Apple make another announcement: The company was switching to Intel processing chips for all new Macs.

UP TO SPEED

Carbon, Cocoa, and Classic (RIP)

There are two chief kinds of Mac OS X–compatible programs, known by the geeks as *Carbon* and *Cocoa* programs. These terms refer to the programming tools that were used to create them, which also have a small effect on how well they run in Mac OS X. Page 188 covers them in more detail, but the point is that this chapter describes how Carbon and Cocoa programs work—these are true Mac OS X programs.

Now, until Leopard (Mac OS X) came along, there was a third software category. Older Macs (pre-Intel Macs) could

also run the very old, pre-2001 operating system known as Mac OS 9, and all of its programs. Mac OS X came with a built-in Mac OS 9 *simulator* called Classic.

A handful of G4 Leopard-capable Mac models could still *restart* into Mac OS 9, which was better than nothing.

But Classic is gone, and Snow Leopard doesn't run on pre-Intel Macs. Snow Leopard is all Mac OS X, all the time, making life simpler for Apple—and more complicated for anyone who used to rely on some of those older programs.

Greater speed was the upside—but only if you ran Intel-rewritten programs. That's right: All the world's Mac programs would have to be rewritten *again*.

Eventually, the dust settled, the world forgave Apple for its fickle leadership, and Mac OS X and its programs have finally reached a stable period.

For now, anyway.

Opening Mac OS X Programs

You can launch (open) a program in any of several ways:

- Click a program's icon once on the Dock, the Sidebar, or the Finder toolbar.

- Use Spotlight. Hit ⌘-space bar, type the first letters of the program's name, and then press Return or Enter.

- Double-click an application's icon in the Finder.

- If you've added the Applications folder to your Dock (or, better yet, a folder containing aliases of only the programs you *use*), click the Dock icon to open the pop-up fan, grid, or list of icons. Then click the program you want (or even type the first few letters of its name and then press Return).

- Highlight an application icon and then press ⌘-O (short for File→Open) or ⌘-down arrow.

- Use the submenus of the menu's Recent Items→Applications command.

FREQUENTLY ASKED QUESTION

What's with the Big "Duh"?

So, I've just installed Snow Leopard, I'm all excited, and I double-click an Excel document. And now the Mac asks me: "You are opening Microsoft Excel for the first time. Do you want to continue?" Well, HELLO! I double-clicked the icon, didn't I? Does Apple think I'm some kind of idiot?

It's not you Apple's worried about. It's the silent parade of evil hackers, lurking out there in Internet Land, waiting for the right moment to bring down the Mac.

See, spyware authors have to be sneaky about how they install their stuff on your computer. You wouldn't be so stupid as to double-click an application called Spyware Installer™, of course. So the spyware tricks you into running its installer. In the Windows world, it commandeers a

certain document type (like MP3 or JPEG), reassigning it to its installer. You innocently double-click some document, but an unanticipated program opens—and you've just opened Pandora's box.

In Mac OS X, that can't happen. When double-clicking some document opens a program for the first time, this dialog box appears, just to let you know what's about to happen. If the program that's about to open isn't the one you were expecting, well, you've got a chance to back out of it.

And if it *is* the program you were expecting, click Continue. You won't be asked again about this version of this particular program.

Note: Mac OS X stores a list of your recently used programs in a text file called *com.apple.recentitems.plist*, located in your Home folder→Library→Preferences folder. And with about a dollar, that information will buy you a cup of coffee in most restaurants.

- Open a *document* icon in any of these ways, or drag a document onto the icon of a program that can open it (whether in the Dock, the Finder toolbar, the Sidebar, or a folder window).

UP TO SPEED

When Programs Are Actually Folders

Mac OS X programs don't seem to have 50,000 support files strewn across your hard drive. Most programs just sit there, naked and shivering, in your Applications folder—seemingly unaccompanied by libraries, dictionaries, foreign language components, and other support files and folders.

The question is: Where did all those support files go?

Mac OS X features *packages* or *bundles*, which are folders that behave like single files. Every properly written Mac OS X program looks like a single, double-clickable application icon. Yet to the Mac, it's actually a folder that contains both the actual application icon and all its hidden support files. (Even documents can be packages, including iDVD project files, Keynote files, and some TextEdit documents.)

If you'd like to prove this to yourself, try this experiment. Choose Go→Applications. See the Calculator program? Control-click it or right-click it. From the shortcut menu, choose Show Package Contents. You're asking Mac OS X to show you what's inside the Calculator's "application icon" folder.

The Calculator package window opens, revealing a Contents folder you've never seen before. If you open this folder, you'll find a handful of strange-looking, Unix-named folders and files that are, behind the scenes, pieces of the Calculator program itself.

The application-as-folder trick is convenient for you, of course, because it means you're generally free to move the application to a different window—or uninstall the program by dragging this single icon to the Trash—without worrying that you're leaving behind its entourage of support files. It's also convenient for programmers, because they can update certain aspects of their applications just by replacing one of these component files, without having to rewrite the entire program.

You can even try out this programmery benefit for yourself. In the case of the Calculator and many other Mac OS X programs, the Resources folder contains individual graphics files—PDF or TIFF files—that serve as the graphic elements you see when using the program. For example, the file *lcd.tiff* in the Calculator's Resources folder contains the image of the calculator's screen (where the numbers appear as you punch the calculator number buttons).

Using a graphics program, you can change the background of this light-yellow calculator screen to, say, light blue. The next time you double-click Calculator—which you now realize is actually a folder behind the scenes—you'll see your modified calculator design.

(P.S. There *are* still hundreds or thousands of support files that *aren't* embedded within the program's icon. They're sitting in your Library→Application Support folder, organized by software company.)

Tip: If you press Option as you open an application (or anything else) in the Finder, you automatically close the window that contains its icon. Later, when you return to the Finder, you find a neat, clean desktop—no loitering windows.

When you open a program, the Mac reads its computer code, which lies on your hard drive's surface, and feeds it quickly into RAM (memory). During this brief interval, the icon of the opening program jumps up and down eagerly in your Dock.

Tip: Want to see *multithreading* in action? Launch a program that takes a long time to open—that is, whose icon in the Dock does a lot of bouncing.

You don't have to wait for the application to finish bouncing—you're wasting perfectly good computing time. Just switch to another program and get to work; the newly opened program keeps right on launching in the background. Multithreading means that Mac OS X can crunch more than one process at a time.

What happens next depends on the program you're using. Most present you with a new, blank, untitled document. Some, like iDVD, automatically open the last file you worked on. Some, like FileMaker and PowerPoint, ask if you want to open an existing document or create a new one. And a few oddball programs don't open any window at all when first opened.

The Application Menu

In each case, however, the very first menu after the appears with bold lettering and identifies the program you're using. It might say iTunes, or Microsoft Word, or Stickies.

This Application menu (Figure 5-1) offers a number of commands pertaining to the entire program and its windows, including About, Quit, and Hide.

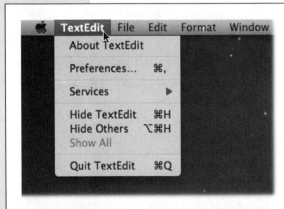

Figure 5-1:
The first menu in every program lets you know, at a glance, which program you're actually in. It also offers overall program commands like Quit and Hide.

Quitting Programs

You quit a program by pressing ⌘-Q, the keyboard equivalent of the Quit command. (In Mac OS X, the Quit command is at the bottom of the Application menu.)

But Mac OS X offers two much more fun ways to quit a program:

- Control-click or right-click a program's Dock icon to make its shortcut menu appear. Then choose Quit. (Or, if you do the *click-and-hold* thing on a program's Dock icon, a Quit button appears just above your cursor.)

- When you've pressed ⌘-Tab to summon the "heads-up display" of open programs, type the letter Q without releasing the ⌘ key. The highlighted program quits without further ado.

Snow Leopard Spots: You may notice that programs seem to quit a lot faster than they used to—a difference that's especially noticeable when you're shutting down your Mac (since quitting apps was what took the most time).

That's because, to save time, Snow Leopard doesn't quit programs the way it used to—it *kills* them. It checks to see if they have unsaved documents or un-backed-up preference-setting changes first, of course. But if not, it issues a *kill* command to them, which terminates them instantly, saving you a couple of seconds each. (Programmers have to write their apps to "listen" for this command, so don't worry—it's all perfectly safe.)

Force Quitting Programs

Mac OS X is a rock-solid operating system, but that doesn't mean that *programs* never screw up. Individual programs are as likely as ever to freeze—or, rather, to *hang* (to lock up and display the "spinning beach ball of death" cursor). In such cases, you have no choice but to *force quit* the program—the computer equivalent of terminating it with a blunt instrument.

Doing so doesn't destabilize your Mac; you don't have to restart it. In fact, you can usually reopen the very same program and get on with your life.

You can force quit a stuck program in any of several ways:

- Click-and-hold on the program's Dock icon. That triggers the Exposé function, of course, but it also offers a Quit button just above your cursor. Press the Option key to make the button say Force Quit (Figure 5-2, left). Click it.

- Control-click (right-click) its Dock icon. Once the shortcut menu appears, press Option so that the Quit command now says Force Quit (Figure 5-2, right). Bingo— that program is outta here.

- Press Option-⌘-Esc, the traditional Mac force quit keystroke, or choose →Force Quit. Either way, proceed as shown in Figure 5-2.

Again, force quitting is not bad for your Mac. The only downside to force quitting a program is that you lose any unsaved changes to your open documents, along with any preference settings you may have changed while the program was open.

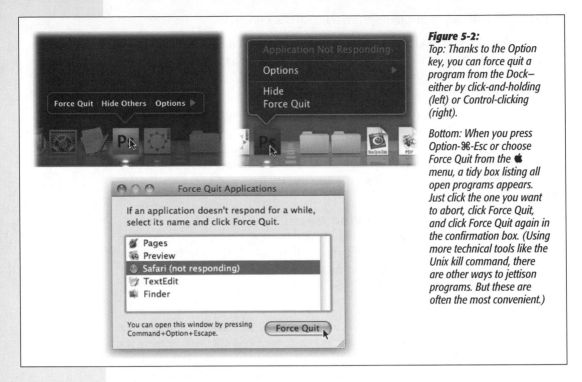

Figure 5-2:
Top: Thanks to the Option key, you can force quit a program from the Dock— either by click-and-holding (left) or Control-clicking (right).

Bottom: When you press Option-⌘-Esc or choose Force Quit from the menu, a tidy box listing all open programs appears. Just click the one you want to abort, click Force Quit, and click Force Quit again in the confirmation box. (Using more technical tools like the Unix kill command, there are other ways to jettison programs. But these are often the most convenient.)

The "Heads-Up" Program Switcher

Only one program can be in front, or active, at a time.

To make a different program active, you could click or double-click its icon (in the Dock, the Applications folder, or whatever). But the fastest method is often to use the ⌘-Tab keystroke (Figure 5-3)—or, if you have a laptop, drag *four fingers* horizontally across your trackpad (page 348).

Figure 5-3:
Apple calls this row of open program icons a "heads-up display," named after the projected data screens on a Navy jet windshield that lets pilots avoid having to look down at their instruments.

You can use this feature in three different ways, which are well worth learning:

- If you keep the ⌘ key pressed, each press of the Tab key highlights the Dock icon of another program, in left-to-right Dock order. Release both keys when you reach the one you want. Mac OS X brings the corresponding program to the front. (To move *backward* through the open programs, press *Shift*-⌘-Tab.)

- If you leave the ⌘ key pressed, you can choose a program by clicking its icon with your mouse, or by pressing the ← or → keys.

- A single press of ⌘-Tab takes you to the program you used most recently, and another, separate ⌘-Tab bounces back to the program you started in.

  Imagine, for example, that you're doing a lot of switching between two programs, like your Web browser and your email program. If you have five other programs open, you don't want to waste your time ⌘-Tabbing your way through all open programs just to get back to your Web browser.

Tip: Here's a related keystroke, equally awesome. If you press ⌘-tilde (the ~ key next to the number 1), you switch to the next window in the *same* program.

Exposé: Death to Window Clutter

In its day, the concept of overlapping windows on the screen was brilliant, innovative, and extremely effective. (Apple borrowed this idea—well, bought it in a stock swap—from a research lab called Xerox PARC.) In that era before digital cameras, MP3 files, and the Web, managing windows was easy this way; after all, you had only about three of them.

These days, however, managing all the open windows in all the open programs can be like herding cats. Off you go, burrowing through the microscopic pop-up menus of your Dock, trying to find the window you want. And heaven help you if you need to duck back to the desktop—to find a newly downloaded file, for example, or eject a disk. You'll have to fight your way through 50,000 other windows on your way to the bottom of the "deck."

Exposé represents the first fresh look at this problem in decades. The concept is delicious: With the one mouse click or keystroke, Mac OS X shrinks all windows in all programs to a size that fits on the screen (Figure 5-4), like index cards on a bulletin board. You click the one you want, and you're there. It's fast, efficient, animated, and a lot of fun.

Now, this is going to get very mind-blowing very fast, so read slowly and keep your shoulders relaxed.

There are actually three different Exposé modes. One shows you miniatures of *all* windows in *all* programs; one shows you miniatures of all the windows in *just one program;* and one hides *all windows in all programs* so you can see the desktop.

Each of these three modes, moreover, can be triggered using different combinations of the mouse and keyboard. The following pages will cover all of them, but of course you're not expected to learn all that. Just find the *one* trigger that seems most convenient, and stick with it.

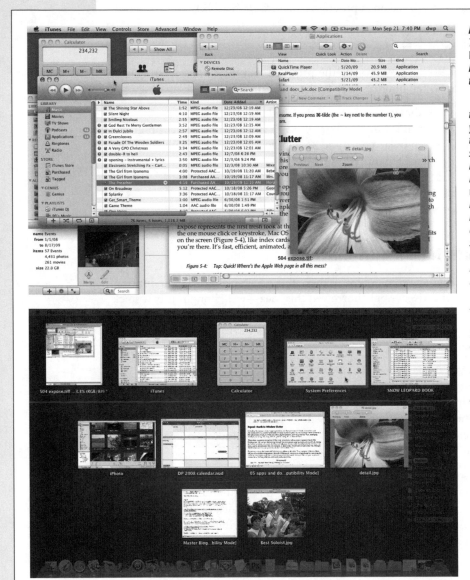

Figure 5-4:

Top: Quick! Where's System Preferences in all this mess?

Bottom: With a tap of the F3 key, you can spot that window, shrunken but not overlapped. Each thumbnail window offers a label to help you identify it. These aren't static snapshots of the windows at the moment you Exposé'd them. They're live, still-updating windows, as you'll discover if one of them contains a playing QuickTime movie or a Web page that's still loading. If you're not pointing to a window, tapping F3 again turns off Exposé without changing anything; if you're pointing to a window, tapping F3 again brings it forward.

Snow Leopard Spots: Before Snow Leopard came along, every window in Exposé was the same size. Big windows looked too shrunken, and small windows were ridiculously large. Now their thumbnails are sized to represent their actual sizes.

The thumbnails appear in a more structured grid, now, too. And they have labels! You can read each window's name under the thumbnail image.

All-Apps Exposé

The first and most famous Exposé method is shown in Figure 5-4. *Every* window in *every* program is arrayed before you, nothing covered up, nothing hidden. It's a great way to get your bearings in a hurry.

Here are the best ways to get this effect:

- **Current keyboards: Press F3 (▣).** On recent Apple laptop and desktop keyboards—aluminum with very flat, thin keys poking up—the F3 key is dedicated to Exposé. It's even painted with a special Exposé logo (▣). Tap that key to get the all-apps Exposé effect.

Note: There are other key combinations available, too. See the box on page 158 for the built-in alternative—but you can use the System Preferences→Keyboard→Keyboard Shortcuts panel to make up any keystroke you want.

- **Plastic keyboards: Press F9.** On older keyboards, the white or black plastic ones, press F9 instead.

- **Laptops: Swipe downward with four fingers.** Sounds contrived, it's true. But giving your trackpad a four-finger swipe is a quick and easy way to trigger all-apps Exposé. (Then you can get back to what you were doing by swiping *upward* with four fingers.)

Note: Older Mac laptops don't have multitouch trackpads and therefore don't offer this four-finger option. To find out if yours is eligible—and to make sure the four-finger swiping feature is turned on—open System Preferences→Trackpad. Confirm that there's a list of gestures at the left side of the panel, as shown on page 225.

As you can read later in this section, you can also trigger all-apps Exposé by pressing special buttons on your mouse, or by flinging the cursor into a specified corner of the screen. But start with baby steps.

To exit Exposé, click one of the miniaturized windows, or repeat any of the Exposé triggers.

Snow Leopard Spots: If you've *minimized* a program's windows, they now show up in Exposé, too—as miniatures below a fine horizontal line. You can see the effect in Figure 5-4.

One-App Exposé

A second Exposé function is designed to present miniatures of all windows *only in the program you're using*—great when you're Web browsing or word processing. All the program's windows spread out, and shrink if necessary, so you can click the one you want (Figure 5-5, top).

Here's how Apple intends most people to trigger this option:

- **Current keyboards: Press Control-F3.** That's the keystroke on current laptops and desktops, the ones with aluminum keyboards.

Tip: As noted in the box below, you can also press Fn-F10, or with some tweaking, F10 alone. Or you can change the keystroke altogether as described on page 179.

- **Plastic keyboards: Press F10.**

- **Use Dock Exposé.** That is, click the program's Dock icon and hold the button down for half a second.

  This feature, new in Snow Leopard, has one chief advantage over the keystroke method: You can Exposé-ize any program's windows, not just the one you're using at the moment.

TROUBLESHOOTING MOMENT

A Tedious Side Note about the Aluminum Apple Keyboards

In the beginning, you could trigger the three Exposé modes described on these pages with three simple keystrokes: F9, F10, and F11.

Then the new-style aluminum keyboards and laptops came along. On these, Apple devoted the F3 key to Exposé functions—and reassigned the F9, F10, and F11 keys to speaker-volume control!

You *can* make them operate Exposé as in the days of yore— by adding the Fn key. That is: Fn-F9 for all-apps Exposé, Fn-F10 for one-app Exposé, and Fn-F11 for desktop Exposé. (Details on the Fn key appear on page 223.)

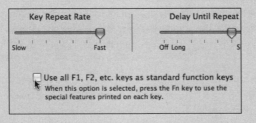

So here's the point: On modern Macs, you have a choice of two Exposé keystroke suites: the F3 key (by itself, with Control, and with ⌘)—or the Fn key plus F9, F10, and F11.

Actually, it's even more complicated than that. If you find yourself using *Exposé* more than you use the volume keys, you can get rid of the requirement to press Fn. Open System Preferences→Keyboard. Here you'll find a checkbox that reverses this logic. It's called "Use all F1, F2, etc. keys as standard function keys."

If that checkbox is *on,* then you can use F9, F10, and F11 to trigger Exposé. Now you need the Fn key only when you want those keys to adjust the *volume.*

Desktop Exposé

The third flavor of Exposé is surprisingly handy. It sends *all* windows in *all* programs cowering to the edges of your screen, revealing the desktop beneath in all its uncluttered splendor (Figure 5-5, bottom).

Here's the keystroke scheme:

- **Current keyboards: Press ⌘-F3.** That's the trigger for current aluminum keyboards and laptops.

Note: Once again, you can also press Fn-11, or (if you set it up) F11 by itself. See the box on the facing page.

- **Plastic keyboards: Press F11.**

The windows fly off to the edges of the screen, where they remain—forever, or until you tap the keystroke again, click a visible window edge, double-click an icon, or take some other window-selection step.

This is a spectacular opportunity to save headache and hassle in situations like these:

- You're writing an email message, and you want to attach a file. Tap the desktop Exposé keystroke, root around in the Finder until you locate the file you want. Begin to drag it, and then, without releasing the mouse button, tap the desktop Exposé keystroke again to bring back your email window. (Or drag the attachment directly onto your email program's icon on the Dock and pause until its window thumbnails appear.)

  Move your cursor, with the file in mid-drag, directly over the outgoing message window; release the cursor to create the attachment. You've just added an attachment from the desktop in one smooth motion.

Tip: You can apply the same life-changing shortcut to dragging a graphic into a page-layout program, a folder of photos into iPhoto, a sound or graphic into iMovie, and so on.

- You want to open a different document. For many people, having access to the entire Finder beats the pants off having to use the Open dialog box. Double-clicking the icon you want automatically opens it and turns off Exposé.

- You're on the Web, and you want to see if some file has finished downloading. Trigger desktop Exposé to survey the situation on your desktop.

If the layer of open programs is the atmosphere, the Finder is the earth below—and the ability to teleport you back and forth is a huge timesaver.

Tip: You can switch among the three Exposé modes (all-apps, one-app, or desktop), even after you've triggered one. For example, if you click-and-hold a Dock icon to shrink only *that* program's windows, you can then press ⌘-F3 to see the desktop, and then press F3 to shrink *all* programs' windows.

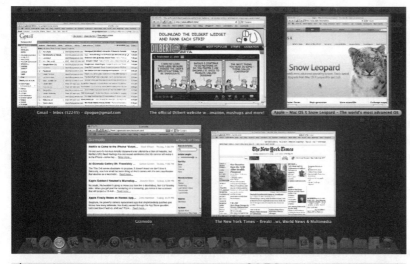

Figure 5-5:
Top: When you trigger one-app Exposé, you get a clear shot at any window in the current program (Safari, in this example). In the meantime, the rest of your screen attractively dims, as though someone has just shined a floodlight onto the windows of the program in question. It's a stunning effect.

Bottom: Trigger desktop Exposé when you need to duck back to the desktop for a quick administrative chore. Here's your chance to find a file, throw something away, eject a disk, or whatever, without having to disturb your application windows.

In either case, tap the same function key again to turn off Exposé. Or click one of the window edges, which you can see peeking out from all four edges of the screen.

Exposé Tip-O-Rama

Just having your world o' windows spread out like index cards is magic enough. But these windows are *live*. You can work with them. Let us count the ways.

- **Tab through Exposé'd apps.** Once you've started one-app Exposé, and a program's windows are arrayed before you, tap the Tab key to switch to the *next* running program. All *its* windows spring to the fore. Tab, Tab, Tab through all your open programs. (Shift-Tab, as usual, cycles through the programs in the opposite direction.)

Exposé: Death to Window Clutter

Tip: You can also switch to another app's micro-windows by clicking its Dock icon.

- **Tab out of all-apps Exposé.** Suppose you pressed F3 (all-apps Exposé), but you decide that what you really meant to do was press Control-F3 to see only *one* program's windows. The solution is to press the Tab key, which switches you *into* one-app mode, displaying only one program's miniaturized windows. At this point, you can press Tab or Shift-Tab to cycle through the open programs.

- **Enter Exposé from the heads-up display.** Page 154 describes the heads-up display—the Mac OS X application switcher, the row of "these are your open programs" icons—which appears when you press ⌘-Tab.

  The cool thing is that once you've got that heads-up display open, you can press ↑ or ↓ to enter Exposé for whatever program's icon is highlighted! From there, release the keys and hit Tab to cycle through your open apps.

- **Change Exposé'd apps using the heads-up display.** Here's another way to change programs once you're in one-app Exposé: Press ⌘-Tab to bring up the heads-up display (yes, even while your windows are shrunken). Tab your way through the program icons (Figure 5-5) until the one you want is selected, and then release the keys. That program's windows spring to the front, still miniaturized and arrayed for your selection pleasure.

- **Hold down instead of two presses.** Most of the time, you'll probably use Exposé in two steps. You'll tap the keystroke once to get the windows out of the way, and tap it again to bring them back (if, indeed, you haven't *clicked* a window to bring them back).

  In some cases, though, you may find it easier to hold down the relevant key. For example, hold down ⌘-F3 to see if a file is finished copying to the desktop, then release the keys to bring back all of the windows. (Actually, you can let go of the ⌘ key as soon as you've entered Exposé.) For quick window-clearing situations, that method saves you the step of having to press the key a second time to turn off Exposé.

- **Use the spring-loaded Dock.** This trick is great when you want to drop a file from one program into a particular window belonging to another.

  The most common example: You want to add an attachment to an outgoing email message. In the Finder, locate the file's icon. Drag it directly onto your email program's Dock icon—and pause with your finger still on the button. After a half second, Exposé happens, showing all your email program's open windows. Now continue your drag onto the miniaturized window of the outgoing message so it's highlighted, tap the space bar to open it, and release. Presto! The file is attached.

This trick also works great when you want to drop a photo into a newsletter, for example, or a text clipping into a word processing document.

- **Sort the windows.** That's right: In Snow Leopard, you can now *sort* the windows as they appear on the screen. Press ⌘-1 to sort the window names alphabetically, or ⌘-2 to sort them according to the programs they belong to.

Exposé Meets Quick Look

The trouble with miniaturized windows is that, well, they're miniaturized. The more windows you've Exposé'd, the smaller they are, and the harder it is to see what's in them.

Fortunately, your old friend Quick Look (page 54) is standing by to help.

Once you've got shrunken windows on the screen (using all-apps Exposé or one-app Exposé), tap your arrow keys to highlight a window (or point with your mouse without clicking). You'll see a bright-blue border move from window to window.

At any point, you can press the space bar to make that one window return to life size. You haven't really activated it—you can't edit it—but at least you can see it at full size.

And here's the very cool part. Once you've triggered Quick Look like this, you can press the arrow keys to zap *other* mini windows back to full size, without having to exit Quick Look. Or, again, point to other windows without clicking. Each zooms in to 100 percent size. (All of this is much easier to do than to imagine.)

You can keep examining your windows at full size until you spot the one you're after; now tap Return or Enter (or click the mouse in the window) to exit Quick Look *and* Exposé. You've just opened that window, and you're ready to roll.

More Triggers for Exposé

Exposé is wonderful and all, but the standard keys for triggering its three functions may leave something to be desired. For one thing, they might already be "taken" by other functions in your programs (like Microsoft Word) or even by your computer. For another thing, those keys are at the top of the keyboard where your typing fingers aren't used to going, and you may have to hunt to make sure you're pressing the right one.

Fortunately, you can reassign the Exposé functions to a huge range of other keys, with or without modifiers like Shift, Control, and Option. To view your options, choose →System Preferences and then click the Exposé & Spaces icon (Figure 5-6).

Here, you'll discover that you can trigger Exposé's functions in any of three ways:

Screen corners

The four pop-up menus (Figure 5-6) represent the four corners of your screen. Using these menus, you can assign an Exposé trigger to each corner; for example, if you choose Desktop from the first pop-up menu, when your pointer hits the upper-left corner of the screen, you'll hide all windows and expose the desktop. (To make the windows come back, click any visible edge of a window, highlight a window thumbnail and press Return, or twitch the cursor back into the same corner.)

Depending on the size of your screen, this option can feel awkward at first. But if you've run out of keystrokes that aren't assigned to other functions, be glad that Apple offers you this alternative.

Note: In previous versions of Mac OS X, of course, whipping the pointer into a corner was one good way to turn on your *screen saver.* Apple hasn't forgotten about that, which is why you'll also find commands called Start Screen Saver and Disable Screen Saver in the pop-up menus. Apple wants to make sure you don't get confused and assign two different functions to the same corner.

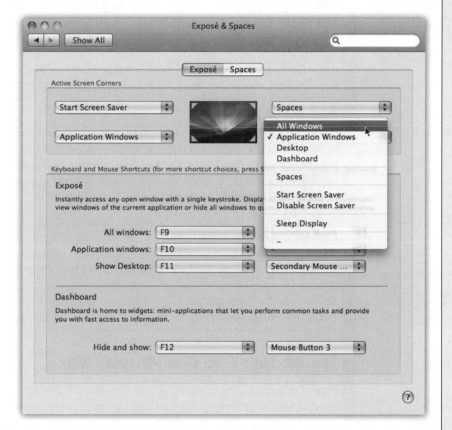

Figure 5-6:
You can trigger Exposé in any of three ways: by twitching your cursor into a certain corner of the screen (top), pressing a key (lower left), or by clicking the extra buttons on a multibutton mouse (lower right), including Apple's Mighty Mouse. Of course, there's nothing to stop you from setting up all three ways, so you can press in some situations and twitch or click in others.

Keystrokes

Also in the Exposé preferences, you'll find three pop-up menus—"All windows," "Application windows," and "Show Desktop"—that correspond to the three functions of Exposé as described above. (The fourth pop-up menu, Dashboard, is described at the end of this chapter.) You can't assign *any* old keystroke to Exposé, but you have far more options than the puny F9, F10, and F11 keys (or the variations on F3).

Within each pop-up menu, for example, you'll discover that all your F-keys— F1, F2, F3, and so on—are available as triggers. If, while the pop-up menu is open, you press one or more of your modifier keys (Shift, Option, Control, or ⌘), all these F-key choices *change* to reflect the key you're pressing; now the pop-up menu says Shift-F1, Shift-F2, Shift-F3, and so on. That's how you can make *Shift*-F1 trigger the hide-all-windows function, for example.

These pop-up menus also contain choices like Left Shift, which refers to the Shift key on the left side of your keyboard. That is, instead of pressing F9 to make all your windows shrink, you could simply tap the Shift key.

Note: This is only an example. Repeat: This is only an example. *Actually* using the Shift key to shrink all your windows is a terrible, terrible idea, as you'll quickly discover the next time you try to type a capital letter. This feature is intended exclusively for hunt-and-peck typists who never use the Shift key on one side.

If you have a laptop, you'll also find out that you can tap the Fn key *alone* for Exposé— and this time, it's a *great* choice, because Fn otherwise has very little direction in life.)

Multiple-button mouse clicks

If your mouse has more than one button, you see a second column of pop-up menus in System Preferences. Each pop-up menu offers choices like Right Mouse Button, Middle Mouse Button, and so on. Use these pop-up menus to assign the three Exposé modes (or Dashboard) to the various clickers on your mouse: right-click to hide *all* windows, left-side click to reveal the desktop, and so on.

Note, by the way, that on a laptop, for example, the wording isn't "right mouse button"—it's "secondary mouse button." Which means "right-click." Which means that on a laptop, you can set it up so that a "right-click" *trackpad gesture* triggers Exposé. See page 224 for all the different ways you can trigger a right-click.

Tip: No matter how you trigger Exposé, try holding down the Shift key as you do it. You'll enjoy watching all your windows shift around with Mac OS X's patented slow-motion animation, which can be quite a sight.

Spaces: Your Free Quad-Display Mac

Exposé makes a big impression, for sure. But Mac OS X offers another radical step forward in window management that you may even come to prefer. It's called Spaces.

This feature gives you two, four, six, eight, or even 16 *full-size monitors.* Ordinarily, of course, attaching so many screens to a single computer would be a massively expensive proposition, not to mention the number it would do on your living space and personal relationships.

Fortunately, Spaces monitors are *virtual.* They exist only in the Mac's little head. You see only one at a time; you switch using a keystroke, a menu, or the mouse.

Just because the Spaces screens are simulated doesn't mean they're not useful, though. You can dedicate each one to a different program or *kind* of program. Screen 1 might contain your email and chat windows, arranged just the way you like them. Screen 2 can hold Photoshop, with an open document and the palettes carefully arrayed. On Screen 3: your Web browser in full-screen mode.

You can also have the *same* program running on multiple screens—but different documents or projects open on each one.

Now, virtual screens aren't a new idea—this sort of software has been available for years. But it's never before been a standard feature of a consumer operating system, and rarely has it been executed with such finesse.

Turning On Spaces

To "install" your new monitors, start by choosing →System Preferences. Click the Exposé & Spaces icon, and then click the Spaces tab. You see something like Figure 5-7, top.

The setup ritual goes like this:

- **Turn Spaces on.** The "Enable Spaces" checkbox is the master on/off switch.

- **Add the menulet.** Turn on "Show Spaces in menu bar" to make a menu of your virtual screens appear in the menu bar (Figure 5-7, bottom). It not only lets you switch screens, but the numeral on it also reminds you which screen you're *on.*

Tip: Consider turning on this option, if only at first, as a safety net. Otherwise, if you don't remember the keystroke for switching screens, you might lose one of your programs on another screen and not be able to find it!

- **Add rows or columns.** Click the **+** and **−** buttons to add rows or columns of virtual monitors. There's a difference between rows and columns, by the way. Not only will you eventually learn to sense where your various window setups live, but you can also move from one screen to another by bumping the mouse against the corresponding edge of your *current* screen—and you'll need to know which edge.

- **Set up program auto-screen assignments.** Spaces becomes truly useful only when you make it part of your routine. You'll eventually memorize where everything is: Web stuff, top left. Email, top right. Photoshop, lower left. Finder with Applications folder open, lower right.

  For that reason, you can use the controls in the center of the System Preferences pane to specify which screen certain programs automatically go to when they open. Click the **+** button to view your Applications folder. Double-click a program's icon to make it appear in the list. Now use the pop-up menu in the Space column to indicate which space you want this program to live on, as shown in Figure 5-7, bottom.

Tip: You can also choose All Spaces, meaning that this program's windows are available on *every* virtual screen. That's handy if it's something you use constantly, like a stock ticker or your phone-book program.

To make a program stop opening into a certain screen, click its name, and then click the — button.

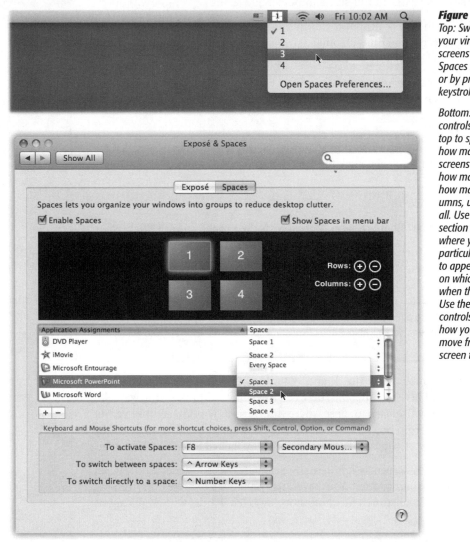

Figure 5-7:
*Top: Switch among
your virtual
screens using the
Spaces menulet,
or by pressing a
keystroke.*

*Bottom: Use the
controls at the
top to specify
how many virtual
screens you want—
how many rows,
how many col-
umns, up to 16 in
all. Use the middle
section to specify
where you want
particular programs
to appear (that is,
on which screen)
when they open.
Use the bottom
controls to set up
how you want to
move from one
screen to another.*

- **Set up keyboard or mouse triggers.** Once you've got your majestic array of Cineplex displays assembled, you need a way to move among them.

Spaces comes set up with the Control key as the "I'm switching screens" key. For example, press Control-↑ to move up one screen, Control-→ to move one screen to the right, and so on. Or, if you have tons of screens, you can jump to one by number (as indicated in the map shown in Figure 5-7): Control-1, Control-4, Control-9, or whatever.

You're welcome to change these keyboard assignments, however, especially if you're already using the Control key for other functions. Use the two bottom pop-up menus.

For example, suppose you want to switch screens by pressing the Option key rather than Control. In that case, you'd open the "To switch between Spaces" pop-up menu, press Option, and choose "⌥ Arrow Keys." (In these pop-up menus, ⌥ means the Option key, ⇧ is the Shift key, and ^ means Control.)

Tip: The pop-up menu at the bottom of the window, "To activate Spaces," lets you choose a keystroke that opens up the master map of all your screens. (See Figure 5-9.)

Using Spaces

Once you've got Spaces set up and turned on, the fun begins. Start by moving to the virtual screen you want. Here are some ways to do that:

- Choose a virtual screen's number from the Spaces menulet, shown in Figure 5-7.

- Press Control-arrow key, or whatever keystroke you've set up as described above. Or hold down Control and keep tapping the arrow key to scroll through all your screens.

- Press Control-number key to jump to a screen without having to scroll.

- Use the heads-up switcher (page 154), or the Dock, to select a program; Spaces switches to the proper screen automatically.

Tip: If a program's windows are scattered on different screens, you can click that program's Dock icon repeatedly to jump from window to window. (On the other hand, the window-switching keystroke ⌘-~ works only within a single screen. It never takes you from one virtual screen to another.)

Figure 5-8:
This display appears momentarily when you switch screens. The arrow shows you the screens you're moving to and from.

You can even move diagonally. While pressing Control, press two arrow keys on your keyboard at once (like ↓ and →).

When you make a switch, you see a flash of animation as one screen flies away and another appears. You also see the display shown in Figure 5-8 to help you orient yourself among your magnificent array of virtual monitors.

Now that you're "on" the screen you want, open programs and arrange windows onto it as usual.

The big picture

Here's yet another window-controlling keystroke: Fn-F8. It opens up a gigantic miniature (if there is such a thing) of your entire Spaces universe (Figure 5-9).

Clicking the Spaces icon in the Dock brings up the same display.

Tip: You can change that keystroke to something simpler. Method 1: You can do away with the Fn key if you turn on "Use all F1, F2, etc. keys as standard function keys" in System Preferences→Keyboard (page 223), or if you have an older, plastic Apple keyboard or laptop. In those cases, F8 alone does the trick.

Method 2: Choose a completely different keystroke right there in System Preferences, as already described.

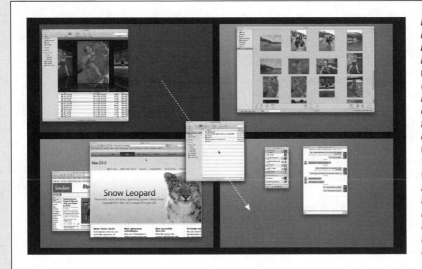

Figure 5-9:
Press Fn-F8, or click Spaces in your Dock, to open this live master view of all the windows on all the screens. (The windows update in real time—if you're in a chat or playing a movie, for example.) You can actually drag individual windows from one of these "window panes" (actually virtual screens) to another. In fact, you can even use the Exposé keystrokes to make all the windows on all the screens visible at once, for ease in moving them around the screens.

So what can you do here?

- **Get oriented.** Especially at first, it's easy to become disoriented among your screens. You could have sworn you opened your favorite Web site—where the heck is it? Pressing F8 gives you an instant readout of where all your windows are sitting at the moment.

- **Switch screens.** Click any "pane" of the big-picture view to jump to the screen. Or just press its number on your keyboard (4 to open the fourth screen, for example).

- **Reorder the screens.** Using any blank background spot as a handle, you can drag the actual panes of the big-picture view around to rearrange them. If you decide that your email screen should really be at top left, drag it there.

- **Move windows around.** Here's the real power of the big-picture view. As shown in Figure 5-9, you can actually drag windows from one screen to another. You can use any part of the window as a handle, not just the title bar.

Tip: If you press Shift as you drag, then you move *all* windows that belong to the same program simultaneously.

- **Hit an Exposé keystroke.** You can actually use the Exposé keyboard shortcuts (F3 on modern keyboards, for example) *while* you're in the big-picture view.

  Yes, this gets kind of meta, but it's useful when you're trying to arrange your windows and programs among your screens. Once you're in the F8 big-picture view, for example, you can hit F3 to see all windows on all screens scurry apart, so that nothing is covered up. Then start dragging windows onto different screens as necessary.

Moving windows among screens

One way to move a particular window to a different screen is to drag it in big-picture view, as shown in Figure 5-9.

But there are two other ways that don't require entering the F8 big-picture view:

- Drag a window (using its title bar as a handle) all the way to the edge of the screen. Stay there with the mouse button still down. After about a second, you'll see the adjacent screen slide into view; you've just moved the window.

- Click anywhere inside a window, and keep the mouse button down. Now press your screen-switching keystroke (Control-←, for example, or Control-3). You've just moved the window to the designated screen.

To be sure, these are power-user techniques that may not come naturally. But the Fn-F8 big-picture view is always waiting should you become befuddled.

Tip: What if you're using Spaces, and you want to drag something from one screen (like a photo in iPhoto) into a window that's on a different screen (like an outgoing email message)?

Two ways; take your pick. First, you can start dragging whatever it is—and then, in mid-drag, press Fn-F8 to open the big-picture view, and complete the drag directly onto the other Space (and even into the relevant window *in* that Space).

Another approach: Start dragging. With the mouse button still down, press ⌘-Tab to open the application switcher. Continue the drag onto the *icon* of the receiving program, and still keep the mouse button down. Mac OS X switches to the appropriate virtual screen automatically.

Hiding Programs the Old-Fashioned Way

When it comes to getting windows out of your way, nothing can touch Exposé and Spaces for speed and entertainment value. Once you've mastered those features, the traditional rituals of hiding windows will seem charmingly quaint. "When I was your age," you'll tell your grandchildren, "we used to have to *hold down the Option key* to hide windows!"

But you know the drill at software companies: They giveth, but they never taketh away. All the old techniques are still around for the benefit of Mac fans who use them by force of habit.

Hiding the Program You're Using

For the purposes of this discussion, when a program is *hidden,* all of its windows, tool palettes, and button bars disappear. You can bring them back only by bringing the program to the front again (by clicking its Dock icon again, for example).

If your aim is to hide only the frontmost program, Mac OS X offers a whole raft of approaches. Many of them involve the Option key, as listed here:

- **Option-click any visible portion of the desktop.** The program you were in vanishes, along with all its windows.

- **Option-click any other program's icon on the Dock.** You open that program (or bring all its windows to the front) *and* hide all the windows of the one you were using.

- **Option-click any visible portion of another program's windows.** Once again, you switch programs, hiding the one you were using at the time.

- **From the Application menu, choose Hide iPhoto (or whatever the program is).** The Application menu is the boldfaced menu that bears the program's name.

- **From the program's Dock icon shortcut menu, choose Hide.** You open the short-cut menu, of course, by Control-clicking (or right-clicking). You also get a Hide button if you click-and-hold on the Dock icon for half a second.

- **When you've highlighted a program's icon by pressing ⌘-Tab to rotate through the running programs, press the letter H key.** The program hides itself instantly. Leave the ⌘ key down the whole time, and after pressing the H, press Tab again to move on to the next program. If you release the keys while "stopped" on the program instead, you'll bring it forward rather than hiding it.

- **Press ⌘-H.** This may be the easiest and most useful trick of all (although it doesn't work in a few oddball programs). Doing so hides the program you're in; you then "fall down" into the next running program.

Tip: Consider this radical, timesaving proposal: *Never quit* the programs you use frequently. Instead, simply hit ⌘-H whenever you're finished working in a program. That way, the next time you need it, the program launches with zero wait time.

There's a limit to this principle; if you have only 1 gigabyte of memory and you keep 20 programs open, and one of them is Photoshop, you'll incur a speed penalty. In more moderate situations, though, Mac OS X's virtual-memory scheme is so good that there's almost no downside to leaving your programs open *all the time.*

To un-hide a program and its windows, click its Dock icon again, choose the Show All command in the Application menu, or press ⌘-Tab to summon the heads-up application display.

Tip: The Dock continues to display the icons of all running programs without any indication that you've hidden them. Fortunately, that's easy enough to fix. All you need is the shareware program TinkerTool, which is described on page 657. It offers a simple checkbox that makes hidden programs appear with transparent Dock icons.

Hiding All Other Programs

Choosing Hide Others from your program's Application menu means, of course, "Hide the windows of every program but this one." It even hides your Finder (desktop) windows, although desktop icons remain visible.

Better yet, there's a keystroke for this command: Option-⌘-H. That's one small step for keystrokes, one giant leap for productivity geeks.

Tip: If you Control-click or right-click a program's Dock icon, you get its shortcut menu, including a Hide command. If you press Option, it changes to say Hide Others. It's a lot more work than the methods described above, but, you know. One strives for thoroughness.

If this trick interests you, you might also enjoy its corollary, described next.

The Bring-Forward, Hide-All-Others Trick

Here's a terrific technique that lets you bring one program to the front (along with all its open windows), and hide all other windows of all *other* open programs—all with one click.

You might think of it as Hero mode, or Front-and-Center mode, or Clear My Calendar mode.

In any case, the trick is to Option-⌘-click the lucky program's icon on the Dock. As it jumps to the fore, all other windows on your Mac are instantly hidden. (You can bring them back, of course, by clicking the appropriate Dock icons.)

Hiding (Minimizing) Individual Windows

You can also hide or show *individual windows* of a single program. In fact, Apple must believe that hiding a window will become one of your favorite activities, because it offers at least four ways to do so:

- Choose Window→Minimize Window, if your program offers such a command, or press ⌘-M.

- Click the Minimize button on the window's title bar.

- Double-click the window's title bar. (If this doesn't work, choose →System Preferences→Appearance. Make sure "Double-click a window's title bar to minimize" is turned on.)

In any case, the affected window shrinks down until it becomes a new icon in the right side of the Dock. Click that icon to bring the window back.

For more details, tips, and tricks on minimizing windows, see page 24.

NOSTALGIA CORNER

Window Layering

Mac OS X takes a layered approach to your programs' windows. They're not *all* in front or *all* in back; it's entirely possible to wind up with the windows of different programs sandwiched and layered, front to back.

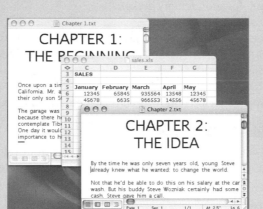

Suppose, for example, you have Microsoft Excel in the foreground but Word in the background. If you click within a visible portion of a background window, you bring only that window of Word to the front.

The remedy for this situation, if it bothers you, is the Window→Bring All to Front command, which appears in the Finder and many other programs. It brings all a program's windows to the front. (You can do the same thing by simply clicking the program's Dock icon, or using the ⌘-Tab "heads-up" display.)

In the Finder, if you prefer, you can also use the Window→Arrange in Front command. To reveal it, press Option as you open the Window menu. (What used to say "Bring All to Front" changes to say "Arrange in Front.") Mac OS X responds by *cascading* all open Finder windows, stacking them diagonally, overlapping them so that only their title bars are visible.

Layered windows shine when you're comparing two documents in two different programs, because it frees you of the window clutter of other open documents. But the time will come when you're ready to bring *all* a background program's windows to the front. Get into the habit of clicking its Dock icon, or pressing ⌘-Tab to select its icon, rather than clicking inside one window. When you do that, all open windows in that application come forward, from wherever they may be.

How Documents Know Their Parents

Every operating system needs a mechanism to associate documents with the applications that created them. When you double-click a Microsoft Word document icon, for example, it's clear that you want Microsoft Word to launch and open the document.

So how does Mac OS X know how to find a document's mommy?

It actually has two different mechanisms.

- **File name extensions.** A *file name extension* is a suffix following a period in the file's name, as in *Letter to Mom.doc.* (It's usually three letters long, but doesn't have to be.) These play a role in determining which documents open into which programs.

  That's how Windows identifies its documents, too. If you double-click something called memo.doc, it opens in Microsoft Word. If you double-click memo.wri, it opens in Microsoft Write, and so on.

Note: Mac OS X comes set to hide most file name extensions, on the premise that they make the operating system look more technical and threatening. If you'd like to see them, however, choose Finder→Preferences, click the Advanced button, and then turn on "Show all file extensions." Now examine a few of your documents; you'll see that their names now display the previously hidden suffixes.

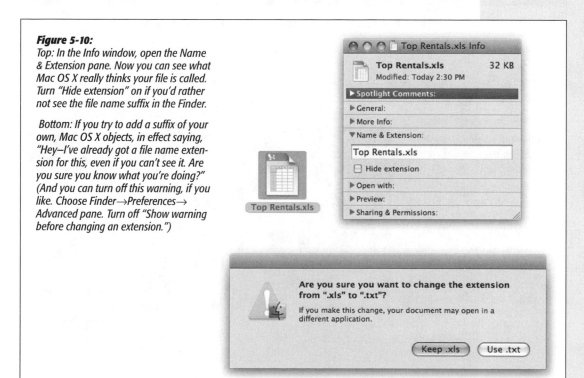

Figure 5-10:
Top: In the Info window, open the Name & Extension pane. Now you can see what Mac OS X really thinks your file is called. Turn "Hide extension" on if you'd rather not see the file name suffix in the Finder.

Bottom: If you try to add a suffix of your own, Mac OS X objects, in effect saying, "Hey—I've already got a file name extension for this, even if you can't see it. Are you sure you know what you're doing?" (And you can turn off this warning, if you like. Choose Finder→Preferences→ Advanced pane. Turn off "Show warning before changing an extension.")

You can hide or show these suffixes on an icon-at-a-time basis, too (or a clump-at-a-time basis). Just highlight the icon or icons you want to affect, and then choose File→Get Info. In the resulting Info window, proceed as shown in Figure 5-10.

- **Your preferences.** If you've used the "Always Open with" command to *specify* which program opens your document (described next), that's the one that opens; this preference *overrides* the file name extension system. Snow Leopard memorizes that new pairing in an internal Unix database. (If you're a Unix geek, you can actually open and inspect that database.)

Snow Leopard Spots: Mac OS X no longer recognizes the invisible, four-letter *Type and Creator codes* that had been a mainstay of program-document relationships since the Mac OS 9 days. The Creator code identified the program; the Type code specified the document's file format: GIF, JPEG, TIFF, and so on. (Apple used to monitor and track these codes, in conjunction with the various Mac software companies, so that no two creator codes were alike.) Apparently Apple thought that two different parent-document systems was plenty already.

It's possible to live a long and happy life without knowing anything about these suffixes and relationships. Indeed, the vast majority of Mac fans may never even encounter them. But if you're prepared for a little bit of technical bushwhacking, you may discover

---

GEM IN THE ROUGH

Using the Dock or Sidebar for Drag-and-Drop

The Mac is smart about the relationship between documents and applications. If you double-click a TextEdit document icon, for example, TextEdit opens automatically and shows you the document.

But it's occasionally useful to open a document using a program *other* than the one that created it. Perhaps, as is often the case with downloaded Internet graphics, you don't *have* the program that created it, or you don't know which one was used. This technique is also useful if you want to open a Read Me file into your word processor, such as Word, instead of the usual TextEdit program.

In such cases, the Dock is handy: Just drag the mystery document onto one of the Dock's tiles, as shown here. Do-

ing so forces the program to open the document—if it can. (Dragging onto a program's icon in the Sidebar or even the Finder toolbar works just as well.)

Incidentally, in general only the Dock icons of programs that can, in fact, open the file you're dragging become highlighted. The others just shrug indifferently or even scoot aside, thinking you're trying to drag the file *into* the Dock.

Pressing Option-⌘ as you drag forces Dock icons to be more tolerant. Now *all* of them "light up" as your document touches them, indicating that they'll *try* to open your file. Even so, a "could not be opened" error message may result. As they say in Cupertino, sometimes what a can really needs is a can opener.

---

that understanding document-program relationships can be useful in troubleshooting, keeping your files private, and appreciating how Mac OS X works.

Reassigning Documents to Programs

Unfortunately, Type and Creator codes aren't of much use when you encounter a document created by a program you don't have. If someone emails you a MIDI file (a file-exchange format for music) that she exported from the Finale sheet-music program, you won't be able to open it by double-clicking, unless you, too, have Finale installed. Even if you have a different sheet-music program on your hard drive, just double-clicking the MIDI file won't, by itself, open it.

File name extensions, meanwhile, have problems of their own. File name extensions are even less likely to pinpoint which parent program should open a particular document. Suppose you've downloaded a graphic called Sunset.jpg. Well, almost any program these days can open a JPEG graphic—Photoshop, Word, Preview, Safari, and so on. How does Mac OS X know which of these programs to open when you double-click the file?

Fortunately, *you* can decide. You can *reassign* a document (or all documents of its kind) to a specific program. Here's the rundown.

Reassigning a certain document—just once

Double-clicking a graphics file generally opens it in Preview, the graphics viewer included with Mac OS X. Most of the time, that's a perfectly good arrangement. But Preview has only limited editing powers. What if you decide to edit a graphics file more substantially? You'd want it to open, just this once, into a different program—Photoshop Elements, for example.

To do so, you must access the Open With command. You can find it in two places:

- Highlight the icon, and then choose File→Open With.

- Control-click (or right-click) the file's icon. Or, in a Finder window, highlight the icon and then open the ✿ menu. In the shortcut menu, choose Open With.

  Study the submenu for a moment (Figure 5-11, top). The program whose name says "(default)" indicates which program usually opens this kind of document. From this pop-up menu, choose the name of the program you'd rather open this particular file, right now, just this once.

Reassigning a certain document—permanently

After opening a TIFF file in, say, Photoshop Elements for editing, you haven't really made any changes in the fabric of your Mac universe. The next time you double-click that file, it opens once again in Preview.

If you wish this particular file would *always* open in Photoshop Elements, the steps are slightly different. In fact, there are three different ways:

• In the Choose an Application dialog box (the one that appears when you double-click a document whose "parent" program isn't clear), turn on "Always Open With" (shown at bottom in Figure 5-11).

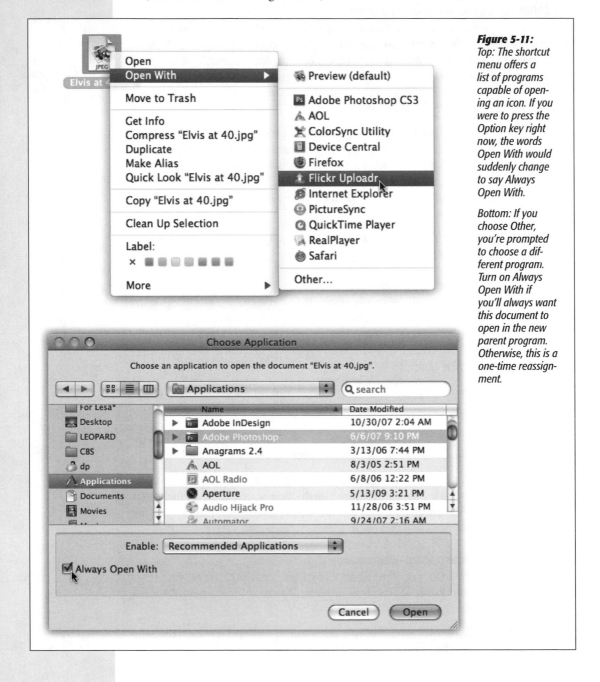

- Start out with one of the previously described techniques (File→Open With, or Control-click/right-click the file's icon and choose Open With)—but after you see the menu, press the Option key, too. Before your very eyes, the Open With command changes to say *Always* Open With.

- Highlight the icon, and then choose File→Get Info. Open the "Open with" panel. Choose a new "parent" program's name from the pop-up menu. You'll see that the word "(default)" changes position, now tacking itself onto the name of the program you've chosen.

Tip: You can use a similar trick to reassign the parenthood of a whole *flock* of selected icons at once. Once you've selected them, keep the Option key pressed as you choose File→Show Inspector. In the "Open with" section of this specialized Get Info window, choose a new program from the pop-up menu. The message at the top of the window—"22 items," for example—reminds you that you're changing the whole batch at once.

Reassigning all documents of one type

So much for reassigning one document (or a group of documents) at a time. What if you're writing, say, a book about Mac OS X, and you've been taking a lot of screenshots? Mac OS X saves each captured screen illustration as a graphics file in something called PNG format. That's all fine, except that every time you double-click one of these, it opens into Preview, where you can't paint out unwanted details.

You could reassign all these files, one at a time, to a different program, but your grandchildren would have grandchildren by the time you finish. In this case, you want to tell Mac OS X, "For heaven's sake, make *all* PNG files open in Photoshop from now on!"

To make it happen, start by highlighting *any* PNG file. Choose File→Get Info. (The shortcut menus won't help you in this case.) Open the "Open with" panel.

From its pop-up menu, choose the program you want to open this kind of document from now on. (If the one you prefer isn't listed, use the Other option, which opens the Choose an Application dialog box so you can navigate to the one you want. Find and double-click the program.)

This time, follow up by clicking Change All beneath the pop-up menu. (This button is dimmed until you've actually selected a different program from the pop-up menu.) Mac OS X asks you to confirm by clicking Continue or pressing Return.

From now on, double-clicking any similar kind of document opens it in the newly selected program.

Keyboard Control

Mac OS X offers a fantastic feature for anyone who believes life is too short: keyboard-controllable menus, dialog boxes, pop-up menus, and even Dock pop-up menus. You can operate every menu in every program without the mouse.

In fact, you can operate every control in every dialog box from the keyboard, including pop-up menus and checkboxes. And you can even redefine many of the built-in Mac OS X keystrokes, like Shift-⌘-3 to capture the screen as a graphic.

In fact, you can even add or change *any menu command in any program*. If you're a keyboard-shortcut lover, your cup runneth over.

Here are some of the ways you can control your Mac mouselessly. In the following descriptions, you'll encounter the factory settings for the keystrokes that do the magic—but as you'll see in a moment, you can change these key combos to anything you like. (The System Preferences→Keyboard→Keyboard Shortcuts tab contains the on/off switches for these features.)

Note: On modern-day, aluminum keyboards, the keystrokes described below may not work unless you also press the Fn key simultaneously.

If that seems just a *tad* clumsy, you can eliminate the Fn-key requirement either by using the "Use all F1, F2, etc. keys as standard function keys" option described in the box on page 223—or by choosing a different keystroke altogether (page 179).

Control the Menus

When you press Control-F2, the menu is highlighted. At this point, you can "walk" to another menu by pressing the ← or → keys (or Tab and Shift-Tab). When you reach the menu you want, open it by pressing ↓, space, Return, or Enter.

Walk down the commands in the menu by pressing ↑ or ↓, or jump directly to a command in the menu by typing the first couple of letters of its name. Finally, "click" a menu command by pressing Enter, Return, or the space bar.

You can also close the menu without making a selection by pressing Esc or ⌘-period.

Control the Dock

Once you've pressed Control-F3, you can highlight *any* icon on the Dock by pressing the appropriate arrow keys (or, once again, Tab and Shift-Tab).

Then, once you've highlighted a Dock icon, you "click it" by pressing Return or the space bar. Again, if you change your mind, press Esc or ⌘-period.

Tip: Once you've highlighted a disk or folder icon, you can press the ↑ or ↓ keys to make its shortcut menu appear. (If you've positioned the Dock vertically, use ← or → instead!)

Cycle Through Your Windows

Every time you press Control-F4, you bring the next window forward, eventually cycling through *every window in every open program*. Add the Shift key to cycle through them in the opposite order.

You may remember that Mac OS X offers a different keystroke for cycling through the different windows in your *current* program (it's ⌘-~, the tilde symbol at the upper-left of your keyboard). Control-F4, on the other hand, tours all windows in *all* programs. Both keystrokes are useful in different situations.

Control the Toolbar

This one is on the unpredictable side, but it more or less works in most programs that display a Mac OS X–style toolbar: the Finder, System Preferences, and so on.

When you press Control-F5, you highlight the first button on that toolbar. Move the "focus" by pressing the arrow keys or Tab and Shift-Tab. Then tap Return or the space bar to "click" the highlighted button.

Control Tool Palettes

In a few programs that feature floating tool palettes, you can highlight the frontmost palette by pressing Control-F6. At this point, use the arrow keys to highlight the various buttons on the palette. You can see the effect when, for example, you're editing text in TextEdit and you've also opened the Font palette. Pressing Control-F6 highlights the Font palette, taking the "focus" off your document.

Control Menulets

Here's a Snow Leopard gem you may not have heard about: You can now operate *menulets*—those menu-bar status indicators for your speaker volume, wireless networks, and so on—from the keyboard, too.

This time, the trick is to hit Control-F8. That highlights the leftmost Apple menulet. Now you can use your ← and → arrow keys to move around the menu bar; when you've highlighted the one you want, press Return or the space bar to "click" that menu and open it.

Control Dialog Boxes

You can also navigate and manipulate any *dialog box* from the keyboard.

See the dialog box shown in Figure 5-12? If you turn on "All controls" at the bottom, then pressing the Tab key highlights the next control of any type, whatever it may be—radio button, pop-up menu, and so on. Press the space bar to "click" a button or open a pop-up menu. Once a menu is open, use the arrow keys (or type letter keys) to highlight commands on it, and the space bar to "click" your choice.

Tip: Press Control-arrow keys to "click" the different tabs of a dialog box.

Changing a Menu Keyboard Shortcut

Suppose you love iPhoto (and who doesn't?). But one thing drives you crazy: The Revert to Original command, which discards all the changes you've ever made since taking the photo, has no keyboard equivalent. You must trek up to the menu bar every time you need that command.

This is why Mac OS X lets you add keyboard shortcuts to menu commands that lack them—or change the command in programs whose key assignments break with tradition. (It works in any program that uses the standard Mac OS X menu software, which rules out Microsoft Word and the other Office programs.) Here's the routine:

1. **Choose →System Preferences→Keyboard. Click the Keyboard Shortcuts tab.**

    You're shown a list of all of Mac OS X's built-in keyboard assignments.

2. **Click the + button just beneath the list.**

    The dialog box shown in Figure 5-12 appears.

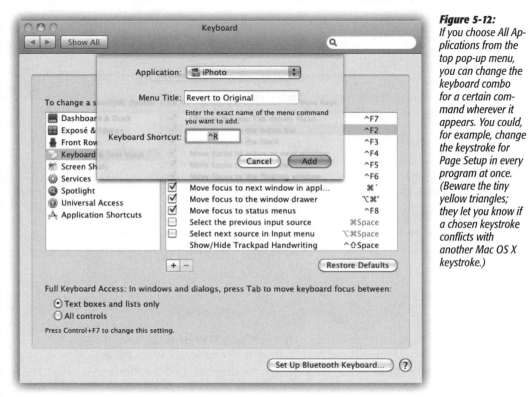

Figure 5-12:
If you choose All Applications from the top pop-up menu, you can change the keyboard combo for a certain command wherever it appears. You could, for example, change the keystroke for Page Setup in every program at once. (Beware the tiny yellow triangles; they let you know if a chosen keystroke conflicts with another Mac OS X keystroke.)

3. **Indicate which program needs behavior modification.**

    In this example, you'd choose iPhoto from the Application pop-up menu. (If the program's name doesn't appear in the pop-up menu, choose Other; navigate to, and double-click, the program you want.)

4. **Carefully type in the name of the menu command whose keyboard shortcut you want to change or add.**

Type it *exactly* as it appears in the menu, complete with capitalization and the little ellipsis (…) that may follow it. (You make the ellipsis character by pressing Option-semicolon.)

5. **Click in the Keyboard Shortcut box. Press the new or revised key combo you want.**

For example, press Control-R for iPhoto's Revert to Original command. You'll see the Mac's notation of your keystroke appear in the Keyboard Shortcut box—unless, of course, the combo you selected is already in use within that program. In that case, you hear only an error sound that means "Try again."

6. **Click Add.**

The dialog box closes. By scrolling down in your Keyboard Shortcuts list, you'll see that the keystroke you selected has now been written down for posterity under the appropriate program's flippy triangle. (To get rid of it, click its name and then click the **–** button beneath the list.)

The next time you open the program you edited, you'll see that the new keystroke is in place.

Tip: To delete or change one of your custom menu shortcuts, open System Preferences→Keyboard→Keyboard Shortcuts. Click Application Shortcuts in the list at left. Click the command you'd like to edit. Press Delete to get rid of it; or, to try a different key combo, click where the existing keyboard shortcut appears, and then press a new one.

Redefining a Snow Leopard Keystroke

As you've no doubt become painfully aware, there are *hundreds* of keyboard combinations for the various Mac OS X functions and settings. That's good, because keyboard shortcuts are efficient and quicker than using the mouse. But that's also bad, because there's no *way* you'll be able to remember all of them—and some of most useful shortcuts are ridiculous, multikey affairs that you'll never remember at all.

Snow Leopard comes with a completely overhauled keyboard-shortcut center, shown in Figure 5-13. Here, you can look over all of the common Mac OS X hidden keyboard functions—for Exposé, Spotlight, Spaces, the Dashboard, the Dock, and many others—and *change them*.

Here's how it goes:

1. **Choose →System Preferences. Click Keyboard. Click the Keyboard Shortcuts tab.**

You arrive at the dialog box shown in Figure 5-13.

2. **In the left-side list, click the category or function you want.**

Your choices include Dashboard & Dock, Exposé & Spaces, Front Row, Keyboard & Text Input, and so on. When you click a category name, you see the available keyboard shortcuts.

Tip: You don't have to be content with *changing* one of these keyboard shortcuts. You can also *turn it off* by clicking the corresponding checkbox. That's great if one of Apple's predefined keystrokes—for a function you don't even use—is interfering with one in a program you like.

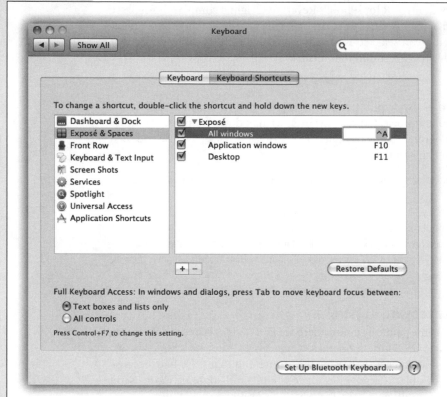

Figure 5-13:
The new keyboard shortcut center in Snow Leopard lets you redefine the keystrokes that trigger many basic Mac OS X features, menu commands in your programs, and software you've built yourself using Automator (Chapter 7).

3. **Click the command you want to change. Then click the current keyboard combination.**

   Suppose, for example, that you wished that the All-Apps Exposé keystroke were something easier to remember, like Control-A. So in step 2, you'd click Exposé & Spaces. In this step, you'd click "All windows," as shown in Figure 5-13. Then you'd click where it currently says F9.

4. **Press a new key combination.**

   In this example, you'd press Control-A.

   Be careful, though. Mac OS X keystrokes take precedence over *all others.* So if you choose a keystroke like ⌘-P for something, well, by golly, you'll no longer be able to use ⌘-P to print anything in any of your programs. Think before you assign. Run a couple of tests afterward.

The Save and Open Dialog Boxes

When you choose File→Save, you're asked where you want the new document stored on your hard drive. The resulting dialog box is a miniature Finder. All the skills you've picked up working at the desktop come into play here.

To give it a try, launch any program that has a Save or Export command—TextEdit, for example. Type a couple of words, and then choose File→Save. The Save sheet appears (Figure 5-14).

Tip: In Mac OS X, a quick glance at the Close button in the upper-left corner of a document window tells you whether it's been saved. When a small dot appears in the red button, it means you've made changes to the document that you haven't saved yet. (Time to press ⌘-S!) The dot disappears as soon as you save your work.

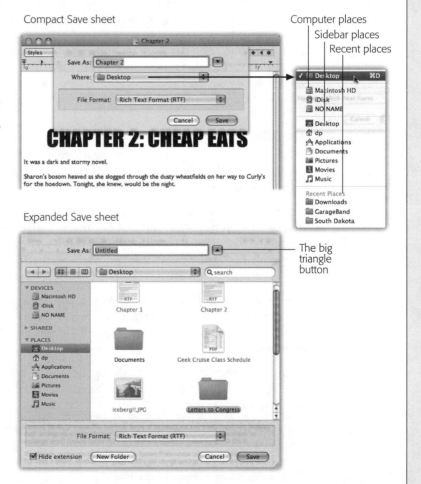

Figure 5-14:
Top: The Save dialog box, or sheet, often appears in its compact form.

Right (inset): If you open the Where pop-up menu, you'll find that Mac OS X lists all the places it thinks you might want to save your new document: on the hard drive or iDisk, in a folder you've put into your Sidebar, or into a folder you've recently opened.

Bottom: If you want to choose a different folder or create a new folder, click the ▼button shown above to expand the dialog box. Here, you see the equivalent of the Finder—with a choice of icon, list, or column view. Even the Sidebar is here, complete with access to other disks on the network.

Compact Save sheet

Computer places
Sidebar places
Recent places

Expanded Save sheet

The big triangle button

Sheets

In the days of operating systems gone by, the Save dialog box appeared dead center on the screen, where it commandeered your entire operation. Moreover, because it seemed stuck to your *screen* rather than to a particular *document,* you couldn't actually tell which document you were saving—a real problem when you quit out of a program that had three unsaved documents open.

SuperTip: Even in the Save or Open dialog box, you can highlight an icon (or several) and then press ⌘-I. You switch back to the Finder, where the Get Info box is waiting with the date, size, and other details about the selected icons.

In most Mac OS X programs, there's no mystery regarding which document you're saving, because a little Save dialog box called a *sheet* slides directly out of the document's title bar.

Better still, this little Save box is a sticky note attached *to the document.* It stays there, neatly attached and waiting, even if you switch to another program, another document, the desktop, or wherever. When you finally return to the document, the Save sheet is still there, waiting for you to type a file name and save the document.

Tip: In most programs, you can enlarge the Save or Open dialog box by dragging the ribbed lower-right corner. You can also adjust the width of the Sidebar by dragging its right edge.

The Mini Finder

Of course *you,* O savvy reader, have probably never saved a document into some deeply nested folder by accident, never to see it again. But millions of novices (and even a few experts) have fallen into this trap.

When the Save sheet appears, a pop-up menu shows you precisely where Mac OS X proposes to put your newly created document: usually in the Documents folder of your own Home folder. For many people, this is an excellent suggestion. If you keep everything in your Documents folder, it will be extremely easy to find, and you'll be able to back up your work just by dragging that single folder to a backup disk.

As shown at top in Figure 5-14, the Where pop-up menu gives you direct access to some other places you might want to save a newly created file. (The keystrokes for the most important folders work here, too—Shift-⌘-H for your Home folder, for example.)

In any case, when you save a file, the options in the Where pop-up menu have you covered 90 percent of the time. Most people work with a limited set of folders for active documents.

But when you want to save a new document into a new folder, or when you want to navigate to a folder that isn't listed in the Where pop-up menu, all is not lost. Click the ▾ button identified in Figure 5-14. The Save sheet expands into a very familiar sight: a miniature version of the Finder.

There's your Sidebar, complete with access to the other computers on your network. There are the Back/Forward buttons. There are your little buttons for icon, list, and column views.

Tip: In column view, your first instinct should be to widen this window, making more columns available. Do so by carefully dragging the lower-right corner of the dialog box. Mac OS X remembers the size for this Save sheet independently in each program.

And in list view, how's this for a tip? If you Control-click (or right-click) one of the column headings, like Name or Date Modified, you get a secret pop-up menu of column names: Last Opened, Size, Kind, Label, and so on. That's right: You can customize the list view *within* an Open or Save dialog box. You can sort, too, by clicking one of the column headings, just as at the desktop.

Most of the familiar Finder navigation shortcuts work here, too. For example, press the ← and → keys to navigate the columns, or the ↑ and ↓ keys to highlight the disk and folder names *within* a column. Once you've highlighted a column, you can also type to select the first letters of disk or folder names.

In fact, you can use Quick Look (page 54) in the Open and Save dialog box, too. Highlight any file or folder in the list and tap the Space bar to view it in a full-size window.

When you're finished playing around, open the folder where you want to save your newly created document, and then click Save to store it there.

Snow Leopard Spots: Here's one of the weirdest new tricks in Mac OS X 10.6.

When the Open or Save dialog box is open before you, you can press Shift-⌘-period (.) to make all of your Mac's *hidden* files appear. (As a Unix-based outfit, Mac OS X is crawling with these invisible files, which are of primary interest to technical types.) Press that keystroke again to hide the hidden files once again. Fun for geeks!

If you use a non-American number-formatting system (where one thousand is 1.000, for example), use Shift-⌘-comma instead.

Alternatively, click New Folder (or press the usual New Folder keystroke, Shift-⌘-N) to create a new folder *inside* the folder you're looking at. (If you're in column view, then the new folder appears inside whichever folder is highlighted.)

You'll be asked to type the new name for the folder. After you've done so, click Create (or press Return). The new folder appears and opens before you, empty. You can now proceed with saving your new document into it, if you like.

The next time you save a new document, the Save sheet reappears in whatever condition you left it. That is, if you used column view the last time, it's still in column view. At any time, you can collapse it into simplified view, shown at top in Figure 5-14, by clicking the ▲ button to the right of the Where pop-up menu.

Spotlight

The Search box at the top of the Open and Save dialog box is a clone of the Finder's Search box (Chapter 3). Press ⌘-F to make your insertion point jump there. Type a few letters of the name of the file or folder you're looking for, and up it pops, regardless of its actual hard-disk location.

Your savings: five minutes of burrowing through folders to find it, and several pages of reading about how to navigate the Save and Open boxes.

Insta-Jumping to a Folder Location

Whether you're using the mini-sheet or the expanded view, you can save yourself some folder-burrowing time by following the tip shown in Figure 5-15. This feature is totally undocumented—but well worth learning.

Tip: If, when the Save box is in its expanded condition, you click the name of an existing file, Mac OS X thoughtfully copies the *name* of the clicked file into the Save As: text box (which otherwise said "Untitled" or was blank).

This trick can save you time when you're saving a second document with a slightly modified name (*Oprah and Me: The Inside Story, Chapter 1* and then *Oprah and Me: The Inside Story, Chapter 2*). It's also useful if you want to *replace* the original file with the new one you're saving. Instead of having to type out the entire name of the file, you can just click it.

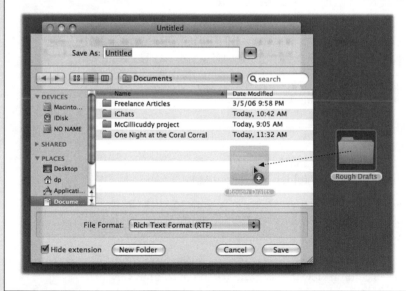

Figure 5-15:
The quickest way to specify a folder location is to drag the icon of any folder or disk from your desktop directly into the Save or Open sheet. Mac OS X instantly displays the contents of that folder or disk. You'll see by the Where pop-up menu that Mac OS X has indeed understood your intention.

The File Format Pop-up Menu

The Save dialog box in many programs offers a pop-up menu of file formats below the Save As box. Use this menu when preparing a document for use by somebody else—somebody whose computer doesn't have the same software. For example, if you've used a graphics program to prepare a photograph for use on the Web, this menu is where you specify JPEG format (the standard Web format for photos).

The Open File Dialog Box

The dialog box that appears when you choose File→Open is almost identical to the expanded Save File sheet. Because you encounter it only when you're opening an existing file, this dialog box lacks the Save button, file name field, and so on.

Note: Furthermore, the Open dialog box gives you access only to disks, folders, and documents that you can actually open at this moment. For example, when you're using GarageBand, picture files show up dimmed.

Figure 5-16:
The new Media Browser is built right into the Open dialog box. That is, you get miniature listings of your iTunes, iPhoto, and movie files right in the Sidebar, for convenience in importing them into (for example) Keynote, PowerPoint, or a Web design program.

But the Open box adds a new Sidebar category called Media (see Figure 5-16), which gives you direct access to all your photos, music, and movies. Apple figures you might want to import these items *into* a document you're working on.

Most of the other Save File dialog box controls are equally useful here. That handy Spotlight search bar is still there, only a ⌘-F away. Once again, you can begin your navigation by seeing what's on the desktop (press ⌘-D) or in your Home folder (Shift-⌘-H). Once again, you can find a folder or disk by beginning your quest with the Sidebar, and then navigate using icon, list, or column view. And once again, you can drag a folder, disk, or file icon off your desktop directly into the dialog box to specify where you want to look. (If you drag a *file* icon, you're shown the folder that contains it.)

When you've finally located the file you want to open, do so by double-clicking it or highlighting it (which you can do from the keyboard), and then pressing Return, Enter, or ⌘-O.

In general, most people don't encounter the Open File dialog box nearly as often as the Save File dialog box. That's because the Mac offers many more convenient ways to *open* a file—double-clicking its icon in the Finder, choosing its name from →Recent Items, and so on—but only a single way to *save* a new file.

Two Kinds of Programs: Cocoa and Carbon

Mac OS X was supposed to make life simpler. It was supposed to eliminate the confusion and complexity that the old Mac OS had accumulated over the years—and replace it with a smooth, simple, solid system.

Someday, that's exactly what Mac OS X will be. For the moment, however, you're stuck with running two different kinds of programs, each with different characteristics: *Cocoa and Carbon*.

The explanation involves a little bit of history and a little bit of logic. To take full advantage of Mac OS X's considerable technical benefits, software companies had to write new programs for it from scratch. So what should Apple have done—sent out an email to the authors of the 18,000 existing Mac programs, suggesting that they throw out their programs and rewrite them from the bottom up?

FREQUENTLY ASKED QUESTION

The Return of Classic?

Are you kidding me? Classic is gone? No more Mac OS 9 at all? But I need to run a couple of old programs!

Yes, the Classic mode—which, until Leopard, let you run older Mac OS 9 programs in a sort of simulation mode—is gone. You can run *only* Mac OS X programs in Mac OS X.

Or at least that's what Apple wants you to think. Truth is, there's a sneaky way to run Mac OS 9 programs, even in

Leopard: a little something called SheepShaver. It's an open-source Mac OS 9 emulator, meaning that it's been written by volunteer collaborators across the Internet.

SheepShaver is difficult to install and isn't what you'd call rock-solid. But it's good to know that, someday, when you absolutely, positively have to run that old program, you're not entirely out of luck.

At most big software companies, that suggestion would wind up on the Joke of the Week bulletin board.

Instead, Apple gave software companies a break. It wrote Mac OS X to let programmers and software companies choose precisely how much work they wanted to put into compatibility with the new system. There are two levels:

- **Update the existing programs (Carbon).** If programmers were willing to put *some* effort into getting with the Mac OS X program, they could simply adapt, or update, their existing software.

  The resulting software looks and feels almost like a true Mac OS X program—you get the crash protection, the good looks, the cool-looking graphics, the Save sheets, and so on—but behind the scenes, the bulk of the computer programming is the same as it was in Mac OS 9. These are what Apple calls Carbonized programs, named for the technology (Carbon) that permits them to run on Mac OS X.

  To this day, many famous Mac programs have simply been Carbonized: AppleWorks, Photoshop versions before CS3, FileMaker, Microsoft Office, and so on.

Snow Leopard Spots: Believe it or not, the Finder itself was a Carbon program until Snow Leopard came along. Yes, it took six years, but Apple finally rewrote the Finder from scratch as a true-blue Cocoa program. Tell *that* to your Windows buddies who call Snow Leopard nothing more than a "service pack."

Most Carbonized programs don't offer all the features available to Mac OS X, however. In the following pages, you'll discover which Mac OS X goodies you sacrifice when using programs adapted this way.

On the other hand, such software offers a feature that software companies like a lot: A Carbon program is a lot easier to write concurrently with a Windows version of the same software. A Cocoa program, by contrast, is almost certainly locked into Mac-only Land.

- **Write new programs from scratch (Cocoa).** As Mac OS X becomes more popular, more software companies create new programs exclusively for it. The geeks call such programs *Cocoa* applications. Although they look exactly like Carbonized programs, they feel a little bit more smooth and solid. And they offer a number of special features that Carbonized programs don't offer.

  These days, almost all the programs that come on every Mac are true Cocoa applications, including iMovie, iPhoto, iDVD, Safari, iChat, TextEdit, Stickies, Mail, Address Book, and so on.

The Cocoa Difference

Here are some of the advantages Cocoa programs offer. It's worth reading—not to make you drool about a future when all Mac programs will fall into this category, but to help clear up any confusion you may have about why certain features seem to be present only occasionally.

Note: The following features appear in almost all Cocoa programs. That's not to say that you'll *never* see these features in Carbonized programs; the occasional Carbon program may offer one of these features or another. That's because programmers have to do quite a bit of work to bring them into Carbon applications—and almost none to include them in Cocoa ones.

The Font Panel

The Mac has always been the designer's preferred computer, and Mac OS X only strengthens its position. For one thing, Mac OS X comes with over 200 absolutely beautiful fonts that Apple licensed from commercial type companies.

When you use a Carbon program, you usually access these fonts the same way as always: using a Font menu. But when you use a Cocoa program, you get the Font *panel*, which makes it far easier to organize, search, and use your font collection. Chapter 14 describes fonts, and the Font panel, in more detail.

Title Bar Tricks

You may remember from Chapter 2 that the title bar of every Finder window harbors a secret pop-up menu. When you Control-click it (or right-click it, or ⌘-click it), you're shown a little folder ladder that delineates your current position in your folder hierarchy. You may also remember that the tiny icon just to the left of the window's name is actually a handle you can drag to move a folder into a different window.

In Cocoa programs, you get the same features in *document* windows, as shown back in Figure 2-5 (page 76). (This feature is available in many Carbonized programs, but it isn't a sure thing.) By dragging the tiny document icon next to the document's name, you can perform stunts like dragging that little icon to the desktop, or to the Dock icon of a different program for opening—right from your document's title bar.

Toolbar Tricks

The toolbar is an increasingly common sight at the top of modern application windows. In any thoughtfully written program, the Customize Toolbar command lets you determine how you want this toolbar to show up—with icons, as icons with text labels beneath them, with text labels alone to save window space, and so on.

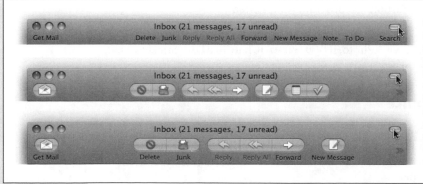

Figure 5-17:
By ⌘-clicking this button repeatedly, you can cycle among toolbar styles. In Mail, for example, you can cycle among six different toolbar styles: with icons and labels (large and small); with icons only (large and small); and with text labels only (large and small).

But in many Cocoa programs—including the Finder, OmniWeb, Mail, Address Book, and Xcode—there's a much faster way to switch among these toolbar styles: Just ⌘-click the white button shown in Figure 5-17.

Secret Keyboard Shortcuts

For the most part, it's possible to ignore the Unix that beats within the heart of Mac OS X. But every now and then, a refreshing reminder pokes its head up through the fields of gradient gray—and here's one of them.

Although you'll never see it mentioned in the instruction manuals for Cocoa applications (if there even were such things as instruction manuals anymore), most of them respond to certain keystrokes left over from the NeXT operating system, which was Mac OS X's ancestor. If you're a card-carrying number of KIAFTMA (the Keyboard Is Always Faster than the Mouse Association), you'll love these additional keyboard navigation strokes:

- **Control-A.** Moves your insertion point to the beginning of the paragraph. (*Mnemonic:* A = beginning of the Alphabet.)

- **Control-E.** Deposits your insertion point at the end of the paragraph. (*Mnemonic:* E = End.)

- **Control-D.** Forward delete (deletes the letter to the *right* of the insertion point).

- **Control-K.** Instantly deletes all text from the insertion point to the right end of the line. (*Mnemonic:* K = Kills the rest of the line.)

- **Control-O.** Inserts a paragraph break, much like Return, but leaves the insertion point where it was, above the break. This is the ideal trick for breaking a paragraph in half when you've just thought of a better ending for the first part. (*Mnemonic:* O = "Oh, I just thought of a better ending for the first part!")

- **Control-T.** Moves the insertion point one letter to the right—and along with it, drags whichever letter was to its left. (*Mnemonic:* T = Transpose letters.)

- **Option-Delete.** Deletes the entire word to the left of the insertion point. When you're typing along in a hurry and you discover that you've just made a typo, this is the keystroke you want. It's much faster to nuke the previous word and retype it than to fiddle around with the mouse and the insertion point just to fix one letter.

Four additional keystrokes duplicate the functions of the arrow keys. Still, as long as you've got your pinky on that Control key…

- **Control-B, Control-F.** Moves the insertion point one character to the left or right, just like the left and right arrow keys. (*Mnemonic:* Back, Forward).

- **Control-N, Control-P.** Moves the insertion point one row down or up, like the down and up arrow keys. (*Mnemonic:* Next, Previous).

Cool Text-Selection Tricks

By holding down certain keys while dragging through text in a Cocoa program, you gain some wild and wacky text-selection powers, (especially useful in, for example, TextEdit and Pages):

- **Highlight only one column** out of several by Option-dragging. Instead of highlighting all the text, margin to margin, you get only the text within your selection rectangle.

- **Highlight several passages simultaneously** by ⌘-dragging. Each time you ⌘-drag, you highlight another block of text, even though the earlier blocks are still selected (see Figure 5-18).

Tip: In most Cocoa programs, you can combine these two tricks. That is, you can select multiple, arbitrary (not full-page-width) blocks of text by pressing both Option and ⌘ as you drag.

Figure 5-18:
The beauty of being able to select multiple blobs of text is that you can format all of them simultaneously (making them bold, for example) with one click. You can also copy the selected portions; when you paste into a different document, you get a tidy excerpt containing only the parts you wanted, all run together.

Background Window Control

The ⌘ key unlocks a slick trick in Cocoa programs: It lets you operate the buttons and controls of an inactive background window without bringing it to the front. You can operate a background window's resize box, buttons, pop-up menus, and scroll bars, all while another window is in front of it. In fact, you can even *drag through text* in a background window—and then drag and drop it into the foreground window. (Freaky!)

In every case, the secret is simply to keep ⌘ pressed as you click or drag.

Universal Apps (Intel Macs) and Rosetta

By the end of 2006, Apple had switched its entire Macintosh product line over to Intel's Core Duo processors (the successor to the Pentium).

Yes, *that* Intel. The company that Mac partisans had derided for years as part of the Dark Side. The company that Steve Jobs routinely belittled in his demonstrations of PowerPC chips (which IBM and Motorola supplied to Apple for more than a decade). The company whose marketing mascot Apple lit on fire in a 1996 attack ad on TV.

Why the change? Apple's computers can only be as fast as the chips inside them, and the chips IBM had in the works just weren't keeping up with the industry. As one editorial put it, "Apple's doing a U-turn out of a dead-end road."

And sure enough, Intel-based Macs start up and run much faster than the old Macs, thanks to the endless march of speed improvements in the chip-making world. And thanks to that Intel chip, today's Macs can even run Microsoft Windows and all the thousands of Windows programs. (Chapter 8 has details.)

At the time, though, there was a small glitch: Existing Mac software didn't *run* on Intel chips.

Apple asked the world's software companies to rewrite their programs *yet again*, after already having dragged them through the Mac OS 9-to-Mac OS X transition only a few years earlier.

Fortunately, the transition wasn't as gruesome as you might expect. First, Apple had already secretly recompiled (reworked) Mac OS X itself to run on Intel chips, beginning with Mac OS X 10.4.4.

Furthermore, Apple wrote an invisible translation program, code-named Rosetta, that permits the existing library of Mac OS X programs—Photoshop, Word, and so on—to run, unmodified, on Intel Macs. They do not, however, run especially fast on Intel Macs. In fact, many of them run *slower* than they did on pre-Intel Macs.

Snow Leopard Spots: When you install Snow Leopard, as described in Appendix A, you have the option to install Rosetta, so you'll have it just in case you want to run a pre-Intel program. (All software that's still on the market has long since been updated to the so-called Universal versions–that is, Intel-compatible. But plenty of older programs, long since abandoned, or whose software companies have gone under, are still around.)

But if it's too late to install Rosetta along with Snow Leopard, don't worry. When the day comes that you *try* to run a pre-Intel program, Snow Leopard offers to grab Rosetta for you. It says: "To open BeeKeeper Pro, you need to install Rosetta. Would you like to install it now?" When you click Install, Snow Leopard downloads it for you automatically.

To make their programs perform at *full speed* on Intel-based Macs, programmers had to update their wares. It took a couple of years, but eventually every major and minor software company still in the Mac business did indeed convert their programs into

Universal binaries—programs that run equally well on PowerPC- *and* Intel-based Macs with a double-click on the very same Finder icon.

As you may have heard, Snow Leopard—and future versions of Mac OS X—will run only on Intel Macs. So Rosetta, Universal binaries, and the term "PowerPC" will slowly fade into the sunset.

UP TO SPEED

A Little Bit About 64 Bits

It's one of the most-advertised features of Snow Leopard: The thing is now almost completely 64-bit.

Right. 64-what?

If you want your eyes to glaze over, you can read the details on 64-bit computing in Wikipedia. But the normal-person's version goes like this:

For decades, the roadways for memory and information passed through Macs or Windows PCs were 32 "lanes" wide—they could manage 32 chunks of data at once. It seemed like plenty at the time. But as programs and even documents grew enormous, and computers came with the capacity to have more and more memory installed, engineers began to dream of 64-lane circuitry.

In the short term, the most visible effect of having a 64-bit computer is that you can install a lot more memory. Today's top-of-the-line Mac Pro, for example, is limited to 32 GB of RAM. That once seemed like a lot, but don't say that to today's video editors, game designers, and number-crunchy engineers.

A 64-bit computer, though, can have just a tad bit more: 16 *million* gigs, to be precise. (That's 16 exabytes, in case you were wondering. And that's a theoretical number; no modern personal computer even has that many RAM slots.)

Eventually, there may be other benefits to a 64-bit Mac. Programs can be rewritten to run faster. Security can be better, too. Unfortunately, getting there requires rewriting huge chunks of the operating system—and all your programs.

Almost all of Snow Leopard is 64-bit software. You may have some older, non-Apple programs that aren't, but fortunately, they still run without a problem. That's because the kernel of Snow Leopard, the underlying heart of it, still runs in 32-bit mode (yes, even on 64-bit processors), to accommodate all those older programs.

Even so, Snow Leopard runs 64-bit programs seamlessly. On certain Macs, you can make Snow Leopard boot into pure 64-bit mode by holding down the 6 and 4 keys as the computer is starting up. It's not a great idea, though, because all your 32-bit applications will crash.

Ordinarily, you never have to worry about any of this stuff. Every kind of program runs in the right mode automatically. Here and there, though, you'll bump your head on this 32-bit/64-bit difference. You'll try to open something—an old PICT graphic you want to see in Preview, for example, or an add-on System Preferences pane from another company—and you'll see a message telling you to deliberately command your modern, 64-bit app (Preview or System Preferences) to run in the older, 32-bit mode.

To do that, highlight the program's icon. Press ⌘-I (Get Info). Turn on "Open in 32-bit mode." Now you'll be able to run that older software.

Over time, these messages will become less frequent, as more of the world's Mac software is released in 64-bit versions. But in the meantime, you'll be ready.

In the meantime, you have only two indications that you're using a program originally designed for PowerPC-based Macs: First, you'll see a notation in the program's Get Info window (see Figure 5-19). Second, you'll probably discover that the program isn't as fast as it used to be.

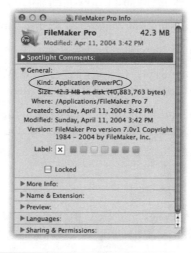
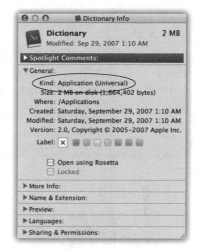

Figure 5-19:
Here's a quick way to tell if a program is an old one that will run slowly on an Intel Mac (instead of a Universal or Intel one that won't require the Rosetta software translation). Highlight its icon and choose File→Get Info. Near the top, you see either "Application: PowerPC" (old and slow), "Application: Intel" (runs only on Intel Macs), or "Application: Universal" (runs fast on both Intel and PowerPC machines).

If all this talk about architectures and chips makes your brain hurt, you can at least take comfort in one fact: No matter which kind of Mac you've got Snow Leopard installed on, every feature, tip, and trick you learn from this book works exactly the same.

Installing Mac OS X Programs

In general, new programs arrive on your Mac via one of two avenues: on a CD or DVD, or via an Internet download. The CD method is slightly simpler; see "Performing the Installation" later in this section.

For help installing downloaded programs, on the other hand, read on.

.sit, .zip, .tar, .gz, and .dmg

Programs you download from the Internet generally arrive in a specially encoded, compressed form. (And unless you've changed the settings, they arrive in the Downloads folder on your Dock.)

The downloaded file's name usually has one of these file name extensions:

- **.sit** indicates a *StuffIt* file, the standard Macintosh file-compression format of years gone by.

- **.zip** is the standard Windows compression file format. And because Snow Leopard has a built-in Compress command right in the File menu (and *doesn't* come with StuffIt Expander), .zip is the *new* standard Macintosh compression format. It certainly makes life easier for people who have to exchange files with the Windows crowd.

- **.tar** is short for *tape archive,* an ancient Unix utility that combines (but doesn't compress) several files into a single icon, for simplicity in sending.

- **.gz** is short for *gzip,* a standard Unix compression format.

- **.tar.gz** or **.tgz** represents one *compressed* archive containing *several* files.

- **.dmg** is a disk image, described below.

Fortunately, if you use Safari (Chapter 20) as your Web browser, you don't have to worry about all this, because it automatically unzips and unstuffs them.

If you use some other browser, *StuffIt Expander* can turn all of them back into usable form when you download a file. (StuffIt Expander doesn't come with Mac OS X, but

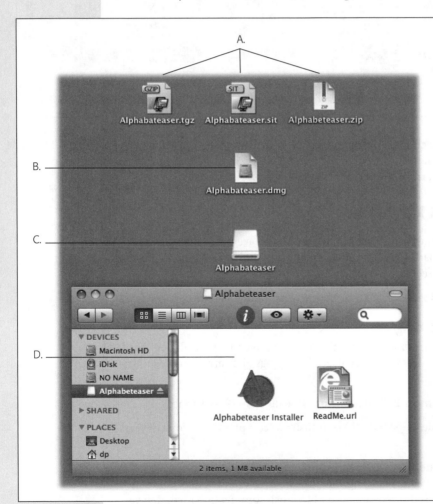

Figure 5-20:
Downloading a new program from the Internet may strew your desktop or Downloads folder with icons. A: These are the original downloaded files. Delete them after they're decompressed. B: The compressed file turns into this .dmg file. Double-click it to "mount" the disk image (if it didn't appear automatically). C: And now, the disk image itself. Double-click it to open the software installer window. (Dismiss the message that warns you that the software came from the Internet.) "Eject" it after the installation is complete. D: Here's the actual software installer window. Drag the software's icon to your Applications folder, or double-click the installer, if you see one here. After the installation is complete, you can delete all this stuff (except maybe the .dmg file, if you think you might want to install the software again later).

you can download it for free from, for example, this book's "Missing CD" page at *www.missingmanuals.com.*)

Disk Images (.dmg files)

Once you've unzipped a downloaded program, it often takes the form of a disk image file, whose name ends with the letters *.dmg* (second from top in Figure 5-20). Some files arrive as disk images straight from the Web, too, without having been compressed first.

Disk images are extremely common in Mac OS X. All you have to do is double-click the .dmg icon. After a moment, it magically turns into a disk icon on your desktop, which you can work with just as though it's a real disk (third from top in Figure 5-20). For example:

- Double-click it to open it. The software you downloaded is inside.

- Remove it from your desktop by dragging it to the Trash (whose icon turns into a big silver ⏏ key as you drag), highlighting it and pressing ⌘-E (the shortcut for File→Eject), clicking its ⏏ button in the Sidebar, or Control-clicking (right-clicking) it, and then choosing Eject from the shortcut menu.

You've still got the original .dmg file you downloaded, so you're not really saying goodbye to the disk image forever.

FREQUENTLY ASKED QUESTION

Submit to Apple

What the—I was working along in Safari, and all of a sudden it just vanished! Poof! And all I got was this lousy dialog box about "submitting to Apple." What's going on?

Apple is trying to assimilate you.

Or, more accurately, it's trying to enlist your help in ferreting out all the little glitches that make modern computing so much fun. If you're willing to click the Submit Report button and type a few comments ("I was just running Word, minding my own business, and when I clicked the Print toolbar button, the whole thing just crashed"), then Apple will add your report to the thousands flowing in from everyone else.

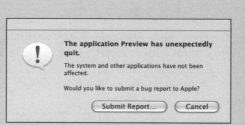

The idea is that when its programmers get a moment, they'll study these reports, track down the patterns ("Hmm, we've received 50,000 reports about that Print button in Word"), and then chase down the software company responsible—and, presumably, get a fix underway.

The report you submit is full of technical info that helps the programmers figure out what was happening at the time of the crash, but no personal information goes along for the ride. So if you feel like doing some good for your fellow Mac fans, by all means submit the report (via the Internet) whenever you're offered the chance.

Cleaning Up after Decompression

When you've finished unzipping or unstuffing a downloaded file, you may have several icons on your desktop or in the Downloads folder. Some are useful; some you're free to trash:

- **The original compressed file.** It's safe to throw away the .sit, .tar, .gz, or .tgz file you originally downloaded (after it's decompressed, of course).

- **The .dmg file.** Once you've turned it into an actual disk-drive icon, installed the software from it, and "ejected" the disk-drive icon, you can delete the .dmg file. Keep it only if you think you might need to reinstall the software someday.

Note: If you try to trash the .dmg file *before* removing the disk-drive icon from the screen, you'll get a "file in use" error message when you try to empty the Trash.

- **The disk image itself.** This final icon, the one that contains the actual software or its installer (third from top in Figure 5-20), doesn't exist as a file on your hard drive. It's a phantom drive, held in memory, that will go away by itself when you log out. So after installing its software, feel free to drag it to the Trash (or highlight it and press ⌘-E to "eject" it).

Performing the Installation

Once you've got a disk icon on your desktop—either a pseudo-disk from a disk image or a CD or DVD you've inserted—you're ready to install the software. You can install many Mac OS X programs just by dragging their icons or folders to your hard drive (usually the Applications folder). Others offer a traditional installer program that requires you to double-click, read and accept a license agreement, and so on.

In both cases, *where* you decide to install the new program is suddenly a big issue. You have two alternatives:

- **The Applications folder.** Most programs, of course, sit in your Applications folder. Most of the time, this is where you'll want to install new programs. Putting them in the Applications folder makes them available to anyone who uses the Mac.

Note: You can't put anything in your Applications folder unless you have an Administrator account, as described on page 464.

- **Your Home folder.** Suppose you share your Mac with other people, as described in Chapter 12. If that's your situation, you may occasionally want to install a program privately, reserving it for your own use only. In that case, just install or drag it into your Home folder, or a folder inside it. When other people log onto the machine, they won't even know you've installed that new program, since it doesn't show up in the Applications folder.

  If you don't have an Administrator account, in fact, this is your only option for installing new programs.

Uninstalling Software

In Mac OS X, there's generally no Uninstall program, and no Add/Remove Programs window. To uninstall a program, you just drag it (or its folder) from the Applications folder (or wherever it is) to the Trash.

Some programs leave harmless scraps of themselves behind; to check for them, look for preference files or folders bearing the dearly departed program's name in your

---

UP TO SPEED

The Color Picker

Here and there—in System Preferences, iMovie, TextEdit, Microsoft Office, and many other programs—Mac OS X offers you the opportunity to choose a *color* for some element: for your desktop background, a window, and so on.

The dialog box that appears offers a miniature color lab that lets you dial in any color in the Mac's rainbow—several color labs, actually, arrayed across the top, each designed to make color choosing easier in certain circumstances:

Color wheel. Drag the scroll bar vertically to adjust the brightness, and then drag your cursor around the ball to pick the shade.

Color sliders. From the pop-up menu, choose the color-mixing method you prefer. *CMYK* stands for cyan, magenta, yellow, and black. People in the printing industry will feel immediately at home, because these four colors are the component inks for color printing. (These people may also be able to explain why *K* stands for *black*.)

RGB is how a TV or computer monitor thinks of colors: as proportions of red, green, and blue light. *Gray Scale* means shades of gray, like a black-and-white TV. And *HSB* stands for Hue, Saturation, and Brightness—a favorite color-specifying scheme in scientific circles.

In each case, just drag the sliders to mix up the color you want, or type in the percentages of each component.

Color palettes. This option presents canned sets of color swatches. They're primarily for programmers who want

quick access to the standard colors in Mac OS X. The Web Safe Colors list is useful for Web designers, too; they can tell whether a color will display properly on other computers.

Image palettes. Here's the visible rainbow arrayed yet another way: in cloudy, color-arranged streaks. (Cool Tip: If you drag a graphics file directly into the dialog box, it appears in the spectrum's place. That's a handy trick if you're trying to identify the color of a certain spot of an image, for example. And don't miss the pop-up button at the bottom of the dialog box, which offers a few other stunts.)

Crayons. Now *this* is a good user interface. You can click each crayon to see its color name: Mocha, Fern, Cayenne, and so on. (Some interior decorator in Cupertino had a field day naming these crayons.)

In any of these color pickers, you can also "sample" a color that's outside the dialog box—a color you found on a Web page, for example. Just click the magnifying-glass icon, and then move your cursor around the screen. You'll see the sliders and numbers change inside the dialog box automatically when you click.

Finally, note that you can store frequently used (or frequently admired) colors in the tiny palette squares at the bottom. To do that, drag the big rectangular color swatch (next to the magnifying glass) directly down into one of the little squares, where it will stay fresh for weeks.

If you don't have space for all the colors you want at the bottom of the window, you can drag the small circular dot down to make room for more.

Library folders (especially in Application Support) and your Home→Library→Preferences folder.

Dashboard

As you know, the essence of using Mac OS X is running *programs*, which often produce *documents*. In Mac OS X, however, there's a third category: a set of weird, hybrid entities that Apple calls *widgets*. They appear, all at once, floating in front of your other windows, when you press the F4 (⊙) key. Welcome to the Dashboard (Figure 5-21).

Note: The keystroke is F4 if you have a current Apple keyboard–the thin aluminum one on a laptop or desktop Mac. In fact, you can see a tiny Dashboard logo ⊙ painted right on the key.

On older, plastic keyboards, the keystroke is usually F12. Or, on laptops where F12 is the key, you have to hold down the Fn key (lower-left corner).

In either case, you can change the Dashboard keystroke to whatever you like, as described below.

Figure 5-21:
When you summon the Dashboard, you get a fleet of floating miniprograms that convey or convert all kinds of useful information. They appear and disappear all at once, on a tinted translucent sheet that floats in front of all your other windows. You get rid of Dashboard either by pressing the same key again (F12 or whatever) or by clicking anywhere on the screen except on a widget.

What are these weird, hybrid entities, anyway? They're not really programs, because they don't create documents or have Dock icons (although Dashboard itself has a Dock icon). They're certainly not documents, because you can't name or save them. What they most resemble, actually, is little Web pages. They're meant to display information, much of it from the Internet, and they're written using Web programming languages like HTML and JavaScript.

Mastering the basics of Dashboard won't take you long at all:

- **To move a widget,** drag it around the screen. (Click anywhere but on a button, menu, or text box.)

- **To close a widget,** press the Option key as you move the mouse across the widget's face. You'll see the ⊗ button appear at the widget's top-left corner; click it.

Tip: If the Widget bar is open (as described below), every widget displays its ⊗ close button. You don't need the Option key.

- **To open a closed widget,** click the circled ⊕ button at the bottom of the screen. Now the entire screen image slides upward by about an inch to make room for the Widget bar: a "perforated metal" tray containing the full array of widgets, even the ones that aren't currently on the screen (Figure 5-22). Open one by clicking its icon.

Figure 5-22:
You'll probably have to scroll the Widget bar, by clicking the arrows at either end, to see all the widgets. When you're finished opening new widgets, close the Widget bar by clicking the ⊗ button at the left side of your screen.

On Macs with newish graphics cards, a new widget appears by splashing down into the center of your screen, sending realistic pond ripples across the liquidy glass of your screen. These widgets really know how to make an appearance, don't they?

- **To hide one of Apple's widgets,** or to delete one you've installed yourself, use the Widget widget described below.

- **To rearrange your widgets as they appear in the Widget bar,** open your hard drive→Library→Widgets folder. Here you'll find the icons for the standard Apple Dashboard widgets. To rearrange them, you have to rename them; they appear on the Widget bar in alphabetical order. (You can also remove a widget for good by deleting it from this folder, if you must.)

Tip: The Dashboard icon also appears in your Dock, just in case you forget the F4 keystroke. On the other hand, if you prefer the keystroke, you can remove the icon from your Dock to make room for more important stuff. Control-click (or right-click) the icon and, from the shortcut menu, choose Remove from Dock.

Dashboard Tips

Dashboard is crawling with cool tips and tricks. Here are a few of the biggies:

- If you just *click* an icon on the Widget bar, the widget appears right in the middle of your screen. But if you *drag* the widget's icon off the bar, you can deposit it anywhere you like.

- There's a great keystroke that opens and closes the Widget bar: ⌘-equal sign (=). (This keystroke may be different on non-U.S. keyboard layouts.)

- To refresh a certain widget—for example, to update its information from the Internet—click it and press ⌘-R. The widget instantly *twist-scrambles* itself into a sort of ice-cream swirl (you've got to see it to believe it) and then untwists to reveal the new data.

- You can open more than one copy of the same widget. Just click its icon more than once in the Widget bar. You wind up with multiple copies of it on your screen: three World Clocks, two Stock Trackers, or whatever. That's a useful trick when, for example, you want to track the time or weather in more than one city, or when you maintain two different stock portfolios.

- If you keep the Shift key pressed when you summon Dashboard, the widgets fly onto the screen in gorgeous, translucent, 3-D *slow motion*. Aren't you just glad to be alive?

Dashboard Preferences

To change the Dashboard keystroke to something other than F4 or F12, choose ⬤→ System Preferences, and then click Keyboard→Keyboard Shortcuts.

FREQUENTLY ASKED QUESTION

Unchained Widgets

I love the widgets, but I wish they weren't locked away in their own Mac OS X "layer." I'd like to work with the Calculator widget, for example, while I'm doing an Excel spreadsheet, without having to send the spreadsheet to the background.

No problem. What you want is Amnesty Widget Browser, a shareware program you can download from, among other places, this book's "Missing CD" page at *www.missingmanuals.com.*

It adds a new menu-bar icon that, when opened, lists all your widgets by name. You can now open them individually—and, more importantly, without sending your other programs to the background. You've just freed your widgets from the translucent layer where they've been imprisoned.

Tip: For faster service, Control-click (right-click) the Dashboard icon on the Dock. Choose Dashboard Preferences from the shortcut menu.

Here, you'll discover that you can choose almost any other keyboard combination to summon and dismiss the Dashboard, or even choose a screen corner that, when your mouse lands there, acts as the Dashboard trigger. This works exactly as described on page 163.

Note: Yes, yes, you can also change the Dashboard keystroke on the new Keyboard→Keyboard Shortcuts pane of System Preferences. But if you use the Exposé & Spaces pane instead, then you can set up a screen corner or a mouse button to trigger Dashboard—not just a keyboard combo.

Widget Catalog

Here's a rundown of the 20 standard widgets that come preinstalled in Snow Leopard. True, they look awfully simple, but some of them harbor a few secrets.

The Widget widget

This widget is designed to manage all your *other* widgets (Figure 5-23). It's the easiest way to hide a widget (that is, get it out of Dashboard but leave it on your Mac, in case you change your mind later) or to uninstall it altogether. It has three functions:

- **Use the checkboxes to hide or show widgets.** You may as well hide the ones you never use.

- **Click the − button to delete a widget for good.** You're not allowed to delete Apple's widgets—only ones you've downloaded and installed yourself.

Figure 5-23:
The Widget widget (whose icon appears at lower left in Figure 5-22) opens up this list of widgets. Turn off a checkmark to hide a widget, or click − to completely uninstall any widget you installed yourself. The ones whose boxes aren't checked are the ones that no longer appear on the Widget bar.

• **Click More Widgets to browse the catalog.** You go right to Apple's Widgets Web page, where *thousands* of new widgets await your downloading pleasure, as described later in this section. (This command is also available from the shortcut menu of the Dashboard Dock icon, by the way.)

Tip: Drag the lower-right ribbed bar to make the Widget widget taller or shorter.

Address Book

The concept behind this widget, of course, is to give you faster access to your own address book. (Trudging off to the actual Address Book program takes way too long when you just want to look up a number.) It's filled with clickable shortcuts. For example:

• **Search box.** Type a few letters of somebody's name here. As you type, the widget fills with matching names from the Address Book program.

Tip: Actually, it shows you entries with text that match *any part* of each person's "card," not just names. For example, you could type *212* to find everyone with that area code, or *cherr* to find someone whose name you've forgotten—but you know she lives on Cherrystone Avenue.

When you spot the name of the person you're looking for, click it to open that person's full Rolodex card.

• **Phone number.** Click it to fill your screen with the phone number, big enough that you could see from outer space. Or at least from across the room as you dial the number on your desk phone, which is the real point.

• **Email address.** Click to fire up your email program, complete with a fresh outgoing message already addressed to this person. All you have to do is type your message and click Send.

• **Mailing address.** Clicking the mailing address fires up your Web browser and takes you to MapQuest.com, already opened up to a map that reveals the pinpoint location of the specified address. Very, very slick.

Business (a.k.a. Yellow Pages)

A Yellow Pages of every business and organization in the entire United States wouldn't be especially compact. In fact, it would probably occupy your entire living room. And yet think of the convenience! You could instantly find the closest Chinese restaurant, hospital, or all-night drugstore in a strange city.

Well, now you can, thanks to Business. Into the text box, type whatever it is you're looking for, exactly as though it's a heading in the Yellow Pages business directory. You could type *drugstore, cleaning service, health club, tailor, library,* or whatever. Alternatively, click the triangular down arrow next to this box to see a list of services the widget already knows about.

The widget shoots out the query to the Internet and, after a moment, provides a list of local businesses that match, including phone numbers and addresses. (Click the arrow at the bottom of the window to see the next set of results.)

The contact information is clickable, by the way. Click the name of the place to open a Web page revealing more information, the phone number to enlarge it for dialing, or the address to see where this place is on a MapQuest map.

Note: Before Business can show you a list of local businesses, it has to know what you mean by *local*—in other words, where you are. Now, your Mac may already know where you live. It can extract this information from your original Mac OS X installation, for example, or from the Address Book program (if you've filled in a card for yourself).

But if it doesn't seem to know where you are—or if you're traveling with a laptop—you have to tell it. Perform any random search using the widget (*Banks,* for example). At the bottom of the results window, you'll see the ❶ button. Click it to rotate the widget; on the "back," you can specify a city and state or ZIP code, how many listings you want per "page," and how many miles away a business has to be to qualify. Then click Done.

Calculator

Here's your basic four-function pocket calculator, with one-number memory storage. Begin by clicking it to make it active—which basically means that any typing you do on the number keys gets intercepted by this little calculator. (Pressing the number keys is much faster than clicking the onscreen numbers.)

There's not a lot to this calculator; if you need scientific and hexadecimal features, or even square root functions, use the regular Calculator program described on page 354.

Dictionary

Apple has provided about 65,000 different ways to access its built-in dictionary/thesaurus, and here's another one. You click either the word Dictionary or Thesaurus, type the word you want, and press Return. Instantly, a handy definitions panel drops down. Use the ▲ and ▼buttons in the upper-left corner to walk through your most recent lookups, and the pop-up menu to specify whether you want to search the dictionary, the thesaurus, or the Apple terminology glossary.

Tip: Once you've looked up a word, you can look up new words by typing only the first few letters. (You don't even have to press Return.) The Dictionary or Thesaurus automatically displays the definition for the first matching word.

If you click the ❶ button in the lower-left corner, the panel spins around to reveal, in addition to a font-size control, the Oxford American Dictionaries logo. Someday when you're feeling curious, click it. You wind up firing up the Oxford University Press Web page.

Tip: See how the first letter of your word appears in a special rounded tab at the left edge of the panel? If you click that letter, you get to see the word you looked up in its alphabetical context among all the other words in the dictionary. It's a neat way to check for additional word forms, to see if perhaps you've misspelled the word, or to scrabble your way out of a tight situation when you're playing the word game "ghost" with someone.

ESPN

This widget shows the current or final scores of college and professional sports games. (If the game hasn't started yet, you see the start time.) Click the ❶ button to choose the sport you want to track. Click the News button to see headlines—and click a headline to visit ESPN's full article online.

Flight Tracker

This handy widget lets you find out which flights fly between which cities—and if the flight is already en route, shows you where it is on the map, how high it's flying, how fast, and whether or not it's going to be on time.

This may look like a small window, but there's a lot going on here:

- **Flight Finder.** If you're planning a trip, the widget can show you a list of flights that match your itinerary. Use the pop-up menus to specify the arrival and departure cities, and which airline you want to study, if any. (Actually, it's usually faster to *type* the name of the city into the box, if you know how to spell it, or, better yet, its three-digit airport code.) Then click Find Flights, or press Return or Enter.

Figure 5-24:
Top: Most of the time, Flight Tracker is like a teeny, tiny travel agent, capable of showing you which flights connect to which cities. But if one of the flights is marked "En route," double-click it.

Bottom: You see an actual map of its progress, as shown here. You also get to see its speed and estimated arrival status (early, late, or on time), and even which terminal it will use upon landing. If you click the plane, you can zoom in on it.

After a moment, the right side of the screen becomes a scrolling list of flights that match your query. You can see the flight number, the departure and arrival time, and the name of the airline.

This is a great tool when a friend or relative is flying in and you're unsure of the flight number, airline, or arrival time.

- **Flight Tracker.** Most of the time, the status column of the results says "Scheduled," meaning that you're looking at some future flight. Every now and then, however, you get lucky, and it says "En route." This is where things get really fun: Double-click that row of results to see the plane's actual position on a national or international map (Figure 5-24).

Tip: If you click the little **❶** button before performing a flight search, the panel flips around to reveal the logo of the company that supplies the flight data. Click the logo to open its Web page.

Google

This one's nothing but a standalone Google search bar. Type a search phrase into it, hit Return or Enter, and presto: You're in your Web browser, staring at the Google search results.

iCal

Sure, you can always find out today's date by clicking the clock on your menu bar. But this one is so much nicer looking. And besides, you can use this calendar to look ahead or back, or to check your schedule for the day. As you click this widget, it cycles through three degrees of expansion; see Figure 5-25.

Tip: Press Shift as you click to see the panels expanding or collapsing in slow motion.

Figure 5-25:
Click the "today's date" panel to expand the second panel, which shows the month. (Click ◄ and ► to move a month at a time.) Click a third time to reveal whatever's on the calendar for the remainder of the day, as recorded in iCal.

iTunes

This glossy-looking controller is a remote control for the iTunes music player. It's intended for people who listen to music while they work all day and have no greater music-management needs than starting and stopping the music (see Figure 5-26). Of course, you can perform all the same functions in iTunes itself, in the miniatur-

---

ized iTunes window, or even using the iTunes Dock icon. But on a Mac with a lot of windows open, with the phone ringing and the baby crying, you may find it quicker to pause the music by hitting F4, and then clicking the Pause button on this widget.

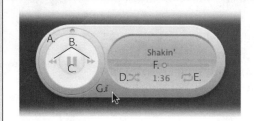

Figure 5-26:
The little iTunes widget is filled with clickable areas. (A) Volume ring. (B) Next song/previous song. (C) Play/Stop. (D) Shuffle (random playback order) on/off. (E) Loop this song on/off. (F) Scroll bar (click to jump around in the song). (G) Click this button to make the widget appear to flip around. On the back, you'll see a pop-up menu that lets you change your playlist, as you've created it in iTunes.

Movies

Look up the local movie-theater listings for any day this week—without having to endure the hassle of the newspaper, the hellish touchtone labyrinth of a phone system, or the flashing ads of a Web site.

When you open this widget, you see a miniature movie poster that changes to a different current movie every 3 seconds. At any point, you can click the poster itself to see what's on the back of the widget (Figure 5-27).

In the left column, you get a scrolling list of movies in your area. The one whose poster you clicked is highlighted, but you can click any one of them to see, at bottom, all the details: release date, rating, length, cast, genre, a plot synopsis, and a link to the preview (trailer). (After you've watched the trailer, click the left-pointing arrow button at the lower-left corner of the widget.)

The center column lists the theaters near you where the selected movie is playing. Click a theater to see the movie showtimes in the right column.

Tip: So how does the widget know what's "near you?" Because you've told it. You've clicked the ❶ button to flip the widget around to the back, where you can input your ZIP code or your city and state.

(And yes, it's true: You've now seen *three faces* of this two-dimensional widget. It's got a front, a back, and a *back* of the back.)

Incidentally, you're not stuck with this "Choose a movie, and we'll show you the theaters" view. See at the top left, where the title "Movies Theaters" appears? Click the word Theaters to reverse the logic. Now you're in "Choose a theater, and we'll show you what movies are playing there" mode. This view is much better when, for example, there's only one theater that's really nearby, and you want to know what your options are there.

Tip: To return to the original cycling movie-poster display, click an empty part of the title bar.

People (a.k.a. White Pages)

This widget is worth its weight in silicon. It's a White Pages for the entire United States, all in a tiny widget. Specify as much information as you know—the last name and state (or ZIP code) at a minimum—and press Return or Enter. In a moment, the widget shows you a list of every matching name, complete with phone number and street address.

Click the phone number to display it in gigantic numbers, large enough to see while dialing across the room (or across town); click the address for a Web page that shows this person's house on a map; and click the ❶ button to limit searches to a certain number of miles from the specified city, state, or ZIP code.

Figure 5-27:
Top: The Movies widget starts out with a slideshow of movie posters.

Bottom: On the back, you can read about current movies in theaters, find out which theaters they're in, and see today's showtimes. The pop-up menu at upper right lets you see the schedule for Today, Tomorrow, and the following four days.

Ski Report

As though you couldn't guess: This widget is for skiers. Click the ❶ button and type the ski resort you're considering visiting. Type in its name (like *Vail, CO* or *Okemo, VT*), and then press Return.

Once the widget displays the correct mountain name, click Done and wait as the widget summons the current ski conditions from the Internet and displays them—temperature, base snow depth, surface conditions, and so on—in handy icon form.

Stickies

Stickies is a virtual Post-it note that lets you type out random scraps of text—a phone number, a Web address, a grocery list, or whatever.

Of course, Mac OS X already comes with a popular Stickies program (page 396). So why did Apple duplicate it in Dashboard? Simple—because you can call this one up with a tap on the F4 key, making it faster to open.

On the other hand, this Stickies isn't quite as flexible as the application Stickies. For example, you can't resize the page. And to add a second or a third note, you have to click the **+** button at the bottom of the screen to reveal the Widget bar, and then click the Stickies icon for each new page.

On the *other* other hand, this Stickies isn't quite as bare-bones as you might think. If you click the little ❶ button at the bottom-right corner, the note spins around to reveal, on the back, the choice of paper colors, fonts, and font sizes.

Stocks

Hey, day traders, this one's for you. This widget lets you build a stock portfolio and watch it rise and fall throughout the day (Figure 5-28).

To set up your portfolio, click the little ❶ button at the bottom of the window. The widget flips around, revealing the configuration page on the back:

- **Add a stock to your list** by typing its name or stock abbreviation into the box at the top; then click the **+** button, or press Return or Enter. If there's only one possible match—Microsoft, for example—the widget adds it to the list instantly. If there's some question about what you typed, or several possible matches, you'll see a pop-up menu listing the alternatives, so you can click the one you want.

- **Remove a stock from the list** by clicking its name and then clicking Remove.

Tip: Ordinarily, the widget displays the ups and downs of each stock as a dollar amount ("+.92" means up 92 cents, for example). But if you turn on "Show change as a percentage," you see these changes represented as percentages of their previous values.

But why bother? Once you're looking at the actual stock statistics, you can switch between dollar and percentage values just by clicking any one of the red or green up/down status buttons.

Click Done to return to the original stock display. Here's your list of stocks, their current prices (well, current as of 20 minutes ago), and the amount they've changed—green if they're up, red if they're down. Click a stock's name to see its chart displayed at the bottom. (You control the time scale by clicking one of the little buttons above the graph: "1d" means one day, "3m" means three months, "1y" means one year, and so on.)

Finally, if you double-click the name of the stock, you fly into your Web browser to view a much more detailed stock-analysis page courtesy of Quote.com (Lycos Finance).

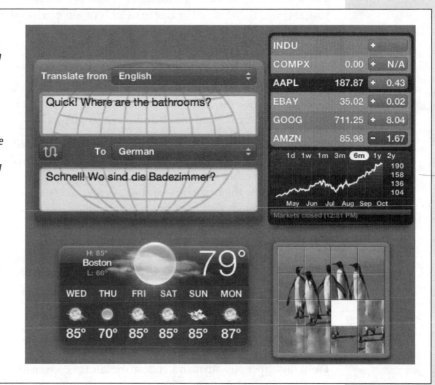

Figure 5-28:
More of Apple's built-in widgets. Clockwise from top left: Translation, Stocks, Tile Game, and Weather.

(The Tile game comes with a photo of a snow leopard, but shown here is a different photo, to prove that you can drag a new graphic into the Tile game.)

Tile Game

For generations, Microsoft Windows has had its Solitaire game—and for generations, the Mac had the Tile Game. The idea, of course, is to click the squares of the puzzle, using logic to rearrange them back into the original sequence, so that the put-together photograph reappears.

Tip: The widget starts you out with a handsome photo of a snow leopard—get it?—but you can substitute any photo you like.

To pull this off, begin by exiting the Dashboard. Go find the photo you prefer (on the desktop or in iPhoto, for example). Now begin dragging it in any direction. While the mouse is still down, press F4 (or whatever your Dashboard keystroke is)—and drop the dragged graphic directly on the Tile Game puzzle. You've just replaced the existing graphic with your new one. (Figure 5-28 shows an example.)

The first time you use the Tile Game, click inside it to trigger the animated tile-scrambling process. Click a second time to stop the scrambling; in other words, Apple leaves it to you to decide just how difficult (how scrambled) the puzzle is.

And what should you do if you get frustrated and give up, or you miss the old leopard photo? Just open the Widget bar and open a fresh copy of the Tile Game.

Translation

The next time you travel, go somewhere that has wireless Internet access wherever you go (yeah, right). You'll be able to use this module to translate your utterances—or those of the natives—to and from 13 languages.

Just choose the language direction you want from the "from" and "to" pop-up menus, and then type the word, sentence, or paragraph into the "Translate From" box. In a flash, the bottom of the window shows the translation, as shown at top left in Figure 5-28. (Don't click the curvy double-headed arrow button to perform the translation; that button means "Swap the To and From languages.")

Of course, these translations are performed by automated software robots on the Web. As a result, they're not nearly as accurate as what you'd get from a paid professional. On the other hand, when you're standing in the middle of a strange city and you don't know the language—and you desperately need to express yourself—what Dashboard provides may just be good enough.

Tip: Your first instinct may be to assume that this module is designed for translating things you want to say into the local language. However, you may find it even more useful for translating foreign-language paragraphs—from email or Web pages, for example—into your *own* language so that you can read them.

Unit Converter

No matter what units you're trying to convert—meters, grams, inches, miles per hour—the Unit Converter widget is ready.

From the upper pop-up menu, choose the kind of conversion you want: Temperature, Area, Weight, or whatever. (Take a moment to enjoy the clever graphic at the top of the window that helps identify the measurement you've selected.)

Use the lower pair of pop-up menus to specify which units you want to convert to and from, like Celsius to Fahrenheit. Then type in either the starting or ending measurement. To convert 48 degrees Celsius to Fahrenheit, for example, type *48* into the Celsius box. You don't have to click anything or press any key; the conversion is performed for you instantly and automatically as you type.

Never let it be said that technology isn't marching forward.

Tip: Unit Converter is especially amazing when it comes to *currency* conversions—from pesos to American dollars, for example—because it actually does its homework. It goes online to download up-to-the-minute currency rates to ensure that the conversion is accurate.

Weather

This famous Dashboard module shows a handy current-conditions display for your city (or any other city) and, if you choose, even offers a six-day forecast (Figure 5-28, lower left).

Before you get started, the most important step is to click the ❶ button at the lower-right corner. The widget flips around, and on the back panel, you'll see where you can specify your city and state or ZIP code. You can also specify whether you prefer degrees Celsius or degrees Fahrenheit, and whether you want the six-day forecast to show both highs and lows. (It ordinarily shows only the highs.) Click Done.

Now the front of the widget displays the name of your town, today's predicted high and low, the current temperature, and a graphic representation of the sky conditions (sunny, cloudy, rainy, and so on). Click anywhere to reveal the six-day forecast.

Tip: Evidently, the Weather widget team members at Apple were really proud of their artwork. Lest you miss out on seeing all the beautiful weather graphics, they've given you a secret keystroke that reveals all 19 of the gorgeous and witty sky-weather graphics.

All you have to do is hold down ⌘ and Option as you click repeatedly on the widget. You'll see that, for the town of Nowhere, the weather changes every time you click.

Web Clips

Web Clips let you make your *own* widgets with one click. This particular widget, however, is nothing more than a little ad for the Web Clips feature—and a reminder that you must start your Web Clips adventure in Safari, not Dashboard. See "Web Clips," page 215.

World Clock

Sure, this clock shows the current time, but your menu bar does that. The neat part is that you can open up several of these clocks—click World Clock in the Widget bar repeatedly—and set each one up to show the time in a different city. The result looks like the row of clocks in a hotel lobby, making you look Swiss and precise.

To specify which city's time appears on the clock, click the ❶ button at the lower-right corner. The widget flips around, revealing the pop-up menus that let you choose a continent and city.

More Widgets

The best part of the Dashboard is that it's expandable. *Thousands* of new widgets, written by other people, are available on the Web: games, chat and email notifiers, gas-price reporters, calculators and translators, news and sports updaters, finance and health trackers, and on and on.

To see Apple's current list of goodies, use one of these tactics:

• **The short way.** Control-click (or right-click) the Dashboard icon in the Dock. From the shortcut menu, choose More Widgets.

• **The long way.** Click the Manage Widgets button that appears whenever the Widgets bar is exposed; when the Widgets widget opens, click More Widgets.

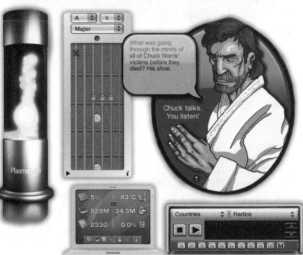

Figure 5-29:
Widgets could, in theory, harbor viruses, so Mac OS X is extremely cautious in downloading them.

Top: When you try to download a widget, the Mac asks if you're sure.

Middle: After you download a widget and confirm your intention, you meet this test-drive mode for newly downloaded widgets. It's a way to play with new widgets before you actually commit to adding them to your system. Play with the widget, and then click Keep to install it (or Delete, if you think it's evil).

Bottom: Not all good things come from Apple. Here's a representative sample of widgets written by other people. From top left: Plasma Tube, Guitar Chords, Chuck Norris Facts, World Radio, and MiniStat 2 (details about your Mac at the moment).

Either way, you go to the Apple Dashboard downloads page. (Alternatively, check a Mac-downloads Web site like *www.versiontracker.com* for an even more complete selection.)

Some of the most intriguing widget offerings include the Yahoo Local Traffic widget (gives you the traffic conditions in your area), Air Traffic Control (identifies wireless AirPort base stations within range of your laptop), and TV Tracker (shows you could be watching on TV right now instead of working). There are also FedEx package trackers, joke-of-the-day widgets, comic-strip-of-the-day widgets, and many other varieties. (See Figure 5-29, bottom.)

Installing a widget

When you download a widget, Mac OS X is smart enough to install it automatically. First, though, it offers you a trial run, as shown in Figure 5-29.

If you click Keep, Mac OS X copies it into your Home→Library→Widgets folder. Only you will see that Dashboard widget, because it's been copied into the Widgets folder of *your account*. Anyone else who has an account on this Mac won't see it.

Unless, of course, you copy or move that widget into the Library→Widgets folder (that is, begin with the Library folder in your main hard drive window). The contents of *that* Widgets folder are available to all account holders.

Web Clips: Make Your Own Widgets

You don't have to be satisfied with Apple's 20 widgets *or* the several thousand that other people have written. You can make a Dashboard widget of your own—in about three clicks.

Web clips exploit an inescapable characteristic of widgets: An awful lot of them exist to deliver real-time information from the Web. That's the point of the Ski Report widget, Weather, Stocks, Flight Tracker, ESPN, and so on.

But what if your interest isn't skiing, stocks, or sports? What if it's *The New York Times* front page? Or the bestselling children's books on Amazon? Or the most-viewed video on YouTube? Or some cool Flash game you wish you could summon with the touch of a key?

That's the beauty of Web clips, a joint venture of Dashboard and the Safari Web browser. They let you turn *any section of any Web page* into a Dashboard widget that updates itself every time you open it. It's like having a real-time keyhole peek at all your favorite Web sites at once.

Creating a Web Clip Widget

Here's how you go about creating a do-it-yourself widget:

1. **Open Safari.**

   Safari is the Mac's Web browser. It's in your Applications folder.

2. **Go to the Web page that contains the information you want to snip. Choose File→Open in Dashboard.**

   The screen goes dark, with only a small window of white. As you move your cursor around the page, the small white rectangle conveniently snaps to fit the various rectangular sections of the page.

   As shown in Figure 5-30, your job is to make a frame around the part of the page that usually shows the information you want. If the Web site ever redesigns its pages, it'll wreck your widget—but what the heck. It takes only 5 seconds to make it again.

Clip button   Adjust handles

Figure 5-30:
Drag the little round handles to make the white box just big enough to surround the part of the page you want to enshrine. Or drag inside the box to move the whole thing.

3. **Adjust the corner or side handles to enclose the piece of page you want. When you're finished, click Add, or press Return or Enter.**

   Now Dashboard opens automatically. But wait—what's this? There's a new widget here that wasn't here before.

   At this point, you can dress up your widget, adding a little polish to this raw clipping you've ripped out of a Web page. Click the ❶ button that appears when you move your mouse to the lower-right corner. The widget flips around to reveal the controls shown in Figure 5-31.

   Here, you can click one of the frame styles to give your widget a better-looking border.

   If you click Edit, the widget flips around to face you again, and here's where it gets weird: You can reposition your widget's contents as though they're a window on the Web page that's visible behind it. Drag the widget contents in any direction within the frame, or resize the frame using the lower-right resize handle. Click Done.

You can make as many Web-clip widgets as you want.

But here's a big screaming caution: If you close one of these homemade widgets, it's gone forever (or at least until you recreate it). They're never represented as icons on the Widget bar, as ordinary widgets are.

Ah, well—easy come, easy go, right?

Note: If you're of the programmer persuasion—if you're handy in JavaScript and HTML, for example—it's much easier to write custom widgets than ever before. (Not just Web-clip widgets, *real* widgets.)

That's because Snow Leopard comes with Dashcode, an easy-to-use widget-assembly environment. You'll find the installer for it on your Snow Leopard installation DVD (in the Optional Installs→XCode Tools folder), and you'll find tutorials and examples by typing *dashcode tutorial* into Google.

Figure 5-31:
Top: Click a frame style to give your widget better-looking edges. If the widget plays sound, it keeps playing sound when you close the Dashboard unless you turn on "Play audio in Dashboard only."

Bottom: Click Edit to return to the front of the widget, where you can adjust its position on the underlying Web page.

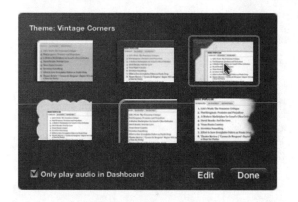

Entering Data, Moving Data, & Time Machine

The original 1984 Mac didn't make jaws drop because of its speed, price, or sleek looks. What amazed people was the simplicity and elegance of the user interface. At some point in every Apple demo, the presenter copied a graphic drawn in a painting program (MacPaint) and pasted it directly into a word processor (MacWrite), where it appeared neatly nestled between typed paragraphs of text.

We take these examples of data input and data exchange for granted today. But in those days, that little stunt struck people like a thunderbolt. After all, if this little computer let you copy and paste between different programs, it could probably do anything.

Today, the Mac is even more adept at helping you enter, move, and share your hard-won data. Mac OS X offers several ways to move information within a single document, between documents, between programs, and even between the Mac and Windows computers. This chapter leads you through this broad cycle of data: from entering it with the mouse and keyboard, to moving it around, to backing it up.

The Macintosh Keyboard

All through this book, you'll find references to certain keys on Apple's keyboards. "Hold down the ⏏ key," you might read, or "Press Control-F2." If you're coming from Mac OS 9, from Windows, or even from a typewriter, you might be a bit befuddled. (The reader email generated by previous editions of this book made that quite clear. "The alphabet has 26 letters," one went. "Why do I need 101 keys?")

To make any attempt at an explanation even more complicated, Apple's keyboards keep changing. The one you're using right now is probably one of these models:

- **The current keyboard,** where the keys are flat little jobbers that poke up through square holes in the aluminum (Figure 6-1). That's what you get on current laptops, wired keyboards, and Bluetooth wireless keyboards.

- **The older, plastic desktop keyboard,** or the white or black plastic laptop one.

Figure 6-1:
On the top row of aluminum Mac keyboards, the F-keys have dual functions. Ordinarily, tapping the F1 through F4 keys correspond to Screen Dimmer, Screen Brighter, Exposé, and Dashboard. Pressing the Fn key in the corner changes their personalities.

Here, then, is a guided tour of the non-typewriter keys on the modern Mac keyboard:

Tip: To see closeups of Apple's current wired and wireless keyboards, visit www.apple.com/keyboards.

- **Fn.** How are you supposed to pronounce Fn? Not "function," certainly; after all, the F-keys on the top row are already known as function keys. And not "fun"; goodness knows, the Fn key isn't particularly hilarious to press.

  What it *does*, though, is quite clear: It changes the purpose of certain keys. That's a big deal on laptops, which don't have nearly as many keys as desktop keyboards. So for some of the less commonly used functions, you're supposed to press Fn and a regular key. (For example, Fn turns the ↑ key into a Page Up key, which scrolls upward by one screenful.)

Note: On most Mac keyboards, the Fn key is in the lower-left corner. The exception is the full-size Apple desktop keyboard (the one with a numeric keypad); there, the Fn key is in the little block of keys between the letter keys and the number pad.

You'll find many more Fn examples in the following paragraphs.

- **Numeric keypad.** The number-pad keys do exactly the same thing as the numbers at the top of the keyboard. But with practice, typing things like phone numbers and prices is much faster with the number pad, since you don't have to look down at what you're doing.

Now, at first glance, only desktop keyboards appear to have these blocks of number keys. But on some older Mac laptops, you may see that the numbers 0 through 9 have actually been painted onto a block of *letter* keys near the right side. (1, 2, and 3 are J, K, and L, for example.)

You can turn those letter keys into their numeric alter egos in either of two ways. First, you can press the NumLock key at the top of the keyboard, which turns the numbers on and keeps them on until you press NumLock again. Or, for just a couple of quick numbers, you can hold down the Fn key with your left hand.

Eventually, Apple eliminated this embedded-keyboard effect from its laptops, having discovered that almost nobody was using it.

- ☼, ☀ (**F1, F2**). These keys control the brightness of your screen. Usually, you can tone it down a bit when you're in a dark room, or when you want to save laptop battery power; you'll want to crank it up in the sun.

- ▦ (**F3**). This one fires up Exposé, the handy window-management feature described on page 155.

- ☺ (**F4**). Tap this key to open Dashboard, the archipelago of tiny, single-purpose widgets like Weather, Stocks, and Movies. The end of Chapter 5 describes Dashboard in detail.

- ⁙, ⁛ (**F5, F6**). Most recent Mac laptops have light-up *keys,* which is very handy indeed when you're typing in the dark. The key lights are supposed to come on automatically when it's dark out, but you can also control the illumination yourself by tapping these keys. (On most other Macs, the F5 and F6 keys aren't assigned to anything. They're free for you to use as you see fit.)

- ◄◄, ►‖, and ►► (**F7, F8, F9**). These keys work in the programs you'd expect: iTunes, QuickTime Player, DVD Player, and other programs where it's handy to have Rewind, Play/Pause, and Fast-forward buttons.

Tip: Tap the ◄◄ or ►► key to skip to the previous or next track or chapter. Hold it down to rewind or fast-forward.

Weirdly, the ►‖ key is hard-wired to open the iTunes program. And no, you can't change that assignment! (Fortunately, when you're already in a playback program like DVD Player or QuickTime Player, the key resumes its duties as the Play/Pause control.)

- ◄, ◄), ◄)) (**F10, F11, F12**). These three keys control your speaker volume. The ◄ key means Mute; tap it once to cut off the sound completely, and again to restore its previous level. Tap the ◄) repeatedly to make the sound level lower, the ◄)) key to make it louder.

With each tap, you see a big white version of each key's symbol on your screen, and you hear a little audio pop—your Mac's little nod to let you know it understands your efforts. (Press Shift to silence the pop sound.)

- ⏏. This is the Eject key. When there's a CD or DVD in your Mac, tap this key to make the computer spit it out. If your Mac has a DVD *tray* (rather than just a slot), then hold down this button for about a second to make the tray slide open.

- **Home, End.** "Home" and "End" mean "jump to the top or bottom of the window." If you're looking at a list of files, the Home and End keys jump to the top or bottom of the list. In iPhoto, they jump to the first or last photo in your collection. In iMovie, the Home key rewinds your movie to the very beginning. In Safari, it's the top or bottom of the Web page.

  (In Word, they jump to the beginning or end of the line. But then again, Microsoft has always had its own ways of doing things.)

  On keyboards without a dedicated block of number keys, you get these functions by holding down Fn as you tap the ← and → keys.

- **Pg Up, Pg Down.** These keys scroll up or down by one screenful. The idea is to let you scroll through word processing documents, Web pages, and lists without having to use the mouse.

  On keyboards without a numeric keypad, you get these functions by pressing Fn plus the ↑ and ↓ keys.

- **Clear.** Clear (on the full-size desktop keyboard only) gets rid of whatever you've highlighted, but without putting a copy on the invisible Clipboard, as the Cut command would do.

- **Esc.** Esc stands for Escape, and it means "cancel." It's fantastically useful. It closes dialog boxes, closes menus, and exits special modes like Quick Look, Front Row, slideshows, screen savers, and so on. Get to know it.

- **Delete.** The backspace key.

- ⌦. Many a Mac fan goes for years without discovering the handiness of this delightful little key: the Forward Delete key. Whereas Delete backspaces over whatever letter is just to the *left* of the insertion point, this one (labeled Del on older keyboards) deletes whatever is just to the *right* of the insertion point. It really comes in handy when, for example, you've clicked into some text to make an edit—but wound up planting your cursor in just the wrong place.

  The full-size Apple keyboard has a dedicated key for this. On all other keyboards, you get this function by holding down Fn as you tap the regular Delete key.

- **Return and Enter.** In almost all programs, these keys do the same thing: wrap your typing to the next line. When a dialog box is on the screen, tapping the Return or Enter key is the same as clicking the confirmation button (like OK or Done). Very few programs treat these keys differently, although Microsoft Excel is one of them.

- ⌘. This key triggers keyboard shortcuts for menu items.

- **Control.** The Control key triggers shortcut menus, described on page 224.

- **Option.** The Option key (labeled Alt on keyboards in some countries) is sort of a "miscellaneous" key. It's the equivalent of the Alt key in Windows.

  It lets you access secret features—you'll find them described all through this book—and type special symbols. For example, you press Option-4 to get the ¢ symbol and Option-y to get the ¥ (yen) symbol.

- **Help.** In the Finder, Microsoft programs, and a few other places, this key opens up the electronic help screens. But you guessed that.

The Complicated Story of the Function Keys

As the previous section makes clear, the F-keys at the top of modern Mac keyboards come with predefined functions. They control screen brightness, keyboard brightness, speaker volume, music playback, and so on.

But they didn't always. Before Apple gave F9, F10, and F11 to the fast-forward and speaker-volume functions, those keys controlled the Exposé window-management function described in Chapter 5.

So the question is: What if you don't *want* to trigger the hardware features of these keys? What if you want pressing F1 to mean "F1" (which opens the Help window in some programs)? What if you want F9, F10, and F11 to control Exposé's three modes, as they once did?

For that purpose, you're supposed to press the Fn key. The Fn key (lower-left on small keyboards, center block of keys on the big ones) switches the function of the function keys. In other words, pressing Fn *and* F10 triggers an Exposé feature, even though the key has a Mute symbol (◄) painted on it.

But here's the thing: What if you decide that you use those F-keys for software features (like Cut, Copy, Paste, and Exposé) *more often* than the hardware features (like brightness and volume)?

In that case, you can reverse the logic, so that pressing the F-keys *alone* triggers software functions, and they govern brightness and audio only when you're pressing Fn.

To do that, choose →System Preferences→Keyboard. Turn on the checkbox "Use all F1, F2, etc. keys as standard function keys."

And that's it. From now on, you press the Fn key to get the functions painted on the keys (◂◂, ▸❙❙, ▸▸, ◂, ◂)), ◂))), ☼, ☼, and so on).

Figure 6-2:
A shortcut menu is one that pops out of something you're clicking—an icon, a button, a folder. The beauty of a shortcut menu is that its commands are contextual. They bring up useful commands in exactly the spots where they're most useful, in menus that are relevant only to what you're clicking.

Notes on Right-Clicking

Apple isn't too proud to steal good ideas from Microsoft; goodness knows, Microsoft has stolen enough from Apple. So in Snow Leopard, *shortcut menus* are more important than ever (Figure 6-2).

They're so important, in fact, that it's worth this ink and this paper to explain the different ways you can trigger a "right-click" (or a *secondary click,* as Apple calls it, because not all these methods actually involve a second mouse button, and it doesn't *have* to be the right one):

- **Control-click.** For years, you could open the shortcut menu of something on the Mac screen by Control-clicking it—and you still can. That is, while pressing the Control key (bottom row), click the mouse on your target.

- **Right-click.** Experienced computer fans have always preferred the one-handed method: right-clicking. That is, clicking something by pressing the *right* mouse button on a two-button mouse.

"Ah, but that's what's always driven me nuts about Apple," goes the common refrain. "Their refusal to get rid of their stupid one-button mouse!"

Well, not so fast.

First of all, you can attach any old $6 USB two-button mouse to the Mac, and it'll work flawlessly. Recycle the one from your old PC, if you like.

Furthermore, if you've bought a desktop Mac since late 2005, you probably already *have* a two-button mouse—but you might not realize it. Take a look: Is it a white, shiny plastic capsule with tiny, gray scrolling track-pea on the far end? Then you have a Mighty Mouse, and it has a *secret* right mouse button. It doesn't work until you ask for it.

To do that, choose →System Preferences. Click Mouse. There, in all its splendor, is a diagram of the Mighty Mouse. (There's a picture on page 340.)

Your job is to choose Secondary Button from the pop-up menu that identifies the right side of the mouse. (The reason it's not called a "right button" is because left-handers might prefer to reverse the right and left functions.)

From now on, even though there aren't two visible mouse buttons, your Mighty Mouse does, in fact, register a left-click or a right-click depending on which side of the mouse you push down. It works a lot more easily than it sounds like it would.

- **Use the trackpad (old way).** If you have a Mac laptop, you can "right-click" right there on the trackpad.

Figure 6-3:
The Trackpad pane of System Preferences looks different depending on your laptop model. But this one shows the two ways to get a "right-click."

To do that, point to whatever you want to click. Rest two fingers on the trackpad—and then click. (You turn this feature on and off in System Preferences→Trackpad, where you can also see a little video on how to do it.

- **Use the trackpad (new way).** Two fingers plus thumb? That *is* quite a lot of digits just to get a right-click, and Apple knows it. So on the latest Mac laptops, you can "right-click" by clicking either the lower-right or lower-left corner of the trackpad—one finger only.

(Your laptop is eligible if it has no separate clicker button. Instead, the *whole trackpad surface* is a clicker. You turn on this clicking method in System Preferences→Trackpad, as shown in Figure 6-3.)

Power Typing in Snow Leopard

Something strange has been quietly taking place at Apple: *Typing* has been getting a lot of attention.

It began when Apple created a *system-wide* spelling checker. For the first time in computer history, the *operating system* took over spelling fixes. You didn't have to maintain a separate spelling checker for each program you used. Now there's just one, and it works in most Apple programs: TextEdit, Stickies, iChat, Mail, iCal, Safari, Pages, iPhoto, iMovie, and so on. Add a word to the dictionary in one program, and it's available to all the others.

In Mac OS X 10.5 (Leopard), Apple added a grammar checker.

Now, in Snow Leopard, there's much more. There's text substitution, where you type *addr* and the system types out "Irwina P. McGillicuddy, 1293 Eastport Lane, Harborvilletown, MA, 02552." (The same system auto-corrects common typos like *teh* instead of *the.*) There's also a case-flipping feature that can change selected text to ALL CAPS, all lowercase, or First Letter Capped. Both of these new features are available in most Apple programs and in any other programs that tap into Mac OS X's built-in text processing circuitry (although not, alas, Microsoft programs).

The Mac OS X Spelling and Grammar Checker

Mac OS X can give you live, interactive spelling and grammar checking, just as in Microsoft Word and other word processors. That is, misspelled words or badly written sentences or fragments get flagged (with a dashed red underline for spelling problems and a green one for grammar problems) the moment you type them. Here's the crash course:

- **Check the spelling of one word:** Highlight the word. Choose Edit→Spelling and Grammar→Show Spelling and Grammar. The spell-check dialog box opens, with the proposed corrections visible.

- **Check spelling as you type.** Choose Edit→Spelling and Grammar→Check Spelling While Typing. (If Check Grammar With Spelling is turned on in the same submenu, you'll get a grammar check, too.)

Now, as you type, you'll see those red and green underlines on words the Mac thinks represent spelling or grammar mistakes. To fix one, Control-click (right-click) the underlined word, and proceed as shown in Figure 6-4.

Tip: In TextEdit, you can tell the Mac you always want the error-underlining turned on for all new documents from now on. Choose TextEdit→Preferences, click New Document, and then turn on "Check spelling as you type."

Figure 6-4:
You're never more than a Control-click (or right-click) away from more accurate spelling. Once you Control-click a questionable word, the suggestions of Apple's built-in dictionary appear right in the shortcut menu, along with the Learn and Ignore commands.

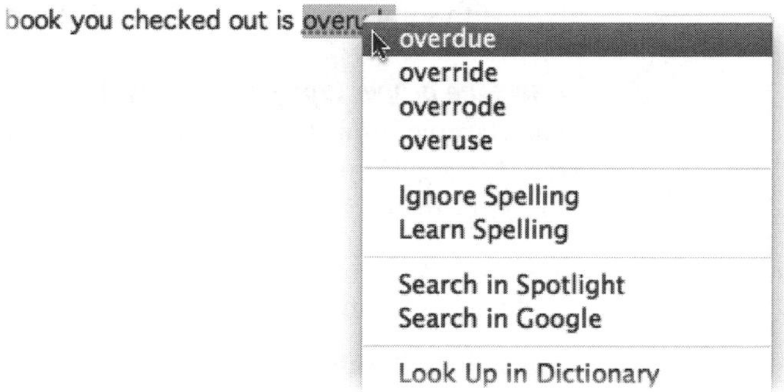

book you checked out is overd...

> overdue
> override
> overrode
> overuse
>
> Ignore Spelling
> Learn Spelling
>
> Search in Spotlight
> Search in Google
>
> Look Up in Dictionary

- **Check spelling after the document is finished.** Choose Edit→Spelling and Grammar→Show Spelling and Grammar (or press ⌘-:). The Spelling dialog box appears. The first error it spots appears in the top box, with the proposed corrections in the bottom one.

  If you like one of Apple's proposals, click it and then click Change. If the word was correct already (for example, the guy's last name really is Teh), then click Find Next ("leave the word as I typed it"), Ignore ("it's OK everywhere in this document"), or Learn ("never flag this word again").

  Handily enough, you can also click Define to look up a highlighted word (one of the spelling suggestions, for example) in the Mac's built-in Dictionary app. Also handily enough, the spelling checker is smart enough to maintain different spelling checkers (dictionaries) for different languages—and to recognize, within a single document, which language you're using!

- **Fix spelling as you type.** Note the difference. *Checking* your spelling just means "finding the misspelled words." *Fixing* means autocorrecting the errors as they occur, as you type. You might not even notice that it's happening!

  This most tantalizing option is Edit→Spelling and Grammar→Correct Spelling Automatically. And sure enough, when this option is turned on, common typos like *teh* and *frmo* and *dont* get fixed as you type; you don't have to do anything to make it happen.

It's not perfect. It doesn't correct all errors (or even most of them). It occasionally even corrects a word you didn't mean to have corrected, like turning *brb* (Internet shorthand for "be right back") into *bribe*, or *arent* into *arrant*. (When it makes a mistake, hit ⌘-Z, the Undo command, to restore what you typed.) And sometimes it doesn't make the change until you're halfway through the sentence.

Still, though. Kind of cool.

Text Substitution (Abbreviation Expansion)

This one's kind of cool: a new Snow Leopard feature that auto-replaces *one* thing you type with something else. Why? Because it can do any of these things.

Insert the proper typographical symbols

For example, Snow Leopard can insert attractive "curly quotes" automatically as you type "straight ones," or em dashes—like this—when you type two hyphens (--like that). It can also insert properly typeset fractions (like ½) when you type 1/2.

You can see the list of built-in substitutions—and create your own—in the System Preferences→Language & Text→Text tab, as shown in Figure 6-5.

Apple doesn't want to drive you nuts, though, so it makes sure *you're* sure you really want these swappings to take place. So you have to turn on each of these features

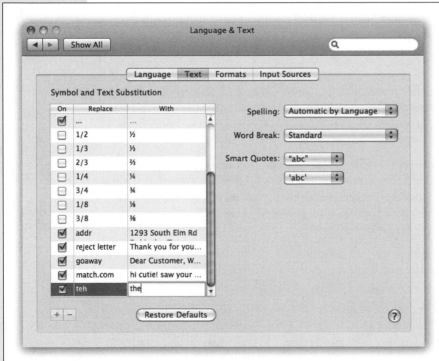

Figure 6-5:
This is where you can manage Mac OS X's typographic substitutions. You can see already that typing common fractions are set to turn into typographically fancy ones as you type them. But you can add all kinds of auto-typo-corrections and even boilerplate text paragraphs.

manually, in each program. (These commands are available anywhere you do a *lot* of typing, like TextEdit, Mail, and Stickies.)

- **Auto-quotes.** To make the quotes curlify themselves, choose Edit→Substitutions→ Smart Quotes, so that a checkmark appears.

Note: In System Preferences→Language & Text→Text tab, you can specify which kind of fancy quotation mark you prefer: «this kind,» „this kind," or whatever. You international thing, you!

- **Auto-dashes.** To turn double hyphens into these (—) long dashes, choose Edit→ Substitutions→Smart Dashes, so that a checkmark appears.

- **Smart links.** There's also an option to create Smart Links, where any Web address you type turns into a blue, underlined, *clickable* link to a Web page. Turn on Edit→Substitutions→Smart Links.

Tip: You can also choose Edit→Substitutions→Show Substitutions to make a floating panel appear, complete with on/off checkboxes for all these features.

Replace abbreviations with much longer phrases

That is, you can program *addr* to type your entire return address. Create two-letter abbreviations for big legal or technical words you have to type a lot. Set up *goaway* to type out a polite rejection letter for use in email. And so on.

This feature has been in Microsoft Office forever (called AutoCorrect), and it's always been available as a shareware add-on (TypeIt4Me and TextExpander, for example). But now it's built right into most Apple programs, plus any others that use Apple's text-input plumbing.

You build your list of abbreviations in the System Preferences→Language & Text→Text tab, shown in Figure 6-5. See the list at left? Click the **+** button to create a new row in the scrolling table of substitutions.

FREQUENTLY ASKED QUESTION

Smart Copy and Paste

Hey, I saw one more auto-fix feature in the Edit→Substitutions submenu: "Smart Copy/Paste." What's that about?

It's about spaces.

Ordinarily, when you cut or copy a word out of a sentence and then paste it into a new one, you have some cleanup to do. You leave an extra space behind, and you have to *add* a space after the word when you paste.

Smart Copy/Paste simply cleans up these spaces for you. If you cut a word out of a sentence, only *one* space gets left between the words where it used to be. And when you paste text, a space is added on either side automatically— but only one.

Click in the left column and type the abbreviation you want (for example, *addr*). Click in the right column and type, or paste, the text you want Mac OS X to type instead.

Tip: Don't be shy—you're not limited to short snippets. The replacement text can be pages long, which is handy if you're a lawyer and you build your contracts out of boilerplate chunks of canned text.

You can even create multiple paragraphs—but not by hitting Return when you want a new line; no, hitting Return means, "I'm finished entering this text" and closes up the box. Instead, press Option-Return when you want a paragraph break.

Here again, you have to explicitly *turn on* the text-replacement feature in each program (TextEdit, Mail, Stickies, and so on). To do that, choose Edit→Substitutions→Text Replacement, so that a checkmark appears.

That's it! Now, whenever you type one of the abbreviations you've set up, the Mac instantly replaces it with your substituted text.

Case Swapping

The final new chunk in Snow Leopard's text-massaging tool chest is case swapping—that is, changing text you've already typed (or pasted) from ALL CAPS to lowercase or Just First Letters Capitalized.

This one's simple: Select the text you want to change, and then choose from the Edit→Transformations submenu. Your options are Make Upper Case (all caps), Make Lower Case (no caps), and Capitalize (first letters, like a movie title).

GEM IN THE ROUGH

The Least-Known Typing Feature of Mac OS X

This may come as a shock if you think you know your Mac pretty well, but here goes: Mac OS X actually offers system-wide autocomplete of big words, just like the iPhone.

We're not talking about the spelling checker, and we're not talking about text substitution. We're talking, you start typing a word, and the Mac finishes it for you. It's ideal when you're in a hurry, when you're not sure how to finish a word (is it *independance* or *independence?)*, or when you're trying to solve a crossword

Dear Harold,

It has come to our attention

> attention
> attention's
> attentional
> attentions
> attentions'
> attentive
> attentively
> attentiveness
> attentiveness'

puzzle. It works in all the standard Mac programs (TextEdit, Mail, Safari, Pages, and so on).

Once you've begun typing a word, press either F5 or Option-Esc to produce the list of possible word completions, as shown here. If the Mac correctly anticipates the rest of the word, great; press Tab, Return, or the space bar to accept the suggestion, and then keep right on typing. If it guesses wrong, you can either select a different word in the list (using the mouse or the arrow keys), or tap Esc and continue typing.

Keep that in mind the next time some raving lunatic SENDS YOU AN EMAIL THAT WAS TYPED ENTIRELY WITH THE CAPS LOCK KEY DOWN.

The Many Languages of Mac OS X Text

Apple has always taken pride in its language-friendliness, and Snow Leopard is no exception. You can shift from language to language on the fly, as you type, even in midsentence—without reinstalling the operating system or even restarting the computer.

Figure 6-6:
Top: This is the list of the 18 "system localizations" that you get with a standard Mac OS X installation.

Bottom: Here's Safari running in Dutch. Actually understanding Dutch would be useful at a time like this—but even if you don't, it can't help but brighten up your work day to choose commands like Spraak-functie or Knip. (Alas, your success with this trick varies by program.)

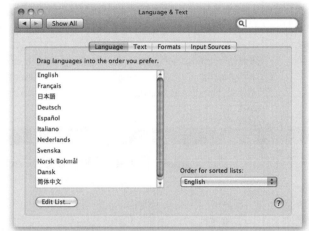

First, tell your Mac which languages you'd like to have available. Open System Preferences→Language & Text. On the Language tab, you see a listing of the different languages the Mac can switch into, in the corresponding languages—Français, Español, and so on. Just drag one of the languages to the top of the list to select it as the target language, as shown in Figure 6-6.

Snow Leopard Spots: In Snow Leopard, you can mix English with right-to-left languages like Hebrew and Arabic. There's even a split-cursor option that makes the pointer flip directions at the boundary between right-to-left and left-to-right text.

Now launch Safari, TextEdit, Mail, or Stickies. Every menu, button, and dialog box is now in the new language you selected! If you log out and back in (or restart) at this point, the entire Finder will be in the new language, too.

Note: Programs differ widely in their "language awareness." If you use a language beyond the 18 in the list, adding it (with the Edit List button) ensures that its relevant features will be available in all programs. (You may still have to add additional language software to make your menus and dialog boxes change.)

GEM IN THE ROUGH

Draw Those Chinese Characters

In Apple's demos, it was one of the coolest features of Snow Leopard: If you want to write in Chinese, you can now *draw* the characters you want, right on your laptop's trackpad. (This trick requires a recent Mac laptop, one of the multitouch models.)

To set this up, turn on Chinese–Simplified, choose the Chinese writing system you prefer, and turn on Trackpad Handwriting, in the System Preferences→Language & Text→Input Sources pane.

Then, when you're actually writing, use the flag (Input) menulet to choose Pinyin–Simplified (or whichever system you like). Now press Shift-Control-space bar to make the writing panel appear, as shown here.

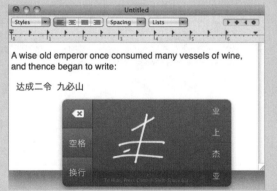

The trick here is to understand that the panel is a *full map* of your trackpad. You can't move the panel. Draw your character by dragging across the trackpad; white lines appear as you go.

On both sides of the on-screen panel, you see the Mac's interpretations of your character; to choose one, tap the corresponding spot on the *outside edges* of your actual trackpad. (Or, to delete your most recent line, tap the upper-left corner of your trackpad.) The Mac drops the character into your document.

Press Shift-Control-space bar again to hide the panel, and shake your head in wonder.

Formats Tab

Of course, if you're *really* French (for example), you'll also want to make these changes:

- On the Formats tab, choose your French-speaking country from the Region pop-up menu, so that time and date formats, number punctuation, and currency symbols also conform to your local customs. (Turn on "Show all regions," if necessary.)

For example, the decimal and thousands separator characters for displaying large numbers differ from country to country. (The number 25,600.99, for example, would be written as 25 600,99 in France, and as 25.600,99 in Spain.) And what appears to an American to be July 4 (the notation 7/4), to a European indicates April 7.

GEM IN THE ROUGH

The Character Palette

There you are, two-thirds of the way through your local matchmaker newsletter, when it hits you that you need a heart symbol. Right now.

You know there's one in one of your symbol fonts, but you're not about to type every single key combo until you produce the heart symbol. You can't help wishing there was an easier way to find those special symbols that hide among your fonts—fancy brackets, math symbols, special stars and asterisks, and so on.

The Keyboard Viewer (next page) is one solution. But there's a better one: the Character Palette. To make it appear, choose Edit→Special Characters.

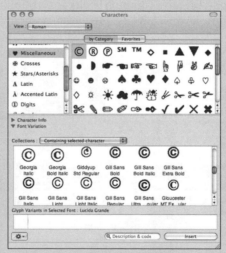

Most Cocoa programs have this command. If yours doesn't, here's the long way: Open System Preferences, click the International icon, click the Input Menu tab, and turn on the Character Palette checkbox.

You've just installed the Keyboard menulet.

Next time you're word processing or doing page layout, choose Show Character Palette from this menu.

The resulting window rounds up all symbols from all your fonts at once. To find a particular symbol, click the "by Category" tab, and then click the various category headings: Arrows, Stars/Asterisks, Math, and so on. Or, for an even more mind-blowing assortment (musical notes, Braille…), choose All Characters from the View pop-up menu.

You can preview variations of the same symbol by opening the Font Variation triangle. You can also use the Search box to find a symbol by name: "heart" or "yen" or "asterisk," for example. When you find the symbol you want, double-click it.

If you're using a Cocoa program, the correct symbol pops into your document. (If not, you may get the correct character in the wrong font. In that case, change the font of the inserted character manually. To find out what font it came from, click the Font Variation flippy triangle to see the font name.)

If, for some reason, Apple's preprogrammed settings aren't right for your region, you'll see Customize buttons that let you override them.

• Choose the French *keyboard layout* from the Input Menu tab, as explained on page 234.

Tip: Every program capable of switching languages is also clogging up your hard drive with a lot of language files you'll never use. A program like DeLocalizer can sweep through all your programs and delete those files, leaving your software in perfect condition but more svelte. You can get DeLocalizer from this book's "Missing CD" page at *www.missingmanuals.com*.

Input Menu Tab

While the Mac can display many different languages, *typing* in those languages is another matter. The symbols you use when you're typing in Swedish aren't the same as when you're typing in English. Apple solved this problem by creating different *keyboard layouts,* one for each language. Each rearranges the letters that appear when you press the keys. For example, when you use the Swedish layout and press the semicolon key, you don't get a semicolon (;)—you get an ö.

Apple even includes a Dvorak layout—a scientific rearrangement of the standard layout that puts the most common letters directly under your fingertips on the home row. Fans of the Dvorak layout claim greater accuracy, better speed, and less fatigue.

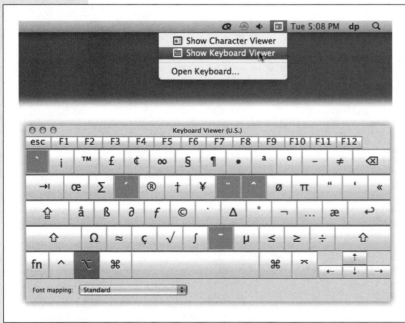

Figure 6-7:
*How do you make a π
symbol? Top: Open Keyboard
Viewer by choosing its name
from the keyboard (flag)
menulet.*

*Bottom: Keyboard Viewer
reveals the answer. When
you press the Option key, the
Keyboard Viewer keyboard
shows that the pi character
(π) is mapped to the P key.
To insert the symbol into an
open document, just click
it in the Keyboard Viewer
window.*

Use the list in the Input Menu pane to indicate which keyboard layout you want. If you select anything in the list, "Show input menu in menu bar" turns on automatically. A tiny flag icon appears in your menu bar—a keyboard *menulet* that lets you switch from one layout to another just by choosing its name. (To preview a certain keyboard arrangement, launch the Keyboard Viewer program described next.)

Snow Leopard Spots: In Snow Leopard, the icon of the Input menulet changes. If you've selected a different language, it becomes a colorful flag to show the currently selected language. If you haven't turned on any additional languages, though, it takes on the look of the Character Palette, described on page 233.

Keyboard Viewer: The Return of Key Caps

Keyboard Viewer, which is descended from the Key Caps program of old, consists of a single window containing a tiny onscreen keyboard (Figure 6-7). When you hold down any of the modifier keys on your keyboard (like ⌘, Option, Shift, or Control), you can see exactly which keys produce which characters. The point, of course, is to help you learn which keys to press when you need special symbols or non-English characters, such as © or ¢, in each font.

Note: Keyboard Viewer shows only the symbols you can produce by typing keystrokes. A font may contain thousands of other characters that can't actually be typed; the Character Palette (page 233) is the only way to access these other symbols.

It's a great tool—if you can find it.

Here's how. Open System Preferences→Language & Text, click Input Sources, and turn on Keyboard & Character Viewer at the top of the list. The window shown at top in Figure 6-7 appears. (Thereafter, you'll be able to choose its name from the Input menulet at the top of the screen, as shown at top in Figure 6-7.)

To see the effect of pressing the modifier keys, either click the onscreen keys or press them on your actual keyboard. The corresponding keys on the onscreen keyboard light up as they're pressed.

Snow Leopard Spots: You're not stuck viewing the characters in a 12-point font size—a good thing, because some of them are hard to read when displayed that small. You can make the Keyboard Viewer window as large as you want—fill the screen with it, why don't you?—by clicking its Zoom button or dragging its lower-right corner. That will magnify the Keyboard Viewer window and its font size.

Data Detectors

Here's a cool step-saver, something no other operating system offers—a little something Apple likes to call *data detectors.*

In short, Mac OS X recognizes commonly used bits of information that may appear in your text: a physical address, a phone number, a date and time, and so on. With one quick click, you can send that information into the appropriate Mac OS X program, like iCal, Address Book, or your Web browser (for looking up an address on a map).

Here's how it works: When you spot a name, address, date, or time, point to it without clicking. Mail draws a dotted rectangle around it. Control-click inside the rectangle, or right-click, or click the pop-up ▼ at the right side.

As shown in Figure 6-8, a shortcut menu appears. Its contents vary depending on what you're pointing to:

- **A mailing address.** You can choose Show Map from the shortcut menu; your Web browser opens automatically and shows you that address on a Google map.

Figure 6-8:
Mail can detect street addresses, phone numbers, dates, and times. When it spots something you may want to add to another program, like Address Book or iCal, it draws a dotted line around the info when you point to it without clicking. Click the little ▼ to get a shortcut menu for further options—like automatically adding the address to your Address Book program or seeing the address pinpointed on a Google map.

Alternatively, you can choose Create New Contact (to add an Address Book entry for this address) or Add to Existing Contact (if the *person* is in your Address Book—just not the *address*). Like magic, a little editing box sprouts out of the data-detected rectangle, prefilled with the information from the message, so that you can approve it.

Tip: In Mail, if you highlight some text in the message and then click the pop-up ▼ menu, Mail also fills in the Notes field in this person's Address Book entry with the highlighted text. Wicked cool.

- **A date and time.** The shortcut menu offers two useful commands. Create New iCal Event opens Mac OS X's calendar program and creates a new appointment at the date and time identified in the message. It's up to you to type a name for the date, set an alarm, and do all the other appointment-setting things described in Chapter 10.

Tip: If, while working in iCal, you ever forget where this event came from, double-click it. In the Info balloon, you'll see a link that takes you right back to the original Mail message that started it all.

If you choose Show This Date in iCal, though, you go to iCal, which opens directly to the specified date and/or time. The logic of this feature is overwhelming; after all, when someone emails you to ask if you're free for drinks next Thursday at 10, what's the first thing you usually want to do? Check your calendar, of course.

- **A phone number.** As with mailing addresses, the shortcut menu here offers you things like Create New Contact and Add to Existing Contact. The third one, Large Type, is great when you want to call this person right now—it displays the phone number in *huge* type, filling your screen, so you can see it from across your mansion.

- **A flight number.** There's a new data detector in Mac OS X 10.6: flights. When you highlight flight information in a text document (for example, "AA 152"), the data detector offers a Show Flight Information command. It opens the Flights widget of Dashboard, so you can see the flight's departure time, arrival time, and other details. It works only if the airline is represented as a two-letter code, and as of Mac OS X 10.6.1, only in Mail and iChat.

Moving Data Between Documents

You can't paste a picture into your Web browser, and you can't paste MIDI music information into your word processor. But you can put graphics into your word processor, paste movies into your database, insert text into GraphicConverter, and combine a surprising variety of seemingly dissimilar kinds of data.

GEM IN THE ROUGH

Styled Text

When you copy text from, for example, Microsoft Word, and then paste it into another program, such as Mail, you may be pleasantly surprised to note that the formatting of that text—bold, italic, font (size, color, and so on)—appears intact in Mail. You're witnessing one of the Mac's most useful but underpublicized features: its support for *styled text* on the Clipboard.

Almost all Mac OS X–compatible programs transfer the formatting along with the copied text. Every time you paste formatted text copied from one of these programs, the pasted material appears with the same typographical characteristics it had in the original program. Over time, this tiny timesaver spares us years' worth of cumulative reformatting effort—yet another tiny favor the noble Macintosh does mankind.

Cut, Copy, and Paste

The original copy-and-paste procedure of 1984—putting a graphic into a word processor—has come a long way. Most experienced Mac fans have learned to trigger the Cut, Copy, and Paste commands from the keyboard, quickly and without even thinking. Here's how the process works:

1. **Highlight some material in a document.**

   Drag through some text in a word processor, for example, or highlight graphics, music, movie, database, or spreadsheet information, depending on the program you're using.

2. **Use either the Edit→Cut or the Edit→Copy command.**

   Or press the keyboard shortcuts ⌘-X (for Cut—think of the X as a pair of scissors) or ⌘-C (for Copy). The Macintosh memorizes the highlighted material, socking it away on an invisible storage pad called the Clipboard. If you chose Copy, nothing visible happens. If you chose Cut, the highlighted material disappears from the original document.

   At this point, most Mac fans take it on faith that the Cut or Copy command actually worked. But if you're in doubt, switch to the Finder (by clicking its Dock icon, for example), and then choose Edit→Show Clipboard. The Clipboard window appears, showing whatever you've copied.

3. **Click to indicate where you want the material to reappear.**

   This may entail switching to a different program, a different document, or simply a different place in the same document.

4. **Choose the Edit→Paste command (⌘-V).**

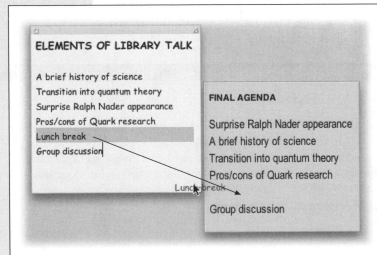

Figure 6-9:
To use drag-and-drop, highlight some material. Click anywhere in the highlighted area and press the mouse button for about half a second. Now, with the button still pressed, drag to another place in the document, into a different window, or into a different application. As your cursor enters the target window, a shaded outline appears inside the window's boundaries—the Mac's way of letting you know it understands your intention. When you release the mouse, the highlighted material appears instantly in its new location.

The copy of the material you had originally highlighted now appears at your insertion point—*if* you're pasting into a program that can accept that kind of information. (You won't have much luck pasting, say, a movie clip into Quicken.)

The most recently cut or copied material remains on your Clipboard even after you paste, making it possible to paste the same blob repeatedly. Such a trick can be useful when, for example, you've designed a business card in your drawing program and want to duplicate it enough times to fill a letter-sized printout. On the other hand, whenever you next copy or cut something, whatever was already on the Clipboard is lost forever.

Drag-and-Drop

As useful and popular as it is, the Copy/Paste routine doesn't win any awards for speed. After all, it requires four steps. In many cases, you can replace that routine with the far more direct (and enjoyable) drag-and-drop method. Figure 6-9 illustrates how this works.

Note: Most Cocoa programs (page 188) require you to press the mouse button for a split second before beginning to drag.

Virtually every Mac OS X program works with the drag-and-drop technique, including TextEdit, Stickies, Mail, Sherlock, QuickTime Player, Preview, iMovie, iPhoto, and Apple System Profiler, not to mention other popular programs like Microsoft applications, America Online, and so on.

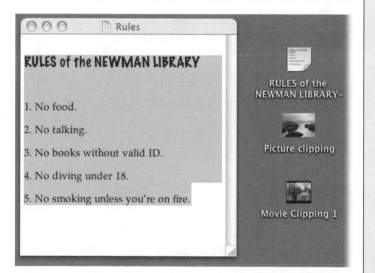

Figure 6-10:
When you drag material out of the document window and onto the desktop, you get a clipping file. Its icon depends on the kind of material contained within: (from top) text clipping, picture clipping, or movie clipping. (For easy identification, Mac OS X conveniently titles text clippings by the first line of the text contained inside.) You can view a clipping just by double-clicking it, so that it opens into its own window (left).

RULES of the NEWMAN LIBRARY

1. No food.

2. No talking.

3. No books without valid ID.

4. No diving under 18.

5. No smoking unless you're on fire.

RULES of the NEWMAN LIBRARY~

Picture clipping

Movie Clipping 1

When to use drag-and-drop

As shown in Figure 6-9, drag-and-drop is ideal for transferring material between windows or between programs—from a Web page into Photoshop, for example. It's especially useful when you've already copied something valuable to your Clipboard, since drag-and-drop doesn't involve (and doesn't erase) the Clipboard.

Its most popular use, however, is rearranging text within a single document. In Word or Pages, for example, you can rearrange entire sections, paragraphs, sentences, or even individual letters, just by dragging them—a wonderfully efficient editing technique.

Tip: When you use drag-and-drop to move text within a document, the Mac moves the highlighted text, deleting the highlighted material from its original location. If you press Option as you drag, however, you make a copy of the highlighted text.

Drag-and-drop to the desktop

You can also use drag-and-drop in the one program you use every single day: the Finder itself. As shown in Figure 6-10, you can drag text, graphics, sounds, and even movie clips out of your document windows and directly onto the desktop. Graphics and movies turn into ordinary graphics or movie files; text becomes an icon called a *clipping file*.

Snow Leopard Spots: Nobody seems to mention it—not even Apple—but clipping files have been greatly upgraded in Snow Leopard. For example, you can now examine a clipping's contents using Quick Look—just select its icon and then tap the space bar.

Second, you can double-click a clipping file and then select a portion of the text to copy (in the past, you could copy only the entire contents). Note, too, that an open clipping has a fully functional title bar. You can even ⌘-click the title to see the usual pop-up list of folders-within-folders, so you know where the thing is sitting on your hard drive.

When you drag a clipping from your desktop *back* into an application window, the material in that clipping reappears. Drag-and-drop, in other words, lets you treat your desktop itself as a giant, computer-wide pasteboard—an area where you can temporarily stash pieces of text or graphics as you work.

Tip: When the material you drag to the desktop contains nothing but an Internet address, such as an email address or Web page URL, Mac OS X gives it a special icon and a special function: an Internet location file. See page 693 for details.

Export/Import

When it comes to transferring large chunks of information—especially address books, spreadsheet cells, and database records—from one program to another, none of the data-transfer methods described so far in this chapter does the trick. For these purposes, use the Export and Import commands found in the File menu of almost every database, spreadsheet, email, and address-book program. (In some programs, the Save As command serves this function.)

These Export/Import commands aren't part of Mac OS X, so the manuals (if any) of the applications in question should be your source for instructions. For now, however, the power and convenience of this feature are worth noting—it means that your four years' worth of collected addresses in, say, some old email program can find its way into a newer program, like Address Book, in a matter of minutes.

Exchanging Data with Other Macs

Considering how many ways there are to move files back and forth between Macs, it seems almost comical that anybody complained when Apple discontinued built-in floppy disk drives. Here's a catalog of the different ways you can move your files from one computer to another, including some that might not have occurred to you.

By Email

Best for small files. High on convenience; computers can be in different countries.

Tip: Of course, the problem with email is that it generally can't handle file attachments larger than 5 or 10 megabytes. You can easily get around that limitation using a free Web site like Sendthisfile.com, which can handle enormous files by sending the recipient only a link to them by email.

By Network

With about $50 worth of equipment (or $200, if you want to go wireless), you can connect your Macs together into a *network*. Once you've done so, you can keep an icon for each Mac's hard drive on your screen. You can open files from the other drives, copy stuff back and forth—anything you would do with your own disk. Step-by-step instructions are in Chapter 13.

Best for files of any size, when the computers are in the same building.

Tip: And for $0, you can create an ad hoc network, meaning a tiny wireless network between just two computers (or a handful). Great when you're in the car somewhere, or in the airport waiting lounge, or a hotel lobby, and someone says, "Hey, can I have a copy of that?" Details are on page 512.

By iDisk

One of the principal virtues of a MobileMe account (Chapter 18) is the iDisk, which is basically like a hard drive on the Internet. You can pull it into the screen of any computer, Mac or PC, and copy files to or from it. It therefore makes a very convenient way station for transferring files of any size; there's even a feature that lets you *email* anything on your iDisk to anyone without worrying about file size.

The only inconvenience, really, is the $100 a year you'll have to pay for MobileMe.

By CD or DVD

You can always burn your files onto a blank CD or DVD and then carry or mail it to the recipient. Awfully slow and clumsy, but does result in a safety copy of whatever you're transferring.

FireWire Disk Mode (Target Disk Mode)

FireWire Disk Mode is a brilliant but little-known Macintosh-only feature that lets you turn one Mac into an external hard drive for another. This is by far the fastest method yet for transferring a lot of data—even faster than copying files over a network. It's extremely useful in any of these situations:

- **You're traveling with a laptop.** You want to copy your life onto it from your main Mac, including your entire 2 GB email folder and project files, before taking it on a trip, and then unload it when you return.

- **You have a new Mac.** You want to copy everything off the old one, without having to wait all night.

- **One Mac won't start up.** You want to repair it using another Mac as a "front end."

Unfortunately, not all Macs have FireWire anymore; on some laptops, Apple made the tragic mistake of eliminating it. If you're not so unfortunate, you can use FireWire like this. (In the following steps, suppose your main Mac is an iMac and you want to use a MacBook as an external hard drive for it.)

1. **Using a FireWire cable, connect the FireWire jacks of both computers.**

   For this trick, you need a *6-pin* FireWire cable—*not* the one that connects a camcorder to a Mac. The one you need has the same large connector on both ends.

Note: *If both Macs have Apple's FireWire 800 jacks, use a 9-pin FireWire cable instead for much greater speed. If only one Mac has a FireWire 800 jack, use that computer's traditional FireWire 400 connector instead. Otherwise, you need either a special FireWire 800–to–FireWire 400 cable, or the 400-to-800 adapter that came with your Mac.*

---

2. **On the MacBook, choose ** →System Preferences. Click Startup Disk.**

   The Startup Disk panel opens.

3. **Click Target Disk Mode. In the confirmation box, click Restart.**

   The MacBook turns off, then on again. A giant yellow FireWire icon (􀯑) bounces around the laptop screen.

   Now take a look at the iMac's screen: Sure enough, there's the MacBook's hard drive icon on the desktop. You're ready to copy files onto or off of it, at extremely high speeds, and go on with your life.

4. **When you're finished working with the MacBook, eject it from the iMac's screen as you would any disk. Then turn off the laptop by pressing the power button.**

The next time you turn on the MacBook, it'll start up from its own copy of Mac OS X, even if the FireWire cable is still attached. (You can disconnect the cable whenever you please.)

Note: The steps above describe the Snow Leopard method of setting up Target Disk Mode. But the old way still works, too.

Leave the iMac turned on, but shut down the MacBook. (Make sure it's plugged in. You wouldn't want the battery to die in the middle of this process.) Now turn the MacBook on again, but hold down the T key immediately after the chime. After a moment, you see the big yellow Y-shaped FireWire icon on the laptop screen, and the laptop's hard drive shows up on the iMac's desktop. Continue from step 4 above.

This method is arguably quicker because you don't have to open up System Preferences.

Via the iPod

An iPod is an extremely fine music player with enormous capacity. That's because it contains an actual hard drive (or a bunch of memory) that stores the songs.

But because the modern iPod has a USB connector, most models make dandy portable hard drives for everyday files, too—not just music.

To set the iPod up for data transfer, proceed like this:

1. **Connect the iPod to your Mac with its white USB cable. Open iTunes. Click the iPod icon in the left-side Source list.**

   The iPod Summary screen appears.

2. **Turn on "Enable disk use."**

   A dialog box warns you that even when you're just syncing up your music collection (and not using the iPod as a hard drive for files), you have to manually eject the iPod after each use.

3. **Click OK, and then OK again.**

   After a moment, you see the iPod's icon appear on your desktop.

Now you've got yourself a multigigabyte external hard drive. Just drag your files onto or off the iPod icon, exactly as though it's a disk (which it is). The iPod automatically keeps your data files separate from your music files; your files won't be touched when you update your music collection from iTunes.

Whenever you're finished using the iPod as a hard drive, eject it in any of the usual ways. For example, in the Finder, drag its icon to the Trash, or Control-click it and choose Eject from the shortcut menu.

Via Flash Drive

A *flash drive,* also called a thumb drive, is a tiny keychain-like doodad that plugs into your USB port. Inside is little more than a big chunk of RAM (memory) that acts like a miniature hard drive. When the flash drive is plugged into your Mac, its icon shows up on the desktop as a disk. Use it as a tiny, 8-gigabyte hard drive (or whatever size you've bought).

The beauty of a flash drive is that it works instantly and automatically with any Mac *or* any Windows machine, without any software installation or configuration. It's small and light enough to carry around on your keychain… and it's *so darned cool.* If you regularly transfer documents between Macs or between Macs and PCs, a flash drive will change your life.

Via Bluetooth

Bluetooth is a long-delayed, but promising, cable-elimination technology. It's designed to let Bluetooth-equipped gadgets communicate within about 30 feet, using radio signals.

Bluetooth comes built into most computers and cellphones, plus the occasional printer, pocket organizer, even camera or camcorder.

Bluetooth is built into all recent Macs. It's ready, therefore, to connect with Apple's wireless keyboard and mouse; to get on the Internet using a Bluetooth cellphone as a cordless modem; and to transfer files through the air to similarly equipped gear.

Bluetooth isn't especially fast—in fact, it's pretty slow. (You get transfer speeds of 30 to 50 K per second, depending on the distance.) But when you consider the time you'd have taken for wiring, passwords, and configuration using any other connection method, you may find that Bluetooth wins, at least in casual, spur-of-the-moment, airport-seat situations.

And when you consider that Bluetooth works no matter what the gadget—Mac, Windows, cellphone—you can see it has tremendous potential as a universal file-exchange translator, too.

Note: For more detail on configuring your Mac for Bluetooth connections, see page 316.

Sending a file

To shoot a file or two across the airwaves to a fellow Bluetooth-equipped Mac fan, first *pair* your Mac with the other Bluetooth machine, as described on page 316. In System Preferences→Bluetooth, make sure your Mac is Discoverable. *Discoverable* means "Other Bluetooth gadgets can see me." (Check the receiving gadget, too, to make sure *it's* in Discoverable mode.) Then you're ready to send:

1. **From the Bluetooth ✱ menulet (Figure 6-11, top), choose Send File.**

   If you don't *have* the Bluetooth menulet on your menu bar, open System Preferences. Click Bluetooth, and turn on "Show Bluetooth status in the menu bar."

After a moment, the Select File to Send dialog box appears. (You've actually suc-
ceeded in opening a program called Bluetooth File Exchange, which sits in your
Applications→Utilities folder.)

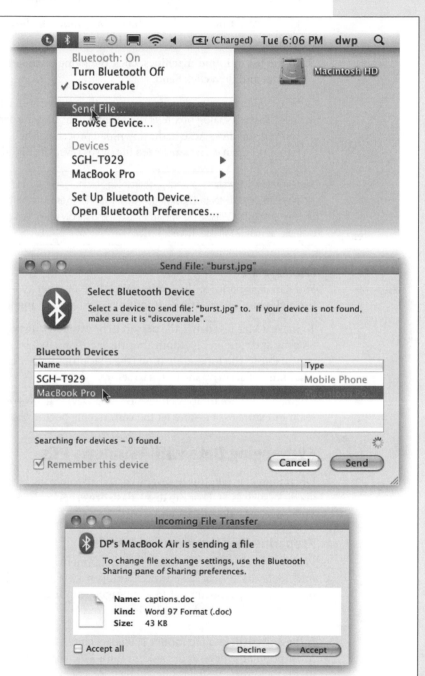

Figure 6-11:
*Top: Once your Mac is
paired with the other
gadget, it's super-easy
to shoot a file to it wirelessly. In this example,
you'll start by choosing
Send File. (But you could
save the second step by
choosing the gadget's
name from this menulet
and then Send File from
the submenu.)*

*Middle: OK. The Mac is
saying: "Send this file
to what gadget?" Click
the one you want. (If the
device isn't in "discoverable" mode, then no
other Bluetooth gizmos
can see it.)*

*Bottom: This is the
view from the receiving
machine (a Mac, in this
case). "Someone's send-
ing you a file. Do you
want it?"*

2. **Navigate to, and select, the files you want to send.**

If you're trying to send a bunch of them, you may find it easier to drag their icons onto the Bluetooth File Exchange icon in your Applications→Utilities folder.

Either way, a new Send File dialog box appears, showing the list of Bluetooth machines within range (Figure 6-11, middle).

3. **In the list of found machines, click the name of the one you want to send your files to, and then click Send.**

What happens now depends on how the receiving machine has been set up. In most cases, a dialog box tells the receiver that files are arriving (Figure 6-11, bottom); if she clicks Accept, the download proceeds. She's then offered the chance to either (a) open each transferred file or (b) reveal its highlighted icon in the Finder.

Tip: In System Preferences→Sharing→Bluetooth Sharing, you can control what happens when someone sends you files via Bluetooth. Usually, you'll want your Mac to ask whether or not to accept these files. (That's what the option "Ask What to Do" means.) You can also specify where you want received files to wind up—for example, in your Downloads folder.

Fetching a file

You can also perform this entire procedure in reverse. That is, you can go fishing through your buddies' files without her explicitly having to send anything.

To make a Mac invadable, the person to be invaded must open System Preferences→ Sharing and turn on Bluetooth Sharing. Here's also where she can specify what folder is available to you for examination (the Mac proposes her Home→Public folder), and what kind of security she wants to set up.

Then all you have to do is choose Browse Device from your own menulet (you can see it in Figure 6-11)—and let the rummaging begin!

Exchanging Data with Windows PCs

Documents can take one of several roads between your Mac and a Windows machine: via disk (such as a CD or Zip disk), flash drive, network, email, Bluetooth, iPod, iDisk, Web page, FTP download, and so on.

Preparing the Document for Transfer

Without special adapters, you can't plug an American appliance into a European power outlet, play a CD on a cassette deck, or open a Macintosh file in Windows. Therefore, before sending a document to a colleague who uses Windows, you must be able to answer "yes" to both of the questions below.

Is the document in a file format Windows understands?

Most popular programs are sold in both Mac and Windows flavors, and the documents they create are freely interchangeable. For example, documents created by recent versions of Word, Excel, PowerPoint, FileMaker, FreeHand, Illustrator, Photoshop, Dreamweaver, and many other Mac programs don't need any conversion. The corresponding Windows versions of those programs open such documents with nary a hiccup.

Files in standard exchange formats don't need conversion, either. These formats include JPEG (digital photos), GIF (cartoon/logo graphics on Web pages), HTML (raw Web page documents), Rich Text Format (a word-processor exchange format that maintains bold, italic, and other formatting), plain text (no formatting at all), QIF (Quicken Interchange Format), MIDI files (for music), and so on.

But what about documents made by Mac programs that don't exist on the typical Windows PC hard drive, like Keynote or Pages? You certainly can't count on your recipient having it.

Do your recipients the favor of first saving such documents into one of those exchange formats. In Pages, for example, choose File→Export; in the resulting dialog box, click Word. Click Next. Now name this special version of the document (complete with the *.doc* suffix), and then click Save.

Does the file have the correct filename suffix?

Every document on your hard drive has some kind of tag to tell the computer what program is supposed to open it: either a pair of invisible four-letter codes or a filename suffix like *.doc*.

Microsoft Windows uses *only* the latter system for identifying documents. Here are some of the most common such codes:

Kind of document	Suffix	Example
Microsoft Word (old)	.doc	Letter to Mom.doc
Microsoft Word (latest)	.docx	Letter to Mom.docx
Excel	.xls or .xlsx	Profit Projection.xls
PowerPoint	.ppt	Slide Show.ppt
JPEG photo	.jpg	Baby Portrait.jpg
GIF graphic	.gif	Logo.gif
Web page	.htm	index.htm

The beauty of Mac OS X is that most programs add these file name suffixes automatically and invisibly, every time you save a new document. You and your Windows comrades can freely exchange documents without ever worrying about this former snag in the Macintosh/Windows relationship.

Notes on Disk Swapping

Once you've created a document destined for a Windows machine, your next challenge is to get it *onto* that machine. One way is to put the file on a disk—a CD you've burned, for example—which you then hand to the Windows owner.

Macs and PCs format *hard drives* differently. The Mac can read Windows disks (which use unappetizingly named formatting schemes like FAT32 and NTFS), but Windows can't read Mac hard drives.

CDs, DVDs, and flash drives use the same format on both kinds of computers, though, so you should have very little problem moving these between machines. Chapter 11 has details on disc burning.

Network Notes

Mac OS X can "see" shared disks and folders on Windows PCs that are on the same network. Complete instructions are in Chapter 13.

Via the Internet

Chapter 22 offers details on FTP and Web sharing, two ways to make your Mac available to other computers—Windows PCs or not—on the Internet.

Time Machine

As the old saying goes, there are two kinds of people: those who have a regular backup system—and those who *will*.

You'll get that grisly joke immediately if you've ever known the pain that comes with deleting the wrong folder by accident, or making changes that you regret, or worst of all, having your hard drive die. All those photos, all that music you've bought online, all your email—gone.

Yet the odds are overwhelming that, at this moment, you do not have a complete, current, automated backup of your Mac. Despite about a thousand warnings, articles, and cautionary tales a year, guess how many do? About *four percent*. Everybody else is flying without a net.

If you don't have much to back up—you don't have much in the way of photos, music, or movies—you can get by with burning copies of stuff onto blank CDs or DVDs (Chapter 11) or using the MobileMe Backup program described at the end of this chapter. But those methods leave most of your Mac unprotected: all your programs and settings, not to mention Mac OS X itself.

What you really want, of course, is a backup that's rock-solid, complete, and *automatic*. You don't want to have to remember to do a backup, to insert a tape, to find a cartridge. You just want to know that you're safe.

That's the idea behind Time Machine, a marquee feature of Mac OS X. It's a silent, set-it-and-forget-it piece of peace of mind. You sleep easy, knowing there's a safety copy of your *entire* system: your system files, programs, settings, music, pictures, videos, document files—*everything*. If your luck runs out, you'll be *so* happy you set Time Machine up.

Setting up Time Machine

Here's the bad news: Time Machine requires a second hard drive. That's the only way to create a completely safe, automatic backup of your *entire* main hard drive.

That second hard drive can take any of these forms:

- An external USB or FireWire hard drive.

- An Apple Time Capsule. That's an AirPort wireless base station/network backup hard drive in one; it's available in gigantic capacities.

- Another internal hard drive.

- A partition of any one of those drives.

- The hard drive of another Leopard or Snow Leopard Mac on the network. You must first mount its drive on your screen (Chapter 13).

Tip: It's perfectly OK to back up several Macs onto the same external hard drive, as long as it's got enough room. You can also back up onto a hard drive that has other stuff on it, although of course that means you'll have less room for Time Machine backups.

In all cases, the backup disk must be bigger than the drive you're backing up (preferably *much* bigger).

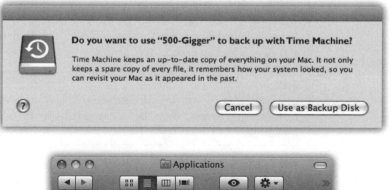

Figure 6-12:
Top: The Mac has just encountered a second hard drive. Time Machine still works if there's other stuff on the drive, but life is simpler if you don't use that drive for anything but Time Machine. The more space Time Machine has to work with, the further back in time you'll be able to go to recover deleted or mangled files.

Bottom: The backup has begun. You know that because you see both a progress message and the ↻ symbol that appears next to the backup drive's name in your Sidebar.

Here's what you *can't* use as the backup disk: an iPod, an iDisk, a removable disk (like a CD or flash drive), or your startup drive.

> **Note:** The backup drive must be a standard Mac-formatted hard drive. That's a gotcha that befalls many a Mac fan who buys a new hard drive for backup purposes; many new drives come in Windows format, which Time Machine doesn't recognize.
>
> To make a new, empty drive like this ready for Time Machine, open Disk Utility (page 414). Click the drive's name, click the Erase tab, choose Mac OS Extended (Journaled) from the Volume Format pop-up menu, and then click Erase.

Sure, it sounds like an Apple plot to sell more hard drives. But you'd be surprised at how cheap hard drives are. At this writing, you can buy a 1-*terabyte* hard drive (1,000 gigabytes) for $75, for goodness' sake—and hard drive prices-per-gigabyte go only down.

The first time the Mac sees your second hard drive, it invites you to use it as Time Machine's backup drive (Figure 6-12, top). That could be the moment you connect an external drive, or the first time you turn on the Mac after installing an internal drive.

If you click Use as Backup Disk, you're taken immediately to the Time Machine pane of System Preferences (Figure 6-12, bottom). It shows that Time Machine is now on, your backup disk has been selected, and the copying process has begun. The Mac copies *everything* on your hard drive, including Mac OS X itself, all your programs, and everyone's Home folders.

Your total involvement has been *one click*. And that, ladies and gentlemen, is the easiest setup for a backup program in history.

> **Note:** Time Machine doesn't use any compression or encoding; it's copying your files exactly as they sit on your hard drive, for maximum safety and recoverability. On the other hand, it does save some space on the backup drive, because it doesn't bother copying cache files, temporary files, and other files you'll never need to restore.

Now go away and let the Mac do its thing. The first backup can take hours as the Mac duplicates your entire internal hard drive onto the second drive. The Mac may feel drugged during this time.

> **Snow Leopard Spots:** This first backup is much faster in Snow Leopard than it was before. It might take two hours instead of all night, for example. Subsequent Time Machine backups are much faster, too, especially in the "preparing backup" stage. (Maybe best of all: Stopping a Time Machine backup—for example, if you feel that it's slowing down your Mac—is much faster, too.)

How the Backups Work

From now on, Time Machine quietly and automatically checks your Mac once per hour. If any file, folder, or setting has changed, it gets backed up at the end of the hour. These follow-up backups, of course, take very little time, since Time Machine backs up only what's changed.

So, should disaster strike, the only files you can lose are those you've changed within the past 59 minutes.

Tip: And even then, you can force more frequent backups if you want to. Just choose Back Up Now from the Time Machine menulet. Or choose Back Up Now from the shortcut menu of the Dock's Time Machine icon.

You can pause the backup the same way—if you need to use the backup drive for another quick task, for example. Open System Preferences→Time Machine and turn the big switch Off. Don't forget to turn the backing-up on again when you're finished.

By the end of the day, you'll have 24 hourly backups on that second disk, all taking up space. So at day's end, Time Machine replaces that huge stash with a single *daily* backup. You can no longer rewind your system to 3:00 p.m. last Monday, but you can rewind to the way it was at the *end* of that day.

Similarly, after a month, Time Machine replaces all those 30 dailies (for example) with four weekly backups. Now you may not be able to rewind to October 24, but you can rewind to November 1. (Apple assumes it won't take you a whole week to notice that your hard drive has crashed.)

FREQUENTLY ASKED QUESTION

The End of Time

What does Time Machine do when my backup drive gets full?

Good question. The whole idea of Time Machine is that it preserves multiple backups, so that you can rewind a window or a drive not just to *a* backup, but to *any* date in the past. The bigger the hard drive, the further back those monthly backups are preserved.

Eventually, of course, your backup drive runs out of space. At that point, Time Machine notifies you and offers you a choice: "Your backup disk is now full. The oldest remaining backup disk is…" (and then the date).

You can keep using that drive; Time Machine will begin deleting the oldest backups to make room for newer ones.

Or you can install a new Time Machine backup drive. New backups will go on that one; your older backups will still be available on the original drive.

If you ever need to retrieve files or folders from the older disk, Control-click (right-click) the Time Machine icon in the Dock; from the shortcut menu, choose Browse Other Time Machine Disks. In the list of disks, choose the older one. Then click the Time Machine icon on the Dock to enter the Restore mode.

Tip: You can see these backups, if you want. Open your backup drive, open the Backups.backupdb folder, and open the folder named for your computer. Inside, you'll find a huge list of backup folders, bearing names like 2010-03-22-155831. That's the backup from March 22, 2010 at 15:58 (that is, 3:58 p.m.) and 31 seconds.

Figure 6-13:
Use the big On/Off switch to shut off all Time Machine activity, although it would be hard to imagine why you'd want to risk it. You can click Choose Backup Disk to choose a different hard drive to represent the mirror of your main drive (after the first one is full, for example).

The point is that Time Machine doesn't just keep *one* copy of your stuff. It keeps *multiple* backups. It remembers how things were in every folder—not just yesterday, but last week, last month, and so on. It keeps on making new snapshots of your hard drive until the backup drive is full.

At that point, the oldest ones get deleted to make room for new ones.

Tip: Ordinarily, Time Machine alerts you when it has to start deleting old backups. If you'd rather have it just do it without bothering you, open System Preferences, click Time Machine, click Options, and then turn off "Warn when old backups are deleted."

By the way, if a backup is interrupted—if you shut down the Mac, put it to sleep, or take your laptop on the road—no big deal. Time Machine resumes automatically the next time you're home and connected.

Changing Time Machine Settings

Time Machine has four faces. There's the application itself, which sits in your Applications folder; open it only when you want to enter Restore mode. There's its Dock icon, which also enters Restore mode, but which has a shortcut menu containing useful commands like Back Up Now (and Stop Backing Up).

There's the Time Machine menulet, which may be the handiest of all. It identifies the time and date of the most recent backup; offers Back Up Now/Stop Backing Up commands; and has direct access to Time Machine's restore mode and preferences pane.

Tip: If you Option-click the Time Machine menulet, you get a secret new command: Browse Other Time Machine Disks. Yes, it's perfectly possible to back up onto multiple hard drives—to keep one offsite so you won't be hosed in case of fire, flood, or burglary, for example—and this is how. (Control-clicking the Time Machine icon on the Dock is another way to get this command.)

Finally, there's its System Preferences pane, where you adjust its settings (Figure 6-13). To see it, choose →System Preferences→Time Machine. Or choose Time Machine Preferences from Time Machine's Dock icon or menulet.

POWER USERS' CLINIC

Declaring Stuff Off-Limits to Time Machine

The whole point of Time Machine is to have a backup of your *entire* hard drive. That's how most people use it.

It's conceivable, though, that you might want to exclude some files or folders from the Time Machine treatment. There are two reasons.

First, you might not want certain, ahem, *private* materials to be part of your incriminating data trail.

Second, you might want to save space on the backup drive, either because it's not as big as your main drive or because you'd rather dedicate its space to *more* backups of the *essential* stuff. For example, you might decide not to back up your collection of downloaded TV shows, since video files are enormous. Or maybe you use an online photo-sharing Web site as a backup for all your photos, so you don't think it's necessary to include those in the Time Machine backup.

To eliminate certain icons from the backup, open the Time Machine pane of System Preferences. Click Options.

In the resulting list, click the **+** button; navigate your hard drive, and then select the files or folders you don't want backed up. Or just find their actual icons in the Finder and *drag* them into the list here. (Use the **−** button to *remove* items from the list, thereby excluding them from the excluded list.)

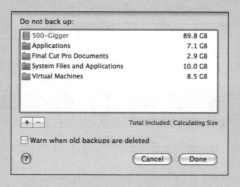

If you're strapped for disk space, one logical candidate to exclude is the System folder on your main hard drive—that is, Mac OS X itself. After all, if you lose your hard drive, you already *have* a copy of Mac OS X: the original installation DVD. (Of course, it doesn't have all the Apple updates that may have come out since the original version.)

When you add the System folder to the exclusion list, Time Machine makes another space-saving offer: "Would you like to also exclude other files installed with Mac OS X, such as system applications and UNIX tools?"

Agreeing (by clicking Exclude All System Files) saves you another several gigabytes of backup space.

Recovering Lost or Changed Files

All right, you've got Time Machine on the job. You sleep easy at night, confident that your life's in order—and your stuff's backed up.

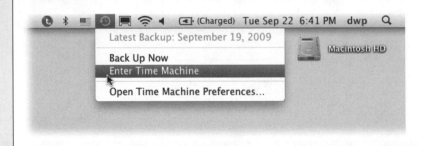

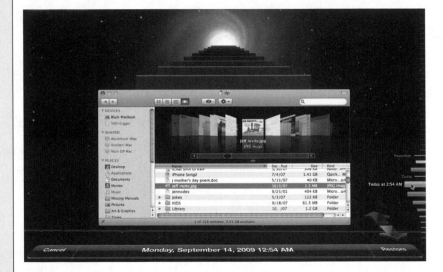

Figure 6-14:
Top: Choose Enter Time Machine from the menulet. (If you don't see this menulet, turn on "Show Time Machine status in the menu bar," shown in Figure 6-13.)

Bottom: This is the big payoff for all your efforts. The familiar desktop slides down, dropping away like a curtain. For the first time, you get to see what's been behind the desktop all this time. Turns out it's outer space. Time Machine shows you dozens of copies of the Finder window, representing its condition at each backup, stretching back to the past.

Then, one day, it happens: Your hard drive crashes. Or you can't find a file or folder you know you had. Or you save a document and then wish you could go back to an earlier draft. Some kind of disaster—sunspots, clueless spouse, overtired self—has befallen your files. This is Time Machine's big moment.

Start by pinpointing what you're looking for, in one of these two ways:

- Open the disk or folder window where the missing or changed item was.

- Type what you're looking for into the Search box at the top of any Finder window. Click the location button that makes the most sense: "This Mac" or the name of the window you're in.

In the case of deleted files or folders, the search will probably come up empty; that's totally OK.

Now click the Time Machine icon on the Dock, or choose Enter Time Machine from the menulet (Figure 6-14, top). Don't look away; you'll miss the show.

Your desktop *slides down the screen* like a curtain that's been dropped from above. And it reveals…outer space. This is it, the ultimate Apple eye candy: an animated starry universe, with bits of stardust and meteors occasionally flying outward from the massive nebula at the center.

Front and center is your Finder window—or, rather, dozens of them, stretching back in time (Figure 6-14, bottom). Each is a snapshot of that window at the time of a Time Machine backup.

You have four ways to peruse your backup universe:

- Click individual windows to see what's in them.

- Drag your cursor through the timeline at the right side. It's like a master dial that flies through the windows into the past.

- Click one of the two big, flat perspective arrows. The one pointing into the past means "Jump directly to the most recent window version that's *different* from the way it is right now."

  In other words, it's often a waste of time to go flipping through the windows one at a time, because your missing or changed file might have been missing or changed for the past 25 backups (or whatever). What you want to know is the last time the contents of this window *changed*. And that's what the big flat arrows do. They jump from one *changed* version of this window to another. (Or, if you began with a search, the arrow takes you to the most recent version backup with a matching result.)

- Use the Search box in the corner of the window. You can search for whatever you're missing in the current backup.

  As you go, the very bottom of the screen identifies where you are in time—that is, which backup you're examining.

Tip: OK, it's all very dazzling and all. But if you're technically inclined, you don't have to sit still for the big show. Just open the backup disk itself, whose icon appears on your desktop. Inside, you'll find nested folders, neatly representing every computer, every backup, every day and every hour—which you can rummage through by hand.

In many ways, the recovery mode is just like the Finder. You can't actually open, edit, rename, or reorganize anything here. But you can use Quick Look (page 54) to inspect the documents, to make sure you've got the right version. And you can use icon, list, column, or Cover Flow view to sort through the files you're seeing.

If you're trying to recover an older *version* of a file or folder, highlight it and then click the flat arrow button that's pointing away from you; Time Machine skips back to the most recent version that's *different* from the current one.

If you're trying to restore a deleted file or folder that you've now located, highlight it and then click Restore (lower-right). The Mac OS X desktop rises again from the

Figure 6-15:
The Time Machine version of iPhoto is a weird, simplified, viewing-only version. You can't do much here besides browse your backups—but when you're in dire straits, that's enough.

bottom of the screen, there's a moment of copying, and then presto: The lost file or folder is back in the window where it belonged.

Note: Time Machine prides itself not just on recovering files and folders, but also on putting them back where they belong.

If you recover a different version of something that's still there, Mac OS X asks if you want to replace it with the recovered version.

And if you're recovering a document whose original folder no longer exists, Time Machine automatically re-creates the folder so that the recovered item feels at home.

Recovering from iPhoto, Address Book, and Mail
The Finder isn't the only program that's hooked into Time Machine's magic. iPhoto, Address Book, and Mail work with Time Machine, too. Other software companies can also revise their own applications to work with it.

In other words, if you want to recover certain photos, addresses, or email messages that have been deleted, you don't start in the Finder; you start in iPhoto, Address Book, or Mail.

Then click the Time Machine icon on the Dock. Once again, you enter the starry recovery mode—but this time, you're facing a strange, disembodied, stripped-down copy of iPhoto, Address Book, or Mail (Figure 6-15).

Tip: Alternatively, in iPhoto, you can also choose File→Browse Backups to enter recovery mode.

You're ready to find your missing data. Click the Jump Back arrow to open the most recent version of your photo library, address book file, or email stash that's different from what you've got now. (You can also use the timeline on the right if you remember the date when things went wrong.)

Tip: If you're looking for something particular, specify that before you start clicking. For example, select the iPhoto Event or album first, or type a name into the Address Book search box.

At this point, you can select individual photos (or albums, or events), Address Book entries, or email messages to restore; just click the Restore button.

Often, though, you'd rather reinstate the *entire* iPhoto library, Address Book file, or email collection from the backup. That's what the Restore All button is for.

If you click it, the experience is slightly different. iPhoto asks if you're sure you want to replace your iPhoto library. Address Book may discover a lot of duplicate name-and-address entries and invite you to step through them, deciding which ones "win" (the old or the new).

Note: When you finish restoring in Mail, you'll find the restored messages in the On My Mac→Time Machine→Recovered folder at the left side of the window.

UP TO SPEED

MobileMe Backup

Time Machine is by far the most complete, effortless, and automatic, way to keep your data life safe.

There's an older method, though, one that's available only to members of MobileMe, Apple's $100-a-year suite of Internet services.

MobileMe membership includes access to a program called Backup, which can give you another automatic backup system for a subset of your files—your most important ones. The beauty of this method is that the backup is *offsite*, so

(unlike Time Machine) it's safe even if fire, flood, or burglary destroys your backup drive.

If you're interested in this oddball little program, you can download it here: *http://bit.ly/ZQMz0*. (At the moment, anyway. Apple is clearly interested in phasing out this program, and may pull it at any time.) Instructions are in the free downloadable PDF appendix to this chapter, called "MobileMe Backup." It's available on this book's "Missing CD" page at *www.missingmanuals.com*.

Recovering the entire hard drive

Every hard drive will die at some point. You just hope it won't happen while *you* own the computer.

But the great gods of technology have a mean-spirited sense of humor, and hard drives do die. But you, as a Time Machine aficionado, won't care. You'll just repair or replace the hard drive, and then proceed as follows:

1. **Connect the Time Machine backup disk to the Mac. Insert the Snow Leopard installation DVD. Double-click the Install Mac OS X icon.**

   The Mac OS X installer opens up as though it's going to lead you through the process of putting Snow Leopard on the new, empty hard drive. But don't fall for it.

2. **At the Welcome screen, choose Utilities→Restore System from Backup.**

   The Restore Your System dialog box appears.

3. **Click Continue.**

   Now you're shown a list of Time Machine backup disks. You probably have only one.

4. **Click your Time Machine backup disk. In the list of backups, click the most recent one.**

   The installer goes about copying *everything* from the backup disk onto your new, empty hard drive. When it's all over, you'll have a perfect working system, just the way it was before your series of unfortunate events.

Tip: You can use these steps to rewind to a previous version of Mac OS X 10.6, too—for example, after you install an Apple software update (10.6.2, say) and discover that it "breaks" a favorite program.

Beware, however: Restoring your earlier version also *erases any files* you've created or changed since you installed the update. Back them up manually before you proceed!

Then follow the steps above; when you're asked to choose a backup to restore, choose the most recent one. When it's all over, copy the latest files (the ones that you manually backed up) back onto the hard drive.

Recovering to another Mac

Weirdly enough, you can also use Time Machine as a glorified data bucket that carries your world from one computer to another. You can bring over some or part of any Time Machine backup to a totally different Mac.

On the new machine, connect your backup disk. In the Applications→Utilities folder, open the program called Migration Assistant. On the first screen, click "From a Time Machine backup." The subsequent screens invite you to choose which backup, which Home folder, and which elements (applications, settings, files) you want to bring over. (You can use the Snow Leopard installation DVD for this purpose, too, as described above.)

Frequently Asked Questions

Time Machine is a very different kind of backup program, and a real departure for longtime Mac addicts. A few questions, therefore, are bound to come up—like these:

- **Can I back up more than one Mac onto the same disk?** Yes. Each Mac's backup is stored in a separate folder on that disk.

- **Does the backup disk have to be dedicated to Time Machine?** No. It can have other files and folders on it. Keep in mind, though, that the more space that's available, the further back your backup trail can go.

- **Can I use more than one backup disk—like one at the office and one at home?** Yes. Just use the Time Machine panel of System Preferences (or the Time Machine Dock icon's shortcut menu) to select the new backup drive each time you switch.

- **Can I delete something for good, from all the backups at once?** Yes. Click the Time Machine icon on the Dock to enter the Restore (outer-space) mode. Find and select the file or folder you want to obliterate. From the ✿ menu, choose Delete From All Backups. (Sneaky, huh? That command is never in the ✿ menu *except* when you're in Time Machine restoring mode.)

- **Can Time Machine back up other hard drives besides the main internal one?** Yes. Open System Preferences→Time Machine. Click Options. Your secondary drives are listed here on the excluded-items list. If you want them backed up, too, then *remove* them from the list (click the drive name and then click the **–** button.)

- **Anything else you want to get off your chest?** Yes. Time Machine has trouble in two situations:

FUTURE NOSTALGIA

The Rapidly Sinking iSync

iSync is an attractive, simple program that was originally designed to keep the calendars and phone lists on your various computers, Palm organizer, cellphone, and even your iPod in perfect synchronization, sparing you the headache of the modern age: inputting the same information over and over again.

Bit by bit, though, Apple has been relieving iSync of its responsibilities. You now sync your iPod through iTunes. In Snow Leopard, iSync no longer recognizes Palm organizers or phones. And iSync never did talk to BlackBerrys or Windows cellphones.

There are still some cellphones that can sync with iSync, however. Apple lists them at *www.apple.com/isync/devices.html.*

(Hint: They're mostly Nokia, Motorola, Samsung, and Sony Ericcson phones.) If your phone isn't on The List, then don't miss *www.taniwha.org.uk,* a Web page loaded with drivers and installation instructions for specific phone models.

But if you have one of the chosen phone models, iSync can keep it up to date with your Mac's other's calendar, Address Book, and to-do list, either via a USB cable or wirelessly using Bluetooth. It requires a certain amount of technical setup (creating a phone profile, pairing the phone with your Mac, opening iSync, choosing Device→Add Device, and finally selecting the phone). You'll find detailed instructions in the iSync Help screens.

First, FileVault (page 497). If you've encrypted your Home folder using FileVault, then Time Machine can back up your Home folder *only* when you've logged out. And when things go wrong, it can recover only your *entire* Home folder (not individual files or folders). It scarcely seems worth the trouble.

Finally, remember that Time Machine backs up *entire* files at a time—not pieces of files. If you edit huge, multigigabyte files like video files, therefore, keep in mind that each giant file gets recopied to the backup drive every time you change it. That is, one 2-gig video file that you work on all day could wind up occupying 48 gigabytes on the backup drive by the end of the day. Consider adding these files to the exclusion list, as described above.

Services, Automator, & AppleScript

A pple's specialty has always been taking complex, expensive technologies and somehow making them simple, attractive, and magical. They've done it with video editing, digital photos, DVD authoring, wireless networking, Web design, music production, podcasting—you name it.

Popularizing one particular task, however, has continued to elude Apple: *programming*.

Through the years, Apple has introduced various new technologies for helping novices write their own software:

- **AppleScript** was the first Apple tool for automating your Mac. You type out English-like commands in a text file called a *script*, one command per line, and click Run to have your Mac carry out the result (Figure 7-1, bottom).

  AppleScript is a power user's dream come true, but it's still a programming language. If you want to automate even a simple custom job like converting music files to MP3s, you have to get your hands dirty hunting for the AppleScript command that does exactly what you want—and that can be a real pain.

- **Automator** is a newer program that lets you create your own programs by assembling a series of visual building blocks called *actions*. Drag actions into the right order, click a big Run button, and your Mac faithfully runs through the list of steps you've given it (Figure 7-1, top).

  You have a list of preprogrammed actions at your fingertips, so you never have to do any coding or learn any programming language. Creating the little software robots (called *workflows)* is exceptionally easy.

On the other hand, your selection of building blocks is limited to what other programmers have already written, so Automator workflows are limited in what they can do. You can't automate a complex newspaper layout using Automator alone, for example, because nobody has written the building-block actions necessary to control all the stages of newspaper production.

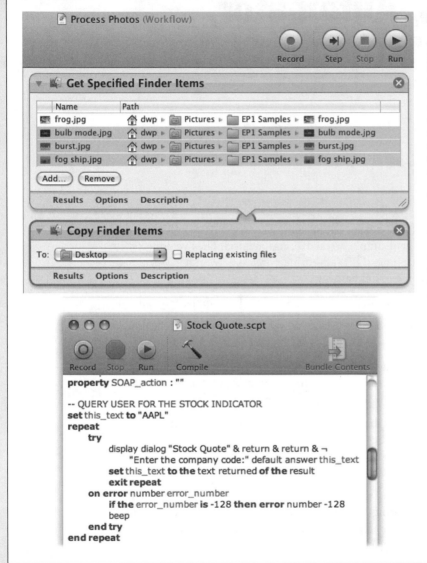

Figure 7-1:
The two faces of Mac automation. Top: Automator uses a visual, step-by-step metaphor for automation; the down-pointing arrows indicate how each building block "feeds" its result into the next action. You can usually tell what an Automator workflow does at a glance.

Bottom: Script Editor (the program you use to write and edit Apple-Script code) is geekier. There's a good amount of programmerese here, and you have to know basic AppleScript syntax before you can begin to understand this script—let alone write your own.

For novices, the most exciting feature might be Watch Me Do mode. It lets you just *do* what you want Automator to learn, as Automator watches and memorizes each keystroke, mouse click, and menu selection. Later, Automator can replay those steps faithfully, like a true-blue macro program.

- **Services** have been completely overhauled in Snow Leopard. These are smart, handy commands, available in most Mac programs and in shortcut menus in the Finder. It's a place to *list* those Automator and AppleScript apps you've created, making them available everywhere—along with a couple of dozen ready-made ones from Apple.

This chapter covers these three build-your-own software technologies: Services, Automator, and AppleScript. True, the latter two require some technical ability. But even if you consider yourself a technophobe, at least read the section about Services. Some real gems await you, and you don't have to do anything but click them.

Services

Apple has always dreamed of a software architecture that would let you mix and match features from different programs—the Mac's spell checker in Microsoft Word, the drawing tools of PowerPoint in your email, and so on. (Remember Apple's OpenDoc software project? Neither does anybody else.)

For several generations of Mac OS X, a menu called Services sat in every single program's Application menu, listing such interchangeable functions. And for all those years, most people pretty much ignored them.

That's because the Services menu was *baffling*. It listed all kinds of weird commands. Most of them, most of the time, were dimmed and unavailable. None of them were described or explained anywhere. They sort of felt like a mistake.

In Snow Leopard, Apple gave Services an extreme makeover, in hopes of making them useful again. They're still a *little* baffling, but there have been some forward strides.

For starters, Services commands are now contextual, meaning that they show up only when relevant; when a photo is selected, the text-related commands don't appear.

They can appear in many more places, too:

- The Services submenu, which is in the Application menu of every single program.

- The shortcut menu that appears when you Control-click (or right-click) a Finder icon.

- The shortcut menu that appears when you Control-click (or right-click) highlighted text in a Services-compatible program.

- The ✿ menu at the top of a Finder window.

Figure 7-2 shows what the Services menu looks like when you've highlighted some text in TextEdit.

You can now turn off Services you never use (in System Preferences), thereby hiding them, and you can even assign your own keystrokes to the Services you do use. Finally, you can very easily create your *own* Services menu items, using Automator.

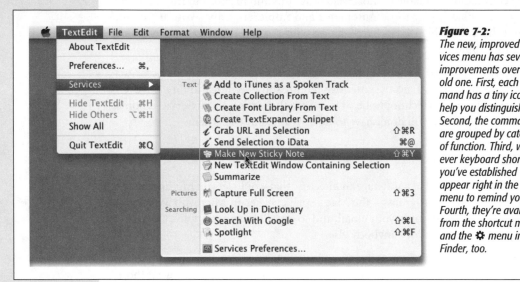

Figure 7-2:
The new, improved Services menu has several improvements over the old one. First, each command has a tiny icon to help you distinguish it. Second, the commands are grouped by category of function. Third, whatever keyboard shortcuts you've established appear right in the menu to remind you. Fourth, they're available from the shortcut menus and the ✿ menu in the Finder, too.

Now, Services *still* aren't first-class Mac citizens. They show up in most of the everyday Apple programs (Safari, Mail, TextEdit, iChat, Stickies, Terminal, and so on). But weirdly enough, they're not available in any of the commercial Apple programs, like iLife (iPhoto, iMovie, iDVD, GarageBand), iWork (Pages, Keynote, Numbers), or the professional apps like Aperture and Final Cut.

Even so, with any luck, the new "appear only when relevant" approach will give Services another shot at stardom.

Seven Services that Come in Handy

If you visit System Preferences→Keyboard→Keyboard Shortcuts, you see that Snow Leopard comes with a big set of starter Services. A lot of them are turned off at the outset (see the checkboxes?). That's because a lot of them are fairly obscure or technical.

If you'd like a complete catalog of what they are and what they do, download the free bonus PDF appendix to this chapter from this book's page at *www.missingmanuals. com*.

In the meantime, here are some examples of what you can do using the built-in Services. These examples also illustrate some of the different ways you can trigger these commands.

Drop in screenshots as you type

You're trying to explain to your mom, or your teacher, or your boss, how to connect to another Mac on the network. What you *really* need to create is an illustrated step-by-step guide.

So you open TextEdit and type up the first step. When it comes time to pop in an illustration, you Control-click (or right-click) the spot on the page; from the shortcut menu, you choose Capture Selection From Screen.

A message appears: "Drag over the portion of the screen you want to capture." You do so, and *snap!*—a picture of the screen area you selected appears right in your document. You continue on that way, typing and illustrating as you go.

One-click desktop picture

Someone just sent you the most *wicked* cool digital photo. It's sitting on your desktop.

So you Control-click (or right-click) it. From the shortcut menu, you choose Set Desktop Picture. *Bam!*—that picture is now your desktop wallpaper, saving you a clunky trip to System Preferences.

Note: In the shortcut menus, Services commands appear at the bottom. If there are more than four of them, they get grouped into a submenu called Services.

Text-to-email, in one step

You're reading on the Web, and you find an article that *totally* settles the argument you've been having with your buddy. You select the text. From the Safari→Services menu, you choose New Email With Selection.

Bing! Your Mac opens the Mail program and pastes the highlighted text into the body of a new outgoing email message. You're saved the trouble of copying, launching Mail, creating a new message, and pasting.

Text to a spoken iTunes track

You like to read *The New York Times'* main stories in the morning, but there's never time before work. Or you're supposed to read some document before school. It hits you: Too bad you couldn't *listen* to these documents, read to you on your iPod or iPhone as you exercise or commute.

Now you can. In Safari, TextEdit, Mail, or wherever, select the text you want converted to audio. Control-click (or right-click) it. From the shortcut menu, choose Add to iTunes as Spoken Track.

Zap! In a flash, you'll find a new file called Text to Speech in your iTunes Library, ready to sync to your iPod or iPhone. It's an *audio file* of someone reading the article aloud. (That someone, of course, is Alex, one of the Mac's built-in digital voices.)

Make a new sticky note

You find a phone number, address, Web address, sage proverb, whatever, in an email message, a TextEdit document, on the Web. You highlight it and then press Shift-⌘-Y. *Pow!*—it's now pasted into a new yellow sticky note in Stickies.

(Shift-⌘-Y, it turns out, is the keyboard shortcut for the Make New Sticky Note command in Services. Any Services command can have a keystroke, and you can change them at will—including this one. See page 179.)

Shorten a long-winded writer

Someone has sent you a speech or proposal or breakup letter. You haven't got time for the pain. "Just gimme the executive summary," you mutter to yourself.

So you highlight all the text, Control-click (or right-click) it, and choose Summarize. *Bing!* Your Mac analyzes the sentences you've highlighted and, after a moment, launches Summary Service. This little program, which you probably never even knew you had, displays a greatly shortened version of the original text. Figure 7-3 offers details.

Note: Lots of add-on Mac programs stock the Services menu with commands of their own. Skype, for example, adds options like Call, Send Message, and Send SMS, so you can call or text someone right from a phone number you encounter in a text document or on the Web. QuicKeys, RealPlayer, iData, Google Quick Search, and many other programs add to the Services menu, too.

More Great Examples from Downloadable Services

The preceding pages describe the best of the *built-in* Services. But there are hundreds more available on the Web.

Consider visiting *www.macosxautomation.com*, for example. That's a Web site maintained by veteran automation fans for the benefit of anyone who's interested. Here, when you click Services, you can find a Download page filled with useful, ready-made services. A few examples:

- **New Disk Image with Selection.** Highlight a folder or a group of icons. Choose this command from the ✿ menu—presto, a new disk image file (.dmg) containing the selected Finder items.

- **Send Photo to Everyone in the Picture.** You choose some photos in iPhoto, and then select this command from the Services menu. The Mac creates a new outgoing message in Mail, containing the selected iPhoto images, addressed to the people *in* the selected images, as determined by iPhoto's Faces feature.

- **Change File Type.** Highlight some photo files in a Finder window. From the ✿ menu, choose this command. It auto-converts them to the new graphics-file format of your choice.

- **Encrypt File.** Highlight a PDF document in the Finder, and then choose this command from the ⚙ menu or the file's shortcut menu. You get duplicates of the PDF files, encrypted with a password you supply, with the word "(encrypted)" appended to their names.

Clearly, there's all kinds of fun (and utility) to be found in Services.

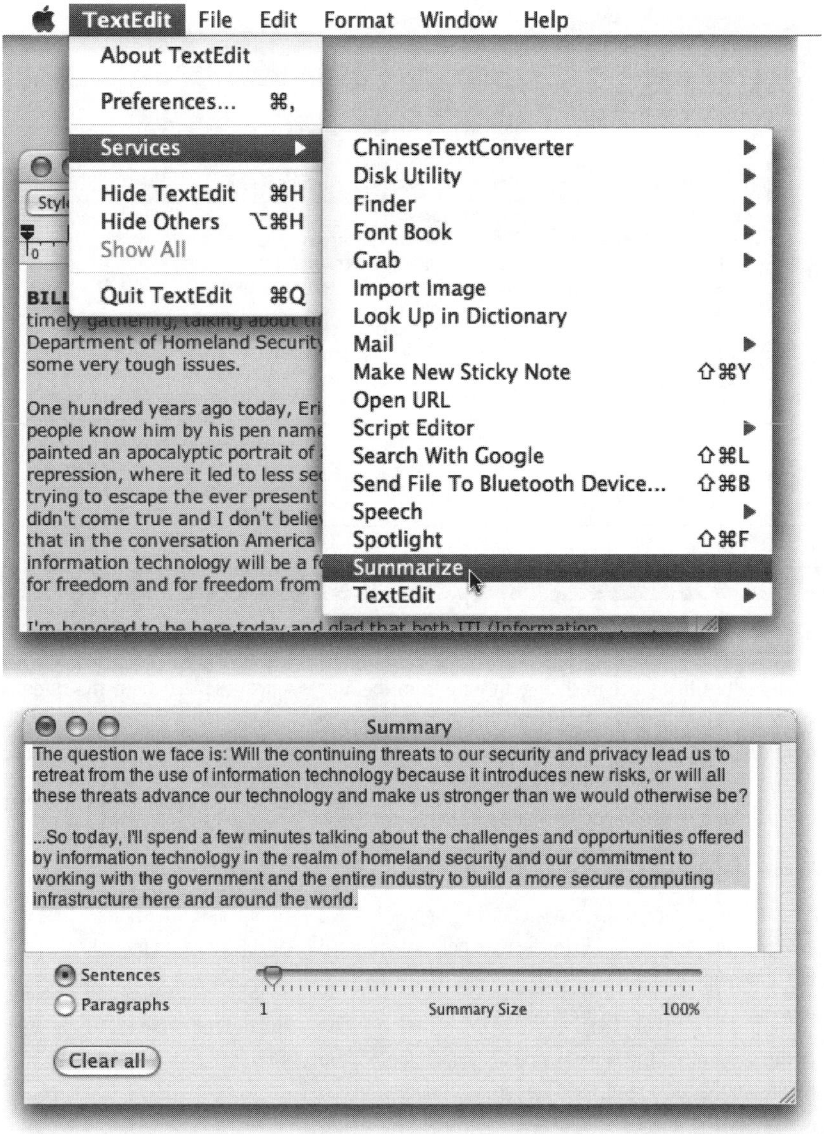

Figure 7-3:
Use the Summarize command to create a one-paragraph summary (bottom) of a longer passage (top). Once the summary appears in the Summary Service program, you can make it more or less concise by dragging the Summary Size slider. You can also ask it to display the most statistically relevant paragraphs instead of sentences, just by clicking the appropriate radio button at the lower left. (Bear in mind that Summary Service doesn't do any creative rewriting; even Mac OS X can't come up with something coherent if the original wasn't. Instead, Summary Service chooses the most statistically significant sentences to include in the summary.)

Turning Them On and Off—and Adding Keyboard Shortcuts

The Services command center is in the System Preferences→Keyboard→Keyboard Shortcuts pane. (You can also get there by choosing Services→Services Preferences from any program's Application menu.)

Here, turn the checkboxes on or off to choose which Services you want available.

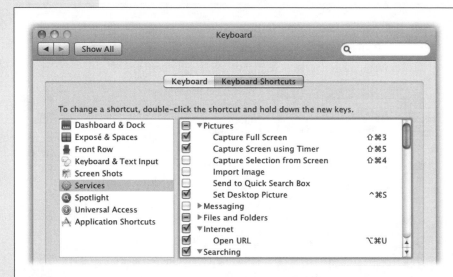

Figure 7-4:
Here's the Services command center. You can purge your shortcut menus and Services menus of the useless Services by turning off their checkboxes. You can also assign (or change) keyboard shortcuts. Click a Service's name and then press Return to open the Keyboard Shortcut box; then press the desired keystroke on your keyboard.

GEM IN THE ROUGH

Open Any Program with a Keystroke

It's a feature that's been achingly missing from the Mac since Day One: assigning keyboard shortcuts to *opening programs.* You couldn't set up Control-W to bring up Microsoft Word, Control-S to open Safari, and so on. (At least not without the help of add-on shareware.)

In Snow Leopard, for the first time, you can.

First, use Automator, described later in this chapter, to build a simple, one-step workflow. The first and only action should be Launch Application. Use its pop-up menu to specify *which* program you want to open from the keyboard.

At the very top of the workflow pane, change the pop-up menus so that they read, "Service receives no input in any

application" (where the underlined phrases are pop-up menus). That "any application" part is important; otherwise, your keystroke will work in only one program.

Save the result and name it "Open Word," or "Open Address Book," or whatever you like.

Finally, open System Preferences→Keyboard→Keyboard Shortcuts. Click Services. Give your new Service a keystroke as described on page 179.

And that's it! You've just created a keystroke that can open the desired program—using only Mac OS X's built-in tools. Hurrah!

Handier still, you can double-click to the right of a Service's name and then press a keyboard combination. That will become its new keyboard shortcut, available system-wide. (The usual caveats apply: Any keystroke you make up *here* overrides the same keystrokes that your programs may use for themselves, so be careful.)

Automator

Automator is the Mac OS X program that lets you create your *own* little programs—and your own Services, if you like. Like most programs on your Mac, it sits waiting in your Applications folder. Double-click its icon to open it for the first time. (Automator's robot icon is supposedly named Otto. Get it? Otto Matic? Stop, you're killing us!)

Seven Startup Templates

As you'll soon discover, building an Automator workflow is a satisfying intellectual exercise and a delicious talent to acquire. But if the point of all the effort is to create a timesaving, step-saving software robot, you'll need some way to *trigger* it—to run it, just the way you run an email program or a Web browser.

Fortunately, you can save a workflow as a regular, double-clickable application, if you like, or turn it into a Service, as described above, or embed it in shortcut menus all over your Mac. In fact, when you fire up Automator, the first thing it wants to know is: What *is* the desired destination for this workflow?

You're offered seven options in the template screen shown in Figure 7-5:

Figure 7-5:
Automator has seven choices for the final form of your workflow.

If you're not sure which format you'll want to use for a particular workflow, choose Workflow for now. Later, if you change your mind about the final product of your masterpiece—for example, you realize it would have been better as a Service or an iCal Alarm—you can create a blank document in one of the other types, then drag the actions from your saved workflow into the new, blank project.

- **Workflow.** An Automator Workflow file (with file name extension *.workflow*) is what you create if you want to study and refine your project. It's not the best format for *using* your homemade app, though, because to run it, you have to open Automator and click the Run button.

- **Application.** A workflow saved as an application has all the benefits associated with normal Mac OS X programs. You can double-click its Finder icon to launch it, drag it to the Dock for one-click launching, or just leave it in your Applications folder, nestled among all the "professional" programs.

So why wouldn't you just save your workflows as applications *all* the time? First, workflow applications are *much* larger than workflow documents—as much as 20 times larger. That's worth remembering if you plan to distribute your workflows online or via email.

Also, when a workflow application runs, it doesn't give you access to the Workflow log (see the box on page 284)—a big downside if you want to monitor the progress of your workflow in minute detail. Instead, you get a dinky action indicator in the menu bar, as shown in Figure 7-6.

Figure 7-6:
The three-part menu-bar indicator tells you that the workflow application is, in fact, running (the spinning progress indicator)—and, more specifically, which action is running (the text next to it). If you want to cancel a workflow halfway through, click the Stop sign.

Finally, it's a pain to edit a workflow application if something goes wrong; you have to open the whole thing in Automator and resave it.

- **Service.** Ahhh, now we're talking. Yes, that's right: You can now build your own Services, as described above—and give them all the privileges of Apple's own Services. One sample benefit: You can assign your own keyboard shortcuts to them, as described on page 179.

The beauty of Automator-created Services is that they show up *instantly* in all the places where Services show up: in the Services menu, in the shortcut menu that appears when you right-click a Finder icon or selected text, and in the Finder's ✿ menu—all ready to use. In other words, enhancing and debugging your workflow is incredibly easy, because it's immediately ready to try out in the "real world" of your Mac.

- **Folder Action.** *Folder Actions* are workflows that run automatically when you do something to a *folder* in the Finder—opening it, say, or adding files to it. Folder Actions are extremely powerful for image processing, network backup jobs, and much more, but they're also extremely complicated. For an explanation of the ins and outs, read this chapter's bonus AppleScript appendix (on this book's "Missing CD" page at *www.missingmanuals.com*).

- **Print Plugin.** Print Workflows show up as menu items inside the Print dialog box's PDF menu (page 563). If you save a workflow as a Print Workflow plug-in, you can easily run the workflow on a document you're about to print—applying a ColorSync filter to the document to compensate for slight discolorations, for example.

- **iCal Alarm** is a powerful plug-in format that lets you schedule workflows to run at specific times. When you save a workflow in this format, iCal opens and creates a new event named after your plug-in; you're supposed to drag and edit this event to whatever time and day you want the workflow to run. (You can even use iCal's "repeat" pop-up menu to have the workflow run every day, week, and so on.)

  This is a fantastic tool. If you have a workflow that plays an iTunes song, for example, you can easily build an alarm clock using nothing more than iCal alarms.

- **Image Capture Plugin.** Image Capture is a program for importing photos from a camera or scanner (page 379). If you save a workflow as an Image Capture plug-in, you can choose to run the workflow whenever you import new photos—so you can easily shrink the new images to a smaller size, for example.

- You can click these icons one at a time to read capsule descriptions. You don't have to make a choice now, though; you can click Close to get rid of these template offerings, build a workflow now, and then decide what to do with it later.

Now, go forth and automate!

Tip: You can find extra Automator resources, including useful workflows and actions, at sites like *www.automatorworld.com, www.automatoractions.com,* and of course *www.macosxautomation.com.*

Automator Tour

Once you've chosen a finished format for the workflow you're about to create, you wind up in Automator itself. A tour may be in order:

Toolbar

At the top of the Automator window, the toolbar offers five fairly self-explanatory buttons. From left to right (Figure 7-7):

- **Hide Library.** This button hides the entire left Library pane of Automator, where all the prefab building-block steps are listed. You wind up with one big Workflow pane.

- **Media.** Click to open the standard Media Browser box that pops up all over Mac OS X. You can drag your music, photos, or movies from the Media Browser directly into the Workflow pane, *or* into an action itself (one with a matching data type, of course) to use that media in your workflow.

Tip: Media from the Media Browser isn't all you can add to Automator. You can also drag files—text documents, media, folders, and so on—straight from the Finder into your workflow, saving you the hassle of having to search for them in Automator.

- **Record.** Click to enter Watch Me Do mode, where Automator memorizes the steps that you perform manually (page 286).

- **Skip, Stop, Run.** These buttons control playback of the workflow you're building.

Tip: To save screen space, you can hide the entire Automator toolbar by choosing View→Toolbar, or by clicking the capsule-shaped button in the upper-right corner of the window. (You can bring the toolbar back by choosing View→Show Toolbar or clicking the pill button again.)

While the toolbar is hidden (and even when it's visible), you can still start and stop playback by choosing Workflow→Run (⌘-R) and Workflow→Stop (⌘-period).

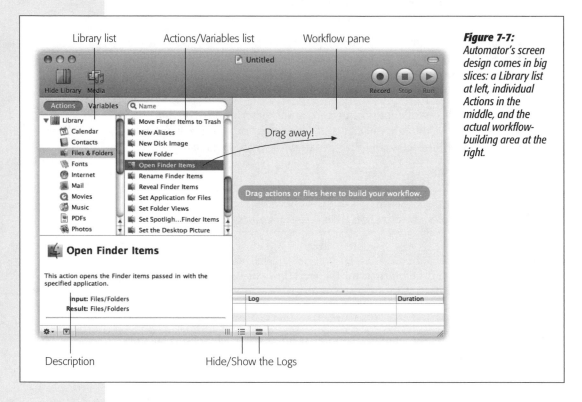

Figure 7-7:
Automator's screen design comes in big slices: a Library list at left, individual Actions in the middle, and the actual workflow-building area at the right.

Library pane

The Library pane is the entire left section of the Automator window. It includes the Search box, Library list, Description field, and the list of Actions or Variables. These are described on the following pages.

Tip: You can resize either of Automator's left-side columns (Library and Actions) by dragging the vertical divider lines between them.

Search box

Like Mac OS X's other Search boxes, this one works in real time—it displays matching actions or variables as you type.

If you start by selecting a folder in the Library list at left, you're telling Automator, "Search only within this folder of actions or variables." If you want to search for actions that can process files in the Finder, for example, click Files & Folders in the Library list, and then type *file* in the Search box.

Tip: You can ⌘-click to select several folders and then search all of them simultaneously.

Or, to search *all* of Automator's folders, click Library at the top of the Library list before searching. (That's the best way to find an action or variable if you're not sure what folder it's in.)

Your search results appear in the Actions/Variables list, ranked by relevance to your search terms. You can begin dragging actions directly into the Workflow pane at the right side to build a workflow, as described shortly.

Click the ⊗ button in the Search box to return to the complete list of actions or variables.

Library

Above the Library list, two buttons appear that govern what's displayed in the Library pane:

- **Actions.** When you click Actions, the Library lists all the features and data that Automator actions can control: Files & Folders, Music, Photos, Text, and so on. When you click a folder, the Actions list on the right shows every action related to that type of data. For example, when you click Photos in the left-side list, the right-side list of actions offers steps like Flip Images, Crop Images, and so on.

  When you find an action you want to use in your workflow, drag it to the right into the large Workflow pane.

- **Variables.** *Variables* are memorized info chunks that you can reuse in an Automator workflow, exactly as in real programming languages. The Variables list is divided into categories like Date & Time (today's date, today's month, and so on), Locations (the paths to various folders on your Mac), and User (your name, phone number, and other information).

  Later in this chapter, you'll see how it's useful to incorporate these information tidbits into your workflows.

Note: Variables whose icons look like a boxed V are variables that you can change. For example, you can change the formatting of the "Current time" variable by double-clicking it.

Variables with ✿ icons are predefined and unchangeable.

Description field

When you click an action or variable in the list, the Description box provides some terse, superficial information on how to use it. You might see what the action does, what kind of data it expects to receive from the previous action (*input*), and what the action sends on to the following action (*result*).

If the variable is editable (it has a V icon), you get to see what parts of it you can change.

Tip: To save space, you can hide the Description field by clicking the ▾ button on the bottom edge of the window. Click it again to bring the Description field back.

✿ button

The ✿ button in the lower-left corner of the window is a pop-up menu. Its four commands let you create and delete customizable collections called *groups* and *smart groups*. They behave exactly like playlists and smart playlists in iTunes. For example, you can create a group that holds the actions you use most often, so you don't have to keep hunting for them.

Smart groups are constantly updated with actions that match the criteria you set for that smart group. (They're available only for actions, not variables.) For example, you can create a smart group that lists only actions that work with iPhoto, or actions with input types that contain the word "image." Add more criteria by clicking the + button.

Tip: Automator's Library list comes with three factory-installed smart groups: Most Relevant, which displays all the actions relevant to the action you have selected in the Workflow pane; Most Used, which displays the actions you've used the most in your workflows; and Recently Added, which displays actions added by newly installed applications, for example, or actions you downloaded and added yourself.

Workflow pane

The Workflow pane is Automator's kitchen. It's where you put your actions in whatever order you want, set any action-specific preferences, and fry them all up in a pan.

The Workflow pane also shows how the information from one action gets piped into another, creating a stream of information. That's how the Workflow pane differentiates Automator from the dozens of non-visual, programming-based automation tools out there. Figure 7-8 shows what a piece of a workflow might look like in the Workflow pane.

When you drag an action out of the Actions list into the Workflow pane, any surrounding actions scoot aside to make room.

Tip: If you double-click an action in the Actions list, Automator inserts it at the bottom of the Workflow pane. (Pressing Return when an action is highlighted does the same thing.)

Log viewer

Under the Workflow pane on the left are two tiny buttons, identified in Figure 7-8. They hide and show two useful pop-up panels that contain *logs* (mini-reports): the Workflow log, which shows which actions ran successfully, which failed (if any), what each action did, and so on; and the Variables log (Figure 7-9), which shows all the variables used in your workflow. When you run the workflow, the Value list shows you what information was stored in each variable after the workflow finishes.

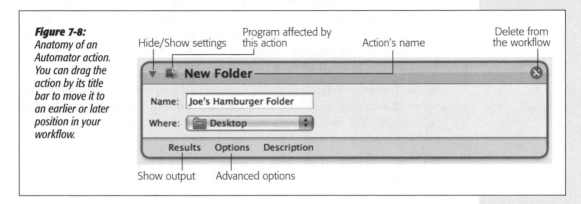

Figure 7-8:
Anatomy of an Automator action. You can drag the action by its title bar to move it to an earlier or later position in your workflow.

Hide/Show settings Program affected by this action Action's name Delete from the workflow

Show output Advanced options

Opening existing workflows

Automator comes with four prebuilt workflows that show off its capabilities. Find them by clicking Help→Open Examples Folder; open one of these workflows for inspection by double-clicking it.

Tip: In Snow Leopard, you don't actually have to open an Automator document to see how it's set up. Simply select a workflow in the Finder and hit the space bar to activate Quick Look (page 54), which gives you a preview of the entire workflow—actions and all.

(This doesn't work on workflows saved in the old Mac OS X 10.4 format, though, at least not until you open them and re-save them in Snow Leopard.)

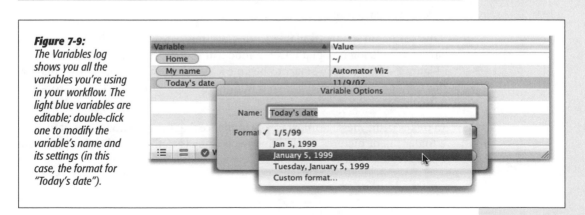

Figure 7-9:
The Variables log shows you all the variables you're using in your workflow. The light blue variables are editable; double-click one to modify the variable's name and its settings (in this case, the format for "Today's date").

To many people's surprise, the included workflows are quite useful:

- **Process Images** applies special visual effects to whatever photos you specify in the workflow. No, people haven't exactly been clamoring for an automated way to create mirror-image camera shots, but this workflow does show you the basics of batch-processing photos. You can use it as a template for building your own "Convert to JPEG" or "Scale to 640 × 480 pixels" workflow, for example.

- **Import MobileMe Photo Album into iPhoto** works only if you have a MobileMe account (Chapter 18). It slurps the photos from a photo album you've previously posted on your MobileMe site (say, while you were on vacation) and copies them into iPhoto. From there, you can view a full-screen slideshow of the images, or even edit them and post them *back* onto your MobileMe site.

- **Display Trailers in Safari** is intended to show you how you can create workflows that work with Web addresses. This one sneaks out to Apple's popular movie-previews Web site, rounds up the list of the latest movie ads, and opens each in a new Web-browser tab.

- **Copy Unread Mail to iPod Notes** copies any new Mail messages into your iPod's text-notes folder. Later, when you're on the train to work, you can pull out your iPod and read whatever mail you didn't get to at home.

Tip: There are two more great Automator examples at the Ground Zero of Automator, *www.macosxautomation.com.* "Welcome to the Party!" for example, cleverly demos two new features of Automator—variables and the Loop action—by showing you how to create a workflow that takes photos of your friends and turns them into a cool, party-ready screen saver.

Understanding a Workflow

Before you build your own workflows, it's a good idea to understand how actions work together to process information. Here's a step-by-step analysis of the Process Images workflow described above (Figure 7-10), which will give you deeper insight into building your *own* workflows.

1. **Ask for Confirmation.**

   This common action, available in the Utilities category (in the Library list), produces a dialog box that tells the innocent bystander what's about to happen (Figure 7-11). It's often smart to begin each of your *own* workflows with a box like this, to remind yourself (or your minimum-wage minions) what the workflow actually does.

   In this case, the message informs your audience that the workflow is about to open a folder full of pictures, apply some wacko effects to them, and then open them up in Preview to display the results.

Tip: If you want the dialog box to appear with a bright warning sign—to inform you, for example, that you're about to erase your entire hard drive—click the robot icon in the upper-left corner of the Ask for Confirmation action. Automator swaps in a robot-with-yellow-triangle icon.

Keep in mind, too, that the entire Ask for Confirmation action is 100 percent customizable. Not only can you change the text that appears in the dialog box—you can even change the names of the Cancel and OK buttons.

Figure 7-10:
The Process Images workflow consists of only five actions. (The first action, which just displays an explanatory dialog box, shouldn't even count.) Still, this simple action does in 10 seconds what would take most humans at least 5 minutes: applying the same photo effect to several images.

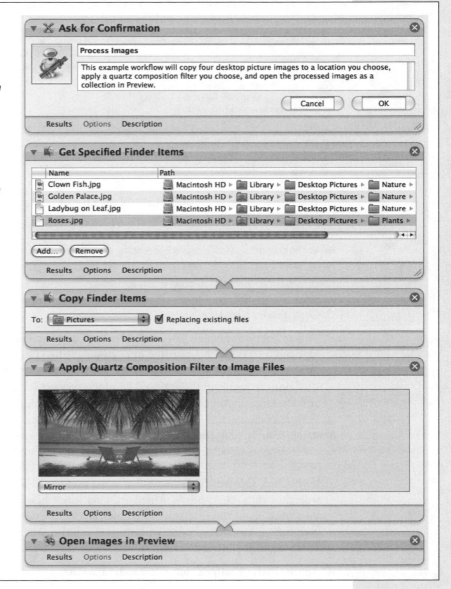

2. Get Specified Finder Items.

The next step in the Process Images workflow comes from the Files & Folders Library category. Here's where you specify which files you want your workflow to operate on. You can use the Add and Remove buttons to edit the list—to add your own images to be mirrored, for example—or you can drag files straight from the Finder into this list.

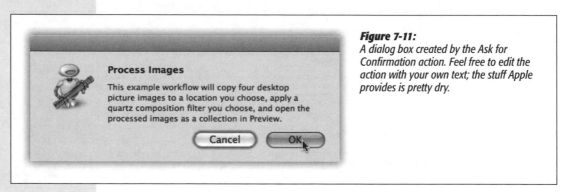

Figure 7-11:
A dialog box created by the Ask for Confirmation action. Feel free to edit the action with your own text; the stuff Apple provides is pretty dry.

When this action is finished, it passes on a list of files and/or folders to the next action, ready for further processing.

Note: This example workflow always operates on the same set of four files. But if you were to substitute the Files & Folders→Ask for Finder Items action instead, Automator would ask which files to process each time you ran the workflow, which is a heck of a lot more useful.

3. Copy Finder Items.

This is a very important Files & Folders action: It makes a *copy* of the specified files and folders (in this case, the ones you identified in step 2) so you don't gum up the originals. You can change where you want the copies stored by editing the "To" pop-up menu in the action. The menu lists obvious locations like Pictures and Desktop, or you can choose Other to select any folder you like.

Note: The "Replacing existing files" checkbox tells Automator that, if there are old files in the Pictures folder with the same names as your new files, you want to delete the old files automatically.

If you click Options in the action, you see that the "Show this action when the workflow runs" checkbox is turned on. That way, when your workflow runs, Automator will ask where to store the copies, so that the destination can be different each time. Otherwise, the files will automatically be copied to whatever folder you select in the pop-up menu right now.

4. Apply Quartz Composition Filter to Image Files.

This action (which came from the Photos category folder) processes the newly duplicated images from step 3; in this case, it applies a mirror filter to them. The action then passes the newly mirrored images on to step 5. If you prefer, you can choose a different filter from the pop-up menu—to make the image look like a comic-book drawing, for example—instead of applying the mirror filter.

Note: The Quartz Composition Filter, a piece of Mac OS X's Quartz display technology, can modify images and photos in real time. Photo Booth uses this technology, which is why many of Photo Booth's effects are also in the action's Filter pop-up menu. (See *http://developer.apple.com/graphicsimaging/quartz* for the incredibly nerdy details on Quartz.)

Since "Show this action when the workflow runs" under Options is turned on, you'll have the chance to choose a different filter each time this workflow runs.

(By the way, the image of the beach is intended to demonstrate the filter's effect; it's not actually one of your photos.)

Tip: The big box on the right side of the action isn't there because Apple had nothing to fill the space. Certain filters have settings you can modify, which appear in that box. The Glow filter, for example, lets you specify how much glow you want applied to the image(s).

---

5. **Open Images in Preview.**

   This final action, which also comes from the Photos category, takes the post-filter images from step 4 and opens them in Preview. From there, you can flip, resize, or resave the images.

Try running the workflow by clicking Run. The bottom of the Workflow pane tells you which step of the workflow is running at the moment. As each action finishes, a green checkmark appears in its lower-left corner.

Note: If something goes wrong while your workflow is running (or if you click Cancel in a dialog box), your workflow stops in its tracks. To identify the offending step, look for the red X in an action's lower-left corner, or check the Log.

Unfortunately, if your workflow shuts down in the middle, you can't restart it from there. When you click Run the next time, the workflow plays from the beginning.

Building Your Own Workflow

You could spend all day playing with the workflows Apple gives you, making minor tweaks and seeing how they affect the workflow's progress. You could even download more preassembled workflows from *www.automatorworld.com*, *http://macscripter.net*, or *www.macosxautomation.com*, if you were so inclined.

Still, those options don't give you the kind of hands-on experience you need to automate your Mac on your own.

That's why the following pages walk you through building two different Automator workflows from scratch. Along the way, you'll learn several tricks that you'll find handy when you start building your own workflows.

Tip: If you're feeling lazy, you can download the completed workflow projects from this book's "Missing CD" page at *www.missingmanuals.com*.

Send a File Attachment from the Desktop

Wouldn't it be cool if you could just click a file's icon in the Finder—and choose "Send This File as an Email Attachment" right from its shortcut menu? One step, instead of the tedious business of opening your mail program, creating a new message, clicking Attach, finding the file, choosing it, and so on. Windows has had this feature for years, and it's absolutely indispensable.

And now you can have it, too. A couple of steps in Automator, and this little gem is yours forever.

1. **In Automator, choose File→New (or press ⌘-N).**

   The templates dialog box appears (shown back in Figure 7-5).

2. **Double-click Service.**

   You want this puppy to be available from any Finder icon's shortcut menu—and that's the beauty of the Service.

   You wind up with a new panel at the top of the workflow, bearing the peculiar legend, "Service receives selected text in any application" (where the underlined phrases are pop-up menus).

   Remember, Services are contextual; they're smart enough to know when to show up in your menus. That's the purpose of these two pop-up menus: to let you specify when your new Service should appear. In this case, you want the menu to appear only if you've opened the shortcut menu for a *file icon,* in *the Finder.*

3. **From the first pop-up menu, choose "files or folders." From the second, choose Finder (Figure 7-12, top).**

   In future experiments, you could choose, from the first menu, "image files," "PDF files," "movie files," or whatever; the Service would then appear only when you've right-clicked *that* kind of file.

   OK: You've now established what kind of file the Service will work on, and in which program. Now you have to tell Automator what you want to *do* with that file: attach it to a new, outgoing email message.

4. **In the Library list at left, click the Mail category.**

   (Make sure the Actions button is clicked above the list.) You've just narrowed down the list of available actions to those that pertain to Apple's email program.

5. **From the Actions column, drag the action called New Mail Message into the Workflow pane.**

(Use the Search box at the top if you don't feel like reading through the list of Actions.)

Figure 7-12:
Top: You want this Service to appear in your shortcut menus only when you've right-clicked a file or folder, and only in the Finder. If you have more than one email account, you can select the one you'd like to send the message from in the pop-up menu at the bottom of this window. You can also specify, in advance, an addressee, subject line, body, and so on.

Bottom: Once you've saved your Service, your Send As Attachment command is ready to go! Control-click (or right-click) any icon in the Finder to see it and trigger it. Just address, click Send, and your message is on its way. (You could even add the Send Outgoing Messages action to the end of your workflow to do this step automatically.)

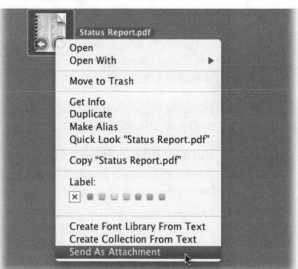

If you leave this action as it is, your workflow will autocreate an *empty, unaddressed* outgoing mail message; you'll fill in the recipient name, subject line, and so on, when you run it. Which is fine.

But you could, if you liked, take a moment now to *pre-specify* the recipient, subject, and body message for your new email message—great if you have to send the same stuff to the same people every week, for example. (You can even add an email address straight from your Address Book. Just click the address-card button in the upper-right corner.)

Tip: If you use Microsoft Entourage for your email instead of Mail, you'll notice that your Library list offers actions for operating Entourage by remote control, too. So in this step, you'd drag the Create New Entourage Mail Message instead of Create New Message.

If you look at the description for this action, you'll see that the Input accepts "(Files/Folders, Text)." It explains that if a file is passed from the previous action, it will automatically be attached to the email.

6. **Choose File→Save. In the dialog box, name your new Service command. Click Save.**

You can call it "Send As Attachment," or "Send By Email," or "Send This Baby Off!" Whatever you like.

That's actually all there is to it. Now for the testing. Switch to the Finder and Control-click (or right-click) any file icon (Figure 7-12, bottom). From the shortcut menu, choose Send As Attachment (or whatever you called your Service).

Tip: If there are more than four Services at the bottom of the shortcut menu, your new command will be added to a submenu called Services. If you'd rather avoid this extra step–preferring a longer list of Services right there in the shortcut menu–then download the free Services Menu Items Utility from this book's "Missing CD" page at *www.missingmanuals.com*. It lets you stack up to 25 Services in the shortcut menu without segregating them into a Services submenu.

Instantly, the Mac opens your email program and creates a new outgoing message—with your selected file already attached. You just saved about 35 steps.

Burn an iPhoto Picture CD

iPhoto is a fantastic program for organizing digital photos. It even has its own photo-backup feature, which burns selected albums' photos to a blank CD or DVD.

However, those backup discs maintain iPhoto's complex and user-hostile Library folder structure. That's great if you expect one day to restore the backup *to iPhoto,* because the backup maintains all your keywords, ratings, albums, comments, and other iPhoto data.

But it's not so great if you want to hand the CD or DVD to anyone who *doesn't* use iPhoto (like an OS 9 or Windows person), because they'll have a devil of a time figuring out where the photos *are* in the convoluted Library folder structure.

If you build an Automator workflow to back up your photos instead, you (a) can burn a disc containing *only* the photos in one simple folder; (b) have more control over which photos are backed up; and (c) learn even more tricks for automating sophisticated operations. Figure 7-13 shows what the final workflow looks like.

Here's how to put it together:

1. **Create a new Automator workflow (⌘-N).**

   The template screen appears. In this example, you'll create a standalone, double-clickable program. You're a programmer now, baby! (Well, sort of.)

2. **Double-click Application.**

   You arrive at the main workflow-construction area.

3. **Click the Photos category folder. In the list of available actions, find Ask for Photos. Drag it into the empty workflow area.**

   Your newly hatched workflow, when it runs, will begin by asking you which photos you want to back up.

Figure 7-13:
Top: The first action presents a dialog box telling you what this workflow does.

Middle: The second action lets you select from your iPhoto Library the images you want to back up.

Bottom: The last action, in a single step, burns those images onto a CD or DVD. It works regardless of whether your Mac has an internal or external burner. Try that simplicity on a PC!

Tip: What you really want is to round up only the latest batch of photos—since your last backup, for example. Fortunately, one of the actions in the Photos folder is called Find iPhoto Items, and it lets you specify a time period like "Within the last 2 weeks." It would be perfect for this workflow—if it weren't so buggy. (For example, it finds multiple copies of each photo.)

For best results, then, create a Smart Album in iPhoto that lets you filter photos based on certain criteria—all your photos taken in the past two months, for example. When you run the workflow, you can choose that album to back up, so that you get only the most recent shots.

4. **In the Library list, click the Utilities folder. Drag the Ask for Confirmation action into the Workflow pane, above the Ask for Photos action. Fill in the text as shown at the top of Figure 7-13.**

Be sure to drag it *above* the Ask for Photos action so it's the first thing that happens when you run your workflow. Now you've just directed Automator to begin its work by displaying a dialog box (Figure 7-14).

Back Up Selected iPhoto Pictures

This workflow lets you select images from your
iPhoto Library and burn them onto a CD or DVD.

Cancel   OK

Figure 7-14:
The explanatory dialog box from the iPhoto Backup workflow. Making the dialog box appear is optional, but it's helpful if you come back to your workflow in a few months and forget what it's supposed to do.

FREQUENTLY ASKED QUESTION

Checking a Workflow's Progress

Some of these actions take their sweet time. Is there some progress bar that will tell me how far along my workflow is?

Actually, Automator provides two ways to check on the status of your workflow: the simple way (call it "the Indicator") and the Workflow log.

The Indicator lies in the lower-left corner of the Automator window, next to the Log buttons. When your workflow is running, a little status message appears here to tell you exactly which action is running at the moment. You can use that information, along with some common sense, to figure out how close your workflow is to being finished. If the workflow has run its course, the Indicator says, "Workflow completed."

(You can also identify whatever action is running at this moment, thanks to the spinning-sprocket indicator in its lower-left corner. But if you have a tall stack of actions, you might not be able to see the action that's currently running. The list doesn't automatically scroll.)

The Workflow log is even more powerful. Activate it by clicking the list-like button in the bottom-right corner of the Workflow pane (or by hitting Option-⌘-L). It tells you when each action begins and ends, and it also displays geeky data-conversion information (like when Mac OS X is turning "image files" into plain-vanilla Finder files). And unlike the Indicator, the Workflow log keeps its information around even after your workflow is finished—so you can see how long your entire workflow took to run, for example.

5. **Drag the "Burn a Disc" action to the bottom of the Workflow pane.**

   Just to make this extra nice, why not make an options box pop up at the time of burning?

6. **Click Options, and turn on "Show this action when the workflow runs."**

   The options box will ask you to name the CD, choose a burning speed, and so on.

7. **In the Disc Name field of the Burn a Disc action, type "iPhoto Backup from "** **(that's a space after "from").**

   This is going to be the proposed name for the CD.

8. **Click Variables above the Library list.**

   Those variables are about to come in handy. You're going to complete the phrase "iPhoto Backup from" with whatever the date of the backup is.

9. **Click the Date & Time folder in the Library list. Drag the "Today's date" variable into the Disc Name field after "from."**

   The CD or DVD's name will be something like "iPhoto Backup from 4/9/10," making it easy for you to see *when* you made the backup disk. The date automatically changes whenever you run the workflow.

10. **Choose File→Save. Type a name for your new program (like *Back Up This Month's iPhoto Pix to CD),* and save it wherever you like (on the desktop, for example).**

    Now try it out. Double-click your newly forged program; your workflow springs into action, asking you to specify the photos you want, asking for a blank disc, and then burning it!

Doing More with Automator

Automator is not a static, this-or-nothing program: It's a versatile, *expandable* tool with ever-increasing potential. There are two especially good ways to increase Automator's power beyond using the factory-installed actions: adding more actions yourself, and using the new Watch Me Do feature.

Getting more action(s)

Automator comes with dozens of actions, but you're bound—eventually—to find yourself wishing there were a few more. Perhaps you'd like some Automator actions to control non-Apple programs like Photoshop, or you'd just like to have a few extra actions to control Mac OS X itself.

Fortunately, Automator can handle actions written by non-Apple programmers, too. Just visit any of the Web sites devoted to Automator actions (like *www.automatorworld. com* or *www.macosxautomation.com*), and download any actions you'd like.

If the action's programmers did their jobs right, you can just download the action, run the installer, and sit back and watch as Mac OS X unpacks, copies, and installs the action automatically. The next time you open Automator, the new action will be listed in the correct folder in the Library list.

If, on the other hand, the action's programmer did not create a self-installing action, you may have to manually double-click the .dmg, .sit, or .zip file you downloaded. Inside the folder or disk image that results, you should find a file ending in .action. Drag that file into either your Home→Library→Automator folder (to install the action for use under only your account) or to your Library→Automator folder (to install the action for all users on your Mac). In either case, if this is the first time you're installing an Automator action by hand, you may have to create the folder yourself.

Once in Automator, you can use your new actions just as you'd use the ones that came bundled with your Mac: dragging and dropping them in whatever order you want, customizing their settings, and so on.

Before you run any new actions, though, look at the Description field to discover the actions' inputs and outputs. With that information in hand, you'll never accidentally connect, say, your new Sauté Vegetables action to an unrelated action like Burn a Disc.

And finally, if you're interested in writing your own Automator actions (warning: programming experience necessary), visit *http://developer.apple.com/documentation/ AppleApplications/Conceptual/AutomatorConcepts/Automator.html* for an introduction.

Watch Me Do mode

Sometimes, you'll run into a task that Automator can't accomplish with *any* action, no matter how nicely you ask: opening multiple folders of bookmarks in several Safari windows, for example, or automating some no-name program that doesn't know anything about Automator and doesn't come with any actions.

Enter Watch Me Do. In this mode, you click a Record button. The Automator window disappears, and a black "Automator: Recording" window takes its place. From now until you hit the Stop button, every mouse click and keystroke is *recorded*, step by step, into Automator. Later, you can survey the list of steps you took and clean them up.

When you run the workflow, your mouse actually moves to reproduce your clicks, and the Mac actually types the same keystrokes you did. It's like watching a ghost control your computer, or maybe a really annoying little brother who won't stop mimicking you.

You can even manipulate the individual steps—delete one, for example, edit the play-back speed, or change how long it takes before the step "times out" (gives up).

It's far easier to create workflows using Watch Me Do than having to drag the correct actions into the correct sequence; you're leaving even more of the programming to Automator.

Unfortunately, there are drawbacks to Watch Me Do, too:

- The conditions on the screen when you run the action must be *identical* to the way they were when you recorded. If some window isn't the same size, or in the same position, or if some button isn't where it used to be, the workflow derails.

- Watch Me Do relies on the Mac's accessibility features—the same ones that form the guts of VoiceOver and other tools for the disabled—and different programs have been "accessibilitized" to wildly varying degrees. You can record and play back steps that involve System Preferences with amazing success, for example. But operating other programs can be hopeless.

That's why Watch Me Do may seem incredibly flaky. For best results, use keystrokes and keyboard shortcuts as much as possible, and avoid the mouse.

Here's an example:

Change your startup disk

If you use Boot Camp to run Windows on your Mac (Chapter 8), you may find yourself having to open the Startup Disk pane of System Preferences with alarming frequency. And unfortunately, there's no Change Startup Disk action in Automator to make that job less repetitive.

Fortunately, Watch Me Do *can* automate the process, so you can switch your startup disk with one click on an Automator-created application on your desktop or Dock. Creating the workflow is simple:

1. **Create a new workflow (⌘-N). Double-click Application in the template-selection panel.**

   Since you're just going to work with Watch Me Do, you won't be messing with any predefined actions this time.

2. **Click the Record button.**

   The Automator window disappears, and the black Recording window pops up. Everything you do is being recorded right into Automator.

3. **Click System Preferences in the Dock.**

   If System Preferences isn't in your Dock, put it there before beginning the recording. (It's in your Applications folder.) Choosing its name from the menu generally doesn't work, thanks to some typical Watch Me Do flakiness.

4. **In System Preferences, click Startup Disk, and then click either your Windows partition or your Mac partition.**

   Later, you can create a second workflow to choose your other disk, if you want.

5. **Click Restart. In the confirmation box, click Restart again.**

   Don't worry; you're not actually going to restart right now. Instead, Automator pops to the front, nagging you about the fact that it has an open document with unsaved changes—that is, the workflow you're in the middle of making!

6. **Click Cancel.**

Now Mac OS X tells you that Automator canceled the restart you had asked for. Which, of course, you already know.

7. **Click OK. Click Stop in the Recording window.**

The Automator window reopens with a new Watch Me Do action in your workflow (Figure 7-15). The Events list shows you everything you did, step by step—right down to the clicking of the OK button in step 7. And *that* step should *not* be part of the workflow.

8. **Click the final step in the workflow action (which says "Click the 'OK' button") and press Delete.**

When you run the workflow, you'll see your cursor magically move from one step to the next, all by itself (well, with a *little* help from Automator). It repeats every hesitation, misstep, and pause in your original mouse motion. Fortunately, you can speed up a particular step by up to 10 times using the Speed slider (also shown in Figure 7-15).

All in all, the mantra to use when dealing with Automator and Watch Me Do is simple: If you can perform a task with a specific action, *use the action.* Use the Watch Me Do mode sparingly.

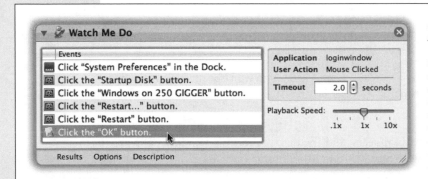

Figure 7-15:
After you've recorded a Watch Me Do workflow, the steps you took appear here. You can drag them up or down to rearrange them; click one and press Delete to eliminate it; or adjust the Playback Speed slider. For now, delete the unnecessary "Click OK" step.

The Script Menu, Resurrected

Hey, what happened to the Scripts menu? There were some pretty cool little tools in there!

It's still there. Both the Script menu and the 100 sample scripts that were in it are still available in Snow Leopard. There are some pretty cool scripts in there, too, like the one that spits out a handy typeface sampler to tack on your wall (so you can remember what each of your fonts looks like).

To resurrect them, open the AppleScript Editor program in your Utilities folder. Choose AppleScript→Preferences, and turn on "Show Script menu in menu bar."

Then download the free bonus PDF Appendix to this chapter, "What's in the Script Menu," and have some fun. It's on this book's "Missing CD" page at *www.missingmanuals.com*.

AppleScript

AppleScript is a powerful computer language that's been around since the days of Mac OS 7. Despite its maturity, however, AppleScript is often criticized by seasoned Mac programmers for being too simple, too easy to learn, and too much like English.

Of course, those are precisely the traits you *want* in a computer language—assuming, of course, that you want to use a computer language at all. If you're an everyday Mac fan—as opposed to some computer-science Ph.D.—AppleScript is by far the easiest programming language to use for automating your Mac.

You can think of AppleScript programs (called *scripts*) as software robots. A simple AppleScript might perform some daily task, like backing up your Documents folder. A more complex script can be pages long. In professional printing and publishing, where AppleScript has hard-core fans, a script might connect to a photographer's hard drive elsewhere on the Internet, download a photo from a predetermined folder, color-correct it in Photoshop, import it into a specified page-layout document, print a proof copy, and send a notification email to the editor—automatically.

Even if you're not aware of it, you use the technology that underlies AppleScript all the time. Behind the scenes, numerous components of your Mac communicate by sending *Apple Events,* which are messages bearing instructions or data that your programs send to one another. When you use the Show Original command for an alias, or the Get Info command for a file or folder, an Apple Event tells the Finder how to respond.

AppleScript has several important advantages over Automator—not least of which is its even greater power. It comes with a dedicated program just for writing out these scripts. It's the AppleScript Editor program that's sitting in your Applications→Utilities folder. (It was called Script Editor before Snow Leopard.)

Still, AppleScript is a *very* deep subject—so deep, in fact, that you'd need an entire book to do it justice. This chapter is an appetizer; a book like *AppleScript: The Missing Manual* is the seven-course meal.

Tip: You can also download an entire chapter about AppleScript—the chapter that appeared in the previous edition of this book—from this book's "Missing CD" page at *www.missingmanuals.com*.

Two Sample AppleScripts

Here are a couple of very simple AppleScripts, just to give you a taste.

Open a folder

The first one opens your Applications folder. Sure, you can do that in the Finder easily enough, but this one works no matter what program you're in.

Open up AppleScript Editor (which is in your Applications→Utilities folder). Type this:

```
tell application "Finder"
activate
open folder "Applications" of the startup disk
end tell
```

The result looks like Figure 7-16.

Now try it. Click the Run button. The first thing AppleScript Editor does is check your script for typos and syntax; if all is well, you'll see the script format itself, putting the verbs in bold, indenting pairs of matched commands, and so on. If that part went well, the script runs—and your Applications folder appears before you. Woo-hoo!

Now you can save your script (File→Save); choose Application as the file type. In the unlikely event that this were an actual *useful* script, instead of a lame sample, you could stash the new program on your Dock for anytime access.

So what do those commands mean? Here's the rundown:

Figure 7-16:
If you've never seen an AppleScript before, you may be surprised at how simple it looks. As you can probably guess from the commands in the window, this script simply opens the Applications folder in the Finder.

- **tell application "Finder"** tells Mac OS X which program is supposed to obey the following commands.

- **activate** brings the Finder to the foreground, much as you would by clicking its Dock icon.

- **open folder "Applications" of the startup disk** tells the Finder to open a new window, displaying the Applications folder on your main hard drive.

- **end tell** directs the Finder to go about its regular business, ignoring further AppleScript commands.

Tip: You can also edit this script to suit your needs. Try replacing "Applications" with "Users," for example, to make the script open the Users folder instead.

The metronome script

Mac OS X comes stocked with dozens of programs—everything but the kitchen sink. All right, everything but the kitchen sink and a *metronome.* How are you ever going to play the piano in even rhythm without a steady clicking sound provided by your Mac? Sure, sure, you can use GarageBand's metronome in a pinch, but that's like using an industrial pile driver to kill an ant.

Instead, you can use AppleScript to do the job for you. Open a new document in Script Editor (File→New, or ⌘-N), and type this:

```
display dialog "Welcome to the AppleScript Metronome"
set bpm to the text returned of (display dialog ¬
"How many beats per minute?" default answer 60)
set pauseBetweenBeeps to (60 / bpm)
repeat
beep
delay pauseBetweenBeeps
end repeat
```

Note: Don't actually type the ¬ character. That's programmerese for, "This is really all supposed to be on the same line, but I ran out of space on the page."

When you run this script, you see a dialog box that asks how many beats per minute you want the metronome to tick. Whatever number you type (for example, *120)* gets stored in a variable—a temporary holding tank within the script—that you've named *bpm.*

Next, the script calculates how long it must pause between beeps, and puts that fraction of a second into the "pauseBetweenBeeps." If you told the script to beep 120 times per minute, for example, "pauseBetweenBeeps" would be 0.5, since the script would have to pause half a second between beeps.

Finally, the script creates an endlessly repeating loop: beeping, pausing for the proper period, and then repeating.

Click Run to test out your script, and click Stop when you've had enough beeping.

AppleScript vs. Automator

AppleScript has hundreds and hundreds of uses: automating layout workflows that are too complicated for Automator, controlling programs that Automator doesn't recognize, and programming things that Automator can't handle.

Yet if all you do is look at AppleScript as a second choice to Automator, you're missing out on a lot of power. Truth is, AppleScript lets you do more than Automator will probably let you do in the next 10 *years;* it's just a lot geekier.

In the end, stick with Automator for simple things. If you need to use AppleScript to automate some aspect of your Mac, though, take pride; you're stepping up to a true power tool. (You can even combine the two, building AppleScripts right into your Automator workflows, thanks to the Run AppleScript action.)

Happy automating!

Windows on Macintosh

The very moment Apple announced in 2006 that all new Mac models would come with Intel chips inside, the geeks and the bloggers started going nuts. "Let's see," they thought. "Macs and PCs now use exactly the same memory, hard drives, monitors, mice, keyboards, networking protocols, *and processors.* By our calculations, it ought to be possible make a Mac run Windows!"

Now, some in the Cult of Macintosh were baffled by the very idea. Who on earth, they asked, wants to pollute the magnificence of the Mac with a headache like Windows?

Lots of people, as it turns out. Think of all the potential switchers who are tempted by the Mac's sleek looks yet worry about leaving Windows behind entirely. Or the people who love Apple's iLife programs but have jobs that rely on Microsoft Access, Outlook, or some other piece of Windows corporateware. Even true-blue Mac fans have occasionally looked longingly at the Windows-only games, Web sites, palmtop sync software, or movie download services they thought they'd never be able to use.

So hackers set about trying to make Windows run on Intel Macs almost immediately. But they were wasting their time; within weeks, Apple did the job for them—by inventing Boot Camp.

Actually, today, there are two ways to run Windows on a Mac with an Intel chip:

- **Restart it in Boot Camp.** Boot Camp is a little Apple program that lets you *restart* your Mac into Windows.

  At that point, it's a full-blown Windows PC, with no trace of the Mac on the screen. It runs at 100 percent of the speed of a real PC, because it is one. Compatibility with Windows software is excellent. The only drag is that you have to restart the Mac *again* to return to the familiar world of Mac OS X.

Snow Leopard Spots: What's cool, though, is that even when you're running Windows, you can still access your Mac files and folders, as described below. That's new in 10.6.

- **Run Windows in a window.** For $80 or so, you can eliminate the Boot Camp Bummer—the business of having to restart the Mac every time you want to switch its operating-system personality. You can buy a program like Parallels, VMWare Fusion, or VirtualBox, which let you run Windows *in a window*.

You're still running Mac OS X, and all your Mac files and programs are still available. But you've got a parallel universe—Microsoft Windows—running in a window simultaneously.

Compared with Boot Camp, this *virtualization software* offers only 90 percent of the speed and 90 percent of the software compatibility. But for thousands of people, the convenience of eliminating all those restarts—and gaining the freedom to copy and paste documents between Mac OS X and Windows programs—makes the Windows-in-a-window solution nearly irresistible.

Tip: There's nothing wrong with using both on the same Mac, by the way. In fact, the Parallels-type programs can use the same copy of Windows as Boot Camp, so you save disk space and don't have to manage two different Windows worlds.

Both techniques require you to provide your own copy of Windows. And both are described on the following pages.

Note: Remember, running Windows smoothly and quickly requires a Mac with an Intel chip inside. To find out if yours has one, choose ⌘→About This Mac. In the resulting dialog box, you'll see, next to the label Processor, either "Intel" something or "PowerPC."

FREQUENTLY ASKED QUESTION

The Virus Question

Doesn't running Windows on my Mac mean I'll be exposed to the nightmare of viruses and spyware, just like the rest of the Windows world?

As a matter of fact, yes.

If you install Windows on your Mac, you should also install Windows antivirus and antispyware software to protect that half of the computer. The world is crawling with commercial programs that do the job. There are also lots of free programs, like Microsoft Defender for spyware, and either AVG Antivirus (*www.free.grisoft.com*) or Avast Antivirus (*www.avast.com*) for viruses.

The good news is that even if your Windows installation gets infected, the Mac side of your computer is unaffected. Just as Mac OS X can't run Windows-only software like, say, Dragon NaturallySpeaking, it also can't run Windows virus software.

Some people, therefore, run Windows naked—*without* virus protection (especially when using Windows-in-a-window programs like Parallels and VMWare Fusion). If a virus does strike, no big deal; they just drag the infected copy of Windows to the Trash and install a fresh one!

Boot Camp

To set up Boot Camp, you need the proper ingredients:

- **An Intel-based Mac.** All Mac models introduced in 2006 and later have Intel chips inside. If you're not sure, choose →About This Mac; if the Processor line says something about Intel, you're good to go.

- **A copy of Windows XP, Windows Vista, or Windows 7.** Windows XP needs Service Pack 2. If you have an earlier copy, you're not *totally* out of luck, but you'll need a hacky approach that you can find online. Let Google be your friend.

  For Windows Vista or Windows 7, you need the Home Basic, Home Premium, Business, or Ultimate Edition. In both cases, an upgrade disc won't work; you need a full-installation copy. Also, Boot Camp requires the normal 32-bit editions of Windows.

Note: The fancy 64-bit versions of Vista and Windows 7 work only on recent Mac models. To find out if yours is eligible, see *http://support.apple.com/kb/HT1846*.

- **At least 10 gigs of free hard drive space** on your built-in hard drive, or a second internal drive. (You can't install Windows on an external drive using Boot Camp.)

- **A wired keyboard and mouse,** at least for the installation process. You can use a Bluetooth keyboard and mouse once the installation is complete.

Then you're ready to proceed.

Installing Boot Camp

Open your Applications→Utilities folder. Inside, open the program called Boot Camp Assistant.

Phase 1: Partition your drive

On the Introduction screen, you can print the instruction booklet, if you like (although the following pages contain the essential info). There's a lot of good, conservative legalese in that booklet: the importance of backing up your whole Mac before you begin, for example.

When you click Continue, you get the dialog box shown in Figure 8-1—the most interesting part of the whole process.

You're being asked to *partition*—subdivide—your hard drive (which can't already be partitioned), setting aside a certain amount of space that will hold your copy of Windows and all the PC software you decide to install. This partitioning process doesn't involve erasing your whole hard drive; all your stuff is perfectly safe.

The dialog box offers handy buttons like Divide Equally and Use 32 GB, but it also lets you drag a space-divider handle, as shown in Figure 8-1, to divide up your drive space between the Mac and Windows sides. Use your experience using Windows on a real PC, if you have one, to decide how big your Windows "hard drive" should be.

Most people choose to dedicate a swath of the main internal hard drive to the Windows partition. But if you have a second internal hard drive, you can also choose one of these options:

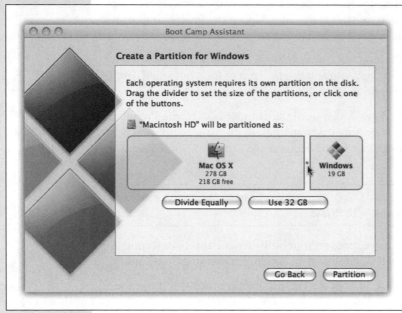

Figure 8-1:
How much hard drive space do you want to dedicate to your "PC"? It's not an idle question; whatever you give Windows is no longer available for your Mac. Drag the vertical handle between the Mac and Windows sides of this diagram.

- **Create a Second Partition.** The Boot Camp Assistant carves out a Windows partition from *that* drive.

- **Erase Disk and Create a Single Partition for Windows.** Just what it says.

POWER USERS' CLINIC

The Skinny on FAT32

If you're installing Windows XP and you choose an amount less than 32 gigabytes, you have a choice of two formatting schemes for your Windows "hard drive."

FAT32 may sound unappetizing, but it will give you one very cool feature that the other available format (NT File System) doesn't: the ability to drag files back and forth from the Windows side to the Mac side. (This works only when you've started up the computer in Mac OS X. When you're in Windows, you'll be able to see and open files on the Mac side of the hard drive, although you won't be able to edit them where they are. At least not without a commercial program like MacDrive [*www.macdrive.com*].)

If you choose a partition size *greater* than 32 GB, or if you're installing Windows Vista or Windows 7, then you *must* use NTFS. It's a more modern, flexible formatting scheme—it offers goodies like file-by-file access permissions, built-in file compression and encryption, journaling (page 832), and so on.

But on a Boot Camp Mac, NTFS has a drawback. When you're running from the Mac side, you'll be able to see what's on the Windows partition, but you won't be able to add, remove, or change any files.

Phase 2: Install Windows

On the Start Windows Installation screen, you're supposed to—hey!—start the Windows installation. Grab your Windows CD or DVD and slip it into the Mac. Its installer goes to work immediately.

Following the "I agree to whatever Microsoft's lawyers say" screen, Microsoft's installer asks which partition you want to put Windows on. It's *really* important to pick the right one. Play your cards wrong, and you could erase your whole *Mac* partition. So:

- **Windows XP.** Choose the partition (by pressing the up or down arrow keys) that's usually called "C: Partition3 <BOOTCAMP>."

  When you press Enter, you may now encounter another frightening-looking screen. Here, Windows invites you to format the new partition.

  If your Windows partition is less than 32 gigs, you get to choose between FAT32 or NTFS —a decision that, presumably, you've already made, having read the box on the facing page. Proceed as shown in Figure 8-2.

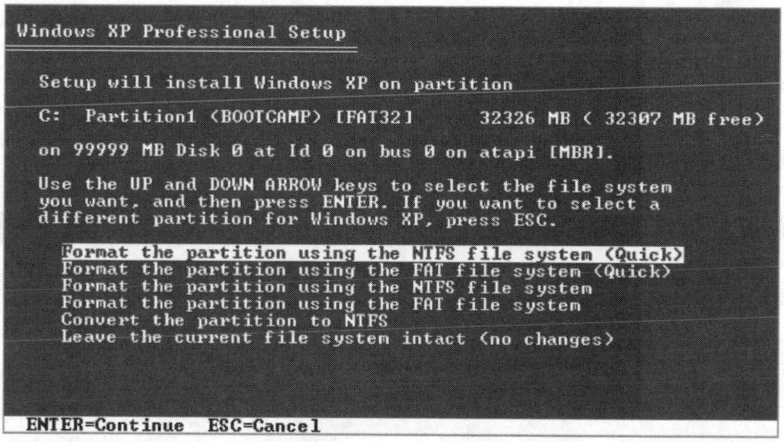

Figure 8-2:
Use the arrow keys to highlight either "Format the partition using the NTFS file system (Quick)" or "Format the partition using the FAT file system (Quick)." Then press Enter. On the following screen, type F to confirm the formatting, then Enter to confirm the whole thing.

```
Windows XP Professional Setup

  Setup will install Windows XP on partition

  C: Partition1 <BOOTCAMP> [FAT32]        32326 MB ( 32307 MB free)

  on 99999 MB Disk 0 at Id 0 on bus 0 on atapi [MBR].

  Use the UP and DOWN ARROW keys to select the file system
  you want, and then press ENTER. If you want to select a
  different partition for Windows XP, press ESC.

  Format the partition using the NTFS file system (Quick)
  Format the partition using the FAT file system (Quick)
  Format the partition using the NTFS file system
  Format the partition using the FAT file system
  Convert the partition to NTFS
  Leave the current file system intact (no changes)


  ENTER=Continue   ESC=Cancel
```

- **Windows Vista, Windows 7.** Choose the one called "Disk 0 Partition 3 BOOT-CAMP."

  Then click "Drive options (advanced)," click Format, click OK, and finally click Next. Your Windows partition is now formatted for NTFS, like it or not.

Now your Mac looks just like a PC that's having Windows installed. Be patient; sit around for half an hour as the Windows installer flits about, restarts, does what it has to do.

Phase 3: Install the drivers

When it's all over, a crazy, disorienting sight presents itself: your Mac, running Windows. There's no trace of the familiar desktop, Dock, or menu; it's Windows now, baby.

Walk through the Windows setup screens, creating an account, setting the time, and so on.

At this point, your Mac is actually a true Windows PC. You can install and run Windows programs, utilities, and even games; you'll discover that they run *really* fast and well.

But as Windows veterans know, every hardware feature of Windows requires a *driver*—a piece of software that tells the machine how to communicate with its own monitor, networking card, speakers, and so on. And it probably goes without saying that Windows doesn't include any drivers for *Apple's* hardware components.

That's why, at this point, you're supposed to insert your Mac OS X installation DVD; it contains all the drivers for the Mac's graphics card, Ethernet and AirPort networking, audio input and output, AirPort wireless antenna, iSight camera, brightness and volume keys, eject key, multitouch trackpad gestures, and Bluetooth transmitter. When this is all over, your white Apple remote control will even work to operate iTunes for Windows.

(It also installs a new Control Panel icon and system-tray pop-up menu, as described later in this chapter.)

WORKAROUND WORKSHOP

How to Right-Click

Every Windows computer comes with a *two*-button mouse. The left button clicks normally; the right button summons a shortcut menu containing commands for whatever you clicked. The Mac has shortcut menus, too, of course, but they're not quite as necessary as they are in Windows, where the shortcut menu is often the *only* place you'll find a certain command.

So when you're running Windows on your Mac, how are you supposed to right-click?

Well, you could get yourself a two-button mouse, of course. It works fine on a Mac (in Windows *or* in Mac OS X). In fact, most desktop Macs sold since 2006 come *with* a two-button mouse, called the Mighty Mouse. It doesn't *appear* to have two buttons, but you can actually click two different spots on its sloping far side. See page 340 for instructions on

turning this feature on. The Mighty Mouse works fine for right-clicking in Windows.

If you have a recent Mac laptop, you can trigger a right-click using a sneaky trick: Put *two* fingertips on the trackpad, and then click the button. (That's an option you can turn on or off in the Trackpad panel of System Preferences.)

Alternatively, if that's too much to learn, just highlight whatever you want to right-click and then press Shift-F10.

If you're stuck with a one-button Mac mouse, and none of these options works for you, use the Apple Mouse Utility program for Windows. (You can download it from this book's "Missing CD" page at *www.missingmanuals.com.*) It lets you Control-click to simulate a right-click while you're running Windows.

Note: Unbeknownst to you, the Snow Leopard DVD is actually a dual-mode disc. When you insert it into a Mac running Mac OS X, it appears as the Snow Leopard installer you know and love. But when you slip it into a PC, its secret Windows partition appears—and automatically opens the Mac driver installer!

When you insert the Mac OS X disc, the driver installer opens and begins work automatically. Click past the Welcome and License Agreement screens, and then click Install. You'll see a lot of dialog boxes come and go; just leave it alone (and don't click Cancel).

A few words of advice:

- If the installation seems to stall, Windows may be waiting for you to click OK or Next in a window that's hidden behind other windows. Inspect the taskbar and look behind open windows.

- Windows XP concludes by presenting the Found New Hardware Wizard. Go ahead and agree to update your drivers.

When it's all over, a dialog box asks you to restart the computer; click Restart. When the machine comes to, it's a much more functional Windows Mac. (And it has an online Boot Camp Help window waiting for you on the screen.)

Forth and Back, Windows/Mac

From now on, your main interaction with Boot Camp will be telling it what kind of computer you want your Mac to be today: a Windows machine or a Mac.

Presumably, though, you'll prefer one operating system *most* of the time. Figure 8-3 (top and middle) shows how you specify your favorite.

Tip: If you're running Windows and you just want to get back to Mac OS X right now, you don't have to bother with all the steps shown in Figure 8-3. Instead, click the Boot Camp system-tray icon and, from the shortcut menu, choose Restart in Mac OS X.

From now on, each time you turn on the Mac, it starts up in the operating system you've selected.

If you ever need to switch—when you need Windows just for one quick job, for example—press the Option key as the Mac is starting up. You'll see something like the icons shown in Figure 8-3 (bottom).

Tip: For nerds only: When you're running Windows, you can now reboot in Mac OS X just by typing a command at the Windows command line (Start→All Programs→Accessories→Command Prompt). Type this, exactly as shown, and then tap Enter. *c:\progra~1\Bootca~1\bootcamp.exe -StartupDisk "Mac OS" Shutdown /r /t 0*

Keyboard Translation Guide

Now, if you really want to learn about Windows, you need *Windows XP: The Missing Manual* (available in Home and Pro editions), *Windows Vista: The Missing Manual,* or *Windows 7: The Missing Manual.*

But suggesting that you go buy *another* book would be tacky. So here's just enough to get by.

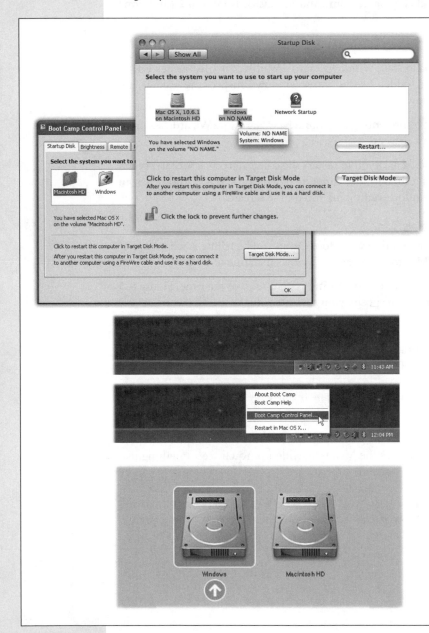

Figure 8-3:

Top: To choose your preferred operating system—the one that starts up automatically unless you intervene—choose ⬧→System Preferences. Click Startup Disk, and then click the icon for either Mac OS X or Windows. Next, either click Restart (if you want to switch right now) or close the panel. The identical controls are available when you're running Windows, thanks to the new Boot Camp Control Panel.

Middle: To open the Boot Camp Control Panel, choose its name from its new icon in the Windows system tray.

Bottom: This display, known as the Startup Manager, appears when you press Option during startup. It displays all the disk icons, or disk partitions, that contain bootable operating systems. Just click the name of the partition you want, and then click the Continue arrow.

First of all, a Mac keyboard and a Windows keyboard aren't the same. Each has keys that would strike the other as extremely goofy. Still, you can trigger almost any keystroke Windows is expecting by substituting special Apple-keystrokes, like this:

Windows keystroke	Apple keystroke
Control-Alt-Delete	Control-Option-Delete
Alt	Option
Backspace	Delete
Delete (forward delete)	⌦ (on laptops, Fn-Delete)
Enter	Return or Enter
Num lock	Clear (laptops; Fn-F6)
Print Screen	F14 (laptops: Fn-F11)
Print active window	Option-F14 (laptops: Option-Fn-F11)
⊞ key	⌘

The keyboard shortcuts in your programs are *mostly* the same as on the Mac, but you have to substitute the Ctrl key for the ⌘ key. So in Windows programs, Copy, Save, and Print are Ctrl-C, Ctrl-S, and Ctrl-P.

Similarly, the Alt key is the Windows equivalent of the Option key.

Tip: You know that awesome two-finger scrolling trick on Mac laptops (page 347)? Guess what? It works when you're running Windows, too.

Accessing Mac Files from the Dark Side—and Vice Versa

One nice feature in Snow Leopard: When you've started up in one operating system, it's much easier to access documents that "belong" to the other one. For example:

- When you're running Mac OS X, you can get to the documents you created while you were running Windows, which is a huge convenience. Just double-click the Windows disk icon (called NO NAME or Untitled), and then navigate to the Documents and Settings→[your account name]→My Documents (or Desktop).

  If you formatted your Windows XP partition using the FAT format as described earlier, you can copy files to *or* from this partition, and even open them up for editing on the Mac side. If you used NTFS, though, you can only copy them *to* the Mac side, or open them without the ability to edit them.

Tip: Actually, there's no reason your Windows "drive" has to be called NO NAME or Untitled. You can rename it as you would any other icon, either in Windows or in Mac OS X. (That's if you used the FAT format. If you used NTFS, you can't change the name in Mac OS X.)

- When you're running Windows, you can get to your Mac documents, too (this is the part that's new in Snow Leopard). Click Start→Computer. In the resulting window, you'll see an icon representing your Mac's hard-drive partition. Open it up.

You can see and open these files. But if you want to edit them, you have to copy them to your Windows world first—onto the desktop, for example, or into a folder. (The Mac partition is "read-only" in this way, Apple says, to avoid the possibility that your Mac stuff could get contaminated by Windows viruses.)

Tip: If you did want to edit Mac files from within Windows, one solution is to buy a $50 program called MacDrive (*www.mediafour.com*). Another solution: Use a disk that both Mac OS X and Windows "see," and keep your shared files on that. A flash drive works beautifully for this. So does your iDisk (page 691) or a shared drive on the network.

Windows in a Window

The problem with Boot Camp is that every time you switch to or from Windows, you have to close down everything you were working on and restart the computer—and reverse the process when you're done. You lose two or three minutes each way. And you can't copy and paste between Mac and Windows programs.

There is another way: an $80 utility called Parallels Desktop for Mac OS X (*www.parallels.com*) and its rival, VMWare Fusion (*www.vmware.com*). These programs let you run Windows and Mac OS X *simultaneously*; Windows hangs out in a window of its own, while the Mac is running Mac OS X (Figure 8-4). You're getting about 90

UP TO SPEED

Removing Windows

Maybe you're a switcher who held onto Windows because you were worried that you'd need it. Maybe you're finished with the project, the job, or the phase of life that required you to use Windows on your Mac. But one way or another, there may come a time when you want to get rid of your Windows installation and reclaim all the hard drive space it was using.

Not only can you do that, but the process won't touch anything that's already on the Mac side. You don't have to erase your entire hard drive or anything—Snow Leopard simply erases what's on the Windows partition of your hard drive, and then adds that disk space back to your main, *Mac* partition.

To do this, start by making sure you've rescued anything worth saving from the Windows side of your computer—it's about to be erased.

Start up in Mac OS X, quit all open programs, and make sure

nobody's logged in but you. Now open up the Boot Camp Assistant program in your Applications→Utilities folder.

On the welcome screen, click "Restore the startup disk to a single volume," and then click Continue. That's all there is to it.

Special notes for special setups: If you installed Windows on a separate hard drive, rather than a partition of your *main* hard drive, don't bother with all this. Just erase the Windows hard drive using Disk Utility, as described in Chapter 10, and format it as a Mac drive.

On the other hand, if your Mac has more than one internal hard drive and you created a Windows partition on one of them (rather than taking it over completely), then open Boot Camp Assistant as described above. This time, though, click "Create or remove a Windows partition," click Continue, click the Windows disk, and then click "Restore to a single Mac OS partition."

---

percent of Boot Camp's Windows speed—not fast enough for 3-D games, but plenty fast for just about everything else.

Once again, you have to supply your own copy of Windows for the installation process. This time, though, it can be any version of Windows, all the way back to Windows 3.1—or even Linux, FreeBSD, Solaris, OS/2, or MS-DOS.

Having virtualization software on your Mac is a beautiful thing. You can be working on a design in iWork, duck into a Microsoft Access database (Windows only), look up an address, copy it, and paste it back into the Mac program.

And what if you can't decide whether to use Boot Camp (fast and feature-complete, but requires restarting) or Parallels/Fusion (fast and no restarting, but no 3-D games)? No problem—install both. They coexist beautifully on a single Mac and can even use the same copy of Windows.

Together, they turn the Macintosh into the Uni-Computer: the single machine that can run nearly 100 percent of the world's software catalog.

Virtualization Tip-O-Rama

Mastering Parallels or Fusion means mastering Windows, of course, but it also means mastering these tips:

Figure 8-4:
The strangest sight you ever did see: Mac OS X and Windows XP. On the same screen. At the same time. Courtesy of VMWare Fusion. Parallels is very similar.

- You don't *have* to run Windows in a window. With one keystroke, you can make your Windows simulator cover the entire screen. You're still actually running two operating systems at once, but the whole Mac world is hidden for the moment so you can exploit your full screen. Just choose View→Full Screen.

Tip: Or use the keystroke Alt-Enter (Parallels) or Ctrl-⌘-Return (Fusion) to enter and exit Full Screen mode.

- Conversely, both Parallels and Fusion offer something called *Coherence* or *Unity* mode, in which there's no trace of the Windows desktop. Instead, each Windows program floats in its own disembodied window, just like a Mac program; the Mac OS X desktop lies reassuringly in the background.

Tip: In Fusion's Unity mode, you can access your Computer, Documents, Network, Control Panel, Search, and Run commands right from Fusion's Dock icon or launch palette, so you won't even care that there's no Start menu.

In Parallels, press Alt+Ctrl+Shift to enter or exit Coherence mode. In Fusion, hit Ctrl-⌘-U for Unity mode.

Tip: In Fusion, in Unity view, you can use the usual Mac keystrokes for Cut, Copy, and Paste within Windows applications (⌘-X, ⌘-C, and ⌘-V). In Parallels, on the other hand, you can remap all Windows Control-key shortcuts to the ⌘ key in Preferences.

- To send the "three-fingered salute" when things have locked up in Windows (usually Ctrl+Alt+Delete), press Control-Option-D (Fusion) or Ctrl+Fn+Alt+Delete (Parallels). Or use the Send Ctrl-Alt-Delete command in the menus.

- You can drag files back and forth between the Mac and Windows universes. Just drag icons into, or out of, the Windows window.

POWER USERS' CLINIC

Beyond the Big Names

Parallels and VMWare Fusion are bloodthirsty rivals. New versions tumble out with alarming frequency, each designed to one-up its rival.

Both also let you specify which program—Mac *or* Windows—opens when you double-click documents of specific types (like .jpeg or .doc). That's yet another way Windows becomes a full player on the Mac team.

Still, these aren't the only options. A program called Virtual-Box (*www.virtualbox.org*) is not as polished or full-featured as its big-name rivals, but it's not as expensive, either; in fact, it's free. That's because it's open-source software, meaning that programmers around the world volunteer to collaborate on it.

Finally, several efforts are afoot to create software that lets you run Windows software *without Windows.* The most promising one is a $60 program called CrossOver (*www. codeweavers.com*).

Sure enough, CrossOver-compatible Windows programs open up and run in Mac OS X just as though they were real Mac programs—without your having to own, install, or fire up a copy of Windows itself.

Unfortunately, the list of compatible programs is tiny; fewer than 20 Windows programs work flawlessly in CrossOver. The list of programs that *mostly* work is longer, though, so check the list on CrossOver's Web site to see if what you need is CrossOver-friendly.

- If you have a one-button mouse, you can "right-click" in Parallels by Control-Shift-clicking. In Fusion, Control-click instead. On Mac laptops, you can right-click by putting two fingers on the trackpad as you click.

- When you quit the virtualization program, you're not really "shutting down" the PC; you're just *suspending* it, or putting it to sleep. When you double-click the Parallels/VMWare icon again, everything in your Windows world is exactly as you left it.

- Your entire Windows universe of files, folders, and programs is represented by a single file on your hard drive. In Parallels, it's in your Home→Library→Parallels folder. In Fusion, it's in your Home→Documents→Virtual Machines folder.

  That's super convenient, because it means you can back up your entire Windows "computer" by dragging a single icon to another drive. And if your Windows world ever gets a virus or spyware infestation, you can drag the entire thing to the Trash—and restore Windows from that clean backup.

Life with Microsoft Exchange

In the corporate world, Microsoft Exchange is the 800-pound gorilla. It's the networking software that runs the email, address book, and calendars for hundreds or thousands of employees. All of this communicates with a central master database whose heart beats away in some closet or back room at your company's headquarters.

For years, Macs have been second-class citizens in Corporate America. As long as they couldn't talk to the Exchange brain, they weren't much use outside of the graphic-design department. (You could buy add-on software or muck about with workarounds, but you always felt like a weirdo.)

In Snow Leopard, for the first time, Exchange compatibility is built in. In iCal, your company's Exchange calendar shows up. In Address Book, your company's names and addresses show up. In Mail, you can get all your corporate email. Best of all, this information shows up side by side with your own personal data, so you can have it all in one place. All the conveniences of Snow Leopard now apply to your corporate email: Spotlight, Quick Look, data detectors, and so on.

The irony is that Mac OS X now comes with built-in Exchange compatibility—and Microsoft Windows *doesn't.* (You have to buy Microsoft Outlook separately.)

If you're lucky—that is, if your company is using Exchange 2007 or later—setting this up could not be easier.

Connecting to Exchange

To connect to your company's Exchange system, open Mail (Chapter 19). Choose Mail→Preferences. Click the **+** below the list of email accounts; proceed as shown in Figure 8-5.

When you click Continue, one of two things happen:

- You're treated to a message that says, "Mail found a server account for the email address you provided. The following account will be set up on your computer." You're all set.

  That box offers an "Also set up" item featuring two delicious checkboxes: "Address Book contacts" and "iCal calendars." Hard to think why you'd want to turn these off; they'll do all the work for you.

- Your Mac doesn't find the server. In that case, either (a) your company doesn't use Exchange 2007 or later or (b) your network geek hasn't turned on Exchange *Autodiscovery*. In that case, you have no choice but to call that person over to your desk and either (a) harangue him for not turning on Autodiscovery or (b) have him fill in the server address and other boxes by hand.

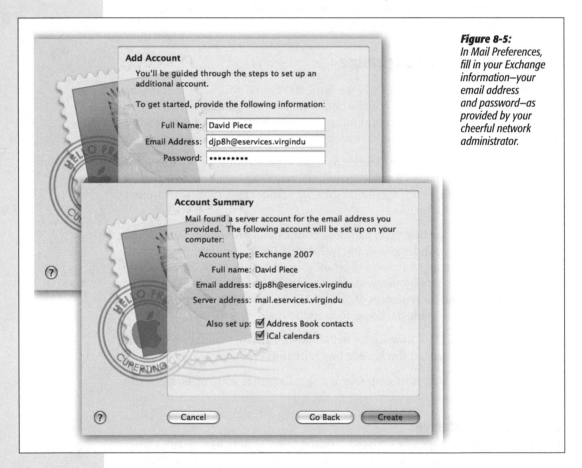

Figure 8-5:
In Mail Preferences, fill in your Exchange information—your email address and password—as provided by your cheerful network administrator.

Note: Here's a tip for the network administrator who gets to fill in this information, courtesy of Apple: "Enter the fully qualified domain name for the organization's Exchange Client Access Server (CAS). (For example, exchange01.example.com, not exchange01.) Note that the CAS doesn't necessarily share the same address as the Outlook Web Access (OWA) Server—although they often do. Http prefixes are not required." Hope you know what that means.

Exchange in Mail

Once everything's set up, open Mail. If you have a lot of mail, it may take a moment (or several) for Mail to synchronize with the Exchange server and display your messages. But it gets there eventually.

Your Exchange account appears with its own heading, beneath your personal accounts (Figure 8-6).

Now you can send and receive email, create notes and to-do items, respond to emailed invitations, and so on. All the Mail features described in Chapter 19 are ready to go: Spotlight can search all your accounts simultaneously, Smart Folders can round up messages from one account or all of them, Quick Look can show you attachments without your having to open them in a separate program, and so on.

Figure 8-6:
Once everything's hooked up, a new heading appears in Mail (left), iCal (middle), and Address Book (right), named after your Exchange account. That's your corporate life, which you can hide and show at will.

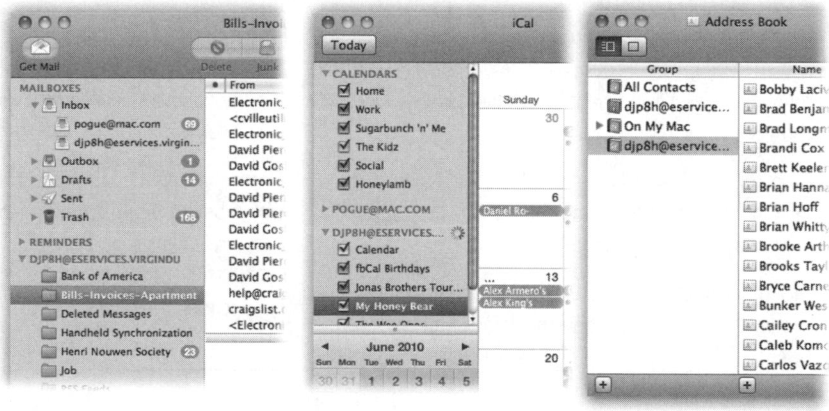

Exchange in Address Book

Your company's Global Address Lists show up in Address Book (Chapter 19) in a "folder" on the left side called Exchange, as shown at right in Figure 8-6. You can work with them just as you would your own addresses: Put them in groups, click an address to see where it is in Google Maps, and so on. When you're addressing an email message or a calendar invitation, the autocomplete feature now proposes names from both your personal and corporate address books.

Exchange in iCal

Your corporate appointments now show up in the Mac's calendar program (Chapter 10), neatly filed under their own heading. Each appointment category shows up with its own checkbox, as usual, so you can hide and show them as you see fit—even when they're mixed right in with your personal agenda.

The big payoff here is scheduling meetings. When you click "add invitees" for an appointment (page 367), iCal can show you a graph of your coworkers' free time, and open slots for your conference room, so you can find a time when they're free.

GEM IN THE ROUGH

Delegating Your Calendars

Once you're all Exchanged up, you can even *delegate* your calendar—that is, permit someone else on your corporate network to see (and, if you wish, edit) them from across the network. That's handy when you're a busy executive and you want your personal assistant to help you manage your busy life, or when you're going to be out of town and you've authorized a trusted minion to carry on with your calendar in your absence.

(This is not the same as *publishing* your calendar as described in Chapter 10. Your Exchange calendar isn't actually going to move. It'll sit right there on the server—you're just giving someone else access to it.)

To set this up, choose iCal→Preferences→Accounts. (If you have more than one account, choose the one you want to share from the Accounts list.)

Click Delegation. Click Edit. On the Manage Account Access screen, click **+**, and then type the name of the person you

want to share your calendar with. You can also specify how much access you want that person to have; "Read Only" means they can just see your life, and "Read & Write" means they can actually edit it. You can grant different levels of access to your calendar and your Tasks list.

Finally, click Done.

Now change hats. Suppose you're the minion—er, trusted assistant.

On your Mac, choose iCal→Preferences→Accounts. Click the account that's been shared with you. Click **+**; type your boss's name.

Finally, turn on the Show checkbox. Close the Preferences dialog box to return to the main iCal display. Here, your boss's calendars (appointment categories) show up in the left-side list; turn on the checkboxes of the ones you want to appear on the calendar grid

---

Part Three: The Components of Mac OS X

3

System Preferences

The hub of Mac customization is System Preferences, the modern-day successor to the old Control Panel (Windows) or Control Panels (previous Mac systems). Some of its panels are extremely important, because their settings determine whether or not you can connect to a network or go online to exchange email. Others handle the more cosmetic aspects of customizing Mac OS X.

This chapter guides you through the entire System Preferences program, panel by panel.

Tip: Only a system administrator (page 464) can change settings that affect everyone who shares a certain machine: its Internet settings, Energy Saver settings, and so on. If you see a bunch of controls that are dimmed and unavailable, now you know why.

A tiny padlock in the lower-left corner of a panel is the other telltale sign. If you, a nonadministrator, would like to edit some settings, then call an administrator over to your Mac and ask him to click the lock, input his password, and supervise your tweaks.

The System Preferences Window

You can open System Preferences in dozens of ways:

- Choose its name from the menu.

- Click its icon in the Dock.

- Press Option-volume key (◀, ◀», or ◀») on the top row of the keyboard), Option-brightness keys (☀ or ☀), or on laptops that have them, Option-keyboard-brightness keys (:-: or :·:). These tricks open the Sound and Displays panes, but you can then click Show All or press ⌘-L to see the full spread.

- If you know the name of the System Preferences panel you want, it's often quicker to use Spotlight. To open Energy Saver, for example, hit ⌘-space, type *ener,* and then press ⌘-Return. See Chapter 3 for more on operating Spotlight from the keyboard.

- Here's a new method in Snow Leopard that saves you a couple of steps. Turns out that if you put the System Preferences icon in your *Dock* (Chapter 4), you can open it *and* jump to a particular preference panel in one smooth move: Use your mouse to click-and-hold the System Preferences icon. You get a pop-up menu of every single System Preferences panel.

Suppose, then, that by hook or by crook, you've figured out how to open System Preferences. You'll notice that, at first, the rows of icons are grouped according to function: Personal, Hardware, and so on (Figure 9-1, top). But you can also view them in tidy alphabetical order, as shown at bottom in Figure 9-1. That can spare you the ritual of hunting through various rows just to find a certain panel icon whose name you

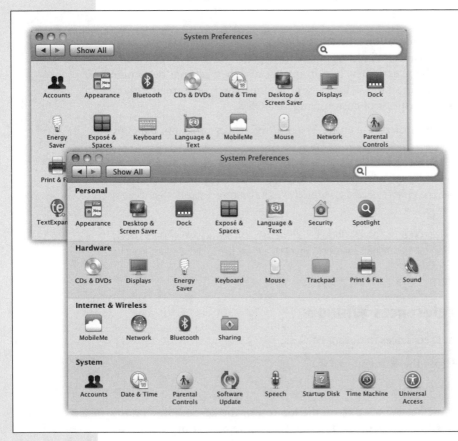

Figure 9-1:
You can view your System Preferences icons alphabetically (top), rather than in rows of arbitrary categories (bottom); just choose View→Organize Alphabetically. This approach not only saves space, but also makes finding a certain panel much easier, because you don't need to worry about which category it's in.

already know. (Quick, without looking: Which row is Date & Time in?) This chapter describes the various panels following this alphabetical arrangement.

Either way, when you click one of the icons, the corresponding controls appear in the main System Preferences window. To access a different preference pane, you have a number of options:

- **Fast:** When System Preferences first opens, the insertion point is blinking in the new System Preferences search box. (If the insertion point is *not* blinking there, press ⌘-F.) Type a few letters of *volume, resolution, wallpaper, wireless,* or whatever feature you want to adjust. In a literal illustration of Spotlight's power, the System Preferences window darkens *except* for the icons where you'll find relevant controls (Figure 9-2). Click the name or icon of the one that looks the most promising.

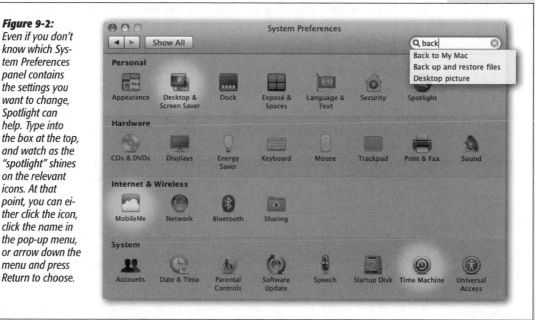

Figure 9-2:
Even if you don't know which System Preferences panel contains the settings you want to change, Spotlight can help. Type into the box at the top, and watch as the "spotlight" shines on the relevant icons. At that point, you can either click the icon, click the name in the pop-up menu, or arrow down the menu and press Return to choose.

- **Faster:** Click the Show All icon in the upper-left corner of the window (or press ⌘-L, a shortcut worth learning). Then click the icon of the new panel you want.

- **Fastest:** Choose any panel's name from the View menu—or from the System Preferences Dock icon pop-up menu described above.

Note: Once System Preferences is actually open, the click-and-hold thing no longer produces the list of all preference panes. Instead, you need to Control-click (or right-click) the System Preferences Dock icon to get that menu.

Here, then, is your grand tour of all 27 of Snow Leopard's built-in System Preferences panes. (You may have a couple more or fewer, depending on whether you have a laptop or a desktop Mac. And if you've installed any non-Apple panes, they appear in their own row of System Preferences, called Other.)

Accounts

This is the master list of people who are allowed to log into your Mac. It's where you can adjust their passwords, startup pictures, self-opening startup items, permissions to use various features of the Mac, and other security tools. All of this is described in Chapter 12.

Appearance

This panel is mostly about how things look on the screen: windows, menus, buttons, scroll bars, and fonts. Nothing you find here lets you perform any *radical* surgery on the overall Mac OS X look—but you can tweak certain settings to match your personal style.

Changing Colors

Two pop-up menus let you crank up or tone down Mac OS X's overall colorfulness:

- **Appearance.** Choose between Blue and Graphite. Blue refers to Mac OS X's factory setting—bright, candy-colored scroll-bar handles, progress bars,  menu, and pulsing OK buttons—and those shiny red, yellow, and green buttons in the corner of every window. If you, like some graphics professionals, find all this circus-poster coloring a bit distracting, then choose Graphite, which renders all those interface elements in various shades of gray.

- **Highlight color.** When you drag your cursor across text, its background changes color to indicate that you've selected it. Exactly what color the background becomes is up to you—just choose the shade you want using the pop-up menu. The Highlight color also affects such subtleties as the lines on the inside of a window as you drag an icon into it.

If you choose Other, the Color Picker palette appears, from which you can choose any color your Mac is capable of displaying (page 199).

Tweaking the Scroll Bars

The two sets of radio buttons control the scroll-bar arrow buttons of all your windows. You can keep these arrows together at one end of the scroll bar, or you can split them up so the "up" arrow sits at the top of the scroll bar and the "down" arrow is at the bottom. (Horizontal scroll bars are similarly affected.) For details on the "Jump to the next page" and "Jump to here" options, see page 31.

Tip: And what if you want the ultimate convenience: both arrows at both ends of the scroll bar? You just need a moment alone with TinkerTool, described on page 657.

You can also turn on these checkboxes:

- **Use smooth scrolling.** This option affects only one tiny situation: when you click (or hold the cursor down) inside the empty area of the scroll bar (not on the handle, and not on the arrow buttons). And it makes only one tiny change: Instead of jumping abruptly from screen to screen, the window lurches with slight accelerations and decelerations, so that the paragraph you're eyeing never jumps suddenly out of view.

- **Minimize when double-clicking a window title bar.** This option provides another way to minimize a window. In addition to the tiny yellow Minimize button at the upper-left corner of the window, you now have a much bigger target—the entire title bar.

Number of Recent Items

Just how many of your recently opened documents and applications do you want the Mac to show using the Recent Items command in the menu? Pick a number from the pop-up menus. For example, you might choose 30 for documents, 20 for programs, and 5 for servers.

Font Smoothing Style

The Mac's built in text-smoothing (*antialiasing*) feature is supposed to produce smoother, more commercial-looking text anywhere it appears on your Mac: in word processing documents, email messages, Web pages, and so on.

Experiment with the on/off checkbox—"Use LCD font smoothing when available," for example—to see how you like the effect. Either way, it's fairly subtle. (See Figure 9-3.) Furthermore, unlike most System Preferences, this one has no effect until the next time you open the program in question. In the Finder, for example, you won't notice the difference until you log out and log back in again.

Figure 9-3:
Top: The same 24-point type with text smoothing turned on (top) and off, shown magnified for your inspection pleasure. In Snow Leopard, you no longer get a choice of degrees of smoothing—it's just on or off.

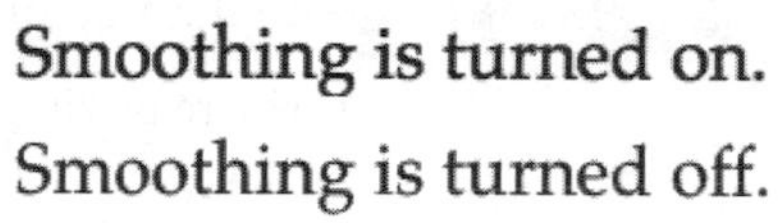

Smoothing is turned on.

Smoothing is turned off.

Turning Off Smoothing on Tiny Fonts

At smaller type sizes (10-point and smaller), you might find that text is actually *less* readable with font smoothing turned on. It all depends upon the font, the size, your monitor, and your taste. For that reason, this pop-up menu lets you choose a cutoff point. If you choose 12 here, for example, then 12-point (and smaller) type still appears crisp and sharp; only larger type, such as headlines, displays the graceful edge smoothing. You can choose a size cutoff as low as 4-point.

(None of these settings affect your printouts, only the onscreen display.)

Bluetooth

Bluetooth is a short-range, low-power, wireless *cable-elimination* technology. It's designed to connect gadgets in pairings that make sense, like cellphone+earpiece, wireless keyboard+Mac, or Mac+cellphone (to connect to the Internet or to transmit files).

Now, you wouldn't want the guy in the next cubicle to be able to operate *your* Mac using *his* Bluetooth keyboard. So the first step in any Bluetooth relationship is *pairing*, where you formally introduce the two gadgets that will be communicating. Here's how that goes:

1. **Open System Preferences→Bluetooth.**

   Make sure the On checkbox is turned on. (The only reason to turn it off is to save laptop battery power.) Also make sure Discoverable is turned on; that makes the Mac "visible" to other Bluetooth gadgets in range.

2. **Click the + button below the list at left.**

   The Bluetooth Setup Assistant opens. After a moment, it displays the names of all Bluetooth gadgets it can sniff out: nearby headsets, laptops, cellphones, and so on. Usually, it finds the one you're trying to pair.

3. **Click the gadget you want to connect to, and then click Continue.**

   If you're pairing a mobile phone or something else that has a keypad or keyboard, the Mac now displays a large, eight-digit *passcode*. It's like a password, except you'll have to input it only this once, to confirm that *you* are the true owner of both the Mac and the gadget. (If it weren't for this passcode business, some guy next to you at the airport could enjoy free laptop Internet access through the cellphone in *your* pocket.)

   At this point, your phone or palmtop displays a message to the effect that you have 30 seconds to type that passcode. Do it. When the gadget asks if you want to pair with the Mac and connect to it, say yes.

   If you're pairing a phone or palmtop, the Mac now asks *which* sorts of Bluetooth syncing you want to do. For example, it can copy your iCal appointments, as well as your Address Book, to the phone or palmtop.

   (Or, if there are *no* kinds of Bluetooth syncing that your Mac can do with the gadget—for example, unless your cellphone offers Bluetooth file transfers, there may be nothing it can accomplish by talking to your Mac—an error message tells you that, too.)

Tip: A few Bluetooth phones, including the iPhone, can even get your laptop onto the Internet via the cellular airwaves. No WiFi required—the phone never even leaves your pocket, and your laptop can get online wherever there's a cellphone signal.

This is a special setup, however, involving signing up with your cell carrier (and paying an additional monthly fee). If you've signed up, then turn on the third option here ("Access the Internet").

When it's all over, the new gadget is listed in the left-side panel, in the list of Bluetooth cellphones, headsets, and other stuff that you've previously introduced to this Mac. Click the **+** button to open the Bluetooth Setup Assistant again, or the **−** button to delete one of the listed items.

Advanced Options

If you click Advanced, you arrive at a pop-up panel with a few more tweaky Bluetoothisms:

Figure 9-4:
Top: This System Preferences panel reveals a list of every Bluetooth gadget your Mac knows about. Click a Bluetooth device to see details.

Middle: The Bluetooth Setup Assistant scans the area for Bluetooth gadgets and, after a moment, lists them. Click one, and then click Continue.

Bottom: Where security is an issue, the Assistant offers you the chance to pair your Bluetooth device with the Mac. To prove that you're really the owner of both the laptop and the phone, the Mac displays a one-time password, which you have 30 seconds to type into the phone. Once that's done, you're free to use the phone's Internet connection without any further muss, fuss, or passwords.

- **Open Bluetooth Assistant at startup when no input device is present.** Here's where you can tell the Bluetooth Setup Assistant to open up automatically when the Mac thinks no keyboard and mouse are attached (because it assumes that you have a wireless Bluetooth keyboard and mouse that have yet to be set up).

- **Allow Bluetooth devices to wake this computer.** Turn this on if you want to be able to wake up a sleeping Mac when you press a key, just like a wired keyboard does.

- **Prompt for all incoming audio requests.** The Mac will let you know if your Bluetooth cellphone, music player, or another music gadget tries to connect.

- **Share my Internet connection with other Bluetooth devices.** Pretty obscure—but when the future arrives, Mac OS X will be ready. The PAN service referred to in the description of this item lets your Mac, which presumably has a wired or WiFi Internet connection, share that connection with Bluetooth gadgets (like palmtops) that *don't* have an Internet connection.

- **Serial ports.** This list identifies which simulated connections are present at the moment. It's a reference to those different Bluetooth *profiles* (features) that various gadgets can handle. They include **Bluetooth File Transfer** (other people with Bluetooth Macs can see a list of what's in your Public folder and help themselves; see page 246), **Bluetooth File Exchange** (other people can send files to you using Bluetooth; page 244), **Bluetooth-PDA-Sync** (personal digital assistants—that is, Palm organizers—can sync with your Mac via Bluetooth); and so on.

Tip: If you Option-click the Bluetooth menulet (✷), you get a couple of lines of secret Bluetooth details. The menu reveals the name of your Mac, as it will appear to other Bluetooth wireless gadgets; the On/Off status of Bluetooth on your Mac; and the version of Bluetooth you're running.

CDs & DVDs

This handy pane (Figure 9-5) lets you tell the Mac what it should do when it detects that you've inserted a CD or DVD. For example, when you insert a music CD, you probably want iTunes (Chapter 11) to open automatically so you can listen to the CD or convert its musical contents to MP3 or AAC files on your hard drive. Similarly, when you insert a picture CD (such as a Kodak Photo CD), you probably want iPhoto to open in readiness to import the pictures from the CD into your photo

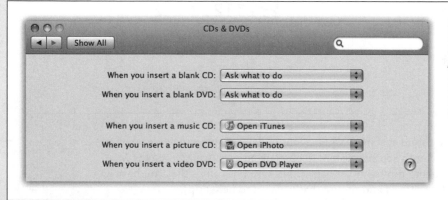

Figure 9-5:
You can tell the Mac exactly which program to launch when you insert each kind of disc, or tell it to do nothing at all.

collection. And when you insert a DVD from Blockbuster, you want the Mac's DVD Player program to open.

For each kind of disc (blank CD, blank DVD, music CD, picture CD, or video DVD), the pop-up menu lets you choose options like these:

- **Ask what to do.** A dialog box appears that asks what you want to do with the newly inserted disc.

- **Open (iDVD, iTunes, iPhoto, DVD Player…).** The Mac can open a certain program automatically when you insert the disc. When the day comes that somebody writes a better music player than iTunes, or a better digital shoebox than iPhoto, then you can use the "Open other application" option.

- **Run script.** If you've become handy writing or downloading AppleScript programs (Chapter 7), you can schedule one of your own scripts to take over from here. For example, you can set things up so that inserting a blank CD automatically copies your Home folder onto it for backup purposes.

- **Ignore.** The Mac won't do anything when you insert a disc except display its icon on the desktop. (If it's a blank disc, the Mac does nothing at all.)

System Preferences: Under the Hood

The entire System Preferences program is nothing more than a series of graphical front ends for underlying Unix settings. (If you know Unix and feel so inclined you can, in fact, bypass the System Preferences panel completely. Using the *defaults* command, you can use Mac OS X's Terminal program to make any of the changes described in this chapter—and many others.)

The individual Preferences panes are represented by *package* icons (page 151) in your various Library folders. For example, icons in the basic Snow Leopard set are in System→Library→PreferencePanes. Mac OS X also looks for preferences modules in the Network→Library→PreferencePanes folder, if there is one.

(All of this is handy to remember when the day comes that you want to *delete* a Preferences pane.)

Now suppose you've downloaded some new Preferences module and you want to install it. Just double-clicking a downloaded System Preferences pane does the trick.

If you prefer manual control, you can put a downloaded module into your Home→Library→PreferencePanes folder. The beauty of this arrangement, of course, is that everyone who shares the Mac now can see a different assortment of customized Preference panes.

If you're an administrator, you can create a PreferencePanes folder in the Mac's main Library folder so that everyone with an account on the Mac (Chapter 12) can access your newly added panes.

When you install some new System Preferences pane like TinkerTool, Adobe Version Cue, or TiVo Desktop, it takes the form of a new icon in one of those four PreferencePanes folders. (If you ever want to remove one, Control-click it and choose Remove Preference Pane from the shortcut menu.)

Within the System Preferences program, any new panes you add in this way appear in a new row of icons labeled Other (when you're viewing System Preferences in Category view).

Date & Time

Your Mac's conception of what time it is can be very important. Every file you create or save is stamped with this time, and every email you send or receive is marked with this time. As you might expect, setting your Mac's clock is what the Date & Time pane is all about.

Date & Time Tab

Click the Date & Time tab. If your Mac is online, turn on "Set date & time automatically" and be done with it. Your Mac sets its own clock by consulting a highly accurate scientific clock on the Internet. (No need to worry about daylight saving time, either; the time servers take that into account.)

Tip: If you have a full-time Internet connection (cable modem or DSL, for example), you may as well leave this checkbox turned on, so your Mac's clock is always correct. If you connect to the Internet by dial-up modem, however, turn off the checkbox, so your Mac won't keep trying to dial spontaneously at all hours of the night.

If you're not online and have no prospect of getting there, you can also set the date and time manually. To change the month, day, or year, click the digit that needs changing and then either (a) type a new number or (b) click the little arrow buttons. Press the Tab key to highlight the next number. (You can also specify the day of the month by clicking a date on the minicalendar.)

To set the time of day, use the same technique—or, for more geeky fun, you can set the time by dragging the hour, minute, or second hands on the analog clock. Finally, click Save. (If you get carried away with dragging the clock hands around and lose track of the *real* time, click the Revert button to restore the panel settings.)

Tip: If you're frustrated that the Mac is showing you the 24-hour "military time" on your menu bar (that is, 17:30 instead of 5:30 p.m.)—or that it isn't showing military time when you'd like it to—click the Clock tab and turn "Use a 24-hour clock" on or off.

Note, however, that this affects only the menu bar clock. If you'd like to reformat the menu bar clock and all other dates (like the ones that show when your files were modified in list views), click the Open Language & Text button at the bottom of the Date & Time pane. Once there, click the Formats tab. There you'll see a Customize button for Times, which leads you to a whole new world of time-format customization. You can drag elements of the current time (Hour, Minute, Second, Millisecond, and so on) into any order you like, and separate them with any desired punctuation. This way, you can set up your date displays in (for example) the European format, expressing April 13 as 13/4 instead of 4/13).

Time Zone Tab

You'd be surprised how important it is to set the time zone for your Mac. If you don't do so, the email and documents you send out—and the Mac's conception of what documents are older and newer—could be hopelessly skewed.

You can teach your Mac where it lives by using what may be Snow Leopard's snazziest new feature: its ability to set its own time zone *automatically*. That's an especially useful feature if you're a laptop warrior who travels a lot.

Just turn on "Set time zone automatically using current location" (Figure 9-6). If possible, the Mac will think for a moment and then, before your eyes, drop a pin onto the world map to represent your location—and set the time zone automatically. (The world map goes black-and-white to show that you can no longer set your location manually.)

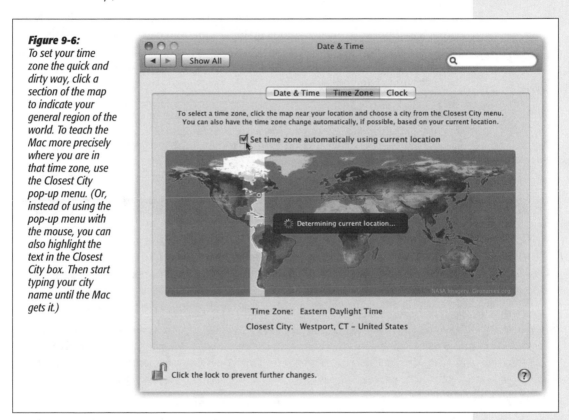

Figure 9-6:
To set your time zone the quick and dirty way, click a section of the map to indicate your general region of the world. To teach the Mac more precisely where you are in that time zone, use the Closest City pop-up menu. (Or, instead of using the pop-up menu with the mouse, you can also highlight the text in the Closest City box. Then start typing your city name until the Mac gets it.)

Often, you'll be told that the Mac is "Unable to determine current location at this time." In that case, specify your location manually, as shown in Figure 9-6.

Clock Tab

In the Clock pane, you can specify whether or not you want the current time to appear, at all times, at the right end of your menu bar. You can choose between two different clock styles: digital (3:53 p.m.) or analog (a round clock face). You also get several other options that govern this digital clock display: the display of seconds, whether or not you want to include designations for a.m. and p.m., the day of the week, a blinking colon, and the option to use a 24-hour clock.

Tip: At the bottom of the dialog box, you'll find a feature called "Announce the time." At the intervals you specify, the Mac can speak, out loud, the current time: "It's 10 o'clock." If you tend to get so immersed in "working" that you lose track of time, Mac OS X just removed your last excuse.

In Snow Leopard, there's a handy new feature: For the first time since the birth of Mac OS X, the menu-bar clock can show not just the time, not just the day of the week, but also today's *date*. Turn on the "Show the day of the week" and "Show date" checkboxes if you want to see, for example, "Wed May 5 7:32 PM" on your menu bar.

If you decide you don't need all that information—if your menu bar is crowded enough as it is—you can always look up today's day and date just by *clicking* the time on your menu bar. A menu drops down revealing the complete date. The menu also lets you switch between digital and analog clock types and provides a shortcut to the Date & Time preferences pane.

Tip: This one's for Unix geeks only. You can also set the date and time from within Terminal (Chapter 16). Use *sudo* (page 639), type *date yyyymmddhhmm.ss,* and press Enter. (Of course, replace that code with the actual date and time you want, such as *201004051755.00* for April 5, 2010, 5:55 p.m.) You might find this method faster than the System Preferences route.

FREQUENTLY ASKED QUESTION

How the Mac Knows Where You Are

OK, I'll bite. To set my time zone automatically, the Mac has to know where I am. It doesn't have GPS. So how does it do that?

Metropolitan areas today are blanketed by overlapping WiFi signals. At a typical Manhattan intersection, you might be in range of 20 base stations. Each one broadcasts its own name and unique network address (its *MAC address*—nothing to do with Mac computers) once every second. Although you'd need to be within 150 feet or so to actually get onto the Internet, a laptop or phone can detect this beacon signal from up to 1,500 feet away.

A company called Skyhook had a huge idea: Suppose you could correlate all those beacon signals with their physical locations. Why, you'd be able to simulate GPS—without the GPS!

So for five years, 500 full-time Skyhook employees have been driving every road, lane, and highway in major cities around the world, measuring all those WiFi signals, noting their network addresses and locations. (Neither these vans nor the Mac ever has to *connect* to these base stations. They're just reading the one-way beacon signals.)

So far, Skyhook's database knows about 50 million hot spots—and the precise longitude and latitude of each. The company licenses this information to companies, like Apple, who want to build location services into their gadgets.

To figure out where it is, the Mac sniffs around for WiFi base stations. If it finds any, it transmits their IDs back to Skyhook, which looks up those network addresses—and sends coordinates back to the Mac over the Internet.

That accuracy is good only to within 100 feet at best, and of course the Skyhook system fails completely once you're out of populated areas—or whenever your Mac doesn't have WiFi or an Internet connection. On the other hand, it works fast, and it works indoors, which GPS definitely doesn't.

Desktop & Screen Saver

This panel offers two ways to show off Mac OS X's glamorous graphics features: *desktop pictures* and *screen savers*.

Desktop Pictures

Mac OS X comes with several ready-to-use collections of desktop pictures, ranging from *National Geographic*–style nature photos to plain solid colors. To install a new background picture, first choose one of the image categories in the list at the left side of the window, as shown in Figure 9-7.

Figure 9-7:
Using the list of picture sources at left, you can preview an entire folder of your own images before installing one specific image as your new desktop picture. Use the + button to select a folder of assorted graphics—or, if you're an iPhoto veteran, click an iPhoto album name, as shown here. Clicking one of the thumbnails installs the corresponding picture on the desktop.

Your choices include Desktop Pictures (muted, soft-focus swishes and swirls), Nature (bugs, water, snow leopard, outer space), Plants (flowers, soft-focus leaves), Black & White (breathtaking monochrome shots), Abstract (swishes and swirls with wild colors), Patterns (a pair of fabric close-ups), or Solid Colors (simple grays, blues, and greens).

Using your own pictures

Of course, you may feel that decorating your Mac desktop is much more fun if you use one of your *own* pictures. You can use any digital photo, scanned image, or graphic you want in almost any graphics format (JPEG, PICT, GIF, TIFF, Photoshop, and—just in case you hope to master your digital camera by dangling its electronic instruction manual in front of your nose each morning—even PDF).

That's why icons for your own Pictures folder and iPhoto albums also appear here, along with a **+** button that lets you choose *any* folder of pictures. When you click one of these icons, you see thumbnail versions of its contents in the main screen to its right. Just click the thumbnail of any picture to apply it immediately to the desktop. (There's no need to remove the previously installed picture first.)

Tip: If there's one certain picture you like, but it's not in any of the listed sources, you can drag its image file onto the well (the miniature desktop displayed in the Desktop panel). A thumbnail of your picture instantly appears in the well and, a moment later, the picture is plastered across your monitor.

Making the picture fit

No matter which source you use to choose a photo of your own, you have one more issue to deal with. Unless you've gone to the trouble of editing your chosen photo so that it matches the precise dimensions of your screen (1280×854 pixels, for example), it probably isn't exactly the same size as your screen.

Tip: The top 23 pixels of your graphic are partly obscured by Snow Leopard's translucent menu bar—something to remember when you prepare the graphic. Then again, you can also make the menu bar stop being translucent—by turning off the "Translucent menu bar" checkbox shown in Figure 9-7.

Fortunately, Mac OS X offers a number of solutions to this problem. Using the pop-up menu just to the right of the desktop preview well, you can choose any of these options:

- **Fit to Screen.** Your photo appears as large as possible without distortion or cropping. If the photo doesn't precisely match the proportions of your screen, you get "letterbox bars" on the sides or at top and bottom. (Use the swatch button just to the right of the pop-up menu to specify a color for those letterbox bars.)

- **Fill Screen.** Enlarges or reduces the image so that it fills every inch of the desktop without distortion. Parts may get chopped off. At least this option never distorts the picture, as the "Stretch" option does (below).

- **Stretch to Fill Screen.** Makes your picture fit the screen exactly, come hell or high water. Larger pictures may be squished vertically or horizontally as necessary, and small pictures are drastically blown up *and* squished, usually with grisly results.

- **Center.** Centers the photo neatly on the screen. The margins of the picture may be chopped off.

  If the picture is smaller than the screen, it sits smack in the center of the monitor at actual size, leaving a swath of empty border all the way around. As a remedy, Apple provides a color-swatch button next to the pop-up menu (also shown in Figure 9-7). When you click it, the Color Picker appears (page 199), so that you can specify the color in which to frame your little picture.

- **Tile.** This option makes your picture repeat over and over until the multiple images fill the entire monitor. (If your picture is larger than the screen, no such tiling takes place. You see only the top center chunk of the image.)

Auto picture-changing

The novelty of any desktop picture, no matter how interesting, is likely to fade after several months of all-day viewing. That's why the randomizing function is so delightful.

Turn on "Change picture" at the bottom of the dialog box. From the pop-up menu, specify when you want your background picture to change: "Every day," "Every 15 minutes," or, if you're *really* having trouble staying awake at your Mac, "Every 5 seconds." (The option called "When waking from sleep" refers to the *Mac* waking from sleep, not its owner.)

Finally, turn on "Random order," if you like. If you leave it off, your desktop pictures change in alphabetical order by file name.

That's all there is to it. Now, at the intervals you specified, your desktop picture changes automatically, smoothly cross-fading between the pictures in your chosen source folder like a slideshow. You may never want to open another window, because you'll hate to block your view of the show.

Screen Saver

On the Screen Saver panel, you can create your own screen-saver slideshows—an absolute must if you have an Apple Cinema Display and a cool Manhattan loft apartment.

Tip: Of course, a screen saver doesn't really save your screen. LCD flat-panel screens, the only kind Apple sells, are incapable of "burning in" a stationary image of the sort that originally inspired the creation of screen savers years ago.

No, these screen savers offer two unrelated functions. First, they mask what's on your screen from passersby whenever you leave your desk. Second, they're kind of fun.

When you click a module's name in the Screen Savers list, you see a mini version of it playing back in the Preview screen. Click Test to give the module a dry run on your full monitor screen.

When you've had enough of the preview, just move the mouse or press any key. You return to the Screen Saver panel.

Apple provides a few displays to get you started, in two categories: Apple and Pictures.

Apple

- **Arabesque.** Your brain will go crazy trying to make sense of the patterns of small circles as they come and go, shrink and grow. But forget it; this module is all just drugged-out randomness.

• **Computer Name.** This display shows nothing more than the Apple logo and the computer's name, faintly displayed on the monitor. (These elements shift position every few minutes—it just isn't very fast.) Apple probably imagined that this feature would let corporate supervisors glance over at the screens of unattended Macs to find out who was not at their desks.

• **Flurry.** You get flaming, colorful, undulating arms of fire, which resemble a cross between an octopus and somebody arc welding in the dark. If you click the Options button, you can control how many streams of fire appear at once, the thickness of the arms, the speed of movement, and the colors.

• **iTunes Artwork.** Somebody put a lot of work into the album covers for the CDs whose music you own—so why not enjoy them as art? This module builds a gigantic mosaic of album art from *your* music collection, if you have one. The tiles periodically flip around, just to keep the image changing. (The Options button lets you specify how many rows of album-art squares appear, and how often the tiles flip.)

• **RSS Visualizer.** Here, buried 43 layers deep in the operating system, is one of Mac OS X's most spectacular and useful features: the RSS Visualizer. When this screen saver kicks in, it shows a jaw-dropping, 3-D display of headlines (news and other items) slurped in from the Safari Web browser's *RSS reader.* (RSS items, short for Really Simple Syndication or Rich Site Summary, are like a cross between email messages and Web pages—they're Web items that get sent directly to you. Details in Chapter 20.)

After the introductory swinging-around-an-invisible-3-D-pole-against-a-swirling-blue-sky-background sequence, the screen saver displays one news blurb at a time. Each remains on the screen just long enough for you to get the point of the headline. Beneath, in small type, is the tantalizing instruction, "Press the '3' key to continue." (It's a different number key for each headline.) If you do, indeed, tap the designated key, you leave the screen saver, fire up Safari, and wind up on a Web page that contains the complete article you requested.

The whole thing is gorgeous, informative, and deeply hypnotic. Do not use while operating heavy equipment.

Tip: Click Options to specify which Web site's RSS feed you want displayed.

• **Shell.** Five swirling fireworky spinners, centered around a bigger one.

• **Spectrum.** This one's for people who prefer not to have anything specific on their screens, like photos or text; instead, it fills the screen with a solid color that gradually shifts to other glowing rainbow hues.

• **Word of the Day.** A parade of interesting words drawn from the Dictionary program. You're invited to tap the D key to open the dictionary to that entry to read more. Build your word power!

Tip: Click Options to specify which dictionary you want: the standard New Oxford American, or the Japanese one.

Pictures

The screen savers in this category are all based on the slideshowy presentation of photos. You can choose from three presentations of pictures in whatever photo group you choose, as represented by the three Display Style buttons just below the screen-saver preview.

- **Slideshow** displays one photo at a time; they slowly zoom and cut into each other.

Tip: If you click Options, you get choices like "Present slides in random order" (instead of the order they appear in Apple's photo folder, or yours); "Cross-fade between slides" (instead of just cutting abruptly); "Zoom back and forth" (that is, slowly enlarge or shrink each photo to keep it interesting); "Crop slides to fit on screen" (instead of exposing letterbox bars of empty desktop if the photo's shape doesn't match the screen's); and "Keep slides centered" (instead of panning gracefully across).

- **Collage** sends individual photos spinning randomly onto the "table," where they lie until the screen is full.

Tip: This time, the Options button offers the "Present slides in random order" button, plus a "Collage style" pop-up menu that lets you add each photo's name and date to its white, Polaroid-style border.

- **Mosaic** will blow your mind; see Figure 9-8.

Tip: Click the Options button to specify the speed of the receding, the number of photos that become pixels of the larger photo, and whether or not you want the composite photos to appear in random order.

In any case, all these photo-show options are available for whatever photo set you choose from the list at left. These are your choices:

- **Abstract, Beach, Cosmos, Forest, Nature Patterns, Paper Shadow.** Abstract features psychedelic swirls of modern art. In the Beach, Cosmos, Forest, and Nature screen savers, you see a series of tropical ocean scenes, deep space objects, lush rain forests, and leaf/flower shots. Paper Shadow is a slideshow of undulating, curling, black-and-white shadowy abstract forms.

  Each creates an amazingly dramatic, almost cinematic experience, worthy of setting up to "play" during dinner parties like the lava lamps of the '70s.

Tip: You can also create a screen saver from any folder full of photos on your hard drive. Click the **+** button and choose Add Folder of Pictures. The folder you select turns into a self-playing slideshow, complete with spectacular zooming and dissolving effects.

- **iPhoto albums.** If you're using iPhoto to organize your digital photos, you'll see its familiar album and Event lists here, making it a snap to choose any of your own photo collections for use as a screen saver.

Snow Leopard Spots: A new option debuts here: Flagged. It displays only the photos you've flagged in iPhoto—which you do by clicking a photo and pressing ⌘-period—which gives you more freedom than having to choose one prepared album or another.

Figure 9-8:
This feeble four-frame sample will have to represent, on this frozen page, the stunning animated pull-out that is the Mosaic screen saver.

It starts with one photo (top); your "camera" pulls back farther and farther, revealing that that photo is just one in a grid—a huge grid—that's comprised of all your photos.

As you pull even further back, each photo appears so small that it becomes only one dot of another photo—from the same collection!

And then that one starts shrinking, and the cycle repeats, on and on into infinity.

- **MobileMe albums.** One of the perks of paying $100 per year for a MobileMe membership is the ability to create slideshows online. If you've published some of them, their names show up here.

  Weirder yet, you can also enjoy a screen saver composed of photos from *somebody else's* MobileMe gallery. ("Oh, look, honey, here's some shots of Uncle Jed's crops this summer!")

  Click the **+** button and choose MobileMe Gallery. You're asked which member's slideshow collection you want to view and how you want it to appear (Figure 9-9).

Tip: If you click the **+** button and choose RSS Feed, can also specify an RSS feed's address. The idea, of course, is that you'd specify a photo RSS feed's address here, like the ones generated by iPhoto.

If you set up more than one MobileMe and RSS-feed address here, the screen saver presents them as sequential slideshows. Drag them up or down the list to change their order.

Figure 9-9:
Once you enter a MobileMe member's name, you're shown that person's list of public photo albums. At this point, you can also specify how you want the screen saver to look: Turn off the crossfade between slides, crop the slides so they fit on the screen, present the slides in random order, and so on.)

Whichever screen-saver module you use, you have two further options:

- **Use random screen saver.** If you can't decide which one of the modules to use, turn on this checkbox. The Mac chooses a different module each time your screen saver kicks in.

- **Show with clock.** This option just superimposes the current time on whatever screen saver you've selected. You'd be surprised at how handy it can be to use your Mac as a giant digital clock when you're getting coffee across the room.

Activating the screen saver

You can control when your screen saver takes over in a couple of ways:

- **After a period of inactivity.** Using the "Start screen saver" slider, you can set the amount of time that has to pass without keyboard or mouse activity before the screen saver starts. The duration can be as short as 3 minutes or as long as 2 hours, or you can drag the slider to Never to prevent the screen saver from ever turning on by itself.

Tip: The screensaver can auto-lock your Mac after a few minutes (and require the password to get back in)—a great security safety net when you wander away from your desk. See page 501.

Figure 9-10:
Click the Hot Corners button to open this "sheet," which lets you designate certain corners of your screen as instant-activation spots, or never-come-on spots. Sliding the mouse to the Start Screen Saver corner, for example, turns on your screen saver right away.

GEM IN THE ROUGH

Secrets of the Screen Saver Modules

The canned screen saver modules are stored in your System→Library→Screen Savers folder. If you Control-click (right-click) one of the icons inside and choose Show Package Contents from the shortcut menu, you'll find a Contents→Resources folder that contains the individual image files for each module (the outer space photos for the Cosmos screen saver, for example).

Why bother? Because some of these spectacular photos make really good desktop pictures. You're free to copy them out of the Resources folder for that purpose.

- **When you park your cursor in the corner of the screen.** If you click the Hot Corners button, you see that you can turn each corner of your monitor into a *hot corner* (Figure 9-10).

Tip: You can find dozens more screen saver modules from Apple. To look them over, click the **+** button below the list; choose Browse Screen Savers. You're taken to *www.apple.com/downloads/macosx/icons_ screensavers*, where you can choose from a selection of amazing add-on screensaver modules. (The older ones may not be compatible with Snow Leopard's new 64-bit design, however.)

Displays

Displays is the center of operations for all your monitor settings. Here, you set your monitor's *resolution*, determine how many colors are displayed onscreen, and calibrate color balance and brightness.

Tip: You can open up this panel with a quick keystroke from any program on the Mac. Just press Option as you tap one of the screen-brightness keys on the top row of your keyboard.

The specific controls depend on the kind of monitor you're using, but here are the ones you'll most likely see:

Display Tab

This tab is the main headquarters for your screen controls. It governs these settings:

- **Resolutions.** All Mac screens today can make the screen picture larger or smaller, thus accommodating different kinds of work. You perform this magnification or reduction by switching among different *resolutions* (measurements of the number of dots that compose the screen). The Resolutions list displays the various resolution settings your monitor can accommodate: 800×600, 1024×768, and so on.

When you use a low-resolution setting, such as 800×600, the dots of your screen image get larger, thus enlarging (zooming in on) the picture—but showing a smaller slice of the page. Use this setting when playing a small QuickTime movie, for example, so that it fills more of the screen. (Lower resolutions usually look blurry on flat-panel screens, though.) At higher resolutions, such as 1280×800,

---

FREQUENTLY ASKED QUESTION

Blurry Flat-Panel Screens

Yucko! I tried the 800×600 setting on my laptop, and everything got all blurry and big! How do I fix it?

On any flat-panel screen—not just laptop screens—only one resolution setting looks really great: the maximum one. That's what geeks call the native *resolution of that screen.*

That's because on flat-panel screens, every pixel is a fixed size. At lower resolutions, the Mac does what it can to blur together adjacent pixels, but the effect is fuzzy and unsatisfying. (On a bulky CRT monitor, the electron gun can actually make the pixels larger or smaller, so you don't have this problem.)

---

the screen dots get smaller, making your windows and icons smaller, but showing more overall area. Use this kind of setting when working on two-page spreads in your page-layout program, for example.

Tip: You can adjust the resolution of your monitor without having to open System Preferences. Just turn on "Show displays in menu bar," which adds a Displays pop-up menu (a menulet) to the right end of your menu bar for quick adjustments. (If you choose Number of Recent Items–did Apple really mean for this command to say that?–then you can adjust how many common resolutions are listed in this menulet.)

- **Colors, Refresh Rate, Brightness, Contrast.** If you're still using a CRT screen—that is, not a flat panel—these additional controls appear. **Colors** specifies how many colors your screen can display (256, Thousands, and so on)—an option that's here only for nostalgia's sake, since no normal person would deliberately want photos to look *worse.* **Refresh Rate** controls how many times per second your screen image is repainted by your monitor's electron gun. Choose a setting that minimizes flicker. Finally, the **Brightness and Contrast** sliders let you make the screen look good in the prevailing lighting conditions.

  Of course, most Apple keyboards have brightness-adjustment *keys,* so these software controls are included just for the sake of completeness.

- **Automatically adjust brightness as ambient light changes.** This option appears only if you have a Mac laptop with a light-up keyboard. In that case, your laptop's light sensor also dims the screen automatically in dark rooms—*if* this checkbox is turned on. (Of course, you can always adjust the keyboard lighting manually, by tapping the .:. and .:. keys.)

Geometry Tab

This pane appears only on Macs with those increasingly rare CRT (that is, non-flat) screens. It lets you adjust the position, size, and angle of the screen image on the glass itself—controls that can be useful in counteracting distortion in aging monitors.

Arrangement Tab

From the dawn of the color-monitor era, Macs have had a terrific feature: the ability to exploit multiple monitors all plugged into the computer at the same time. Any Mac with a video-output jack (laptops, iMacs), or any Mac with a second or third video card (Power Macs, Mac Pros), can project the same thing on both screens (*mirror mode*); that's useful in a classroom when the "external monitor" is a projector.

Tip: The standard video card in a Mac Pro has jacks for two monitors. By installing more video cards, you can get up to six monitors going at once.

But it's equally useful to make one monitor act as an *extension* of the next. For example, you might have your Photoshop image window on your big monitor but keep all the Photoshop controls and tool palettes on a smaller screen. Your cursor passes from one screen to another as it crosses the boundary.

You don't have to shut down the Mac to hook up another monitor. Just hook up the monitor or projector and then choose Detect Displays from the Displays *menulet.*

When you open System Preferences, you see a different Displays window on each screen, so that you can change the color and resolution settings independently for each. Your Displays menulet shows two sets of resolutions, too, one for each screen.

If your Mac can show different images on each screen, then your Displays panel offers an Arrangement tab, showing a miniature version of each monitor. By dragging these icons around relative to each other, you can specify how you want the second monitor's image "attached" to the first. Most people position the second monitor's image to the right of the first, but you're also free to position it on the left, above, below, or even directly on top of the first monitor's icon (the last of which produces a video-mirroring setup). For the least likelihood of going insane, consider placing the real-world monitor into the same position.

For committed multiple-monitor fanatics, the fun doesn't stop there. See the microscopic menu bar on the first-monitor icon? You can drag that tiny strip onto a different monitor icon, if you like, to tell Displays where you'd like your menu bar to appear. (And check out how most screen savers correctly show different stuff on each monitor!)

Color Tab

This pane offers a list of *color profiles* for your monitor (or, if you turn off "Show profiles for this display only," for *all* monitors). Each profile represents colors slightly differently—a big deal for designers and photo types. See page 572 for more on color profiles.

When you click Calibrate, the Display Calibrator Assistant opens to walk you through a series of six screens, presenting various brightness and color-balance settings in each screen. You pick the settings that look best to you; at the end of the process, you save your monitor tweaks as a ColorSync profile, which ColorSync-savvy programs can use to adjust your display for improved color accuracy.

Snow Leopard Spots: Speaking of options that only color nerds will appreciate: The standard gamma (contrast) setting in Snow Leopard has been changed from 1.8 to 2.2. That is, the overall contrast has been boosted to a level that matches Windows and most TV sets. Supposedly that's something that graphics pros had been clamoring for. If you prefer the older look, click the Calibrate button; in the Display Calibration Assistant that appears, you have a gamma choice on the very first options screen.

Dock

See Chapter 4 for details on the Dock and its System Preferences pane.

Energy Saver

The Energy Saver program helps you and your Mac in a number of ways. By blacking out the screen after a period of inactivity, it prolongs the life of your monitor. By putting the Mac to sleep half an hour after you've stopped using it, Energy Saver cuts down on electricity costs and pollution. On a laptop, Energy Saver extends the length of the battery charge by controlling the activity of the hard drive and screen.

Best of all, this pane offers the option to have your computer turn off each night automatically—and turn on again at a specified time in anticipation of your arrival at the desk.

Sleep Sliders

The Energy Saver controls are different on a laptop Mac and a desktop Mac, but both present a pair of sliders (Figure 9-11).

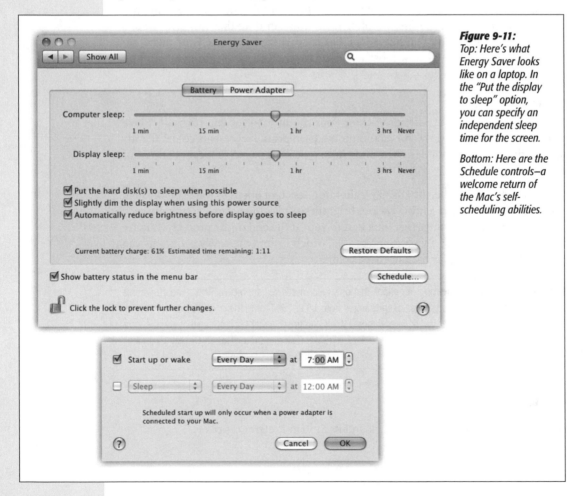

Figure 9-11:
Top: Here's what Energy Saver looks like on a laptop. In the "Put the display to sleep" option, you can specify an independent sleep time for the screen.

Bottom: Here are the Schedule controls—a welcome return of the Mac's self-scheduling abilities.

The top slider controls when the Mac will automatically go to sleep—anywhere from 1 minute after your last activity to Never. (Activity can be mouse movement, keyboard action, or Internet data transfer; Energy Saver won't put your Mac to sleep in the middle of a download.)

At that time, the screen goes dark, the hard drive stops spinning, and your processor chip slows to a crawl. Your Mac is now in *sleep* mode, using only a fraction of its usual electricity consumption. To wake it up when you return to your desk, press any key. Everything you were working on, including open programs and documents, is still onscreen, exactly as it was. (To turn off this automatic sleep feature entirely, drag the slider to Never.)

The second slider controls when the *screen* goes black to save power. These days, there's really only one good reason to put the screen to sleep independently of the Mac itself: so that your Mac can run its standard middle-of-the-night maintenance routines, even while the screen is off to save power.

Checkbox Options

Below the sliders, you see a selection of additional power-related options:

- **Put the hard disk(s) to sleep when possible.** This saves even more juice—and noise—by letting your drives stop spinning when not in use. The downside is a longer pause when you return to work and wake the thing up, because it takes a few seconds for your hard drive to "spin up" again.

- **Wake for network access.** This option lets you access a sleeping Mac from across the network. How is that possible? See the box on the next page.

Note: The wording of this option reflects how your Mac can connect to a network. If it can connect either over an Ethernet cable or a wireless hot spot, it says, "Wake for network access." If it's not a wireless Mac, you'll see, "Wake for Ethernet network access." If it's a MacBook Air without an Ethernet adapter, it says, "Wake for AirPort network access." On a laptop, the "wake" feature is available only when the machine's lid is left open and you're plugged into a power outlet.

- **Allow power button to put the computer to sleep.** On desktop Macs, it can be handy to sleep the Mac just by tapping its ⏻ button.

- **Start up automatically after a power failure.** This is a good option if you leave your Mac unattended and access it remotely, or if you use it as a network file server or Web server. It ensures that, if there's even a momentary blackout that shuts down your Mac, it starts itself right back up again when the juice returns. (On a laptop, it's available only when you're adjusting Power Adapter mode.)

- **Slightly dim the display when using this power source.** You see this checkbox only when you're adjusting the settings for battery-power mode on a laptop. It means "Don't use full brightness, so I can save power."

- **Automatically reduce the brightness of the display before display sleep.** When this option is on for your laptop, the screen doesn't just go black suddenly after the designated period of inactivity; instead, it goes to half brightness as a sort of drowsy mode that lets you know full sleep is coming soon.

- **Show battery status in the menu bar.** This on/off switch (laptops only) controls the battery menulet described in the box on the facing page.

Note: On a laptop, notice the two tabs at the top of the dialog box. They let you create different settings for the two states of life for a laptop, when it's plugged in (Power Adapter) and when it's running on battery power (Battery). That's important, because on a laptop, every drop of battery power counts.

However, Snow Leopard no longer offers a choice of battery-power "profiles," like Better Energy Savings and Better Performance. Simpler is better, right?

Scheduled Startup and Shutdown

By clicking the Schedule button, you can set up the Mac to shut itself down and turn itself back on automatically (Figure 9-11, bottom).

If you work 9 to 5, for example, you can set the office Mac to turn itself on at 8:45 a.m. and shut itself down at 5:30 p.m.—an arrangement that conserves electricity, saves money, and reduces pollution, but doesn't inconvenience you in the least. In fact, you may come to forget that you've set up the Mac this way, since you'll never actually see it turn itself off.

GEM IN THE ROUGH

Auto-Wake for Network Access

You should put your Mac to sleep as much as possible; you'll save power, money, and pollution. Unfortunately, a sleeping Mac is useless on the network. For example, you can't access files on it from another machine.

A new Snow Leopard feature called Wake on Demand, however, gives you the best of both worlds. It keeps a sleeping Mac available on the network, so you can wake it up remotely when you need it.

How can it do that? Is it sleeping, or isn't it?

Yes, it's sleeping. But before it dozes off, it hands off its list of available network services—file sharing, screen sharing, iTunes Library sharing, printer sharing, and so on—to your Apple wireless base station. The base station becomes your sleeping Mac's agent, continuing to broadcast the available

features of the sleeping Mac (via Apple's Bonjour networking technology) to the rest of the network.

To make this work, you need an AirPort Extreme wireless base station or a Time Capsule, running the latest Apple firmware. If you're using a WPA or WPA2 password on your base station or Time Capsule, it can't be in "bridge mode" (you'd know if you'd turned that on). Only Macs made since late 2008 can be awakened over a *wireless* network (all Macs can be awakened over an Ethernet wired network). To find out if yours is eligible, open System Profiler (page 427); under the Network heading, click AirPort and look to see if "Wake on Wireless" is listed as "Supported."

(Longtime Mac nuts may observe that "Wake for network access" has been available in Energy Saver for years. That older method, however, worked only on wired networks, not wireless.)

Note: The Mac doesn't shut down automatically if you've left unsaved documents open onscreen. It will go to sleep, though.

Exposé & Spaces

Exposé and Spaces, the two ingenious window- and screen-management features of Mac OS X, are described in detail in Chapter 5—and so is this joint-venture control panel.

Keyboard

The changes you make on this panel are tiny but can have a cumulatively big impact on your daily typing routine. The options have been organized on two panes.

Keyboard

In Snow Leopard, Apple has continued its annual shuffling around of the controls for the keyboard, mouse, and trackpad (which, believe it or not, all used to be in a single System Preferences pane). On this pane, you have:

GEM IN THE ROUGH

Mysteries of the Battery Menulet

If you've got a laptop, don't miss the checkbox in Energy Saver called "Show battery status in the menu bar." It puts a handy status indicator in the menu bar (⊏⊐) that keeps you informed of your battery's life.

When used as a menu, this menulet lets you choose between displaying the actual number of minutes left until a battery is depleted, the percentage of battery life that remains, or a visual emptying-battery icon.

If you've opted to view the numeric version, you may notice that sometimes the number, or the percentage, is in parentheses, like this: (78%). That's your signal that the laptop is plugged in and charging; you're seeing the number of minutes left until the battery is fully recharged (or the percentage of full charge you've achieved so far). Either way, the readout is counting down (or up) to that joyous moment.

If you're seeing only the battery icon (no text) in the menu bar, here's what the readouts mean:

Power cord in the battery: The laptop is plugged in, and the battery is 100 percent charged. Ready to roll, Captain!

Lightning bolt in the battery: The laptop is plugged in, but the battery is still charging.

Superimposed X: The laptop is plugged in, but the battery isn't in right, it's missing, or it isn't getting a charge for some other reason.

Emptying black battery: The laptop is running off of battery power and has at least 25 percent power left. (The width of the bar reveals how much charge is left.)

Emptying red battery: You're running off of battery power, and you have less than 25 percent charge remaining.

A nearly invisible red bar means you have less than 9 minutes left. Save those documents, buddy.

(Snow Leopard tip: If you Option-click the menulet, you see a health report for your battery. It might say, for example, "Condition: Good." When the condition needs your attention—when it says "Service Battery," "Replace Soon," "Replace Now," or "Check Battery"—you don't have to press Option. You'll see that message every time you open the menulet.)

- **Key Repeat Rate, Delay Until Repeat.** You're probably too young to remember the antique once known as the *typewriter*. On some electric versions of this machine, you could hold down the letter X key to type a series of XXXXXXXs—ideal for crossing something out in a contract, for example.

  On the Mac, *every* key behaves this way. Hold down any key long enough, and it starts spitting out repetitions, making it easy to type, for example, "No WAAAAAAAY!" or "You go, girrrrrrrrl!" These two sliders govern this behavior. On the right: a slider that determines how long you must hold down the key before it starts repeating (to prevent triggering repetitions accidentally, in other words). On the left: a slider that governs how fast each key spits out letters once the spitting has begun.

- **Use all F1, F2, etc. keys as standard function keys.** This option appears *only* on laptops and aluminum-keyboard Macs. It's complicated, so read page 223 slowly.

- **Illuminate keyboard in low light conditions.** This setting appears only if your Mac's keyboard does, in fact, light up when you're working in the dark—a showy feature of many Mac laptops. You can specify that you want the internal lighting to shut off after a period of inactivity (to save power when you've wandered away, for example), or you can turn the lighting off altogether. (You can always adjust the keyboard brightness manually, of course, by tapping the ⚬⚬⚬ and ⚬⚬⚬ keys.)

- **Show Keyboard & Character Viewer in menu bar.** You can read all about these special symbol-generating windows on page 233. For years, the on/off switch for these handy tools has been buried in the International pane of System Preferences; in Snow Leopard, there's a duplicate on/off switch here, for your convenience.

- **Modifier Keys.** This button lets you turn off, or remap, the functions of the Option, Caps Lock, Control, and ⌘ keys. It's for Unix programmers whose pinkies can't adjust to the Mac's modifier-key layout—and for anyone who keeps hitting Caps Lock by accident during everyday typing.

Keyboard Shortcuts

This pane is new in Snow Leopard—and pretty neat. It lets you make up new keystrokes for just about any function on the Mac, from capturing a screenshot to operating the Dock, triggering one of the Services, or operating a menu in any program from the keyboard. You can come up with keyboard combinations that, for example, are easier to remember, harder to trigger by accident, or easier to hit with one hand.

Step-by-step instructions for using this pane appear on page 179.

Language & Text

The primary job of this pane, formerly called International, is to set up your Mac to work in other languages. If you bought your Mac with a *localized* operating system—a version that already runs in your own language—and you're already using the only language, number format, and keyboard layout you'll ever need, then you can ignore most of this panel. But when it comes to showing off Mac OS X to your friends and loved ones, the "wow" factor on the Mac's polyglot features is huge. Details appear on page 231.

MobileMe

This panel is of no value unless you've signed up for a MobileMe account. See Chapter 18 for details.

Mouse

This pane, newly split apart from the Keyboard & Mouse panel that kicked around the Mac OS for decades, looks different depending on what kind of mouse (if any) is attached to your Mac.

Tracking Speed, Double-Click Speed

It may surprise you that the cursor on the screen doesn't move 5 inches when you move the mouse 5 inches on the desk. Instead, the cursor moves farther when you move the mouse faster.

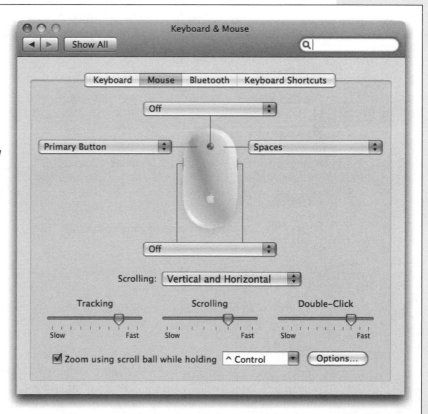

Figure 9-12:
This enormous photographic display shows up only if you have the Mighty Mouse, Apple's "two-button" mouse. The pop-up menus let you program the right, left, and side buttons. They offer functions like opening Dashboard, triggering Exposé, and so on.

This is also where you can turn the right-clicking feature on (just choose Secondary Button from the appropriate pop-up menu)—or swap the right- and left-click buttons' functions.

How *much* farther depends on how you set the first slider here. The Fast setting is nice if you have an enormous monitor, since you don't need an equally large mouse pad to get from one corner to another. The Slow setting, on the other hand, forces you to pick up and put down the mouse frequently as you scoot across the screen. It offers very little acceleration, but it can be great for highly detailed work like pixel-by-pixel editing in Photoshop.

The Double-Click Speed setting specifies how much time you have to complete a double-click. If you click too slowly—beyond the time you've allotted yourself with this slider—the Mac "hears" two *single* clicks instead.

Snow Leopard Spots: If you have a real mouse attached, you also see the magnificent "Zoom using scroll wheel while holding Control" checkbox at the bottom of this pane. What this means is that you can magnify the entire screen, zooming in, by turning the little ball or wheel atop your mouse while you press the Control key. It's great for reading tiny type, examining photos up close, and so on.

The Mighty Mouse

If you have an Apple Mighty Mouse—the white mouse that has come with desktop Macs since 2005—then the Mouse pane is a much fancier affair (Figure 9-12).

On a laptop without any mouse attached, the Mouse pane still appears in System Preferences—but its sole function is to help you "pair" your Mac with a wireless Bluetooth mouse.

Network

See Chapters 13 and 18 for the settings you need to plug in for networking.

Parental Controls

These controls are described at length in Chapter 12.

Print & Fax

Chapter 14 describes printing and faxing in detail. This panel offers a centralized list of the printers you've introduced to the Mac.

Security

See Chapter 12 for details on locking up your Mac.

Sharing

Mac OS X is an upstanding network citizen, flexible enough to share its contents with other Macs, Windows PCs, people dialing in from the road, and so on. On this panel, you'll find on/off switches for each of these sharing channels.

In this book, many of these features are covered in other chapters. For example, **Screen Sharing** and **File Sharing** are in Chapter 13; **Printer Sharing** and **Fax Sharing** are in Chapter 14; **Web Sharing** and **Remote Login** are in Chapter 22; **Internet Sharing** is in Chapter 18.

Here's a quick rundown on the other items:

- **DVD or CD Sharing.** This feature was added to accommodate the MacBook Air laptop, which doesn't have a built-in CD/DVD drive. When you turn on this option, any MacBook Airs on the network can "see," and borrow, your Mac's DVD drive, for the purposes of installing new software or running Mac disk-repair software. (Your drive shows up under the Remote Disc heading in the Air's Sidebar.)

- **Remote Management.** Lets someone else control your Mac using Apple Remote Desktop, a popular add-on program for teachers.

- **Remote Apple Events.** Lets AppleScript gurus (Chapter 7) send commands to Macs across the network.

- **Xgrid Sharing.** Xgrid is powerful software that lets you divide up a complex computational task—like computer animation or huge scientific calculations—among a whole bunch of Macs on your network, so that they automatically work on the problem when they're otherwise sitting idle. If you're intrigued, visit *http://developer.apple.com/hardware/hpc/xgrid_intro.html*.

- **Bluetooth Sharing.** This pane lets you set up Bluetooth file sharing, a way for other people near you to shoot files over to (or receive files from) your laptop—without muss, fuss, or passwords. Page 244 has the details.

Software Update

Whenever Apple improves or fixes some piece of Mac OS X or some Apple-branded program, the Software Update program can notify you, download the update, and install it into your system automatically. These updates may include new versions of programs like iPhoto and iMovie; drivers for newly released printers, scanners, cameras, and such; bug fixes and security patches; and so on.

Software Update doesn't download the new software without asking your permission first and explicitly telling you what it plans to install, as shown in Figure 9-13.

Scheduled Check Tab

For maximum effortlessness, turn on the "Check for updates" checkbox and then select a frequency from the pop-up menu—daily, weekly, or monthly. If you also turn on "Download updates automatically," you'll still be notified before anything gets installed, but you won't have to wait for the downloading—the deed will already be done.

(If you've had "Check for updates" turned off, you can always click the Check Now button to force Mac OS X to report in to see if new patches are available.)

Installed Software

Software Update also keeps a meticulous log of everything it drops into your system. On this tab, you see them listed, for your reference pleasure.

Figure 9-13:
When Software Update finds an appropriate software morsel, it presents a simple message: "Software updates are available for your computer. Do you want to install them?"

You could click install, if you're the trusting short. But it's informative to click Show Details instead.

Doing so expands the box to what's pictured here; you can click each proposed update and read about it.

Storing Apple Software Updates

The great unspoken migraine of Software Update is this: If you ever reinstall Mac OS X from its original DVD (when you install a new hard drive or move to a new computer, for example), you'll have to download and install all relevant updates again. That is, if your Mac came with Mac OS X 10.6 and iPhoto 8.0.1, you'll have to re-download and install the 10.6.1 update, the iPhoto 8.0.2 update, and so on.

Fortunately, although you can't skip the reinstallation process, you can skip the download step—because the Mac preserves the update installers as they arrive. They wind up in your Macintosh HD→Library→Receipts folder.

Later, you can reinstall your downloaded updates at any time simply by double-clicking each installer.

Tip: In your Macintosh HD→Library→Receipts folder, you'll find a liberal handful of .pkg files that have been downloaded by Software Update.

Most of these are nothing more than receipts that help Mac OS X understand which updaters you've already downloaded and installed. They make intriguing reading, but their primary practical use is finding out whether or not you've installed, for example, the 10.6.1 update.

Sound

Using the panes of the Sound panel, you can configure the sound system of your Mac in any of several ways.

Tip: Here's a quick way to jump directly to the Sound panel of System Preferences—from the keyboard, without ever having to open System Preferences or click Sound. Just press Option as you tap the ◀, ◀), or ◀)) key on the top row of your Apple keyboard.

Sound Effects Tab

"Sound effects" means *error beeps*—the sound you hear when the Mac wants your attention, or when you click someplace you shouldn't.

Just click the sound of your choice to make it your default system beep. Most of the canned choices here are funny and clever, yet subdued enough to be of practical value as alert sounds (Figure 9-14). As for the other controls on the Sound Effects panel, they include these:

- **Alert volume slider.** Some Mac fans are confused by the fact that even when they drag this slider all the way to the left, the sound from games and music CDs still plays at full volume.

  The actual *main* volume slider for your Mac is the "Output volume" slider at the bottom of the Sound pane. The "Alert volume" slider is *just* for error beeps; Apple was kind enough to let you adjust the volume of these error beeps independently.

- **Play user interface sound effects.** This option produces a few subtle sound effects during certain Finder operations: when you drag something off the Dock, into the Trash, or into a folder, or when the Finder finishes a file-copying job.

- **Play feedback when volume is changed.** Each time you press one of the volume keys (◀, ◀), ◀))), the Mac beeps to help you gauge the current volume.

  That's all fine when you're working at home. But more than one person has been humiliated in an important meeting when the Mac made a sudden, inappropriately loud sonic outburst—and then amplified that embarrassment by furiously and repeatedly pressing the volume-down key, beeping all the way.

  If you turn off this checkbox, the Mac won't make any sound at all as you adjust its volume. Instead, you'll see only a visual representation of the steadily decreasing (or increasing) volume level.

Tip: The Shift key reverses the logic. So if you have "Play feedback" turned on, holding down Shift as you tap the volume keys makes them silent. If it's turned off, you can force the volume-gauging beeps to play by pressing Shift as you tap the volume keys.

- **Play Front Row sound effects.** You can read about Front Row, which turns your screen into a giant multimedia directory for your entire Mac, in Chapter 15. All this option does is silence the little clicks and whooshes that liven up the proceedings when you operate Front Row's menus.

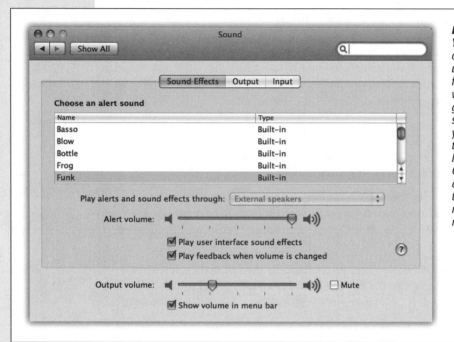

Figure 9-14:
You can adjust your overall speaker volume independently from the alert-beep volume, thank goodness. Tip nerds should note that you can also adjust the alert volume by holding down the Option key as you drag the handle in the speaker-volume menulet (on your menu bar).

Output Tab

"Output" means speakers or headphones. For most people, this pane offers nothing useful except the Balance slider, with which you can set the balance between your Mac's left and right stereo speakers. The "Select a device" wording seems to imply that you can choose which speakers you want to use for playback. But Internal Speakers is generally the only choice, even if you have external speakers. (The Mac uses your external speakers automatically when they're plugged in.)

A visit to this pane is necessary, however, if you want to use USB speakers or a Bluetooth or USB phone headset. Choose its name from the list.

Snow Leopard Spots: Mac OS X now remembers your volume setting for headphones independently.

Input Tab

This panel lets you specify which sound source you want the Mac to "listen to," if you have more than one connected: external microphone, internal microphone, line input, USB headset, or whatever. It also lets you adjust the sensitivity of that microphone—its *input volume*—by dragging the slider and watching the real-time Input level meter above it change as you speak. Put another way, it's a quick way to see if your microphone is working.

The "Use ambient noise reduction" is great if you make podcasts or use dictation software. It turns any mike into what amounts to a noise-canceling microphone, deadening the background noise while you're recording.

Snow Leopard Spots: Here's a much quicker way to change your audio input or output: Press Option as you click the ◀⁾ menulet. You get a secret pop-up menu that lists your various microphones, speakers, and headphones, so you can switch things without a visit to System Preferences.

If you'd prefer even more control over your Mac's sound inputs and outputs, don't miss the rewritten Audio/MIDI Setup program in your Applications→Utilities folder.

Speech

Your Mac's ability to speak—and be spoken to—is described in juicy detail starting on page 593.

Spotlight

Here's how you tell the Mac (a) which categories of files and information you want the Spotlight search feature to search, (b) which folders you *don't* want searched, for privacy reasons, and (c) which key combination you want to use for summoning the Spotlight menu or dialog box. Details are in Chapter 3.

Startup Disk

Use this panel to pick the System Folder your Mac will use the next time it starts up—when you're swapping between Mac OS X and Windows (running with Boot Camp), for example. Check out the details in Chapter 8.

Time Machine

Here's the master on/off switch and options panel for Time Machine, which is described in Chapter 6.

Trackpad

This panel, present only on laptops, keeps growing with each successive MacBook generation. (It's shown in Figure 6-3 on page 225.)

At the top, you find duplicates of the same Tracking Speed and Double-Click Speed sliders described under "Mouse" earlier in this chapter—but these let you establish independent tracking and clicking speeds for the *trackpad*. (There's even a new Scrolling slider, too, so you can control how fast the Mac scrolls a document when you drag two fingers down the trackpad.)

Trackpad Gestures

You may love your Mac laptop now, but wait until you find out about these special features. They make your laptop *crazy* better. It turns out you can point, click, scroll, right-click, rotate things, enlarge things, hide windows, and switch programs—all on the trackpad itself, without a mouse and without ever having to lift your fingers.

Apple keeps adding new "gestures" with each new laptop, so yours may not offer all these options. But here's what you might see. (If you point to one of these items without clicking, a movie illustrates each of these maneuvers right on the screen.)

Snow Leopard Spots: In Snow Leopard, all Mac laptops that have multi-touch trackpads can handle the three-finger and four-finger gestures described below. (For a while there, those gestures were available only on the latest models, the ones with no separate clicker button below the trackpad.)

One Finger

- **Tap to Click.** Usually, you touch your laptop's trackpad only to move the cursor. For clicking and dragging, you're supposed to use the clicking button *beneath* the trackpad (or, on the latest models, click the trackpad surface itself).

  Many people find, however, that it's more direct to tap and drag directly on the trackpad, using the same finger that's been moving the cursor. That's the purpose of this checkbox. When it's on, you can tap the trackpad surface to register a mouse click at the location of the cursor. Double-tap to double-click.

- **Dragging.** This option lets you move icons, highlight text, or pull down menus—in other words, to drag, not just click—using the trackpad.

  Start by tapping twice on the trackpad, then *immediately* after the second tap, begin dragging your finger. (If you don't start moving promptly, the laptop assumes that you were double-clicking.) You can stroke the trackpad repeatedly to continue your movement, as long as your finger never leaves the trackpad surface for more than about a second. When you "let go," the drag is considered complete.

- **Drag Lock.** If you worry that you're going to "drop" what you're dragging if you stop moving your finger, turn on this option instead. Once again, begin your drag by double-clicking, then move your finger immediately after the second click.

  When this option is on, however, you can take your sweet time in continuing the movement. In between strokes of the trackpad, you can take your finger off the laptop for as long as you like. You can take a phone call, a shower, or a vacation; the Mac still thinks that you're in the middle of a drag. Only when you tap *again* does the laptop consider the drag a done deal.

Two Fingers

- **Scroll.** This one is *sweet.* You have to try it to believe it. It means that dragging *two* fingers across your trackpad scrolls whatever window is open, just as though you had slid over to the scroll bar and clicked there. Except doing it with your two fingers, right in place, is infinitely faster and less fussy. You even get a Scrolling *Speed* slider.

- **Rotate.** Place two fingers on the trackpad, and then twist them around an invisible center point, to rotate a photo or a PDF document. This doesn't work in all programs or in all circumstances, but it's great for turning images upright in the Finder, Preview, iPhoto, Image Capture, and so on.

- **Pinch Open & Close.** If you've used an iPhone, this one will seem familiar. What it means is, "Put two fingers on the trackpad and spread them apart to *enlarge* what's on the screen. Slide two fingers *together* to shrink it down again." It doesn't work in every program—it affects icons on the desktop, pictures in Preview and iPhoto, text in Safari, and so on—but it's great when it does.

- **Screen zoom.** Here's another irresistible feature. It lets you zoom into the screen image, magnifying the whole thing, just by dragging two fingers up or down the trackpad while you're pressing the Control key. You can zoom in so far that the word "zoom" in 12-point type fills the entire monitor.

  This feature comes in handy with amazing frequency. It's great for reading Web pages in tiny type, or enlarging Web movies, or studying the dot-by-dot construction of a button or icon that you admire. Just Control-drag upward to zoom in, and Control-drag downward to zoom out again.

  You can click Options to customize this feature. For example, you can substitute the Option or ⌘ key, if Control isn't working out for you. Furthermore, you can specify how you want to scroll around within your zoomed-in screen image. The factory setting, "Continuously with pointer," is actually pretty frustrating; the whole screen shifts around whenever you move the cursor. ("So the pointer is at or near the center of the image" is very similar.) "Only when the pointer reaches an edge" is a lot less annoying, and lets you *use* the cursor (to click buttons, for example) without sending the entire screen image darting away from you.

Tip: Also in the Options box: the ability to turn off the pixel-smoothing feature that adds a certain blurriness to the zoomed-in image—and a reminder that you can press Option-⌘-\ (backslash) to turn it on or off.

- **Secondary click.** This means "right-click." Right-clicking is a huge deal on the Mac; it unleashes useful features just about everywhere.

  On all Mac laptops, you can trigger a right-click by clicking with your thumb while resting your index and middle fingers on the trackpad.

  On the latest laptops—the ones with no separate clicker button—there's another option: a pop-up menu that lets you designate a certain trackpad corner (bottom right, for example) as the right-click spot. Clicking there triggers a right-click—to open a shortcut menu, for example. Weird, but wonderful.

Three Fingers

- **Swipe to Navigate.** Drag three fingers horizontally across the trackpad to skip to the next or previous page or image in a batch. Here again, this feature doesn't work in all programs, but it's great for flipping through images or PDF pages in Preview or iPhoto.

Four Fingers

- **Swipe Up/Down for Exposé.** A four-finger swipe *up* the trackpad triggers the "Show desktop" function of Exposé. A four-finger drag *downward* triggers the "Show all windows" function instead. Swipe the opposite direction to restore the windows.

- **Swipe Left/Right to Switch Applications.** A four-finger swipe left or right makes the ⌘-Tab program switcher appear (page 154) so that you can point to a different program's icon and switch to it with a click.

Universal Access

The Universal Access panel is designed for people who type with one hand, find it difficult to use a mouse, or have trouble seeing or hearing. (These features can also be handy when the mouse is broken or missing.)

Accessibility is a huge focus for Apple, and in Snow Leopard, there are more features than ever for disabled people, including compatibility with Braille screens (yes, there is such a thing). In fact, there's a whole Apple Web site dedicated to explaining all these features: *www.apple.com/macosx/accessibility.*

Here, though, is an overview of the noteworthiest features.

Seeing Tab (Magnifying the Screen)

If you have trouble seeing the screen, then boy, does Mac OS X have features for you (Figure 9-15).

VoiceOver

One option is VoiceOver, which makes the Mac *read out loud* every bit of text that's on the screen. The impressively enhanced Snow Leopard version of VoiceOver is described on page 603.

Zoom

Another quick solution is to reduce your monitor's *resolution*—thus magnifying the image—using the Displays panel described earlier in this chapter. If you have a 17-inch or larger monitor set to, say, 640 × 480, the result is a greatly magnified picture. That method doesn't give you much flexibility, however, and it's a hassle to adjust.

If you agree, then try the Zoom feature that appears here; it lets you enlarge the area surrounding your cursor in any increment.

Tip: If you have a laptop, just using the Control-key trackpad trick described on page 347 is a far faster and easier way to magnify the screen. If you have a mouse, turning the wheel or trackpea while pressing Control is also much faster. Both of those features work even when this one is turned Off.

To make it work, press Option-⌘-8 as you're working. Or, if the Seeing panel is open, click On in the Zoom section. That's the master switch.

No zooming actually takes place, however, until you press Option-⌘-plus sign (to zoom in) or Option-⌘-minus sign (to zoom out). With each press, the entire screen image gets larger or smaller, creating a virtual monitor that follows your cursor around the screen.

Display (inverted colors)

While you're at it, pressing Control-Option-⌘-8, or clicking the "Switch to Black on White" button, inverts the colors of the screen, so that text appears white on black—an effect that some people find easier to read. (This option also freaks out many Mac

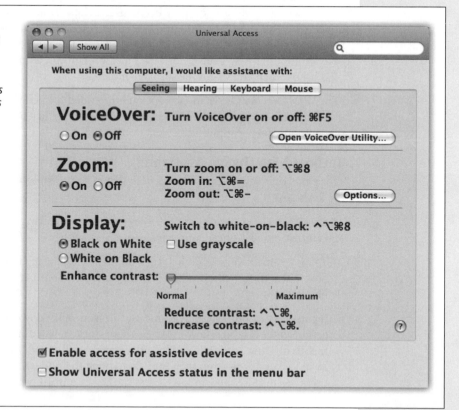

Figure 9-15:
You'll be amazed at just how much you can zoom into the Mac's screen using this Universal Access pane. In fact, there's nothing to stop you from zooming in so far that a single pixel fills the entire monitor. (That may not be especially useful for people with limited vision, but it can be handy for graphic designers learning how to reproduce a certain icon, dot by dot.)

fans who turn it on by *mistake*, somehow pressing Control-Option-⌘-8 by accident during everyday work. They think the Mac's expensive monitor has just gone loco. Now you know better.)

Tip: There's also a button called Use Grayscale, which banishes all color from your screen. This is another feature designed to improve text clarity, but it's also a dandy way to see how a color document will look when printed on a monochrome laser printer.

No matter which color mode you choose, the "Enhance contrast" slider is another option that can help. It makes blacks blacker and whites whiter, further eliminating in-between shades and thereby making the screen easier to see. (If the Universal Access panel doesn't happen to be open, you can always use the keystrokes Control-Option-⌘-< and Control-Option-⌘-> to decrease or increase contrast.)

Hearing Tab (Flashing the Screen)

If you have trouble hearing the Mac's sounds, the obvious solution is to increase the volume, which is why this panel offers a direct link to the Sound preferences pane.

Fortunately, hearing your computer usually isn't critical (except when working in music and audio, of course). The only time audio is especially important is when the Mac tries to get your attention by beeping. For those situations, turn on "Flash the screen when an alert sound occurs" (an effect you can try out by clicking the Flash Screen button). Now you'll see a white flash across the entire monitor whenever the Mac would otherwise beep—not a bad idea on laptops, actually, so that you don't miss beeps when you've got the speakers muted.

(The "Play stereo audio as mono" option is intended for people with hearing loss in one ear. This way, you won't miss any of the musical mix just because you're listening through only one headphone.)

Keyboard Tab (Typing Assistance)

This panel offers two clever features designed to help people who have trouble using the keyboard.

- **Sticky Keys** lets you press multiple-key shortcuts (involving keys like Shift, Option, Control, and ⌘) one at a time instead of all together.

  To make Sticky Keys work, first turn on the master switch at the top of the dialog box. Then go to work on the Mac, triggering keyboard commands as shown in Figure 9-16.

  If you press a modifier key *twice*, meanwhile, you lock it down. (Its onscreen symbol gets brighter to let you know.) When a key is locked, you can use it for several commands in a row. For example, if a folder icon is highlighted, you could double-press ⌘ to lock it down—and then type O (to open the folder), look around, and then press W (to close the window). Press the ⌘ key a third time to "un-press" it.

Tip: The checkbox called "Press the Shift key five times to turn Sticky Keys on or off" gives you the flexibility of turning Sticky Keys on and off at will, without even taking a trip to System Preferences. Whenever you want to turn on Sticky Keys, press the Shift key five times in succession. You'll hear a special clacking sound effect alerting you that you just turned on Sticky Keys. (Repeat the five presses to turn Sticky Keys off again.)

- **Slow Keys,** on the other hand, doesn't register a key press at all until you've held down the key for more than a second or so—a feature designed to screen out accidental key presses.

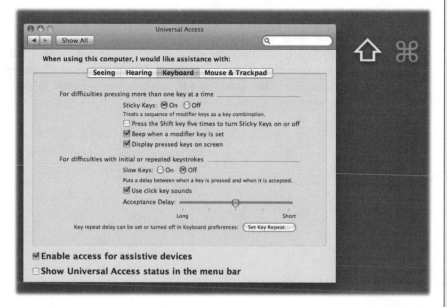

Figure 9-16:
Whenever you want to press a multiple-key keystroke like Shift-⌘-D, press them one at a time. You'll see ghost images of these keys superimposed on your screen, as though to show you which keystrokes you've added to your temporary collection. To "unpress" a key you've already pressed, press it again twice.

If "Use click key sounds" is turned on, you'll hear a little typing sound each time you press a key—but none of these key presses registers unless you hold the key down for a moment. (Use the Acceptance Delay slider to govern this threshold.)

You hear a different sound when the Mac actually accepts the key press—and, of course, you see the letter you typed appear onscreen.

Mouse & Trackpad Tab (Cursor Control from the Keyboard)

Mouse Keys is designed to help people who can't use the mouse—or who want more precision when working in graphics programs. It lets you click, drag, and otherwise manipulate the cursor by pressing the keys on your numeric keypad. (It's not very useful on keyboards that don't *have* separate numeric keypads, like laptops.)

When Mouse Keys is turned on, the 5 key acts as the clicker—hold it down for a moment to "click the mouse," do that twice to double-click, and so on. Hold down the 0 key to lock down the mouse button, and the period key to unlock it. (The amount of time you have to hold them down depends on how you've set the Initial Delay slider.)

Move the cursor around the screen by pressing the eight keys that surround the 5 key. (For example, hold down the 9 key to move the cursor diagonally up and to the right.) If you hold one of these keys down continuously, the cursor, after a pause, begins to move smoothly in that direction—according to the way you've adjusted the sliders called Initial Delay and Maximum Speed.

Tip: The checkbox called "Press the Option key five times to turn Mouse Keys on or off" saves you the trouble of opening System Preferences.

At the bottom of this window, you'll find the Cursor Size slider. It's a godsend not only to people with failing vision, but also to anyone using one of Apple's large, super-high-resolution screens; as the pixel density increases, the arrow cursor gets smaller and smaller. This slider lets you make the arrow cursor larger—much larger, if you like—making it much easier to see.

The Free Programs

R ight out of the box, Mac OS X comes with a healthy assortment of about 50 freebies: programs for sending email, writing documents, doing math, even playing games. Some have been around for years. Others, though, have been given extreme makeovers in Snow Leopard. They're designed not only to show off some of Mac OS X's most dramatic technologies, but also to let you get real work done without having to invest in additional software.

Your Free Mac OS X Programs

A broad assortment of programs sits in the Applications folder in the main hard drive window, and another couple dozen less frequently used apps await in the Applications→Utilities folder.

This chapter guides you through every item in your new software library, one program at a time. (Of course, your Applications list may vary. Apple might have blessed your particular Mac model with some bonus programs, or you may have downloaded or installed some on your own.)

Tip: A reminder: You can jump straight to the Applications folder in the Finder by pressing Shift-⌘-A (the shortcut for Go→Applications), or by clicking the Applications folder icon in the Sidebar. You might consider adding the Application folder's icon to the Dock, too, so you can access it no matter what program you're in. Shift-⌘-U (or Go→Utilities) takes you, of course, to the Utilities folder.

Address Book

The Address Book is a database that stores names, addresses, email addresses, phone numbers, and other contact information. See page 735.

Automator

This software-robot program is introduced in Chapter 7.

Calculator

The Calculator is much more than a simple four-function memory calculator. It can also act as a scientific calculator for students and scientists, a conversion calculator for metric and U.S. measures, and even a currency calculator for world travelers.

The little Calculator widget in the Dashboard is quicker to open, but the standalone Calculator program is far more powerful. For example:

- Calculator has three modes: Basic, Advanced, and Programmer (Figure 10-1). Switch among them by choosing from the View menu (or pressing ⌘-1 for Basic, ⌘-2 for Advanced, or ⌘-3 for Programmer).

Tip: You can also cycle among the three modes by repeatedly clicking what, on most windows, is the Zoom button (the green round dot at upper left). It's a first for the Mac—a Zoom button that changes function each time you click it—but it's kind of neat.

- You can operate Calculator by clicking the onscreen buttons, but it's much easier to press the corresponding number and symbol keys on your keyboard.

- As you go, you can make Calculator speak each key you press. The Mac's voice ensures that you don't mistype as you keep your eyes on the receipts in front of you, typing by touch.

    Just choose Speech→Speak Button Pressed to turn this feature on or off. (You choose *which* voice does the talking in the Speech panel of System Preferences.)

Tip: If you have a pre-2008 laptop, you probably have an embedded numeric keypad, superimposed on the right side of the keyboard and labeled on the keys in a different color ink. When you press the Fn key in the lower-left corner of the keyboard, typing these keys produces the numbers instead of the letters. (You can also press the NumLock key to stay in number mode, so you don't have to keep pressing Fn.)

- Press the C key to clear the calculator display.

- Once you've calculated a result, you can copy it (using Edit→Copy, or ⌘-C) and paste it directly into another program.

- Calculator even offers Reverse Polish Notation (RPN), a system of entering numbers that's popular with some mathematicians, programmers, and engineers, because it lets them omit parentheses. Choose View→RPN to turn it on and off.

Tip: How cool is this? In most programs, you don't need Calculator or even a Dashboard widget. Just highlight an equation (like 56*32.1-517) right in your document, and press ⌘-Shift-8. Presto—Mac OS X replaces the equation with the right answer. This trick works in TextEdit, Mail, Entourage, FileMaker, and many other programs.

And if you ever find that it doesn't work, remember that the Spotlight menu is now a calculator, too. Type or paste an equation into the Spotlight search box; instantly, the answer appears in the results menu.

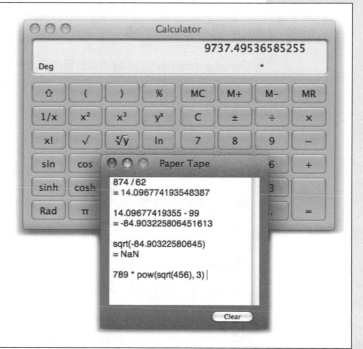

Figure 10-1:
The Calculator program offers a four-function Basic mode, a full-blown scientific calculator mode, and a programmer's calculator (shown here, and capable of hex, octal, decimal, and binary notation). The first two modes offer a "paper tape" feature (View→Show Paper Tape) that lets you correct errors made way back in a calculation. To edit one of the numbers on the paper tape, drag through it, retype, and then click Recalculate Totals. You can also save the tape as a text file by choosing File→Save Tape As, or print it by selecting File→Print Tape.

Conversions

Calculator is more than a calculator; it's also a conversion program. No matter what units you're trying to convert—meters, grams, inches, miles per hour, money—Calculator is ready.

Now, the truth is, the Units Converter widget in Dashboard is simpler and better than this older Calculator feature. But if you've already got Calculator open, here's the drill:

1. **Clear the calculator (for example, type the letter C on your keyboard). Type in the starting measurement.**

   To convert 48 degrees Celsius to Fahrenheit, for example, type *48*.

2. **From the Convert menu, choose the kind of conversion you want.**

   In this case, choose Temperature. When you're done choosing, a dialog box appears.

3. **Use the pop-up menus to specify which units you want to convert to and from.**

   To convert Celsius to Fahrenheit, choose Celsius from the first pop-up menu, and Fahrenheit from the second.

4. **Click OK.**

   That's it. The Calculator displays the result—in degrees Fahrenheit, in this example.

The next time you want to make this kind of calculation, you can skip steps 2, 3, and 4. Instead, just choose your desired conversion from the Convert→Recent Conversions submenu.

Calculator is especially amazing when it comes to *currency* conversions—from pesos to American dollars, for example—because it actually does its homework. It goes online to download up-to-the-minute currency rates to ensure that the conversion is accurate. (Choose Convert→Update Currency Exchange Rates.)

Tip: If you're working with big numbers, don't forget to turn on View→Show Thousands Separators. Calculator will add commas (like 1,242,939) to help you read your big numbers more easily.

Chess

Mac OS X comes with only one game, but it's a beauty (Figure 10-2). It's a traditional chess game played on a gorgeously rendered board with a set of realistic 3-D pieces.

Note: The program is actually a sophisticated Unix-based chess program, Sjeng Chess, that Apple packaged up in a new wrapper.

Playing a Game of Chess

When you launch Chess, you're presented with a fresh, new game that's set up in Human vs. Computer mode—meaning that you, the Human (light-colored pieces) get to play against the Computer (your Mac, on the dark side). Drag the chess piece of your choice into position on the board, and the game is afoot.

If you choose Game→New Game, however, you're offered a pop-up menu with choices like Human vs. Computer, Human vs. Human, and so on. If you switch the pop-up menu to Computer vs. Human, you and your Mac trade places; the Mac takes the white side of the board and opens the game with the first move, and you play the black side.

Tip: The same New Game dialog box also offers a pop-up menu called Variant, which offers three other chess-like games: Crazyhouse, Suicide, and Losers. The Chess help screens (choose Help→Chess Help, and then click "Starting a new chess game") explain these variations.

Figure 10-2:
You don't have to be terribly exact about grabbing the chess pieces when it's time to make your move. Just click anywhere within a piece's current square to drag it into a new position on the board (shown here in its Marble incarnation). And how did this chess board get rotated like this? Because you can grab a corner of the board and rotate it in 3-D space. Cool!

Francis – Computer (White to Move)

On some night when the video store is closed and you're desperate for entertainment, you might also want to try the Computer vs. Computer option, which pits your Mac against itself. Pour yourself a beer, open a bag of chips, and settle in to watch until someone—either the Mac or the Mac—gains victory.

Chess Prefs

Choose Chess→Preferences to find some useful controls like these:

- **Style.** Apple has gone nuts with the computer-generated materials options in this program. (Is it a coincidence that Steve Jobs is also the CEO of Pixar, the computer-animation company?)

  In any case, you can choose all kinds of wacky materials for the look of your game board—Wood, Metal, Marble, or *Grass* (?)—and for your playing pieces (Wood, Metal, Marble, or *Fur*).

- **Computer Plays.** Use this slider to determine how frustrated you want to get when trying to win at Chess. The farther you drag the slider toward the Stronger side, the more calculations the computer runs before making its next move—and, thus, the harder it gets for you to outthink it. At the Faster setting, Chess won't spend more than 5 seconds ruminating over possible moves. Drag the slider all the way to the right, however, and the program may analyze *each move* for as long as 10 fun-filled hours. This hardest setting, of course, makes it all but impossible to win a game (which may stretch on for a week or more anyway).

  Choosing the Faster setting makes it only mildly impossible.

- **Speech.** The two checkboxes here let you play Chess using the Mac's built-in voice-recognition features, *telling* your chess pieces where to go instead of dragging them, and listening to the Mac tell you which moves it's making. Page 593 has the details.

Tip: If your Chess-playing skills are less than optimal, the Moves menu will become your fast friend. The three commands tucked away there undo your last move (great for recovering from a blunder), suggest a move when you don't have a clue what to do next, and display your opponent's previous move (in case you failed to notice what the computer just did).

Studying Your Games

You can choose Game→Save Game to save any game in progress, so you can resume it later.

To analyze the moves making up a game, use the Game Log command, which displays the history of your game, move by move. A typical move would be recorded as "Nb8 – c6," meaning the knight on the b8 square moved to the c6 square. Equipped with a Chess list document, you could re-create an entire game, move by move.

Tip: If you open this window before you begin a new game, you can see the game log fill in the moves as they happen.

Dashboard

Dashboard, described in Chapter 5, is a true-blue, double-clickable application. As a result, you can remove its icon from your Dock, if you like.

Dictionary

For word nerds everywhere, the Dictionary (and thesaurus) is a blessing—a handy way to look up word definitions, pronunciations, and synonyms. To be precise, Snow Leopard comes with electronic versions of multiple reference works in one:

- The entire New Oxford American Dictionary.

- The complete Oxford American Writers Thesaurus.

Snow Leopard Spots: Snow Leopard comes with the second edition of the Oxford American. You'll note that its entries give you a lot more examples, background, and tables that help to differentiate fine shades of meaning (look up "weak" for an example).

- A dictionary of Apple terms, from "A/UX" to "widget." (Apparently there aren't any Apple terms that begin with X, Y, or Z.)

- Wikipedia. Of course, this famous open-source, citizen-created encyclopedia isn't actually on your Mac. All Dictionary does is give you an easy way to search the *online* version, and display the results right in the comfy Dictionary window.

- A Japanese dictionary, thesaurus, and Japanese-to-English translation dictionary.

Tip: You don't ordinarily see the Japanese reference books. You have to turn them on in Dictionary→ Preferences.

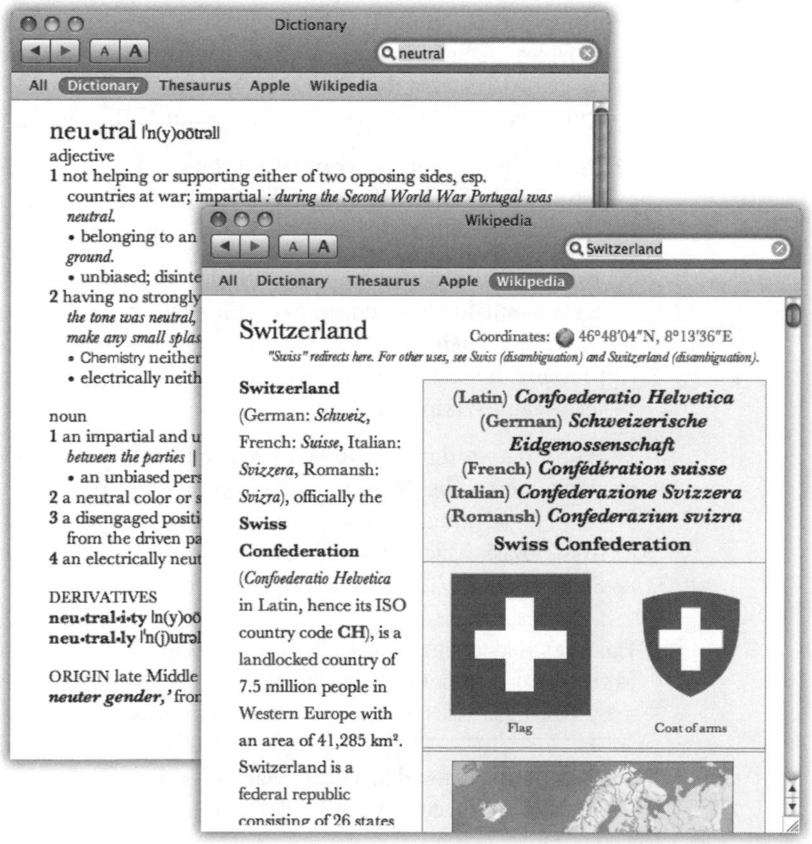

Figure 10-3:
When you open the Dictionary, it generally assumes that you want a word's definition (top left). If you prefer to see the Wikipedia entry (lower right) at startup time instead, for example, choose Dictionary→Preferences—and drag Wikipedia upward so that it precedes New Oxford American Dictionary. That's all there is to it!

Mac OS X also comes with about a million ways to look up a word:

- **Double-click the Dictionary icon.** You get the window shown at top in Figure 10-3. As you type into the Spotlight-y search box, you home in on matching words; double-click a word, or highlight it and press Return, to view a full, typographically elegant definition, complete with sample sentence and pronunciation guide.

Tip: And if you don't recognize a word in the definition, click that word to look up its definition. (Each word turns blue and underlined when you point to it, as a reminder.) You can then double-click again in that definition—and on, and on, and on.

(You can then use the History menu, the ◄ and ► buttons on the toolbar, or the ⌘-[and ⌘-] keystrokes to go back and forward in your chain of lookups.)

It's worth exploring the Dictionary→Preferences dialog box, by the way. There, you can choose U.S. or British pronunciations and adjust the font size.

- **Press F12.** Yes, the Dictionary is one of the widgets in Dashboard (page 205).

- **Control-click (right-click) a highlighted word in a Cocoa program.** From the shortcut menu, choose Look Up in Dictionary. The Dictionary program opens to that word. (Or visit the Dictionary's Preferences box and choose "Open Dictionary panel." Now you get a panel that pops out of the highlighted word instead.)

- **Use the** *dict://* **prefix in your Web browser.** This might sound a little odd, but it's actually ultra-convenient, because it puts the dictionary right where you're most likely to need it: on the Web.

  Turns out that you can look up a word (for example, *preposterous)* by typing *dict:// preposterous* into the address bar—the spot where you'd normally type *http://www. whatever.* When you hit Return, Mac OS X opens Dictionary automatically and presents the search results from all of its resources (dictionary, thesaurus, Apple terms, and Wikipedia).

- **Point to a word in a basic Mac program, and then press Control-⌘-D.** That keystroke makes the definition panel sprout right from the word you were pointing to. (The advantage here, of course, is that you don't have to highlight the word first.) "Basic Mac program," in this case, means one of the Apple standards: Mail, Stickies, Safari, TextEdit, iChat, and so on.

Tip: Here's a trick for the informationally thirsty Mac fan (or speed reader). Once you've invoked the Control-⌘-D keystroke, keep the Control and ⌘ keys pressed. Now drag the cursor across the text. As you push the mouse around, the definition pops up for every word you touch.

- **Highlight to a word in a basic Mac program, and then press Shift-⌘-L.** That's the keyboard shortcut for the Look Up in Dictionary *Service* (see Chapter 7).

The *front matter* of the Oxford American Dictionary (the reference pages at the beginning) is here, too. It includes some delicious writers' tools, including guides to spelling, grammar, capitalization, punctuation, chemical elements, and clichés, along with the full text of the Declaration of Independence and the U.S. Constitution. Just choose Go→Front/Back Matter—and marvel that your Mac comes with a built-in college English course.

Tip: Got a big screen or poor eyesight? Then bump up the type size. Dictionary's toolbar has bigger/smaller buttons, and there's a Font Size pop-up menu in the Preferences window.

DVD Player

DVD Player, your Mac's built-in movie projector, is described in Chapter 11.

Font Book

For details on this font-management program, see Chapter 14.

Front Row

This full-screen multimedia playback program is now part of Mac OS X; it's available even on Macs that *didn't* come with Apple's slim white remote control. Chapter 15 has details.

GarageBand

GarageBand, Apple's do-it-yourself music construction kit, isn't actually part of Mac OS X. If you have a copy, that's because it's part of the iLife suite that comes on every new Mac (along with iMovie, iPhoto, and iWeb). There's a crash-course bonus chapter on this book's "Missing CD" page at *www.missingmanuals.com*.

iCal

In many ways, iCal is not so different from those "Hunks of the Midwest Police Stations" paper calendars people leave hanging on the walls for months past their natural life span.

Tip: iCal's Dock icon displays today's date—even when iCal isn't running.

But iCal offers several advantages over paper calendars. For example:

• It can automate the process of entering repeating events, such as weekly staff meetings or gym workouts.

- iCal can give you a gentle nudge (with a sound, a dialog box, or even an email) when an important appointment is approaching.

- iCal can share information with your Address Book program, with Mail, with your iPod or iPhone, with other Macs, with "published" calendars on the Internet, or with a Palm organizer. Some of these features require one of those MobileMe accounts described in Chapter 18. But iCal also works fine on a single Mac, even without an Internet connection.

- iCal can subscribe to other people's calendars. For example, you can subscribe to your spouse's calendar, thereby finding out when you've been committed to after-dinner drinks on the night of the big game on TV.

Snow Leopard Spots: You can now tell iCal to display your online calendars from Google and Yahoo—without requiring hacks, add-on software, or weeks of fasting.

iCal can now display your company's Exchange calendar, too. For those details, see Chapter 8.

Working with Views

When you open iCal, you see something like Figure 10-4. By clicking one of the View buttons above the calendar, you can switch among these views:

- **Day** shows the appointments for a single day in the main calendar area, broken down by time slot.

Figure 10-4:
In iCal, the miniature navigation calendar (lower left) provides an overview of adjacent months. You can jump to a different week or day by clicking the ◄ and ► buttons, and then clicking within the numbers. Double-click any appointment to see the summary balloon shown here. You can hide the To Do list either by using the Window→Hide To Dos command or by clicking the thumbtack button in the lower-right corner.

If you choose iCal→Preferences, you can specify what hours constitute a workday. This is ideal both for those annoying power-life people who get up at 5 a.m. for two hours of calisthenics and the more reasonable people who sleep until 11 a.m.

Tip: iCal provides three quick ways to get to the current day's date. Click Today (upper-left corner), choose View→Go to Today, or press ⌘-T.

- **Week** fills the main display area with seven columns, reflecting the current week. (You can establish a five-day work week instead in iCal→Preferences.)

Tip: If you double-click the date above the calendar, you open the day view for that day.

- **Month** shows the entire month that contains the current date (Figure 10-4). Double-click a date number to open the day view for that date.

  To save space, iCal generally doesn't show you the *times* of your appointments in Month view. If you'd like to see them anyway, choose iCal→Preferences, click General, and turn on "Show time in month view."

Tip: If your mouse has a scroll wheel, you can use it to great advantage in iCal. For example, when entering a date, turning the wheel lets you jump forward or backward in time. It also lets you change the priority level of a To Do item you're entering, or even tweak the time zone as you're setting it.

In any of the views, *double-click* an appointment to see more about it. The very first time you do that, you get the summary balloon shown in Figure 10-4. If you want to make changes, you can then click the Edit button to open a more detailed view.

Tip: In Week or Day view, iCal sprouts a handy horizontal line that shows where you are in time right now. (Look in the hours-of-the-day "ruler" down the left side of the window to see this line's little red bulb.) A nice touch, and a handy visual aid that can tell you at a glance when you're already late for something.

Making an Appointment

The basic iCal calendar is easy to figure out. After all, with the exception of one unfortunate Gregorian incident, we've been using calendars successfully for centuries.

Even so, there are two ways to record a new appointment: a simple way and a more flexible, elaborate way.

The easy way

You can quickly record an appointment using any of several techniques, listed here in order of decreasing efficiency:

- In Month view, double-click a blank spot on the date you want. A pop-up info balloon appears (Figure 10-5), where you type the details for your new appointment.

- In Day or Week view, double-click the starting time to create a one-hour appointment. Or drag vertically through the time slots that represent the appointment's duration. Either way, type the event's name inside the newly created colored box.

- Choose File→New Event (or press ⌘-N). A new appointment appears on the currently selected day, regardless of the current view.

- In any view, Control-click or right-click a date and choose New Event from the shortcut menu.

Unless you use the drag-over-hours method, a new event believes itself to be one hour long. But in Day or Week view, you can adjust its duration by dragging the bottom edge vertically. Drag the dark top bar up or down to adjust the start time.

In many cases, that's all there is to it. You have just specified the day, time, and title of the appointment. Now you can get on with your life.

Tip: If this Edit balloon is blocking a part of the calendar you need to see, no biggie: Just drag the balloon out of the way, using any blank spot as a handle.

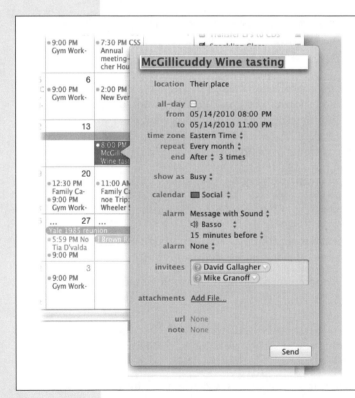

Figure 10-5:
All the details for an appointment sprout right out of the appointment itself in this balloon/box. Tab your way to an organized life.

The long way

The information balloon shown in Figure 10-5 appears when you double-click a Month-view square, or double-click any existing appointment.

Snow Leopard Spots: After you've already edited an appointment once, the full info balloon is a little more effort to open; double-clicking an event produces only the summary balloon shown in Figure 10-4.

The short way to open the full balloon is to click the appointment and then press ⌘-E (which is short for Edit→Edit Event). The long way is to double-click the appointment to get the summary balloon and then click Edit inside it.

But the best solution to this problem is to avail yourself of the new Snow Leopard option in iCal→Preferences→Advanced. It's the checkbox called "Open events in separate windows." Now when you double-click an appointment in iCal, it opens immediately into a full-size Details window, saving you that intermediate step forever. (You can close the window with a quick ⌘-W.)

For each appointment, you can Tab your way to the following information areas:

- **subject.** That's the large, bold type at the top—the name of your appointment. For example, you might type *Fly to Phoenix.*

- **location.** This field makes a lot of sense; if you think about it, almost everyone needs to record *where* a meeting is to take place. You might type a reminder for yourself like *My place,* a specific address like *212 East 23,* or some other helpful information like a contact phone number or flight number.

- **all-day.** An "all-day" event, of course, refers to something that has no specific time of day associated with it: a holiday, a birthday, a book deadline. When you turn on this box, you see the name of the appointment jump to the top of the iCal screen, in the area reserved for this kind of thing.

- **from, to.** You can adjust the times shown here by typing, clicking buttons, or both. Press Tab to jump from one setting to another, and from there to the hours and minutes of the starting time.

   For example, start by clicking the hour, then increase or decrease this number either by pressing ↑ and ↓ or by typing a number. Press Tab to highlight the minutes and repeat the arrow-buttons-or-keys business. Finally, press Tab to highlight the AM/PM indicator, and type either *A* or *P*—or press ↑ or ↓—to change it, if necessary.

Tip: If you specify a different ending date, a banner appears across the top of the calendar.

- **time zone.** This option appears only after you choose iCal→Preferences→Advanced and then turn on "Turn on time zone support." And you would do *that* only if you plan to be traveling on the day this appointment comes to pass.

Once you've done that, a time zone pop-up menu appears. It starts out with "America/New York" (or whatever your Mac's usual time zone is); if you choose Other, a tiny world map appears. Click the time zone that represents where you'll be when this appointment comes due. From the shortcut menu, choose the major city that's in the same zone you'll be in.

Tip: The time zone pop-up menu remembers each new city you select. The next time you travel to a city you've visited before, you won't have to do that clicking-the-world-map business.

Now, when you arrive in the distant city, use the time zone pop-up menu at the top-right corner of the iCal window to tell iCal where you are. You'll see all of iCal's appointments jump, like magic, to their correct new time slots.

- **repeat.** The pop-up menu here contains common options for recurring events: every day, every week, and so on. It starts out saying None.

Once you've made a selection, you get an *end* pop-up menu that lets you specify when this event should *stop* repeating. If you choose "Never," you're stuck seeing this event repeating on your calendar until the end of time (a good choice for recording, say, your anniversary, especially if your spouse might be consulting the same calendar). You can also turn on "After" (a certain number of times), which is a useful option for car and mortgage payments. And if you choose "On date," you can specify the date that the repetitions come to an end; use this option to indicate the last day of school, for example.

"Custom" lets you specify repeat schedules like "First Monday of the month" or "Every two weeks."

- **show as (busy/free/tentative/"out of office").** This little item, new in Snow Leopard, shows up only if you've subscribed to an Internet-based calendar (in geek-speak, a CalDAV server) or you've hooked up to your company's Exchange calendar (Chapter 8). It communicates to your colleagues when you might be available for meetings.

Note: If your calendar comes from a CalDAV server, then your only options are "busy" and "free." The factory setting for most appointments is "busy," but for all-day events it's "free." Which is logical; just because it's International Gecko Appreciation Day doesn't mean you're not available for meetings (rats!).

You might think: "Well, *duh*—if I've got something on the calendar, then I'm obviously busy!" But not necessarily. Some iCal entries might just be placeholders, reminders to self, TV shows you wanted to watch, appointments you'd be willing to change—not things that would necessarily render you unavailable if a better invitation should come along.

- **calendar.** A *calendar,* in iCal's confusing terminology, is a subset—a category—into which you can place various appointments. You can create one for yourself, another for family-only events, another for book-club appointments, and so on.

Later, you'll be able to hide and show these categories at will, adding or removing them from iCal with a single click. Details begin on page 370.

Tip: Use this same pop-up menu to change an appointment's category. If you filed something in "Company Memos" that should have been in "Sweet Nothings for Honey-Poo," then open the event's information balloon and reassign it. Quick.

- **alarm.** This pop-up menu tells iCal how to notify you when a certain appointment is about to begin. iCal can send any of four kinds of flags to get your attention. It can display a message on the screen (with a sound, if you like), send you an email, run a script of the sort described in Chapter 7, or open a file on your hard drive. (You could use this unusual option to ensure that you don't forget a work deadline by flinging the relevant document open in front of your face at the eleventh hour.)

  Once you've specified an alarm mechanism, a new pop-up menu appears to let you specify how much advance notice you want for this particular appointment. If it's a TV show you'd like to watch, you might set up a reminder five minutes before airtime. If it's a birthday, you might set up a two-day warning to give yourself enough time to buy a present. In fact, you can set up more than one alarm for the same appointment, each with its own advance-warning interval.

Tip: In iCal→Preferences→Advanced, you can opt to prevent alarms from going off—a good checkbox to inspect before you give a presentation in front of 2,000 people. There's also an option to stifle alarms except when iCal is open. In other words, just quitting iCal is enough to ensure that those alarms won't interrupt whatever you're doing.

- **invitees.** If the appointment is a meeting or some other gathering, you can type the participants' names here. If a name is already in your Address Book program, iCal proposes autocompleting the name for you.

  If you separate several names with commas, iCal automatically turns each into a shaded oval pop-up button. You can click it for a pop-up menu of commands like Remove Attendee and Send Email. (That last option appears only if the person in your Address Book has an email address, or if you typed a name *with* an email address in brackets, like this: *Chris Smith <chris@yahoo.com>.*)

  Once you've specified some attendees, a Send button appears in the Info box. If you click it, iCal fires up Mail and prepares ready-to-send messages, each with an *iCal.ics* attachment: a calendar-program invitation file. See the box on page 368.

- **attachments.** This new option lets you fasten a file to the appointment. It can be anything: a photo of the person you're meeting, a document to finish by that deadline, the song that was playing the first time you met this person—whatever.

- **url.** A *URL* is a Uniform Resource Locator, better known as a Web address, like *www.apple.com*. If there's a URL relevant to this appointment, by all means type

---

it here. Type more than one, if it'll help you; just be sure to separate them with a comma.

- **note.** Here's your chance to customize your calendar event. You can type, paste, or drag any text you like in the note area—driving directions, contact phone numbers, a call history, or whatever.

Your newly scheduled event now shows up on the calendar, complete with the color coding that corresponds to the calendar category you've assigned.

What to Do with an Appointment

Once you've entrusted your agenda to iCal, you can start putting it to work. iCal is only too pleased to remind you (via pop-up messages) of your events, reschedule them, print them out, and so on. Here are a few of the possibilities:

Editing events

To edit a calendar event's details, you have to open its Info balloon, as described in Figure 10-5.

Tip: If you just want to change an event's name, Option-double-click it right in place.

And if you want to change only an appointment's "calendar" category, Control-click (or right-click) anywhere on the appointment and, from the resulting shortcut menu, choose the category you want.

In both cases, you bypass the need to open the Info balloon.

UP TO SPEED

Inviting Guests

The truth is, this business of automatic invitations to iCal events hasn't really caught on yet. Unless you've hooked up iCal to your company's Exchange server (Chapter 8), the invitations system is still fairly complicated, and it requires compatible software on the receivers' end.

When you click Send at the bottom of the info balloon, your guests receive your invitation. If they use iCal, the invitation appears in their Notifications panel. (To open the Notifications panel, click the tiny envelope icon in the lower-left corner of the window.) They can click Accept, Decline, or Maybe.

In *your* Notifications window, *you* then see the status of each invitee's name: a checkmark for Accepted, an X for Declined, a ? for Maybe, and an arrow for Not Yet Responded.

(Your guests, meanwhile, will be delighted to find that the appointment automatically appears on their calendars once they commit.)

Now, suppose you send an invitation to your sister, who doesn't have a Mac. She just gets an email message that says, "Chris Smith has invited you to the event: Company Hoedown, scheduled for February 02, 2010 at 3:00 PM. To accept or decline this invitation, click the link below." Unfortunately, there generally *is* no link. She just has to know to open the .ics attachment.

If she uses a calendar program that understands this attachment, the appointment appears on her calendar, and her RSVP shows up in your iCal Notification panel.

You don't have to bother with this if all you want to do is *reschedule* an event, however, as described next.

Rescheduling events

If an event in your life gets rescheduled, you can drag an appointment block vertically in a day- or week-view column to make it later or earlier the same day, or horizontally to another date in any view. (If you reschedule a recurring event, iCal asks if you want to change only *this* occurrence, or this *and* all future ones.)

If something is postponed for, say, a month or two, you're in trouble, since you can't drag an appointment beyond its month window. You have no choice but to open the Info balloon and edit the starting and ending dates or times—or just cut and paste the event to a different date.

Lengthening or shortening events

If a scheduled meeting becomes shorter or your lunch hour becomes a lunch hour-and-a-half (in your dreams), changing the length of the representative calendar event is as easy as dragging the bottom border of its block in any column view (see Figure 10-6).

Tip: In week view, if you've grabbed the bottom edge of an appointment's block so that the cursor changes, you can drag horizontally to make an appointment cross the midnight line and extend into a second day.

Figure 10-6:
You can resize any iCal calendar event just by dragging its bottom border. As your cursor touches the bottom edge of a calendar event, it turns into a double-headed arrow. You can now drag the event's edge to make it take up more or less time on your calendar.

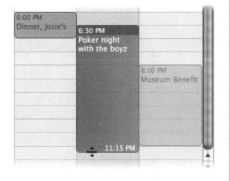

Printing events

To commit your calendar to paper, choose File→Print, or press ⌘-P. The resulting Print dialog box lets you include only a certain range of dates, only events on certain calendars, with or without To Do lists or mini-month calendars, and so on.

Deleting events

To delete an appointment, just select it and then press the Delete key. If you delete a recurring event (like a weekly meeting), iCal asks whether you want to delete only that particular instance of the event, or the whole series from that point forward.

Searching for Events

You should recognize the oval text box at the top of the iCal screen immediately: It's almost identical to the Spotlight box. This search box is designed to let you hide all appointments except those matching what you type into it. Figure 10-7 has the details.

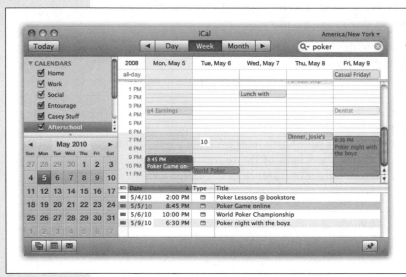

Figure 10-7:
As you type into the search box (top right), iCal builds a little search-results list at the bottom of the window. Double-click any row of the list to jump to and highlight the corresponding event on the calendar and open up its summary balloon.

The "Calendar" Category Concept

Just as iTunes has *playlists* that let you organize songs into subsets and iPhoto has *albums* that let you organize photos into subsets, iCal has *calendars* that let you organize appointments into subsets. They can be anything you like. One person might have calendars called Home, Work, and TV Reminders. Another might have Me, Spouse 'n' Me, and Whole Family. A small business could have categories called Deductible Travel, R&D, and R&R.

To create a calendar, double-click any white space in the Calendar list (below the existing calendars), or click the **+** button at the lower-left corner of the iCal window. Type a name that defines the category in your mind.

Tip: Click a calendar name before you create an appointment. That way, the appointment will already belong to the correct calendar.

To change the color-coding of your category, Control-click (right-click) its name; from the shortcut menu, choose Get Info. The Calendar Info box appears. Here, you can change the name, color, or description of this category—or turn off alarms for this category.

You assign an appointment to one of these categories using the pop-up menu on its Info balloon, or by Control-clicking (right-clicking) an event and choosing a calendar name from the shortcut menu. After that, you can hide or show an entire category of appointments at once just by turning on or off the appropriate checkbox in the Calendars list.

Tip: iCal also has calendar groups: calendar containers that consolidate the appointments from several other calendars. Super-calendars like this make it easier to manage, hide, show, print, and search subsets of your appointments.

To create a calendar group, choose File→New Calendar Group. Name the resulting item in the Calendar list; for the most part, it behaves like any other calendar. Drag other calendar names onto it to include them. Click the flippy triangle to hide or show the component calendars.

"Publishing" Calendars to the Web

One of iCal's best features is its ability to post your calendar on the Web, so that other people (or you, on a different computer) can subscribe to it, which adds *your* appointments to *their* calendars. If you have a MobileMe account, then anyone with a Web browser can also *view* your calendar, right online.

For example, you might use this feature to post the meeting schedule for a club that you manage, or to share the agenda for a series of upcoming financial meetings that all of your coworkers will need to consult.

Publishing

Begin by clicking the calendar category you want in the left-side list. (iCal can publish only one calendar category at a time. If you want to publish more than one calendar, create a calendar *group*.)

Then choose Calendar→Publish; the dialog box shown at top in Figure 10-8 appears. This is where you customize how your saved calendar is going to look and work. You can even turn on "Publish changes automatically," so whenever you edit the calendar,

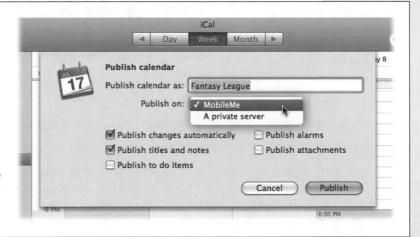

Figure 10-8:
If you click "Publish on: MobileMe," iCal posts the actual, viewable calendar on the Web, as shown in Figure 10-9. If you choose "a private server," you have the freedom to upload the calendar to your own personal Web site, if it's WebDAV-compatible (ask your Web-hosting company). Your fans will be able to download the calendar, but not view it online.

iCal connects to the Internet and updates the calendar automatically. (Otherwise, you'll have to choose Calendar→Refresh every time you want to update the Web copy.)

While you're at it, you can include To Do items, notes, and even alarms with the published calendar.

When you click Publish, your Mac connects to the Web and then shows you the Web address (the URL) of the finished page, complete with a Send Mail button that lets you fire the URL off to your colleagues.

Subscribing

If somebody else has published a calendar, you can subscribe to it by choosing Calendar→Subscribe. In the Subscribe to Calendar dialog box, type in the Internet address you received from the person who published the calendar. Alternatively, click the Subscribe button on any iCal Web page (Figure 10-9, lower left).

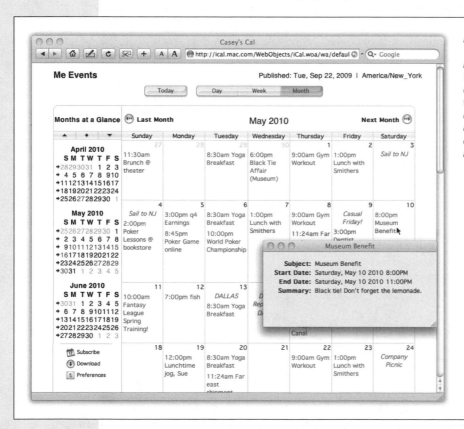

Figure 10-9:
Your calendar is now live on the Web. Your visitors can control the view, switch dates, double-click an appointment for details—it's like iCal Live!

Either way, you can also specify how often you want your own copy to be updated (assuming you have a full-time Internet connection) and whether or not you want to be bothered with the publisher's alarms and notes.

When it's all over, you see a new "calendar" category in your left-side list, representing the published appointments.

Tip: Want to try it out right now? Visit *www.icalshare.com*, a worldwide clearinghouse for sets of iCal appointments. You can subscribe to calendars for shuttle launches, Mac trade shows, National Hockey League teams, NASCAR races, soccer matches, the *Iron Chef* and *Survivor* TV shows, holidays, and much more. You'll never suffer from empty-calendar syndrome again.

Google and Yahoo Calendars

If you maintain a calendar online—at *www.google.com/calendar* or *http://calendar.yahoo.com*, for example, you may take particular pleasure in discovering how easy it is to bring those appointments into iCal. It's one handy way to keep, for example, a husband's and wife's appointments visible on each other's calendars.

Setting this up is ridiculously easy in Snow Leopard (see Figure 10-10).

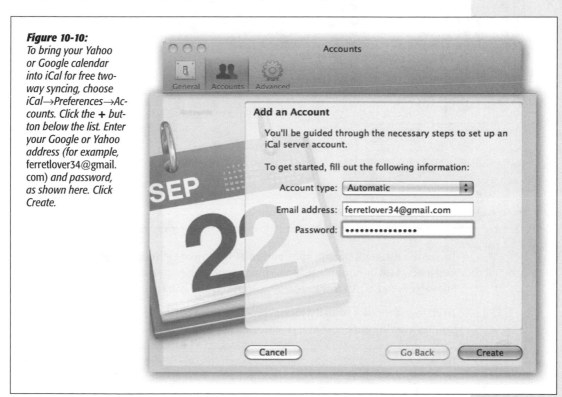

Figure 10-10:
To bring your Yahoo or Google calendar into iCal for free two-way syncing, choose iCal→Preferences→Accounts. Click the + button below the list. Enter your Google or Yahoo address (for example, ferretlover34@gmail.com) and password, as shown here. Click Create.

In a minute or so, you'll see all your Google or Yahoo appointments show up in iCal. (Each Web calendar has its own heading in the left-side list.) Better yet: It's a two-way sync; changes you make to these events in iCal show up on the Web, too.

To Do Lists

iCal's Tasks feature lets you make a To Do list and shepherds you along by giving you gentle reminders, if you so desire (Figure 10-11). What's nice is that Mac OS X maintains a single To Do list, which shows up in both iCal and Mail.

Sorting pop-up   Priority pop-ups

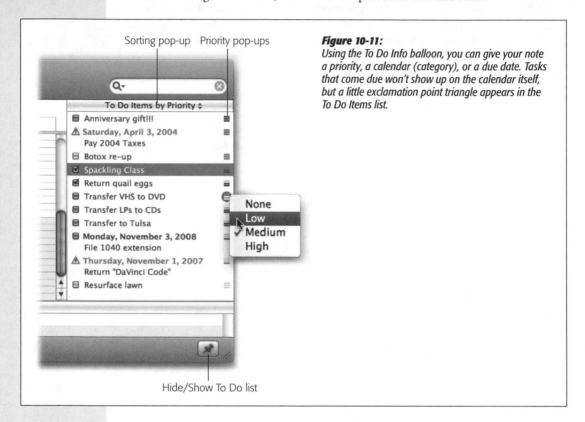

Figure 10-11:
Using the To Do Info balloon, you can give your note a priority, a calendar (category), or a due date. Tasks that come due won't show up on the calendar itself, but a little exclamation point triangle appears in the To Do Items list.

Hide/Show To Do list

To see the list, click the pushpin button at the lower-right corner of the iCal screen. Add a new task by double-clicking a blank spot in the list that appears, or by choosing File→New To Do. After the new item appears, you can type to name it.

To change the task's priority, alarm, repeating pattern, and so on, double-click it. An Info balloon appears, just as it does for an appointment.

Tip: Actually, there's a faster way to change a To Do item's priority—click the tiny three-line ribbed handle at the right side of the list. Turns out it's a shortcut menu that lets you choose Low, Medium, or High priority (or None).

To sort the list (by priority, for example), use the pop-up menu at the top of the To Do list. To delete a task, click it and then press the Delete key.

Tip: You have lots of control over what happens to a task listing after you check it off. In iCal→Preferences, for example, you can make tasks auto-hide or auto-delete themselves after, say, a week or a month. (And if you asked them to auto-hide themselves, you can make them reappear temporarily using the Show All Completed Items command in the pop-up menu at the top of the To Do list.)

iChat

Details on the iChat instant-messaging program can be found in Chapter 21.

iDVD

iDVD isn't really part of Mac OS X, although you probably have a copy of it; as part of the iLife software suite, iDVD comes free on every new Mac. iDVD lets you turn your digital photos or camcorder movies into DVDs that work on almost any DVD player, complete with menus, slideshow controls, and other navigation features. iDVD handles the technology; you control the style.

For a primer on iDVD, see the free, downloadable iLife appendix to this chapter, available on this book's "Missing CD" page at *www.missingmanuals.com.*

Image Capture

This unsung little program, completely redesigned in Snow Leopard, was originally designed to download pictures from a camera and then process them automatically (turning them into a Web page, scaling them to emailable size, and so on). Of course, after Image Capture's birth, iPhoto came along, generally blowing its predecessor out of the water.

Even so, Apple includes Image Capture with Mac OS X for these reasons:

- Image Capture is a smaller, faster app for downloading all or only *some* pictures from your camera (Figure 10-12). iPhoto can do that nowadays, but sometimes that's like using a bulldozer to get out a splinter.

- Image Capture can grab images from Mac OS X–compatible scanners, too, not just digital cameras.

- Image Capture can download your *sounds* (like voice notes) from a digital still camera; iPhoto can't.

- Image Capture can share your camera or scanner on the network.

- Image Capture can turn a compatible digital camera into a Webcam, broadcasting whatever it "sees" to anyone on your office network—or the whole Internet. Similarly, it can share a scanner with all the networked Macs in your office.

You can open Image Capture in either of two ways: You can simply double-click its icon in your Applications folder, or you can set it up to open automatically whenever you connect a digital camera and turn it on. To set up that arrangement, open Image Capture manually. Using the "Connecting this camera opens:" pop-up menu, choose Image Capture.

Snow Leopard Spots: For the first time, you can now specify which program on your Mac opens when you connect a camera independently for each camera. For example, you can set it up so that when you connect your fancy SLR camera, Aperture opens; when you connect your spouse's pocket camera, iPhoto opens; and when you connect your iPhone, Image Capture opens, so you can quickly grab the best shots and email them directly.

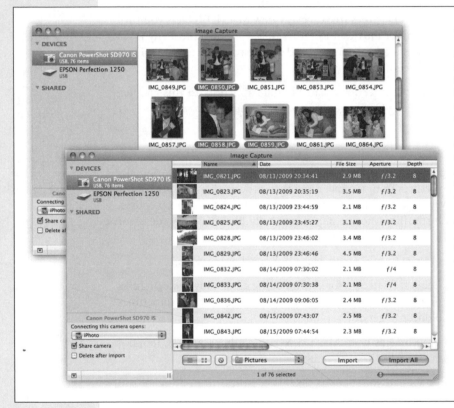

Figure 10-12:
Top: In some ways, Image Capture is like a mini iPhoto; use the slider in the lower right to change the thumbnail sizes. Use the "Delete after import" checkbox (lower-left) if you want your camera's card erased after you slurp in its photos. You can choose the individual pictures you want to download, rotate selected shots (using the buttons at the top), or delete shots from the camera.

Bottom: List view gives you a table of details about the photos to be imported.

Once Image Capture is open, it looks like Figure 10-12. Its controls, once buried in menus and Preferences dialog boxes, have, in Snow Leopard, all been brought out to the main window so they're readily available.

When you connect your camera, cellphone, or scanner, its name appears in the left-side list. To begin, click it. After a moment, Image Capture displays all the photos on the camera's card, in either list view or icon view (your choice).

Import To:

Use this pop-up menu to specify what happens to the imported pictures. Image Capture proposes putting photos, sounds, and movies from the camera into your Home folder's Pictures, Music, and Movies folders, respectively. But you can specify any folder (choose Other from the pop-up menu).

Furthermore, there are some other very cool options here:

- **iPhoto.** Neat that you can direct photos from your camera *to* iPhoto *via* Image Capture. Might come in handy when you didn't *expect* to want to load photos into your permanent collection, but change your mind when you actually look them over in Image Capture.

- **Preview** opens the fresh pictures in Preview so you can get a better (and bigger) look at them.

- **Mail** sends the pix directly into the Mac's email program, which can be very handy when the whole point of getting the photos off the camera is to send them off to friends.

- **Build web page** creates an actual, and very attractive, Web page of your downloaded shots. Against a dark gray background, you get thumbnail images of the pictures in a Web page document called index.html. Just click one of the small images to view it at full size, exactly as your Web site visitors will be able to do once this page is actually on the Web. (Getting it online is up to you.)

Note: Image Capture puts the Web page files in a Home folder→Pictures→Webpage on [today's date and time] folder. It contains the graphics files incorporated into this HTML document; you can post the whole thing on your Web site, if you like.

Image Capture automatically opens up this page in your Web browser, proud of its work.

- **MakePDF.** What is MakePDF? It's a little Snow Leopard app you didn't even know you had.

When you choose this option, you wind up with what looks like a Preview window, showing thumbnails of your photos. If you choose Save right now, you'll get a beautiful full-color PDF of the selected photos, ready to print out and then, presumably, to cut apart with scissors or a paper cutter. But if you use the Layout menu, you can choose different layouts for your photos: 3×5, 4×6, 8×10, and so on.

And what if a photo doesn't precisely fit the proportions you've selected? The Crop commands in the Layout menu (for example, "Crop to 4×6") center each photo within the specified shape, and then trim the outer borders if necessary. The Fit commands, on the other hand, *shrink* the photo as necessary to fit into the specified dimensions, sometimes leaving blank white margins.

Note: The "crop" commands never touch the actual downloaded photos. The downloaded image files themselves retain their full sizes and resolutions.

- **Other.** The beauty of the Image Capture system is that people can, in theory, write additional processing scripts. Once you've written or downloaded them, drop them into your System→Library→Image Capture→Automatic Tasks folder. Then enjoy their presence in the newly enhanced Import To pop-up menu.

Tip: You can set up Image Capture to download everything on the camera automatically when you connect it. No muss, no options, no fuss.

To do that, connect the camera. Click its name in the Devices list. Then, from the "Connecting this camera opens" pop-up menu, choose AutoImporter. From now on, Image Capture downloads all pictures on the camera each time it's connected.

When the downloading process is complete, a little green checkmark appears on the thumbnail of each imported photo.

Import Some, Import All

Clicking Import All, of course, begins the process of downloading the photos to the folder you've selected. A progress dialog box appears, showing you thumbnail images of each picture that flies down the wire.

If you prefer to import only *some* photos, select them first. (In icon view, you click and Shift-click to select a bunch of *consecutive* photos, and ⌘-click to add *individual* photos to the selection. In icon view, you can only click and *Shift*-click to select individual photos.) Then click Import.

Downloading from Across the Network

You're sitting in front of Macintosh #1, but the digital camera or scanner is connected to Macintosh #2 downstairs, elsewhere on the network. What's a Mac fan to do?

All right, that situation may not exactly be the scourge of modern computing. Still, downloading pictures from a camera attached to a different computer can occasionally be useful. In a graphics studio, for example, when a photographer comes back from the field, camera brimming with fresh shots, he can hook up the camera to his Mac so that his editor can peruse the pictures on hers, while he heads home for a shower.

To share your camera on the network, hook it up; then turn on the Share Camera checkbox (lower left). (This trick works with scanners, too.)

On the other Mac (it, too, must be running Snow Leopard), open Image Capture. The shared camera's name appears in the Shared list at left. Click the camera's name. Now you see the photos on that camera, much like what's shown in Figure 10-12; you can view and download the photos exactly as though the camera's connected to *your* Mac.

Image Capture as Spycam

A few newer camera models can actually be *controlled* from the Mac. You can trigger the shutter button from your laptop, for example, without touching the camera and risking jiggling it. (Studio photographers often use this trick.)

Note: The Webcamable cameras include recent Canon PowerShot models, some Kodaks, and several Nikon digital SLRs. In Snow Leopard, you can't operate a camera like this from across the network or Internet—only when the camera is actually attached to your Mac. Sorry, babysittercam fans.

To set this up, connect the camera. Choose File→Take Picture. (If the command is dimmed, then your camera doesn't offer this remote-control feature.)

If you *do* have this feature, a new dialog box appears, showing a preview of what the camera sees. It also offers options that let you control *when* pictures are taken: manually (when you press the space bar or Return key) or automatically at regular intervals.

Scanning

If you own a scanner, chances are good that you won't be needing whatever special scanning software came with it. Instead, Mac OS X gives you two programs that can operate any standard scanner: Image Capture and Preview. In fact, the available controls are identical in both programs.

To scan in Image Capture, turn on your scanner and click its name in the left-side list. Put your photos or documents into the scanner.

Note: You can share a scanner on the network, if you like, by turning on the Share button in the lower-left corner of the window. That's sort of a weird option, though, for two reasons. First, what do you gain by sitting somewhere else in the building? Do you really want to yell or call up to whoever's sitting next to the scanner: "OK! Put in the next photo!"?

Second, don't forget that anyone else on the network will be able to see whatever you're scanning. Embarrassment may result. You've been warned.

Now you have a couple of decisions to make:

- **Separate and straighten?** If you turn on "Detect separate items," Snow Leopard will perform a nifty little stunt indeed: It will check to see if you've put *multiple* items onto the scanner glass, like several small photos. (It looks for rectangular images surrounded by empty white space, so if the photos are overlapping, this feature won't work.)

  If it finds multiple items, Snow Leopard automatically straightens them, compensating for haphazard placement on the glass, and then saves them as individual files.

- **Where to file.** Use the "Scan to" pop-up menu to specify where you want the newly scanned image files to land—in the Pictures folder, for example. You have some other cool options beyond sticking the scans in a folder; you can use the Web page, PDF, iPhoto, and other options described on page 377.

Once you've put a document onto it or into it, click Scan. The scanner heaves to life. After a moment, you see on the screen what's on the glass. It's simultaneously been sent to the folder (or post-processing task) you requested using the "Scan to" pop-up menu.

More power to you

As you can see, Apple has tried to make *basic* scanning as simple as possible: one click. That idiotproof method gives you very few options, however.

If you click Show Details before you scan, though, you get a special panel on the right side of the window that's filled with useful scanning controls (Figure 10-13).

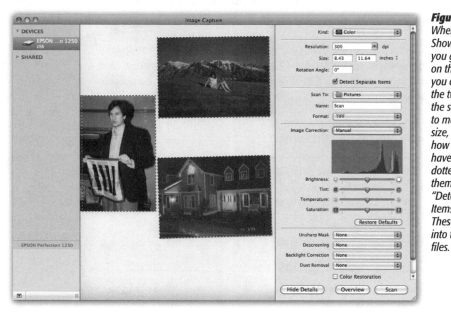

Figure 10-13:
When you use the Show Details button, you get a new panel on the right, where you can specify all the tweaky details for the scan you're about to make: resolution, size, and so on. See how the three photos have individual dotted lines around them? That's because "Detect Separate Items" is turned on. These will be scanned into three separate files.

Here are some of the most useful options:

- **Resolution.** This is the number of tiny scanned dots per inch. 300 is about right for something you plan to print out; 72 is standard for graphics that will be viewed on the screen, like images on a Web page.

- **Name.** Here, specify how you want each image file named when it lands on your hard drive. If it says *Scan,* then the files will be called *Scan 1, Scan 2,* and so on.

- **Format.** Usually, the file format for scanned graphics is TIFF. That's a very high-res format that's ideal if you're scanning precious photos for posterity. But if these images are bound for the Web, you might want to choose JPEG instead; that's the standard Web format.

- **Image Correction.** If you choose Manual from this pop-up menu, then, incredibly, you'll be treated to a whole expando-panel of color correction tools: brightness, tint, saturation, a histogram, and so on.

- **Unsharp Mask.** This option sharpens up any slightly "soft" photos after scanning.

- **Descreening.** Sometimes, when you scan printed photos from a newspaper or magazine, you get a *moiré* effect: a weird rippling pattern in the scanned image that wasn't in the original. This option is supposed to get rid of that ugliness.

- **Dust Removal.** Dust is a common problem in scanned images. This option attempts to eliminate the specks of dust that might mar a photo.

Opening the Details panel has another handy benefit, too: It lets you scan only a *portion* of what's on the scanner glass.

Once you've put the document or photo into the scanner, click Overview. Snow Leopard does a quick pass and displays on the screen whatever's on the glass. You'll see a dotted-line rectangle around the entire scanned image—unless you'd turned on "Detect separate images," in which case you see a dotted-line rectangle around *each* item on the glass.

You can adjust these dotted-line rectangles around until you've enclosed precisely the portion of the image you want scanned. For example, drag the rectangles' corner handles to resize them; drag inside the rectangles to move them; drag the right end of the line inside the rectangle to rotate it; preview the rotation by pressing Control and Option.

Finally, when you think you've got the selection rectangle(s) correctly positioned, click Scan to trigger the actual scan.

Note: These instructions apply to the most common kind of scanner—the flatbed scanner. If you have a scanner with a document feeder—a tray or slot that sucks in one paper document after another from a stack—the instructions are only slightly different.

You may, for example, see a Mode or Scan Mode pop-up menu; if so, choose Document Feeder. You'll want to use the Show Details option described above. You may also be offered a Duplex command (meaning, "scan both sides of the paper"—not all scanners can do this).

---

iMovie, iPhoto

Here's another pair of the iLife apps—not really part of Mac OS X, but kicking around on your Mac because iLife comes with all new Macs.

A basic getting-started chapter for these programs awaits, in free downloadable PDF form, on this book's "Missing CD" page at *www.missingmanuals.com.*

Tip: If that basic guide isn't enough for you, keep in mind that masterfully written, in-depth guides are available in the form of iMovie '09 & iDVD: The Missing Manual and iPhoto '09: The Missing Manual. (Corresponding Missing Manual titles are available for earlier versions of these programs, too.)

---

iSync

See Chapter 6 for details on this file-synchronization software.

iTunes

iTunes is Apple's beloved digital music–library program. Chapter 11 tells all.

Mail

See Chapter 19 for the whole story.

Photo Booth

It may be goofy, it may be pointless, but the Photo Booth program is a bigger time drain than Solitaire, the Web, and *Dancing with the Stars* put together.

It's a match made in heaven for Macs that have a tiny video camera above the screen, but you can also use it with a camcorder, iSight, or Webcam. Just be sure the camera is turned on and hooked up *before* you open Photo Booth. (Photo Booth doesn't even open if your Mac doesn't have *some* kind of camera.)

Open this program and then peer into the camera. Photo Booth acts like a digital mirror, showing whatever the camera sees—that is, you.

But then click the Effects button. You enter a world of special visual effects—and we're talking *very* special. Some make you look like a pinhead, or bulbous, or like a Siamese twin; others simulate Andy Warhol paintings, fisheye lenses, and charcoal sketches (Figure 10-14). In the Snow Leopard version, in fact, there are *four pages* of effects, nine previews on a page; click the left or right arrow buttons, or press ⌘-← or ⌘-→, to see them all. (The last two pages hold *backdrop* effects, described below.)

Some of the effects have sliders that govern their intensity; you'll see them appear when you click the preview.

Still Photos

When you find an effect that looks appealing (or unappealing, depending on your goals here), click the camera button, or press ⌘-T. You see and hear a 3-second countdown, and then *snap!*—your screen flashes white to add illumination, and the resulting photo appears on your screen. Its thumbnail joins the collection at the bottom.

Tip: If that countdown is getting on your nerves, Option-click the camera button. You can get rid of the screen flash, too, by Shift-clicking. Needless to say, if you press Option and Shift, you get neither the countdown nor the flash.

Figure 10-14:
The Photo Booth effects must have been dreamed up one night in the midst of a serious beer party at Apple. They're disturbingly creative. If you decide that you really look best without any help from Apple's warped imagery, click the Normal icon in the center.

Click an effect

Still   4-Up Movie   Effects pages   Finished shots (still, 4-up, movie)

4-Up Photos

If you click the 4-Up button identified in Figure 10-14, then when you click the Camera icon (or press ⌘-T), the 3-2-1 countdown begins, and then Photo Booth snaps *four* consecutive photos in 2 seconds. You can exploit the timing just the way you would in a real photo booth—make four different expressions, horse around, whatever.

The result is a single graphic with four panes, kind of like what you get at a shopping-mall photo booth. (In Photo Booth, they appear rakishly assembled at an angle; but when you export the image, they appear straight, like panes of a window.) Its icon plops into the row of thumbnails at the bottom of the window, just like the single still photos.

Movies

Photo Booth can also record *videos,* complete with those wacky distortion effects. Click the third icon below the screen, the Movie icon (Figure 10-14), and then click the camera button (or press ⌘-T). You get the 3-2-1 countdown—but this time, Photo Booth records a video, with sound, until you click the Stop button or the hard drive is full, whichever comes first. (The little digital counter at left reminds you that you're still filming.) When it's over, the movie's icon appears in the row of thumbnails, ready to play or export.

Or choose Edit→Auto Flip New Photos if you want Photo Booth to do the flipping *for* you from now on.

Exporting Shots and Movies

To look at a photo or movie you've captured, click its thumbnail in the scrolling row at the bottom of the screen. (To return to camera mode, click the camera button.)

Fortunately, these masterpieces of goofiness and distortion aren't locked in Photo Booth forever. You can share them with your adoring public in any of four ways:

- Drag a thumbnail out of the window to your desktop. Or use the File→Reveal in Finder command to see the actual picture or movie files.

Tip: They're in your Home→Pictures→Photo Booth folder. You'll find one JPEG apiece for single shots, four JPEG files for a 4-up, and a .mov movie file for videos.

De-Mirrorizing Your Photos

Technically, Photo Booth acts like a mirror, not a camera. That is, every picture you take is actually flipped, left-to-right. If there's ever text in the picture—something written on your T-shirt, for example—or if you ever examine the way your hair is parted, you'll realize that every image is backwards.

That's why you can click a thumbnail at the bottom of the window and then choose Edit→Flip Photo (⌘-F). You've just made the photo match what a camera would have seen.

- Click Mail to send the photo or movie as an outgoing attachment in Mail.

- Click the iPhoto button to import the shot or movie into iPhoto.

- Click Account Picture to make this photo represent you on the Login screen.

Tip: You can choose one frame of a Photo Booth movie to represent you. As the movie plays, click the Pause button, then drag the scroll-bar handle to freeze the action on the frame you want. Then click Account Picture.

Similarly, you can click your favorite *one pane* of a 4-up image to serve as your account photo—it expands to fill the Photo Booth screen—before clicking Account Picture.

And speaking of interesting headshots: If you export a 4-up image and choose it as your buddy icon in iChat (Chapter 21), you'll get an *animated* buddy icon. That is, your tiny icon cycles among the four images, creating a crude sort of animation. It's sort of annoying, actually, but all the kids are doing it.

GEM IN THE ROUGH

Still and Video Backdrops

Photo Booth and iChat are cousins, and they're closer than ever. One particular feature, in fact, is identical in each: custom backdrops. You can replace the actual, mundane background of your office or den with something far more exciting: a rushing waterfall, for example, or a rider's-eye view of a roller coaster. In fact, you can use any photo or video you want as the background.

It's just like the bluescreen or greenscreen technology that Hollywood uses to put their actors someplace they're not—but without the bluescreen or greenscreen.

To replace your background in Photo Booth, click Effects. The third page of effects offers eight *canned* backgrounds, prepared by Apple for your enjoyment: various spectacular stills (cloudscape, color dots, the moon) and videos (Eiffel Tower plaza, aquarium, roller coaster, tropical beach, Yosemite waterfall).

The final page offers eight *empty* preview squares. You're supposed to drag a still or a video from your desktop (or iPhoto) into these empty squares, making them not so empty.

In any case, prepare the backdrop by clicking one of the preview squares. Photo Booth says, "Please step out of the frame." Do it. Photo Booth is going to memorize what its field of view looks like *without* you in it, so that when you reappear, it can tell *you* apart from your boring office background.

Now, when you record the movie or take the photo, you'll be amazed to discover that Photo Booth has just transplanted you to the far more exotic locale you selected. (Alas, blotches may result if the background includes movement or highly contrasting elements.)

As you set off on your Photo Booth adventures, a note of caution: Keep it away from children. They won't move from Photo Booth for the next 12 years.

Preview

Preview is Mac OS X's scanning software, graphics viewer, fax viewer, and PDF reader. It's always been teeming with features that most Mac owners never even knew were there—but in Snow Leopard, it's been given even more horsepower.

Importing Camera Photos

Preview can import pictures directly from a digital camera (or iPhone), meaning that there are now *three* Snow Leopard apps that can perform that duty. (iPhoto and Image Capture are the other two.) It's sometimes handy to use Preview for this purpose, though, because it has some great tools for photos: color-correction controls, size/resolution options, format conversion, and so on.

The actual importing process, though, is *exactly* like using Image Capture for this purpose. Connect your camera, choose File→Import from [Your Camera's Name], and carry on as described on page 377.

Operating Your Scanner

Preview can also operate a scanner, auto-straighten the scanned images, and export them as PDF files, JPEG graphics, and so on.

This, too, is exactly like using Image Capture to operate your scanner. Only the first step is different. Open Preview, choose File→Import from Scanner→[Your Scanner's Name], and proceed as described on page 379.

Clearly, Apple saved some time by reusing some code.

Multiple Pages, Multiple Views

One hallmark of Preview is its effortless handling of *multiples:* multiple fax pages, multiple PDF files, batches of photos, and so on. The key to understanding the possibilities is mastering the Sidebar, shown in Figure 10-15. The idea is that these thumbnails let you navigate pages or graphics without having to open a rat's nest of individual windows.

Tip: You can drag these thumbnails from one Preview window's Sidebar into another. That's a great way to mix and match pages from different PDF documents into a single new one, for example.

To hide or show the Sidebar, press Shift-⌘-D (or click the Sidebar button in the toolbar, or use the View→Sidebar submenu). Once the Sidebar is open, the four tiny icons at the bottom let you choose among four views:

Tip: You can also change among these four views using the View→Sidebar submenu—or by pressing the keyboard shortcuts Option-⌘-1, 2, 3, and 4.

- **Contact Sheet.** When you choose this view, the *main* window scrolls away, leaving you with a full screen of thumbnail miniatures. It's like a light table where you can look over all the photos or PDF pages at once. Make them bigger or smaller using the slider in the lower left.

- **Thumbnails.** This standard view (Figure 10-15, left) offers a scrolling vertical list of miniature pages or photos. Click one to see it at full size in the main window. Make the thumbnails larger or smaller by dragging the small grabber handle at the bottom of the main window/Sidebar dividing line.

- **Table of Contents.** If you're looking over photos, this option turns the Sidebar into a scrolling list of their names. If you've opened a group of PDFs all at once, you see a list of them. Or, if you have a PDF that contains chapter headings, you see them listed in the Sidebar as, yes, a table of contents.

Figure 10-15:
The Sidebar can display thumbnails (left), a table of contents (right), or annotations, or it can appear as a full-screen array of thumbnail images. Drag the central scroll bar to make the Sidebar bigger; drag the lower-right corner of the Sidebar to make the whole Preview bigger.

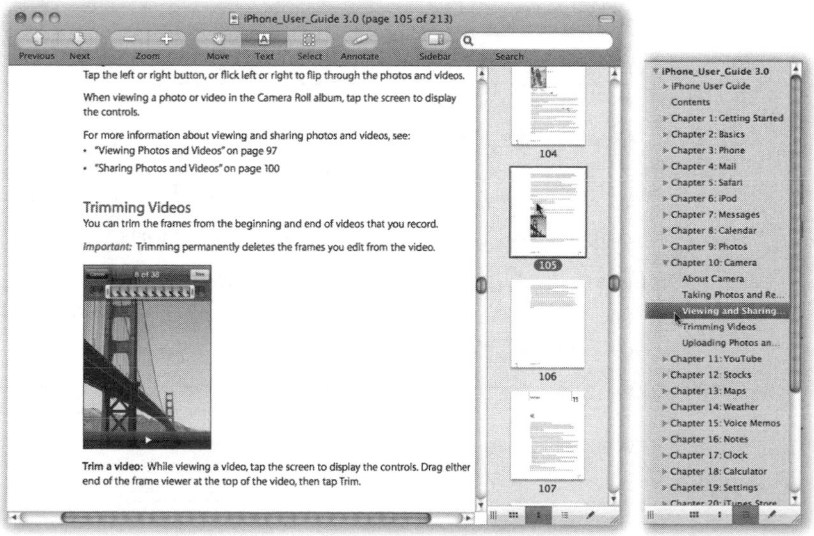

- **Annotations.** Later in this section, you can read about all the ways you can *mark up* a PDF document with notes, underlines, highlighting, and so on. This Sidebar view displays a list of all such annotations, so you can skip directly from one to the next, responding to your editor's worthless sniping far more efficiently.

Preview as Graphics Viewer

Preview, as you're probably starting to figure out, is surprisingly versatile. It can display and manipulate pictures saved in a wide variety of formats, including common graphics formats like JPEG, TIFF, PICT, and GIF; less commonly used formats like BMP, PNG, SGI, TGA, and MacPaint; and even Photoshop, EPS, and PDF graphics. You can even open animated GIFs by adding a Play button to the toolbar, as described on page 395.

Bunches o' graphics

If you highlight a group of image files in the Finder and open them all at once (for example, by pressing ⌘-O), Preview opens the first one, but lists the thumbnails of the whole group in the Sidebar. You can walk through them with the ↑ and ↓ keys, or you can choose View→Slideshow (Shift-⌘-F) to open a full-screen slideshow. (You have to click through the pictures manually, though.)

Tip: You can change the order of the photos just by dragging them around in the Sidebar, in any of its views.

Cropping graphics

To crop graphics in Preview, drag across the part of the graphic that you want to keep. To redraw, drag the round handles on the dotted rectangle; or, to proceed with the crop, choose Tools→Crop. (The keyboard shortcut is ⌘-K.)

If you don't think you'll ever need the original again, save the document. Otherwise, choose File→Save As to spin the cropped image out as a separate file, preserving the original in the process.

Tip: You can also rotate an image—even a PDF document—in 90-degree increments and then flip it vertically or horizontally, using the commands in the Tools menu. In fact, if you select several thumbnails in the Sidebar first, you can rotate or flip them all simultaneously.

Fixing up photos

Preview is no Photoshop, but it's getting closer every year. Let us count the ways:

- **Choose Tools→Inspector.** A floating palette appears. Click the first tab to see the photo's name, when it was taken, its pixel dimensions, and so on. Click the second one for even more geeky photo details, including camera settings like the lens type, ISO setting, focus mode, whether the flash was on, and so on. The third tab lets you add keywords, so you'll be able to search for this image later using Spotlight. (The fourth is for PDF documents only, not photos; it lets you add annotations.)

- **Choose Tools→Adjust Color.** A translucent, floating color-adjustment palette appears, teeming with sliders for brightness, contrast, exposure, saturation (color intensity), temperature and tint (color cast), sharpness, and more. See Figure 10-16.

- **Choose Tools→Adjust Size.** This command lets you adjust a photo's resolution, which comes in handy a lot. For example, you can scale an unwieldy 10-megapixel, gazillion-by-gazillion-pixel shot down to a nice 640 × 480 JPEG that's small enough to send by email. Or you can shrink a photo down so it fits within a desktop window, for use as a window background.

Figure 10-16:
Humble little Preview has grown up into a big, strong mini-Photoshop. You can really fix up a photo if you know what you're doing, using these sliders. Or you can just click the Auto Levels button. It sets all those sliders for you, which generally does an amazing job of making almost any photo look better.

POWER USERS' CLINIC

Scaling and Resampling

When you're fooling around with a picture's size and resolution in the Change Size dialog box, you might find that a couple of the options take a little explaining.

If "Scale proportionally" is turned on, Preview changes the Height number when you change the Width number, and vice versa. In other words, it won't let you change the *shape* of the photo; that's why a little padlock icon appears to bracket the Height and Width boxes.

If "Resample image" is turned off, then Preview adjusts the image's size by making the existing dots bigger or smaller—but never changes the *number* of

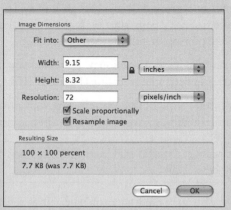

dots. (That's why a padlock bracket links all three boxes together. For example, you can make the image larger—but you'll lower the number of dots per inch.)

If "Resample image" is turned *on,* then you're giving Preview permission to add or subtract pixels as necessary to scale the photo up or down. Of course, it can't create detail that wasn't there in the original, but if you're scaling the picture *up,* it does a decent job of generating new pixels by averaging the colors of the neighboring ones.

There's not much to it. Type in the new print dimensions you want for the photo, in inches or whatever units you choose from the pop-up menu. If you like, you can also change the resolution (the number of pixels per inch) by editing the Resolution box.

Cutting people out of backgrounds

Here's a Photoshoppy feature you would never, ever expect to find in a simple viewer like Preview: You can extract a person (or anything, really) from its background. That's handy when you want to clip yourself out of a group shot to use as your iChat portrait, when you want to paste somebody into a new background, or when you break up with someone and want them out of your photos.

- **Solid backgrounds.** If the background is simple—mostly a solid color or two—you can do this job quickly. Start by making sure the toolbar is visible (⌘-B). From the Select pop-up menu, choose Instant Alpha.

  This feature is extremely weird, but here goes: Click the first background color you want to eliminate. Preview automatically dims out *all* the pixels that match the color you clicked. Click again in another area to add more of the background to the dimmed patch.

  Actually, if you click and *drag* a tiny distance, you'll see sensitivity-percentage numbers appear next to your cursor. They indicate that the more you drag, the more you're expanding the selection to colors *close* to the one you clicked. The proper technique, then, isn't click-click-click; it's drag-drag-drag.

  If you accidentally eat into part of the person or thing that you want to *keep*, Option-drag across it to remove those colors from the selection.

  When it looks like you've successfully isolated the subject from the background, press Return or Enter. There it is, ready to cut or copy.

- **Complex backgrounds.** If the background *isn't* primarily solid colors, the process is a little trickier. Again, start by making sure the toolbar is visible (⌘-B). From the Select pop-up menu, choose Extract Shape.

  Now carefully trace the person or thing that you'll want to extract. Preview marks your tracing with a fat pink line (Figure 10-17).

  You can trace straight lines by releasing your mouse button and clicking the next endpoint. Preview draws a straight line between your last drag and the click.

Tip: If the pink outline is too thick or too thin for your tastes, hold down the **–** or **+** keys to make the entire line grow thinner or thicker.

Don't worry if you're not exact; you'll be able to refine the outline later. (Zoom in for tight corners by pressing ⌘-+.) Continue until you've made a complete closed loop. Or just double-click to say, "Connect where I am now with where I started."

(Hit Esc to erase the line and start over—or give up.)

When you're done, the outline sprouts dotted handles, as shown in Figure 10-17. You can drag them to refine the border's edges. When the outline looks close enough, press Return or Enter.

Figure 10-17:
After your outline is complete, the fat pink outline sprouts a trail of tiny handles. Drag them to refine the edge.

Now you enter the Instant Alpha mode described above. If you see bits of background still showing, dab them with the mouse; they fade into the foggy "not included" area. If you accidentally chopped out a piece of your person, Option-dab. In both cases, Preview includes all pixels of the same color you dabbed, making it easy to remove, for example, a hunk of fabric.

When it all looks good, press Return or Enter. Preview ditches the background, leaving only the outlined person. If you choose File→Save As, you'll have yourself an empty-background picture, ready to import or paste into another program.

Once you've exported the file, congratulate yourself. You've just created a graphic with an *alpha channel*, which, in computer-graphics terms, is a special mask that can be used for transparency or blending. The background that you deleted—the empty white part—appears transparent when you import the graphic into certain graphically sophisticated programs. For example:

- **iMovie '08 or '09.** You can drag your exported graphic directly onto a filmstrip in an iMovie project. The white areas of the exported Preview image become transparent, so whatever video is already in the filmstrip plays through it. Great for opening credits or special effects.

- **Preview.** Yes, Preview itself recognizes incoming alpha channels. So after you cut the background out of Photo A, you can select what's left (press ⌘-A), copy it to the Clipboard (⌘-C), open Photo B, and paste (⌘-V). The visible part of Photo A gets pasted into the background of Photo B.

- **Photoshop, Photoshop Elements.** Of course, these advanced graphics programs recognize alpha channels, too. Paste in your Preview graphic; it appears as a layer, with the existing layers shining through the empty areas.

Tip: Here's a great way to create a banner or headline for your Web page: Create a big, bold-font text block in TextEdit. Choose File→Print; from the PDF pop-up button, choose Open PDF in Preview.

In Preview, crop the document down, and save it as a PNG-format graphic (because PNG recognizes alpha channels). Then use the Instant Alpha feature to dab out the background and the gaps inside the letters. When you import this image to your Web page, you'll find a professional-looking text banner that lets your page's background shine through the empty areas of the lettering.

Converting file formats

Preview doesn't just open all these file formats—it can also convert between most of them. You can pop open some old Mac PICT files and turn them into BMP files for a Windows user, pry open some SGI files created on a Silicon Graphics workstation and turn them into JPEGs for use on your Web site, and so on.

Tip: What's even cooler is you can open raw PostScript files right into Preview, which converts them into PDF files on the spot. You no longer need a PostScript laser printer to print out high-end diagrams and page layouts that come to you as PostScript files. Thanks to Preview, even an inkjet printer can handle them.

All you have to do is open the file you want to convert and choose File→Save As. In the dialog box that appears, choose the new format for the image using the Format pop-up menu (JPEG, TIFF, PNG, or Photoshop, for example). Finally, click Save to export the file.

Preview as PDF Reader

Preview is a nearly full-blown equivalent of Acrobat Reader, the free program used by millions to read PDF documents. It lets you search PDF documents, copy text out of them, add comments, fill in forms, click live hyperlinks, add highlighting, circle certain passages, type in notes—features that used to be available only in Adobe's Acrobat Reader.

Here are the basics:

- Zoom in and out using ⌘-plus and ⌘-minus.

- Use the View→PDF Display submenu to control how the PDF document appears: as two-page spreads; as single scrolling sheets of "paper towel"; with borders that indicate ends of pages; and so on.

- Press the space bar to page through a document (add Shift to page *upward*. The Page Up and Page Down keys do the same thing.)

Tip: Some PDF documents include a table of contents, which you'll see in Preview's Sidebar, complete with flippy triangles that denote major topics or chapter headings (Figure 10-19, right). You can use the ↑ and ↓ keys alone to walk through these chapter headings, and then expand one that looks good by pressing the → key. Collapse it again with the ← key.

In other words, you expand and collapse flippy triangles in Preview just as you do in a Finder list view.

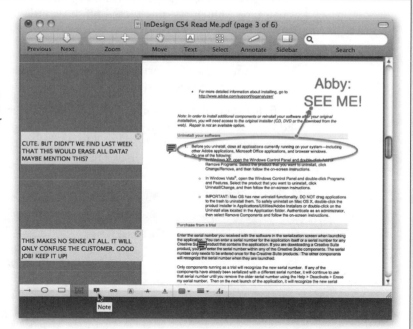

Figure 10-18:
The new Annotation strip at the bottom edge of the Preview window makes it incredibly easy to add different kinds of annotations. This strip appears when you click the Annotate button on the top toolbar, or whenever you've added a marking or a note manually using the Tools→Annotate submenu.

Click the button you want, then drag diagonally to define a rectangle, oval, arrow, or link. Or click to place a Note icon and edit that note in the left margin. You can drag or delete the annotation's little icon, or adjust its look using the Tools→Inspector palette.

- Bookmark your place by choosing Bookmarks→Add Bookmark (⌘-D); type a clever name. In the future, you'll be able to return to that spot by choosing its name from the Bookmarks menu.

- You can type in notes, add clickable links (to Web addresses or other spots in the document), or use circles, arrows, rectangles, strikethrough, underlining, or yellow highlighting to draw your readers' attention to certain sections, as shown in Figure 10-18.

Tip: Preview ordinarily stamps each text note with your name and the date. If you'd rather not have that info added, choose Preview→Preferences, click PDF, and then turn off "Add name to annotations."

These remain living, editable entities even after the document is saved and re-opened. These are full-blown Acrobat annotations; they'll show up when your PDF document is opened by Acrobat Reader or even on Windows PCs.

Tip: You can add circles, arrows, rectangles, and text boxes, even on image files like photos.

- **Turn smoothing on or off to improve readability.** To find the on/off switch, choose Preview→Preferences, and click the PDF tab. Turn on "Smooth line art and text." (Though antialiased text generally looks great, it's sometimes easier to read very small type with antialiasing turned off. It's a little jagged, but clearer nonetheless.)

- **Turn on View→PDF Display→Single Page (or Double Page) Continuous** to scroll through multipage PDF documents in one continuous stream, instead of jumping from page to page when you use the scroll bars.

- **To find a word or phrase somewhere in a PDF document,** press ⌘-F (or choose Edit→Find→Find) to open the Find box—or just type into the ○ box at the top of the Sidebar, if it's open. Proceed as shown in Figure 10-19.

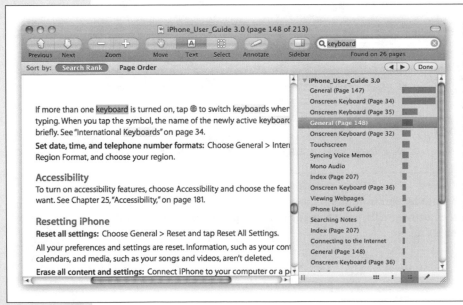

Figure 10-19:
Type into the Search or Find box. Matches appear in the Sidebar, with page numbers; click one to go there. The bar graph shows you how relevant that page is to your search term—how many times that word appears, for example.

- If you want to copy some text out of a PDF document—for pasting into a word processor, for example, where you can edit it—click the Text tool (the letter A on the toolbar) or choose Tools→Text Tool. Now you can drag through some text and then choose Edit→Copy, just as though the PDF document were a Web page. You can even drag across page boundaries.

Snow Leopard Spots: Ordinarily, dragging across text selects the text from one edge of the page to the other, even if the PDF document is laid out in columns. But in Snow Leopard, Preview is a bit smarter. It can tell if you're trying to get the text in only one column, and highlights just that part automatically. (The old Preview could do this, too, but you had to press Option as you dragged.)

- You can save a single page from a PDF as a TIFF file to use it in other graphics, word processing, or page layout programs that might not directly recognize PDF.

    To extract a page, use the usual File→Save As command, making sure to choose the new file format from the pop-up menu. (If you choose a format like Photoshop or JPEG, Preview converts only the currently selected page of your PDF document. That's because there's no such thing as a multipage Photoshop or JPEG graphic. But you already knew that.)

- Add keywords to a graphic or PDF (choose Tools→Show Inspector, click the ⚲ tab, click the **+** button). Later, you'll be able to call up these documents with a quick Spotlight search for those details.

The Toolbar

You can have hours of fun with Preview's toolbar. Exactly as with the Finder toolbar, you can customize it (by choosing View→Customize Toolbar—or by Option-⌘-clicking the upper-right toolbar button), rearrange its icons (by ⌘-dragging them sideways), and remove icons (by ⌘-dragging them downward).

Tip: Unhappy about the full inch of screen space consumed by the toolbar? No problem. Just ⌘-click the toolbar button (the white capsule in the upper-right corner). With each click, you cycle to the next toolbar style: large icons, small icons, no text labels, only text labels, and so on.

QuickTime Player

There's a lot to say about QuickTime player, but it's all in Chapter 15.

Safari

Apple's Web browser harbors enough tips and tricks lurking inside to last you a lifetime. Details in Chapter 20.

Stickies

Stickies creates virtual Post-it notes that you can stick anywhere on your screen—a triumphant software answer to the thousands of people who stick notes on the edges of their actual monitors. Like the Stickies widget in Dashboard, you can open this program with a keystroke (highlight some text, then press Shift-⌘-Y)—but it's a lot more powerful.

You can use Stickies to type quick notes and to-do items, paste in Web addresses or phone numbers you need to remember, or store any other little scraps and snippets of text you come across. Your electronic Post-it notes show up whenever the Stickies program is running (Figure 10-20).

Figure 10-20:
In the old days of the Mac, the notes you created with Stickies were text-only, single-font deals. Today, however, you can use a mix of fonts, text colors, and styles within each note. You can even paste in graphics, sounds, and movies (like PICT, GIF, JPEG, QuickTime, AIFF, whole PDF files, and so on), creating the world's most elaborate reminders and to-do lists.

Creating Sticky Notes

The first time you launch Stickies, a few sample notes appear automatically, describing some of the program's features. You can quickly dispose of each sample by clicking the close button in the upper-left corner of each note or by choosing File→Close (⌘-W). Each time you close a note, a dialog box asks if you want to save it. If you click Don't Save (or press ⌘-D), the note disappears permanently.

To create a new note, choose File→New Note (⌘-N). Then start typing or:

- Drag text in from any other program, such as TextEdit, Mail, or Microsoft Word. Or drag text clippings from the desktop directly into your note. You can also drag a PICT, GIF, JPEG, or TIFF file into a note to add a picture. You can even drag a sound or movie in. (A message asks if you're sure you want to copy the whole whopping QuickTime movie into a little Stickies note.)

- Drag the icon of a PDF file into a note. (Stickies can even accommodate multipage PDF files. At first, you see only the first page, but a scroll bar is available to see the rest.)

- How weird is this? You can even drag a *Microsoft Word* document into a note!

- Choose File→Import and select any plain text file or RTF (Rich Text Format) document to bring it into a note.

- Drag URLs into a note directly from a Web browser's address bar.

Tip: If one particular note contains your most important information—your to-do list, say—you can force it to remain in front of all other windows, even if Stickies itself gets shunted to the background. Just click the note, and then choose Note→Floating Window.

- In TextEdit, Mail, Pages, Safari, iChat, Stickies itself, and other standard Apple programs, you can select a chunk of text and then choose Make New Sticky Note from the program's Services menu, or press Shift-⌘-Y. This command launches Stickies, creates a new note, and fills it with your selected text—all in one step.

Note: All your notes are stored in a file called StickiesDatabase, located in your Home→Library folder. You're free to copy it, pass it along, and so on, just as you would any file.

Have a favorite style for your sticky notes? First create a new note, choosing the color and text style that you like and setting it to the size you prefer. Then choose Note→Use as Default. All new notes you create now appear in the size, font, and color you've chosen.

Growing and Shrinking Notes

Stickies includes a few built-in tricks for managing a deskful of notes:

- There's a small resize handle on the lower-right corner of each note. Drag it to make notes larger or smaller onscreen.

- Use the small triangle in the upper-right corner of each note to zoom and shrink note windows with a single click. The first click collapses a note down to a more compact size. Another click pops the note back open to normal size.

- The best option: Double-click anywhere along the dark strip at the top of each note to collapse it into a compact one-line mininote, as shown in Figure 10-21. You also can collapse a selected note by choosing Window→Miniaturize Window (⌘-M).

Tip: The most efficient way to use Stickies is to keep the notes in their collapsed state, as shown in Figure 10-21. When a note is collapsed, the first line of text shows up in tiny type in the collapsed title bar of the note, so you don't have to expand the note to remember what's in it. And since many—if not most—of your notes can probably be summed up in a couple of words ("Pick up dry cleaning," "Call Mom"), it's possible to keep your sticky notes in their collapsed state permanently.

Figure 10-21:
If the first line of text gets truncated, as in the third note shown here, you can tug the right corner of the note and drag it wider without de-miniaturizing it.

Formatting Notes

Stickies has several word processor-like commands for creating designer sticky notes, with any combination of fonts, colors, and styles. You can also choose from six background colors from the Color menu. For the full scoop on Mac OS X's Font panel, choosing colors, and other typographic finery, see page 569.

Saving Sticky Notes

The notes you create in Stickies last only as long as you keep them open. If you close a note to get it out of the way (and click Don't Save in the confirmation box), it vanishes permanently.

If you want to preserve the information you've stuffed into your notes in a more permanent form, use File→Export Text to save each note as a standalone TextEdit document. When you use the Export Text command, you have the following options:

- **Plain Text**. This option saves your note as a plain text file, with neither formatting nor pictures.

- **RTF** stands for Rich Text Format, a special exchange format that preserves most formatting, including font, style, and color choices. You can open the resulting RTF file in just about any word processor with all of your formatting still intact.

- **RTFD**. RTFD, a strange and powerful variant of RTF, is a Rich Text Format document *with attachments*. How do you "attach" items to an RTFD file? Drag the icon of an actual application (Preview, Calculator, or whatever) or a multipage PDF file, into a sticky note. The icon for the program or document appears in the note, but double-clicking the icon doesn't do anything. When you export the note as an RTFD file, the result is a TextEdit document that has embedded within it the *entire* program or document that you dragged in. The program icon appears just as it did in the sticky note, but if you double-click the icon, the program now actually opens. (For more about RTFD files, see the box on page 406.)

You can also paste a graphic into your sticky note. When you export the note as an RTFD document, the resulting *package* file includes a graphics file of the format that you pasted.

If you don't have embedded programs or documents in your notes, then exported RTFD files are exactly the same as their RTF counterparts.

Tip: You can import the Stickies file from your old Mac OS 9 System Folder. Just choose File→Import Classic Stickies. In the Open File dialog box, navigate to the old System Folder→Preferences→Stickies File document and open it.

System Preferences

This program opens the door to the nerve center of Mac OS X's various user preferences, settings, and options. Chapter 9 covers every option in detail.

TextEdit

TextEdit: It's not just for Read Me files anymore.

TextEdit (Figure 10-22) is a basic word processor—but it's not nearly as basic as it used to be. You can create real documents with real formatting, using style sheets, colors, automatic numbering and bullets, tables, and customized line spacing,

---

UP TO SPEED

The Deal with Microsoft Word

Yes, you read that correctly: Humble TextEdit can open and create Microsoft Word documents! Your savings: the $400 price of Microsoft Office!

Well, sort of.

When you open a Microsoft Word document in TextEdit, most of the formatting comes through alive: bold, italic, font choices, colors, line spacing, alignment, and so on. Even very basic tables make it into TextEdit, although with different column widths.

A lot of Word-specific formatting does not survive crossing the chasm, however: borders, style sheets, footnotes, and the like. Bullets and numbered lists don't make it, either, even though TextEdit can create its own versions of these. And TextEdit doesn't recognize the comments and tracked

changes your collaborators might use to mark up your manuscript.

Saving a TextEdit document as a Word document (File→Save As) is a better bet, because Word understands the many kinds of formatting that TextEdit can produce—including bullets, numbering, and tables. The one disappointment is that Word doesn't recognize any style sheets you've set up in TextEdit. The formatting applied by those style names survives—just not the style names themselves.

Even so, a built-in Word-document editor is a huge, huge step for the Mac OS. It means that in many cases, you can be a first-class citizen on the playing field of American business. Nobody ever needs to know that you're (a) using a Mac, and (b) not using the real Microsoft Word.

---

and—get this—even save the result as a Microsoft Word document. There's even a multiple-level Undo command. If you had to, you could write a novel in TextEdit, and it would look pretty decent.

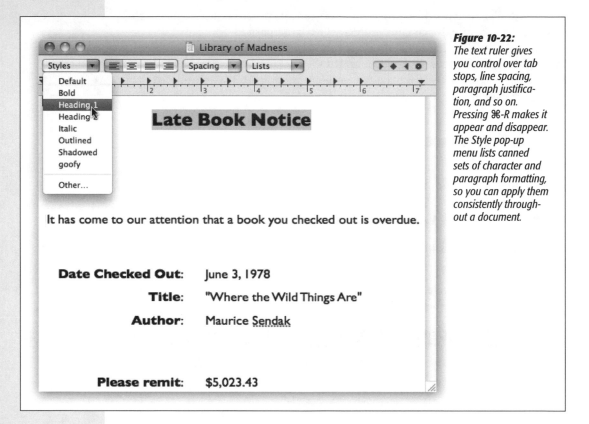

Figure 10-22:
The text ruler gives you control over tab stops, line spacing, paragraph justification, and so on. Pressing ⌘-R makes it appear and disappear. The Style pop-up menu lists canned sets of character and paragraph formatting, so you can apply them consistently throughout a document.

There aren't any new features in TextEdit in Snow Leopard. There is, however, a long list of new text-*editing* features in Snow Leopard: smart links, smart quotes, smart dashes, smart copy/paste, abbreviation expansion, auto-typo correction, data detectors, and so on. They're all described in Chapter 6, and they all work in TextEdit.

TextEdit's Two Personalities

The one confusing aspect of TextEdit is that it's both a *plain text editor* (no formatting; globally compatible) and a true *word processor* (fonts, sizes, styles; compatible with other word processors). You need to keep your wits about you as you edit, because the minute you add formatting to your document, TextEdit no longer lets you save it as a plain text file.

Here's the scheme:

- You can change a plain text document to a formatted one by choosing Format→ Make Rich Text. The ruler appears automatically to remind you that a new world of formatting has just become available.

- Conversely, you can change a formatted document (a Word file you've opened, for example) to a plain text document by choosing Format→Make Plain Text. An alert message appears to point out that you're about to lose all formatting.

- If you know what kind of document you *always* want to create, go to the TextEdit→ Preferences dialog box; on the New Document tab, select Rich Text or Plain Text. That's what you'll get each time you choose File→New.

Tip: Here's also where you can turn on smart links, smart quotes, smart dashes, and the other smart text-processing features described in Chapter 6.

Working in TextEdit

As you begin typing, all the usual word processing rules apply, with a few twists:

- Choose Bold, Italic, and font sizes using the Format→Font submenu, or choose Format→Font→Show Fonts (⌘-T) to open up the standard Mac OS X Font panel. You can even create subscript or superscript, change the color of the text (Format→Font→Show Colors), and so on.

- Common paragraph-alignment options—Align Left, Align Right, Center, Justify— are all available as ruler buttons and also reside in the Format→Text submenu. Adjust the line spacing (single, double, or any fraction or multiple) using the Spacing pop-up menu in the ruler.

- The ruler also offers automatic bulleting and numbering of paragraphs. Just choose the numbering style you prefer from the Lists pop-up menu.

- You can select several non-adjacent bits of text *simultaneously*. To pull this off, highlight your first piece of text by dragging, and then press ⌘ as you use the mouse to select more text. Bingo: You've highlighted two separate chunks of text.

  When you're done selecting bits of text here and there, you can operate on them en masse. For example, you can make them all bold or italic with one fell swoop. You can even use the Cut, Copy, and Paste commands, as described in the next section. When you cut or copy, the command acts upon all your selections at once.

  You can also drag any *one* of the highlighted portions to a new area, confident that the other chunks will come along for the ride. All the selected areas wind up consolidated in their new location.

Tip: If you Option-drag one of the highlighted bits, you copy all selected chunks, leaving the originals in place.

- Similarly, you can use the Find command to highlight a certain term everywhere it appears in a document. To do that, choose Edit→Find→Find (or just press ⌘-F). Fill in the "Find" and "Replace with" boxes—and then press the Control key. The Replace All button changes to say Select All.

Tip: Oh, don't get TextEdit started on secret keystrokes in the Find box. If you press Option, for example, the Replace All button changes to say In Selection (meaning that you'll search-and-replace only the highlighted blob of text).

You can combine the two previous tricks, too. If you press Control and Option, the Replace All button changes to say In Selection—but now you're selecting, not replacing, all occurrences of the search text just within the highlighted block.

- If you Option-drag vertically, you can freely select an arbitrary column of text (not necessarily the entire page width). This technique is very useful when you want to select only one column in a multicolumn layout, or when you want to select the numbers in a list and format them all at once. (As noted earlier, this trick also works in Preview PDF documents.)

POWER USERS' CLINIC

Advanced Typography in TextEdit

If you just sprayed your coffee upon reading the heading of this sidebar, you're forgiven. Advanced typography in TextEdit? Isn't that a little bit like saying "advanced page layout in Note Pad"?

Not at all. TextEdit is a gleaming showcase for Mac OS X's typographical smarts.

Most of the commands in the Format→Font submenu should be familiar to you: Bold, Italic, Underline, and so on. But a few were once found only in expensive page-layout programs like InDesign and QuarkXPress. For example:

Kern. Use these commands, such as Tighten and Loosen, to nudge the letters of the selected text closer together or farther apart— an especially useful feature when you're fiddling with headlines and headings.

There are no controls to set how much you want to kern the text, but you can apply these commands repeatedly to the same text selection to intensify them. If you want your text to be very tight, for example, just keep choosing the Tighten command. The characters creep closer and closer together until they crash into one another.

Ligature. Ligatures are letter pairs, such as fl and ff, that, in fancy typesetting, are often conjoined into special combination characters, as shown here. If you choose Format→ Font→Ligature→Use Default (or Use All), then TextEdit displays these letter pairs with the appropriate ligatures. (This works only if the font you're using has those ligatures built into it. New York, Charcoal, Apple Chancery, and all Adobe Expert fonts do, for example, but many other fonts don't.)

Baseline. The baseline is the imaginary "floor" for text characters in a line of type. You can push text above this line or sink it below the baseline using the Raise and Lower commands in the Baseline submenu. The Superscript and Subscript commands, meanwhile, shift characters far above or below the baseline, so you can write stuff like H_2O.

Character Shape. In a few fonts, such as Adobe Expert fonts, this submenu offers a choice between Traditional Form and specialized type treatments like Small Caps.

Copy Style/Paste Style. If mastering the Styles pop-up menu (described on the facing page) is too much effort, these commands offer another way to copy and paste just the font formatting to other text—the font, color, style, and size, but none of the actual text or paragraph attributes, such as alignment.

Style Sheets

A *style* is a prepackaged collection of formatting attributes that you can apply and reapply with a click of the mouse (bold, 24-point Optima, double-spaced, centered, for instance). You can create as many styles as you need: chapter headings, sidebar styles, and so on. You end up with a collection of custom-tailored styles for each of the repeating elements of your document.

Once you've created your styles, you can apply them as you need them, safe in the knowledge that they'll be consistent throughout the document. During the editing process, if you notice you accidentally styled a *headline* using the *Subhead* style, you can fix the problem by simply reapplying the correct style.

Note: Unlike a real word processor, TextEdit doesn't let you change a style's formatting and thereby update every occurrence of it. You can't search and replace by style, either.

- **Creating a named style.** To create a style, format some text so it looks the way you like it, complete with font, color, line spacing, tab settings, and so on.

  Then, from the Styles pop-up menu in the ruler, choose Other (Figure 10-23, top). Click Add to Favorites, type a name for the style, turn on both checkboxes (Figure 10-23, bottom), and click Add.

Figure 10-23:
Top: Highlight the text you want to format. Then, from the Styles pop-up menu in the ruler, choose Other. With each click of the ▶ button, you summon a snippet of the next chunk of formatting. When you find one you like, you can either click Apply (to zap the highlighted text into submission) or Add To Favorites (to reuse this canned style later). In the latter case, you can give the new style a name (bottom).

- **Applying a style.** Later, when you want to reuse the formatting you set up, highlight some text and then choose the appropriate name from the Styles pop-up menu. TextEdit applies the formatting immediately.

Tip: If you simply click inside a paragraph, applying a style affects only paragraph attributes like line spacing, tab stops, and alignment. If you highlight a random chunk of text instead, applying a style affects only character attributes like the font and type size. If you highlight an entire paragraph, however, both text and paragraph formatting appear.

- **Deleting a style.** To delete a superfluous style, choose Other from the Styles pop-up menu on the ruler. Click the Favorite Styles button, choose the unwanted style's name from the pop-up menu, and then click Remove From Favorites. (Deleting a style doesn't affect any formatting that's already in your document; it just removes the name from the Styles menu.)

- **Copying by example.** In TextEdit, you can also use Option-⌘-C and Option-⌘-V (Format→Copy Style and Format→Paste Style) to grab formatting from one place in your document and reuse it elsewhere. (Of course, you can't apply styles in text-only documents.)

Tables

Tables can make life a heck of a lot easier when you want to create a resumé, agenda, program booklet, list, multiple-choice test, Web page, or another document where numbers, words, and phrases must be aligned across the page. In the bad old days, people did it by pressing the Tab key to line up columns—a technique that turned into a nightmare as soon as you tried to add or delete text. But using a word processor's *table* feature is light-years easier and more flexible, because each row of a table expands to contain whatever you put into it. Everything else in its row remains aligned.

Tip: Tables are also critical for designing Web pages, as any Web designer can tell you. Even though you can't see the table outlines, many a Web page is filled with columns of text that are aligned invisibly by tables. And now that TextEdit can save your work as an HTML document, it's suddenly a viable candidate for designing basic Web pages.

- **Create a table** by choosing Format→Text→Table. The floating Table palette appears (Figure 10-24). Use it to specify how many rows and columns you want. The placeholder table in your document adjusts itself in real time.

- **Format the table** using the other controls in the Table palette. The Alignment controls let you specify how the text in the table cells hugs its border. Cell Border controls the thickness of the line around the selected cells' borders (or, if you enter 0, makes the table walls invisible). The color swatch next to Cell Border specifies the color of the solid lines. The Cell Background controls let you color in the table cells with colors of your choice. (Choose Color Fill from the pop-up menu, and then click the color swatch.) This is an especially valuable option for Web designers.

- **Adjust the rows and columns** by dragging the cell borders.

- **Merge two selected cells** by clicking Merge Cells in the Table palette. Once you've done that, you can use the Split Cell button to split them apart again. (Split Cell doesn't work except in cells you've previously merged.)

- **Nest one table inside a cell of another** by clicking in the cell and then clicking Nest Table. Change the numbers in the Rows and Columns boxes to set up its dimensions.

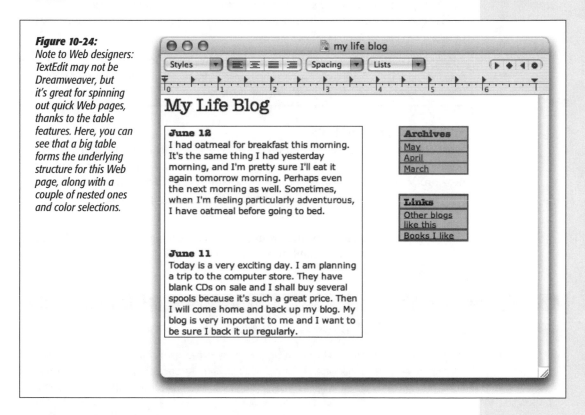

Figure 10-24:
Note to Web designers: TextEdit may not be Dreamweaver, but it's great for spinning out quick Web pages, thanks to the table features. Here, you can see that a big table forms the underlying structure for this Web page, along with a couple of nested ones and color selections.

TextEdit as Web Designer

The new Table palette isn't the only clue that Apple intends TextEdit to be a quick-and-dirty Web page design program. Consider these other tools:

- You can easily add graphics to the page by dragging or pasting them into a document. The program understands TIFF, PICT, JPEG, and GIF formats.

- You can add Web-style hyperlinks by highlighting "Click here" (or whatever the link says), choosing Format→Text→Link, and entering the Web address in the resulting dialog box. Or just drag a link in from Safari, Mail, or another program. (To edit the link later, Control-click it, and then choose Edit Link.)

- To save a document as an HTML (Web page) file, choose File→Save As; from the File Format pop-up menu, choose Web Archive.

- Don't miss the HTML options in TextEdit→Preferences. On the "Open and Save" tab, you can specify what kind of HTML document you want to produce, what cascading style sheets (CSS) setting you want, and whether or not you want TextEdit to include code to preserve blank areas (white space) in your layout.

Tip: When you open a Web page document—that is, an HTML document—TextEdit is faced with a quandary. Should it open up the page as though it's a Web page, interpreting the HTML code as though it's a browser? Or should it reveal the underlying HTML code itself?

Actually, that's up to you. When you choose File→Open, turn on "Ignore rich text commands" to make the document open up as HTML code. (To make this change permanent, turn on the same checkbox on the "Open and Save" pane of the TextEdit→Preferences dialog box.)

The TextEdit Preferences

Most of the settings in the TextEdit Preferences→New Document pane have no effect on documents that are *already* open—only on documents you open or create from now on. Most of the settings are self-explanatory; nonetheless, handy explanatory balloons appear if you point to an option without clicking. Here are a few settings that may not be immediately clear:

- **Font.** If Helvetica 12 doesn't float your boat, you can change TextEdit's starting font. In fact, you can set *two* default fonts—one for Rich Text documents and another one for plain text files.

GEM IN THE ROUGH

Files Within Files Within Files

It's no surprise that you can include formatted text and pictures in a TextEdit document, but here's a shocker: You can also embed an entire program or document within a TextEdit file.

Try this experiment: Create a new TextEdit document in Rich Text mode. Drag a couple of program icons into the TextEdit document. Do the same with some documents that were created using native Mac OS X programs (another TextEdit document, for example).

When you save the file, Mac OS X saves embedded copies of the applications and documents you dragged into the TextEdit document itself. (The TextEdit file is saved in RTFD, a Rich Text Format document with attachments.)

Once you've saved the file, you can double-click any of the icons in it to launch the embedded items. In the TextEdit document shown here, you could launch the Chess, DVD Player, and Mail programs—all right from within the file.

To make things even wilder, it's possible to drag a TextEdit file containing embedded items into another TextEdit file, saving a file within a file within a file.

One important point: The double-clickable icons you create in TextEdit using this method are not aliases or links to your original documents and programs. They're actual, full copies. If you embed a 10 MB program into a TextEdit document, you'll end up with a 10 MB TextEdit file!

Note: By definition, plain text files don't have any formatting. So whatever font you choose here for plain text files is for your viewing pleasure only. If you plan to send the file to anyone else, remember that the font choice won't be saved with the document.

- **Window Size.** These settings have no effect unless you're in Wrap to Window mode, in which the text rewraps to fit the window width, as opposed to Wrap to Page mode. (You choose these options from TextEdit's Format menu.)

  If you *are* in Wrap to Window mode, then these dimensions determine the size of the window that appears each time you create a new TextEdit document.

- **Properties.** These boxes—Author, Company, and Copyright—are some of the tags that Spotlight inspects when it searches your Mac. If you'd like to be able to round up your documents by these characteristics, fill them in here to specify the information you want to use for *most* documents. (To fill them in differently for individual documents, choose File→Show Properties instead.)

- **Options.** These are the on/off switches for the various new Snow Leopard typing aids described in Chapter 6: smart quotes, data detectors, text replacement, and so on.

TextEdit's Other Writing Tools

TextEdit includes a few other very useful document-editing tools:

- **Allow Hyphenation.** When you select this command from the Format menu, TextEdit breaks up words by syllable and inserts hyphens when necessary in order to create more visually pleasing line breaks.

Tip: It's especially important to turn this feature on if your paragraph alignment is set to Justify, or if you create narrow columns of text. If hyphenation is turned off, TextEdit won't break up whole words at the end of a line—even if it leaves big, ugly white gaps between words.

- **Prevent Editing.** When you turn this option on (again, in the Format menu), you're locked out. You can select and copy text to your heart's content, but you can't change anything. Prevent Editing mode can be useful if you want to prevent yourself from making accidental changes to a file, but it's not much of a security feature. (All anyone has to do is choose Format→Allow Editing to regain full editing privileges.)

- **Spelling and Grammar.** These aren't TextEdit features; they're system-wide Mac OS X features, and they're described in Chapter 6.

Time Machine

This marquee feature of Mac OS X is described in Chapter 6.

Utilities: Your Mac OS X Toolbox

The Utilities folder (inside your Applications folder) is home to another batch of freebies: a couple of dozen tools for monitoring, tuning, tweaking, and troubleshooting your Mac.

The truth is, you're likely to use only about six of these utilities. The rest are very specialized gizmos primarily of interest to network administrators or Unix geeks who are obsessed with knowing what kind of computer-code gibberish is going on behind the scenes.

Tip: Even so, Apple obviously noticed that as the sophistication of Mac OS X fans grows, more people open the Utilities folder more often. That's why there's a menu command and a keystroke that can take you there. In the Finder, choose Go→Utilities (Shift-⌘-U).

Activity Monitor

Activity Monitor is designed to let the technologically savvy Mac fan see how much of the Mac's available power is being tapped at any given moment.

The Processes table

Even when you're only running a program or two on your Mac, dozens of computational tasks (*processes*) are going on in the background. The top half of the dialog box, which looks like a table, shows you all the different processes—visible and invisible—that your Mac is handling at the moment.

Check out how many items appear in the Process list, even when you're just staring at the desktop. It's awesome to see just how busy your Mac is! Some are easily recognizable programs (such as Finder), while others are background system-level operations you don't normally see. For each item, you can see the percentage of CPU being used, who's using it (either your account name, someone else's, or *root,* meaning the Mac itself), whether or not it's been written as a 64-bit app, and how much memory it's using.

Or use the pop-up menu above the list to see views like these:

- **All Processes.** This is the complete list of running processes; you'll notice that the vast majority are little Unix applications you never even knew you had.

- **All Processes, Hierarchically.** Sometimes, one process launches another, creating a hierarchy. The big daddy of them all is the process called *launchd.* Here and there, you'll see some other interesting relationships: For example, the Dock launches Dashboard, and InternetSharing opens up a few other processes to do its thing.

- **My Processes.** This list shows only the programs that pertain to *your* world—your login. There are still plenty of unfamiliar items, but they're all running to serve *your* account.

- **Administrator Processes.** These are the processes run by *root*—that is, opened by Snow Leopard itself.

- **Other User Processes.** Here's a list of all *other* processes—"owned" by neither root nor you. Here, you might see the processes being run by another account holder, for example (using Fast User Switching), or people who have connected to this Mac from across a network or the Internet.

- **Active Processes, Inactive Processes.** This differentiates between processes that are actually doing something right now, as opposed to sitting there, waiting for a signal (like a keypress or a mouse click).

- **Windowed Processes.** Now *this* is probably what you were expecting: a list of actual programs with actual English names, like Activity Monitor, Finder, Safari, and Mail. These are the only ones running in actual windows, the only ones that are *visible*, which is what most people probably think of as programs.

The System monitor tabs

At the bottom of Activity Monitor, you're offered five tabs that reveal intimate details about your Mac and its behind-the-scenes efforts (Figure 10-25):

- **CPU.** As you go about your usual Mac business, opening a few programs, dragging a playing QuickTime movie across the screen, playing a game, and so on, you can see the CPU graph rise and fall, depending on how busy you're keeping the CPU. On multiple-processor or multi-core Macs, you see a different bar for each, so you can see how efficiently Mac OS X is distributing the work among them.

Tip: You may also want to watch this graph right in your Dock (choose View→Dock Icon→Show CPU Usage) or in a bar at the edge of your screen (choose Window→Floating CPU Window→Horizontally).

Finally, there's the View→Show CPU History command. It makes a resizable, real-time monitor window float on top of all your other programs, so you can't miss it.

- **System Memory.** Here's a colorful graph that reveals the state of your Mac's RAM at the moment.

  The number below the graph shows how much memory is installed in your Mac. If, when your Mac is running a typical complement of programs, the Wired number plus the Active number nearly equals your total RAM amount, it's time to consider buying more memory. You're suffocating your Mac.

- **Disk Activity.** Even when you're not opening or saving a file, your Mac's hard drive is frequently hard at work, shuffling chunks of program code into and out of memory, for example. Here's where the savvy technician can see exactly how frantic the disk is at the moment.

- **Disk Usage.** This little graph offers one of the quickest ways to check out how full your hard drive is. (If you have more than one drive—say, a flash drive, tape-backup drive, or whatever—choose another drive's name from the pop-up menu.)

- **Network.** Keep an eye on how much data is shooting across your office network with this handy EKG-ish graph.

Figure 10-25:
The many faces of Activity Monitor.

Top: It can be a graph of your processor (CPU) activity, your RAM usage at the moment, your disk capacity, and so on. For most people, only the processes listed here with tiny icons beside their names are actual windowed programs—those with icons in the Finder, the ones you actually interact with.

Don't miss the top-left Quit Process button. It's a convenient way to jettison a locked-up program when all else fails.

Bottom: If you double-click a process's name, you get a three-tab dialog box that offers stunningly complete reams of data (mostly of interest only to programmers) about what that program is up to. (The Open Files and Ports tab, for example, shows you how many files that program has opened, often invisibly.)

AirPort Utility

You use the AirPort Utility to set up and manage AirPort base stations (Apple's wireless WiFi networking routers).

If you click Continue, it presents a series of screens, posing one question at a time: what you want to name the network, what password you want for it, and so on. Once you've followed the steps and answered the questions, your AirPort hardware will be properly configured and ready to use.

AppleScript Editor

This little program, formerly called Script Editor, is where you can type up your own *AppleScripts,* as described at the end of Chapter 7.

Audio MIDI Setup

This program has developed a split personality in Snow Leopard. Its name is now a literal description of its two halves.

- **Audio.** When you first open Audio MIDI Setup, you see a complete summary of the audio inputs and outputs available on your Mac right now. It's a lot like the Sound pane of System Preferences, but with a lot more geeky detail. Here, for example, you can specify the recording level for your Mac's microphone, or even change the audio quality it records.

  For most people, this is all meaningless, because most Macs have only one input (the microphone) and one output (the speakers). But if you're sitting in your darkened music studio, which is humming with high-tech audio gear whose software has been designed to work with this little program, you'll smile when you see this tab.

  There's even a Configure Speakers button, for those audiophilic Mac fans who've attached stereo or even surround-sound speaker systems to their Macs.

Tip: Using the ✿ menu at the bottom of the window, you can turn your various audio inputs (that is, microphones, line inputs, and so on) on or off. You can even direct your Mac's system beeps to pour forth from one set of speakers (like the one built into your Mac), and all other sound, like music, through a different set.

- **MIDI.** MIDI stands for Musical Instrument Digital Interface, a standard "language" for inter-synthesizer communication. It's available to music software companies who have written their wares to capitalize on these tools.

  When you choose Window→Show MIDI Window, you get a window that represents your recording-studio configuration. By clicking Add Device, you create a new icon that represents one of your pieces of gear. Double-click the icon to specify its make and model. Finally, by dragging lines from the "in" and "out" arrows, you teach your Mac and its MIDI software how the various components are wired together.

Bluetooth File Exchange

One of the luxuries of using a Mac that has Bluetooth is the ability to shoot files (to colleagues who own similarly clever gadgets) through the air, up to 30 feet away. Bluetooth File Exchange makes it possible, as described on page 244.

Boot Camp Assistant

This program helps you create (or destroy) a partition of your hard drive to hold a copy of Microsoft Windows. Details in Chapter 8.

ColorSync Utility

If you use ColorSync, then you probably know already that this utility is for people in the high-end color printing business. Its tabs include these two:

- **Profile First Aid.** This tab performs a fairly esoteric task: repairing ColorSync profiles that may be "broken" because they don't strictly conform to the *ICC profile* specifications. (ICC [International Color Consortium] profiles are part of Apple's ColorSync color management system, as described on page 571.) If a profile for your specific monitor or printer doesn't appear in the Profiles tab of this program when it should, Profile First Aid is the tool you need to fix it.

- **Profiles.** This tab lets you review all the ColorSync profiles installed on your system. The area on the right side of the window displays information about each ColorSync profile you select from the list on the left.

The **other tabs** are described on page 571.

Console

Console is a viewer for all of Mac OS X's text logs—the behind-the-scenes, internal Unix status messages being passed between the Mac OS X and other applications.

Opening the Console log is a bit like stepping into an operating room during a complex surgery: You're exposed to stuff the average person just isn't supposed to see. (Typical Console entries: "kCGErrorCannotComplete" or "doGetDisplayTransferByTable.") You can adjust the font and word wrapping using Console's Font menu, but the truth is that the phrase "CGXGetWindowType: Invalid window –1" looks ugly in just about *any* font!

Console isn't useless, however. These messages can be of significant value to programmers who are debugging software or troubleshooting a messy problem, or, occasionally, to someone you've called for tech support.

DigitalColor Meter

DigitalColor Meter can grab the exact color value of any pixel on your screen, which can be helpful when matching colors in Web page construction or other design work. After launching the DigitalColor Meter, just point anywhere on your screen. A magnified view appears in the meter window, and the RGB (red-green-blue) color value of the pixels appears in the meter window. You can display the color values as RGB percentages or actual values, in Hex form (which is how colors are defined in HTML; white is represented as #FFFFFF, for example), and in several other formats.

Here are some tips for using the DigitalColor Meter to capture color information from your screen:

- To home in on the exact pixel (and color) you want to measure, drag the Aperture Size slider to the smallest size—one pixel. Then use the *arrow keys* to move the aperture to the precise location you want.

- Press Shift-⌘-C (Color→Copy Color as Text) to put on the Clipboard the numeric value of the color you're pointing to.

- Press Shift-⌘-H (Color→Hold Color) to "freeze" the color meter on the color you're pointing to—a handy stunt when you're comparing two colors onscreen. You can point to one color, hold it using Shift-⌘-H, and then move your mouse to the second color. Pressing Shift-⌘-H again releases the hold on the color.

- When the Aperture Size slider is set to view more than one pixel, DigitalColor Meter measures the *average* value of the pixels being examined.

Note: Are you reading this page because you're looking for the Directory app? (You geek!) It's gone in Snow Leopard. Directory, a glorified address-book program intended to be configured by a network administrator, been incorporated into Address Book.

Directory Utility also seems to be missing, but it lives on in a new location. This app, also for network administrators, controls the access that each Mac on a network has to Mac OS X's directory services (special databases that store info about users and servers). Directory Access also governs access to LDAP directories (Internet or intranet-based "white pages" for Internet addresses). To find it, open System Preferences→ Accounts→Login Options. Where it says Network Account Server, click Join. You're asked for the address of the network directory you want—and you're offered a button that opens, yes, the old Directory Utility.

Disk Utility

This important program serves two key functions:

- It serves as Mac OS X's own little Norton Utilities: a powerful hard drive administration tool that lets you repair, erase, format, and partition disks. In everyday life, you'll probably use Disk Utility most often for its *Repair Permissions* feature, which solves an uncanny number of weird little Mac OS X glitches. But it's also worth keeping in mind in case you ever find yourself facing a serious disk problem.

- Disk Utility also creates and manages *disk images,* electronic versions of disks or folders that you can exchange electronically with other people.

The following discussion tackles the program's two personalities one at a time.

Disk Utility, the hard drive repair program

Here are some of the tasks you can perform with this half of Disk Utility:

- Repair folders, files, and programs that don't work because you supposedly don't have sufficient "access privileges." This is by far the most common use of Disk Utility, not to mention the most reliable and satisfying. Using the Repair Disk Permissions button fixes an *astonishing* range of bizarre Mac OS X problems, from programs that won't open to menulets that freeze up the works.

- Get size and type information about any disks attached to your Mac.

- Fix disks that won't appear on your desktop or behave properly.

- Completely erase disks—including rewritable CDs and DVDs (such as CD-RW and DVD-RW discs).

- Partition a disk into multiple *volumes* (that is, subdivide a drive so that its segments appear on the desktop with separate disk icons).

Tip: In Snow Leopard, Disk Utility can create or enlarge disk partitions without requiring you to erase the entire hard drive. Details below.

- Set up a *RAID array* (a cluster of separate disks that acts as a single volume).

Note: Disk Utility can perform some of its magic on the startup disk—the disk that's running Mac OS X at the moment. For example, it can check the disk for damage, fix the permissions of the disk, or even adjust its partitions.

But any other operation, like reformatting, erasing, or actually repairing the disk, still requires the Mac to start up from a different disk (your Snow Leopard DVD, for example). Otherwise, it'd be like a surgeon performing an appendectomy on himself—not a great idea.

The left Disk Utility panel lists your hard drive and any other disks in or attached to your Mac at the moment. When you click the name of your hard drive's mechanism, like "74.5 GB Hitachi iC25N0…" (not the "Macintosh HD" partition label below it), you see a panel with five tabs, one for each of the main Disk Utility functions:

- **First Aid.** This is the disk-repair part of Disk Utility, and it does a terrific job at fixing many disk problems. When you're troubleshooting, Disk Utility should always be your first resort.

  To use it, click the icon of a disk and then click either Verify Disk (to get a report on the disk's health) or Repair Disk (which fixes whatever problems the program finds). In other words, First Aid attempts to perform the same healing effects on a sick hard drive as, say, a program like Norton Utilities.

  If Disk First Aid reports that it's unable to fix the problem, *then* it's time to invest in a program like DiskWarrior (*www.alsoft.com*).

You may wind up using the Verify and Repair Disk *Permissions* buttons even more often. Their function is to straighten out problems with the invisible Unix file permissions that keep you from moving, changing, or deleting files or folders. (The occasional software installer can create problems like this.) You'd be surprised how often running one of these permission checks solves little Mac OS X glitches.

Chapter 12 has a much more detailed discussion of permissions.

- **Erase.** Select a disk, choose a format (*always* Mac OS Extended [Journaled], unless you're formatting a disk for use on a Windows machine or an ancient Mac running Mac OS 8.1 or earlier), give it a name, and then click Erase to wipe a disk clean.

- **Partition.** With the Partition tools, you can erase a hard drive in such a way that you subdivide its surface. Each chunk is represented on your screen by another hard drive icon (Figure 10-26).

There are some very good reasons *not* to partition a drive these days: A partitioned hard drive is more difficult to resurrect after a serious crash, requires more navigation when you want to open a particular file, and offers no speed or safety benefits.

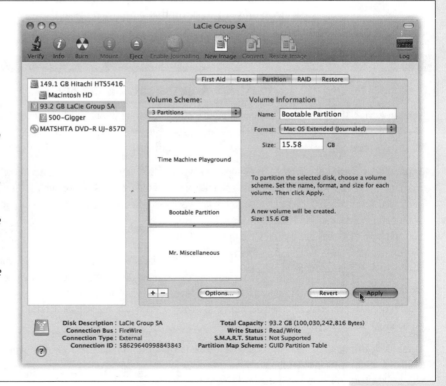

Figure 10-26:
Partitioning your drive with Disk Utility no longer involves erasing it completely. Select the drive you want to partition from the list on the left, and then click the Partition tab. Click the + button for each new partition you want.

Now drag the horizontal dividers in the Volumes map to specify the relative sizes of the partitions you want to create. Assign a name and a format for each partition in the Volume Information area, and then click Apply.

On the other hand, there's one very good reason *to* do it: Partitioning is the only way to use Boot Camp, described in Chapter 8. When you're using Boot Camp, your Mac is a Mac when running off of the first partition, and a Windows PC when starting up from the second one. (But you don't use Disk Utility in that case; use Boot Camp Assistant.)

• **RAID.** RAID stands for Redundant Array of Independent Disks, and refers to a special formatting scheme in which a group of separate disks are configured to work together as one very large, very fast drive. In a RAID array, multiple disks share the job of storing data—a setup that can improve speed and reliability.

Most Mac owners don't use or set up RAID arrays, probably because most Mac owners have only one hard drive (and Disk Utility can't make your startup disk part of a RAID array).

If you're using multiple external hard disks, though, you can use Apple RAID to merge them into one giant disk. Just drag the icons of the relevant disks (or disk partitions) from the left-side list of disks into the main list (where it says, "Drag disks or volumes here to add to set"). Use the RAID Type pop-up menu to specify the RAID format you want to use (Stripe is a popular choice for maximizing disk speed), name your new mega-disk, and then click Create. The result is a single "disk" icon on your desktop that actually represents the combined capacity of all the RAID disks.

POWER USERS' CLINIC

Partition Adjustments on the Fly

You can expand, shrink, or create partitions without having to erase the whole hard drive. If you're into partitioning at all, this is a *huge* convenience.

Expanding a partition. Suppose, for example, that your main hard drive has two partitions: a main one (200 gigs) and a secondary one (50 gigs) that used to hold all your photos and movies. But you've outgrown the second partition and have moved all those photos and movies to their own external hard drive. Wouldn't it be nice to add the newly unoccupied 50 gigs to your main partition?

You can do that without having to erase the whole hard drive. (This process, however, nukes everything on the *second* partition, so make sure you're prepared to lose it all.)

Open Disk Utility. Click the name of the hard drive (for example, "Hitachi HTS541616J9SA00"–*not* "Macintosh HD"). Click Partition. You see a display like the one in Figure 10-26.

Click the second partition (or third, or whatever partition is *just after* the one you want to expand) and then click the – button below the list. Poof! It's gone.

Now you can drag the main partition's bottom edge downward (or type a new size into the Size box), expanding it into the free area. Take a deep breath, and then click Apply.

Shrinking a partition. In Figure 10-26, you can see that a portion of the first partition is lightly shaded. (It's blue in real life.) The blue represents data; you can't shrink a partition so much that it crowds out your files. You can, however, shrink the partition to eliminate empty space. Just drag the lower edge of its map chunk upward.

Creating new partitions. Anytime there's leftover space on the drive, you can create *new* partitions from it.

To do that, click the **+** button, and proceed as described in Figure 10-26.

- **Restore.** This tab lets you make a perfect copy of a disk or a disk image, much like the popular shareware programs Carbon Copy Cloner and SuperDuper. You might find this useful when, for example, you want to make an exact copy of your old Mac's drive on your new one. You can't do that just by copying your old files and folders manually. If you try, you won't get the thousands of *invisible* files that make up Mac OS X. If you use the Restore function, they'll come along for the ride.

  Start by dragging the disk or disk image you want to copy *from* into the Source box. Then drag the icon of the disk you want to copy *to* into the Destination box.

Tip: If you want to copy an online disk image onto one of your disks, you don't have to download it first. Just type its Web address into the Source field. You might find this trick convenient if you keep disk images on your iDisk, for example.

If you turn on Erase Destination, Disk Utility obliterates all the data on your target disk before copying the data. If you leave this checkbox off, however, Disk Utility simply copies everything onto your destination, preserving all your old data in the process. (The Skip Checksum checkbox is available only if you choose to erase your destination disk. If you're confident all the files on the source disk are 100 percent healthy and whole, turn on this checkbox to save time. Otherwise, leave it off for extra safety.)

Finally, click the Restore button. (You might need to type in an administrator password.) Restoring can take a long time for big disks, so go ahead and make yourself a cup of coffee while you're waiting.

Tip: Instead of clicking a disk icon and then clicking the appropriate Disk Utility tab, you can just Control-click (or right-click) a disk's name and choose Information, First Aid, Erase, Partition, RAID, or Restore from the shortcut menu.

Disk Utility, the disk-image program

Disk images are very cool. Each one is a single icon that behaves precisely like an actual disk—a flash drive or hard drive, for example—but can be distributed electronically. For example, a lot of Mac OS X add-on software arrives from your Web download in disk-image form, as shown below.

Disk images are popular for software distribution for a simple reason: Each image file precisely duplicates the original master disk, complete with all the necessary files in all the right places. When a software company sends you a disk image, it ensures that you'll install the software from a disk that *exactly* matches the master disk.

It's important to understand the difference between a *disk-image file* and the *mounted disk* (the one that appears when you double-click the disk image). If you flip back to page 196 and consult Figure 5-20, this distinction should be clear.

Tip: After you double-click a disk image, click Skip in the verification box that appears. If something truly got scrambled during the download, you'll know about it right away—your file won't decompress correctly, or it'll display the wrong icon, for example.

In fact, you can make Disk Utility always skip that verification business, which is a relic from the days of floppy disks. To do so, choose Disk Utility→Preferences, and turn off "Check images on locked media."

You can create disk images, too. Doing so can be very handy in situations like these:

- You want to create a backup of an important CD. By turning it into a disk-image file on your hard drive, you'll always have a safety copy, ready to burn back onto a *new* CD. (This is an essential practice for educational CDs that kids will be handling soon after eating peanut butter and jelly.)

- You want to replicate your entire hard drive—complete with all of its files, programs, folder setups, and so on—onto a new, bigger hard drive (or a new, better Mac), using the Restore feature described earlier.

- You want to back up your entire hard drive, or maybe just a certain chunk of it, onto an iPod or another disk. (Again, you can later use the Restore function to complete the transaction.)

- You bought a game that requires its CD to be in the drive at all times. Many programs like these run equally well off of a mounted disk image that you made from the original CD.

- You want to send somebody else a copy of a disk via the Internet. You simply create a disk image, and then send *that*—preferably in compressed form.

Here's how you make a disk image:

- **To image-ize a disk or partition.** Click the name of the disk in the left-panel list, where you see the disks currently in, or attached to, your Mac. (The topmost item is the name of your *drive*, like "484.0 MB MATSHITA DVD-R" for a DVD drive or "74.5 GB Hitachi" for a hard drive. Beneath that entry, you generally see the name of the actual partition, like "Macintosh HD," or the CD's name as it appears on the screen.)

  Then choose File→New→Disk Image from [whatever the disk or partition's name is].

- **To image-ize a folder.** Choose File→New→Disk Image from Folder. In the Open dialog box, click the folder you want, and then click Image.

Tip: Disk Utility can't turn an individual file into a disk image. But you can put a single file into a folder, and then make a disk image of it.

Either way, the next dialog box (Figure 10-27) offers some fascinating options.

- **Image Format.** If you choose "read/write," your disk image file, when double-clicked, turns into a superb imitation of a hard drive. You can drag files and folders onto it, drag them off of it, change icons' names on it, and so on.

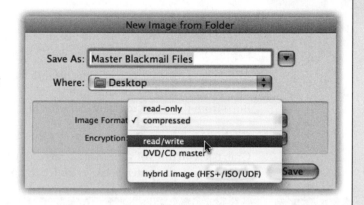

Figure 10-27:
These two pop-up menus let you specify (a) what kind of disk image you want, and (b) whether or not you want it password-protected. The latter option is great when you want to password-protect one folder, without bothering with your entire Home folder.

If you choose "read-only," however, the result behaves more like a CD. You can copy things off of it, but not make any changes to it.

The "compressed" option is best if you intend to send the resulting file by email, post it for Web download, or preserve the disk image on some backup disk for a rainy day. It takes a little longer to create a simulated disk when you double-click the disk image file, but it takes up a lot less disk space than an uncompressed version.

Finally, choose "DVD/CD master" if you're copying a CD or a DVD. The resulting file is a perfect mirror of the original disc, ready for copying onto a blank CD or DVD when the time comes.

- **Encryption.** Here's an easy way to lock private files away into a vault that nobody else can open. If you choose one of these two AES encryption options (choose AES-128, if you value your time), you're asked to assign a password to your new image file. Nobody can open it without the password—not even you. On the other hand, if you save it into your Keychain (page 504), it's not such a disaster if you forget the password.

- **Save As.** Choose a name and location for your new image file. The name you choose here doesn't need to match the original disk or folder name.

When you click Save (or press Return), if you opted to create an encrypted image, you're asked to make up a password at this point.

Otherwise, Disk Utility now creates the image and then *mounts* it—that is, turns the image file into a simulated, yet fully functional, disk icon on your desktop.

When you're finished working with the disk, eject it as you would any disk (Control-click it and choose Eject, for example). Hang onto the .dmg disk image file itself, however. This is the file you'll need to double-click if you ever want to recreate your "simulated disk."

Turning an image into a CD

One of the other most common disk-image tasks is turning a disk image *back* into a CD or DVD—provided your Mac has a CD or DVD burner, of course.

All you have to do is drag the .dmg file into the Disk Utility window, select it, and click the Burn icon on the toolbar (or, alternatively, Control-click the .dmg icon and choose Burn from the shortcut menu). Insert a blank CD or DVD, and then click Burn.

Grab

Grab takes pictures of your Mac's screen, for use when you're writing up instructions, illustrating a computer book, or collecting proof of some secret screen you found

---

GEM IN THE ROUGH

The Sparse Image

One of the coolest Disk Utility features is also one of the most buried.

Turns out you can make a nice, hermetically sealed, password-protected disk image that starts out small but magically increases as you stuff more files into it. If the usual disk image is like a steel bucket—a fixed size forever—a *sparse image* is like an accordion file folder.

Choose File→New→Blank Disk Image. In the resulting dialog box, name the file you're creating (which you'll double-click to make the virtual disk appear), as well as the virtual disk itself.

From the Volume Size pop-up menu, choose the *maximum* size this disk image will ever be. The beautiful part is that it will probably *never* occupy that much disk space; it starts out small and slowly expands only as necessary. But you're setting the maximum here.

From the Encryption pop-up menu, choose one of the two scrambling methods that will password-protect your disk image. Finally, from the Image Format pop-up menu—this is the key step—choose "sparse disk image."

New Blank Image
Save As: Growing Evidence
Where: 📁 Desktop
Volume Name: Disk Image
Volume Size: 2.6 GB (DVD–RAM)
Volume Format: Mac OS Extended (Journaled)
Encryption: 128–bit AES encryption (recommended)
Partition: read/write disk image
Image Format ✓ sparse disk image
sparse bundle disk image
Cancel   Create

Click Create. Make up a password (type it twice); for added security, *don't* store in your Keychain. (If you store it in your Keychain, no password at all will be required to open it by snoopy passersby.) Then click Create.

Now, on your desktop, there's a disk image *file* with the suffix ".sparse-image." It occupies only 26 MB on your hard drive to start with.

Double-click it and enter your password to bring the actual virtual disk icon to your desktop. You can now start filling the disk image up with private stuff. The .sparseimage file will grow automatically to accommodate it—but only as necessary.

---

buried in a game. You can take pictures of the entire screen (press ⌘-Z, which for once in its life does *not* mean Undo) or capture only the contents of a rectangular selection (press Shift-⌘-A). When you're finished, Grab displays your snapshot in a new window, which you can print, close without saving, copy, or save as a TIFF file, ready for emailing or inserting into a manuscript.

Now, as experienced Mac enthusiasts already know, the Mac OS has long had its *own* built-in shortcuts for capturing screenshots: Press Shift-⌘-3 to take a picture of the whole screen, and Shift-⌘-4 to capture a rectangular selection.

Snow Leopard Spots: Don't forget that you can choose different, easier to remember keyboard shortcuts for these functions, if you like. Just open System Preferences→Keyboard→Keyboard Shortcuts, click where it now says Shift-⌘-3 (or whatever), and press the new key combo.

So why use Grab instead? In many cases, you shouldn't. The Shift-⌘-3 and Shift-⌘-4 shortcuts work like a dream. But there are some cases in which it might make more sense to opt for Grab. Here are three:

- Grab can make a *timed* screen capture (choose Capture→Timed Screen, or press Shift-⌘-Z), which lets you enjoy a 10-second delay before the screenshot is actually taken. After you click the Start Timer button, you have an opportunity to activate windows, pull down menus, drag items around, and otherwise set up the shot before Grab shoots the picture.

- When you capture a screenshot using Grab's Selection command, the *size* of your selection is displayed, in pixels, right under the pointer as you drag. If you need to capture a 256-pixel-wide square, for example, you can do so with pinpoint accuracy. (Choose Edit→Inspector to read the dimensions of a screenshot *after* you capture it.)

- With Grab, you have the option of including the cursor in the picture, which is extremely useful when you're showing a menu being pulled down or a button being clicked. (Mac OS X's screenshot keystrokes, by contrast, always eliminate the pointer.) Use the technique described in Figure 10-28 to add the pointer style of your choice to a Grab screenshot.

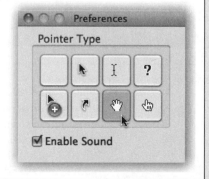

Figure 10-28:
Unlike the Shift-⌘-3 or Shift-⌘-4 keystrokes, Grab lets you include the pointer/cursor in the picture—or hide it. Choose Grab→Preferences and pick one of the eight pointer styles, or choose to keep the pointer hidden by activating the blank button in the upper-left corner.

Tip: Actually, if you're going to write a book or manual about Mac OS X, the program you really need is Snapz Pro X; a trial version is available from this book's "Missing CD" at *www.missingmanuals.com*, among other places. It offers far more flexibility than any of Mac OS X's own screenshot features. For example, you have a choice of file format, you can neatly snip out just one dialog box or window with a single click, and you can capture movies of screen activity with far more flexibility than QuickTime Player offers (Chapter 15).

Grapher

This little unsung app is an amazing piece of work. It lets you create 2-D or 3-D graphs of staggering beauty and complexity.

When you first open Grapher, you're asked to choose what kind of virtual "graph paper" you want: two-dimensional (standard, polar, logarithmic) or three-dimensional (cubic, spherical, cylindrical). Click a name to see a preview; when you're happy with the selection, click Open.

Now the main Grapher window appears (Figure 10-29). Do yourself a favor. Spend a few wow-inducing minutes choosing canned equations from the Examples menu, and watching how Grapher whips up gorgeous, colorful, sometimes animated graphs on the fly.

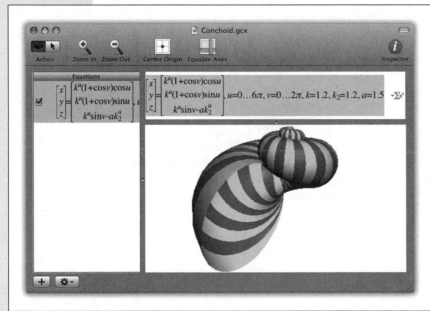

Figure 10-29:
In general, you type equations into Grapher just as you would on paper (like z=2xy). If in doubt, check the online help, which offers enough hints on functions, constants, differential equations, series, and periodic equations to keep the A Beautiful Mind guy busy for days.

When you're ready to plug in an equation of your own, type it into the text box at the top of the window. If you're not such a math hotshot, or you're not sure of the equation format, work from the canned equations and mathematical building blocks that appear when you choose Equation→New Equation from Template or Window→Show Equation Palette (a floating window containing a huge selection of math symbols and constants).

Tip: If you don't know the keystroke that produces a mathematical symbol like π or θ, you can just type *pi* or *theta*. Grapher replaces it with the correct symbol automatically.

Once the graph is up on the screen, you can tailor it like this:

- **To move a 2-D graph** in the window, choose View→Move Tool and then drag; to move a 3-D graph, ⌘-drag it.

- **To rotate a 3-D graph,** drag in any direction. If you add the Option key, you flip the graph around on one axis.

- **To change the colors, line thicknesses, 3-D "walls," and other graphic elements,** click the I button (or choose Window→Show Inspector) to open the formatting palette. The controls you find here vary by graph type, but rest assured that Grapher can accommodate your every visual whim.

- **To change the fonts and sizes,** choose Grapher→Preferences. On the Equations panel, the four sliders let you specify the relative sizes of the text elements. If you click the sample equation, the Font panel appears, so you can fiddle with the type.

- Add your own captions, arrows, ovals, or rectangles using the Object menu.

When it's all over, you can preserve your masterpiece using any of these techniques:

- **Export a graphic** by choosing File→Export.

- **Copy an equation to the Clipboard** by Control-clicking it and choosing Copy As→TIFF (or EPS, or whatever) from the shortcut menu. Now you can paste it into another program.

- **Export an animated graph** by choosing Equation→Create Animation. The resulting dialog box lets you specify how long you want the movie to last (and a lot of other parameters).

Tip: If you Shift-drag the starting or ending images at the bottom, you can change their size.

POWER USERS' CLINIC

For Mathematicians (and Physicists, Scientists, and Students) Only

If you're into math, science, or studying math or science, Grapher is a tremendous addition to Mac OS X. There's a whole lot to it—but if you're just getting started, here are a few features not to miss.

You can calculate values, intercepts, derivatives, and integrals (even indefinite integrals) by using the Equation→Evaluation and Equation→Integration commands.

Some useful ready-made equation components await in the pop-up button at the right side of the equation text box. Using the Sum and Product symbols, for example, you can quickly calculate summations and products.

That same pop-up menu can help you generate piecewise, parametric, and other specialized kinds of graphs (this means you, math students).

- **Finally, click Create Animation.** After a moment, the finished movie appears. If you like it the way it is, choose File→Save As to preserve it on your hard drive for future generations.

Java Preferences

Programmers generally use the Java programming language to create small programs that they then embed into Web pages—animated effects, clocks, calculators, stock tickers, and so on. Your browser automatically downloads and runs such applets (assuming that you have "Enable Java" turned on in your browser).

Your Java folder contains several Java-related tools, which exist primarily for the benefit of Web programmers and Web programs (including Safari).

Keychain Access

Keychain Access memorizes and stores all your secret information—passwords for network access, file servers, FTP sites, Web pages, and other secure items. For instructions on using Keychain Access, see Chapter 12.

Migration Assistant

This little cutie automates the transfer of all your stuff from one Mac to another—your Home folder, network settings, programs, and more. This comes in extremely handy when you buy a newer, better Mac—or when you need Time Machine to recover an entire dead Mac's worth of data. (It can also copy everything over from a secondary hard drive or partition.) The instructions on the screen guide you through the process (see page 820).

Network Utility

The Network Utility gathers information about Web sites and network citizens. It offers a suite of standard Internet tools like NetStat, Ping, Traceroute, Finger, and Whois—advanced tools, to be sure, but ones that even Mac novices may be asked to fire up when calling a technician for Internet help.

Otherwise, you probably won't need to use Network Utility to get your work done. However, Network Utility can be useful when you're performing Internet detective work.

- **Whois** ("who is") can gather an amazing amount of information about the owners of any particular domain (such as *www.apple.com*)—including name and address info, telephone numbers, and administrative contacts. It uses the technique shown in Figure 10-30.

- Use **Ping** to enter a Web address (such as *www.google.com*), and then "ping" (send out a "sonar" signal to) the server to see how long it takes for it to respond to your request. Network Utility reports the response time in milliseconds—a useful test when you're trying to see if a remote server (a Web site, for example) is up and running. (The time it takes for the ping to report back to you also tells you how busy that server is.)

- **Traceroute** lets you track how many "hops" are required for your Mac to communicate with a certain Web server. Just type in the network address or URL, and then click Trace. You'll see that your request actually jumps from one *trunk* of the Internet to another, from router to router, as it makes its way to its destination. You'll learn that a message sometimes crisscrosses the entire country before it arrives at its destination. You can also see how long each leg of the journey took, in milliseconds.

Snow Leopard Spots: At this point in this alphabetic chapter, you used to read about ODBC Administrator. If you have no idea what this program was for, and no corporate system administrator has sat down to explain it to you, then your daily work probably doesn't involve working with corporate ODBC (Open Database Connectivity) databases. No? You've never used it? Maybe that's why Apple got rid of it.

Figure 10-30:
The Whois tool is a powerful part of Network Utility. First enter a domain that you want information about, and then choose a Whois server from the pop-up menu (you might try whois.networksolutions. com). When you click the Whois button, you get a surprisingly revealing report about the owner of the domain, including phone numbers, fax numbers, contact names, and so on.

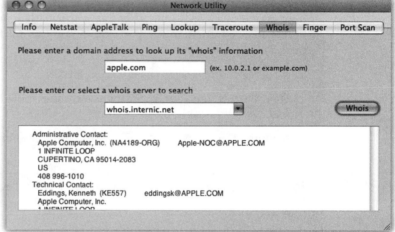

Podcast Capture

This program is a front end for Podcast Producer, a professional-league podcast recording and publishing program that's part of Apple's Mac OS X Server software suite. Unless you work in an office where a Mac OS X Server hums away in a back room, you can toss this program.

RAID Utility

Another program you probably don't need. It's useful only if your office has Mac OS X Server, and only if your Mac has a RAID (multiple-disk system) card installed.

Remote Install Mac OS X

OK, so you bought a MacBook Air laptop. It has no CD/DVD drive. How are you supposed to install Snow Leopard on it, or run a disk testing/repair program?

By "borrowing" another Mac's DVD drive, that's how. To use this little utility, put the CD or DVD into the other Mac; then run Remote Install Mac OS X (on the same Mac). Click Continue. You'll be walked through the process of installing Mac OS X or running your utility program, remotely, across the network to your Air.

Note: To install other kinds of software onto an Air, you don't have to go to all this trouble. You can borrow another Mac's drive much more directly, as described on page 341.

Spaces

Double-clicking this icon is another way of triggering Spaces, the Mac's virtual-screen feature; it's described on page 164.

System Profiler

System Profiler is a great tool for learning exactly what's installed on your Mac and what's not—in terms of both hardware and software. The people who answer the phones on Apple's tech-support line are particularly fond of System Profiler, since the detailed information it reports can be very useful for troubleshooting nasty problems.

There are now three ways to open System Profiler:

- **Slow.** Burrow into your Applications→Utilities folder; double-click System Profiler.

- **Medium.** Choose →About This Mac. In the resulting dialog box, click More Info.

Tip: If you click your Mac OS X version number twice in the About box, you get to see your Mac's serial number!

- **Fast.** Hold down the Option key, which makes the →About This Mac command *change* to say System Profiler. Choose it.

When System Profiler opens, it reports information about your Mac in a list down the left side (Figure 10-31). The details fall into these categories:

- **Hardware.** Click this word to see precisely which model Mac you have, what kind of chip is inside (and how many), how much memory it has, and its serial number.

  If you expand the flippy triangle, you get to see details about which **Memory** slots are filled and the size of the memory module in each slot; what kind of **Disc Burning** your Mac can do (DVD-R, DVD+R, and so on); what **PCI Cards** are installed in your expansion slots; what **Graphics/Displays** circuitry you have (graphics card and monitor); what's attached to your **ATA** bus (internal drives, like your DVD drive and hard drive); what's connected to your **SCSI, USB,** and **FireWire** chains, if anything; and much more.

- **Network.** This section reveals details on your **AirPort Card** (if you have one), what **Modems** you have, what Internet connection **Locations** you've established (page 679), and so on.

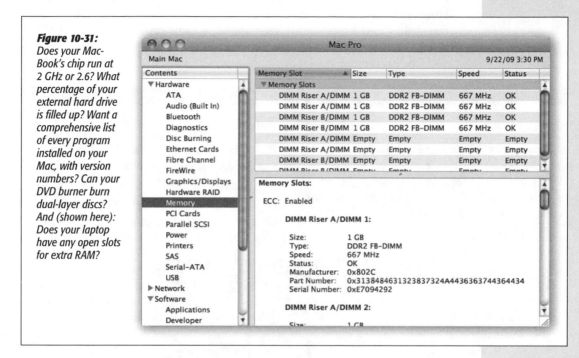

Figure 10-31:
Does your Mac-Book's chip run at 2 GHz or 2.6? What percentage of your external hard drive is filled up? Want a comprehensive list of every program installed on your Mac, with version numbers? Can your DVD burner burn dual-layer discs? And (shown here): Does your laptop have any open slots for extra RAM?

- **Software.** Click this heading to see exactly which version of Mac OS X you have, and what your computer's name is, as far as the network is concerned ("Chris's Computer," for example).

The **Applications** list documents every program on your system, with version information—a quick inventory of what you've installed on your Mac. It's useful for spotting duplicate copies of programs.

Tip: The right-hand column of the Applications list identifies each program as being Universal or PowerPC (or, in rare cases, Intel). (A Universal program can run natively–at full speed–on either Intel-based Macs or earlier models; a PowerPC program runs natively on older Macs, but somewhat slower on Intel Macs because it has to go through the Rosetta translator described on page 193). This list is a handy summary of which programs have been updated for the Intel generation.

Similar information shows up in the **Extensions** panel. In this sense, "extensions" doesn't mean *system* extensions like those that made life a living hell in Mac OS 9 and earlier. In Mac OS X, the term *extensions* refers to a different kind of add-on component to the core system software. Generally, these are drivers for the Mac's various components, which sit in the System→Library→Extensions folder. Whatever's in that folder is what you see listed in this panel.

Other categories include self-explanatory lists like **Fonts, Preference Panes,** and **Startup Items.**

Finally, the **Logs** panel reveals your Mac's secret diary: a record of the traumatic events that it experiences from day to day. (Many of these are the same as those revealed by the Console utility; see page 831.) Some reveal *crash logs,* which are detailed technical descriptions of what went wrong when various programs crashed, and what was stored in memory at the time.

POWER USERS' CLINIC

The Xcode Tools

The Mac OS X DVD includes a special batch of programs, known as the Xcode Tools, primarily for developers (programmers) who write Mac OS X software. You'll need some of these programs if you want to get into some of the more esoteric (or, as some would say, fun) Mac OS X tricks and tips.

To install these tools, open the Optional Installs→Xcode Tools window on the DVD, and then double-click XcodeTools.mpkg. After following the onscreen prompts, you wind up with a new folder called Developer on your hard drive. Its Applications→Utilities folder contains a few programs that are user-friendly enough even for nonprogrammers.

CrashReporterPrefs, for example, lets you tell Mac OS X when to display the "Application Unexpectedly Quit" dialog box. If you choose Server, you'll never see one of those annoying dialog boxes again—perfect if you have a program that just won't stop crashing.

Also, if you open Developer→Applications→Graphics Tools,

you'll find **Quartz Composer Visualizer**. This program lets you build screen savers, animations, and tons of other graphical goodies without writing a single line of code.

Finally, don't miss **Core Image Fun House** (also in Developer→Applications→Graphics Tools). It's intended to be a showcase for Mac OS X's Core Image technologies, which constitute a ready-to-use photo-transformation toolkit that software companies can build into their programs. Fun House lets you apply dozens of mind-blowing visual effects to your images and movies—distortions, color corrections, solar flares, and so on—with nothing more than a few clicks. (If your Mac is fast enough, you can even adjust filters in real time, so you can see the result of your modifications as you make them.) One possibility is shown here.

When you're done psychedelicizing your image, you can export it to a standard JPEG or TIFF image by choosing File→Save As. From there, you can show it off on a Web site, email it to your friends, or make it your desktop background.

Unfortunately, there's not much plain English here to help you understand the crash, or how to avoid it in the future. Most of it runs along the lines of "Exception: EXC_BAD_ACCESS (0x0001); Codes: KERN_INVALID_ADDRESS (0x0001) at 0x2f6b657d." In other words, it's primarily for the benefit of programmers. Still, tech-support staff may occasionally ask to see the information in one of these logs.

Tip: If any of these screens is showing you more or less technical information than you'd like, use the View menu to choose Mini Profile, Basic Profile, or Full Profile.

Saving a report

To create a handsomely formatted report that you can print or save, choose File→Save, and then choose Rich Text Format from the File Format pop-up menu. Note, however, that the resulting report can be well over 100 pages long. In many cases, you're better off simply making a screenshot of the relevant Profiler screen, as described on page 575, or saving the thing as a PDF file (page 552).

Terminal

Terminal opens a terminal window with a *command line interface,* taking you deep into the world of Unix, the operating system on which Mac OS X is based. Chapter 16 offers a crash course on this powerful window into the Mac's shadow operating system.

VoiceOver Utility

For details on this screen-reader software, see page 603.

CDs, DVDs, & iTunes

Apple shocked the world when, in 1998, it introduced the iMac without a floppy disk drive—and proceeded to eliminate the floppy drive from all subsequent Mac models in the following years. Apple argued that the floppy disk was dead: It was too small to serve as a backup disk, and, in the Internet age, it was a redundant method of exchanging files with other computers.

These days, even Windows PC manufacturers have left the floppy drive for dead. Joining it in the great CompUSA in the sky: Zip disks, Jaz disks, SyQuest disks, SuperDisks, Peerless disks…

Disks Today

So what's springing up to take the floppy's place? Let us count the disks.

Hard Drives, iPods

Thanks to the Mac's FireWire or USB jacks, it's easier than ever to attach an external hard drive for extra storage. It would be hard to imagine a more convenient second hard drive than, for example, Apple's iPod. Most models are not only outstanding MP3 music players, but they also double as self-powered, extremely compact, bootable hard drives.

CDs, DVDs

You wouldn't get far in today's computer world without a CD/DVD drive. Most commercial software comes on a CD or DVD—not to mention the music CDs that the Mac can play so expertly.

CD-ROM stands for "compact disc, read-only memory"—in other words, you can't freely add and delete files from one, as you can from a hard drive. But your Mac can also record onto blank CDs, of course, and blank DVDs, too, thanks to a built-in *CD/DVD burner.* A burner can record onto either of two kinds of blank discs:

- **CD-R.** You can fill this type of disc with your own files—once. (The R stands for *recordable.*) The disc can't be erased, although you can add to it (see page 440). Once you've grasped that much, you'll probably also understand the term DVD-R (and the nearly identical "plus" versions, CD+R and DVD+R).

Note: A Snow Leopard Mac can accept either kind of blank disc: the –R type or the +R type. They're technically different, but since your Mac can handle either type, just buy whichever is on sale.

- **CD-RW.** The initials stand for *rewritable;* using Disk Utility, you can erase one of these discs and rerecord it, over and over again. Of course, CD-RW and DVD-RW blank discs are somewhat more expensive than the one-shot kind.

The standard Mac CD/DVD drive can also play DVD movies that you've rented or bought, but you may also occasionally use it for *data* DVDs—that is, DVDs that contain Mac files or software installers.

Every Snow Leopard Mac (except the MacBook Air, of course) contains what Apple calls a SuperDrive. This drive, actually made by a company like Pioneer or Matsushita, can play *and* record CDs *and* DVDs. You could, for example, use blank DVDs as backup disks that hold 4.7 GB or 8.5 GB each. (That's 4.7 gigs for regular blank DVDs, and 8.5 gigs on the newer, more expensive dual-layer blanks. Not all Macs recognize dual-layer DVDs, though. Check your copy of System Profiler, as described on page 426.)

If you've used iMovie to edit your home camcorder footage, you can also save your masterpiece onto one of these DVDs for playback in standard home DVD players— the perfect way to distribute it to friends and family with spectacular quality.

Flash Drives

The most recent invention is among the most convenient: tiny, keychain-sized *flash drives* or *thumb drives,* which plug directly into your USB jack and serve as low-capacity hard drives with no moving parts. Inside, they contain nothing but RAM— pure memory.

Flash drives are fantastic, inexpensive gadgets that hold as much as 128 gigabytes. They work on any Mac or Windows PC and don't require any drivers or special software installation. Ask for one for your birthday.

Disks In, Disks Out

When you insert a disk, its icon shows up in three places (unless you've changed your Finder preferences): on the right side of the screen, in the Computer window, and in the Sidebar. To see what's on a disk you've inserted, double-click its icon.

Note: You can make the Mac work like Windows, if you choose. For example, to open a single window containing the icons of all currently inserted disks, choose Go→Computer (which produces the rough equivalent of the Computer window).

To complete the illusion that you're running Windows, you can even tell Mac OS X not to put disk icons on the desktop at all. Just choose Finder→Preferences, click General, and turn off the four top checkboxes—"Hard disks," "External disks," "CDs, DVDs, and iPods," and "Connected servers." They'll no longer appear on the desktop—only in your Computer window. (You can stop them from appearing in the Sidebar, too, by clicking the Sidebar button in the Finder preferences and turning off the same checkboxes.)

Figure 11-1:
You may see all kinds of disks on the Mac OS X desktop (shown here: hard drive, CD, iPod, iDisk)—or none at all, if you've chosen to hide them using the Finder→Preferences command.

By the way: If you have a MacBook Air (a laptop with no CD/DVD drive), you can still use discs. You can buy Apple's sleek, $100 external USB drive. Or you can use Remote Disc Sharing, a weird little technology that lets the Air access the drive on another computer on the network.

To turn on Remote Disc, visit the other Mac. Open System Preferences→Sharing. Turn on DVD or CD Sharing. (You can even use a Windows PC as the "other Mac," provided you install the disc-sharing control panel that came with your Air.)

Now, any disc you put into that other Mac shows up in the Sidebar on the MacBook Air, labeled Remote Disc. You can double-click it to see the disc-sharing computers on the network, and double-click their icons to access whatever disc is in their borrowed drives. Sneaky, eh?

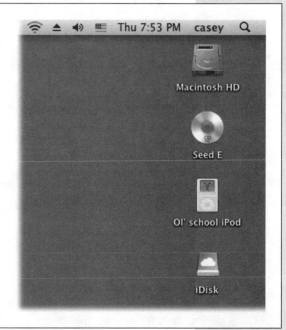

To remove a disk from your Mac, use one of these methods:

- **Hold down the ⏏ key on your keyboard.** Mac keyboards, both on laptops and desktops, have a special Eject key (⏏), usually in the upper-right corner. Hold it down for a moment to make a CD or DVD pop out. (If you don't have an ⏏ key, hold down F12 instead.)

- **Drag its icon onto the Trash icon.** For years, this technique has confused and frightened first-time Mac users. Their typical reaction: Doesn't the Trash mean "delete"? Yes, but only when you drag *file or folder* icons there—not *disk* icons. Dragging a disk icon into the Trash (at the end of the Dock) makes the Mac spit the disk out. (If you drag a *disk image* icon or the icon of a networked disk, this maneuver *unmounts* them—that is, gets them off your screen.)

The instant you begin dragging a disk icon, the Trash icon on the Dock changes form, as though to reassure the novice that dragging a disk icon there will only eject the disk. As you drag, the wastebasket icon morphs into a giant-sized ⏏ logo.

- Highlight the disk icon, and then choose File→Eject (or press ⌘-E). The disk pops out.

- Control-click (or right-click) the disk icon. Choose Eject from the shortcut menu.

- Click the ⏏ button next to a disk's name in the Sidebar.

Any of these techniques also work to get network disks and disk images off your screen.

Snow Leopard Spots: In the bad old days, ejecting a disk, too often, produced a snotty error message to the effect that, "This disk is in use." It would appear when, for example, a document on that disk was still open in one of your programs.

In Snow Leopard, that message appears far less often—and when it does appear, the message tells you exactly which program is still holding onto the disk. You can switch to that program, close whatever document is causing the problem, and then eject the disk.

FREQUENTLY ASKED QUESTION

The Eject Button That Doesn't

When I push the ⏏ key on my keyboard (or the Eject button on my CD-ROM drawer), how come the CD doesn't come out?

There might be any of three things going on. First of all, some file on the disc might be open—that is, in use by one of your programs. You're not allowed to eject the disc until that file is closed.

Second, to prevent accidental pushings, the ⏏ key on the modern Mac keyboard is designed to work only when you hold it down steadily for a second or two. Just tapping it doesn't work.

Third, remember that once you've inserted a disc, the Mac won't let go unless you eject it in one of the official ways.

On Mac models with a CD tray (drawer), pushing the button on the CD-ROM door opens the drawer only when it's empty. If there's a disc in it, you can push that button till doomsday, but the Mac will simply ignore you.

That behavior especially confuses people who are used to working with Windows. (On a Windows PC, pushing the CD button does indeed eject the disc.) But on the Mac, pushing the CD-door button ejects an inserted disc only when the disc wasn't seated properly, or the Mac couldn't read the disc for some other reason, and the disc's icon never appeared onscreen.

The ⏏ key on the modern Mac keyboard, however, isn't so fussy. It pops out whatever CD or DVD is in the drive.

Oh—and if a CD or DVD won't come out at all (and its icon doesn't show up on the desktop), restart the Mac. Keep the mouse button or the F12 key pressed as the Mac restarts to make the disc pop out.

And if even that technique doesn't work, look for a tiny pinhole in or around the slot. Inserting a straightened paper clip, slowly and firmly, will also make the disc pop out.

Startup Disks

When you turn the Mac on, it hunts for a *startup disk*—that is, a disk containing a System folder. If you've ever seen the dispiriting blinking folder icon on a Mac's screen, you know what happens when the Mac *can't* find a startup disk. It blinks like that forever, or until you find and insert a disk with a viable System folder on it.

Creating a Startup Disk

By installing the Mac OS onto a disk—be it a hard drive or a DVD—you can create a startup disk.

Note: Not all external USB disks are capable of starting up the Mac, but any internal hard drive can, and any external FireWire hard drive can.

Selecting a Startup Disk

It's perfectly possible to have more than one startup disk simultaneously attached to your Mac. That's the deal, for example, whenever you've inserted the Mac OS X DVD into your Mac: Both your main hard drive and the DVD contain a System folder, and each is a startup disk. Some veteran Mac fans deliberately create other startup disks—using iPods, for example—so that they can easily start the Mac up from a backup disk, or from a different version of the OS.

Only one System folder can be operational at a time. So how does the Mac know which to use as its startup disk? You make your selection in the Startup Disk pane of System Preferences (Figure 11-2).

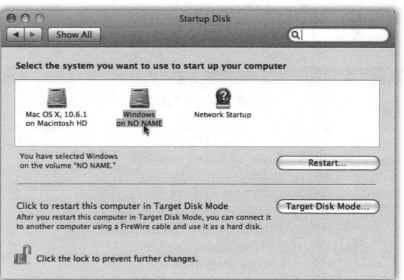

Figure 11-2:
In the Startup Disk pane of System Preferences, the currently selected disk—the one that will be "in force" the next time the machine starts up—is always highlighted. You also see the System folder's version, the name of the drive it's on, and its actual name.

Tip: If you're in a hurry to start the machine up from a different disk, just click the disk icon and then click Restart in the System Preferences window. You don't have to close the System Preferences window first.

Erasing a Disk

Mac OS X doesn't have an Erase Disk command at the desktop. When you want to erase a disk (such as a DVD-RW disc), the only tool Apple gives you is Disk Utility, which sits in your Applications→Utilities folder. This is the same program you use to erase, repair, or subdivide *(partition)* a hard drive.

Once you've opened Disk Utility, click the name of the disk (in the left-side list), click the Erase tab, and then click the Erase button.

You won't be able to do so, though, if:

- The disk is a standard CD-ROM, DVD, a previously recorded CD-R disc, or a disk elsewhere on the network.

- You're trying to erase the startup disk. You can't wipe out the disk that contains the currently running System folder any more than you can paint the floor directly beneath your feet. (To erase your built-in hard drive, for example, you must start up from the Mac OS X DVD.)

Burning CDs and DVDs

You can buy blank CDs incredibly cheaply in bulk—$20 for 100 discs, for example—via the Web. (To find the best prices, visit *www.shopper.com* or *www.buy.com* and search for *blank CD-R.*) Blank DVDs are only slightly more expensive—about $30 for 100.

Burning a CD or DVD is great for backing up stuff, transferring stuff to another computer (even a Windows PC), mailing to somebody, or offloading (archiving) older files to free up hard drive space.

UP TO SPEED

Mac OS Extended Formatting

Whether you use Disk Utility to erase a disk (or when you first install Mac OS X and elect to erase the hard drive in the process), you'll be confronted with a choice between formatting options called Mac OS Extended and UNIX File System (UFS). (Depending on the kind of disk, you may also see an option to create a DOS-formatted disk for use in Windows machines.)

Mac OS Extended or Mac OS Extended (Journaled) refers to the HFS Plus filing system, a disk format that has been proudly maximizing disk space for Mac fans since Mac

OS 8.1. (For a definition of journaling, see page 832.)

Mac OS X still accepts disks that were prepared using the older, Mac OS Standard formatting—the ancient HFS (hierarchical filing system) format—but you can't use one as your startup disk, and any file names longer than 31 characters will appear chopped off.

As for the UNIX File System option, it's exclusively for use on computers that run Unix (the pure variety, not the dressed-up version that is Mac OS X).

You can burn a disc in either of two ways: with the blank disc inserted or without.

Burn Folders: Without the Disc

The *burn folder* is a special folder that you fill up by dragging file and folder icons to it. Then, when you're ready to burn, you just insert the blank disc and go.

The burn-folder concept has a lot going for it:

- **No wasted hard drive space.** When you use a burn folder, you're not using up any additional disk space as you load up a disc with files and folders. Instead, the Mac just sets aside aliases of the files and folders you want to burn. Aliases take up negligible hard drive space. When you finally burn the disc, the designated material is copied directly onto the CD or DVD.

- **Easy reuse.** You can keep a burn folder on your desktop, prestocked with the folders you like to back up. Each time you burn a disc, you get the latest version of those folders' contents, and you're saved the effort of having to gather them each time.

- **Prepare ahead of time.** You can get a CD or DVD ready to burn without having a blank disc on hand.

Here's how you use burn folders:

1. **Create a burn folder.**

   To make a burn folder appear on your desktop, choose File→New Burn Folder. To create one in any other window, Control-click (or right-click) a blank spot inside that window and, from the shortcut menu, choose New Burn Folder.

   Either way, a new folder appears, bearing the universal Mac "burn" symbol (☢).

2. **Rename it.**

   Its name is highlighted, so you can just start typing to rename it. Press Return when you're finished.

3. **Load up the folder by dragging files and folders onto it.**

   If you double-click the burn folder to open its window (Figure 11-3), you'll notice that you're not actually copying huge files. You're simply making a list of aliases.

Tip: At the bottom of the burn folder's window, the "minimum disc size" display keeps track of how much stuff you've loaded up so far, so you can gauge if it will fit on one disc.

---

4. **Decorate the window, if you like.**

   You can choose list view or icon view; you can drag the icons into an arrangement you like; you can change the background color of the window; and so on. One nice feature of the Mac (which is not available on The Other OS) is that the look of a window is preserved when you burn it to CD.

5. **Click the Burn button in the upper-right corner of the window, or choose File→ Burn Disc.**

   The message shown at bottom in Figure 11-3 appears.

Figure 11-3:
Top: A burn folder looks like any ordinary folder—except that it has that radioactive logo on it. You can drag files and folders right into its window; Mac OS X displays only aliases for now, but when you burn the disc, the actual files and folders will be there.

If you open the burn folder, you find an unusual strip across the top. Its most important feature is the Burn button at the right.

Bottom: Ready to proceed, Captain.

6. **Insert a blank disc.**

   If you have a slot-loading Mac, slip the disc into the slot. If your Mac has a sliding CD/DVD tray instead, open it first by pressing the button on the tray, or pressing your ⏏ key for about a second.

Tip: Once you've inserted a CD or DVD into your tray, you can close it either by pushing gently on the tray or by pressing the ⏏ key again.

   One last confirmation box appears, where you can name the disc and choose a burning speed for it.

7. **Click Burn (or press Return).**

   The Mac's laser proceeds to record the CD or DVD, which can take some time. Feel free to switch into another program and continue using your Mac. When it's all over, you have a freshly minted CD or DVD, whose files and folders you can open on any Mac or Windows PC.

When You Have a Blank Disc On Hand

If you have a blank disc ready to go, burning is even simpler.

Start by inserting the disc. After a moment, the Mac displays a dialog box asking, in effect, what you want to do with this blank disc (unless you've fiddled with your preference settings). See Figure 11-4 for instructions.

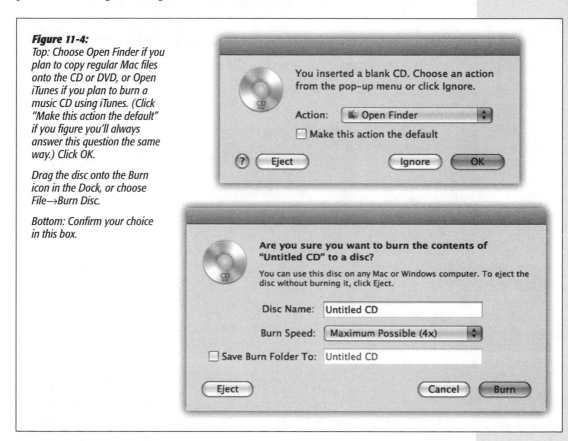

Figure 11-4:
Top: Choose Open Finder if you plan to copy regular Mac files onto the CD or DVD, or Open iTunes if you plan to burn a music CD using iTunes. (Click "Make this action the default" if you figure you'll always answer this question the same way.) Click OK.

Drag the disc onto the Burn icon in the Dock, or choose File→Burn Disc.

Bottom: Confirm your choice in this box.

If you choose Open Finder, the disc's icon appears on the desktop after a moment; its icon also appears in the Sidebar, complete with the Burn symbol (☢).

At this point, you can begin dragging files and folders onto the disc's icon, or (if you double-click the icon) into its window. You can add, remove, reorganize, and rename the files on it just as you would in any standard Finder window. All you're really doing is dragging aliases around; the real files are left untouched on your hard drive. You can also rename the CD or DVD itself just as you would a file or folder.

When the disc's icon contains the files and folders you want to immortalize, do one of these things:

- Choose File→Burn [the disc's name].

- Click the ☢ button next to the disc's name in the Sidebar.

- Click the Burn button in the upper-right corner of the disc's window.

- Drag the disc's icon toward the Trash icon in the Dock. As soon as you begin to drag, the Trash icon turns into the yellow ☢ logo. Drop the disc's icon onto it.

GEM IN THE ROUGH

How to Burn a Multisession CD in Mac OS X

Most people think that once you've burned a CD-R disc, it's done. You can't burn more onto it.

In fact, though, you can use humble old Disk Utility, right there in your Applications→Utilities folder, to burn a single disc as many times as you like. That's right—regular, cheapie CD-R discs, not CD-RW (rewritable).

What you'll create here is a *multisession* disc. Each time you burn more material onto it, you create a new disc icon that will appear separately when you insert the CD. Shown here at top, for example, is a disc that's been burned twice. A folder called Photo-Rabbit was burned to the CD first. Then, a week later, a folder called "Flower pix" was burned onto the same disc, creating a second session (disc icon).

To pull off this stunt, prepare the material you intend to burn the first time. For example, put it all into a folder on your desktop.

Now open Disk Utility. Choose File→New→Disk Image from Folder. When prompted, navigate to, and select, the folder you want to burn, and then click Image.

Type a name for the disk image you're creating. Specify a location (like the Desktop) and then click Save. In this example, suppose it's called PhotoRabbit CD.dmg.

When you're ready to burn, open Disk Utility. Click the Burn icon on the toolbar. Navigate to, and click once, the disk image (PhotoRabbit CD.dmg). Then click Burn.

In the resulting Burn Disc dialog box, click the blue ▼ button at the upper right, if necessary, so that the dialog box is expanded as shown here. Turn on "Leave disc appendable." Click Burn to record the material onto the CD.

When it comes time to add new material to that disc, repeat all the steps given so far. This time, in the dialog box shown here, you'll see that instead of Burn, the lower-right button now says Append. That's your clue that Disk Utility understands what it's about to do: add information to an existing CD, resulting in a second disk icon on the desktop containing only the new material.

You've just created a multisession disc!

You can repeat the process over and over again, adding more and more material to a disc—or at least until it's just about full.

- Control-click (or right-click) the disc's icon; from the shortcut menu, choose Burn [the disc's name].

In any case, the dialog box shown at bottom in Figure 11-4 now appears. Click Burn. When the recording process is over, you'll have yourself a DVD or CD that works in any other Mac or PC.

Here are a few final notes on burning CDs and DVDs at the desktop:

- Not sure what kinds of discs your Mac can burn? Open System Profiler (in your Applications→Utilities folder). Expand the Hardware triangle, and click the Disc Burning category. There it is, plain as day: a list of the formats your machine can read and write (that is, burn). For example, you might see: "CD-Write: -R, -RW. DVD-Write: -R, -RW, +R, +RW."

- In the Finder, you can record only an entire disc at once; you can't add any more files after the first burn. There is a trick, however, that lets you add more to a previously recorded CD-R or DVD-R if you use Disk Utility instead. (Technically, you create a *multisession* disc.) See the box on the facing page.

- If you do a lot of disc burning, a full-fledged CD-burning program like Toast 10 Titanium (*www.roxio.com*) adds myriad additional formatting options that let you make startup CDs, video CDs, and so on.

- When you insert a CD-*RW* or DVD-*RW* disc that you've previously recorded, the box shown at the top in Figure 11-4 doesn't appear. Instead, the disc's icon simply appears on the desktop as though it's an ordinary CD. Before you can copy new files onto it, you must erase it using Disk Utility as described in the previous section.

- The discs that your Mac burns work equally well on Macs and Windows (or Linux) PCs. If you plan to insert a CD or DVD into a PC, however, remember that Windows doesn't permit certain symbols in a Windows filename (\ / : * ? " < > |). You'll run into trouble if any of your file names contain these symbols. In fact, you won't be able to open any folders on your disc that contain illegally named files.

iTunes: The Digital Jukebox

iTunes, in your Applications folder, is the ultimate software jukebox (Figure 11-5). It can play music CDs, tune in to Internet radio stations, load up your iPod music player or iPhone, and play back digital sound files (including the Internet's favorite format, MP3 files) and other popular audio formats. It can also turn selected tracks from your music CDs *into* MP3 files, so that you can store favorite songs on your hard drive to play back anytime—without having to dig up the original.

iTunes also lets you record your own custom audio CDs that contain only the good songs. Finally, of course, iTunes is the shop window for the online iTunes Store, which sells music, TV shows, and movies.

iTunes can also burn *MP3 CDs:* music CDs that fit much more than the usual 74 or 80 minutes of music onto a disc (because they store songs in MP3 format instead of AIFF). Not all CD players can play MP3 discs, however, and the sound quality is slightly lower than standard CDs.

Figure 11-5:
iTunes has become one of the most popular software programs in the world, because it's useful, it's cross-platform, and, of course, it's free.

It's basically a database that lists all of your music, video, and other playables, but it's full of ways to slice, dice, and export that entertainment to other devices.

The first time you run iTunes, you're asked (a) whether you want iTunes to be the program your Mac uses for playing music files from the Internet, (b) whether you want it to ask your permission every time it connects to the Internet, and (c) whether you want the program to scan your Home folder for all music files already on it. (You can decline to have your hard drive scanned at this time. Later, you can always drag it, or any other folder, directly into the iTunes window for automatic scanning.)

Tip: The following pages present a mini-manual on iTunes. For the full scoop, plus coverage of the iPod and the iTunes Store, consult *iPod: The Missing Manual.*

By now, the layout of iTunes should look familiar: a Source list at the left side, acting as a table of contents for the larger window to the right. It's the same layout used in Finder windows (the Sidebar), iPhoto, Image Capture, and other Apple programs.

The major headings in iTunes's list are Library, Store, Devices, Shared, Genius, and Playlists. Here's what they do:

Library

The items in this list represent all your music and videos: Music, Movies, TV Shows, Podcasts, and so on. They include both your own stuff—songs you copied off of music CDs, for example—and material you bought from the iTunes Store online.

Note: When you first open iTunes, it offers to search your hard drive for the kinds of files it can play—every song in formats like MP3, AIFF, WAV, AAC, and Apple Lossless, for example. It then copies all such files into your Home folder→Music→iTunes→iTunes Music folder. But you don't ever need to muck around in there; use iTunes to manage your collection instead.

When you click Music, the main iTunes window is organized much like a Finder window, with columns indicating the song length, artist, album, and so on. As always, you can rearrange these columns by dragging their headings, sort your list by one of these criteria by clicking its heading, reverse the sorting order by clicking the heading a second time, and so on.

Or click one of the three View buttons next to the Search box to display your music as either a grid of thumbnail album covers—or as Cover Flow, which lets you flip through album covers as though they're sitting in a record-store bin.

To find a particular song or video, just type a few letters into the Spotlight-ish Search box above the list. iTunes hides all but the ones that match.

Store

The iTunes Store is easy to figure out. By clicking the tabs across the top of the window, you can search or browse for music (over 11 million songs, classical pieces, and comedy routines); movies (8,000 and counting); TV shows ($2 an episode, with no ads, from over 500 series); iPhone apps (85,000); free podcasts (75,000); audiobooks (30,000); and more. Sure, you may go broke, but at least you'll be entertained.

Besides, there are no monthly fees, and your downloads don't go *poof!* into the ether if you decide to cancel your subscription, as they do with some rival services.

Use the Search Music Store box (top-right corner) to find the songs or performers you're interested in. Double-click a song or video to hear or view a 30-second excerpt. (For audiobooks, you get a 90-second excerpt.)

If you decide to buy a song, you need an Apple account. Click the Sign In button (upper right) and then Create New Account to get started. (If you've ever bought or registered an Apple product on the company's Web site, signed up for AppleCare, ordered an iPhoto book, or have a MobileMe membership, you have an Apple Account already. All you have to do is remember your name—usually your email address—and password.)

When you click the Buy button next to a song's name, iTunes downloads it to your Mac. Behind the scenes, it goes into your Home→Music→iTunes Music folder. But for your purposes, it shows up in the Store→Purchased category in the Source list for convenient access.

Devices

These icons represent other gadgets that iTunes can talk to. If you insert a CD, it shows up here. If you attach an iPod or iPhone, its icon appears here, too. An Apple TV, if you have one, also appears here. Click any one of these icons to see what's on it.

And if you don't have *any* of these things attached, the Devices category doesn't appear at all.

Shared

If you've taken the trouble to set up a home network, you can share songs and playlists with up to five networked computers. You could, for example, tap into your roommates' jazz collection without getting up from your desk, and they can sample the zydeco and tejano tunes from your World Beat playlist. The music you decide to share is streamed over the network to the other computer. In fact, you can even *copy* songs and videos from one machine to the other, so you can enjoy them even when the original computer is turned off.

Note: This Home Share feature even works between Macs and PCs.

To get started, sit at Computer A. Click Home Sharing in the Source list. You're asked for your Apple account information. Click Create Home Share and then Done.

Now, if you open iTunes on Computer B, you'll see Computer A listed in the Shared category at left. Click it to see what's in its copy of iTunes. You can play that stuff—even sitting at Computer B—and even copy it to Computer A. (Just drag the songs or videos you want into the appropriate category—Music, Movies, TV Shows, and so on—at the top of your Source list.)

Note: There's some fine print. Up to five computers can do this Home Share business. They all have to sign in with the same Apple account, and they all have to be on the same network (meaning inside the same building).

Genius

Genius, according to Apple, assembles lists of "songs that sound great together," whatever that means. (It seems to mean "songs that have the same degree of rockiness").

To get started, choose Store→Turn On Genius (unless it's already on). Click a song in your library that you want to serve as the anchor—the "seed" song—that you want to match. Then proceed in one of these three ways:

- **Create a Genius playlist.** Click the ✳ button at lower right. Presto: a new playlist, filed in your Source list under Genius. (Its name is Genius. Pure genius!) Play it to see how iTunes did at matching your original song's feel.

  At the top of the window, you can use the Limit To pop-up menu to specify how many songs are in this playlist; the Refresh button to try again matching your "seed" song; or the Save Playlist button to turn this iTunes guess into a proper playlist.

- **Create a Genius Mix.** There's also such a thing as a Genius *Mix,* which, unlike a playlist, never ends. It's more like a radio station, eternally plucking songs from your collection that all match each other (or, as Apple would say, "sound great together"). Just click Genius Mixes in the Source list; you'll see a couple of starter mixes to get you going. Click one to hear it.

- **Shop for Genius suggestions.** If you click a song name, and then click the tiny, boxed ▶ button to the *right* of the ✳ button, you get a new Genius panel hugging the right side of the iTunes window. It shows other songs and albums from the iTunes store that Apple thinks you'd like, based on whatever song you clicked.

Playlists

Apple recognizes that you may not want to listen to *all* your songs every time you need some tunes. That's why iTunes lets you create *playlists*—folders in the Source list that contain, and play back, only certain songs (or videos). In effect, you can devise your own albums, like one called Party Tunes, another called Blind Date Music, and so on.

Creating playlists

To create a new playlist, click the **+** button in the lower-left corner of the window, or choose File→New Playlist (⌘-N). Alternatively, if you've already highlighted certain songs—by ⌘-clicking them or Shift-clicking them—you can choose File→New Playlist From Selection.

A new playlist appears as an icon in the Source list. You can rename this playlist by double-clicking it, and add songs to it by dragging them out of the main list into the icon.

Tip: Deleting a song from a playlist doesn't delete it from the Library (or your hard drive). Similarly, it's fine to add the same song to as many different playlists as you like, since you're not actually increasing the size of your Library. (You might be starting to pick up a running theme in Apple's software. Playlists work just like albums in iPhoto, or the Sidebar in the Finder.)

Smart playlists

Smart playlists constantly rebuild themselves according to criteria you specify. You might tell one smart playlist to assemble 45 minutes' worth of songs you've rated higher than four stars but rarely listen to, and another to list your most-often-played songs from the '80s.

Tip: To rate a song, make the window wide enough that you can see the Rating column. (If you don't see this column, Control-click any column heading and choose Rating from the list of options.) Then just click the Rating column for a selected song. The appropriate number of stars appears—one, two, three, four, or five—depending on the position of your click. You can change a song's rating as many times as you like—a good thing, considering the short shelf life of a pop hit these days.

To make a smart playlist, choose File→New Smart Playlist (Option-⌘-N)—or just Option-click the **+** button beneath the Source list. The dialog box shown in Figure 11-6 appears. The controls here are designed to set up a search of your music database. Figure 11-6, for example, illustrates how you'd find up to 74 Beatles tunes released between 1965 and 1968—that you've rated three stars or higher and that you've listened to fewer than three times.

When you click OK, your smart playlist is ready to show off. When you click its name in the Source list, the main song list updates itself according to your criteria and any changes in your music collection. (Smart playlists get transferred to your iPod or iPhone but don't continue to update themselves there.)

Audio CDs

If you insert a music CD while iTunes is open, the songs on it immediately show up in the list.

At first, they may appear with the exciting names "Track 01," "Track 02," and so on. But after a moment, iTunes connects to the Internet and compares your CD with the listings at *www.gracenote.com*, a global database of music CDs and their contents. If it finds a match among the thousands of CDs there, it copies the album and song names into iTunes, where they reappear every time you use this particular CD.

FREQUENTLY ASKED QUESTION

Auto-Playing Music CDs

How do I make music CDs automatically play when they're inserted into the Mac?

First, make sure iTunes is slated to open automatically when you insert a music CD. You do that on the CDs & DVDs panel of System Preferences (use the "When you insert a music CD" pop-up menu).

Then all you have to do is make sure iTunes knows to begin playing automatically once it launches. Choose iTunes→Preferences, click the Advanced icon, and then click Importing; from the On CD Insert pop-up menu, choose Begin Playing. Click OK.

From now on, whenever you insert a music CD, iTunes will open automatically and begin playing.

You can play the CD just as you would anything else in iTunes: by tapping the space bar, for example.

Tip: If you connect an iTunes-compatible portable MP3 player to your Mac (the iPod isn't the only one), its name, too, shows up in the left-side Source list. You can add songs to your player (by dragging them onto its icon), rename or reorder them, and so on.

Figure 11-6:
A smart playlist is a powerful search command for your iTunes database. You can set up certain criteria, like the hunt for particular Beatles tunes illustrated here. The "Live updating" checkbox makes iTunes keep this playlist updated as your collection changes, as you change your ratings, as your play count changes, and so on.

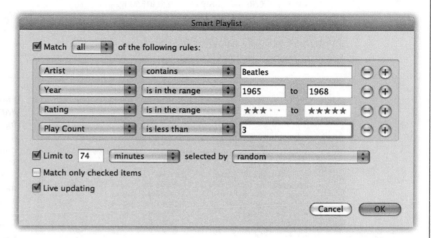

Copying (ripping) CD songs to your hard drive

Once you copy your favorite audio CDs onto your hard drive, you can play them whenever you like, without the original CD.

To *rip* a CD (as aficionados would say) like this, make sure that only the songs you want to capture have checkmarks in the main list. Choose a format for the files you're about to create, if you like—MP3, for example, or AAC (better quality/size tradeoff, but less compatible with other gadgets)—by clicking the Import Settings button (Figure 11-7). Finally, click the Import CD button at the lower-right corner of the window.

When it's all over, you'll find the imported songs listed in your Library. (Click Music in the left-side Source list.) From there, you can drag them into any other "folder" (playlist), as described above.

The iPod and iPhone

Unless you're just off the shuttle from Alpha Centauri, you probably already know that the iPod is Apple's tiny, elegant music player. It, and its cellular pal the iPhone, are designed to integrate seamlessly with iTunes.

All you have to do is connect the iPod or iPhone to the Mac via its white USB cable. The gadget's icon shows up in the iTunes Source list. Click its icon to view its contents—and click the tabs (Music, TV Shows, Podcasts, and so on) to specify what Mac material you'd like copied over to it.

Playing with Playback

To play a song or video, double-click it. Or click iTunes's Play button (▶) or press the space bar. The Mac immediately begins to play the songs whose names have checkmarks in the main list (Figure 11-7), or the CD that's currently in your Mac.

Tip: The central display at the top of the window shows not only the name of the song and album, but also where you are in the song, as represented by the diamond in the horizontal strip. Drag this diamond, or click elsewhere in the strip, to jump around in the song.

To view the current music's sound levels, click the tiny triangle at the left side of this display to see a pulsing VU meter, indicating the various frequencies.

Figure 11-7:
Watch the display at the top of the window to see how long the conversion is going to take, and which song iTunes is working on. As iTunes finishes processing each song, you see a small, circled checkmark next to its name in the main list to remind you that you've got it on board and no longer need the CD in your machine.

As music plays, you can control and manipulate the music and the visuals of your Mac in all kinds of interesting ways. Some people don't move from their Macs for months at a time.

Turning on visuals

Visuals are onscreen light shows that pulse, beat, and dance in sync to the music. The effect is hypnotic and wild. (For real party fun, invite some people who grew up in the '60s to your house to watch.)

To summon this psychedelic display, choose View→Turn On Visuals, or just press ⌘-T. The show begins immediately—although it's much more fun if you choose View→Full Screen (⌘-F) so the show takes over your whole monitor. True, you won't get a lot of work done, but when it comes to stress relief, visuals are a lot cheaper than a hot tub.

If you investigate the View→Visualizer submenu, you'll see that iTunes comes with six different screensavery modules. Each one has secret keystrokes that trigger secret functions. Press the ? key to see a tiny cheat sheet of the available keyboard commands.

Keyboard control

You can control iTunes' music playback using its menus, of course, but the keyboard can be far more efficient. Here are a few of the control keystrokes worth noting:

Function	Keystroke
Play, Pause	space bar or ▸॥ key
Next song/previous song	↑, ↓ or ←, →
Louder, quieter	⌘-↑, ⌘-↓
Rewind, fast-forward	◂◂, ▸▸ keys (or Option-⌘-←, Option-⌘-→)
Eject the CD	⌘-E
Turn Visuals on	⌘-T
Turn Visuals off	⌘-T or mouse click
Full-screen visuals	⌘-F
Exit full-screen visuals	⌘-T, ⌘-F, Esc, or mouse click

Tip: You can also control CD playback from the Dock. Control-click (or right-click) the iTunes icon to produce a pop-up menu offering playback commands like Pause, Next Song, and Previous Song, along with a display that identifies the song currently being played.

Playing with the graphic equalizer

If you choose Window→Equalizer, you get a handsome control console that lets you adjust the strength of each musical frequency independently (Figure 11-8).

WORKAROUND WORKSHOP

iPod Independence

Out of the box, the iPod and iTunes come set for automatic synchronization. That is, as soon as you hook them together, iTunes sends your complete music library (the contents of your Library "folder" in iTunes) to the iPod. The iPod's songs and playlists always match the Mac's.

Apple's idea here was to ensure that you don't use the iPod as a convenient piracy machine. Your iPod gets its music from your Mac, it but can't put its songs *onto* a Mac.

At least that's the theory. But what if your hard drive self-destructs, vaporizing the 945 MP3 files that you've made from your paid-for CD collection? You legally own those

copies. Shouldn't you have the right to retrieve them from your own iPod?

If you believe the answer is yes, a quick search at *www. versiontracker.com* for the word "iPod" will bring up a list of programs like Senuti (iTunes spelled backward, get it?), which let you copy music from the iPod to the Mac.

These programs know that the name of the super-secret music folder on the iPod, called iPod_Control, is invisible, which is why you can't see it on your desktop without the help of these utilities.

Preventing ear-blast syndrome

Here's a clever touch: In iTunes→Preferences→Playback, you see a checkbox called Sound Check. Its function is to keep the playback volume of all songs within the same basic level so you don't have to adjust the volume to compensate for different recorded levels. (This setting, too, gets transferred to your iPod or iPhone.)

Come to think of it, you could while away quite a few happy afternoons just poking through the Preferences dialog box. It grows richer with every successive version of iTunes.

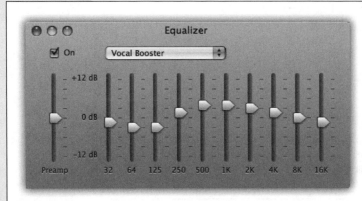

Figure 11-8:
Drag the sliders (bass on the left, treble on the right) to accommodate the strengths and weaknesses of your speakers or headphones (and listening tastes). Or save yourself the trouble—use the pop-up menu above the sliders to choose a canned set of slider positions for Classical, Dance, Jazz, Latin, and so on. These settings even transfer to the iPod.

Burning Music CDs

iTunes can record selected sets of songs, no matter what the original sources, onto a blank CD. When it's all over, you can play the burned CD on a standard CD player, just as you would a CD from the record store—but this time, you hear only the songs you like, in the order you like, with all the annoying ones eliminated.

Start by creating a playlist for the CD you're about to make. Click its icon in the left-side Source list to see the list you've built. Drag songs up or down in the list to change their playback order. Keep these points in mind:

- The readout at the bottom of the list shows how much time the songs will take.

- About 74 or 80 minutes of regular audio files fit on one CD. But if you make an *MP3 CD*, you can fit at least 10 times as much—12 hours of music on a single disc!

  The fine print: Not all CD players can play MP3 CDs (check the manual or the side of the CD player's box). Also note that your MP3 CD can't include songs you've bought on Apple's iTunes music store; iTunes won't convert them into the MP3 format.

  To burn an MP3 CD, see Figure 11-9.

- You can control how many seconds of silence iTunes leaves between tracks on your custom CD, too. Use the Gap Between Songs pop-up menu shown in Figure 11-9.

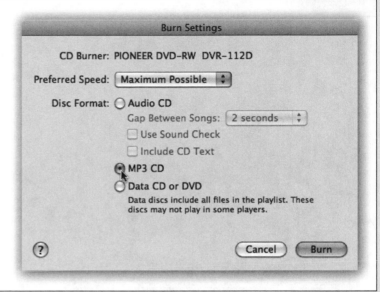

Figure 11-9:
To burn an MP3 CD, click the playlist, insert a blank CD, and then click Burn Disc (lower-right corner of the window). This box appears. Here, you can select MP3 CD. If you're burning a regular audio CD instead, you can specify how much gap you want between the songs.

When everything is set up, click the Burn Disc button in the playlist window. Specify your CD options (Figure 11-9), insert a blank CD into the Mac, and go read a book; the burning process takes some time. Feel free to work in other programs while iTunes chugs away.

DVD Movies

Watching movies on your Mac screen couldn't be simpler: Just insert a movie DVD. The Mac detects that it's a video DVD (as opposed to, say, one that's just filled with files). Then, unless you've fiddled with your preference settings, the DVD Player program opens and begins playing the movie in full-screen mode. (Even the menu bar disappears. To make it reappear, move your cursor to near the top of the screen.)

Note: If DVD Player doesn't open automatically when you insert a DVD movie, you can open it yourself. It's sitting there in your Applications folder. (Then fix the problem, using the CDs & DVDs panel of System Preferences.)

Playing a Movie

Once DVD Player starts playing your movie, you can move your mouse to the bottom of the screen, at any time, to bring up the control bar, which is deconstructed in Figure 11-10.

Figure 11-10:
Top: Even in full-screen mode, you can control the playback and navigate the disc using the translucent pop-up control bar.

Don't miss the scrubber bar at the very bottom. It lets you scroll directly to any spot in the DVD.

Bottom: When you're not in full-screen mode, you get a separate, floating "remote control." It has most of the same controls, but they're arranged with a more 1999 sort of design aesthetic.

Scrubber bar

Languages, Subtitles

Eject DVD

Click to see elapsed time/ time remaining

Picture controls

Exit full screen

Slo Mo
Frame Advance
Return to Movie

Subtitles
Language
Angle

Previous chapter/Next chapter
(Hold to scan backward/forward)

Or just use the keyboard controls, which appear here in this clip 'n' save cheat sheet:

Function	Keystroke
Play, Pause	space bar or ▶❙❙ key
Fast-forward, rewind	◀◀, ▶▶ keys (or Shift⌘-→, Shift-⌘-←); press repeatedly to multiply the speed of scanning
Skip forward/back 5 seconds	Option-⌘-→, Option-⌘-←
Louder, quieter	⌘-↑, ⌘-↓
Mute/Unmute	Option-⌘-↓

Next/previous "chapter"	→, ←
Full-screen mode on/off	⌘-F
Half, normal, maximum size	⌘-1, -2, -3
Eject	⌘-E
Add a bookmark	⌘-= (equal sign)

Language Fun

Most Hollywood DVDs have been programmed with onscreen subtitles to help those with hearing impairments and people sitting in noisy bars. The Subtitle button offers a pop-up menu of alternative languages and subtitle options.

GEM IN THE ROUGH

Internet Radio and Podcasts

Audio CDs and MP3 files aren't the only sources of musical and spoken sound you can listen to as you work. iTunes also lets you tune in to hundreds of Internet-based radio stations, which may turn out to be the most convenient music source of all. They're free, they play 24 hours a day, and their music col-

lections make yours look like a drop in the bucket. You can also download and listen to podcasts, which are like home-made (sometimes *very* homemade), Web-distributed personal radio shows.

For radio, click Radio in the left-side Source list. (If you

don't see Radio there, choose iTunes→Preferences→ General, and turn on Radio.)

In the main list, if you're connected to the Internet, you'll see categories like Blues, Classic Rock, Classical, and so on, as shown here. Click the flippy triangle to see a list of Internet radio stations in that category.

When you see one that looks interesting, double-click it. (The higher the number in the Bit Rate column, the better the sound quality.) Wait a moment for your Mac to connect to

the appropriate Internet site, and then let the music begin!

Without add-on shareware, there's no easy way to capture Internet broadcasts or save them onto your hard drive. You can, however, drag a radio station's name into the Music list (in the Source list), or even a playlist, to make it easier to access later on.

If you discover other Internet radio stations that sound interesting, choose Advanced→Open Stream, type in the station's Web address (URL), and press Return.

To grab a podcast, click iTunes Store in the Source list. At the top of the screen, click Podcasts. Now iTunes lets you browse a vast list of available podcasts. When you click one that looks promising, you'll see that you can either listen to it on the spot, or—and here's the real fun—click Subscribe.

Once you do that, a new icon called Podcasts appears in your Source list; click it to find the latest episodes of the podcasts you've subscribed to. Sync those babies to your iPod or iPhone, and you've got interesting material—or, at least fresh material—to listen to every day of the week.

Tip: For real fun, turn on English subtitles but switch the soundtrack to a foreign language. No matter how trashy the movie you're watching, you'll gain much more respect from your friends and family when you tell them you're watching a foreign film.

Bookmarks and Video Clips

Two DVD Player features are designed to help you flag and return to favorite moments or scenes in a DVD movie.

- **Bookmarks.** Each time you find a spot you'll want to find again later (during playback or when paused), hit ⌘-= (equal sign), or choose Controls→New Bookmark. DVD Player invites you to name the bookmark. You can also accept its proposal of 1:23:15 (or whatever the hours:minutes:seconds count happens to be).

  Once you click OK, you can use the Go→Bookmarks submenu to jump from one bookmark to another.

Tip: Ordinarily, DVD Player is smart enough to begin playing back a movie from the point where you stopped, even if you ejected the DVD in the meantime and three years have gone by.

But when you create a bookmark, the "Name your bookmark" dialog box offers you the chance to define a default bookmark. That means, "Next time you insert this disc, play back from here instead of where I stopped."

Figure 11-11:
When you choose Controls→New Video Clip, this box appears. Find the starting point of the scene you want to capture and then click the upper Set button. Now play or navigate to the end of the scene, and click the lower Set button. When you click Save, you're invited to name the scene. From now on, you can play the scene by choosing from the Go→Video Clips submenu.

- **Video Clips.** A video clip is exactly the same as a bookmark, except that you're supposed to designate a starting point *and* an ending point. (Don't get excited; a video clip isn't a standalone file that's saved on your computer, and you can't send it or share it. It works only within DVD Player.)

Figure 11-11 shows how you create and use a video clip.

Chapter Thumbnails

A standard Hollywood DVD comes programmed with chapters—invisible markers that let you jump from one important scene beginning to the next. To see them in DVD Player, just move your mouse to the top of the screen. A row of chapter thumbnail images appears, which you can click to jump around in.

You can create your own scene thumbnails, too. That might not be an especially tempting feature when you're playing Hollywood DVDs. But on homemade DVDs, made either by you or somebody else, these custom scene markers can be handy signposts.

First choose Window→Chapters (⌘-B) to open the new chapter thumbnail palette. Here you'll find the existing scene breaks, which may or may not already have "poster frame" images (Figure 11-12).

All the action takes place in the Action menu (✿) at the bottom of the panel. For example, it contains the Generate Missing Thumbnails command, for use on DVDs that have chapter breaks but no little poster frames to represent them.

GEM IN THE ROUGH

Picture Controls

Every TV set has picture controls—settings that change the proportions and color of the picture; why not your Mac?

If you click the Picture Settings button on the toolbar (identified in Figure 11-10), you get this little-known floating control. It's actually three dialog boxes in one; if you click the ▶ button in its title bar, you can choose the one you want.

Video Zoom controls the *aspect ratio* (proportions) of the picture. It's handy when the DVD you're playing doesn't quite match the size and shape of your screen. When you turn it On (upper left), you can choose Auto Zoom (the Mac's best fit), or you can adjust

the horizontal and vertical sliders. (The Lock Aspect Ratio checkbox keeps them linked so you don't distort the image.) Or you can use the pop-up menu that starts out saying Manual, and choose a preset, like Widescreen. You can even save your tweakings under a new preset name, for use later on your oddball system.

Video Color adjusts the tint, brightness, contrast, and so on. And **Audio Equalizer** lets you adjust the sound characteristics to suit your particular speakers/ headphones and your particular ears. It works just like the one described in Figure 11-8.

Whether there's a poster frame for a particular chapter or not, you can substitute an image of your own. Find the exact frame of the movie that you think looks better than what's already in the Chapters palette; click the chapter in the palette, and, from the

Figure 11-12:
Double-click a chapter thumbnail to jump to that spot in the video. Use the pop-up menu at the top to switch between chapters, bookmarks, and video clips you've made. And use the ✿ menu at the bottom to manage the chapters' names and images.

FREQUENTLY ASKED QUESTION

Region Changing

The first time I tried to play a DVD, I got this weird message about initializing the region code. What's up with that?

Hollywood generally releases a movie in different parts of the world at different times. A movie may come out on video in the U.S. when it's just hitting screens in Europe. We certainly can't have people watching a DVD before the movie studio says it's OK! That's why many discs are region-locked, so that they play back only on players in certain geographical regions.

As a DVD player in disguise, your Mac is just doing its duty. You can change its region (you'll be offered the chance to do so when you insert a region-locked DVD from another region), but only five times—and then it's frozen forever in the fifth version.

The dialog box shows you which region your DVD is designed for: 1 for the U.S. and Canada; 2 for Japan, Europe, South Africa, and the Middle East; 3 for Southeast and East Asia; 4 for Australia, New Zealand, Pacific Islands, Central America, Mexico, South America, and the Caribbean; 5 for Eastern Europe, Africa, and North Korea; 6 for China; and 8 for airplanes, cruise ships, and so on. Any DVD that you burn yourself is assigned region 0, meaning that it will play anywhere.

(There's no Region 7. Maybe it's reserved for the empty spot in movie executives' hearts.)

✿ pop-up menu, choose Use Current Frame for Thumbnail. Presto: You've replaced the unhelpful (or nonexistent) chapter image with one that works better.

Parental Controls

The parental controls in DVD Player aren't much. You can't say, for example, "Don't play anything rated PG-13 or above"; you have to rate each DVD yourself, one at a time. But they're better than nothing.

Insert the DVD you're worried about. Choose File→Get Disk Info. Click the Parental Controls tab.

Click the 🔒 button and enter your administrator's password. (Unless, of course, your 8-year-old is the administrator of this Mac instead of you, in which case this DVD is the least of your problems.)

GEM IN THE ROUGH

Snow Leopard and Disk Capacity

Snow Leopard was supposed to be the quiet upgrade—the revision without any world-shaking features. Yet in one tiny, quiet way, Snow Leopard's disk-space measuring scheme strikes a huge blow for common sense.

Since the dawn of the metric system, we've used terms like *milli, centi, kilo,* and *mega* to indicate powers of 10. There are 10 millimeters in a centimeter. There are 1,000 kilowatts in a megawatt. And so on.

So how come when it comes to *disk-space* measurements, those convenient prefixes have completely different meanings? There aren't 1,000 megabytes in a gigabyte—there are 1,024!

That's because software engineers, who are binary-thinker types, have always thought in powers of *two*. On a hard drive, Windows and traditional versions of Mac OS X have always reported that there are 1,024 kilobytes in a megabyte, because 1,024 is the closest thing the binary system has to 1,000. (There are, in fact, terms for those power-of-two units: *kibibyte, mebibyte*, and so on. But nobody can say those words with a straight face.)

So you'd pay good money for, say, a 4-gig flash drive—and you'd get it home and find only 3.7 gigabytes available for you to use! The flash drive really does contain 4 billion bytes of space—but your operating system divides that by 1,024 instead of 1,000 to find out how many kilobytes it has. So it shows up appearing to have less space than what you'd

expected. (Of course, the files you put on it are proportionally "smaller," too, but you'd still feel ripped off.)

In Snow Leopard, Apple finally decided that enough was enough: 4 gigs should show up as 4 gigs. So Snow Leopard reports file and disk sizes using the metric system, just as you'd expect. When you buy a 500-gigabyte hard drive, by golly, it will show up as having 500 gigabytes free (minus a little overhead for formatting and stuff).

The only time you'll ever even notice this change is when you shuttle files or disks back and forth between Snow Leopard and some other computer. Files will be reported as a little smaller on Mac OS X 10.5 than on 10.6. A hard drive will seem to have a little more capacity in Snow Leopard than in Windows. And so on.

You're not actually getting any more space. Nothing is being added, taken away, or compressed. If a drive has 30 percent of its free space remaining on Leopard, it will still have 30 percent free in Snow Leopard, even though the number of megabytes is larger— because your files are being reported as larger, too.

In the meantime, though, Snow Leopard spares you that tiny moment of panic when you hook up a new drive—and eliminates that question we've all had at one time or another:

"Why isn't this disk as big as the manufacturer said it would be?"

Now you can select either "Always ask for authorization" or "Always allow to be played," depending on your feelings about the movie. Click OK.

All you've done so far, however, is to specify what happens when you turn on parental controls—and you haven't done that yet. Choosing Features→Enable Parental Control does the trick.

When parental control is turned on, nobody's allowed to watch the "Always ask for authorization" DVDs *unless* they correctly input your administrator's password.

Which nobody knows except you. (Right?)

The Big Picture

Now, watching a movie while sitting in front of your Mac is not exactly the great American movie-watching dream. Fortunately, every recent Mac model has a video-output jack; with the proper cables, you can connect the Mac to your TV for a much more comfortable movie-watching experience.

Just be sure to connect the cable *directly* to the TV. If you connect it to your VCR instead, you'll probably get a horrible, murky, color-shifting picture—the result of the built-in copy-protection circuitry of every VCR.

Or what the heck—just ask for an Apple TV for your birthday.

Part Four:
The Technologies of
Mac OS X

4

Accounts, Parental Controls, & Security

I n an era when *security* is the hottest high-tech buzzword, Apple was smart to make it a focal point for Mac OS X. It was already virus-free and better protected from Internet attacks than Windows. But Mac OS X 10.6 is the most impenetrable Mac system yet, filled with new defenses against the dark arts. This chapter covers the whole range of them.

On the premise that the biggest security threat of all comes from other people in your home or office, though, the most important security feature in Mac OS X is the *accounts* system.

Introducing Accounts

The concept of *user accounts* is central to Mac OS X's security approach. Like the Unix under its skin (and also like Windows), Mac OS X is designed from the ground up to be a *multiple-user* operating system. That is, you can set up your Mac OS X so that everyone must log in—click her name and type her password—when the computer turns on (Figure 12-1).

Upon doing so, you discover the Macintosh universe just as you left it, including these elements:

- Your documents, files, and folders.

- Your preference settings in every program you use: Web browser bookmarks and preferred home page; desktop picture, screen saver, and language; icons on the desktop and in the Dock—and the size and position of the Dock itself; and so on.

- Email account(s), including personal information and mailboxes.

- Your personally installed programs and fonts.

- Your choice of programs that launch automatically at startup.

This system lets different people use it throughout the day without disrupting one another's files and settings. It also protects the Mac from getting fouled up by mischievous (or bumbling) students, employees, and hackers.

If you're the only person who uses your Mac, you can safely skip most of this chapter. The Mac never pauses at startup time to demand the name and password you made up when you installed Mac OS X, because Apple's installer automatically turns on something called *automatic login* (page 483). You *will* be using one of these accounts, though, whether you realize it or not.

Furthermore, when you're stuck in line at the Department of Motor Vehicles, you may find the concepts presented here worth skimming, as certain elements of this multiple-user system may intrude upon your solo activities—and figure in the discussions in this book—from time to time.

Tip: Even if you don't share your Mac with anyone and don't create any other accounts, you might still be tempted to learn about the accounts feature because of its ability to password-protect the entire computer. All you have to do is to turn off the automatic login feature described on page 483. Thereafter, your Mac is protected from unauthorized fiddling when you're away from your desk or if your laptop is stolen.

Figure 12-1:
When you set up several accounts, you don't turn on the Mac so much as sign into it. A command in the menu called Log Out summons this sign-in screen, as does the Accounts menu described later in this chapter. Click your own name, and type your password (if any), to get past this box and into your own stuff.

The First Account

When you first installed Mac OS X, whether it was 10.6 or an earlier version, you were asked for a name and password. You were creating the first *user account* on your Macintosh. Since that fateful day, you may have made a number of changes to your desktop—adjusted the Dock settings, set up your folders and desktop the way you like them, added some bookmarks to your Web browser, and so on—without realizing that you were actually making these changes to only *your account.*

You've probably been saving your documents into your own Home folder, which is the cornerstone of your account. This folder, generally named after you and stashed in the Users folder on your hard drive, stores not only your own work, but also your preference settings for all the programs you use, special fonts you've installed, your own email collection, and so on.

Now then: Suppose you create an account for a second person. When she turns on the computer and signs in, she finds the desktop exactly the way it was factory-installed by Apple—stunning outer-space desktop picture, Dock along the bottom, and so on. She can make the same kinds of changes to the Mac that you've made, but nothing she does affects *your* environment the next time you log in.

In other words, the multiple-accounts feature has two components: first, a convenience element that hides everyone else's junk; and second, a security element that protects both the Mac's system software and everybody's work.

Creating an Account

Suppose somebody new joins your little Mac family—a new worker, student, or love interest, for example. And you want to make that person feel at home on your Mac.

Begin by opening System Preferences (Chapter 9). In the System Preferences window, click Accounts. You have just arrived at the master control center for account creation and management (Figure 12-2).

To create a new account, start by unlocking the Accounts panel. That is, click the 🔒 at lower left, and fill in your own account name and password.

Now you can click the **+** button beneath the list of accounts. The little panel shown at bottom in Figure 12-2 appears.

Phase 1: Choose an Account Type

As though this business of accounts and passwords weren't complicated enough already, Mac OS X offers more *types* of accounts than ever. And you're expected to specify *which* type each person gets at the moment you create an account.

To do that, open the New Account pop-up menu (Figure 12-2, bottom). Its five account types are described on the following pages.

Administrator accounts

If this is your own personal Mac, then just beneath your name on the Accounts pane of System Preferences, it probably says *Admin*. This, as you could probably guess, stands for Administrator.

Figure 12-2:
Top: The screen lists everyone who has an account. From here, you can create new accounts or change passwords. If you're new at this, there's probably just one account listed here: yours. This is the account Mac OS X created when you first installed it. You, the all-wise administrator, have to click the ⏷ to authenticate yourself before you can start making changes.

Bottom: In the account-creation process, the first step is choosing which type of account you want to create.

Because you're the person who originally installed Mac OS X, the Mac assumes you are its *administrator*—the technical wizard in charge of it. You're the teacher, the parent, the resident guru. You're the one who will maintain this Mac. Only an administrator is allowed to:

- Install new programs into the Applications folder.

- Add fonts that everybody can use.

- Make changes to certain System Preferences panes (including Network, Date & Time, Energy Saver, and Startup Disk).

- Use some features of the Disk Utility program.

- Create, move, or delete folders outside of your Home or Shared folder.

- Decide who gets to have accounts on the Mac.

- Open, change, or delete anyone else's files.

- Bypass FileVault using a master password (page 498).

The administrator concept may be new to you, but it's an important pill to swallow. For one thing, you'll find certain settings all over Mac OS X that you can change *only* if you're an administrator—including many in the Accounts pane itself. For another thing, administrator status plays an enormous role when you want to network your Mac to other kinds of computers, as described in the next chapter. And finally, in the bigger picture, the fact that the Mac has an industrial-strength accounts system, just like traditional Unix and recent Windows operating systems, gives it a fighting chance in the corporations of America.

As you create accounts for other people who'll use this Mac, you're offered the opportunity to make each one an administrator just like you. Needless to say, use discretion. Bestow these powers only upon people as responsible and technically masterful as yourself.

Standard accounts

Most people, on most Macs, are ordinary *Standard* account holders (Figure 12-2). These people have everyday access to their own Home folders and to the harmless panes of System Preferences, but most other areas of the Mac are off limits. Mac OS X won't even let them create new folders on the main hard drive, except inside their own Home folders (or in the Shared folder described starting on page 488).

A few of the System Preferences panels display a padlock icon (🔒). If you're a Standard account holder, you can't make changes to these settings without the assistance of an administrator. Fortunately, you aren't required to log out so an administrator can log in and make changes. You can just call the administrator over, click the padlock icon, and let him type in his name and password (if, indeed, he feels comfortable with you making the changes you're about to make).

Managed accounts with Parental Controls

A Managed account is the same thing as a Standard account—except that you've turned on Parental Controls. (These controls are described later in this chapter.) You can turn a Managed account into a Standard account just by turning off Parental Controls, and vice versa.

That is, this account usually has even fewer freedoms—because you've limited the programs this person is allowed to use, for example. Use a Managed account for children or anyone else who needs a Mac with rubber walls.

Sharing Only

This kind of account is extremely useful—*if* your Mac is on a network (Chapter 13). See, ordinarily, you can log in and access the files on your Mac in either of two ways:

- In person, seated in front of it.

- From across the network.

This arrangement was designed with families and schools in mind: lots of people sharing a *single* Mac.

POWER USERS' CLINIC

Creating Groups

Changing permissions settings on a networked Mac, or one with a lot of account holders, is a lot easier if you sweep all your minions into subsets called *groups*.

This process used to require a complicated series of Unixy steps that, if not performed carefully, could seriously foul up your Mac. But in Mac OS X, you can create a group as easily as you'd create an account. And in the same place: the Accounts pane of System Preferences.

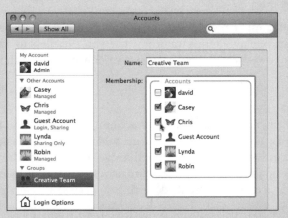

Now click the **+** button as though you're about to create a new account. But from the New Account pop-up menu (shown at bottom in Figure 12-2), choose Group. Type a name for the new group (Accounting, Kids, or whatever), and then click Create Group.

Now you see something like the list shown here: checkboxes for all this Mac's account holders. Turn on the checkboxes for the ones you consider worthy of being part of this group.

Click the tiny 🔒 in the lower-left corner. When prompted, type in your administrator's name and password, and then click OK. The Mac is just making sure that somebody with a clue is at the helm.

You can create as many groups as you like. Later, when it comes time to share a folder or file, you'll save time by choosing a group name instead of setting these permissions one person at a time.

The setup gets a little silly, though, when the people on a home or office network each have their *own* computers. If you wanted your spouse or your sales director to be able to grab some files off of your Mac, you'd have to create full-blown accounts for them on *your* Mac, complete with utterly unnecessary Home folders they'd never use.

That's why the *Sharing Only* account is such a great idea. It's available *only* from across the network. You can't get into it by sitting down at the Mac itself—it has no Home folder!

Finally, of course, Sharing Only account holders can't make any changes to the Mac's settings or programs. (And since these accounts don't have Home folders, you also can't turn on FileVault for them, as described on page 497.)

In other words, a Sharing Only account exists *solely* for the purpose of file sharing on the network, and people can enter their names and passwords *only* from other Macs.

Once you've set up this kind of account, all the file-sharing and screen-sharing goodies described in Chapter 13 become available.

Group

A *group* is just a virtual container that holds the names of other account holders. You might create one for your most trusted colleagues, another for those rambunctious kids, and so on—all in the name of streamlining the *file-sharing privileges* feature described on page 514. The box on the facing page covers groups in more detail.

The Guest account

Mac OS X has always offered a special account called the Guest account. It was great for accommodating visitors, buddies, or anyone else who was just passing through and wanted to use your Mac for a while. If you let such people use the Guest account, your own account remains private and un-messed-with.

Note: The Guest account isn't listed among the account types in the New Account pop-up menu (Figure 12-2). That's because there's only one Guest account; you can't actually create additional ones.

But it's still an account type with specific characteristics. It's sitting right there in the list of accounts, from Day One.

But until Mac OS X 10.5 and 10.6 came along, there was a problem: Any changes your friend made—downloading mail, making Web bookmarks, putting up a raunchy desktop picture—would still be there for the *next* guest to enjoy, unless you painstakingly restored everything back to neutral. The Guest account was like a hotel room shared by successive guests. And *you* were the maid.

Today, any changes your guest makes while using your Mac are automatically erased when he logs out. Files are deleted, email is nuked, setting changes are forgotten. It's like a hotel that gets demolished and rebuilt after each guest departs.

As noted above, the Guest account is permanently listed in the Accounts panel of System Preferences. Ordinarily, though, you don't see it in the Login screen list; if you're ordinarily the only person who uses this Mac, you don't need to have it staring you in the face every day.

So to use the Guest account, bring it to life by turning on "Allow guests to log into this computer." You can even turn on the parental controls described earlier in this chapter by clicking Open Parental Controls, or permit the guest to exchange files with your Mac from across the network (Chapter 13) by turning on "Allow guests to connect to shared folders."

Just remember to warn your vagabond friend that once he logs out, all traces of his visit are wiped out forever. (At least from your *Mac.*)

Phase 2: Name, Password, and Status

All right. So you clicked the **+** button. And from the New Account pop-up menu, you chose the type of account you wanted to create.

Now, on the same starter sheet, it's time to fill in the most critical information about the new account holder:

- **Name.** If it's just the family, this could be "Chris" or "Robin." If it's a corporation or school, you probably want to use both first and last names.

- **Short Name.** You'll quickly discover the value of having a short name—an abbreviation of your actual name—particularly if your name is, say, Alexandra Stephanopoulos.

  When you sign into your Mac in person, you can use either your long or short name. But when you access this Mac by dialing into it or connecting from across the network (as described in the next chapter), use the short version.

  As soon as you tab into this field, the Mac proposes a short name for you. You can replace the suggestion with whatever you like. Technically, it doesn't even have to be shorter than the "long" name, but spaces and most punctuation marks are forbidden.

- **Password, Verify.** Here's where you type this new account holder's password (Figure 12-2). In fact, you're supposed to type it twice, to make sure you didn't introduce a typo the first time. (The Mac displays only dots as you type, to guard against the possibility that somebody is watching over your shoulder.)

  The usual computer book takes this opportunity to stress the importance of a long, complex password—a phrase that isn't in the dictionary, something made up of mixed letters and numbers. This is excellent advice if you create sensitive documents and work in a big corporation.

  But if you share the Mac only with a spouse or a few trusted colleagues in a small office, you may have nothing to hide. You may see the multiple-users feature more as a convenience (keeping your settings and files separate) than as a protector of secrecy and security. In these situations, there's no particular urgency to the mission of thwarting the world's hackers with a convoluted password.

In that case, you may want to consider setting up *no* password—leaving both password blanks empty. Later, whenever you're asked for your password, just leave the Password box blank. You'll be able to log in that much faster each day.

Tip: *Actually, having some password comes in handy if you share files on the network, because Mac A can store your name and password from Mac B—and therefore you can access Mac B without entering your name and password at all. So consider making your password the apostrophe/quote mark—the ' key. It's a real password, so it's enough for Mac A to memorize. Yet when you are asked to enter your password—for example, when you're installing a new program—it's incredibly fast and easy to enter, because it's right next to the Return key.*

- **Password Hint.** If you gave yourself a password, you can leave yourself a hint in this box. If your password is the middle name of the first person who ever kissed you, for example, your hint might be "middle name of the first person who ever kissed me."

  Later, if you forget your password, the Mac will show you this cue to jog your memory.

- **Turn on FileVault protection.** Page 497 has more on this advanced corporate-security feature. (This option isn't available for Sharing Only accounts.)

Snow Leopard Spots: *Two new buttons make their debut on the Account screen: a place to specify your MobileMe account name (just in case you hadn't stumbled onto the MobileMe pane of System Preferences) and a place to create a card for yourself in the Address Book program. This information—who you are—crops up from time to time in Mac OS X. It's what Mail uses as your identity, for example.*

When you finish setting up these essential items, click Create Account. If you left the password boxes empty, the Mac asks for reassurance that you know what you're doing; click OK.

You then return to the Accounts pane, where you see the new account name in the list at the left side.

Here, three final decisions await your wisdom:

- **MobileMe User Name.** Each account holder might well have his own MobileMe account (especially because Apple offers a family-pack deal on these accounts). Since the MobileMe service is growing in importance and features—email address, Web site, iDisk, syncing, Back to My Mac, and so on—it's convenient to associate each account with its own MobileMe name.

- **Enable Parental Controls.** "Parental Controls" refers to the Mac OS X feature that limits what your offspring are allowed to do on this computer—and how much time a day they're allowed to spend glued to the mouse. (You can turn on Parental

---

Controls *only* for Standard/Managed and Guest accounts, even though the checkbox appears for Admin accounts, too.) Details are on page 472.

- **Allow user to administer this computer.** This checkbox lets you turn ordinary, unsuspecting Standard or Managed accounts into Administrator accounts, as described above. You know—when your kid turns 18.

Phase 3: Choose a Picture

The usual Mac OS X sign-in screen (Figure 12-1) displays each account holder's name, accompanied by a little picture.

When you click the sample photo, you get a pop-up menu of Apple-supplied graphics; you can choose one to represent you. It becomes not only your icon on the sign-in screen but also your "card" photo in Mac OS X's Address Book program and your icon in iChat.

If you'd rather supply your *own* graphics file—a digital photo of your own head, for example—then choose Edit Picture from the pop-up menu. As shown in Figure 12-3, you have several options:

- Drag a graphics file directly into the "picture well" (Figure 12-3). Use the cropping slider below the picture to frame it properly.

- Click Choose. You're shown a list of what's on your hard drive. Find and double-click the image you want.

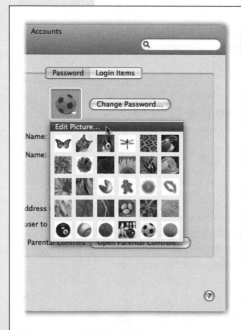

Figure 12-3:
Once you've selected a photo to represent yourself (left), you can adjust its position relative to the square "frame" (right), or adjust its size by dragging the slider. Finally, when the picture looks correctly framed, click Set. (The next time you return to the Images dialog box, you can recall the new image using the Recent Pictures pop-up menu.)

- Take a new picture. If your Mac has a built-in camera above the screen, or if you have an external Webcam or a camcorder hooked up, click the little camera button. The Mac counts down from three with loud beeps to help you get ready and then takes the picture.

In each case, click Set to enshrine your icon forever (or until you feel like picking a different one).

Phase 4: Startup Items

There's one additional setting that your account holders can set up for themselves: which programs or documents open automatically upon login. (This is one decision an administrator *can't* make for other people. It's available only to whoever is logged in at the moment.)

To choose your own crew of self-starters, open System Preferences and click Accounts. Click the Login Items tab. As shown in Figure 12-4, you can now build a list of programs, documents, disks, and other goodies that automatically launch each time you log in. You can even turn on the Hide checkbox for each one so that the program is running in the background at login time, waiting to be called into service with a quick click.

Figure 12-4:
You can add any icon to the list of things you want to start up automatically. Click the + button to summon the Open dialog box where you can find the icon, select it, and then click Choose. Better yet, if you can see the icon in a folder or disk window (or on the desktop), just drag it into this list. To remove an item, click it in the list and then click the – button.

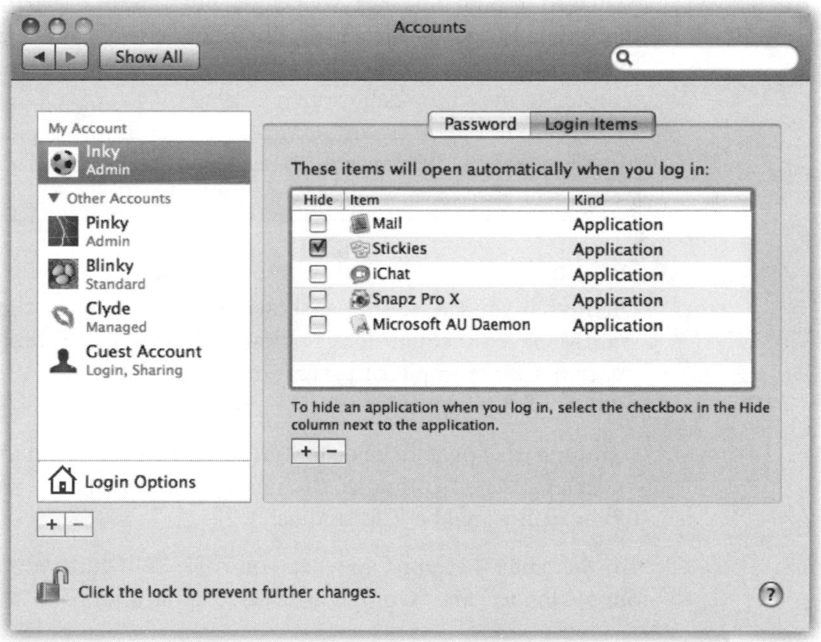

Don't feel obligated to limit this list to programs and documents, by the way. Disks, folders, servers on the network, and other fun icons can also be startup items, so that their windows are open and waiting when you arrive at the Mac each morning.

Tip: Here's a much quicker way to add something to the Login Items list: Control-click (or right-click) its Dock icon and choose "Open at Login" from the shortcut menu.

Parental Controls

If you're setting up a Standard/Managed account, the Parental Controls checkbox affords you the opportunity to shield your Mac—or its very young, very fearful, or very mischievous operator—from confusion and harm. This is a helpful feature to remember when you're setting up accounts for students, young children, or easily intimidated adults. (This checkbox is available for Admin accounts, too, but trying to turn it on produces only a "Silly rabbit—this is for kids!" sort of message.)

You can specify how many hours a day each person is allowed to use the Mac, and declare certain hours (like sleeping hours) off-limits. You can specify exactly who your kids are allowed to communicate with via email (if they use Mail) and instant messaging (if they use iChat), what Web sites they can visit (if they use Safari), what programs they're allowed to use, and even what words they can look up in the Mac OS X Dictionary.

Here are all the ways you can keep your little Managed account holders shielded from the Internet—and themselves. For sanity's sake, the following discussion refers to the Managed account holder as "your child." But some of these controls—notably those in the System category—are equally useful for people of *any* age who feel overwhelmed by the Mac, are inclined to mess it up by not knowing what they're doing, or are tempted to mess it up deliberately.

Note: If you apply any of these options to a Standard account, the account type listed on the Accounts panel changes from "Standard" to "Managed."

System

On this tab, you see the options shown in Figure 12-5. Use these options to limit what your Managed-account flock is allowed to do. You can limit them to using certain programs, for example, or prevent them from burning DVDs, changing settings, or fiddling with your printer setups.

(Limiting what people can do to your Mac when you're not looking is a handy feature under any shared-computer circumstance. But if there's one word tattooed on its forehead, it would be "Classrooms!")

On the panel that pops up when you click Configure, you have two options: "Use Simple Finder" and "Only allow selected applications."

Use Simple Finder

If you're *really* concerned about somebody's ability to survive the Mac—or the Mac's ability to survive them—turn on Use Simple Finder. Then turn on the checkboxes of the programs that person is allowed to use.

Suppose you've been given a Simple Finder account. When you log in, you discover the barren world shown in Figure 12-6. There are only three menus (, Finder, and File), a single onscreen window, no hard drive icon, and a bare-bones Dock. The only folders you can see are in the Dock. They include:

Figure 12-5:
In the Parental Controls window, you can control the capabilities of any account holder on your Mac. In the lower half of the System tab window, you can choose applications and even Dashboard widgets by turning on the boxes next to their names. (Expand the flippy triangles if necessary.) Those are the only programs these account holders will be allowed to use. (The new Search box helps you find certain programs without knowing their categories.)

- **My Applications.** These are aliases of the applications that the administrator approved. They appear on a strange, fixed, icon view, called "pages." List and column views don't exist. As a Simple person, you can't move, rename, delete, sort, or change the display of these icons—you can merely click them. If you have too many to fit on one screen, you get numbered page buttons beneath them, which you can click to move from one set to another.

- **Documents.** Behind the scenes, this is your Home→Documents folder. Of course, as a Simple Finder kind of soul, you don't *have* a visible Home folder. All your stuff goes in here.

• **Shared.** This is the same Shared folder described on page 488. It's provided so that you and other account holders can exchange documents. However, you can't open any of the folders here, only the documents.

Figure 12-6:
The Simple Finder doesn't feel like home—unless you've got one of those spartan, space-age, Dr. Evil–style pads. But it can be just the ticket for less-skilled Mac users, with few options and a basic one-click interface. Every program in the My Applications folder is actually an alias to the real program, which is safely ensconced in the off-limits Applications folder.

• **Trash.** The Trash is here, but you won't use it much. Selecting or dragging any icon is against the rules, so you're left with no obvious means of putting anything into your Trash.

The only programs with their own icons in the Dock are Finder and Dashboard.

Otherwise, you can essentially forget everything else you've read in this book. You can't create folders, move icons, or do much of anything beyond clicking the icons that your benevolent administrator has provided. It's as though Mac OS X moved away and left you the empty house.

• To keep things extra-simple, Mac OS X permits only one window at a time to be open. It's easy to open icons, too, because *one* click opens them, not two.

• The File menu is stunted, offering only a Close Window command. The Finder menu gives you only two options: About Finder and Run Full Finder. (The latter command prompts you for an administrator's user name and password and then turns back into the regular Finder—a handy escape hatch. To return to Simple Finder, just choose Finder→Return to Simple Finder.)

• The menu is *really* bare-bones: You can Log Out, Force Quit, or go to Sleep. That's it.

• There's no trace of Spotlight.

Although the Simple Finder is simple, any program (at least, any that the administrator has permitted) can run from Simple Finder. A program running inside the Simple Finder still has all of its features and complexities—only the Finder has been whittled down to its essence.

In other words, Simple Finder is great for streamlining the Finder, but novices won't get far combating their techno-fear until the world presents us with Simple iMovie, Simple Mail, and Simple Microsoft Word. Still, it's better than nothing.

When Simple people try to save documents, they'll find that although the Save box lists the usual locations (Desktop, Applications, and so on), they can in fact save files only into their own Home folders or subfolders inside them.

Only allow selected applications

By tinkering with the checkboxes here, you can declare certain programs off-limits to this account holder, or turn off his ability to remove Dock icons, burn CDs, and so on.

You can restrict this person's access to the Mac in several different ways:

- **Limit the programs.** At the bottom of the dialog box shown in Figure 12-5, you see a list of all the programs in your Applications folder (an interesting read in its own right). Only checked items show up in the account holder's Applications folder.

Tip: If you don't see a program listed, use the Search box, or drag its icon from the Finder into the window.

If, for instance, you're setting up an account for use in the classroom, you may want to turn off access to programs like Disk Utility, iChat, and Tomb Raider.

- **Limit the features.** When you first create Standard accounts, their holders are free to burn CDs or DVDs, modify what's on the Dock, change their passwords, and view the settings of all System Preferences panels (although they can't *change* all of these settings).

Depending on your situation, you may find it useful to turn off some of these options. In a school lab, for example, you might want to turn off the ability to burn discs (to block software piracy). If you're setting up a Mac for a technophobe, you might want to turn off the ability to change the Dock (so your colleague won't accidentally lose access to his own programs and work).

Content (Dictionary and Web)

"Content," in this case, means "two options we really didn't have any other place to put." Actually, what it *really* means is Dictionary and Safari.

Hide profanity in Dictionary

As you know from Chapter 10, Mac OS X comes with a complete electronic copy of the *New Oxford American Dictionary*. And "complete," in this case, means "it even has swear words."

Turning on "Hide profanity in Dictionary" is like having an Insta-Censor™. It hides most of the naughty words from the dictionary whenever your young account holder is logged in (Figure 12-7).

Figure 12-7:
Something's oddly missing from the Dictionary when Parental Controls are turned on: dirty words.

Web Site Restrictions

This feature is designed to limit which Web sites your kid is allowed to visit.

Frankly, trying to block the racy stuff from the Web is something of a hopeless task; if your kid doesn't manage to get around this blockade by simply using a different browser, then he'll just see the dirty pictures at another kid's house. But at least you can enjoy the illusion of taking a stand, using approaches of three degrees of severity:

- **Allow unrestricted access to Web sites.** In other words, no filtering. Anything goes.

- **Try to limit access to adult Web sites automatically.** Those words—"try to"—are Apple's way of admitting that no filter is foolproof.

  In any case, Mac OS X comes with a built-in database of Web sites that it already knows may be inappropriate for children—and these sites won't appear in Safari while this account holder is logged in. By clicking Customize and then editing the "Always allow" and "Never allow" lists, you can override its decisions on a site-at-a-time basis.

- **Allow access to only these Web sites.** This is the most restrictive approach of all: It's a *whitelist,* a list of the *only* Web sites your youngster is allowed to visit. It's filled with kid-friendly sites like Disney and Discovery Kids, but of course you can edit the list by clicking the **+** and **−** buttons below the list.

Snow Leopard Spots: The Web filter is supposed to be a lot more effective in Snow Leopard. That's because it "now supports auto proxy (PAC) files," whatever they may be.

Mail & iChat

Here, you can build a list of email and chat addresses, corresponding to the people you feel comfortable letting your kid exchange emails and chat with. Click the **+** button below the list, type the address, press Return, lather, rinse, and repeat.

Tip: No, you can't drag cards in from your Address Book; that would be much too simple. But after clicking the **+** button to create a new row in the list (in Edit mode), you can drag just the email address out of an Address Book card you've opened up.

For reasons explained in a moment, turn on "Send permission emails to" and plug in your own email address.

Now then: When your youngster uses Apple's Mail program to send a message to someone who's *not* on the approved list, or tries to iChat with someone not on the list, she gets the message shown at top in Figure 12-8. If she clicks Ask Permission, then *your* copy of Mail shortly receives a permission-request message (Figure 12-8, middle); meanwhile, the outgoing message gets placed in limbo in her Drafts folder.

If you add that person's address to the list of approved correspondents, then the next time your young apprentice clicks the quarantined outgoing message in her Drafts folder, the banner across the top lets her know that all is well—and the message is OK to go out.

Figure 12-8:
Top: If your kid tries to contact someone who's not on the Approved list, she can either give up or click Ask Permission.

Bottom: In the latter case, you'll know about it. If you're convinced that the would-be correspondent is not, in fact, a stalker, you can grant permission by clicking Always Allow. Your young ward gets the good news the next time she visits her Drafts folder, where the message has been awaiting word from you, the Good Parent.

Note: This feature doesn't attempt to stop email or chat using other programs, like Microsoft Entourage or Skype. If you're worried about your efforts being bypassed, block access to those programs using the Forbidden Applications list described above.

When your underling fires up iChat or Mail, she'll discover that her Buddy List is empty except for the people you've identified.

Handling the teenage hissy fit is your problem.

Time Limits

Clever folks, those Apple programmers. They must have kids of their own.

They realize that some parents care about *how much* time their kids spend in front of the Mac, and that some also care about *which* hours (Figure 12-9):

- **How much time.** In the "Weekday time limits" section, turn on "Limit computer use to," and then adjust the slider. A similar slider appears for weekend time limits.

- **Which hours.** In the "Bedtime" section, turn on the checkbox for either "School nights" or "Weekend," and then set the hours of the day (or, rather, night) when the Mac is unavailable to your young account holders.

POWER USERS' CLINIC

Parental Remote Controls

It occurred to somebody at Apple that the new Parental Controls feature might be especially useful in a classroom. That person further realized that it'd be very cool if you could adjust the settings for Macs A, B, C, and D while *seated* at Mac E. That is, the teacher might prefer not to have to scurry from kid's desk to kid's desk to make changes.

And that's why you can operate Parental Controls from another Mac on the same network.

Phase 1: While seated at the first kid's Mac, open System Preferences; open Parental Controls; click the 🔒; enter your password.

Now click the name of the account you want to manage remotely. Then, from the ⚙ menu below the list of accounts, choose Allow Remote Setup. Close System Preferences.

Repeat for each account on each Mac that you'll want to manage from afar.

Phase 2: Go back to your teacher's desk. On your own Mac, choose Go→Connect to Server. In the resulting dialog box, click Browse.

☑ Manage parental controls from another computer
To access this computer to change parental control settings, you need the name and password of an administrator of this computer.

Now you get a list of the other Macs on the network. Click one and enter an administrator's name and password for that Mac.

Now open System Preferences, click Parental Controls, click the 🔒, and then enter your password again. This time, you'll see a section in the Accounts list called Other Computers. Click the account name (on the kid's Mac) whose settings you want to change. Enter the administrator name and password of the remote computer one more time, and off you go!

In other words, this feature may have the smallest pages-to-significance ratio in this entire book. Doesn't take long to explain it, but it could bring the parents of Mac addicts a lot of peace.

Snow Leopard Spots: When Time Limits have been applied, your little rug rats can now check to see how much time they have left to goof off on the Mac before your digital iron fist slams down. When they click the menu-bar clock (where it now says the current time), a menu appears, complete with a readout that says, for example, "Parental Controls: Time Remaining 1:29." Good parenting comes in all forms.

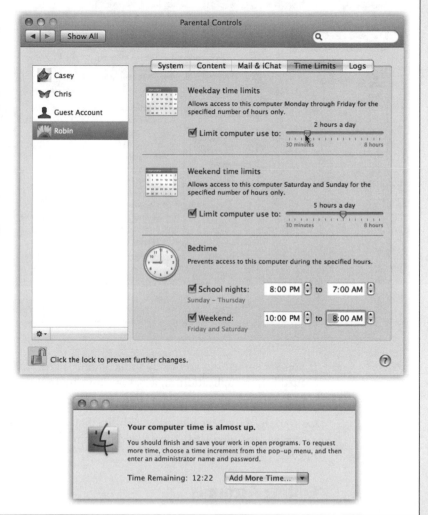

Figure 12-9:
Top: If this account holder tries to log in outside the time limits you specify here, she'll encounter only a box that says, "Computer time limits expired." She'll be offered a pop-up menu that grants her additional time, from 15 minutes to "Rest of the day"—but it requires your parental consent (actually, your parental password) to activate.

Bottom: Similarly, if she's using the Mac as her time winds down, she gets this message. Once again, you, the all-knowing administrator, can grant her more time using this dialog box.

Logs

The final tab of the Parental Controls panel is Big Brother Central. Here's a complete rundown of what your kids have been up to. Its four categories—Websites visited, Websites blocked, Applications, and iChat—are extremely detailed. For example, in Applications, you can see exactly which programs your kids tried to use when, and how much time they spent in each one. Figure 12-10 shows the idea.

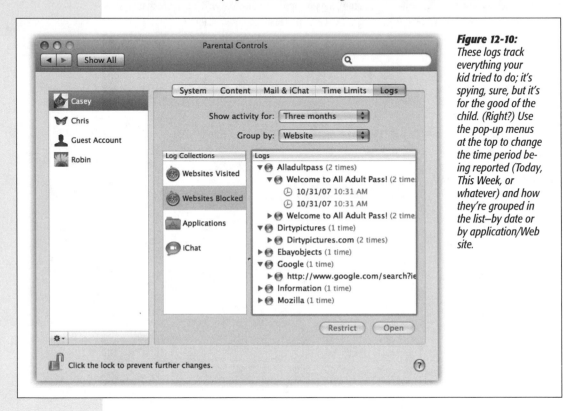

Figure 12-10:
These logs track everything your kid tried to do; it's spying, sure, but it's for the good of the child. (Right?) Use the pop-up menus at the top to change the time period being reported (Today, This Week, or whatever) and how they're grouped in the list—by date or by application/Web site.

If you see something you really think should be off limits—a site in the Websites Visited list, an application, an iChat session with someone—click its name and then click Restrict. You've just nipped *that* one in the bud.

Conversely, if the Mac blocked a Web site that you think is really OK, click its name in the list, and then click Allow. (And if you're wondering what a certain Web page *is,* click it and then click Open.)

Editing Accounts

If you're an administrator, you can change your own account in any way you like.

If you have any other kind of account, though, you can't change anything but your picture and password. If you want to make any other changes, you have to ask an admin to log in, make the changes you want made to your account, and then turn the computer back over to you.

Deleting Accounts

Hey, it happens: Somebody graduates, somebody gets fired, somebody dumps you. Sooner or later, you may need to delete an account from your Mac.

When that time comes, click the account name in the Accounts list and then click the minus-sign button beneath the list. Mac OS X asks what to do with all the dearly departed's files and settings (Figure 12-11):

- **Save the home folder in a disk image.** This option represents the "I'll be back" approach. Mac OS X preserves the deleted account holder's folders on the Mac, in a tidy digital envelope that won't clutter your hard drive and can be reopened in case of emergency.

  In the Users→Deleted Users folder, you find a disk image file (.dmg). If you double-click it, a new, virtual disk icon named for the deleted account appears on your

---

POWER USERS' CLINIC

The Secret Account Options

Anyone who knows Mac OS X very well might object to one sentence in this section: "If you're an administrator, you can change your own account in any way you like."

Because everybody knows that there's one aspect of an account that even an admin can't change: the account's *short name.* Once that's created, it's yours forever, or at least until you delete the account.

Or at least that's what Apple *wants* you to think. There is, however, a secret way to pick a different short name. You can't easily *change* the one you created originally, but you can create *another* one—shorter, more memorable—that *also* works when you're logging in or authenticating yourself.

To find it, Control-click (or right-click) the account's name in the list at the left side of the Accounts panel in System

Preferences. From the shortcut menu, choose Advanced Options.

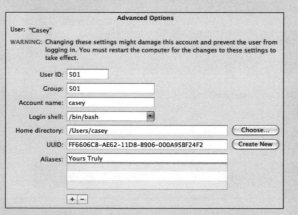

The strange and wonderful Advanced Options panel appears. Right there in the middle is a "Account name" box, but don't edit that; it won't work.

Instead, click the **+** button below the Aliases list. You're offered the chance to type in an *alternative* short name. Do it and then click OK. You can create as many of these aliases as you like.

When it's all over, click OK. The next time you log into your Mac, you can use your new, improved short name instead of the old one.

Rejoice that you lived to see the day.

---

desktop. You can open folders and root through the stuff in this "disk," just as if it were a living, working Home folder.

If fate ever brings that person back into your life, you can use this disk image to reinstate the deleted person's account. Start by creating a brand-new account. Then copy the contents of the folders in the mounted disk image (Documents, Pictures, Desktop, and so on) into the corresponding folders of the new Home folder.

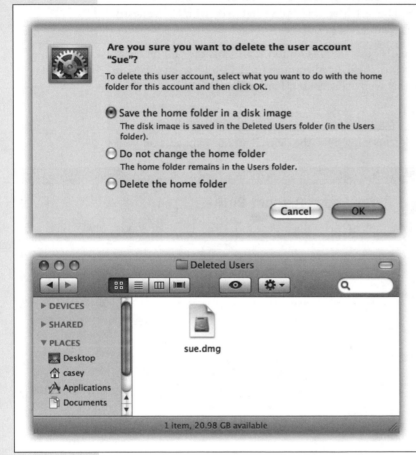

Figure 12-11:
Top: This dialog box lets you know where to find the deleted account's material, should the need arise. Bottom: The files and settings of accounts you deleted live on, in the Users→Deleted Users folder.

- **Do not change the home folder.** This time, Mac OS X removes the *account*, in that it no longer appears in the Login list or in the Accounts panel of System Preferences— but it leaves the *Home folder* right where it is. Use this option if you don't intend to dispose of the dearly departed's belongings right here and now.

- **Delete the home folder.** This button offers the "Hasta la vista, baby" approach. The account and all its files and settings are vaporized forever, on the spot.

Note: If you delete a Shared Only account, you're not offered the chance to preserve the Home folder contents—because a Shared Only account doesn't have a Home folder.

Setting Up the Login Process

Once you've set up more than one account, the dialog box shown in Figure 12-1 appears whenever you turn on the Mac, whenever you choose →Log Out, or whenever the Mac logs you out automatically. But a few extra controls let you, an administrator, set up either more or less security at the login screen—or, put another way, build in less or more convenience.

Open System Preferences, click Accounts, and then click the Login Options button (Figure 12-12). Here are some of the ways you can shape the login experience for greater security (or greater convenience):

- **Automatic login.** This option eliminates the need to sign in at all. It's a timesaving, hassle-free arrangement if only one person uses the Mac, or uses it most of the time.

POWER USERS' CLINIC

Moving Your Home Folder Between Computers

Mac OS X proposes putting all the account holders' Home folders in one special folder (Users) on the main hard drive. But being able to put your Home folder on a different disk can have its advantages, too. If you bring your files back and forth between home and work, for example, you might find it convenient to keep your entire life on an iPod or some other portable disk. In corporate environments, a network administrator may want you to keep your Home folder elsewhere on the Windows network. (Yes, Mac OS X is that compatible.)

You can do it, but it takes a few steps.

Begin by copying your Home folder to the iPod (or wherever). To make absolutely sure you're getting everything in it, use Terminal—described in Chapter 16. Open up a Terminal window and type this command:

```
sudo ditto -rsrc "/Users/casey"
    "/Volumes/path-to-new-folder"
```

Of course, type your own account name instead of "casey," and the actual folder path instead of "path-to-new-folder."

Use the folder-path notation described on page 23.

Now open the Accounts pane of System Preferences. Control-click (or right-click) your account's name; from the shortcut menu, choose Advanced Options.

In the new Advanced Options dialog box, in the Home Directory box, type the folder path to your new home folder—or just click Choose and show Mac OS X where it is.

Now restart the Mac. Log back in, and test the new Home-folder arrangement. If everything is working perfectly, you can delete the original from the internal hard drive.

If your intention is to take the external hard drive back and forth to work, then repeat the procedure on the Mac at work.

Just make sure the external drive is plugged in, powered up, and running before you try to log in; otherwise, the Mac won't be able to find the Home folder at all and will give you an error message.

When you choose an account holder's name from this pop-up menu, you're prompted for his name and password. Type it and click OK.

From now on, the dialog box shown in Figure 12-1 won't appear *at all* at startup time. After turning on the machine, you, the specified account holder, zoom straight to your desktop.

Of course, everybody else must still enter their names and passwords. (And how can they, since the Mac rushes right into the Automatic person's account at startup time? Answer: The Automatic thing happens only at startup time. The usual login screen appears whenever the current account holder logs out—by choosing ➝Log Out, for example.)

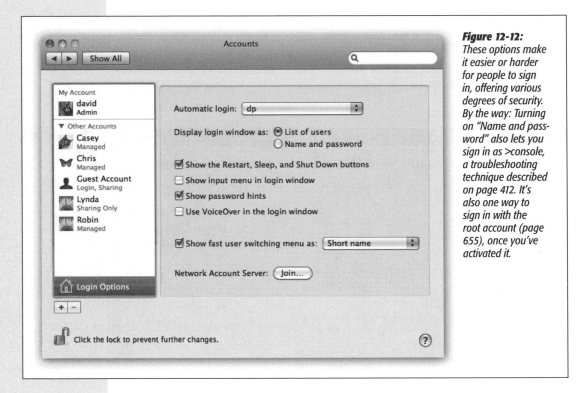

Figure 12-12:
These options make it easier or harder for people to sign in, offering various degrees of security. By the way: Turning on "Name and password" also lets you sign in as >console, a troubleshooting technique described on page 412. It's also one way to sign in with the root account (page 655), once you've activated it.

- **Display login window as.** Under normal circumstances, the login screen presents a list of account holders when you power up the Mac, as shown in Figure 12-1. That's the "List of users" option in action.

If you're especially worried about security, however, you might not even want that list to appear. If you turn on "Name and password," each person who signs in must type both his name (into a blank that appears) *and* his password—a very inconvenient, but more secure, arrangement.

- **Show the Restart, Sleep, and Shut Down buttons.** Truth is, the Mac OS X security system is easy to circumvent. Truly devoted evildoers can bypass the standard login screen in a number of different ways: Restart in FireWire disk mode, restart at the Unix Terminal, and so on. Suddenly, these no-goodniks have full access to every document on the machine, blowing right past all the safeguards you've so carefully established.

One way to thwart them is to use FileVault (page 497). Another is to turn off this checkbox. Now there's no Restart or Shut Down button to tempt mischief-makers. That's plenty of protection in most homes, schools, and workplaces; after all, Mac people tend to be *nice* people.

POWER USERS' CLINIC

The Firmware Password Utility

After all this discussion of security and passwords, it may come as a bit of a shock to learn that enterprising villains can bypass all of Mac OS X's security features in 10 seconds. If you haven't turned on FileVault, their nefarious options include using the Unix console described in Appendix B, using FireWire disk mode, and so on.

But there is one way to secure your Mac completely: by using the very secret, little-known Firmware Password Utility program.

To find it, insert the Snow Leopard DVD. Restart the Mac while pressing down the letter C key, which starts up the Mac from the DVD and launches the Mac OS X installer. On the first screen, choose your language and then click the Next arrow (or hit Return).

On the Install screen, choose Utilities→Firmware Password Utility.

When you run this utility, turn on "Require password to change firmware settings," as shown here. Then make up a

master password that's required to start up from anything but the internal drive.

Next, you're asked for an administrator's password. Finally, a message tells you, "The settings were successfully saved." Restart the Mac.

From now on, whenever you attempt to start up in anything but the usual way, you're asked to type the Open Firmware password. For example, you see it when you press the C key to start up from a CD, or when you press Option to choose a different startup disk or partition.

None of the usual startup-key tricks work. Holding down the C key to start up from a CD, holding down N to start up from a NetBoot server, pressing T to start up in Target Disk Mode, pressing D to start up from the installation DVD in diagnostic mode, pressing ⌘-V to start up in Verbose mode, ⌘-S to start up in Single-user mode, ⌘-Option-P-R to reset the parameter RAM, pressing Option to start up from a different system disk, pressing Shift to enter Safe Boot mode—none of it works without the master Open Firmware Password.

But if you worry that somebody with a pronounced mean streak might restart simply by pulling the plug, then either use FileVault or set the *Open Firmware password,* as described in the box on the previous page.

- **Show Input menu in login window.** If the Input menu (page 234) is available at login time, it means that people who use non-U.S. keyboard layouts and alphabets can use the login features without having to pretend to be American. (It also means that you have a much wider universe of difficult-to-guess passwords, since your password can be in, for example, Japanese characters. Greetings, Mr. Bond-san.)

- **Show password hints.** As described earlier, Mac OS X is kind enough to display your password hint ("middle name of the first person who ever kissed me") after you've typed it wrong three times when trying to log in. Or turn off this feature for an extra layer of security, and the hint will never appear.

- **Use VoiceOver at login window.** The VoiceOver feature (page 603) is all well and good if you're blind. But how are you supposed to log in? Turn on this checkbox, and VoiceOver speaks the features on the Login panel, too.

- **Show fast user switching menu as:** The Fast User Switching feature lets you switch to another account without having to log out of the first one, as described on page 490.

If you do turn on Fast User Switching, a new menu appears at the upper-right corner of your screen, listing all the account holders on the machine. Thanks to this pop-up menu, you can now specify what that menu looks like. It can display the current account holder's full name (Name), the short name (Short Name), or only a generic torso-silhouette icon (Icon) to save space on the menu bar.

Signing In, Logging Out

Once somebody has set up your account, here's what it's like getting into, and out of, a Mac OS X machine. (For the purposes of this discussion, "you" are no longer the administrator—you're one of the students, employees, or family members for whom an account has been set up.)

Identifying Yourself

When you first turn on the Mac—or when the person who last used this computer chooses →Log Out—the login screen shown in Figure 12-1 appears. At this point, you can proceed in any of several ways:

- **Restart.** Click if you need to restart the Mac for some reason. (The Restart and Shut Down buttons don't appear here if the administrator has chosen to hide them as a security precaution.)

- **Shut Down.** Click if you're done for the day, or if sudden panic about the complexity of user accounts makes you want to run away. The computer turns off.

- **Log In.** To sign in, click your account name in the list. If you're a keyboard speed freak, you can also type the first letter or two—or press the up or down arrow keys—until your name is highlighted. Then press Return.

Either way, the password box appears now (if a password is required). If you accidentally click the wrong person's name on the first screen, you can click Back. Otherwise, type your password, and then press Return (or click Log In).

You can try as many times as you want to type the password. With each incorrect guess, the entire dialog box shudders violently from side to side, as though shaking its head "No." If you try unsuccessfully three times, your hint appears—if you've set one up. (If you see a strange ⇪ icon in the password box, guess what? You've got your Caps Lock key on, and the Mac thinks you're typing an all-capitals password.)

Tip: So what happens if you forget your password, and even the Mac's administrator doesn't know it? On your third attempt to type the password correctly, the Mac shows you your password hint (unless the administrator has turned off the Hint option) and a button called Reset Password. When you click it, the Mac asks for the master password (page 498), which the administrator almost certainly knows.

Once that's typed in, you're allowed to make up a new password for your own account (and, presumably, a better hint this time). No harm done.

DON'T PANIC

The Case of the Forgotten Password

Help—I forgot my password! And I never told it to anybody, so even the administrator can't help me!

No problem. Your administrator can simply open up System Preferences, click Accounts, click the name of the person who forgot the password, and then click Reset Password to re-establish the password.

But you don't understand. I am the administrator! And I'm the only account!

Aha—that's a different story. All right, no big deal. At the login screen, type a gibberish password three times. On the last attempt, the Mac will offer you the chance to reset the password. All you have to do is type in your master password (page 498) to prove your credentials.

Um—I never set up a master password.

All right then. That's actually good news, because it means you didn't turn on FileVault. (If you had, and you'd also

forgotten the master password, your account would now be locked away forever.)

Insert the Mac OS X DVD. Restart the Mac while pressing down the letter C key, which starts up the Mac from the DVD and launches the Mac OS X installer. On the first screen, choose your language and then click the Next arrow (or hit Return).

On the Install screen, choose Utilities→Reset Password. When the Reset Password screen appears, click the hard drive that contains Mac OS X. From the first pop-up menu, choose the name of your account. Now make up a new password and type it into both boxes. Click Save, close the window, click the installer, and restart.

And next time, be more careful! Write down your password on a Post-it note and affix it to your monitor. (Joke—that's a joke!)

Once you're in, the world of the Mac looks just the way you left it (or the way an administrator set it up for you). Everything in your Home folder, all your email and bookmarks, your desktop picture and Dock settings—all of it is unique to you. Your Home folder even contains its own Library folder, which maintains a separate (additional) set of fonts and preference settings just for you. Your Applications folder may even have programs that other account holders don't see.

Unless you're an administrator, you're not allowed to install any new programs (or indeed, to put anything at all) into the Applications folder. That folder, after all, is a central software repository for *everybody* who uses the Mac, and the Mac forbids everyday account holders from moving or changing all such universally shared folders.

Logging Out

When you're finished using the Mac, choose →Log Out (or press Shift-⌘-Q). A confirmation message appears; if you click Cancel or press Esc, you return to whatever you were doing. If you click Log Out or press Return, you return to the screen shown in Figure 12-1, and the entire sign-in cycle begins again.

Tip: If you press Option as you choose →Log Out (or as you press Shift-⌘-Q), the confirmation box doesn't appear.

Sharing Across Accounts

It's all fine to say that every account is segregated from all *other* accounts. It's nice to know your stuff is safe from the prying eyes of your coworkers or family.

But what about collaboration? What if you *want* to give some files or folders to another account holder?

You can't just open up someone else's Home folder and drop it in there. Yes, every account holder has a Home folder (all in the Users folder on your hard drive). But if you try to open anybody else's Home folder, you'll see a tiny red ⊘ icon superimposed on almost every folder inside, telling you, "Look, but don't touch."

Fortunately, there are a couple of wormholes between accounts (Figure 12-13):

- **The Shared folder.** Sitting in the Users folder is one folder that doesn't correspond to any particular person: Shared. Everybody can freely access this folder, inserting and extracting files without restriction. It's the common ground among all the account holders on a single Mac. It's Central Park, the farmers market, and the grocery-store bulletin board.

- **The Public folder.** In your Home folder, there's a folder called Public. Anything you copy into it becomes available for inspection or copying (but not changing or deleting) by any other account holder, whether they log into your Mac or sign in from across the network.

- **The Drop Box.** And *inside* your Public folder is another cool little folder: the Drop Box. It exists to let *other* people give files to *you*, discreetly and invisibly to anyone else. That is, people can drop files and folders into your Drop Box, but they can't actually *open* it. This folder, too, is available both locally (in person) and from across the network.

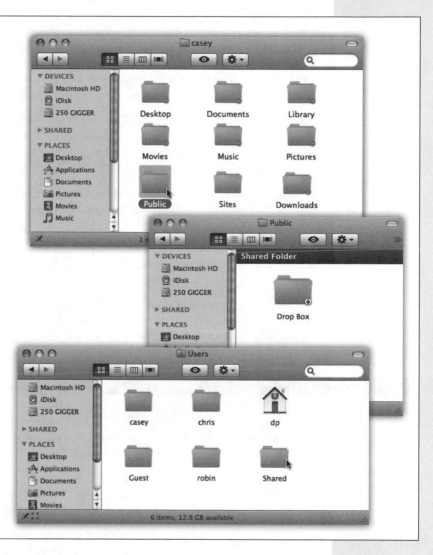

Figure 12-13:

Top: In other people's Home folders, the Public and Sites folders are available for your inspection. These two folders contain stuff that other people have "published" for the benefit of their coworkers.

Middle: In the Public folder is the Drop Box, which serves the opposite purpose. It lets anyone else who uses this Mac hand in files to you; they, however, can't see what's in it.

Bottom: Inside the Users folder (to get there from a Home folder, press ⌘-↑) is the Shared folder, a wormhole connecting all accounts. Everybody has full access to everything inside.

Fast User Switching

The account system described so far in this chapter has its charms. It keeps everyone's stuff separate, it keeps your files safe, and it lets you have the desktop picture of your choice.

Unfortunately, it can go from handy to hassle in one split second. That's when you're logged in, and somebody else wants to duck in just for a second—to check email or a calendar, for example. What are you supposed to do—log out completely, closing all your documents and quitting all your programs, just so the interloper can look something up? Then, afterward, you'd have to log back in and fire up all your stuff again, praying that your inspirational muse hasn't fled in the meantime.

Fortunately, that's all over now. Fast User Switching—a feature modeled on a similar Windows feature, which itself was modeled on a Unix feature—lets Person B log in and use the Mac for a little while. All *your* stuff, Person A, simply slides into the background, still open the way you had it; see Figure 12-14.

When Person B is finished working, you can bring your whole work environment back to the screen without having to reopen anything. All your windows and programs are still open, just as you left them.

To turn on this feature, open the Accounts panel of System Preferences (and click the 🔒, if necessary, to unlock the panel). Click Login Options, and turn on the "Show fast user switching menu as" checkbox. (You can see this option in Figure 12-12.)

The only change you notice immediately is the appearance of your own account name in the upper-right corner of the screen (Figure 12-14, top). You can change what this menu looks like by using the "Show fast user switching menu as" pop-up menu, also shown in Figure 12-12.

Shared Data Files

My wife and my 8-year-old kid share my Mac. Over the years, we've amassed a fabulous collection of MP3 files, but at the moment, I'm the only one who sees them in iTunes. This business of separate environments for every account holder is all well and good, but what about when we want to access the same files—like our iTunes Library?

The problem is that the iTunes Library is stored in the Music folder of just one person. Fortunately, the solution is easy enough.

Whoever is the administrator—probably your 8-year-old— should move the *iTunes Music* folder (currently inside

somebody's iTunes→Music folder) to the Users→Shared folder. Now it's available to everybody.

At this point, each account holder can log in, fire up iTunes, choose iTunes→Preferences→Advanced, and click the Change button to choose the relocated iTunes Music folder in the Shared folder.

From now on, each person will be able to see and access the entire library of iTunes tunes, but will still enjoy the flexibility to build individual playlists.

That's all there is to it. Next time you need a fellow account holder to relinquish control so you can duck in to do a little work, just choose your name from the Accounts menu. Type your password, if one is required, and feel guiltless about the interruption.

Figure 12-14:
Top: The appearance of the Accounts menu lets you know that Fast User Switching is turned on. The circled checkmark indicates people who are already logged in, including those who have been "fast user switched" into the background. The dimmed name shows who's logged in right now.

Bottom: When the screen changes from your account to somebody else's, your entire world slides visibly offscreen as though it's mounted on the side of a rotating cube—a spectacular animation made possible by Mac OS X's Quartz Extreme graphics software.

And now, the finer points of Fast User Switching:

- Depending on how many programs are open and how much memory the Mac has, switching accounts may entail a delay and a good deal of hard drive activity. That's Mac OS X's virtual memory scheme "setting down" what was in memory in *your* account to make room for the incoming account's stuff.

- To exit an open account, choose ⌘→Log Out as usual. Or just choose Login Window from the Accounts menu. It ensures that you can get to your own account no matter whose is running at the moment.

- Weirdly enough, a bunch of account holders can be using the same program simultaneously in their own parallel universes. Even if Microsoft Word was open in your account, Chris, Casey, and Robin can each open the same copy of the same program simultaneously when they fast-switch into their own accounts.

- You can't make changes to accounts (in System Preferences) that are still logged in. Nor, as you'd expect, can you turn off Fast User Switching while other people are logged in. Can't turn on FileVault, either.

- If you try to shut the Mac down or restart it while other people are logged in, a dialog box tells you, "There are currently logged in users who may lose unsaved changes if you shut down this computer." And you're asked to type in an administrator's name and password to establish that you know what the heck you're doing.

  Here's a moral dilemma for the modern age. If you proceed by typing the password and clicking Shut Down, you shut down all accounts that were open in the background *and* any open documents—and if those documents hadn't been saved, any changes are gone forever. If you click Cancel, you can't shut down the Mac until you hunt down the account holders whose stuff is still open in the background so they can log out.

Tip: You can avoid this awkward situation in either of two ways: (1) Trust each other completely, or (2) save all your documents before you let anyone else cut in and send your account to the background.

- Remember the Shared folder (in the Users folder on the hard drive)? It's still the wormhole connecting all accounts. If you want to share a file with another account holder, put it there.

- Your account isn't anesthetized completely when it's switched into the background. In fact, it keeps on doing whatever you set it to doing. If you were downloading some big file, for example, it keeps right on downloading when the next guy logs in.

Five Mac OS X Security Shields

Mac OS X has a spectacular reputation for stability and security. At this writing, not a single Mac OS X virus has emerged—a spectacular feature that makes Windows look like a waste of time. There's no Windows-esque plague of spyware, either (downloaded programs that do something sneaky behind your back). In fact, there isn't *any* Mac spyware.

The usual rap is, "Well, that's because Windows is a much bigger target. What virus writer is going to waste his time on a computer with 8 percent market share?"

That may be part of the reason Mac OS X is virus-free. But Mac OS X has also been built more intelligently from the ground up. Listed below are a few of the many drafty corners of a typical operating system that Apple has solidly plugged:

- The original Windows XP came with five of its *ports* open. Mac OS X has always come from the factory with all of them shut and locked.

Ports are channels that remote computers use to connect to services on your computer: one for instant messaging, one for Windows XP's remote-control feature, and so on. It's fine to have them open if you're expecting visitors. But if you've got an open port that exposes the soft underbelly of your computer without your knowledge, you're in for a world of hurt. Open ports are precisely what permitted viruses like Blaster to infiltrate millions of PCs. Microsoft didn't close those ports until the Windows XP Service Pack 2.

- Whenever a program tried to install itself in the original Windows XP, the operating system went ahead and installed it, potentially without your awareness.

In Mac OS X, that never happens. You're notified at every juncture when anything is trying to install itself on your Mac. In fact, every time you try to download something, either in Safari or Mail, that contains *executable code* (a program, in other words), a dialog box warns you that it could conceivably harbor a virus—even if your download is compressed as a .zip or .sit file (Figure 12-15).

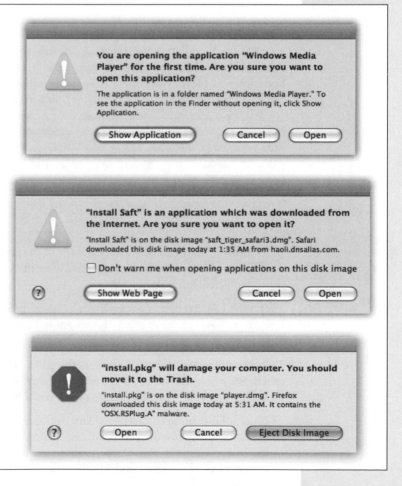

Figure 12-15:
This operating system intends to make darned sure no program ever runs without your knowledge (which is how Windows PCs get viruses and spyware). It tries to protect you, for example, when you double-click a document and the required program opens for the first time (top). It also warns you the first time you double-click any program that came from the Internet (middle). In Snow Leopard , it even checks your downloads against a database of known viruses, and lets you know before it's too late (bottom). Fat chance ever seeing that one, though; Mac viruses come along about as often as the Loch Ness Monster.

• Unlike certain other operating systems, Mac OS X doesn't even let an administrator touch the files that drive the operating system itself without pestering you to provide your password and grant it permission to do so. A Mac OS X virus (if there were such a thing) could theoretically wipe out all your files, but it wouldn't be able to access anyone else's stuff—and it couldn't touch the operating system itself.

• You probably already know about the Finder's Secure Empty Trash option (page 86). But an option on the Erase tab of the Disk Utility program can do the same super-erasing of *all free space* on your hard drive. We're talking not just erasing, but recording gibberish over the spots where your files once were—once, seven times, or *35* times—utterly shattering any hope any hard-disk recovery firm (or spy) might have had of recovering passwords or files from your hard drive.

• Safari's Private Browsing mode means that you can freely visit Web sites without leaving *any* digital tracks—no history, no nothing (page 763).

Those are only a few tiny examples. Here are a few of Mac OS X's big-ticket defenses.

The Firewall

If you have a broadband, always-on connection, you're open to the Internet 24 hours a day. It's theoretically possible for some cretin to use automated hacking software to flood you with files or take control of your machine. Snow Leopard's beefed-up *firewall* feature puts up a barrier to such mischief. To turn it on, click Start on this pane.

Note: You don't need to turn on this firewall if your Mac connects to the Internet through a wired or wireless router (including the AirPort base station). Virtually every router already has a built-in firewall that protects your entire network. (Similarly, if you're using the Mac's Internet Sharing feature, turn on the firewall only for the first Mac, the one connected right to the Internet.)

In short: Use the firewall only if your Mac is connected directly to a cable modem, DSL box, or dial-up modem.

Fortunately, it's not a *complete* barrier. One of the great joys of having a computer is its ability to connect to other computers. Living in a cement crypt is one way to avoid getting infected, but it's not much fun.

Therefore, you can turn the firewall on by opening System Preferences→Security→ Firewall tab and clicking Start. But in Snow Leopard, you can also fine-tune the blockade.

To do that, click Advanced; you see something like Figure 12-16 at top. As you can sort of tell, Snow Leopard now lets you allow or block Internet connections individually for *each program* on your Mac. Here's what you'll find there:

• **Block all incoming connections.** This option might be better known as Paranoid Mode. You're allowed to do email and basic Web surfing and a few other deep-seated services that Mac OS X needs to get by. But all other kinds of network connections are blocked, including screen sharing, iTunes music sharing, and so on. This is a hard-core, meat-fisted firewall that, for most people, is more trouble than it's worth.

- **[List of individual programs.]** If the firewall is on but you haven't turned on "Block all," then the Mac uses this list of individual programs and features to determine what's allowed to accept network connections.

 Above the horizontal line (Figure 12-16, top), features of Mac OS X itself are listed. They get added to this list automatically when you turn them on in System Preferences: File Sharing, Printer Sharing, and so on.

 Non-Apple programs can gain passage through your firewall, too. You can add one to the list manually by clicking the **+** button below the list and choosing it by hand; or you can simply respond to the request box that pops up whenever a new program wants to connect to the Internet (Figure 12-16, bottom).

 In fact, this bombardment of permission requests begins as soon as you turn on the firewall—one permission request for each of your *currently* open programs. Click Allow for each (unless, of course, you see a request for an app called Sneaky-PoisonVirus or something). As you do so, their names get added to the list of programs in this dialog box.

 For each program, you can use the pop-up menu beside its name to specify either "Allow incoming connections" or "Block incoming connections," depending on your level of paranoia.

- **Automatically allow signed software to receive incoming connections.** *Signed* software means programs that Apple recognizes as coming from legitimate companies. Anything from Adobe or Microsoft, for example, has got to be OK, right? (Insert your own wisecrack here.)

Note: OK, technically, a signed program is one whose authenticity is confirmed by a third party—a "certificate authority" company like VeriSign or GoDaddy. A system of invisible keys (security numbers) confirms that the software did indeed come from the creators it claims it came from, no matter how many detours it took to reach you.

One more point: When you explicitly grant permission to a program as described below, you're signing that program.

 If this checkbox is *not* turned on, then each time you run a new program for the first time, you'll be interrupted so the Mac can ask if it's OK to permit Internet connections. The "signed software" box cuts down on the interruptions, since well-known apps are assumed not to be viruses or spyware.

- **Enable Stealth Mode** is designed to slam shut the Mac's back door to the Internet. See, hackers often use automated hacker tools that send out "Are you there?" messages. They're hoping to find computers that are turned on and connected full time to the Internet. If your machine responds, and they can figure out how to get into it, they'll use it, without your knowledge, as a relay station for pumping out spam or masking their hacking footsteps.

Enable Stealth Mode, then, makes your Mac even more invisible on the network; it means your Mac won't respond to the electronic signal called a *ping*. (On the other hand, *you* won't be able to ping your machine, either, when you're on the road and want to know if it's turned on and online.)

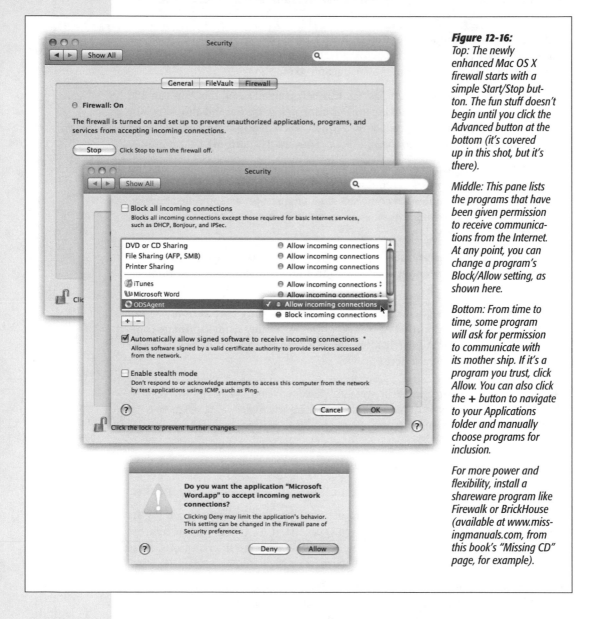

Figure 12-16:
Top: The newly enhanced Mac OS X firewall starts with a simple Start/Stop button. The fun stuff doesn't begin until you click the Advanced button at the bottom (it's covered up in this shot, but it's there).

Middle: This pane lists the programs that have been given permission to receive communications from the Internet. At any point, you can change a program's Block/Allow setting, as shown here.

Bottom: From time to time, some program will ask for permission to communicate with its mother ship. If it's a program you trust, click Allow. You can also click the + button to navigate to your Applications folder and manually choose programs for inclusion.

For more power and flexibility, install a shareware program like Firewalk or BrickHouse (available at www.missingmanuals.com, from this book's "Missing CD" page, for example).

Snow Leopard Spots: You might have noticed that there's no longer an option to turn on firewall logging, which creates a little text file where Mac OS X records every attempt that anyone from the outside makes to infiltrate your Mac. Logging is still available, though—in fact, it's turned on all the time. To view the log, open the Applications→Utilities→Console program. In the left-side list, expand the /private/var/log heading, and click appfirewall.log.

FileVault

The Security pane of System Preferences is one of Mac OS X's most powerful security features. Understanding what it does, however, may take a little slogging.

As you know, the Mac OS X accounts system is designed to keep people out of one another's stuff. Ordinarily, for example, Chris isn't allowed to go rooting through Robin's stuff.

Until FileVault came along, though, there were all kinds of ways to circumvent this protection system. A sneak or a showoff could start up the Mac in FireWire disk mode, for example, or even remove the hard drive and hook it up to a Linux machine or another Mac.

In each case, they'd then be able to run rampant through everybody's files, changing or trashing them with abandon. For people with sensitive or private files, the result was a security hole bigger than Steve Jobs's bank account.

FileVault is an extra line of defense. When you turn on this feature, your Mac automatically *encrypts* (scrambles) everything in your Home folder, using something called AES-128 encryption. (How secure is that? It would take a password-guessing computer *149 trillion years* before hitting pay dirt. Or, in more human terms, slightly longer than two back-to-back Kevin Costner movies.)

This means that unless someone knows (or can figure out) your password, FileVault renders your files unreadable for anyone but you and your computer's administrator—no matter what sneaky tricks they try to pull.

You won't notice much difference when FileVault is turned on. You log in as usual, clicking your name and typing your password. Only a slight pause as you log out indicates that Mac OS X is doing some housekeeping on the encrypted files: freeing up some space and/or backing up your home directory with Time Machine.

Tip: This feature is especially useful for laptop owners. If someone swipes or "borrows" your laptop, they can't get into your stuff without the password.

Here are some things you should know about FileVault's protection:

- **It's useful only if you've logged out.** Once you're logged in, your files are accessible. If you want the protection, log out before you wander away from the Mac. (Or let the screen saver close your account for you; see page 501.)

- **It covers only your Home folder.** Anything in your Applications, System, or Library folders is exempt from protection.

- **An administrator can access your files, too.** According to Mac OS X's caste system, anyone with an administrator's account can theoretically have unhindered access to his peasants' files—even with FileVault on—if that administrator has the master password described below.

- **It keeps other people from *opening* your files, not from deleting them.** It's still possible for someone to trash all your files, without ever seeing what they are. There's not much you can do about this with FileVault on *or* off—all a malicious person needs to do is start deleting the encrypted files, and your data is gone. (FileVault works by encrypting your Home folder into 8-megabyte chunks.)

- **Shared folders in your Home folder will no longer be available on the network.** That is, any folders you've shared won't be available to your coworkers *except* when you're at your Mac and logged in.

- **Backup programs may throw a tizzy.** FileVault's job is to "stuff" and "unstuff" your Home folder as you log in and out. Backup programs that work by backing up files and folders that have changed since the last backup may therefore get very confused.

Even Time Machine (Chapter 6) doesn't always play well with FileVault. For one thing, it can copy the encrypted Home folder only when it's closed—that is, when you're logged off. So you don't get the continuous hourly backups that everyone else gets.

Similarly, in times of tragedy, Time Machine can restore only your *entire* Home folder; you can't recover individual documents or folders in it.

FREQUENTLY ASKED QUESTION

Password Hell

With the introduction of the master password, you now have quite a few different passwords to keep straight. Each one, however, has a specific purpose:

Account password. You type this password in at the normal login screen. You can't get into anyone else's account with it–only yours. Entering this password unlocks FileVault, too.

Administrator password. You're asked to enter this password whenever you try to install new software or modify certain system settings. If you're the only one who uses your computer (or you're the one who controls it), your administrator password *is* your account password. Otherwise, you're

supposed to go find an administrator (the parent, teacher, or guru who set up your account to begin with) and ask that person to type in his name and password once he's assessed what you're trying to do.

Master password. Think of this password as a master key. If anyone with FileVault forgets her account password, the administrator who knows the master password can unlock the account. The master password also lets an administrator change an account's password right at the Login screen, whether FileVault is turned on or not.

Root password. This password is rarely useful for anything other than Unix hackery, as described on page 655.

- **It's only as secure as your password.** If someone can figure out your account's password, they can bypass FileVault for your account. Even more seriously, if someone can figure out the *master password* (see the box on the facing page), they can bypass FileVault for *every* account on your computer.

- **If you forget your password *and* your administrator forgets the master password, you're toast.** If this happens, your data is *permanently lost.* You have no choice but to erase your hard drive and start from scratch.

To turn FileVault on, proceed like this:

1. **In System Preferences, click Security, and then click FileVault. Click Set Master Password.**

   If you're the first person to try to turn on FileVault, you need to create a *master* password first.

   The master password is an override password that gives an administrator full power to access any account, even without knowing the account holder's password, or to turn off FileVault for any account.

   The thinking goes like this: Yeah, yeah, the peons with Standard accounts forget their *account* passwords all the time. But with FileVault, a forgotten password would mean *the entire Home folder is locked forever*—so Apple gave you, the technically savvy administrator, a back door. (And you, the omniscient administrator, would *never* forget the *master* password—right?)

   When you click Set Master Password, the dialog box shown at top in Figure 12-17 appears.

2. **Click "Turn On FileVault."**

   You'll see an error message if other account holders are simultaneously logged in (using Fast User Switching). Otherwise, you're asked to type your account password. An explanatory dialog box appears offering some options.

   If you select the "Use secure erase" option, Mac OS X works harder when it erases files that you delete, and that makes it harder for the bad guys to obtain the encrypted data even if they kidnap your computer.

   If you select "Use secure virtual memory," then Mac OS X also encrypts the contents of *virtual memory* (page 502). (All accounts share the same virtual-memory files in Mac OS X, so an evil hacker with sophisticated tools could conceivably analyze the virtual-memory files on your Mac to see what's in the documents you have open on the screen.)

Note: You can also turn on FileVault for an account at the moment you create it in System Preferences→ Accounts.

---

3. **Click "Turn On FileVault" again.**

Now Mac OS X logs you out of your own account. (It can't encrypt a folder that's in use.) Some time passes while it converts your Home folder into a protected state, during which you can't do anything but wait.

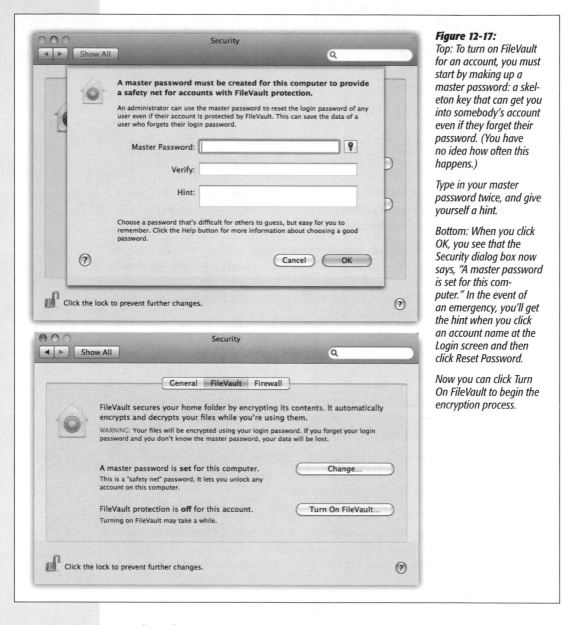

Figure 12-17:
Top: To turn on FileVault for an account, you must start by making up a master password: a skeleton key that can get you into somebody's account even if they forget their password. (You have no idea how often this happens.)

Type in your master password twice, and give yourself a hint.

Bottom: When you click OK, you see that the Security dialog box now says, "A master password is set for this computer." In the event of an emergency, you'll get the hint when you click an account name at the Login screen and then click Reset Password.

Now you can click Turn On FileVault to begin the encryption process.

After a few minutes, you arrive at the standard login window, where you can sign in as usual, confident that your stuff is securely locked away from anyone who tries to get at it when you're not logged in.

Note: To turn off FileVault, open System Preferences, click Security, and then click Turn Off FileVault. Enter your password, and then click OK. (The master password sticks around once you've created it, however, in case you ever want to turn FileVault on again.)

Logout Options

As you read earlier in this chapter, the usual procedure for finishing up a work session is for each person to choose →Log Out. After you confirm your intention to log out, the Login screen appears, ready for the next victim.

But sometimes people forget. You might wander off to the bathroom for a minute, but run into a colleague there who breathlessly begins describing last night's date and proposes finishing the conversation over pizza. The next thing you know, you've left your Mac unattended but logged in, with all your life's secrets accessible to anyone who walks by your desk.

You can prevent that situation using either of two checkboxes, both in the Security→ General panel of System Preferences:

- **Require password immediately after sleep or screen saver begins.** This option gives you a password-protected screen saver that locks your Mac when you wander away. Now, whenever somebody tries to wake up your Mac after the screen saver has appeared (or when the Mac has simply gone to sleep according to your settings in the Energy Saver panel of System Preferences), the "Enter your password" dialog box appears. No password? No access.

Snow Leopard Spots: The pop-up menu here (which starts out saying "immediately") is an awesome enhancement to this feature. Before, the person most inconvenienced by the password requirement was you, not the evil snitch from Accounting; even if you'd just stepped away to the bathroom or the coffee machine, you'd have to unlock the screen saver with your password. It got old fast.

Now, the password requirement can kick in only after you've been away for a more serious amount of time—5 minutes, 15 minutes, an hour, whatever. You can still put the Mac to sleep, or you can still set up your screen saver to kick in sooner than that. But until that time period has passed, you'll be able to wake the machine without having to log in.

(Super-geeky bonus fact: You can use a Unix command in Terminal, described in Chapter 16, to specify any time interval—not just the canned choices in the pop-up menu. The magic command is defaults -currentHost write com.apple.screensaver askForPasswordDelay -int 1800, where the final number specifies how many seconds should elapse before a password is required.)

- **Disable automatic login.** This is just a duplicate of the Automatic Login on/off switch described on page 462. Apple figured that this feature really deserved *some* presence on a control panel called Security.

- **Require a password to unlock each System Preferences pane.** Ordinarily, certain System Preferences changes require an administrator's approval—namely, the ones that affect the entire computer and everyone who uses it, like Date & Time, Accounts, Network, Time Capsule, and Security. If you're *not* an administrator, you can't make changes to these panels until an administrator has typed in his name and password to approve your change.

However, once Mr. Teacher or Ms. Parent has unlocked *one* of those secure preference settings, they're *all* unlocked. Once the administrator leaves your desk, you can go right on making changes to the *other* important panels (Network *and* Time Capsule *and* Security) without the administrator's knowledge.

Unless this "Require a password" box is turned on, that is. In that case, an administrative-account holder has to enter his name and password to approve *each* of those System Preferences panes individually.

- **Log out after __ minutes of inactivity.** You can make the Mac sign out of your account completely if it figures out that you've wandered off (and it's been, say, 15 minutes since the last time you touched the mouse or keyboard). Anyone who shows up at your Mac will find only the standard Login screen.

Note: Beware! If there are open, unsaved documents at the moment of truth, the Mac can't log you out.

- **Use secure virtual memory.** *Virtual memory* is a trick that computers use to keep a lot of programs open at once—more, in fact, than they technically have enough memory (RAM) for. How do they manage to keep so many software balls in the air? Easy: They set some of them down on the hard drive.

When you bring Photoshop to the front, Mac OS X frees up the necessary memory for it by storing some of the *background* programs' code on the hard drive. When you switch back to, say, Safari, Mac OS X swaps Photoshop for the Safari code it needs from the hard drive, so that the frontmost program always has full command of your actual memory.

Sophisticated software snoopers could, in theory, sneak up to the Mac while you're logged in but away from your desk. Using a built-in Unix command called *strings,* the no-goodniks could actually *read* what's stored on the hard drive in that virtual-memory swap file—in particular, your passwords.

But this checkbox takes away all their fun; it encrypts your virtual memory swap file so nobody can read it. (You may also find that it slows down your Mac, though, especially when you switch from one program to another.)

- **Disable Location Services.** Location Services means "knowing where I am." It's the new Snow Leopard feature that lets a laptop figure out its own time zone, for example (page 322).

Every time a program wants to use your current location for its own feature, you'll be asked about it. But if you want to rule out any possibility that someone, or some software, can find out where you are, then turn on this box.

Note: Once you grant permission to a program to access the Mac's location information, that program never asks you again. Click Reset Warnings if you want to start over—if you want every program to ask you again if it's allowed to use your location information, as though for the first time.

- **Disable remote control infrared receiver.** You can operate the playback functions of laptops and iMacs with a remote control, like Apple's tiny white one. (For example, that's how you'd control movie, music, and slideshow playback in Front Row, a program described in Chapter 15.)

  If you're worried about some smart-aleck high-school kid interfering by, for example, summoning Front Row when you're trying to crunch some numbers, then turn this on. Now the Mac turns a deaf eye and ear to remote-control signals.

Note: The Pair button here is handy when more than one Apple product is responding to remote-control signals—two different Macs sitting next to each other, for example, or one Mac and an Apple TV. Click Pair to "marry" one particular remote with this particular Mac.

The Password Assistant

Plenty of software features require you to make up a password: Web sites, accounts, networked disks, and so on. No wonder most people wind up trying to use the same password in as many situations as possible. Worse, they use something easily guessable like their names, kids' names, spouse's names, and so on. Even regular English words aren't very secure, because hackers routinely use *dictionary attacks*—software that tries to guess your password by running through every word in the dictionary—to break in.

To prevent evildoers from guessing your passwords, Mac OS X comes with a good-password suggestion feature called the Password Assistant. It cheerfully generates one suggestion after another for impossible-to-guess passwords. (*recharges8@exchange-ability,* anyone?)

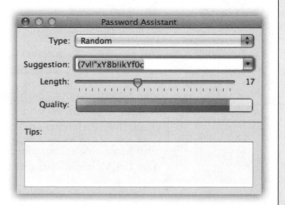

Figure 12-18:
Anyplace you're supposed to make up a password, including in the Accounts pane of System Preferences, a key icon appears. When you click it, the Password Assistant opens. Use the pop-up menu and the Length slider to specify how long and unguessable the password is. The Quality graph shows you just how tough it is to crack this password.

(In the Type pop-up menu, you might wonder about FIPS-181. It stands for the Federal Information Processing Standards Publication 181, which sets forth the U.S. government's standard for password-generating algorithms.)

Fortunately, *you* won't have to remember most of them, thanks to the Keychain password-memorizing feature described at the end of this chapter. (The only password you have to memorize is your account password.)

See Figure 12-18 for details on the Password Assistant.

The Keychain

The information explosion of the computer age may translate into bargains, power, and efficiency, but as noted above, it carries with it a colossal annoyance: the proliferation of *passwords* we have to memorize. Shared folders on the network, Web sites, your iDisk, FTP sites—each requires another password.

Apple has done the world a mighty favor with its *Keychain* feature. Whenever you log into Mac OS X and type in your password, you've typed the master code that tells the computer, "It's really me. I'm at my computer now." From that moment on, the Mac *automatically* fills in every password blank you encounter, whether it's a Web site in Safari or Opera, a shared disk on your network, a wireless network, an encrypted disk image, or an FTP program like Transmit or RBrowser. With only a few exceptions, you can safely forget *all* your passwords except your login password.

These days, all kinds of programs and services know about the Keychain and offer to store your passwords there. For example:

- In Safari, whenever you type your name and password for a certain Web page and then click OK, a dialog box asks: "Would you like to save this password?" (See Figure 12-19, top.)

Note: This offer is valid only if, in Safari→Preferences→AutoFill tab, "User names and passwords" is turned on. If not, the "Would you?" message never appears.

Note, too, that some Web sites use a nonstandard login system that also doesn't produce the "Would you?" message. Unless the Web site provides its own "Remember me" or "Store my password" option, you're out of luck; you'll have to type in this information with every visit.

- When you connect to a shared folder or disk on the network, the opportunity to save the password in your Keychain is equally obvious (Figure 12-20, bottom).

- You also see a "Remember password (add to Keychain)" option when you create an encrypted disk image using Disk Utility.

- Mac email programs, like Mail and Entourage, store your email account passwords in your Keychain. So do FTP (file-transfer) programs like RBrowser and Fetch; check their Preferences dialog boxes.

- Your MobileMe account information is stored in the Keychain, too (as you entered it on the MobileMe pane of System Preferences).

- A "Remember password" option appears when you type in the password for a wireless network or AirPort base station.

- The iTunes program memorizes your Apple Music Store password, too.

Tip: If you're a MobileMe subscriber (Chapter 18), the MobileMe service can even synchronize your Keychain with other Macs. (Open System Preferences→MobileMe→Sync to set it up.) All your Macs will contain the identical Keychain—so they will know and auto-enter your passwords, too. Life gets simpler yet.

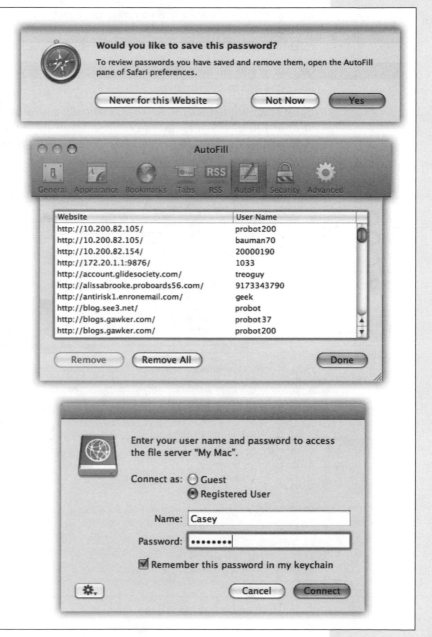

Figure 12-19:
Top: Safari is one of several Internet-based programs that offer to store your passwords in the Keychain; just click Yes. The next time you visit this Web page, you'll find your name and password already typed in.

Middle: At any time, you can see a complete list of the memorized Web passwords by choosing Safari→Preferences, clicking AutoFill, and then clicking the Edit button next to "User names and passwords." This is also where you can delete a password, thus making Safari forget it.

Bottom: When you connect to a server (a shared disk or folder on the network), just turn on "Remember this password in my keychain."

Locking and unlocking the Keychain

If you work alone, the Keychain is automatic, invisible, and generally wonderful. Log-in is the only time you have to type a password. After that, the Mac figures, "Hey, I know it's you; you proved it by entering your account password. That ID is good enough for me. I'll fill in all your other passwords automatically." In Apple parlance, you've *unlocked* your Keychain just by logging in.

But there may be times when you want the Keychain to *stop* filling in all your passwords, perhaps only temporarily. Maybe you work in an office where someone else might sit down at your Mac while you're getting a candy bar.

Of course, you can have Mac OS X lock your Mac—Keychain and all—after a specified period of inactivity (page 501).

But if you want to lock the Keychain *manually,* so that no passwords are autofilled in until you unlock it again, you can use any of these methods. Each requires the Keychain Access program (in your Applications→Utilities folder):

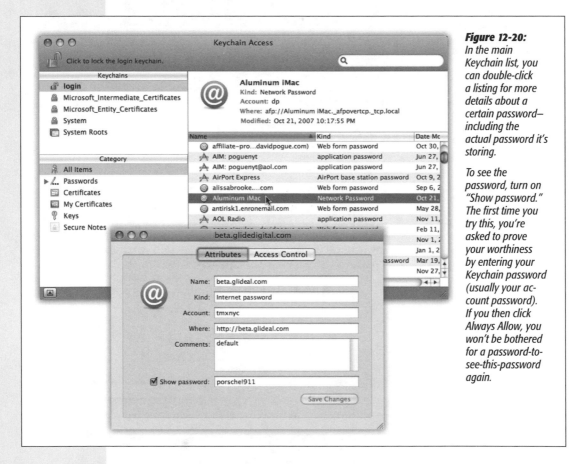

Figure 12-20:
In the main Keychain list, you can double-click a listing for more details about a certain password—including the actual password it's storing.

To see the password, turn on "Show password." The first time you try this, you're asked to prove your worthiness by entering your Keychain password (usually your account password). If you then click Always Allow, you won't be bothered for a password-to-see-this-password again.

- **Lock the Keychain manually.** In the Keychain Access program, choose File→Lock Keychain [Your Name] (⌘-L), or just click the big padlock at upper left. Click the 🔒 button in the toolbar of the Keychain Access window (Figure 12-20).

- **Choose Lock Keychain [Your Name] from the Keychain menulet.** To put the Keychain menulet on your menu bar, open Keychain Access, choose Keychain Access→Preferences→General. Turn on Show Status in Menu Bar.

- **Lock the Keychain automatically.** In the Keychain Access program, choose Edit→Change Settings for Keychain [your name]. The resulting dialog box lets you set up the Keychain to lock itself, say, 5 minutes after the last time you used your Mac, or whenever the Mac goes to sleep. When you return to the Mac, you're asked to re-enter your account password in order to unlock the Keychain, restoring your automatic-password feature.

Whenever the Keychain is locked, Mac OS X no longer fills in your passwords.

Note: As noted above, you unlock your Keychain using the same password you use to log into Mac OS X, but that's just a convenience. If you're really worried about security, you can choose Edit→Change Password for Keychain [your name], thereby establishing a different password for your Keychain, so that it no longer matches your login password.

Of course, doing so also turns off the automatic-Keychain-unlocking-when-you-log-in feature.

Managing Keychain

To take a look at your Keychain, open the Keychain Access program. By clicking one of the password rows, you get to see its attributes—name, kind, account, and so on (Figure 12-20).

Tip: The primary purpose of the Keychain is, of course, to type in passwords for you automatically. However, it's also an excellent place to record all kinds of private information just for your own reference: credit card numbers, ATM numbers, and so on. Simply choose File→New Password Item (if it's a name and password) or File→New Secure Note (if you just want to type a blob of very, very private text).

No, the Mac won't type them in for you automatically anywhere, but it does maintain them in one central location that is, itself, password-protected.

Multiple Keychains

By choosing File→New Keychain, you can create more than one Keychain, each with its own master password. On one hand, this might defeat the simplicity goal of the Keychain. On the other hand, it's conceivable that you might want to encrypt all your business documents with one master password and all your personal stuff with another, for example.

If you do have more than one Keychain, you can view all of them by clicking the little Show Keychains button at the lower-left corner of the Keychain Access window; now you see a list of all your Keychains (including some maintained by Microsoft Office and Mac OS X itself). Click their names to switch among them.

Keychain files

Keychains are represented by separate files in your Home→Library→Keychains folder. Knowing that can be handy when you want to delete a Keychain or copy it to another Mac—your laptop, for example. (Then again, the File→Export command may be even more convenient.)

Networking, File Sharing, & Screen Sharing

Networks are awesome. Once you've got a network, you can copy files from one machine to another—even between Windows PCs and Macs—just as you'd drag files between folders on your own Mac. You can send little messages to other people's screens. Everyone on the network can consult the same database or calendar, or listen to the same iTunes music collection. You can play games over the network. You can share a single printer or cable modem among all the Macs in the office. You can connect to the network from wherever you are in the world, using the Internet as the world's longest extension cord back to your office.

In Snow Leopard, you can even do *screen sharing,* which means that you, the wise computer whiz, can see what's on the screen of your pathetic, floundering relative or buddy elsewhere on the network. You can seize control of the other Mac's mouse and keyboard. You can troubleshoot, fiddle with settings, and so on. It's the next best thing to being there—often, a lot *better* than being there.

This chapter concerns itself with *local* networking—setting up a network in your home or small office. But don't miss its sibling, Chapter 18, which is about hooking up to the somewhat larger network called the Internet.

Wiring the Network

Most people connect their computers using one of two connection systems: Ethernet or WiFi (which Apple calls AirPort).

Ethernet Networks

Every Mac (except the MacBook Air) and every network-ready laser printer has an Ethernet jack (Figure 13-1). If you connect all the Macs and Ethernet printers in your small office to a central *Ethernet hub* or *router*—a compact, inexpensive box with jacks for five, 10, or even more computers and printers—you've got yourself a very fast, very reliable network. (Most people wind up hiding the hub in a closet and running the wiring either along the edges of the room or inside the walls.) You can buy Ethernet cables, plus the hub, at any computer store or, less expensively, from an Internet-based mail-order house; none of this stuff is Mac-specific.

Tip: If you want to connect only two Macs—say, your laptop and your desktop machine—you don't need an Ethernet hub. Instead, you just need a standard Ethernet cable. Run it directly between the Ethernet jacks of the two computers. (You don't need a special crossover Ethernet cable, as you did with Macs of old.) Then connect the Macs as described in the box on page 512.

Or don't use Ethernet at all; just use a FireWire cable or a person-to-person AirPort network.

Ethernet jack   Ethernet hub

Figure 13-1:
Every Mac except the Air has a built-in Ethernet jack (left). It looks like an overweight telephone jack. It connects to an Ethernet router or hub (right) via an Ethernet cable (also known as Cat 5 or Cat 6), which ends in what looks like an overweight telephone-wire plug (also known as an RJ-45 connector).

Ethernet is the best networking system for many offices. It's fast, easy, and cheap.

AirPort Networks

WiFi, known to the geeks as 802.11 and to Apple fans as AirPort, means wireless networking. It's the technology that lets laptops the world over get online at high speed in any WiFi "hot spot." Hot spots are everywhere these days: in homes, offices, coffee shops (notably Starbucks), hotels, airports, and thousands of other places.

Tip: At *www.jiwire.com,* you can type in an address or a city and learn exactly where to find the closest WiFi hot spots.

When you're in a WiFi hot spot, your Mac has a very fast connection to the Internet, as though it's connected to a cable modem or DSL.

AirPort circuitry comes preinstalled in every Mac laptop, iMac, and Mac Mini, and you can order it built into a Mac Pro.

This circuitry lets your machine connect to your network and the Internet without any wires at all. You just have to be within about 150 feet of a *base station* or *access* point (as Windows people call it), which must in turn be physically connected to your network and Internet connection.

If you think about it, the AirPort system is a lot like a cordless phone, where the base station is, well, the base station, and the Mac is the handset.

The base station can take any of these forms:

- **AirPort base station.** Apple's sleek, white, squarish or rounded base stations ($100 to $180) permit as many as 50 computers to connect simultaneously.

  The less expensive one, the AirPort Express, is so small it looks like a small white power adapter. It also has a USB jack so you can share a USB printer on the network. It can serve up to 10 computers at once.

- **A Time Capsule.** This Apple gizmo is exactly the same as the AirPort base station except that it also contains a huge hard drive so that it can back up your Macs automatically over the wired or wireless network.

UP TO SPEED

AirPort a, b, g, and n: Regular or Supersized?

In the short history of wireless networking, WiFi gear has come in several variants, bearing the absurdly user-hostile names *802.11b, 802.11g, 802.11a, 802.11n,* and so on.

The difference involves the technical specs of the wireless signal. Original AirPort uses the 802.11b standard; AirPort Extreme uses 802.11g; the current AirPort cards and base stations use 802.11n.

So what's the difference? Equipment bearing the "b" label transfers data through the air at up to 11 megabits per second; the "g" system is almost five times as fast (54 megabits a second); and "n" is supposed to be four times as fast as *that*.

(Traditionally, geeks measure network speeds in mega*bits*, not mega*bytes*. If you're more familiar with megabytes, though, here's a translation: The older AirPort gear has a top speed of 1.4 megabytes per second, versus more than 6 megabytes per second for the AirPort Extreme stuff.)

(Oh, and while we're using parentheses here: The only place you'll get the quoted speeds out of this gear is on the moon. Here on earth, signal strength is affected by pesky things like air, furniture, walls, floors, wiring, phone interference, and antenna angle. Speed and signal strength diminish proportionally as you move away from the base station.)

Now, each successive version of the WiFi base station/laptop circuitry standard is backward-compatible. For example, you can buy a new, 802.11n base station, and still connect to it from your ancient 802.11g PowerBook. You won't get any greater speed, of course—that would require a laptop with an 802.11n transmitter—but you'll enjoy the greater range in your house.

It's important to understand, though, that even the most expensive, top-tier cable modem or DSL service delivers Internet information at only about *half* a megabyte per second. The bottleneck is the Internet connection, not your network. Don't buy newer AirPort gear thinking that you're going to speed up your email and Web activity.

Instead, the speed boost you get with AirPort Extreme is useful *only* for transferring files between computers and gadgets on your own network (like the bandwidth-hungry Apple TV)—and playing networkable games.

And one more note: All WiFi gear works together, no matter what kind of computer you have. There's no such thing as a "Windows" wireless network or a "Macintosh" wireless network. Macs can use non-Apple base stations, Windows PCs can use AirPort base stations, and so on.

- **A wireless broadband router.** Lots of other companies make less expensive WiFi base stations, including Linksys (*www.linksys.com*) and Belkin (*www.belkin.com*). You can plug the base station into an Ethernet router or hub, thus permitting 10 or 20 wireless-equipped computers, including Macs, to join an existing Ethernet network without wiring. (With all due non-fanboyism, however, Apple's base stations and software are infinitely more polished and satisfying to use.)

Tip: It's perfectly possible to plug a WiFi base station into a regular router, too, to accommodate both wired and wireless computers.

- **Another Mac.** Your Mac can also *impersonate* an AirPort base station. In effect, the Mac becomes a software-based base station, and you save yourself the cost of a separate physical base station.

A few, proud people still get online by dialing via modem, which is built into some old AirPort base station models. The base station is plugged into a phone jack. Wireless Macs in the house can get online by triggering the base station to dial by remote control.

Tip: If you connect through a modern router or AirPort base station, you already have a great firewall protecting you. You don't have to turn on Mac OS X's firewall. But remember to turn it on when you escape to the local WiFi coffee shop with your laptop.

For the easiest AirPort network setup, begin by configuring your Mac so that it can go online the wired way, as described in the previous pages. Once it's capable of connecting to the Internet via wires, you can then use the AirPort Utility (in your Applications→Utilities folder) to transmit those Internet settings wirelessly to the base station itself. From then on, the base station's modem or Ethernet jack—not your Mac's—will do the connecting to the Internet.

GEM IN THE ROUGH

Networking Without the Network

In a pinch, you can connect two Macs without any real network at all. You can create an Ethernet connection without a hub or a router—or an AirPort connection without a WiFi base station.

To set up the wired connection, just run a standard Ethernet cable between the Ethernet jacks of the two Macs. (You don't need to use an Ethernet *crossover* cable, as you did in days of old.)

To set up a wireless connection, from your 🛜 menulet, choose Create Network. Make up a name for your little private network, and then click OK. On the second Mac, choose 🛜→Join Network, enter the same private network name, and then click Join.

At this point, your two Macs belong to the same *ad hoc* micro-network. If you've shared some folders on the first Mac, its name (like "Casey's iMac") now appears in the Sidebar of the second Mac. Click it to see what's on it. From here, proceed exactly as described on page 521.

Whether you've set up your own wireless network or want to hop onto somebody else's, Chapter 18 has the full scoop on *joining* WiFi networks.

FireWire Networks

FireWire networks?

You're forgiven for splurting your coffee. Everyone knows that FireWire is great for hooking up a camcorder or a hard drive, and a few people know about FireWire Disk Mode. But not many people realize that FireWire makes a fantastic networking cable, since it's insanely, blisteringly fast. (All right, *gigabit Ethernet* is faster, and so is FireWire 800. But attaining that kind of networking nirvana requires that all your Macs, hubs, and other networking gear are all compatible with gigabit Ethernet or FireWire 800.)

FireWire networking, technically known as *IP over FireWire,* is an unheralded, unsung feature of Mac OS X. But when you have a lot of data to move between Macs—your desktop and your laptop, for example—a casual FireWire network is the way to go. It lets you copy a gigabyte of email, pictures, or video files in a matter of seconds.

Here's how you unleash this secret feature:

1. **Connect two Macs with a FireWire cable.**

   You can't use the one that fits a camcorder. You need a six-pin-to-six-pin cable for traditional FireWire jacks. If you want to use the faster FireWire 800 connection on some of the latest Mac models, you'll need to shop for an even less common cord.

   Both computers can remain turned on; you can even continue to *use* both Macs while they're connected.

2. **Open System Preferences→Network. Click the 🔒 icon and enter your Administrator password. Click the + button below the list of network connections.**

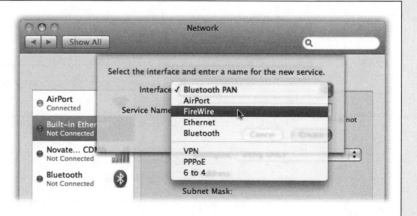

Figure 13-2:
In the Network pane of System Preferences, you can add your FireWire port to the list of network connections. The point of this window, by the way, is that a Mac can maintain simultaneous open network connections— Ethernet, AirPort, FireWire, and dial-up modem. (That's a feature called multihoming.)

The tiny dialog box shown in Figure 13-2 appears, letting you specify what kind of network connection you want to set up.

3. **From the pop-up menu, choose FireWire. Click Create.**

Now your newly created FireWire connection appears in the list.

4. **Repeat steps 2 through 3 on the second Mac.**

By now, it may have dawned on you that you can't actually get *online* via FireWire, since your cable runs directly between two Macs. But you can always turn on Internet Sharing (page 681) on the other Mac.

5. **Quit System Preferences.**

Your Macs are ready to talk—*fast.* Read the following pages for details on sharing files between them.

Tip: Once you've switched on your FireWire connection, you may need to turn File Sharing or Internet Sharing off and on again to make it work.

File Sharing

When you're done wiring (or not wiring, as the case may be), your network is ready. Your Mac should "see" any Ethernet or shared USB printers, in readiness to print (Chapter 14). You can now play network games or use a network calendar. And you can now turn on *File Sharing,* one of the most useful features of all.

In File Sharing, you can summon the icon for a folder or disk attached to another computer on the network, whether it's a Mac or a Windows PC. It shows up in a Finder window, as shown in Figure 13-3.

At this point, you can drag files back and forth, exactly as though the other computer's folder or disk is a hard drive connected to your own machine.

The thing is, it's not easy being Apple. You have to write *one* operating system that's supposed to please *everyone,* from the self-employed first-time computer owner to the network administrator for NASA. You have to design a networking system simple enough for the laptop owner who just wants to copy things to a desktop Mac when returning from a trip, yet secure and flexible enough for the network designer at a large corporation.

Clearly, different people have different attitudes toward the need for security and flexibility.

That's why Snow Leopard offers two ways to share files—a simple and limited way, and a more complicated and flexible way:

- **The simple way: the Public folder.** Every account holder has a Public folder. It's free for anyone else on the network to access. Like a grocery store bulletin board, there's no password required. Super-convenient, super-easy.

There's only one downside, and you may not care about it: You have to move or copy files *into* the Public folder before anyone else can see them. Depending on how many files you want to share, this can get tedious, disrupt your standard organizational structure, and eat up disk space.

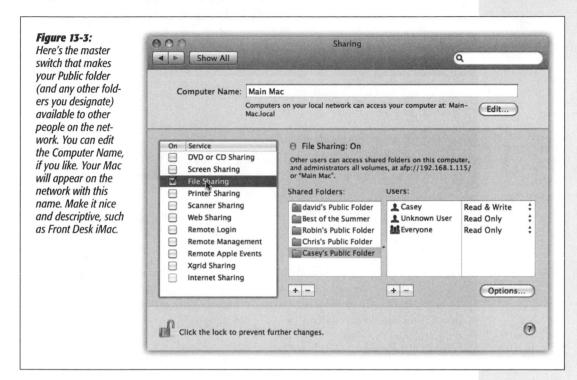

Figure 13-3:
Here's the master switch that makes your Public folder (and any other folders you designate) available to other people on the network. You can edit the Computer Name, if you like. Your Mac will appear on the network with this name. Make it nice and descriptive, such as Front Desk iMac.

- **The flexible way: Any folder.** You can also make *any* file, folder, or disk available for inspection by other people on the network. This method means that you don't have to move files into the Public folder, for starters. It also gives you elaborate control over who is allowed to do what to your files. You might want to permit your company's executives to see *and* edit your documents, but allow the peons in Accounting just to see them. And Andy, that unreliable goofball in Sales? You don't want him even *seeing* what's in your shared folder.

Of course, setting up all those levels of control means more work and more complexity.

Setup: Sharing Through the Public Folder

Inside your Home folder, there's a folder called Public. Inside *everybody's* Home folder is a folder called Public.

Anything you copy into this folder is automatically available to everyone else on the network. They don't need a password, they don't need an account on your Mac—they just have to be on the same network.

To make your Public folder available to your network mates, you have to turn on the File Sharing master switch. Choose →System Preferences, click Sharing, and turn on File Sharing (Figure 13-3).

Now round up the files and folders you want to share with all comers on the network, and drag them into your Home→Public folder. That's all there is to it.

Note: You may notice that there's already something in your Public folder: a folder called Drop Box. It's there so that other people can give you files from across the network, as described later in this chapter.

So now that you've set up Public folder sharing, how are other people supposed to access your Public folder? See page 521.

Setup: Sharing Through Any Folder

If the Public folder method seems too simple and restrictive, then you can graduate to the "share any folder" method. In this scheme, you can make *any* file, folder, or disk available to other people on the network.

This time, you don't have to move your files anywhere; they sit right where you have them. And this time, you can set up elaborate *sharing privileges* (also known as *permissions*) that grant individuals different amounts of access to your files.

This method is more complicated to set up than that Public-folder business. In fact, just to underline its complexity, Apple has created two different setup procedures. You can share one icon at a time by opening its Get Info window; or you can work in a master list of shared items in System Preferences.

The following pages cover both methods.

The Get Info method

Here's how to share a Mac file, disk, or folder disk using its Get Info window.

The following steps assume that you've turned on →System Preferences→Sharing→File Sharing, as shown in Figure 13-3.

1. **Highlight the folder or disk you want to share. Choose File→Get Info.**

   The Get Info dialog box appears (Figure 13-4). Expand the General panel, if it's not already visible.

Note: Sharing an entire disk means that every folder and file on it is available to anyone you give access to. On the other hand, by sharing only a folder or two, you can keep most of the stuff on your hard drive private, out of view of curious network comrades. Sharing only a folder or two does them a favor, too, by making it easier for them to find the files they're supposed to have. This way, they don't have to root through your entire drive looking for the folder they actually need.

---

2. **Turn on "Shared folder."**

   Enter your administrative password, if necessary.

Snow Leopard Spots: New in Mac OS X 10.6: To help you remember what you've made available to other people on the network, a gray banner labeled "Shared Folder" appears across the top of any Finder window that you've shared. It even appears at the top of the Open and Save dialog boxes.

OK, this disk or folder is now shared. But with whom?

3. **Expand the Sharing & Permissions panel, if it's not already visible. Click the 🔒 icon and enter your administrator's password.**

The controls in the Sharing & Permissions area spring to life and become editable. At the bottom of the Info panel is a little table. The first column can display the names of individual account holders, like Casey or Chris, or *groups* of account holders, like Everyone or Accounting Dept.

The second column lists the *privileges* each person or group has for this folder.

Now, the average person has no clue what "privileges" means, and this is why things get a little hairy when you're setting up folder-by-folder permissions. But read on; it's not as bad as it seems.

4. **Edit the table by adding people's names. Then set their access permissions.**

At the moment, your name appears in the Name column, and it probably says Read & Write in the Privilege column. In other words, you're currently the master of this folder. You can put things in, and you can take things out.

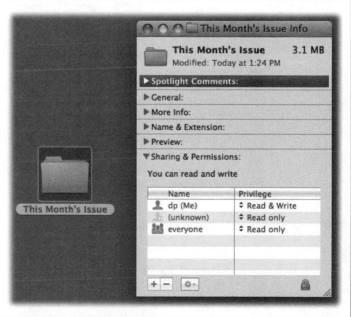

Figure 13-4:
The file-sharing permissions controls are here, in the Get Info box for any file, folder, or disk.

In other words, if you just want to share files with *yourself,* so you can transfer them from one computer to another, you can stop here.

If you want to share files with *other* people, well, note that at the moment, the privileges for "Everyone" is probably set to "Read only." Other people can see this folder, but they can't do anything with it.

Your job is to work through this list of people, specifying *how much* control each person has over the file or folder you're sharing.

To add the name of a person or group, click the **+** button below the list. The people list shown in Figure 13-5 appears.

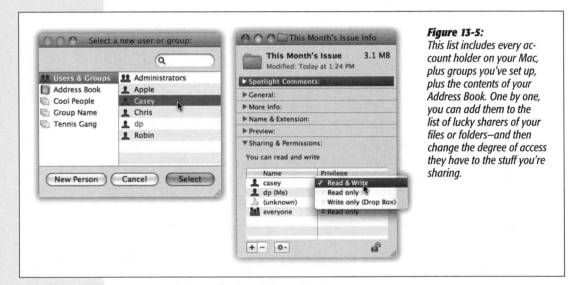

Figure 13-5:
This list includes every account holder on your Mac, plus groups you've set up, plus the contents of your Address Book. One by one, you can add them to the list of lucky sharers of your files or folders—and then change the degree of access they have to the stuff you're sharing.

Now click a name in the list. Then, from the Privilege pop-up menu, choose a permissions setting.

Read & Write has the most access of all. This person, like you, can add, change, or delete any file in the shared folder, or make any changes they like to a document. Give Read & Write permission to people you trust not to mess things up.

Read only means "Look, but don't touch." This person can see what's in the folder (or file) and can copy it, but they can't delete or change the original. It's a good setting for distributing company documents or making source files available to your minions.

Write only (drop box) means that other people can't open the folder at all. They can drop things into it, but it's like dropping icons through a mail slot: The letter disappears into the slot, and then it's too late for them to change their minds. As the folder's owner, you can do what you like with the deposited goodies. This drop-box effect is great when you want students, coworkers, or family members to be able to *turn things in* to you—homework, reports, scandalous diaries—without running the risk that someone else might see those documents. (This option doesn't appear for documents—only disks and folders.)

No access is an option only for "Everyone." It means that other people can see this file or folder's icon but can't do a thing with it.

Tip: Usually, you'll want the privileges for the folder to also apply to everything inside it; it would be a real drag to have to change the sharing privileges of the contents one icon as a time. That's why the ✿ menu at the bottom of the Get Info box has a command called "Apply to enclosed items."

---

5. **Close the Get Info window.**

   Now the folder is ready for invasion from across the network.

The System Preferences method

It's very convenient to turn on sharing one folder at a time, using the Get Info window. But there's another way in, too, one that displays *all* your shared stuff in one handy master list.

To see it, choose →System Preferences. Click Sharing. Click File Sharing (and make sure it's turned on).

Figure 13-6:
Hiding in System Preferences is a list of every file, disk, and folder you've shared. To stop sharing something, click it and click the — button. To share something new, drag its icon off the desktop, or out of its window, directly into the Shared Folders list.

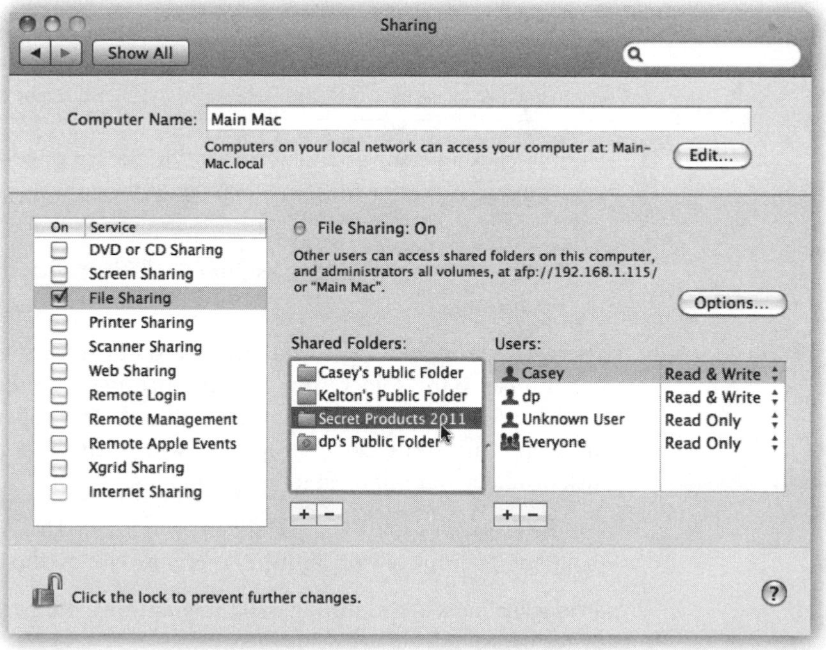

Now you're looking at a slightly different kind of permissions table, shown in Figure 13-6. It has *three* columns:

- **Shared folders.** The first column lists the files, folders, and disks you've shared. You'll probably see that every account's *Public* folder is already listed here, since they're all shared automatically. (You can turn *off* sharing for a Public folder, too, just by clicking it and then clicking the **–** button.)

  But you can add more icons to this list. Either drag them into the list directly from the desktop or a Finder window, or click the **+** sign, navigate to the item you want to share, select it, and then click Add. Either way, that item now appears in the Shared Folders list.

- **Users.** When you click a shared item, the second column sprouts a list of *who* gets to work with it from across the network. You're probably listed here, of course, since it's your stuff. But somebody called Unknown User also appears in this list (a reference to people who sign in as Guests, as described on page 467). There's also a listing here for Everyone, which really means, "everyone *else*"—that is, everyone who's not specifically listed here.

  You can add to this list, too. Click **+** to open the person-selection box shown in Figure 13-5. It lists the other account holders on your Mac, some predefined groups, and the contents of your Address Book.

Note: Most of the Address Book people don't actually have accounts on this Mac, of course. If you choose somebody from this list, you're asked to make up an account password. When you click Create Account, you have actually created a Sharing Only account on your Mac for that person, as described on page 466. When you return to the Accounts pane of System Preferences, you'll see that new person listed.

Double-click a person's name to add her to the list of people who can access this item from over the network, and then set up the appropriate privileges (described next).

To *remove* someone from this list, of course, just click the name and then click the **–** button.

- **Users.** This *third* column lets you specify how much access each person in the *second* column has to this folder. Your choices, once again, are **Read & Write** (full access to change or delete this item's contents); **Read Only** (open or copy, but can't edit or delete); and **Write Only** (**Drop Box**), which lets the person put things *into* this disk or folder, but not open it or see what else is in it.

  For the Everyone group, you also get an option called **No Access,** which means that this item is completely off-limits to everyone else on the network.

And now, having slogged through all these options and permutations, your Mac is ready for invasion from across the network.

Accessing Shared Files

So far in this chapter, you've read about *setting up* a Mac so people at other computers can access its files.

Now comes the payoff: sitting at another computer and *connecting* to the one you set up. There are two ways to go about it: You can use the Sidebar, or you can use the older, more flexible Connect to Server command. The following pages cover both methods.

Connection Method A: Use the Sidebar

Suppose, then, that you're seated in front of your Mac, and you want to see the files on another Mac on the network. Proceed like this:

1. **Open any Finder window.**

   In the Shared category of the Sidebar at the left side of the window, icons for all the computers on the network appear. See Figure 13-7.

Tip: The same Sidebar items show up in the Save and Open dialog boxes of your programs, too, making the entire network available to you for opening and saving files.

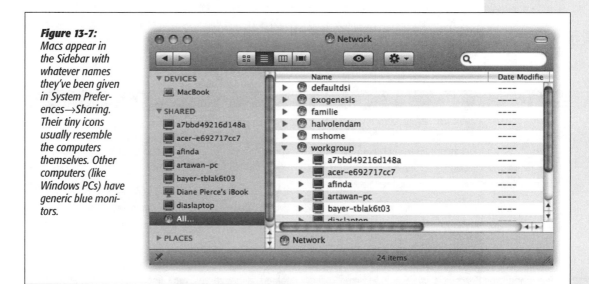

Figure 13-7:
Macs appear in the Sidebar with whatever names they've been given in System Preferences→Sharing. Their tiny icons usually resemble the computers themselves. Other computers (like Windows PCs) have generic blue monitors.

If you *don't* see a certain Mac's icon here, it might be turned off, it might not be on the network, or it might have File Sharing turned off. (And if you don't see any computers at all in the Sidebar, then *your* computer might not be on the network. Or maybe you've turned off the checkboxes for "Connected Servers" and "Bonjour Computers" in Finder→Preferences→Sidebar.)

Snow Leopard Spots: If the other Mac is just asleep, though, it still shows up in the Sidebar, and you can wake it up to get at it. How is that possible? Through the miracle of the new Wake for Network Access feature described on page 335.

If there are a lot of computer icons in the Sidebar, or if you're on a corporate-style network that has sub-chunks like *nodes* or *workgroups*, you may also see an icon called All. Click it to see the full list of network entities that your Mac can see: not just individual Mac, Windows, and Unix machines, but also any "network neighborhoods" (limbs of your network tree). For example, you may see the names of network zones (clusters of machines, as found in big companies and universities).

Or, if you're trying to tap into a Windows machine, open the icon representing the *workgroup* (computer cluster) that contains the machine you want. In small office networks, it's usually called MSHOME or WORKGROUP. In big corporations, these workgroups can be called almost anything—as long as it's no more than 12 letters long with no punctuation. (Thanks, Microsoft.)

If you *do* see icons for workgroups or other network "zones," double-click until you're seeing the icons for individual computers.

Note: If you're a network nerd, you may be interested to note that Mac OS X can "see" servers that use the SMB/CIFS, NFS, FTP, and WebDAV protocols running on Mac OS X Server, AppleShare, Unix, Linux, Novell NetWare, Windows NT, Windows 2000, Windows XP, and Windows Vista servers. But the Sidebar reveals only the shared computers on your subnet (your local, internal office network). (It also shows Back to My Mac if it's set up; see page 543.)

POWER USERS' CLINIC

What You Can See

Precisely which other folders you can see on the remote Mac depend on what kind of account you have there: *Guest, Standard,* or *Administrator.* (See the previous chapter.)

If you're using the Guest account, you can see only the Public and Drop Box folders. The rest of the Mac is invisible and off limits to you.

If you have a Standard account, you can see other people's Public and Drop Box folders, *plus* your own Home folder.

(Of course, those are just the factory settings; somebody could have turned on sharing for additional folders.)

If you're an administrator, you get to see icons for the account-holder folders *and* the hard drive itself to which

you're connecting. In fact, you even get to see the names of any other disks connected to that Mac.

If you, O lucky administrator, open the hard drive, you'll discover that you also have the freedom to see and manipulate the contents of the Applications, Desktop, Library, and Users→Shared folders.

You can even see what folders are in other users' Home folders, although you can't open them or put anything into them.

Finally, as described in the previous chapter, there's the *root user.* This account has complete freedom to move or delete *any file or folder anywhere,* including critical system files that could disable your Mac. Page 655 has the details.

---

2. Click the computer whose files you want to open.

In the main window, you now see the icons for each account holder on that computer: Mom, Dad, Sissy, whatever. If you have an account on the other computer, you'll see a folder representing *your* stuff, too (Figure 13-8).

At this point, the remaining instructions diverge, depending on whether you want to access *other* people's stuff or *your* stuff. That's why there are two alternative versions of step 3 here:

Figure 13-8:
Without requiring any name or password on the other Mac, you have full access to anything the other account holders have left in their Public folders. (There's a Public folder in everyone's Home folder.) Right now, you're considered a Guest.

3a. If you want to access the stuff that somebody else has left for you, double-click that person's Public folder.

Instantly, the icon for that folder appears on your desktop, and an Eject button (⏏) appears beside the computer's name in the Sidebar.

In this situation, you're only a Guest. You don't have to bother with a password. On the other hand, the only thing you can generally see inside the other person's account folder is his Public folder.

Tip: Actually, you might see other folders here—if the account holder has specifically shared them and decided that you're important enough to have access to them, as described on page 516.

One thing you'll find inside the Public folder is the Drop Box folder. This folder exists so that you can *give* files and folders to the other person. You can drop any of your own icons onto the Drop Box folder—but you can't open the Drop Box folder to see what *other* people have put there. It's one-way, like a mail slot in somebody's front door.

If you see anything else at all in the Public folder you've opened, then it's stuff the account holder has copied there for the enjoyment of you and your network mates. You're not allowed to delete anything from the other person's Public folder or make changes to anything in it.

You can, however, open those icons, read them, or even copy them to *your* Mac—and then edit *your* copies.

3b. To access your own Home folder on the other Mac, click it, and then click the Connect As button (Figure 13-9). Sign in as usual.

When the "Connect to the file server" box appears, you're supposed to specify your account name and password (from the Mac you're tapping into). This is the same name and password you'd use to log in if you were actually sitting at that machine.

Type your short user name and password. (If you're not sure what your short user name is, open System Preferences on your home-base Mac, click Accounts, and then click your account name.) And if you didn't set up a password for your account, leave the password box empty.

Tip: The dialog box shown in Figure 13-9 includes the delightful and timesaving "Remember this password in my keychain" option, which makes the Mac memorize your password for a certain disk so you don't have to type it—or even see this dialog box—every darned time you connect. (If you have no password, though, the "Remember password" doesn't work, and you'll have to confront—and press Return to dismiss—the "Connect to the file server" box every time.)

Figure 13-9:
Top: You can sign in to your account on another Mac on the network (even while somebody else is actually using that Mac in person). Click Connect As (top right), and then enter your name and password. Turn on "Remember this password" to speed up the process for next time.

The Action (✿) pop-up menu offers a Change Password command that gives you the opportunity to change your account password on the other machine, just in case you suspect someone saw what you typed.

Bottom: No matter which method you use to connect to a shared folder or disk, its icon shows up in the Sidebar. It's easy to disconnect, thanks to the little ⏏ button.

When you click Connect (or press Return or Enter), your own Home folder on the other Mac appears. Its icon shows up on your desktop, and a little ▲ button appears next to its name. Click it to disconnect.

Tip: Once you've connected to a Mac using your account, the other Mac has a lock on your identity. You'll be able to connect to the other Mac over and over again during this same computing session, without ever having to retype your password.

In the meantime, you can double-click icons to open them, make copies of them, and otherwise manipulate them exactly as though they were icons on your own hard drive. Depending on what permissions you've been given, you can even edit or trash those files.

Tip: There's one significant difference between working with "local" icons and working with those that sit elsewhere on the network. When you delete a file from another Mac on the network, either by pressing the Delete key or by dragging it to the Trash, a message appears to let you know that you're about to delete that item instantly and permanently. It won't simply land in the Trash "folder," awaiting the Empty Trash command.

You can even use Spotlight to find files on that networked disk. If the Mac across the network is running Leopard or Snow Leopard, in fact, you can search for words *inside* its files, just as though you were sitting in front of it. If not, you can still search for text in files' names.

Connection Method B: Connect to Server

The Sidebar method of connecting to networked folders and disks is practically effortless. It involves nothing more than clicking your way through folders—a skill that, in theory, you already know.

GEM IN THE ROUGH

Faster Ways to Connect Next Time

If you expect that you might want to access a shared disk or folder again later, take a moment to make an alias of it. (For example, Control-click it and choose Make Alias from the shortcut menu.)

Next time, you can bring it back to your screen later just by double-clicking the alias. And if you turned on "Remember this password in my keychain," you won't even be asked for your name and password again.

Similarly, if you drag a shared folder into the Dock, you can bring it back to your screen later just by clicking its icon.

You can even drag its icon into the Login Items window described on page 471. Now the disk appears on your desktop *automatically* each time you log in—the most effortless arrangement of all.

But the Sidebar method has its drawbacks. For example, the Sidebar doesn't let you type in a disk's network address. As a result, you can't access any shared disk *on the Internet* (an FTP site, for example), or indeed anywhere beyond your local subnet (your own small network).

Fortunately, there's another way. When you choose Go→Connect to Server, you get the dialog box shown in Figure 13-10. You're supposed to type in the *address* of the shared disk you want.

Figure 13-10:
The Sidebar method of connecting to shared disks and folders is quick and easy, but it doesn't let you connect to certain kinds of disks. The Connect to Server method entails plodding through several dialog boxes and doesn't let you browse for shared disks, but it can find just about every kind of networked disk.

For example, from here you can connect to:

- **Everyday Macs on your network.** If you know the IP address of the Mac you're trying to access (you geek!), you can type nothing but its IP address into the box and then hit Connect.

  And if the other Mac runs Mac OS X 10.2 or later, you can just type its Bonjour (formerly Rendezvous) name: *afp://upstairs-PowerMac.local/*.

Tip: To find out your Mac's IP address, open the Network pane of System Preferences. There, near the top, you'll see a message like this: "AirPort is connected to Tim's Hotspot and has the IP address 192.168.1.113." That's your IP address.

To see your Bonjour address, open the Sharing pane of System Preferences. Click File Sharing. Near the top, you'll see the computer name with ".local" tacked onto its name—and hyphens instead of spaces—like this: Little-MacBook.local.

After you enter your account password and choose the shared disk or folder you want, its icon appears on your desktop and in the Sidebar. You're connected exactly as though you had clicked Connect As (Figure 13-9).

The next time you open the Connect to Server dialog box, Mac OS X remembers that address, as a courtesy to you, and shows it pre-entered in the Address field.

- **Macs across the Internet.** If your Mac has a permanent (static) IP address, the computer itself can be a server, to which you can connect from anywhere in the world via the Internet. Details on this procedure begin on page 802.

- **Windows machines.** Find out the PC's IP address or computer name, and then use this format for the address: *smb://192.168.1.34* or *smb://Cheapo-Dell.*

  After a moment, you're asked to enter your Windows account name and password, and then to choose the name of the shared folder you want. When you click OK, the shared folder appears on your desktop as an icon, ready to use. (More on sharing with Windows PCs later in this chapter.)

Tip: If you know the name of the shared folder, you can add that after a slash, like this: smb://192.168.4.23/ sharedstuff. You save yourself one dialog box.

- **NFS servers.** If you're on a network with Unix machines, you can tap into one of their shared directories using this address format: *nfs://Machine-Name/pathname,* where *Machine-Name* is the computer's name or IP address, and *pathname* is the folder path (page 23) to the shared item you want.

- **FTP servers.** Mac OS X makes it simple to bring *FTP servers* onto your screen, too. (These are the drives, out there on the Internet, that store the files used by Web sites.)

  In the Connect to Server dialog box, type the FTP address of the server you want, like this: *ftp://www.apple.com.* If the site's administrators have permitted *anonymous* access—the equivalent of a Guest account—that's all there is to it. A Finder window pops open, revealing the FTP site's contents.

  If you need a password for the FTP site, however, what you type into the Connect to Server dialog box should incorporate the account name you've been given, like this: *ftp://yourname@www.apple.com.* You'll be asked for your password.

Tip: You can even eliminate that password-dialog box step by using this address format: *ftp:// yourname:yourpassword@www.apple.com.*

Once you type it and press Return, the FTP server appears as a disk icon on your desktop (and in the Sidebar). Its contents appear, too, ready to open or copy.

- **WebDAV server.** This special Web-based shared disk requires a special address format, like this: *http://Computer-Name/pathname.* (Technically, the iDisk is a WebDAV server—but there are far user-friendlier ways to get at it.)

  In each case, once you click OK, you may be asked for your name and password.

And now, some timesaving features in the Connect to Server box:

- Once you've typed a disk's address, you can click **+** to add it to the list of server favorites. The next time you want to connect, you can just double-click its name.

- The clock-icon pop-up menu lists Recent Servers—computers you've accessed recently over the network. If you choose one of them from this pop-up menu, you can skip having to type in an address.

Tip: Like the Sidebar network-browsing method, the Connect to Server command displays each connected computer as an icon in your Sidebar, even within the Open or Save dialog boxes of your programs. You don't have to burrow through the Sidebar's Network icon to open files from them, or save files onto them.

Disconnecting Yourself

When you're finished using a shared disk or folder, you can disconnect from it by clicking the ⏏ icon next to its name in the Sidebar.

GEM IN THE ROUGH

Hello, Bonjour

Throughout this chapter, and throughout this book, you'll encounter rituals in which you're supposed to connect to another Mac, server, or printer by typing in its *IP address* (its unique network address).

But first of all, IP addresses are insanely difficult to memorize (192.179.244.3, anyone?). Second, networks shouldn't require you to deal with them anyway. If a piece of equipment is on the network, it should *announce* its presence, rather than making you specifically *call* for it by name.

Now you can appreciate the beauty of *Bonjour* (formerly Rendezvous), an underlying Mac OS X networking technology that lets networked gadgets detect one another on the network *automatically* and recognize one another's capabilities.

It's Bonjour at work, for example, that makes other Macs' names show up in your iTunes program so you can listen to their music from across the network. Bonjour is also responsible for filling up your Bonjour buddy list in iChat automatically, listing everyone who's on the same office network; for making shared Macs' names show up in the Sidebar's Network icon; and for making the names of modern laser printers from HP, Epson, or Lexmark appear like magic in the list of printers in the Print dialog box.

And if you're lucky enough to have (a) a TiVo Series 2 (or later) video recorder for your television, (b) a home network that connects it with your Mac, and (c) TiVo's Home Networking Option, then you already know that your Mac's name magically appears on the TiVo screen. This allows you to play your iTunes music, or put on a slide show of your iPhoto pictures, right on the TV. Once again, it's Bonjour at work.

It's even more tantalizing to contemplate the future of Bonjour. To quote *www.zeroconf.org,* whose underlying technology forms the basis of Bonjour:

"The long-term goal of Zeroconf is to enable the creation of entirely new kinds of networked products, products that today would simply not be commercially viable because of the inconvenience and support costs involved in setting up, configuring, and maintaining a network to allow them to operate."

But that's just the beginning. If electronics companies show interest (and some have already), you may someday be able to connect the TV, stereo, and DVD player with just a couple of Ethernet cables, instead of a rat's nest of audio and video cables.

For most of us, that day can't come soon enough.

Disconnecting Others

In Mac OS X, you really have to work if you want to know whether other people on the network are accessing *your* Mac. You have to choose System Preferences→Sharing→File Sharing→Options. There you'll see something like, "Number of users connected: 1."

Maybe that's because there's nothing to worry about. You certainly have nothing to fear from a security standpoint, since you control what they can see on your Mac. Nor will you experience much computer slowdown as you work, thanks to Mac OS X's prodigious multitasking features.

Still, if you're feeling particularly antisocial, you can slam shut the door to your Mac. Just open System Preferences→Sharing and turn off File Sharing.

If anybody is, in fact, connected to your Mac at the time (*from* a Mac), you see the dialog box in Figure 13-11. If not, your Mac instantly becomes an island once again.

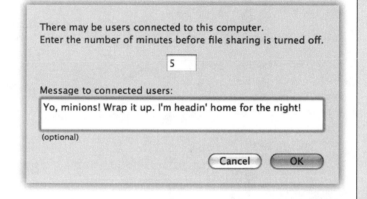

Figure 13-11:
This dialog box asks you how much notice you want to give your coworkers that they're about to be disconnected, and what message to send them before the ax falls.

There may be users connected to this computer.
Enter the number of minutes before file sharing is turned off.

5

Message to connected users:

Yo, minions! Wrap it up. I'm headin' home for the night!

(optional)

Cancel   OK

Networking with Windows

Microsoft Windows may dominate the corporate market, but there *are* Macs in the offices of America —and there *are* PCs in homes. Fortunately, Macs and Windows PCs can see each other on the network, with no special software (or talent) required.

In fact, you can go in either direction. Your Mac can see shared folders on the Windows PC, and a Windows PC can see shared folders on your Mac.

It goes like this.

Seated at the Mac, Seeing the PC

Suppose you have a Windows PC and a Mac on the same wired or wireless network. Here's how you get the Mac and PC chatting:

1. **On your Windows PC, share some files.**

   This isn't really a book about Windows networking (thank heaven), but here are the basics.

   Just as on the Mac, there are two ways to share files in Windows. One of them is super-simple: You just copy the files you want to share into a central, fully accessible folder. No passwords, accounts, or other steps are required.

TROUBLESHOOTING MOMENT

Windows 7 Hell

In Windows 7, Microsoft gutted the networking software and replaced it with something it considers better. Unfortunately, it's also incompatible with Mac file sharing.

You can fix it, though.

First, make sure you've shared everything you want to share on the Windows 7 machine. For example, suppose you want to share your entire Personal folder (the equivalent of the Mac's Home folder).

To do that, choose Start→ [your name]. In the window that opens, choose "Share with"→"Specific people." In the resulting dialog box, you'll see that *you* are already permitted to access this folder, as shown here; unless you want to add someone else, just click Share, then Done.

Now, on the Mac, in the Finder, choose Go→Connect to Server. Type *smb://SuperDell,* or whatever your PC's name is. (And how do you find *that* out? Open the Start menu; right-click Computer; from the shortcut menu, choose Properties. You'll see the Computer Name in the middle of the dialog box.)

On the Mac, after typing the PC's name, click Connect. After a moment, you're asked for your account name and password, as it appears on the *PC.* Enter these credentials—turn on "Remember my password" if you want to be spared this rigamarole the next time—and then click Connect.

Now you're shown a list of disks and folders you shared on the Windows PC. Double-click the one you want. Presto: It appears in a Finder window, ready to access!

(If you discover you can copy stuff *out* of these folders but can't put stuff *into* them, it's because you didn't turn on Full Control for yourself, as described above.)

Finally, for heaven's sake, make an alias of the Windows folder or disk on the Mac so you can just double-click to open it the next time!

In **Windows XP,** that special folder is the Shared Documents folder, which you can find by choosing Start→My Computer. Share it on the network as shown in Figure 13-12, top.

In **Windows Vista,** it's the Public folder, which appears in the Navigation pane of every Explorer window. (In Vista, there's one Public folder for the whole *computer,* not one per account holder.)

In **Windows 7,** there's a Public folder in each of your libraries. That is, there's a Public Documents, Public Pictures, Public Music, and so on.

Figure 13-12:
Top: To share a folder in Windows, right-click it, choose Properties, and then turn on "Share this folder on the network." In the "Share name" box, type a name for the folder as it will appear on the network. (No spaces are allowed).

Bottom: Back in the safety of Mac OS X, click the PC's name in the Sidebar. (If it's part of a workgroup, click All, and then your workgroup name first. And if you still don't see the PC's name, see the box on the next page.)

Next, click the name of the shared computer. If the files you need are in a Shared Documents or Public folder, no password is required. You see the contents of the PC's Shared Documents folder or Public folder, as shown here. Now it's just like file sharing with another Mac.

If you want access to any other shared folder, click Connect As, and see Figure 13-13.

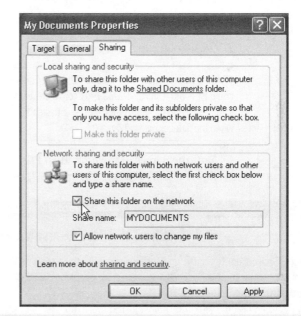

The second, more complicated method is the "share any folder" method, just as in Leopard. In XP or Vista, you right-click the folder you want to share, choose Properties from the shortcut menu, click the Sharing tab, and turn on "Share this folder on the network" (Figure 13-12, top). In Windows 7, use the Share With menu at the top of any folder's window. See the box on page 530 for more details.

Repeat for any other folders you want to make available to your Mac.

2. On the Mac, open any Finder window.

The shared PCs may appear as individual computer names in the Sidebar, or you may have to click the All icon to see the icons of their *workgroups* (network clusters—an effect shown on page 521). Unless you or a network administrator changed it, the workgroup name is probably MSHOME or WORKGROUP. Double-click the workgroup name you want.

Tip: You can also access the shared PC via the Connect to Server command, as described on page 525. You could type into it *smb://192.168.1.103* (or whatever the PC's IP address is) or *smb://SuperDell* (or whatever its name is) and hit Return—and then skip to step 5. In fact, using the Connect to Server method often works when the Sidebar method doesn't.

Now the names of the individual PCs on the network appear in your Finder window. (If you're running Windows 7, see the box on page 536.)

TROUBLESHOOTING MOMENT

When the Mac Doesn't See the PC

If your PC's icon doesn't show up on the Mac at all, it's probably because the Mac doesn't know anything about Windows *workgroups.* And even a lowly home PC is part of a workgroup (a corporate cluster), whether it knows it or not. And until your Mac is part of that very tiny club, it won't be able to see your PCs, and they won't be able to see it.

So if you're having no luck with this whole Mac-PC thing, try this. First, find out what your PC thinks its workgroup is. It's usually either WORKGROUP or MSHOME. Click Start. Right-click the word Computer; from the shortcut menu, choose Properties. In the resulting info screen, you'll see the workgroup's name.

Now, on the Mac, open System Preferences. Click Network. Click the connection you're using (like AirPort or Ethernet). Click Advanced. Click WINS.

Now you see the peculiar controls shown here. Type the workgroup name into the box (if indeed it's not already a choice in the Workgroup pop-up menu). Click OK, and then click Apply.

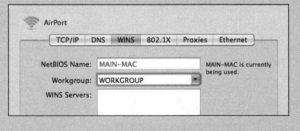

Now your Windows PC shows up in the Sidebar, like magic.

Still having trouble? Open System Preferences→Security→Firewall. Make sure your Mac's firewall is either turned off or at least not set to "Block all incoming connections."

---

3. **Double-click the name of the computer you want.**

If you're using one of the simple file-sharing methods on the PC, as described above, that's all there is to it. The contents of the Shared Documents or Public folder now appear on your Mac screen. You can work with them just as you would your own files.

If you're not using one of those simple methods, and you want access to individual shared folders, read on.

Note: In Windows XP Pro, the next step won't work unless you turn off Simple File Sharing. To do that, choose Tools→Folder Options in any Explorer window. Click the View tab and turn off "Use simple file sharing."

---

4. **Click Connect As.**

This button appears in the top-right corner of the Finder window; you can see it at bottom in Figure 13-12.

Now you're asked for your name and password (Figure 13-13, top).

Figure 13-13:
Top: The PC wants to make sure you're authorized to visit it. If the terminology here seems a bit geeky by Apple standards, no wonder–this is Microsoft Windows' lingo you're seeing, not Apple's. Fortunately, you see this box only the very first time you access a certain Windows folder or disk; after that, you see only the box shown below.

Bottom: Here, you see a list of shared folders on the PC. Choose the one you want to connect to, and then click OK. Like magic, the Windows folder shows up on your Mac screen, ready to use!

5. Enter the name and password for your account on the PC, and then click OK.

At long last, the contents of the shared folder on the Windows machine appear in your Finder window, just as though you'd tapped into another Mac (Figure 13-13, bottom). The icon of the shared folder appears on your desktop, too, and an Eject button (⏏) appears next to the PC's name in your Sidebar.

From here, it's a simple matter to drag files between the machines, open Word documents on the PC using Word for the Mac, and so on—exactly like you're hooked into another Mac.

Seated at the PC, Seeing the Mac

Cross-platformers, rejoice: Mac OS X lets you share files in *both directions.* Not only can your Mac see other PCs on the network, but they can see the Mac, too.

On the Mac, open →System Preferences→Sharing. Click File Sharing (make sure File Sharing is turned on), and then click Options to open the dialog box shown in Figure 13-14.

Turn on "Share files and folders using SMB (Windows)." Below that checkbox, you see a list of all the accounts on your Mac. Turn on the checkboxes to specify *which* Mac user accounts you want to be able to access. You must type in each person's password, too. Click Done.

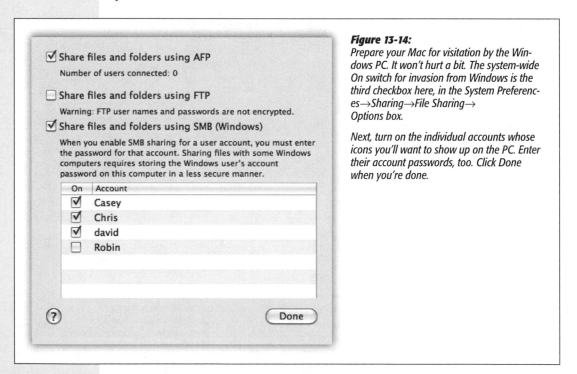

Figure 13-14:
Prepare your Mac for visitation by the Windows PC. It won't hurt a bit. The system-wide On switch for invasion from Windows is the third checkbox here, in the System Preferences→Sharing→File Sharing→ Options box.

Next, turn on the individual accounts whose icons you'll want to show up on the PC. Enter their account passwords, too. Click Done when you're done.

Before you close System Preferences, study the line near the middle of the window, where it says something like: "Other users can access your computer at afp://192.168.1.108 or MacBook-Pro." You'll need one of these addresses shortly.

Now, on **Windows XP,** open My Network Places; in **Windows Vista,** choose Start→ Network; in **Windows 7,** expand the Network heading in the sidebar of any desktop window. If you've sacrificed the proper animals to the networking gods, your Mac's icon should appear by itself in the network window, as shown in Figure 13-15, top.

Note: If you don't see your Mac here, proceed immediately to the boxes on pages 532 and 536.

Double-click the Mac's icon. Public-folder stuff is available immediately. Otherwise, you have to sign in with your Mac account name and password; Figure 13-15, middle, has the details.

Figure 13-15:
Top: Double-click the icon of the Mac you want to visit from your Windows machine (Vista is shown here).

Middle: Type your Mac's name in all capitals (or its IP address), then a backslash, and then your Mac account short name. (You can find out your Mac's name on the Sharing pane of System Preferences.)

Enter your Mac account's password, too. Turn on "Remember my password" if you plan to do this again someday. Click OK.

Bottom: Here's your Mac Home folder—in Windows! Open it up to find all your stuff.

In the final window, you see your actual Home folder—on a Windows PC! You're ready to open its files, copy them back and forth, or whatever (Figure 13-15, bottom).

If your Mac's icon *doesn't* appear, and you've read the box on page 532, wait a minute or two. Try restarting the PC. In Windows XP, try clicking "Microsoft Windows Network" or "View workgroup computers" in the task pane.

If your Mac still doesn't show up, you'll have to add it the hard way. In the address bar of any Windows window, type *macbook-pro\chris* (but substitute your Mac's actual computer name and your short account name), taking care to use backslashes, not normal / slashes. You can also type your Mac's IP address in place of its computer name.

In the future, you won't have to do so much burrowing; your Mac's icon should appear automatically in the My Network Places or Network window.

More Mac-Windows Connections

The direct Mac-to-Windows file-sharing feature of Mac OS X is by far the easiest way to access each other's files. But it's not the only way. Page 244 offers a long list of other options, from flash drives to the iDisk.

Screen Sharing

The prayers of baffled beginners and exasperated experts everywhere have now been answered. Now, when the novice needs help from the guru, the guru doesn't have to run all the way downstairs or down the hall to assist. Thanks to Snow Leopard's

---

TROUBLESHOOTING MOMENT

When Windows 7 Can't See the Mac

If you're sitting at your PC and you want to bring the Mac onto your screen, things generally don't go quite as smoothly as they did with Windows XP or Vista. Windows 7 uses a different security method, which the Mac doesn't know about.

You can solve the problem, though, if you slog through an ugly but one-time procedure. It involves making some tweaky, geeky settings in a corner of Windows most people never see.

Click Start→Control Panel. Change the view to Small Icons; double-click Administrative Tools→Local Security Policy.

In the list at left, expand the Local Policies "folder"; click Security Options. In the list at right, hunt down the line called "Network security: LAN Manager authentication level." Double-click it. In the resulting dialog box, change the pop-up menu to say "Send LM & NTLM - use NTLMv2 session if negotiated." (It's not necessary to understand what the hell Microsoft is talking about. Just do it.)

Click OK.

Now, in the same list, find and double-click "Network security: Minimum session security for NTLM SSP Based (including secure RPC) Clients." Turn off "Require 128-bit encryption," and then click OK.

Restart the PC. When it comes to, your Mac's icon shows up in the Sidebar of any desktop window on the PC. Click it to see what's in it.

---

screen-sharing feature, you can see exactly what's on the screen of another Mac, from across the network—and even seize control of the other Mac's mouse and keyboard (with the newbie's permission, of course).

(Anyone who's ever tried to help someone troubleshoot over the phone knows *exactly* what this means. If you haven't, this small example may suffice: "OK, open the Apple menu and choose 'About This Mac.' " Pause. "What's the Apple menu?")

Nor is playing Bail-Out-the-Newbie the only situation when screen sharing is useful. It's also great for collaborating on a document, showing something to someone for approval, or just freaking each other out. It can also be handy when *you* are the owner of both Macs (a laptop and a desktop, for example), and you want to run a program that you don't have on the Mac that's in front of you. For example, you might want to adjust the playlist selection on the upstairs Mac that's connected to your sound system.

Or maybe you just want to keep an eye on what your kids are doing on the Macs upstairs in their rooms.

The controlling person can do *everything* on the controlled Mac, including running programs, messing around with the folders and files, and even shutting it down.

Snow Leopard Spots: In fact, screen sharing has been enhanced in one especially juicy way in Mac OS X 10.6: Now you can press keystrokes on your Mac—⌘-Tab, ⌘-space, ⌘-Option-Escape, and so on—to trigger the corresponding functions on the other Mac. (In Mac OS X 10.5, your own Mac intercepted these keystrokes.)

If you want a keystroke to affect your own Mac, first click your own Desktop, or click into a different window on your own Mac.

Mac OS X is crawling with different ways to use screen sharing. You can do it over a network, over the Internet, and even during an iChat chat.

Truth is, the iChat method, described in Chapter 21, is much simpler and better than the small-network method described here. It doesn't require names or passwords, it's easy to flip back between seeing the other guy's screen and your own, and you can transfer files by dragging them from your screen to the other guy's (or vice versa).

Then again, the small-network method described here is built right into the Finder, doesn't require logging into iChat, and doesn't require Leopard or Snow Leopard running on both computers.

Mac #1: Give Permission in Advance

As always, trying to understand meta concepts like seeing one Mac's screen on the monitor of another can get confusing fast. So in this example, suppose that you want to take control of Mac #1 while seated at Mac #2.

Now, it would be a chaotic world (although greatly entertaining) if any Mac could randomly take control of any other Mac. Fortunately, though, nobody can share your screen or take control of your Mac without your explicit permission.

To give such permission, choose →System Preferences→Sharing, and then turn on Screen Sharing.

Note: If a message appears to the effect that "Screen Sharing is currently being controlled by the Remote Management service," turn off the Remote Management checkbox and then try again.

At this point, there are three levels of security to protect your Mac against unauthorized remote-control mischief:

- **Secure.** If you select All Users, *anyone with an account on your Mac* will be able to tap in and take control any time they like, even when you're not around. They'll just have to enter the same name and password they'd use if they were sitting in front of your machine.

  If "anyone" means "you and your spouse" or "you and the other two fourth-grade teachers," then that's probably perfectly fine.

- **Securer.** For greater security, though, you can limit who's allowed to stop in. Click "Only these users" and then click the **+** sign. A small panel appears, listing everyone with an account on your Mac. Choose the ones you trust not to mess things up while you're away from your Mac (Figure 13-16).

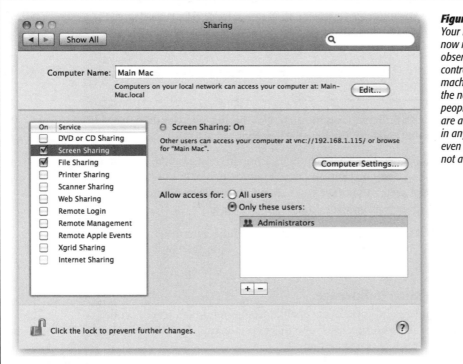

Figure 13-16:
Your Mac is now ready to be observed and even controlled by other machines across the network. The people listed here are allowed to tap in anytime they like, even when you're not at your machine.

- **Securest.** If you click "Only these users" and then don't add *anyone* to the list, then only people who have Administrator accounts on your Mac (page 464) can tap into your screen.

Alternatively, if you're only a *little* bit of a Scrooge, you can set things up so that they can request permission to share your screen—as long as you're sitting in front of your Mac at the time and feeling generous.

To set this up, click Computer Settings and then turn on "Anyone may request permission to share screen." Now your fans will have to request permission to enter, and you'll have to grant it (by clicking OK on the screen), in real time, while you're there to watch what they're doing.

Mac #2: Take Control

All right, Mac #1 has been prepared for invasion. Now suppose you're the person on the other end. You're the guru, or the parent, or whoever wants to take control.

Sit at Mac #2 elsewhere on your home or office network. Open a Finder window. Expand the Sharing list in the Sidebar, if necessary, so that you see the icon of Mac #1.

When you click that Mac's icon, the dark strip at the top of the main window displays a button that wasn't there before: Share Screen. Proceed as shown in Figure 13-17.

Tip: In theory, you can also connect from across the Internet, assuming you left your Mac at home turned on and connected to a broadband modem, and assuming you've worked through the port-forwarding issue described on page 796.

In this case, though, you'd begin by choosing Go→Connect to Server in the Finder; in the Connect to Server box, type in *vnc://123.456.78.90* (or whatever your home Mac's public IP address is). The rest of the steps are the same.

If you've signed in successfully, or if permission is granted, then a weird and wonderful sight appears. As shown in Figure 13-18, your screen now fills with a *second* screen—from the other Mac. You have full keyboard and mouse control to work with that other machine exactly as though you were sitting in front of it.

Well, maybe not *exactly.* There are a few caveats.

- **Mismatched screen sizes.** If the other screen is *smaller* than yours, no big deal. It floats at actual size on your monitor, with room to spare. But if it's the same size as yours or larger, then the other Mac's screen gets shrunken down to fit in a window.

  If you'd prefer to see it at actual size, choose View→Turn Scaling Off. Of course, now you have to *scroll* in the Screen Sharing window to see the whole image.

Tip: Another way to turn scaling on and off is to click the first button on the Screen Sharing toolbar (Figure 13-18).

CHAPTER 13: NETWORKING, FILE SHARING, & SCREEN SHARING

• **The speed-vs.-blurriness issue.** Remember, you're asking the other Mac to pump its video display across the network—and that takes time. Entire milliseconds of time, in fact.

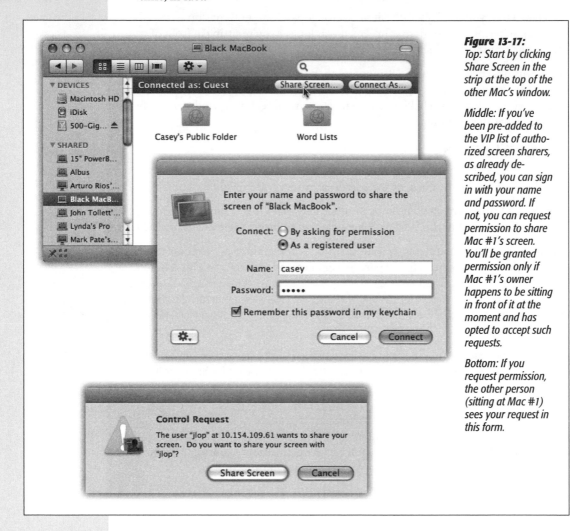

Figure 13-17:
Top: Start by clicking Share Screen in the strip at the top of the other Mac's window.

Middle: If you've been pre-added to the VIP list of authorized screen sharers, as already described, you can sign in with your name and password. If not, you can request permission to share Mac #1's screen. You'll be granted permission only if Mac #1's owner happens to be sitting in front of it at the moment and has opted to accept such requests.

Bottom: If you request permission, the other person (sitting at Mac #1) sees your request in this form.

So ordinarily, the Mac uses something called *adaptive quality,* which just means that the screen gets blurry when you scroll, quit a program, or do anything else that creates a sudden change in the picture. You can turn off this feature by choosing View→Full Quality. Now you get full sharpness all the time—but things take longer to scroll, appear, and disappear.

• **Manage the Clipboard.** Believe it or not, you can actually *copy and paste* material from the remote-controlled Mac to your own—or the other way—thanks to a freaky little wormhole in the time-space continuum.

Just make the Screen Sharing toolbar visible (you can see it in Figure 13-18). Click the *second* button on it to copy the faraway Mac's Clipboard contents onto *your* Clipboard. Or click the *third* button to put what's on *your* Clipboard onto the *other* Mac's Clipboard. Breathe slowly and drink plenty of fluids, and your brain won't explode.

Note: Unfortunately, there's no way to transfer files while screen sharing—only material you've copied out of documents. Use the iChat method described in Chapter 21 if you want to exchange files.

Figure 13-18:
Don't be alarmed. You're looking at the other Mac's desktop in a window on your Mac desktop. You have keyboard and mouse control, and so does the other guy (if he's there); when you're really bored, you can play King of the Cursor. (Note the Screen Sharing toolbar, which has been made visible by choosing View→Show Toolbar.)

• **Quitting.** When you hit the ⌘-Q keystroke, you *don't* quit Screen Sharing; you quit whatever program is *running* on the other Mac! So when you're finished having your way with the other computer, choose Screen Sharing→Quit Screen Sharing to return to your own desktop (and your own sanity).

Variations on Screen Sharing

The steps above guide you through screen sharing between two Leopard or Snow Leopard Macs. But screen-sharing is based on a standard technology called VNC, and Mac OS X is bristling with different permutations.

Screen sharing through iChat

Two people who both have Mac OS X 10.5 or later can perform exactly the same screen-sharing stunt *over the Internet*. No accounts, passwords, or setup are required—only the granting of permission by the other guy. Just initiate an iChat chat, and then proceed as described on page 789. It's really awesome.

Screen sharing with a pre-Leopard Mac

Both Macs don't have to be running Mac OS X 10.5 or 10.6 to use screen sharing. As it turns out, Mac OS X 10.3 and 10.4 are capable of sharing their screens, too—it's just that the on/off switch has a different name. Figure 13-19 has details.

Once you've turned on Apple Remote Desktop on the older Mac, as shown in Figure 13-19, you can sit at your Leopard/Snow Leopard Mac and take control by clicking Share Screen in the Sidebar, exactly as described above.

Note: At this point, the screen sharing is one-way: Your modern Mac can see the older Mac's screen. If you want the older Mac to access your Mac's screen, return to the box shown in Figure 13-19. Turn on "VNC viewers may control screen with password," and make up a password. Now download the free Chicken of the VNC software; it's available from this book's "Missing CD" page at *www.missingmanuals.com*. Use it to access the Snow Leopard Mac; the box on page 544 has more details on this concept.

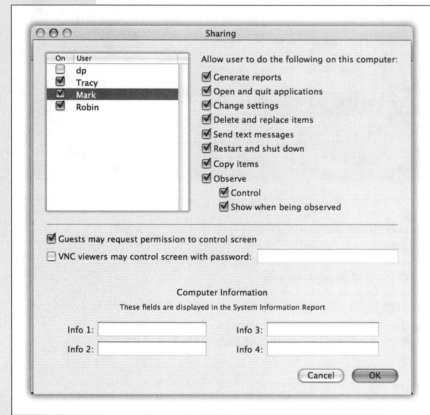

Figure 13-19:
On pre-10.5 Macs, there's no option for Screen Sharing in the Sharing pane of System Preferences. There is one, however, called Apple Remote Desktop—and that's the one that permits screen sharing with 10.5 and 10.6 machines. When you click it, you're offered many of the same options that Snow Leopard offers. More, in fact.

Screen sharing the manual way

Screen Sharing is an actual, double-clickable program, with its own icon on your Mac. (It's in the System→Library→CoreServices folder.) When you double-click it, you can type in the public IP address (page 796) or domain name of the computer you want to connect to, and presto: You're connected!

Screen sharing with Back to My Mac

"Back to My Mac" is intended to simplify the nightmare of remote networking. It works only if:

- You're a MobileMe member.

- You have at least two Macs, both running Leopard or Snow Leopard.

- On each one, you've entered your MobileMe information into the MobileMe pane of System Preferences, and logged in.

Once that's all in place, your Macs behave exactly as though they're on the same home network, even though they can be thousands of miles apart across the network.

To set it up, proceed as shown in Figure 13-20.

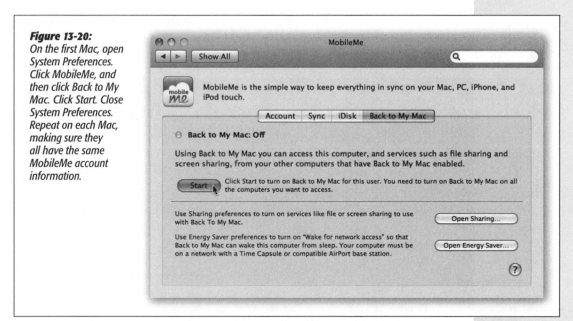

Figure 13-20:
On the first Mac, open System Preferences. Click MobileMe, and then click Back to My Mac. Click Start. Close System Preferences. Repeat on each Mac, making sure they all have the same MobileMe account information.

Now, on each Mac you'll want to "visit" from afar, open the System Preferences→Sharing pane and turn on File Sharing and/or Screen Sharing.

Then, on your laptop in New Zealand, you see an entry for Back to My Mac in the Sharing section of your Sidebar. Click to see the icon of your Mac back at home. At this point, you can connect to it for file sharing by clicking Connect As (page 524), or take control of it by clicking Share Screen (page 539).

In theory, Back to My Mac spares you an awful long visit to networking hell (including the port-forwarding headache described on page 796), because Apple has done all the configuration work for you.

Note: Lots of people can't get Back to My Mac to work. Apple says the problems are related to (a) firewalls, (b) port-forwarding issues, and (c) router incompatibilities. Apple also says you'll have the best luck on networks that involve only an AirPort base station—and not a hardware router.

All the technical details are available online. Go to *http://search.info.apple.com* and do a search for *306672*. (That's the article number that explains the Back to My Mac issues.)

More Dialing In from the Road

If you're one of the several million lucky people who have full-time Internet connections—in other words, cable modem or DSL accounts—a special thrill awaits. You can connect to your Mac from anywhere in the world via the Internet. If you have a laptop, you don't need to worry when you discover you've left a critical file on your desktop Mac at home.

Mac OS X offers several ways to connect to your Mac from a distant location, including file sharing over the Internet, Back to My Mac, virtual private networking, FTP, and SSH (secure shell). Chapter 22 has the details.

GEM IN THE ROUGH

Screen Sharing with Windows and Other Oddball Machines

The beauty of Apple's screen-sharing technology is that it isn't *Apple's* screen-sharing technology. It's a popular, open standard called VNC (Virtual Network Computing).

Once you've turned on Screen Sharing on your Mac, any computer on earth with a free VNC client program—sort of a viewer program—can pop onto your machine for a screen share. VNC clients are available for Windows, Linux, pre-Leopard Macs, and even some cellphones.

To prepare your Mac for invasion, open the Sharing pane of System Preferences. Click Screen Sharing, and then click

Computer Settings. Turn on "VNC viewers may control screen with password," and make up a password. (VNC doesn't know anything about Mac OS X account passwords, so you're making up one password for sharing your *whole* Mac.)

Give that password to the lucky few who have your trust. Let them plug your Mac's public IP address (page 526) into their VNC clients—or let them connect over your office network, using the address displayed on the Screen Sharing pane ("vnc:// MacBook-Pro," for example)—and let the sharing begin.

Printing, Faxing, Fonts, & Graphics

The Macintosh may be only the 8 percent solution in the mainstream business world, but in the graphics and printing industries, it's the 800-pound gorilla. You'd better believe that when Apple designed Mac OS X, it worked very hard to keep its graphics and printing fans happy.

This chapter tackles printing, faxing, fonts, graphics, ColorSync, and PDF files, which Mac OS X uses as an everyday exchange format—one of the biggest perks in Mac OS X.

Mac Meets Printer

One of the most attractive features of Snow Leopard is that it takes up so much less space on your hard drive. Overall, this operating system is *half* the size of the previous version.

As it turns out, though, a substantial chunk of that savings comes from printer drivers. Mac OS X used to come preloaded with the printing software for every conceivable printer model from every conceivable printer company— Epson, HP, Lexmark, Canon, and others, several gigabytes' worth. Clearly, most people wound up with about 900 wads of printing software they'd never use.

When you install Snow Leopard, though, you get *only* the printer drivers for the printers you actually have, or are nearby on the network. If you ever encounter a different printer model later, Mac OS X downloads it for you on the spot.

Note: If you don't have an Internet connection, you can also install all those hundreds of other drivers from the Snow Leopard DVD. Just click Customize on the first screen of the installer, as described in Appendix A.

Setting Up a Printer

Setting up a printer for the first time is incredibly easy. The first time you want to print something, follow this guide:

1. **Connect the printer to the Mac, and then turn the printer on.**

   Inkjet printers connect to your USB jack. Laser printers hook up either to your USB jack or to your network (Ethernet or wireless).

2. **Open the document you want to print. Choose File→Print. In the Print dialog box, choose your printer's name from the Printer pop-up menu (or one of its submenus, if any, like Nearby Printers).**

   Cool! Wasn't that easy? Very nice how the Mac autodiscovers, autoconfigures, and autolists almost any USB, FireWire, Bluetooth, or Bonjour (Rendezvous) printer.

   Have a nice afternoon. The End.

   Oh—unless your printer *isn't* listed in the Printer pop-up menu. In that case, read on.

Note: "Nearby Printers" refers to printers that aren't connected directly to your Mac but are accessible anyway: a printer connected to an Apple Time Capsule or AirPort base station, certain network printers that speak Bonjour (page 528), or printers connected to other Macs that you've shared, as described later in this chapter.

---

3. **From the Printer pop-up menu, choose Add Printer (Figure 14-1, top).**

   A special setup window opens (Figure 14-1, bottom), which is even better at auto-detecting printers available to your Mac. If you see the printer's name here, click it, and then click Add (Figure 14-1, bottom).

   You're all set. Have a good time.

   Unless, of course, your printer *still* isn't showing up. Proceed to step 4.

4. **Click the icon for the kind of printer you have: Default, IP, or Windows.**

   Default usually does the trick, especially if you have an inkjet printer. Choose **IP** if you have a network printer that's not showing up in Default—especially if you have an old AppleTalk printer (see the box on page 548). And choose **Windows** if there's a Windows-only printer out there on your office network.

   After a moment, the names of any printers that are turned on and connected appear in the printer list. For most people, that means only one printer—but one's enough.

5. Click the name of the printer you want to use.

As an optional step, you can open the Print Using pop-up menu at the bottom of the dialog box. Choose "Select a driver to use," and then, in the list that appears, choose your particular printer's model name, if you can find it. That's how your Mac knows what printing features to offer you when the time comes: double-sided, legal size, second paper tray, and so on.

Figure 14-1:
Top: To introduce your Mac to a new printer, try to print something—and then choose Add Printer from this pop-up menu. Bottom: Your Mac should automatically "see" any printers that are hooked up and turned on. Click the one you want, and then click Add.

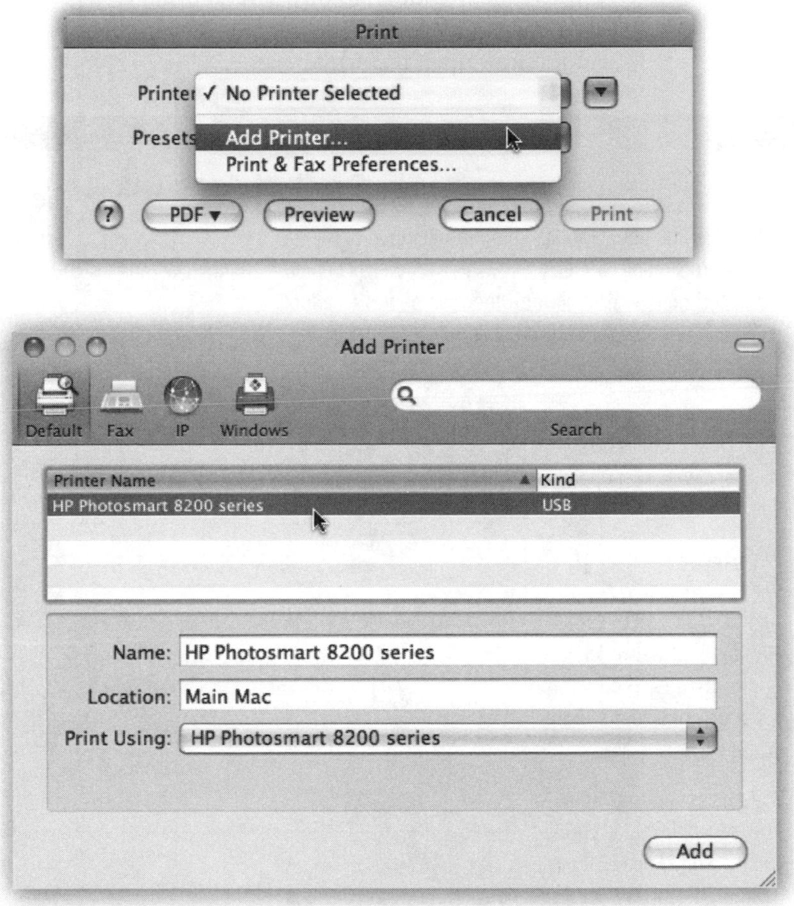

6. Click Add.

After a moment, you return to the main Printer Browser window (Figure 14-1, top), where your printer now appears. You're ready to print.

Note: If you still don't see your printer's name show up, ask yourself: Is my Mac on a corporate network? Does the network have an LPR (Line Printer Remote) printer? If you and your company's network nerd determine that the printer you want to use is, in fact, an LPR printer, click IP Printing at the top of the Printer Browser dialog box. Fill in the appropriate IP address and other settings, as directed by your cheerful network administrator.

The Printer List

If you're lucky enough to own several printers, repeat the steps above for each one. Eventually, you'll have introduced the Mac to all the printers available to it, so all their names show up in the printer list.

TROUBLESHOOTING MOMENT

The Death of AppleTalk

Like most 800-pound-gorilla computer companies, Apple can be a frustrating partner. It throws its hairy weight behind some technology, gets all the other companies to adopt it—and then moves on to something else.

That's why AppleTalk is no longer with us, much to the dismay of thousands of Mac fans who own Apple-Talk printers.

AppleTalk was a networking system that was part of the Mac since 1984. Hundreds of networkable printer models, especially laser printers, used this scheme to talk to Macs.

If yours is among them, you can still make your printer work. Follow steps 1 through 4 of "Setting Up a Printer" on these pages; in step 4, choose IP.

From the Protocol pop-up menu, choose HP Jetdirect—Socket (if you have an HP laser printer), or Internet Printing Protocol (IPP) (for most other laser printers). If you and your company's network expert determine that the printer

you want to use is, in fact, an LPR printer, then choose Line Printer Daemon instead.

In any of these cases, you now have to fill in the *IP address* (network address) of the printer. On some printers, you can call up this information on the screen. On others, you have to print out that printer's configuration or test page. (On many HP laser printers, you do that by holding down a button while the printer turns on.) There's no solution to this except to cuddle up with the manual—or, faster yet, Google it ("HP LaserJet 1300 configuration page").

Once you've filled in the IP address, you can make up a name for this printer ("HP Hulk") and a location ("Next to the water cooler"), if you like. The "Print using:" pop-up menu is supposed to fill itself in with the correct printer-driver information; if it doesn't, you can choose the printer model (or, in a pinch, a very similar one) manually.

Click Add. You're off and printing!

To see the printer list so far, open System Preferences→Print & Fax. You can have all kinds of fun here:

- **Choose a default printer.** As indicated by the Default Printer pop-up menu, Mac OS X intends, conveniently enough, to use whichever printer you used for the last printout for the next one. Most people, after all, don't switch printers much.

    Still, you can choose one particular printer from this pop-up menu to set it as the default printer—the one the Mac uses unless you intervene by choosing from the Printer pop-up menu in the Print dialog box (Figure 14-1).

- **Create desktop printer icons.** *This* handy, little-known feature gives you drag-and-drop access to your printers.

    From the Print & Fax pane of System Preferences, just drag a printer's icon out of the window and onto the desktop (or wherever you like). Repeat for your other printers. From now on, you can print a document on a certain printer just by dragging the document's icon onto the appropriate printer desktop icon.

- **Check the ink level.** Click a printer, then click Options & Supplies, to see how your inkjet ink or laser-printer toner level is. That way, you won't be caught short when you're on a deadline and your printer is out of ink.

Snow Leopard Spots: You now get a bright yellow "low ink" warning in the dialog box that appears when you print (Figure 14-3).

Making the Printout

The experience of printing depends on the printer you're using—laser printer, inkjet, or whatever. In every case, however, all the printing options hide behind two commands: File→Page Setup, which you need to adjust only occasionally, and File→Print, which you generally use every time you print. You'll find these two commands in almost every Macintosh program.

Page Setup

The Page Setup box lets you specify some key characteristics about the document you're going to print: orientation, paper dimensions, and so on; see Figure 14-2.

The options here vary by program and printer. The Page Setup options for an Epson inkjet, for example, differ dramatically from those for a laser printer. Only your printer's user manual can tell you exactly what these choices do.

Tip: You configure the Page Setup settings independently in each program you use. And by the way, to change the default paper size for all new documents, choose Save As Default from the Settings pop-up menu. (Mac fans in the UK: You're welcome.)

The Print Command

Although you can grow to a ripe old age without ever seeing the Page Setup dialog box, you can't miss the Print dialog box. It appears, like it or not, whenever you choose File→Print in one of your programs.

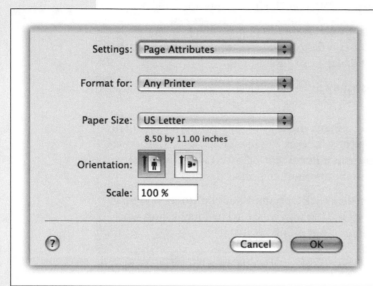

Figure 14-2:
Here in Page Setup are the controls you need to print a document rotated sideways on the page, so it prints "the long way." The Scale control, which lets you reduce or enlarge your document, can be handy if the program you're using doesn't offer such a control. And the Paper Size pop-up menu, of course, specifies the size of the paper you're printing on—US Letter, US Legal, envelopes, or one of the standard European or Japanese paper sizes (A4 and B5).

Once again, the options you encounter depend on the printer you're using. They also depend on whether or not you *expand* the dialog box by clicking the ▼ button; doing so reveals a *lot* of useful options, including a handy preview; see Figure 14-3.

Note: The exact layout of this expanded Print dialog box differs by program, but most modern ones resemble Figure 14-3.

If you expand the box, here's what you may find:

• **Printer.** If you have more than one printer connected to your Mac, you can indicate which you want to use for a particular printout by choosing its name from this pop-up menu.

• **Presets.** Here's a way to preserve your favorite print settings: Once you've proceeded through this dialog box, specifying the number of copies, which printer trays you want the paper taken from, and so on, you can choose Save As from the pop-up menu, and then assign your settings set a name (like "Borderless, 2 copies"). Thereafter, you'll be able to recreate that elaborate suite of settings simply by choosing its name from this pop-up menu.

- **Copies.** Type the number of copies you want printed. The Collated checkbox controls the printing order for the various pages. For example, if you print two copies of a three-page document, the Mac generally prints the pages in this order: 1, 2, 3, 1, 2, 3. If you turn off Collated, on the other hand, it prints in this order: 1, 1, 2, 2, 3, 3.

- **Pages.** You don't have to print an entire document—you can print, say, only pages 2 through 15.

Tip: You don't have to type numbers into both the From and To boxes. If you leave the first box blank, the Mac assumes you mean "from page 1." If you leave the second box blank, the Mac understands you mean "to the end." To print only the first three pages, in other words, leave the first box blank and type 3 into the second box. (These page numbers refer to the physical pages you're printing, not to any fancy numbering you've set up in your word processor. As far as the Print dialog box is concerned, the first printed page is page 1, even if you've told your word processor to label it page 455.)

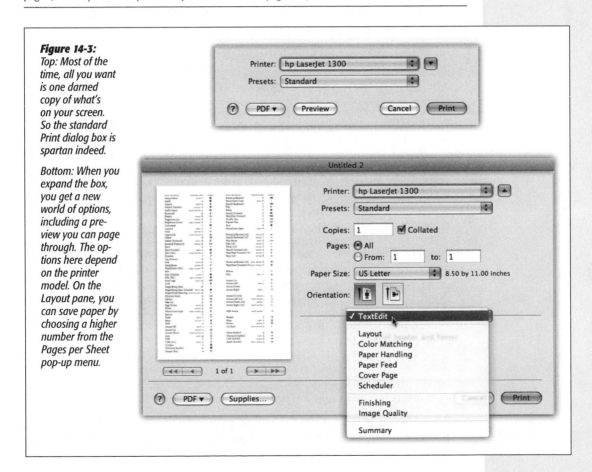

Figure 14-3:
Top: Most of the time, all you want is one darned copy of what's on your screen. So the standard Print dialog box is spartan indeed.

Bottom: When you expand the box, you get a new world of options, including a preview you can page through. The options here depend on the printer model. On the Layout pane, you can save paper by choosing a higher number from the Pages per Sheet pop-up menu.

- **Paper Size, Orientation.** Somebody at Apple finally realized how frustrating it was to have to open the Page Setup dialog box to change the paper-size and orientation settings, and then open the Print dialog box for other settings. Now, in most programs, these controls are duplicated right in the Print dialog box for your convenience.

- **PDF.** A *PDF* file, of course, is an Adobe Acrobat document—a file that any Mac, Windows, Linux, or Unix user can view, read, and print using either Preview or the free Acrobat Reader (included with every PC and Mac operating system).

  You can easily save any document as a PDF file instead of printing it—a truly beautiful feature that saves paper, ink, and time. The document remains on your hard drive, and the text inside is even searchable using Spotlight.

  But that's just the beginning. Apple has added a long list of additional PDF options (like password-protected PDFs, emailed ones, and so on). It faced a design quandary: How could it offer a new list of PDF-related options without junking up the Print dialog box?

  Its solution was a strange little item called a pop-up *button,* shown in Figure 14-3, top. Use it like a pop-up menu. The command you'll use most often is probably Save as PDF, which turns the printout into a PDF file instead of sending it to the printer. For details on the other PDF-related options here, see page 562.

- **Preview.** This button provides a print-preview function to almost every Mac OS X program on earth, which, in the course of your life, could save huge swaths of the Brazilian rain forest and a swimming pool's worth of ink in wasted printouts.

  Technically, the Preview button sends your printout to Preview, the program. Preview lets you zoom in or zoom out, rotate, or otherwise process your preview. When you're satisfied with how it looks, you can print it (File→Print), cancel it (File→Close), or turn it into a PDF file (File→Save as PDF).

- **Supplies.** This feature will strike you either as blissfully convenient or disgustingly mercenary: a button that takes you directly to a Web page where you can buy new cartridges for your specific printer model. In Snow Leopard, it turns yellow and sprouts a "Low Ink" exclamation point when your cartridges are running low.

If you examine the unnamed pop-up menu just below the Presets pop-up menu, you find dozens of additional options. They depend on your printer model and the program you're using at the moment, but here are some typical choices:

- **Layout.** As described in Figure 14-3, you can save paper and ink or toner cartridges by printing several miniature "pages" on a single sheet of paper.

- **Paper Handling.** You can opt to print out your pages in reverse order so they stack correctly, or you can print just odd or even pages so you can run them through again for double-sided printing.

- **Paper Feed.** If you chose the correct printer model when setting up your printer, then this screen "knows about" your printer's various paper trays. Here's where you specify which pages you want to come from which paper tray. (By far the most popular use for this feature is printing the first page of a letter on company letterhead and the following pages on blank paper from a second tray.)

- **Cover Page.** Yes, that throwaway info page has made its way from the fax world into the hard-copy world.

- **Scheduler.** This option lets you specify *when* you want your document to print. If you're a freelancer, sitting at home with an inkjet on your desk, you might not immediately grasp why anyone wouldn't want the printouts *right now.* But try printing a 400-page catalog in a big office where other people on the network might conceivably resent you for tying up the laser printer all afternoon, and you'll get the idea.

- **ColorSync.** Most color printers offer this panel, where you can adjust the color settings—to add a little more red, perhaps. This is also where you indicate whose *color-matching system* you want to use: Apple's ColorSync, your printer manufacturer's, or none at all.

Then, below the light gray line in this pop-up menu, you'll find a few options that are unique to the chosen printer or program. Some HP printers, for example, offer Cover Page, Finishing, and other choices. Other likely guest commands:

- **Quality & Media** (inkjet printers only). Here's where you specify the print quality you want, the kind of paper you're printing on, and so on. (The name of this panel varies by manufacturer.)

- **[Program Name].** Whichever program you're using—Mail, Word, AppleWorks, or anything else—may offer its own special printing options on this screen.

- **Summary.** This command summons a text summary of all your settings so far.

Tip: Here's one for the technically inclined. Open your Web browser and enter this address: *http://127.0.0.1:631.* You find yourself at a secret "front end" for CUPS (Common Unix Printing System), the underlying printing technology for Mac OS X. This trick lets your Mac communicate with a huge array of older printers that don't yet have Mac OS X drivers. Using this administration screen, you can print a test page, stop your printer in its tracks, manage your networked printers and print jobs, and more—a very slick trick.

Printing

When all your settings look good, click Print (or press Return) to send your printout to the printer.

Managing Printouts

After you've used the Print command, you can either sit there until the paper emerges from the printer, or you can *manage* the printouts-in-waiting. That option is attractive primarily to people who do a lot of printing, have connections to a lot of printers, or share printers with many other people.

Start by opening the printer's window. If you're already in the process of printing, just click the printer's Dock icon. If not, open →System Preferences→Print & Fax, click the printer's name, and then click Open Print Queue.

At this point, you see something like Figure 14-4: The printouts that will soon be sliding out of your printer appear in a tidy list.

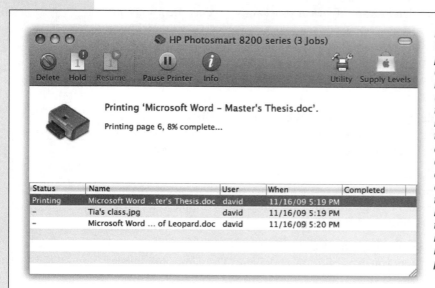

Figure 14-4:
Waiting printouts appear in this window. You can sort the list by clicking the column headings (Name or Status), make the columns wider or narrower by dragging the column-heading dividers horizontally, or reverse the sorting order by clicking the column name a second time. The Supply Level button opens a graph that shows how much ink each cartridge has remaining (certain printer models only).

Here are some of the ways in which you can control these waiting printouts, which Apple collectively calls the *print queue*:

- **Delete them.** By clicking an icon, or ⌘-clicking several, and then clicking the Delete toolbar button, you remove items from the list of waiting printouts. Now they won't print.

- **Pause them.** By highlighting a printout and then clicking the Hold button, you pause that printout. It doesn't print out until you highlight it again and then click the Resume button. (Other documents continue to print.) This pausing business could be useful when, for example, you need time to check or refill the printer, or when you're just about to print your letter of resignation as your boss drops by. (Maybe to offer you a promotion.)

- **Halt them all.** You can stop all printouts from a printer by clicking Pause Printer. (They resume when you click the button again, which now says Resume Printer.)

You can't rearrange printouts by dragging them in the queue list. But remember that you can resequence the printing order by choosing the Scheduler option; you can also drag waiting printouts *between* these lists, shifting them from one printer to another.

Tip: As you now know, the icon for a printer's queue window appears automatically in the Dock when you print. But it also stays in the Dock for the rest of the day; it doesn't disappear when the printing is complete.

If you wish it would, Control-click (or right-click) the printer's Dock icon; from the shortcut menu, choose Auto Quit.

Printer Sharing

Printer sharing is for people (or offices) with more than one Mac, connected to a network, who'd rather not buy a separate printer for each machine. Instead, you connect the printer to one Mac, flip a couple of software switches, and then boom: The other Macs on the network can send their printouts to the printer without actually being attached to it—even wirelessly attached, if they're on an AirPort network.

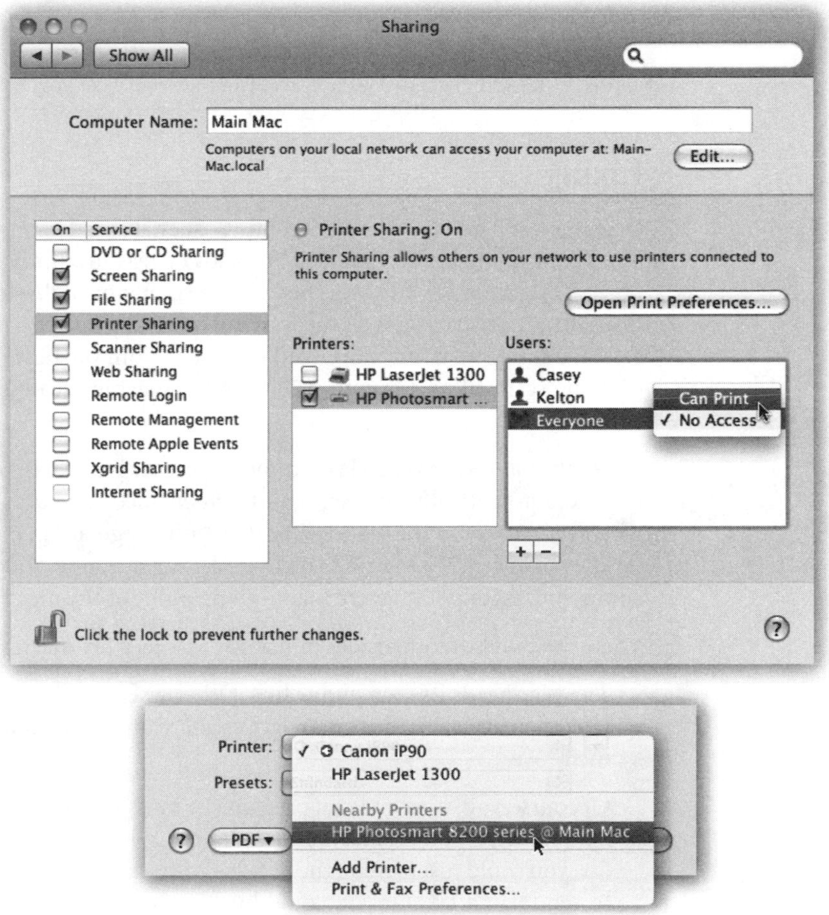

Figure 14-5:
Top: On the Mac with the printer, open the Sharing panel of System Preferences. Turn on Printer Sharing, and turn on the checkboxes for the printers you want to share. Switch to the Print & Fax pane, and turn on the "Share this printer" checkbox for the printer(s) you want to share.

Bottom: To use a shared printer elsewhere on the network, open the document you want to print, and then choose File→Print. In the Print dialog box, the shared printer is clearly identified under the Nearby Printers heading.

Note: Of course, this feature is most useful when you're sharing printers that can hook up to only one Mac at a time, like USB inkjet photo printers. Office laser printers are often designed to be networked from Day One.

Setting up printer sharing is easy; see Figure 14-5, top. Then, to make a printout from across the network, see the instructions in Figure 14-5, bottom.

Snow Leopard Spots: In Mac OS X 10.6, you can control which account holders on your network are allowed to use the printer you've shared. You know that idiot in Accounting who's always using up your cartridges by printing 200-page documents? Cut that sucker off! Just add the lucky guests' names to the Users column in System Preferences→Sharing→Printer Sharing, as shown in Figure 14-5.

If your PC-wielding friends install Bonjour for Windows (a free download from this book's "Missing CD" page at *www.missingmanuals.com*), they can even print to your Mac's shared printer, too.

Tip: Of course, your Mac (the one attached to the printer) must be turned on in order for the other computers to print. In part, that's because the documents-in-waiting from other people pile up on your hard drive.

Faxing

If faxing is still part of your work routine—hey, it could happen—then using the Mac as a fax machine is a terrific idea, for a lot of reasons. It saves money on paper and fax cartridges, and spares you the expense of buying a physical fax machine. Faxing from the Mac also eliminates the wasteful ritual of printing something out just so you can feed it into a fax machine. And faxes sent from the heart of Mac OS X—instead of being scanned by a crummy 200-dpi fax-machine scanner—look terrific on the receiving end.

Here's the basic idea: When faxes come in, you can read them on the screen, have them printed automatically, or even have them emailed to you so that you can get them wherever you are in the world. (Try *that* with a regular fax machine.) And sending a fax is even easier on a Mac than on a regular fax machine: You just use the File→Print command, exactly like you're making a printout of the onscreen document.

There are only two downsides of using a Mac as a fax machine:

• **The Mac needs its own phone line.** Otherwise, your Mac, answering each incoming call, will give friends and relatives a screaming earful when they call to express their love.

Of course, you can avoid that prerequisite by using your Mac exclusively for *sending* faxes, so that it doesn't answer the phone. Or if you need to receive the occasional fax, you could just turn on the fax-receiving feature only when somebody is about to send you a fax. Or you could buy an automated fax/voice splitter that sends voice lines to the phone and incoming faxes to the Mac.

But in general, the Mac-as-fax works best if it has its own line.

- **You can't fax from a book or magazine.** The one big limitation of Mac-based faxing is that you can only transmit documents that are, in fact, *on the computer*. That pretty much rules out faxing notes scribbled on a legal pad, clippings from *People* magazine, and so on, unless you scan them in first.

Setting Up Faxing

Apple no longer builds fax modems into new Macs—not even laptops. Therefore, if you have a fax modem at all, it probably takes one of these forms:

- Apple's external dangly Apple USB Fax/Modem ($50). As soon as it's plugged into a USB port, a dialog box lets you know that the Mac "sees" it, and offers to take you directly to System Preferences, where its name appears in the Printers list (Figure 14-6).

- A multifunction printer with a fax feature. Set it up as a printer, as described earlier in this chapter. Then click its name in the list at System Preferences→Print & Fax, and proceed as shown in Figure 14-6.

Figure 14-6:
If your new modem says "Not configured," you just have to type in your fax number and click Apply. If you're smart, you'll also turn on "Show fax status in menu bar." It installs a fax menulet that lets you monitor and control your fax sending and receiving. You're ready to fax!

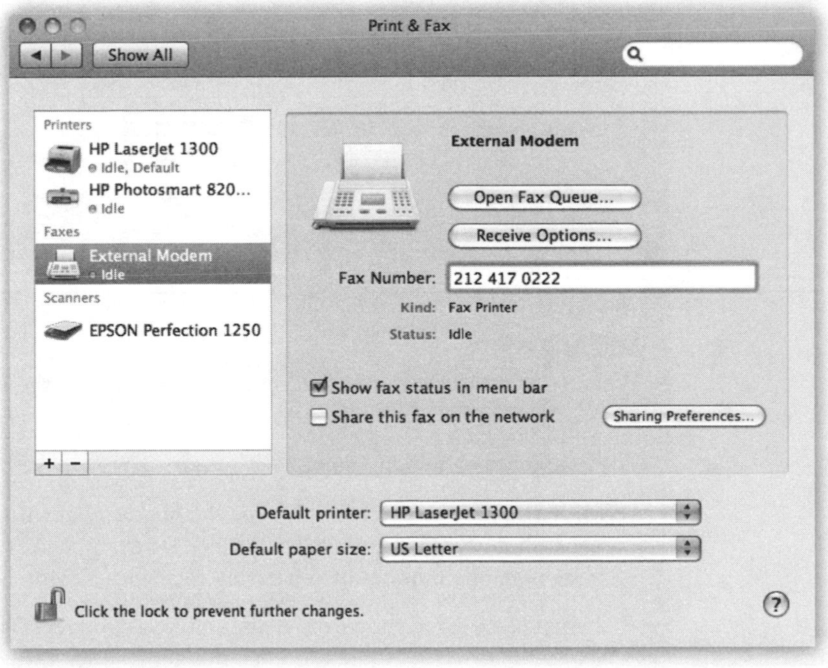

If you intend to *receive* faxes, then click Receive Options and turn on "Receive faxes on this computer." Then specify how soon the fax machine should pick up the call (after how many rings—you don't want it answering calls before *you* have a chance).

Finally, you can say how you want to handle incoming faxes, as described in Figure 14-7.

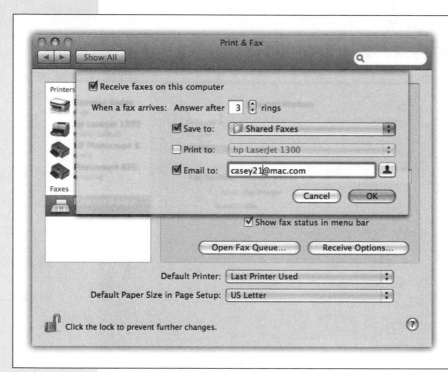

Figure 14-7:
When your Mac answers the fax line, it can do three things with the incoming fax. Option 1: Save it as a PDF file that you open with Preview. (The Mac proposes saving these files into the Users→ Shared→Shared Faxes folder, but you can set up a more convenient folder.) Option 2: Print it out automatically, just like a real fax machine. Option 3: Email it to you, so you can get your faxes even when you're not home (and so you can forward the fax easily).

Sending a Fax

When you're ready to send a fax, choose File→Print. In the Print dialog box (Figure 14-3), open the PDF pop-up button and then choose Fax PDF.

The dialog box shown in Figure 14-8 appears. Here are the boxes you can fill in:

- **To.** If you like, you can simply type the fax number into the To box, exactly the way it should be dialed: *1-212-553-2999,* for example. You can send a single fax to more than one number by separating each with a comma and a space.

  If you fax the same people often, though, you're better off adding their names and fax numbers to the Address Book (Chapter 19). That way, you can click the little silhouette button to the right of the To box and choose the recipient, as shown in Figure 14-8.

Tip: The Address Book feature doesn't work when you're sending from Microsoft Word or Excel. But here's a workaround: choose File→Print, then click Preview, then send the fax from there (File→Print again).

- **Settings.** Most of the time, fiddling with the printing pop-up menu isn't relevant to sending a fax. (ColorSync? On a black-and-white fax? Get real!) But the standard printing controls are here for your convenience. You can use the Scheduler pane to specify a time for your outgoing fax, the Layout pane to print more than one "page" per sheet, and so on.

- **Use Cover Page, Subject, Message.** If you turn on this checkbox, you're allowed to type a little message into the Subject and Message boxes.

  Beware! Don't press the Return key to add a blank line to your message. Mac OS X thinks you intend to "click" the Fax button—and off it goes!

Tip: Choosing Save as PDF from the little PDF pop-up button, at this moment, is your only chance to keep a copy of the fax you're sending.

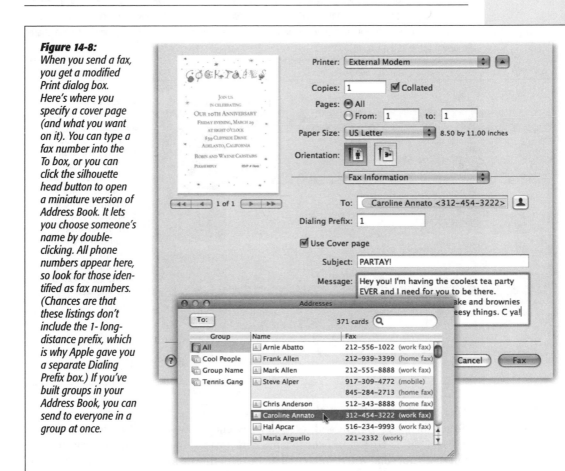

Figure 14-8:
When you send a fax, you get a modified Print dialog box. Here's where you specify a cover page (and what you want on it). You can type a fax number into the To box, or you can click the silhouette head button to open a miniature version of Address Book. It lets you choose someone's name by double-clicking. All phone numbers appear here, so look for those identified as fax numbers. (Chances are that these listings don't include the 1- long-distance prefix, which is why Apple gave you a separate Dialing Prefix box.) If you've built groups in your Address Book, you can send to everyone in a group at once.

Sending

When everything looks good, hit the Fax button. Although it may look like nothing is happening, check your Dock, where the icon for your fax/modem has appeared. If you click it, you'll see a clone of the dialog box shown in Figure 14-4, indicating the progress of your fax. Here you can pause the faxing, delete it, or hold it, exactly as you would a printout. (Your Fax menulet, if you've installed it, also keeps you apprised of the fax's progress; see Figure 14-9.)

Once the connection sounds are complete, you don't hear anything, see anything, or receive any notice that the fax was successful. (If your fax was *not* successfully sent for some reason, the modem's window automatically reschedules the fax to go out in 5 minutes.)

Tip: On a network, only one Mac has to be connected to a phone line. On that Mac, open System Preferences, click Sharing, turn on Printer Sharing, and turn on the checkbox for your fax modem. From now on, other Macs on the network can send out faxes via the one that has a phone line! (They'll see the shared modem listed in the Fax dialog box.)

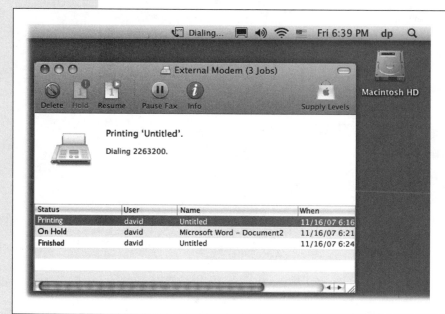

Figure 14-9:
The Fax menulet (top) says "Dialing...Connecting..." and so on. Click to see the Hang Up Now command. The Fax queue shows the faxes that are currently sending or scheduled to go out later. To see which documents you've successfully sent, and when they went out, choose Jobs→Show Complete Jobs.

Checking the log, checking the queue

To see the log of all sent and received faxes, choose →System Preferences→Print & Fax. Double-click your fax/modem's name; its fax-management window appears, but that's not what you're interested in. Instead, choose Jobs→Show Completed Jobs. You get a status window that looks a lot like the one for a printer.

Receiving a Fax

A Mac that's been set up to answer calls does a very good impersonation of a fax machine. You don't even have to be logged in to get faxes, although the Mac does have to be turned on. In System Preferences→Energy Saver→Options, turn on "Wake when modem detects a ring" to prevent your Mac from being asleep at the big moment.

When a fax call comes in, the Mac answers it after the number of rings you've specified. Then it treats the incoming fax image in the way you've specified in System Preferences: by sending it to your email program, printing it automatically, or just saving it as a PDF file in a folder you've specified.

PDF Files

Sooner or later, almost everyone with a personal computer encounters PDF (portable document format) files. Many a software manual, Read Me file, and downloadable "white paper" comes in this format. Until recently, you needed the free program called Acrobat Reader if you hoped to open or print these files. Windows devotees still do.

PDF files, however, are one of Mac OS X's common forms of currency. In fact, you can turn *any document* (in any program with a Print command) into a PDF file—a trick that once required the $250 program called Adobe Acrobat Distiller. (Maybe Apple should advertise: "Buy Acrobat for $250, get Mac OS X free—and $120 cash back!")

Note: All right, that joke about a free copy of Acrobat is an exaggeration. Mac OS X alone creates screen-optimized PDF files: compact, easy-to-email files that look good onscreen but don't have high enough resolution for professional printing. For high-end purposes and more optimization for specific uses (Web, fancy press machines, and so on), you still need a program like Adobe Acrobat, Illustrator, or InDesign.

But why would you want to do so? What's the big deal about PDF in Mac OS X? Consider these advantages:

- **Other people see your layout.** When you distribute PDF files to other people, they see precisely the same fonts, colors, page design, and other elements that you put in your original document. And here's the kicker: They get to see all of this even if they don't *have* the fonts or the software you used to create the document. (Contrast with the alternative: Say you're sending somebody a Microsoft Word document. If your correspondent doesn't have precisely the same fonts you have, then he'll see a screwy layout. And if he doesn't have Word or a program that can open Word files, he'll see nothing at all.)

- **It's universal.** PDF files are very common in the Macintosh, Windows, Unix/Linux, and even smartphone worlds. When you create a PDF file, you can distribute it (by email, for example) without worrying about what kinds of computers your correspondents are using.

- **It has very high resolution.** PDF files can print at the maximum quality of any printer. A PDF file prints great both on cheapo inkjets and on high-quality image-setting gear at professional print shops. (Right now, in fact, you're looking at a PDF file that was printed at a publishing plant.)

- **You can search it.** A PDF file may look like a captured graphic, but behind the scenes, its text is still text; Spotlight can find a PDF in a haystack in a matter of seconds. That's an especially handy feature when you work with electronic software manuals in PDF format.

Opening PDF Files

There's nothing to opening up a PDF file: Just double-click it. Preview takes over from there and opens the PDF file on your screen.

Creating PDF Files

Opening, schmopening—what's really exciting in Mac OS X is the ability to create your *own* PDF files. The easiest way is to click the PDF pop-up button in the standard Print dialog box (Figure 14-10). When you click it, you're offered a world of interesting PDF-creation possibilities:

- **Save as PDF.** Mac OS X saves your printout-to-be to the disk as a PDF document instead of printing it.

- **Save PDF as PostScript.** You get a PostScript file instead of a PDF. (PostScript is a format preferred by some designers and print shops. It consists of highly precise "what to draw" instructions for PostScript laser printers.)

- **Fax PDF** *faxes* a document instead of printing it, as described on the preceding pages.

- **Mail PDF** generates a PDF and then attaches it to an outgoing message in Mail. Great for exchanging layout-intensive documents with collaborators who don't have the same fonts, layout software, or taste as you.

- **Save as PDF-X** creates a specialized PDF format, popular in the printing industry, that's extra compact because it contains the minimum data needed to print the document.

- **Save PDF to iPhoto** creates a PDF version of the document and then exports it to iPhoto. That's not such a bad idea; iPhoto is great at managing and finding any kind of graphics documents, including PDFs.

Tip: Remember that once you send a document or layout to iPhoto, you can turn it into a custom-printed book, calendar, greeting card, or postcard.

- **Save PDF to Web Receipts Folder** is one of the simplest and sweetest features in all of Mac OS X.

You use it when you've just ordered something on a Web site and the "Print This Receipt" screen is staring you in the face. Don't waste paper and ink (and, later, time trying to find it!). Instead, use this command. You get a perfectly usable PDF version, stored in your Home→Documents→Web Receipts folder, where you can use Spotlight to find it later, when you need to consult or print it because your gray-market goods never arrived.

- **Edit Menu** lets you prune this very list to remove the options you never use.

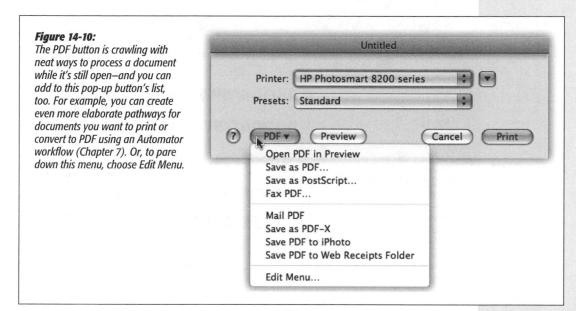

Figure 14-10:
The PDF button is crawling with neat ways to process a document while it's still open—and you can add to this pop-up button's list, too. For example, you can create even more elaborate pathways for documents you want to print or convert to PDF using an Automator workflow (Chapter 7). Or, to pare down this menu, choose Edit Menu.

Fonts—and Font Book

Mac OS X type is all smooth, all the time. Fonts in Mac OS X's formats—called TrueType, PostScript Type 1, and OpenType—always look smooth onscreen and in printouts, no matter what the point size.

Mac OS X also comes with a program that's *just* for installing, removing, inspecting, and organizing fonts. It's called Font Book (Figure 14-11), and it's in your Applications folder.

Where Fonts Live

Brace yourself. In Mac OS X, there are *three* Fonts folders. The fonts you actually see listed in the Fonts menus and Fonts panels of your programs are combinations of these Fonts folders' contents.

They include:

- **Your private fonts (your Home folder→Library→Fonts).** This Fonts folder sits right inside your own Home folder. You're free to add your own custom fonts to this folder. Go wild—it's your font collection and yours alone. Nobody else who uses the Mac can use these fonts; they'll never even know you have them.

- **Main font collection (Library→Fonts).** Any fonts in this folder are available to everyone to use in every program. (As with most features that affect everybody who shares your Macintosh, however, only people with Administrator accounts can change the contents of this folder.)

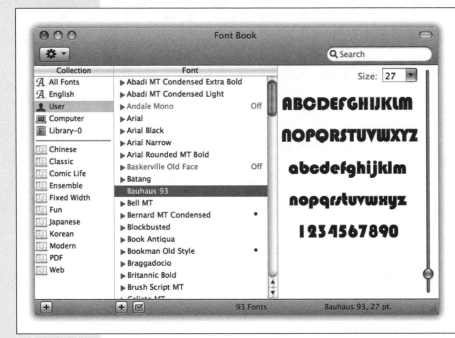

Figure 14-11:
Each account holder can have a separate set of fonts; your set is represented by the User icon. You can drag fonts and font families between the various Fonts folders represented here—from your User account folder to the Computer icon, for example, making them available to all account holders.

- **Essential system fonts (System→Library→Fonts).** This folder contains the 35 fonts that the Mac itself needs: the typefaces you see in your menus, dialog boxes, icons, and so on. You can open this folder to *see* these font suitcases, but you can't do anything with them, such as open, move, or add to them. Remember that, for stability reasons, the System folder is sealed under glass forever. Only the *superuser* (page 639) can touch these files—and even that person would be foolish to do so.

With the exception of the essential system fonts, you'll find an icon representing each of these locations in your Font Book program, described next.

Note: And just to make life even more exciting, Adobe's software installers may donate even more fonts to your cause, in yet another folder: your Home→Application Support folder.

Font Book: Installing and Managing Fonts

One of the biggest perks of Mac OS X is its preinstalled collection of over 50 great-looking fonts—"over $1,000 worth," according to Apple, which licensed many of them from type companies. In short, fewer Mac users than ever will wind up buying and installing new fonts.

Snow Leopard Spots: In fact, Mac OS X 10.6 comes with four new fonts: Menlo, a new monospace font for use in programs like Terminal; Chalkduster, which looks like handwriting on a blackboard; and Heiti and Hiragino Sans (for Asian languages).

But when you do buy or download new fonts, you're in luck. There's no limit to the number of fonts you can install.

Looking over your fonts

Right off the bat, Font Book is great for looking at samples of each typeface. Click Computer, for example, click the first font name, and then press the ↓ key. As you walk down the list, the rightmost panel shows you a sample of each font (Figure 14-11).

You can also click any font family's flippy triangle (or highlight its name and then press →) to see the font *variations* it includes: Italic, Bold, and so on.

Tip: When you first open Font Book, the actual text of the typeface preview (in the right panel) is pretty generic. Don't miss the Preview menu, though. It lets you substitute a full display of every character (choose Repertoire)—or, if you choose Custom, it lets you type your own text.

Printing a reference sheet

It's easy to print yourself a handy, whole-font sampler of any font. Click its name and then choose File→Print. In the Print dialog box, click the ▼ button to expand the dialog box, if necessary.

As shown in Figure 14-12, you can use the Report Type pop-up menu to choose from three reference-sheet styles:

- **Catalog** prints the alphabet twice (uppercase and lowercase) and the numbers in each selected font; use the Sample Size slider to control the size. This style is the most compact, because more than one print sample fits on each sheet of paper.

- **Repertoire** prints a grid that contains every single character in the font. This report may take more than one page per font.

- **Waterfall** prints the alphabet over and over again, with increasing type sizes, until the page is full. You can control which sizes appear using the Sample Sizes list.

When everything looks good, click Print.

Eliminating duplicates

Since your Mac accesses up to three folders containing fonts, you might wonder what happens in the case of *conflicts*. For example, suppose you have two slightly different fonts, both called Optima, which came from different type companies and are housed in different Fonts folders on your system. Which font do you actually get when you use it in your documents?

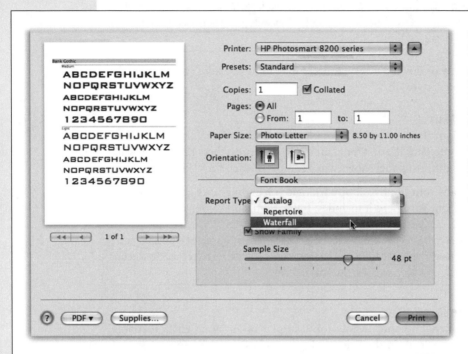

Figure 14-12:
From the Report Type pop-up menu, choose the style you want. The preview screen shows you each one before you commit it to paper. Type-size controls always appear in the lower right.

The scheme is actually fairly simple: Mac OS X proceeds down the list of Fonts folders in the order shown on page 563, beginning with your own home Fonts folder. It acknowledges the existence of only the *first* duplicated font it finds.

If you'd rather have more control, open Font Book. A bullet (•) next to a font's name is Font Book's charming way of trying to tell you that you've got copies of the same font in more than one of your Fonts folders. You might have one version of Comic Sans in your own Home→Library→Fonts folder, for example, and another in your Mac's main Fonts folder.

Click the one you want to keep, and then choose Edit→Resolve Duplicates. Font Book turns off all *other* copies, and the bullet disappears.

Adding, removing, and hiding fonts

Here's what you can do with Font Book:

- **Install a font.** When you double-click a font file's icon in the Finder, Font Book opens and presents the typeface for your inspection pleasure. If you like it, click Install Font. You've just installed it into *your account's* Fonts folder so it appears in the Fonts menus of all your programs. (If you'd rather install it so that it appears in *all* account holders' Fonts menus, see Figure 14-11.)

- **Remove a font.** Removing a font from your machine is easy: Highlight it in the Font Book list, and then press the Delete key. (You're asked to confirm the decision.) Before taking such a drastic and permanent step, however, keep in mind that you can simply *disable* (hide) the font instead. Read on.

- **Disable a font.** When you disable a font, you're simply hiding it from your programs. You might want to turn off a font so you can use a different version of it (bearing the same name but from a different type company, for example) or to make your Fonts menus shorter, or to make programs like Microsoft Word start up faster. You can always turn a disabled font back on if you ever need it again.

Tip: How's this for a sweet feature? Mac OS X can activate fonts automatically as you need them. When you open a document that relies on a font it doesn't have, Snow Leopard activates that font and keeps it available until that particular program quits.

Actually, it does better than that. If it doesn't see that font installed, it searches your hard drive on a quest to find the font—and then it asks you if you want it installed so the document will look right.

To disable a font, just click it (or its family name; see Figure 14-11) and then click the checkbox button beneath the list (or press Shift-⌘-D). Confirm your decision by clicking Disable in the confirmation box. (Turn on "Do not ask me again" if you're the confident sort.)

The font's name now appears gray, and the word Off appears next to it, making it absolutely clear what you've just done. (To turn the font on again, highlight its name, and then click the now-empty checkbox button, or press Shift-⌘-D again.)

Note: When you install, remove, disable, or enable a font using Font Book, you see the changes in the Fonts menus and panels of your Cocoa programs immediately. You won't see the changes in open Carbon programs, however, until you quit and reopen them.

Font collections

A *collection,* like the ones listed in the first Font Book column, is a subset of your installed fonts. Apple starts you off with collections called things like PDF (a set of standard fonts used in PDF files) and Web (fonts you're safe using on Web pages— that is, fonts that are very likely to be installed on the Macs or Windows PCs of your Web visitors).

But you can create collections called, for example, Headline or Sans Serif, organized by font type. Or you can create collections like Brochure or Movie Poster, organized by project. Then you can switch these groups of fonts on or off at will, just as though you'd bought a program like Suitcase.

To create a new collection, click the leftmost **+** button to create a new entry in the Collections column, whose name you can edit. Then click one of the font storage locations—User or Computer—and drag fonts or font families onto your newly created collection icon. (Recognize this process from playlists in iTunes, or albums in iPhoto?) Each font can be in as many different collections as you want.

To remove a font from the collection, click its name, and then press Delete. You're not actually removing the font from your Mac, of course—only from the collection.

Tip: Each time you create a new font collection, Mac OS X records its name and contents in a little file in your Home folder→Library→FontCollections folder.

By copying these files into the Users→Shared folder on your hard drive, you can make them available to anyone who uses the Mac. If your sister, for example, copies one of these files from there into her own Home folder→Library→FontCollections folder, she'll see the name of your collection in her own Fonts panel. This way, she can reap the benefits of the effort and care you put into its creation.

Font libraries

Don't get confused; a font *library* is not the same as a font *collection.*

A font library is a set of fonts *outside* Font Book that you can install or uninstall on the fly. They don't have to be in any of your Fonts folders; Font Book can install them from wherever they happen to be sitting on your hard drive (or even on the network). Font Book never copies or moves these font files as you install or remove them from libraries; it simply adds them to your Fonts menus by referencing them right where they sit.

Tip: That can be a handy arrangement if you periodically work on different projects for different clients. Why burden your day-to-day Fonts menu with the 37 fonts used by *Beekeeper Quarterly* magazine, when you need to work with those fonts only four times a year?

Once you've added some fonts to a library, you can even set up collections *within* that library.

To create a library, choose File→New Library; the library appears in the Collection list at the left side of Font Book. Now you can drag fonts into it right from the Finder, or set up collections inside it by highlighting the library's icon and choosing File→New Collection.

Exporting fonts

Next time you submit a design project to a print shop or graphics bureau, you won't have to worry that they won't have the right fonts. It's easy to collect all the fonts you used in a document and then export them to a folder, ready to submit along with your document.

Use the Services→Font Book→Create Collection From Text command. Font Book opens and shows you a new collection it's created, containing all the fonts used in your document. Click the collection, and then choose File→Export Collection. The software prompts you to name and choose a location for the exported fonts folder.

Note: The Create Collection From Text command doesn't work in all programs, but you can always build and export a collection manually.

The Fonts Panel

As noted in Chapter 5, some existing Mac programs have simply been touched up—*Carbonized*, in the lingo—to be Mac OS X–compatible. Choosing fonts in these programs works exactly as it always has on the Mac: You choose a typeface name from the Fonts menu or a formatting palette.

Things get much more interesting when you use the more modern Cocoa programs, like TextEdit, iMovie, Pages, Keynote, Numbers, iPhoto, and Mail. They offer a standard Mac OS X feature called the Fonts panel. If you're seated in front of your Mac OS X machine now, fire up TextEdit or Pages and follow along.

Choosing fonts from the Fonts panel

Suppose you've just highlighted a headline in TextEdit, and now you want to choose an appropriate typeface for it.

In TextEdit, you open the Fonts panel (Figure 14-13) by choosing Format→ Font→Show Fonts (⌘-T). Just as in Font Book, the first column lists your Collections. The second column, Family, shows the names of the actual fonts in your system. The third, Typeface, shows the various style variations—Bold, Italic, Condensed, and so on—available in that type family. (Oblique and Italic are roughly the same thing; Bold, Black, and Ultra are varying degrees of boldface.)

The last column lists a sampling of point sizes. You can use the size slider, choose from the point-size pop-up menu, or type any number into the box at the top of the Size list.

Designing collections and favorites

At the bottom of the Fonts panel, the ✿ menu offers a few useful tools for customizing the standard Fonts panel:

- **Add to Favorites.** To designate a font as one of your favorites, specify a font, style, and size by clicking in the appropriate columns of the Fonts panel. Then use this command.

From now on, whenever you click Favorites in the Collections column, you'll see a list of the typefaces you've specified.

- **Show Preview.** The Fonts panel is great and all that, but you may have noticed that, at least at first, it doesn't actually *show* you the fonts you're working with—something of an oversight in a window designed to help you find your fonts. See Figure 14-13 for details. (Choose this command again—now called Hide Preview—to get rid of this preview.)

Tip: Once you've opened the Preview pane, feel free to click the different sizes, typeface names, and family names to see the various effects.

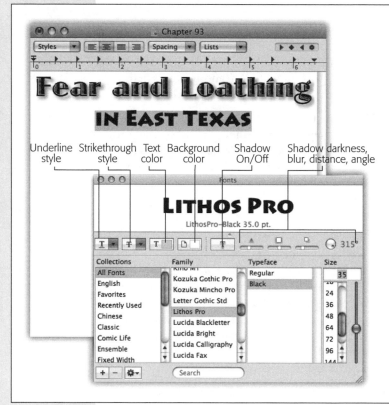

Figure 14-13:
The Fonts panel, generally available only in Cocoa programs, offers elaborate controls over text color, shadow, and underline styles.

See the handy font sample shown here above the font lists? To get it, choose Show Preview from the ✿ pop-up menu. Or use the mousy way: Place your cursor just below the title bar (where it says Fonts) and drag downward.

- **Hide Effects.** The "toolbar" of the Fonts panel lets you create special text effects—colors, shadows, and so on—as shown in Figure 14-13. This command hides that row of pop-up buttons.

- **Color.** Opens the Color Picker (page 199) so you can specify a color for the highlighted text in your document.

- **Characters.** Opens the Character Palette (page 233) so you can choose a symbol without having to remember the crazy keyboard combo that types it.

- **Typography.** Opens the Typography palette (see Figure 14-14).

- **Edit Sizes.** The point sizes listed in the Fonts panel are just suggestions. You can actually type in any point size you want. By choosing this command, in fact, you can edit this list so that the sizes you use most often are only a click away.

- **Manage Fonts.** Opens Font Book, described earlier in this chapter.

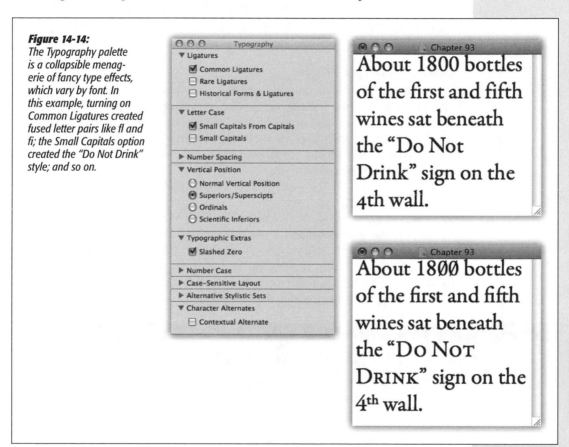

Figure 14-14:
The Typography palette is a collapsible menagerie of fancy type effects, which vary by font. In this example, turning on Common Ligatures created fused letter pairs like fl and fi; the Small Capitals option created the "Do Not Drink" style; and so on.

ColorSync

As you may have discovered through painful experience, computers aren't great with color. Each device you use to create and print digital images "sees" color a little bit differently, which explains why the deep amber captured by your scanner may be rendered as chalky brown on your monitor, yet come out as a fiery orange on your Epson inkjet printer. Since every gadget defines and renders color in its own way, colors are often inconsistent as a print job moves from design to proof to press.

ColorSync attempts to sort out this mess, serving as a translator between all the different pieces of hardware in your workflow. For this to work, each device (scanner, monitor, printer, digital camera, copier, proofer, and so on) has to be calibrated with a unique *ColorSync profile*—a file that tells your Mac exactly how it defines colors. Armed with the knowledge contained in the profiles, the ColorSync software can compensate for the various quirks of the different devices, and even the different kinds of paper they print on.

Most of the people who lose sleep over color fidelity are those who do commercial color scanning and printing, where "off" colors are a big deal. After all, a customer might return a product after discovering, for example, that the actual product color doesn't match the photo on a company's Web site.

Getting ColorSync Profiles

ColorSync profiles for many color printers, scanners, and monitors come built into Mac OS X. When you buy equipment or software from, say, Kodak, Agfa, or Pantone, you may get additional profiles. If your equipment didn't come with a ColorSync profile, visit Profile Central (*www.chromix.com*), where hundreds of model-specific profiles are available for downloading. Put new profiles into the Library→ColorSync→Profiles folder.

Default Profiles

In professional graphics work, a ColorSync profile is often embedded right in a photo, making all this color management automatic. Using the ColorSync Utility program (in Applications→Utilities), you can specify which ColorSync profile each of your gadgets should use. Click the Devices button, open the category for your device (scanner, camera, display, printer, or proofer), click the model you have, and use the Current Profile pop-up menu to assign a profile to it.

GEM IN THE ROUGH

The Coolest Feature?

Deep in the heart of the ColorSync Utility program beats one of the coolest Mac OS X features that nobody's ever discovered.

On the Profiles tab, you can click the name of a color-device profile and view a lab plot of its *gamut* (the colors it's capable of displaying). What you might not realize, however, is that this is a 3-D graph; you can drag its corners to spin it in space.

But that's not the cool part. The tiny triangle in the corner of the graph is a pop-up menu. If you choose "Hold for comparison" and then choose a different color profile, you'll see both lab plots superimposed, revealing the spectrum areas where they overlap—and the yawning gaps where they *can't* display the same colors.

You'll find out, among other things, that some printers can't display nearly as many colors as your monitor can, and that inkjets are much better at depicting, say, cyan than green.

And while we're discussing features you might have missed: You can double-click a profile's name to view a dizzyingly complex scientific description of its elements.

Blue colorant tristimulus, anyone?

Tip: In the Displays pane of System Preferences, you'll find a Color tab. Its Calibrate button is designed to create a profile for your particular monitor in your particular office lighting—all you have to do is answer a few fun questions onscreen and drag a few sliders.

More on ColorSync

If you ache to learn more about ColorSync, you won't find much in Mac OS X's Help system. Instead, search the Web. You'll find Googling *ColorSync* to be a fruitful exercise.

Graphics in Mac OS X

Now you're talking! If you want to see dilated pupils and sweaty palms, just say "graphics" to any Mac OS X junkie.

Yes, Mac OS X has made graphics a huge deal, thanks to its sophisticated Quartz graphics-processing technology. Everywhere you look in Mac OS X, you'll find visual effects that would make any other operating system think about early retirement.

For example: Menus are transparent, and when you release them, they fade away instead of snapping off. You can set Excel 3-D graphs to be slightly transparent so that they don't block other bars in a 3-D graph. When you paste files into windows in icon view, their icons fade into view. When you open an especially long message in Mail, its text fades in from white. When you open a widget in Dashboard, it splashes down with a pond-ripple effect. And when you switch accounts using Fast User Switching, your work environment slides off the screen as though it's pasted on the side of an animated cube.

All these visual goodies owe their existence to Quartz (or its enhanced successor, Quartz Extreme, which is not available on older Macs).

POWER USERS' CLINIC

AppleScript and ColorSync

Using AppleScript, described in Chapter 7, you can harness ColorSync in elaborate ways. Just by dragging document icons onto AppleScript icons, for example, you can embed ColorSync profiles, modify the profiles already incorporated, remove profiles, review the profile information embedded in a graphic, and much more. Better yet, you don't even have to know AppleScript to perform these functions—just use the built-in AppleScripts that come with Mac OS X.

To find them, open the Library→ColorSync→Scripts folder. Unfortunately, there aren't any instructions for using these eight ready-made AppleScripts. Nonetheless, Apple's real hope is that these example scripts will give you a leg up on creating your own AppleScripts (Chapter 7)—that someday you, the print shop operator, will be able to automate your entire color processing routine using AppleScript and ColorSync.

Graphics Formats in Mac OS X

Mac OS X understands dozens of Mac and Windows graphics file formats. Better yet, its Preview program can open such graphics and then export them in a different format, making it an excellent file-conversion program.

You can confidently double-click graphics files—from a digital camera, scanner, or Web download, for example—in any of these formats:

- **PICT files.** For almost 20 years, the PICT file was the graphics format Mac fans were most familiar with. It was the graphics format used by the Macintosh Clipboard, and it was the format created by the Shift-⌘-3 keystroke (see the end of this chapter).

  Unfortunately, no other kinds of computers could open these files, so PICT files gave conniptions to the equipment at printing shops. In Snow Leopard, after all these years, Apple is finally letting PICT slip away. The Preview program can no longer save graphics in the PICT format. It *can* open them, but only when it's running in 32-bit mode (page 194).

- **TIFF files.** The TIFF file format is a high-density, high-quality *bitmap*—that is, the Mac has memorized the color of each tiny dot in the file. Trying to enlarge one is like enlarging a fax: Make it too big, and the image breaks down into visible dots.

  Nonetheless, TIFF files are very popular in the printing industry—most of the graphics in this book, for example, were stored as TIFF files. They print beautifully, work nicely in page-layout programs, and are understood by both Macs and Windows PCs. (They're also pretty big files.)

- **JPEG files.** This format is one of the most popular on the Web, particularly for photos or other high-quality, full-color artwork.

  What makes JPEG files ideal for online use is that they've been compressed (using a program like Photoshop). Just enough of the color data has been thrown out from the original file to make the image a quick download without noticeably affecting its quality.

- **GIF files.** GIF stands for *graphics interchange format.* Today, GIF files are used almost exclusively on the Web, usually for solid-colored graphics like cartoons, headlines, and logos. (A GIF file can have a maximum of 256 colors, which is not even close to the photorealism of, say, JPEG. That's what makes GIF files inappropriate for photographs.)

- **PNG files.** As it turns out, one of the algorithms used by GIF files is, technically speaking, the property of a company called Unisys, which threatened to sue everybody who was creating GIF files. "No problem," said the World Wide Web Consortium. "We'll just come up with our own replacement—a file format that has no legal strings attached." What they created was PNG (for Portable Network Graphics). You can save AppleWorks, Photoshop, and Preview documents in PNG format, and every modern Web browser understands it. Screenshots you take in

Mac OS X (that is, captured images of the screen, as described in the following pages) are in the PNG format.

PNG files don't lose quality when compressed, as JPEG files do. On the other hand, PNG files don't accommodate animation, as GIF files do. And when it comes to photos, they don't offer as impressive a size/quality balance as JPEG.

- **PDF (Acrobat) files.** As noted earlier in this chapter, Mac OS X traffics effortlessly in PDF files, meaning that you can distribute documents you create to almost anyone, confident that they'll be able to open and print your stuff regardless of what kind of computer, fonts, and programs they have.

- **Photoshop files.** If you're a graphic designer or Webmeister, this one is kind of neat: Mac OS X can open (and Preview can even export) actual Photoshop files (except for so-called *16-bit RGB* files and really huge files). In practical terms, the fact that Mac OS X can open and display these files means that you could use a Photoshop masterpiece, complete with layers and transparency, as, for example, a Mac OS X desktop background.

- **BMP.** You can think of this graphics format as the PICT of the Windows world. It's nice that Mac OS X can open (and Preview can export) them, especially because you may occasionally find .bmp files on the Web or attached to email messages.

- **Silicon Graphics, MacPaint, Targ.** Talk about obscure—you could go through your whole life without ever seeing a graphic in one of these formats. Silicon Graphics is, of course, the format created by Silicon Graphics computers. MacPaint is a black-and-white only, 8 × 10-inch maximum, ancient Macintosh graphics format that disappeared from the scene in about 1988. And Targ (Targa) is the file format once used by products from the Truevision Corporation.

Screen-Capture Keystrokes

If you're reading a chapter about printing and graphics, you may someday be interested in creating *screenshots*—printable illustrations of the Mac screen.

Screenshots are a staple of articles, tutorials, and books about the Mac (including this one). Mac OS X has a secret built-in feature that lets you make them—and includes some very cool convenience features.

Here's how to capture various regions of the screen.

The Whole Screen

Press Shift-⌘-3 to create a picture file on your desktop, in PNG format, that depicts the entire screen image. A satisfying camera-shutter sound tells you that you were successful. Each time you press Shift-⌘-3, you get another file on your desktop.

Since the dawn of Mac, these files were named Picture 1, Picture 2, and so on, which wasn't the most enlightening of naming systems. In Snow Leopard, for the first time, the files are named after the current time and date. They're called "Screen shot 2010-01-18 at 5.18.13 PM," "Screen shot 2010-01-18 at 5:18:32 PM," and so on.

You can open these files into Preview or any other graphics program, in readiness for editing, printing, or exporting in a different format.

***

Tip: It doesn't have to be Shift-⌘-3. You can change this keystroke, or any of these screenshot keystrokes, to anything you like. Open System Preferences→Keyboard→Keyboard Shortcuts→Screen Shots. Click the keystroke you want to change, press Return to highlight the current keyboard combo, and then press the new keystroke you prefer.

***

One Section of the Screen

You can capture just a rectangular *region* of the screen by pressing Shift-⌘-4. Your cursor turns into a crosshairs with two tiny digital readouts—the horizontal and vertical coordinates of your cursor on the screen at this moment. (The numbers are pixels, as measured from the upper-left corner of the screen, which has coordinates 0, 0.)

Now drag diagonally across the screen to capture only a rectangular chunk of it. When you drag and release the mouse, you hear the camera-click sound, and the Picture 1 file appears on your desktop as usual—containing only the rectangle you enclosed.

But that's just the beginning. Once you've begun dragging diagonally, while the mouse is still down, you can press any of these keys for special manipulation effects:

- **Space bar.** While you hold down the space bar with one hand, your selection rectangle is frozen in size and shape. With your mouse hand, you can move the cursor with the entire selection rectangle attached, the better to fine-tune your positioning relative to your target.

- **Shift key.** When you hit Shift, you confine the dragging action of your mouse to a single dimension: horizontal or vertical. Which dimension depends on how you move your mouse after you hit Shift.

   For example, suppose you drag out a 2-inch square, and then you pause. With the mouse button still down, you press Shift. If you now continue to drag downward, the selected area maintains a fixed width; you're increasing only the rectangle's height.

- **Option key.** If you hold down Option after beginning to drag, Mac OS X creates a rectangular selection that grows from the center point outward. That is, it treats your initial click as the rectangle's center point, rather than as a diagonal corner.

- **Esc.** If you change your mind about taking a screenshot, tap Esc. The darkened selection area disappears, and you've exited screenshot mode.

A Dialog Box, Menu, Window, or Icon

Why fuss with cleaning up a screenshot after you've taken it? Using this trick, you can neatly snip *one screen element* out from its background.

Make sure the dialog box, menu, window, or icon is visible. Then press Shift-⌘-4. But *instead of* dragging diagonally, tap the space bar.

***

Your cursor turns into a tiny camera (Figure 14-15). Move it so the misty-blue highlighting fills the window or menu you want to capture—and then click. The resulting picture file snips the window or menu neatly from its background.

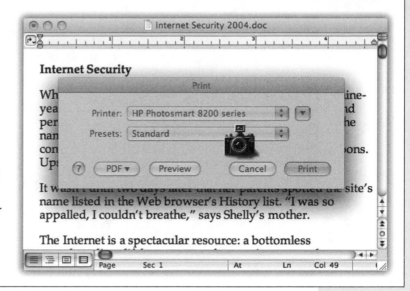

Figure 14-15:
To capture just one dialog box, use the old Camera Cursor trick. That is, invoke Shift-⌘-4 and then tap the space bar to produce the cursor shown here. Click the element you want to snip from its background. (Press the space bar a second time to exit "snip one screen element" mode and return to "drag across an area" mode.) If you ever change your mind about taking any kind of screenshot, press ⌘-period or the Esc key.

Shift-⌘-4 and then the space bar also captures the Dock in one quick snip. Once you've got the camera cursor, just click any *blank* spot in the Dock (between icons).

Tip: If you hold down the Control key as you click or drag (using any of the techniques described above), you copy the screenshot to your Clipboard, ready for pasting, rather than saving it as a new graphics file on your desktop.

Snow Leopard comes with other ways to create screenshots:

- **Grab.** Grab is a program in your Applications→Utilities folder. Grab's chief selling point is its *timer* option, which lets you set up the screen before it takes the shot.

- **Preview.** You can use the File→Take Screen Shot submenu commands to take screenshots (whole screen, selection, just one window) and open the result directly into Preview, rather than dumping the result onto your hard drive. The advantage here is that you can use all of Preview's image-manipulation skills—changing resolution, cropping, annotating, color-adjusting, exporting in various graphics formats—before committing the thing to your hard drive.

- **Services.** The Capture commands in the Services menu (Chapter 7) trigger the same screen-capturing function. They work, however, only when your cursor is in a Cocoa program that accepts pasted graphics (TextEdit, Stickies, Mail, and Pages, for example).

Tip: One picture may be worth a thousand words, but sometimes a video is worth a thousand pictures. Don't forget that QuickTime Player (Chapter 15) can record *video* of your screen activity, for when a single still frame doesn't quite cut it.

Sound, Movies, & Speech

For years, as other computer companies whipped themselves into a frenzy try-ing to market one multimedia computer or another, Mac fans just smiled. Macs have been capable of displaying sound and graphics—no add-on sound, graphics, or video boards required—from day one, years before the word *multimedia* was even coined.

The Mac's superiority at handling sound and video continues in Snow Leopard. QuickTime, for example, the software that plays digital movies and live "streaming" broadcasts from the Internet, has been rewritten completely for better video and cooler controls.

This chapter covers both creative pursuits: creating and using sound, and playing and editing movies.

As a bonus, this chapter also covers Mac OS X's speech features (how to command your Mac by voice, as well as making your Mac talk back); VoiceOver, the newly beefed-up talking-Mac feature for blind people; and Front Row, the full-screen, across-the-room, remote-controlled presentation mode for movies, sounds, photos, and DVDs.

Playing Sounds

You can have a lot of fun with digital sounds—if you know where to find them, where to put them, and how to edit them. You can play almost any kind of digitized sound files, even MP3 files, right in the Finder—if you put their windows into column view or Cover Flow view (or use Quick Look). But that's just the beginning.

Controlling the Volume

Adjusting the volume of your Mac's speakers couldn't be easier: tap the ◄» and ◄»)) keys on your keyboard. (The ◄ key next to them is the Mute button, which instantaneously cuts off all the Mac's sound—a wonderful feature when you find yourself trying to use the Mac surreptitiously in a library or a church.)

Alternatively, you can add the ◄») menulet to your menu bar (Figure 15-1).

Figure 15-1:
The tiny speaker silhouette in the upper-right corner of your screen turns into a volume slider when you click it. To make this sound menulet appear, open the Sound pane of System Preferences and turn on "Show volume in menu bar."

The Output tab of the System Preferences pane, by the way, is designed to let you adjust the left-to-right balance of your stereo speakers, if you have them. The stereo speakers on most Macs that have them (iMacs, laptops) are already perfectly centered, so there's little need to adjust this slider unless you generally list to one side in your chair. (You might find additional controls here if you have extra audio gear—an old iSub subwoofer system, for example.)

Tip: In the Audio MIDI Setup program (in Applications→Utilities), you can set up and configure much fancier speaker setups, including 5.1 and 6.1 surround-sound systems.

Alert Beeps and You

Alert beeps are the quacks, beeps, or trumpet blasts that say, "You can't click here." (Try typing letters into a dialog box where a program expects numbers, for example.)

Choosing an alert beep

To choose one that suits your personal taste, open System Preferences→Sound→Sound Effects. Press the ↑ and ↓ keys to walk through the 14 witty and interesting sound snippets you can use as error beeps. You can also drag the "Alert volume" slider to adjust the error beep volume relative to your Mac's overall speaker setting.

Adding new alert beeps

Mac OS X's error beeps are AIFF sound files, a popular Mac/Windows/Internet sound format—which, as a testimony to its potential for high quality, is also the standard sound-file format for music CDs. (The abbreviation stands for *audio interchange file format.*)

As with fonts, Mac OS X builds the list of error beeps you see in the Sound pane of System Preferences from several folder sources:

- **System→Library→Sounds folder.** This folder contains the basic Mac OS X set. Because it's in the System folder, it's off-limits to manipulation by us meddlesome human beings. You can't easily delete one of the original Mac OS X error beeps or add to this collection.

- **Home folder→Library→Sounds folder.** It's easy enough to add sounds for your own use—just add them to this folder.

- **Library→Sounds folder.** If you, an administrator, want to make a sound file available to all account holders on your Mac (if there are more than one), create a new Sounds folder in the main hard drive window's Library folder. Any sound files you put there now appear in every account holder's list of alert sounds.

The sound files you put into these folders must be in AIFF format, and their names must end with the extension *.aiff* or *.aif.*

Note: Any changes you make to these Sounds folders don't show up in the Sound pane until the next time you open it.

Recording Sound

If you hope to record new sounds, you need a microphone. Your microphone situation depends on the kind of Mac you have:

- **Laptop, iMac, eMac.** You have a built-in microphone, usually a tiny hole near the screen.

- **Mac Pro, Mac Mini.** You can plug in an external USB microphone or use an adapter (such as the iMic, *www.griffintechnology.com*) that accommodates a standard microphone.

The System Preferences→Sound→Input pane lets you choose which sound source you want the Mac to listen to: external USB microphone, built-in microphone, or whatever.

Tip: Actually, there's a quicker way to change audio inputs—if you know the secret. Option-click the ◀)) menulet, if you've installed it. The resulting menu lists all your audio inputs and outputs, making it simple to switch.

Making the Recording

Once you've got your microphone situation taken care of, you need to get your hands on some sound-recording software. Snow Leopard offers a new, especially easy way to record audio: QuickTime Player, which is in your Applications folder. (You can use GarageBand to record sound, too, but that's often like using a pneumatic drill to get out a splinter.)

Choose File→New Audio Recording. Use the pop-up menu to specify the audio quality and sound source (Figure 15-2). Click the round, red Record button and begin to speak; click the square Stop button to finish up. Now you can use the volume slider and the ▶ button to listen to your masterpiece.

Tip: Don't adjust the tiny volume slider in the Audio Recording window unless you're wearing headphones. This slider lets you monitor the sound—and turning it up while the Mac's speakers are live risks producing the hideous shriek known as feedback.

Figure 15-2:
There's a lot going on in this tiny window. The pop-up menu lets you choose audio quality and audio input. At bottom, as you record, you see a VU meter (audio level) and an indication of the recording's length and file size.

Behind the scenes, the Mac has created an AAC audio file called Audio Recording.mov in your Home→Movies folder. (Additional recordings are called Audio Recording 2, 3, 4, and so on.) You can double-click it to open it right back up into QuickTime Player for trimming (page 589). Or, if you think it needs more in-depth editing, you can open it with GarageBand and really go to town.

Note: You can record video in QuickTime Player just as easily. See page 586.

QuickTime Movies

A QuickTime movie is a video file you can play from your hard drive, a CD or DVD, or the Internet. Like any movie, it creates the illusion of motion by flashing many individual frames (photos) per second before your eyes, while also playing a synchronized soundtrack.

QuickTime Player

Thousands of Mac OS X programs can open QuickTime movies, play them back, and sometimes even incorporate them into documents. Among them: Word, FileMaker, Keynote, PowerPoint, Safari, and even the Finder (when you use Quick Look, column view, or Cover Flow view; see Chapter 1).

But the cornerstone of Mac OS X's movie-playback software is QuickTime Player, which sits in your Applications folder (and even comes factory-installed in the Dock). This program, rewritten from scratch for Snow Leopard, is designed not only to play movies and sounds, but also to record and trim them, post them to YouTube or MobileMe, and so on.

Playing movies with QuickTime Player

You can open a movie file by double-clicking it. When QuickTime Player first opens, you get Snow Leopard's very cool, borderless playback window. If you just hit the space bar, you play the movie.

There's a control toolbar at the bottom of the window (Figure 15-3), but it fades away after a few seconds—or immediately, if you push the cursor out of the frame. The toolbar reappears anytime your mouse moves back where it used to be. These are the controls:

- **Volume slider (🔈...🔊).** Click in the slider, or drag the dot, to adjust the volume—although it's actually easier to just tap the ↑ or ↓ keys. Click the 🔈 to mute the audio; click it again to unmute.

FREQUENTLY ASKED QUESTION

QuickTime Player vs. QuickTime Player 7 vs. QuickTime Player Pro

Hey! I had paid $30 to upgrade the old *QuickTime Player to the Pro version, so I could edit videos, copy/paste, combine tracks, export in different formats, stuff like that. I upgraded to Snow Leopard, and now Pro is gone! What's the deal!? Apple just trashed my $30 software?*

Chillax, bro. It's all good.

True enough, the new QuickTime Player is intended to replace the old, free program QuickTime Player (now called QuickTime Player 7) as well as the $30 upgraded version, QuickTime Player Pro. Apple figures: Look, the new app looks better, plays better, uploads movies to YouTube, and does basic editing really well. If you need fancier editing or exporting, well, your Mac came with iMovie, didn't it? You can always use that.

But if you paid $30 to upgrade your old Player to Pro, you might resent having to heave open the lumbering iMovie just for quick copy/paste jobs.

Fortunately, Apple didn't delete your old QuickTime Player Pro; it just moved it into the Applications→Utilities folder when you installed Snow Leopard. There it sits, bearing the new name QuickTime Player 7. If you use it more often than you use the Snow Leopard QuickTime Player, then you can reassign movies so that they open up in Player 7 when double-clicked.

To make things a little more complicated, the old QuickTime Player (non-Pro) is actually still available–in the unlikely event that you prefer its basic playback functions to the new Player's. It's one of the Optional Installs on your Mac OS X installation DVD.

To recap, there are three programs kicking around. **QuickTime Player** in your Applications folder is the new playback/recording program (with trimming and YouTube uploading). **QuickTime Player 7,** if you find it in your Utilities folder, is either your old $30 copy of QuickTime Player Pro, or the old QuickTime Player that you've manually installed from the Mac OS X DVD.

Happy QuickTiming!

Tip: To mute the sound, click the ◄⁾ icon, or press Option-↓. Press Option-↑ to make the volume slider jump to full-blast position.

- **Rewind, Fast-forward** (◄◄, ►►). By clicking one of these buttons, you get to speed through your movie at double speed, backward or forward, complete with sound. Click again for 4X speed, again for 8X.

Snow Leopard Spots: You don't have to keep your mouse button pressed on these buttons, as in the olden days. Just click once and let QuickTime Player do the work. Click ► or tap the space bar to stop scanning.

- **Play/Pause** (►/II). Click ► to start playback, II to pause/stop. Or just tap the space bar for both functions.

Figure 15-3:
The new, improved QuickTime Player displays this control bar only when you move your mouse into its window, or whenever playback is stopped.

- **Scroll bar.** Drag the little diamond, or just click inside its track, to jump to a different spot in the movie. The counters at the beginning and end of the scroll bar tell you, in "hours:minutes:seconds" format, how far your playhead cursor has moved into the movie, and how far you are from the end. (Click the right-hand readout to see the total movie duration.)

Tip: You can also press the ← and → keys to step through the movie one frame at a time. If you press Option-← or Option-→, you jump to the beginning or end of the movie. That's important to know, since there are no longer dedicated Jump to Start/Jump to End buttons on the control bar.

- **Resize handle.** Drag diagonally to make the window bigger or smaller. QuickTime Player always maintains the same *aspect ratio* (relative dimensions) of the original movie, so you won't accidentally squish it.

- **Share button ( ).** Click for a pop-up menu of three choices for passing on this video to your adoring fans: iTunes, YouTube, or MobileMe. The Trim command is here, too. All four of these options are described below.

- **Full Screen ( ).** Click to make the video fill your entire monitor, just as though you'd chosen View→Enter Full Screen.

Snow Leopard Spots: When you enter Full Screen, the movie doesn't begin playing automatically, as it did in the old QuickTime Player. You have to tap the space bar to get the show under way.

Fancy playback tricks

Nobody knows for sure what Apple was thinking when it created some of these additional features—exactly how often do you want your movie to play backward?—but here they are (some of these features are available only in the unlocked Pro version of QuickTime Player):

- **Change the screen size.** As noted above, you can drag the window to any size using the lower-right handle. But the View menu commands—Fit to Screen, Actual Size, Enter Full Screen, and so on—are handy, too.

So what do they all mean? **Actual size** represents the movie on your screen at its real size—no larger. (If it's truly huge, larger than your screen, it may be scaled *smaller* to fit. But that's a rarity.)

Fit to Screen fills your screen without cropping or distorting; the menu bar and other windows remain visible.

Enter Full Screen is especially satisfying, because it turns your entire monitor into a movie playback area; even the menu bar is hidden. And what if the proportions of the movie don't quite match your screen? If you make the menu bar return by pointing to the top of your screen, you can handle this problem using one of the three choices in the View menu:

Fit to Screen, as before, enlarges the video as much as possible *without chopping off the edges.* So you might get black letterbox bars at top/bottom or left/right. **Fill Screen** enlarges the movie to fill your screen completely, even if the edges get chopped off. **Panoramic** squishes the outer edges of the video, distorting them slightly, so that nothing gets chopped off *and* the movie fills the screen.

Making the window larger may also make the movie coarser, because QuickTime Player simply enlarges every dot that was present in the original. Still, when you want to show a movie to a group of people more than a few feet back from the screen, these larger sizes are perfectly effective.

- **Play more than one movie.** You can open several movies at once and run them simultaneously. (Of course, the more movies you try to play at once, the jerkier the playback gets.)

- **Loop the movie.** When you choose View→Loop and then click Play, the movie repeats endlessly until you make it stop.

- **Navigate chapters.** A few movies, like the ones you buy or rent from Apple, come with built-in chapter markers, just like a DVD. As shown in Figure 15-4, they let you jump around in the film at your whim.

Figure 15-4:
Movies from the iTunes store come with built-in chapter markers, which you can click to navigate. To see them, choose View→Show Chapters (⌘-R). In the unlikely event that you encounter a movie with alternate languages or subtitle options, you can turn those on and off from the View menu, too.

Recording Movies with QuickTime Player

For the first time in its history, QuickTime Player now does more than *play* movies; it can also *record* them. Yes, your Mac is now a camcorder, and a darned handy one; you can pop out quick video greetings, gross out your former roommates, impress your coworkers with a dress rehearsal of your pitch, and so on.

Laptops and iMacs, of course, have a video camera built right in, above the screen. If you have another model, you can attach a Web cam, an old iSight camera, or even a FireWire camcorder.

Then open QuickTime Player and choose File→New Video Recording. The preview window appears. Use the pop-up menu shown in Figure 15-5 to specify what mike and camera you want to use (in the unlikely even that you have more than one), what video quality you want, and where you want to store the result.

Figure 15-5:
Use the pop-up menu to set up your flick; check the audio level (reflected by the "sound waves" at the bottom of the control bar). Press space when you're ready to roll!

Then, to record, click the red Record button, or just tap the space bar. Do your schtick. Press space again to stop the recording.

Your new video appears in its own playback window. Check it out, trim it if necessary, then shoot it off to iTunes, MobileMe, or YouTube!

Recording Screen Movies

Now here's a new Snow Leopard feature *nobody* saw coming: You can now record movies *of the screen.*

Why is it useful to capture screen activity as a video? Because you can give little lessons to techno-clueless relatives by sending a mini-tutorial. You can make video podcasts that show how to do things in your software programs. You can preserve Web animations that you used to think you had no way to capture.

There are limitations. QuickTime Player can record only the *entire screen,* not just a part of it. Your movies don't include the sound from the Mac's own speakers, so forget about capturing YouTube videos. (It can record from the *mike,* though, so you can narrate what you're doing.) In other words, it's no match for a dedicated screen-movie-making program like Snapz Pro X.

But who cares? It's fantastically handy.

Tip: If you do want to isolate only part of the screen, you can do that later in iMovie, which came with your Mac. It has a very cool video-cropping tool.

To make a screen recording, choose File→New Screen Recording. Use the pop-up menu on the resulting Screen Recording panel to turn the microphone on or off, to choose a quality setting, and to indicate where you want the finished movie stored.

Finally, click the red Record button, or tap the space bar, then proceed as shown in Figure 15-6.

Figure 15-6:
This odd little warning appears when you tap the space bar. It lets you know that it's going to hide itself so that it won't mess up your screen movie, but that a Stop Recording button will appear in your menu bar. Try the Show Me button. Weird! (Yes, the Stop Recording button will appear in your video.) Click Start Recording once you understand the deal.

When you finally click Stop Recording in the menu bar, or press ⌘-Control-Esc, your movie appears in a regular playback window—a *really big* one—ready to trim or send away to your fans.

Internet Streaming QuickTime

QuickTime Player also lets you view "Internet slideshows," watch a couple of live TV stations, or listen to the radio—all as you work on your Mac, and all at no charge.

Streaming video from your browser

With ever-increasing frequency, Web sites advertise *streaming video* events, such as Apple keynote speeches and the occasional live rock concert. You'll find a note on a

Web page, for example, that says, "Watch the live debate by clicking here on October 15 at 9:00 p.m. EST."

If you do so, you'll sometimes be able to watch it in your browser, and sometimes you'll be transported once again into QuickTime Player, which connects to the appropriate Internet "station" and plays the video in its window. (You can also choose File→Open URL from within QuickTime Player to type in the Web address.)

You don't have much control when watching a live broadcast. You generally can't rewind, and you certainly can't fast-forward. You may be able to pause the broadcast, but when you un-pause, you wind up at the current broadcast moment—not where you stopped.

Snow Leopard Spots: QuickTime Player can now play HTTP streaming video, which is catching on for live broadcasts. One advantage: Because it uses the same "language" as ordinary Web pages, corporate firewalls and grouchy routers are less likely to block this kind of video.

Trimming Video

Like it or not, we live in a short-attention-span world. In this culture of YouTube and digital camera videos, the world has become one gigantic highlights reel.

Maybe that's why the new QuickTime Player comes equipped with a handy Trim command. You still can't cut anything out of the *middle* of a video, but you can very easily trim dead space off the *ends*. Figure 15-7 shows how.

Figure 15-7:
To trim a video, choose Edit→Trim, or press ⌘-T. Drag the yellow handles inward to isolate the chunk you want to preserve. (You can click ▶ or tap the space bar to check your work.) When everything looks good, click Trim or press Return.

Supertip: It's often useful to "see the audio" as you trim, so you can end the clip after someone's fina word, for example. No problem. If you hold down the Option key, you see a graph of the audio (bottom).

Tip: Once you're in Trim mode, the Edit menu sprouts a very cool command: Select All Excluding Silence. It automatically adjusts the yellow trim handles so that they cut out any silent portions of the video (at the beginning or end). That's a handy shortcut if you, like many impromptu videographers, let the camera roll a bit before and after the main event.

You don't have to worry about damaging the original video when trimming—you couldn't modify the original if you tried, because there's no Save command. (But if you've just recorded fresh video, save it before you trim; otherwise, the trim is permanent!)

You can, however, export or upload the shortened video, as described next.

Four Ways to Export Your Video

One of the new QuickTime Player's most important talents is *sharing* a video: posting it directly to YouTube or MobileMe, converting it to the right format for an iPod, iPhone or cellphone, stashing it in iTunes for easy transfer to your iPod/iPhone, or saving it to the hard drive as a double-clickable movie.

Let us count the ways.

Send to iTunes

The main reason you'd want to send your video to iTunes is because you have an iPod, iPhone, or Apple TV. Once it's in iTunes, you can sync your video easily to that other Apple gadget and have it ready to view at all times.

To make this transfer happen, choose Share→iTunes. Or click the 🖻 icon on the control bar and choose iTunes from the pop-up menu.

Either way, you see the dialog box in Figure 15-8. Click the appropriate gadget/screen size, and then click Share. When it's all over, your video will appear safely nestled in iTunes, in the Videos category, ready to watch or sync.

Figure 15-8:
This dialog box gives you three size choices for the movie you're exporting, which correspond to the screen sizes of the three Apple gadgets available. (The Computer option is just there in case you like to play videos right in iTunes, right on the screen. It's dimmed if the original movie isn't big enough to fill the screen.)

Post to MobileMe Gallery

If you're paying $100 a year for a MobileMe account (Chapter 18), a better alternative awaits: You can post your video to your own online gallery. Advantages over YouTube? Simpler, quicker uploading. No 10-minute, 1-gig length or size limit. A much classier presentation online, without blinking ads and juvenile comments. Control over who can see it. Higher quality (even high definition).

Choose Share→YouTube, or click on the control bar and choose MobileMe Gallery from the pop-up menu. Type a name and description, and consider these three options:

- **Include a movie compatible with iPhoto and iPod Touch.** The big-screen movie you're about to post isn't in the right format for people who tune into your MobileMe Gallery on their iPhones and Touches. But if you turn on this checkbox, you generate a shadow version that's correctly sized and formatted for those popular gadgets.

- **Hide movie on my Gallery home page.** In other words, "Don't make this movie public." Nobody will even know this movie exists online unless you send them the unguessable Web address.

- **Allow movie to be downloaded.** Just what it says. If you want to retain control of your movie, leave this off; people will be able to watch it only on your Me gallery. If you want your creation to go viral, on the other hand, then turn this on and hope for the best.

Finally, click Share. QuickTime Player gets right to work sending your video to your MobileMe Gallery. When the progress bar finishes its crawl across the status dialog box, you see a tiny link (Figure 15-9) to the posted video.

Figure 15-9:
When the video is finished uploading to MobileMe, a tiny Web address appears in the progress box. Click it to view your masterpiece online, or send the Web address around to your fans.

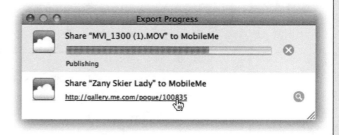

Post to YouTube

When you consider your movie ready for prime time, you can post it to YouTube, the world's most popular and famous Web site for short videos, with a single command. (The movie can't be longer than 10 minutes, or larger than 1 gigabyte.)

Before you begin, though, you have to sign up for a YouTube *account*. It's free, but you have to do it at YouTube.com, and remember the name and password you choose.

Then, with your movie open in QuickTime Player, choose Share→YouTube. (Or click the 📤 icon on the control bar and then choose YouTube from the pop-up menu.) You're asked for your YouTube name and password. If you turn on "Remember this password in my keychain," you won't have to enter it the next time.

Finally, click Sign In. On the next screen (Figure 15-10), type a title and description for the movie. Enter keywords (search categories like "funny" or "sports") so people on YouTube will find your video when they search.

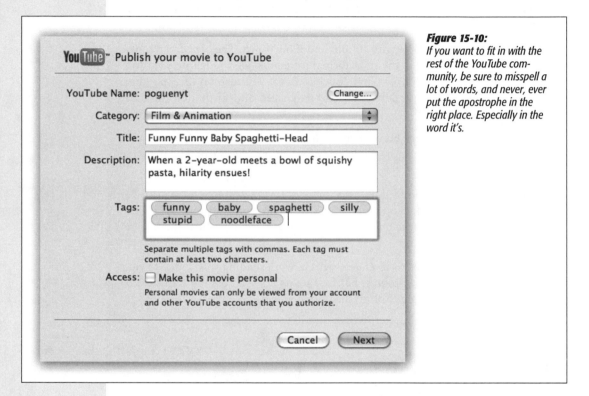

Figure 15-10:
If you want to fit in with the rest of the YouTube community, be sure to misspell a lot of words, and never, ever put the apostrophe in the right place. Especially in the word it's.

Finally, click Next. A final screen appears, warning you not to be naughty. Click Share to finish process. In a few minutes, your video will be live for the whole world to see—no charge.

Saving the finished movie

After you've trimmed a movie (or not), you can choose File→Save As to specify a new name for your edited masterpiece. All you have to do is specify, using the Format pop-up menu, what *size* you want the finished file to be: iPhone, iPod, HD 480p (meaning "standard TV screen"), HD 720p (meaning "hi-def TV"), and so on. Keep in mind that big size on the screen = huge video file that's slow and awkward to transmit online.

Speech Recognition

Although it may surprise many people, the Mac is quite talented when it comes to speech. Its abilities fall into two categories: reading text aloud, using a synthesized voice; and taking commands from your voice.

The Apple marketing machine may have been working too hard when it called this feature "speech recognition"—the Mac OS feature called PlainTalk doesn't take dictation, typing out what you say. (For that, you need a program like iListen, *www.macspeech. com*—or, better yet, Dragon NaturallySpeaking, an amazing dictation program for Windows that you can run in a Mac, as described in Chapter 8.)

Instead, PlainTalk is what's known as a *command-and-control* technology. It lets you open programs, trigger AppleScripts, choose menu commands, trigger keystrokes, and click dialog box buttons and tabs—just by speaking their names.

Few people use PlainTalk speech recognition. But if your Mac has a microphone, PlainTalk is worth at least a 15-minute test drive. It may become a part of your work routine forever.

GEM IN THE ROUGH

QuickTime Virtual Reality

If they live to be 100, most Mac users will probably never encounter a QuickTime VR movie. Maybe that's why the Snow Leopard version of QuickTime Player can't even open these aging-but-cool "panorama movies," whose technology was built into every Mac for a decade.

Fortunately, QuickTime Player 7 is still included with Snow Leopard (see the box on page 583), and it can still play these immersive movies.

The trick is finding a QuickTime VR movie; your safest bet is, as usual, the Web. (The best starting point is Apple's own QuickTime VR page, *www.apple.com/ quicktime/technologies/qtvr.*)

When you open a QuickTime VR movie, you might think at first that you've simply opened a still photo (there's no scroll bar, for example). The trick is to drag your cursor around inside the photo. Doing so rotates the "camera," enabling you to look around you in all directions.

Then try pressing the Shift key to zoom in (move forward) as much as you like. If you go too far, the image becomes too grainy. Press the Control key to zoom out (move backward).

And if you really want to blow your mind, try one of the *cubic* VR movies posted on that Web page. It lets you rotate your view not just side to side, but also up to the sky and down to your feet.

Using the free and commercial tools listed on the Apple Web site (or several that aren't, including PanoTools), you can even make your own QuickTime VR movies—provided you've got a camera, a tripod, and a good deal of patience.

Your First Conversation with the Mac

The on/off switch for speech recognition in Mac OS X is the Speech pane of System Preferences (Figure 15-11). Where you see "Speakable items" (on the Speech Recognition tab), click On.

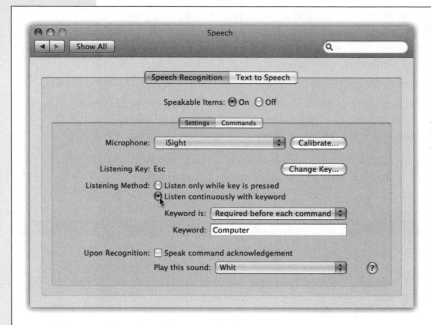

Figure 15-11:
Turn listening on and off here. If you turn on "Listen only while key is pressed," then the Mac pays attention to you only when you're pressing a key (like Esc). As a convenience, it even pauses iTunes playback while you're pressing the key. If you turn on "Listen continuously with keyword," then you have to say a certain keyword to "get its attention" before speaking each command. In the Keyword blank, type the word you want the Mac to listen for as it monitors the sound from your mike.

The Feedback window

Check out your screen: A small, microphone-like floating window now appears (Figure 15-12). The "Esc" in its center indicates the "listen" key—the key you're supposed to hold down when you want the Mac to respond to your voice. (You wouldn't want the Mac listening all the time—even when you said, for example, "Hey, it's cold in here. *Close the window.*" Therefore, the Mac comes set to listen only when you're pressing that key.)

You can specify a different key, if you wish, or eliminate the requirement to press a key altogether, as described in the next section.

When you start talking, you'll also see the Mac's interpretation of what you said written out in a yellow balloon just over the Feedback window.

The Speakable Commands window

The only commands PlainTalk understands are listed in the Speakable Commands window. (If it's not open, see Figure 15-12.) Keeping your eye on this window is essential, because it offers a complete list of everything your Mac understands. As you can see, some of the commands represent shortcuts that would take several steps if you had to perform them manually.

Here are a few examples of what you'll find in the list at first:

- **Phone for [Steve Jobs].** Displays Steve Jobs's phone number in huge digits across your screen—the fastest way yet to look up a number of somebody in your Address Book program.

  You can also say "Chat with Steve Jobs" (or whomever) to begin a new chat session in iChat with that person, "Mail this to Steve Jobs" to send the current document as a Mail attachment, or "Meet with Steve Jobs" to add an iCal appointment with this person's information attached.

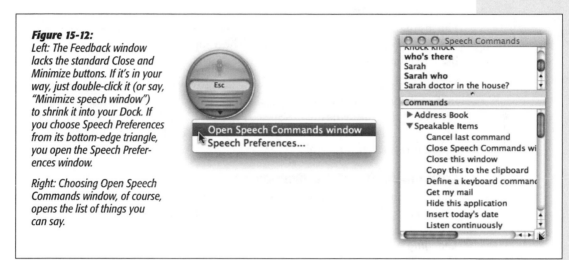

Figure 15-12:
Left: The Feedback window lacks the standard Close and Minimize buttons. If it's in your way, just double-click it (or say, "Minimize speech window") to shrink it into your Dock. If you choose Speech Preferences from its bottom-edge triangle, you open the Speech Preferences window.

Right: Choosing Open Speech Commands window, of course, opens the list of things you can say.

- **Set alarm for 30 minutes.** (You can say any number of minutes or hours—"Set alarm for 2 hours," or whatever.) The Mac asks you to type a little message, which will serve as the iCal dialog box that appears at the specified time.

Tip: Check the complete list of iCal and Address Book commands in the Speech Commands window.

- **Close this window.** Closes the frontmost window instantly.

- **Empty the Trash.** Works only when you're in the Finder.

- **Switch to Safari.** Brings Safari to the front. (Actually, you can say, "Switch to" and then the name of *any* running or recently used program.)

- **Quit all applications.** Saves you the trouble of switching into each program and choosing Quit.

- **Open the Speech Commands window** or **Show me what to say.** Opens the Speech Commands window, of course.

- **What day is it?** Tells you the date.

• **Tell me a joke.** Begins a pathetic/funny knock-knock joke. You've got to play along, providing the "Who's there?" and "So-and-so *who?*" answers.

Mac OS X *updates* the listing in the Speech Commands window in real time, according to the context. When you switch from one program to another, you see a list of the local commands that work in the new program. You'll discover that when you use the "Tell me a joke" command, for example, you don't necessarily have to say, "Who's there?" You can also say, "Stop," "Go away," or "Stop with the jokes!" (It must really be fun to work at Apple.)

Speaking to the Mac

Finish up on the Speech pane of System Preferences. Use the Microphone pop-up menu to specify which microphone you'll be using (if you have a choice). Click Calibrate to adjust its sensitivity.

Now you're ready to begin. While pressing the Esc key (if that's still the one identified in the Feedback window), begin speaking. Speak normally; don't exaggerate or shout. Try one of the commands in the Speakable Commands list—perhaps "What time is it?" If your mike is set up properly, the round Feedback window displays animated sound waves when you speak.

Customizing Speech Recognition

You can tailor the speech recognition feature in two ways: by adjusting the way it looks and operates, and by adding new commands to its vocabulary.

Changing when the Mac listens

Having the microphone "open," listening full-time, is an invitation for disaster. Everyday phone conversations, office chatter, and throat clearings would completely bewilder the software, triggering random commands.

Therefore, you must explicitly *tell* the Mac when you're addressing it. When you first turn on the speech recognition feature, the Mac expects you to alert it by pressing a key, like Esc, when you speak.

Tip: To change the key you hold down when you want the Mac to listen, visit the Speech pane of System Preferences; click the Speech Recognition tab; click Settings; and then click Change Key. A little message prompts you to press the keyboard key you'd prefer to use. Your choices are Esc, Delete, F5 through F12, or the keys on your numeric keypad—with or without the Shift, Control, or Option keys.

If you'd rather not have to press some key whenever you want the computer's attention, click the other option in this pane, "Listen continuously with keyword." Now to get the computer's attention, you must speak the keyword—which you type into the Keyword box—before each command. For example, you might say, "Computer, open AppleWorks," or "Hal, what day is it?"

The word you specify appears in the middle of the round Feedback window.

Note: This method of getting the computer's attention is less reliable than the push-a-key-to-talk system. Especially if you name the computer "Hal." Although that's hilarious in theory, polysyllabic words work better in practice.

By using the "Keyword is" pop-up menu, meanwhile, you can specify how big your window of opportunity is:

- **Optional before commands.** If you work alone in a quiet room, this is the choice for you. It means you don't have to press a key *or* say the Mac's name when issuing a voice command. *Everything you say* is considered a command.

- **Required before each command.** Nothing you say is interpreted as a command unless you say the computer's keyword first, as in, "*Macintosh,* switch to Microsoft Word."

- **Required 15 seconds after last command, Required 30 seconds after last command.** Sometimes you want to issue several commands in a row and would feel foolish saying, "Computer, close all windows. Computer, empty the Trash. Computer, switch to Calculator." When you turn on this option, you can say the keyword just once; all commands you issue in the next 15 or 30 seconds "belong to" that first salutation. The push-to-talk key and the spoken keyword, in this case, serve as a master on/off switch for the Mac's listening mode.

Tip: If you're not using the push-to-talk method, you can still turn speech recognition off temporarily by saying, "Turn on push to talk." (Now the Mac listens to you only when you're pressing the designated key.) When you want to return to listening-all-the-time mode, say, "Listen continuously."

Changing the feedback

Another set of options on the Speech Recognition tab governs what the Mac does when it understands something you've said. For example:

- **Play sound.** The Mac generally makes a sound whenever it recognizes something you've said. Use this pop-up menu to control which of your built-in beeps you want it to use—or choose None.

- **Speak command acknowledgement.** Sometimes the Speech Feedback window shows you a message of its own. When you use the "Empty the Trash" command, for example, text in the Feedback window may inform you that a locked item prevents the emptying. The Mac generally reads this text aloud to you; turn this checkbox off if you'd rather have the Mac be silent.

Triggering menus by voice

On the Speech pane of System Preferences, click the Speech Recognition tab, and then click the Commands minitab. Here you find a list of the command categories that Speakable Items can understand. As you turn each checkbox on or off, watch the Speech Commands window. Giant swaths of commands appear or disappear as you fool with these checkboxes, giving you a good indication as to their function. Here's a rundown:

- **Address Book.** These commands let you look up numbers; add appointments to iCal; set up alarm reminders for yourself; mail things to people; and begin text, audio, or video chats with people whose names are already in your Address Book.

- **Global Speakable Items.** This is the master list of Speakable Items, shown in Figure 15-12.

- **Application-Specific Items.** Certain Mac OS X programs come with preset lists of commands that work only when you're in the relevant program. For example, whenever you're in the Finder, you can say, "Empty the Trash," "Go to my Home directory," "Hide the Dock," "Minimize all windows," "Make a new folder," and so on. When this checkbox is off, the Mac no longer recognizes any of these handy commands.

- **Application Switching.** This is the command category at the bottom half of the Speech Commands list—"Switch to Address Book," "Switch to AOL," and so on.

- **Front Window.** In your Speech Commands window, note the appearance of a new category of commands, called Front Window. The idea here is to provide you with quick speech-recognition access to the most prominent buttons, tabs, and icons in whichever window is before you. Figure 15-13 elaborates on the idea.

- **Menu Bar.** This command lets you open menus (in the menu bar) by speaking their names.

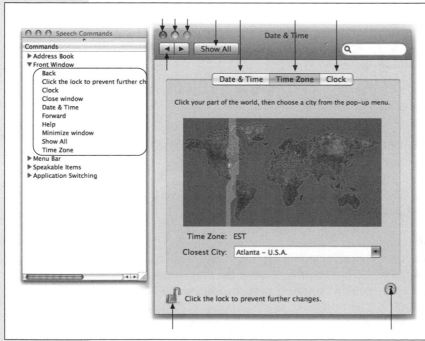

Figure 15-13:
The Front Window commands change automatically to reflect the controls in the frontmost window. For example, in the Date & Time pane of System Preferences, you can say anything in the circled area of the Speech Commands window: the name of any tab or window control (indicated by the arrows). Whenever you say an item, the Mac "clicks" it for you. You can also speak the menus' names to open them.

Once you say its name ("File menu," for example), the menu opens. Now you can say any command in the open menu ("New Playlist," "Save," or whatever). The Menu Bar category of the Speech Commands window changes to remind you of what you can say at any given moment.

The combination of Front Window and Menu Bar commands lets you do quite a bit of work on your Mac without ever needing the mouse or keyboard.

Improving the PlainTalk vocabulary

By putting an alias of a favorite document, folder, disk, or program into your Home→Library→Speakable Items folder, you can teach PlainTalk to recognize its name and open it for you on command. You can name these icons anything you want.

You can also rename the starter set that Apple provides. You'll have the best luck with multiword or polysyllabic names—"Microsoft Word," not just "Word."

One kind of icon PlainTalk can open is an *AppleScript* icon (see Chapter 7). If you open your Home folder→Library→Speech→Speakable Items, you'll discover that most of the built-in Speakable Items icons are, in fact, AppleScript icons. The point is you can make PlainTalk do almost anything you want, especially in the Finder, simply by creating AppleScripts and putting them into the Speakable Items folder.

Application-specific commands

Most of the preinstalled PlainTalk commands work in any program. You can say, for example, "Open iTunes" to launch iTunes from within any program.

However, you can also create commands that work only in a specific program. They sit in your Speakable Items→Application Speakable Items folder, inside individual application-name folders. For example, Mac OS X comes with commands for Safari that include Go Back, Go Forward, and Page Down.

If you get good at AppleScript, you can create your own application-command folders in the Speakable Items→Application Speakable Items folder.

Then open the program for which you want to create special commands and say, "Make this application speakable." The Mac creates a folder for the program in the Speakable Items folder; fill it with the AppleScripts you've created. (Not all programs can be AppleScript-controlled.)

Note: If you give an application-specific icon the same name as one of the global commands, the Mac executes the application-specific one—if that program is running.

PlainTalk tips, tricks, and troubleshooting

When you're creating new commands, click the Helpful Tips button at the lower-right corner of the Commands pane (of the Speech Recognition pane of the Speech pane of System Preferences).

The Mac Reads to You

So far in this chapter, you've read about the Mac's listening ability. But the conversation doesn't have to be one-way; it's even easier to make the Mac *talk*.

In Snow Leopard, most Apple programs have a Start Speaking command built right in: Safari, Mail, TextEdit, iChat, Stickies, Pages, and so on. Just Control-click (or right-click) inside a window full of text and, from the pop-up menu, choose Speech→Start Speaking. How cool is that? Your Mac can read your email or a Web article to you while you're getting dressed.

You can add a Speak command in FileMaker Pro scripts. Mac OS X's Chess and Calculator programs can talk back, too.

But that's kid stuff. Truth is, the Mac can read almost anything you like: text you pass your cursor over, alert messages, menus, and *any text document in any program*. It can speak in your choice of 24 synthesizer voices, ages 8 to 50. Most read with a twangy, charmingly Norwegian accent—all but Alex, Apple's newest voice, which sounds scarily like a professional human voice-over artist.

Note: This text-reading business is not the same thing as the Mac's VoiceOver feature. VoiceOver is designed to read everything on the screen, including pop-up menus, buttons, and other controls, to visually impaired Mac fans (and to permit complete control, mouse-free, of everything). See page 603.

Setting Up the Mac's Voice

To configure the way the Mac talks, revisit the Speech pane of System Preferences. Click the Text to Speech tab at the top of the window. As you can see in Figure 15-14, you can control which of the Mac's voices you want your computer to use, as well as how fast it should speak.

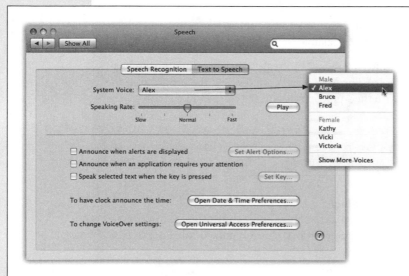

Figure 15-14:
At the outset, you see only six voices—the ones that sound the most human. Choose Show More Voices to see the complete list of 24.

Then, for 15 minutes of hilarity, try clicking the voices in turn to hear sample sentences. Drag the slider to affect how fast each one speaks. (Clearly, Apple's programmers had some fun with this assignment.)

Tip: Five of the voices sing rather than speak. Good News sings to the tune of *Pomp and Circumstance*, otherwise known as the Graduation March. Bad News sings to the tune of Chopin's *Prelude in C Minor*, better known as the Funeral March. Cellos sings to the tune of Grieg's *Peer Gynt* Suite. Pipe Organ sings to the tune of the Alfred Hitchcock TV theme. Bells sings the typical church-bell carillon melody.

In other words, these voices sing whatever words you type to those melodies. (To hear the melody in its entirety, don't use any punctuation.)

Here are all the different occasions when the Mac can talk to you.

Announce when alerts are displayed

If you turn on this checkbox, you can make the Mac read aloud error messages and alert messages that may appear on your screen. If you click the Set Alert Options button, you find these useful controls:

- **Voice.** Use this pop-up menu to specify the voice you want reading your error messages. (It doesn't have to be the same as the standard Mac default voice that's used for other purposes.)

- **Phrase.** Use this pop-up menu to specify which utterance the Mac speaks before the actual error message—for example, "*Excuse me!* The Trash could not be emptied," or "*Attention!* The document could not be printed."

  If you choose "Next in the phrase list" or "Random from the phrase list" from this pop-up menu, you'll never hear the same expletive twice. Better yet, choose Edit Phrase List to open a dialog box where you can specify your own words of frustration. (Apple Computer, Inc., is not liable for any trouble you may get into with people in neighboring cubicles.)

- **Delay.** The ostensible purpose of the Talking Alerts feature is to get your attention if you've wandered away from your Mac—mentally or physically. The chances are slim, but an urgent problem might occur that, if left undetected, could land you in trouble. (A 500-page printout brought to its knees by a paper jam comes to mind.)

  In other words, if you're still sitting in front of your Mac, you may not need the Mac to speak to get your attention; you could simply read the onscreen message. That's why you can set this slider to make the Mac wait, after the error message appears, for up to a minute before trying to flag you with its voice. That way it won't harangue you unnecessarily.

Announce when an application requires your attention

A jumping Dock icon means that the program is trying to get your attention. It might be because your printer is out of paper, or it might be because you've tried to shut down but one program still has open, unsaved documents. In any case, now the Mac can tell you, in so many words, which program needs some loving care.

Speak selected text when the key is pressed

As promised, this is the feature that lets you hear any Web page read to you, any email message, any sticky note—a welcome break for sore eyes. Furthermore, if you do any kind of writing at all, you'll discover the value of having your material read back to you out loud; it's a proofreading technique that reveals all kinds of typos and wordos that you wouldn't catch just by reading, even if you read it 50 times.

The very first time you turn on this checkbox, the Mac prompts you to specify a keystroke. (Later, you can always change the keystroke by clicking Set Key.) Choose a keystroke that doesn't conflict with the program you're using, like Control-T.

Now go to the program where you'd like the reading to happen. Highlight some text (or press ⌘-A to select all of it). Then press the keystroke you specified. The Mac begins reading it aloud immediately. To interrupt the playback, press the same keystroke again.

And be glad you were alive to see the day.

Tip: If you have an iPod or iPhone, your Mac can convert any text or word processing document into a spoken recording so you can listen to it when you're on the go. To pull this off, see page 265.

GEM IN THE ROUGH

Talking to Chess

If your friends and coworkers are, for some reason, still unimpressed by Mac OS X and your mastery of it, invite them over to watch you play a game of chess with your Mac—by talking to it.

(Actually, this feature isn't purely for entertainment: Some chess players prefer to move without looking at the board. By speaking their moves to the computer—and having the computer respond by speaking its own moves—these people can play "blindfolded.")

Open the Chess program. Unless you've turned it off (in Chess→Preferences), the game's speech-recognition feature is already turned on. When it's on, the round Feedback window should be visible onscreen.

To learn how to speak commands in a way that Chess un-

derstands, click the small gray triangle at the bottom of the Speech Feedback window to open the Speech Commands window. As usual, it lists all the commands that Chess can comprehend.

You specify the location of pieces using the grid of numbers and letters that appears along the edges of the chessboard. The white king, for example, starts on square e1 because he's in the first row (1) and the fifth column (e). To move the king forward by one square, you'd say: "King e1 to e2."

As the Speech Commands window should make clear, a few other commands are at your disposal. "Take back move" is one of the most useful. When you're ready to close in for the kill, the syntax is: "Pawn e5 takes f6."

And smile when you say that.

VoiceOver

The Mac has always been able to read stuff on the screen out loud. But Apple has taken this feature light-years farther, turning it into a full-blown *screen reader* for the benefit of people who can't see. VoiceOver doesn't just read every scrap of text it finds on the screen—it also lets you control everything on the screen (menus, buttons, and so on) without ever needing the mouse. And in Snow Leopard, VoiceOver has taken another *enormous* leap forward.

Here's a little bit of what's new:

- **Gestures.** On a Mac with a multitouch trackpad, you can interact with what's visible on the screen by using the trackpad itself as a map of the current window or screen area; VoiceOver speaks whatever's under your finger. You can flick in any direction to move to the next thing on the screen. You hear a sound whenever VoiceOver finds blank spaces on the screen, all in the name of helping you "feel" where everything is.

- **Braille monitors.** Yes, there are actually Braille "displays"—essentially flat, touchable panels with dots that rise through holes in a flat surface as you move the Mac's cursor, permitting you to read what's on the screen. Snow Leopard works with more of these contraptions, including wireless ones, and can broadcast to a classroom full of them simultaneously.

- **VoiceOver Web browsing.** Snow Leopard can read entire Web pages, navigate Web tables, hop from link to link, and so on. You can navigate by pressing arrow keys, using the mouse, or using the trackpad.

- **More flexibility.** Snow Leopard brings more customizability, more settings, and more help getting started, thanks to an interactive tutorial.

Obviously, learning VoiceOver is a *huge* task that can take days or weeks—but if it's your ticket to being able to use a computer at all, you'll probably be happy to have such a full-fledged monster of a program.

A full guide to VoiceOver could easily fill 40 pages—and does. Download the free PDF appendix to this chapter, "VoiceOver: The Missing Manual" from this book's "Missing CD" page at *www.missingmanuals.com*.

Ink: Handwriting Recognition

In the same way that your grandmother turned yesterday's dinner into today's sandwich (and tomorrow's soup), Apple recycled the handwriting technology of its failed Newton handheld and added it to Mac OS X. It's now called Ink, and it does exactly what it used to: turn your handwriting into "typed" text in any program.

You can't very well write directly on your Apple Cinema Display (although that would be cool). So Ink appears in Mac OS X only if you have a graphics tablet, one of those stylus-and-pad devices found generally only on the desks of graphic artists. (Wacom is the best-known tablet company, but there are a couple of others.)

Can Ink really replace the keyboard? Not for anything more than quick notes, that's for sure. But it can be handy when you're Web surfing, sketching, filling in database forms, and so on.

Still, let's face it: You could count the number of people with Wacom digitizing tablets who use them for handwriting input on one hand. And so, to avoid sacrificing any more old-growth trees to this book than absolutely necessary, the how-to for Ink is available as a free downloadable PDF appendix to this chapter. You'll find it on this book's "Missing CD" page at *www.missingmanuals.com*.

Note: Why on earth did Apple go to all this software-writing trouble just to satisfy the tiny community of graphics-tablet owners? That's exactly what the GICPWBAMBDOPTC (Great Internet Confederacy of People Who Believe that Apple Must Be Developing a One-Piece Tablet Computer) wants to know.

Front Row

For a few years there, most new Mac models came with a peculiar accessory: a slim, white remote control, looking for all the world like an iPod that's lost too much weight. If you point it at the Mac and press the remote's Menu button, you're catapulted into the magic world of Front Row, a special overlay that provides access to your music, photos, movies, and DVD player—with super-big fonts and graphics visible from the couch across the room.

The idea, of course, was to turn your Mac into an entertainment system unto itself.

The idea never caught on much. Eventually, Apple stopped including that remote in the box (although you can buy it from Apple). But even today, every Mac laptop, Mac Mini, and iMac responds to that little remote—and Front Row, the software, is built right into Mac OS X. It gets installed on *all* Macs, even the ones that don't have an infrared sensor.

That's because you can operate Front Row entirely from the keyboard—even from across the room, if you have a Bluetooth wireless one. So now even infrared-less Macs like the Mac Pro are invited to the Front Row party.

Front Row looks like the menu system of the Apple TV, if you've ever seen that (Figure 15-15).

Use the arrow keys or the **+** and **−** buttons on the remote to choose the primary activity you're interested in: DVD, Movies, TV Shows, Music, Podcasts, or Photos. Use the space bar or the remote's ▶ button as the Enter key to choose that kind of entertainment.

You'll find, to your delight, that Front Row lets you fire up not only all the music and videos you've got in iTunes, all the photos in iPhoto, and so on, but also all the music, photos, and videos stored on other Macs on your network (assuming you've left iPhoto and iTunes running on those Macs).

The bottom line: Your Mac is now an entertainment center that can be operated from across the room. Bit by bit, Apple is sneaking into the living room—and Front Row is its Trojan horse.

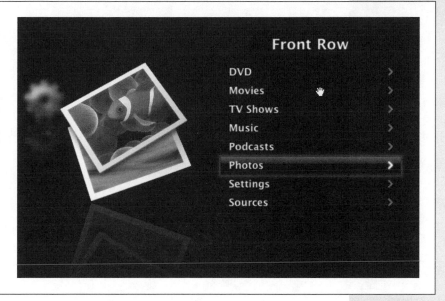

Figure 15-15:
Front Row is all about drilling down through the menu screens, exactly as on an iPod. Start here, on the main menu. Use the center button on your remote, or the space bar on your keyboard, to select a command or category and open the next screen. Keep going like that until you're watching your movies or slideshows, or listening to your music.

Here, then, is the cheat sheet for navigating your Mac's entertainment collections—whether you have a Front Row remote or not.

How to	Using the Remote	Using the Keyboard
Open and close Front Row	Menu	⌘-Esc
Navigate menus and lists	+, −	↑, ↓
Return to a previous menu	Menu	Esc
Select an item in a menu or list	▶ıı	space bar or Return
Play and pause audio or video	▶ıı	space bar or Return
Change volume	+, −	↑, ↓
Go to the next/previous song, photo, or DVD chapter	◄◄/►►ı	→, ←
Rewind/fast-forward (DVD or movie)	◄◄/►►ı (press and hold the button)	→, ← (hold down)

MAC OS X: THE MISSING MANUAL

The Unix Crash Course

As you're certainly aware by now, Mac OS X's resemblance to the original Mac operating system is only superficial. The engine underneath the pretty skin is utterly different. In fact, it's Unix, one of the oldest and most respected operating systems in use today. The first time you see it, you'd swear that Unix has about as much in common with the original Mac OS as a Jeep does with a melon (see Figure 16-1).

What the illustration at the bottom of Figure 16-1 shows, of course, is a *command line interface:* a place where you can type out instructions to the computer. This is a world without icons, menus, or dialog boxes. The mouse is almost useless here.

Surely you can appreciate the irony: The brilliance of the original 1984 Macintosh was that it *eliminated* the command line interface that was still the ruling party on the computers of the day (like Apple II and DOS machines). Most nongeeks sighed with relief, delighted that they'd never have to memorize commands again. Yet here's Mac OS X, Apple's supposedly ultramodern operating system, complete with a command line! What's going on?

Actually, the command line never went away. At universities and corporations worldwide, professional computer nerds kept right on pounding away at the little *C:* or *$* prompts, appreciating the efficiency and power such direct computer control afforded them.

You're forgiven if your reaction to the idea of learning Unix is, "For goodness' sake—can't I finish learning one way to control my new operating system before I have to learn yet another one?"

Absolutely. You never *have* to use Mac OS X's command line. In fact, Apple has swept it far under the rug, obviously expecting that most people will use the beautiful icons and menus of the regular desktop. There are, however, some tasks you can perform *only* at the command line, although fewer with each release of Mac OS X.

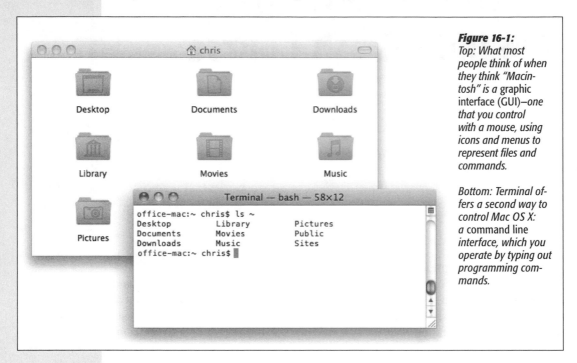

Figure 16-1:
Top: What most people think of when they think "Macintosh" is a graphic interface (GUI)—one that you control with a mouse, using icons and menus to represent files and commands.

Bottom: Terminal offers a second way to control Mac OS X: a command line interface, which you operate by typing out programming commands.

For intermediate or advanced Mac fans with a little time and curiosity, however, the command line opens up a world of possibilities. It lets you access corners of Mac OS X that you can't get to from the regular desktop. It lets you perform certain tasks with much greater speed and efficiency than you'd get by clicking buttons and dragging icons. And it gives you a fascinating glimpse into the minds and moods of people who live and breathe computers.

If you've ever dabbled in Excel macros, experimented with AppleScript, or set up a Mac on a network, you already know the technical level of the material you're about to read. The Unix command line may be *unfamiliar,* but it doesn't have to be especially technical, particularly if you have some "recipes" to follow like the ones in this chapter.

Note: Unix is an entire operating system unto itself. This chapter is designed to help you find your footing and decide whether or not you like the feel of Unix. If you get bit by the bug, see Appendix D for sources of additional Unix info.

Terminal

The keyhole into Mac OS X's Unix innards is a program called Terminal, which sits in your Applications→Utilities folder (see Figure 16-2). Terminal is named after the terminals (computers that consist of only a monitor and keyboard) that still tap into the mainframe computers at some universities and corporations. In the same way, Terminal is just a window that passes along messages to and from the Mac's brain.

The first time you open Terminal, you'll notice that there's not much in its window except the date, time and source of your last login, and the *command line prompt* (Figure 16-2).

UP TO SPEED

Mac OS X's Unix Roots

In 1969, Bell Labs programmer Ken Thompson found himself with some spare time after his main project, an operating system called Multics, was canceled. Bell Labs had withdrawn from the expensive project, disappointed with the results after four years of work.

But Thompson still thought the project—an OS that worked well as a cooperative software-development environment—was a promising idea. Eventually, he and colleague Dennis Ritchie came up with the OS that would soon be called Unix (a pun on Multics). Bell Labs saw the value of Unix, agreed to support further development, and became the first corporation to adopt it.

In the age when Thompson and Ritchie started their work on Unix, most programmers wrote code that would work on only one kind of computer (or even one computer *model*). Unix, however, was one of the first *portable* operating systems; its programs could run on different kinds of computers without having to be completely rewritten. That's because Thompson and Ritchie wrote Unix using a new programming language of their own invention called *C*.

In a language like C, programmers need only write their code once. After that, a software Cuisinart called a *compiler* can convert the newly hatched software into the form a particular computer model can understand.

Unix soon found its way into labs and, thanks to AT&T's low academic licensing fees, universities around the world. Programmers all over the world added to the source code,

fixed bugs, and then passed those modifications around.

In the mid-1970s, the University of California at Berkeley became the site of especially intense Unix development. Students and faculty there improved the Unix *kernel* (the central, essential part of the OS), added features, and wrote new Unix applications. By 1977, they had enough additional software to release their own version of Unix, the first of several *Berkeley Software Distribution* (BSD) versions.

As it happened, the government's Defense Advanced Research Projects Agency (DARPA) was seeking a uniform, portable OS to use for their growing wide-area network, originally called ARPAnet (and now called the Internet).

DARPA liked Unix and agreed to sponsor further research at Berkeley. In January 1983, DARPA changed ARPAnet's networking protocol to TCP/IP—and the Internet was born, running mostly on Unix machines.

Cut to 1985. Steve Jobs left Apple to start NeXT Computer, whose NeXTSTEP operating system was based on BSD Unix. When Apple bought NeXT in 1996, Jobs, NeXTSTEP (eventually renamed OpenStep) and its Terminal program came along with it. The Unix that beats within Mac OS X's heart is just the latest resting place for the OS that Jobs's team developed at NeXT.

So the next time you hear Apple talk about its "new" operating system, remember that its underlying technology is actually over 35 years old.

For user-friendliness fans, Terminal doesn't get off to a very good start; this prompt looks about as technical as computers get. It breaks down like this:

- **OfficeMac:** is the name of your Mac (at least, as Unix thinks of it). It's usually the Mac's Computer Name (as it appears in the Sharing pane of System Preferences), but it's occasionally the name your Mac goes by on the Internet.

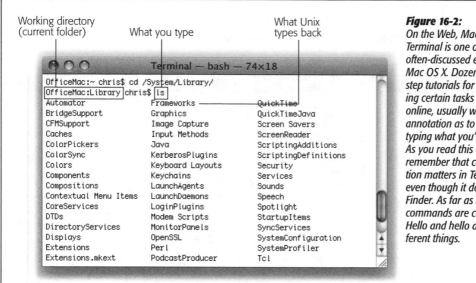

Working directory (current folder)   What you type   What Unix types back

Figure 16-2:
On the Web, Mac OS X's Terminal is one of the most often-discussed elements of Mac OS X. Dozens of step-by-step tutorials for performing certain tasks circulate online, usually without much annotation as to why you're typing what you're typing. As you read this chapter, remember that capitalization matters in Terminal, even though it doesn't in the Finder. As far as most Unix commands are concerned, Hello and hello are two different things.

- **~** indicates what folder you're "in" (Figure 16-2). It denotes the *working directory*—that is, the currently open folder. (Remember, there are no icons on the command line.) Essentially, this notation tells you where you are as you navigate your machine.

  The very first time you try out Terminal, the working directory is set to the symbol ~. That tilde symbol is important shorthand; it means "your own Home folder." It's what you see the first time you start up Terminal, but you'll soon be seeing the names of other folders here—*OfficeMac: /Users* or *OfficeMac: /System/Library,* for example. (More on this slash notation on page 23.)

Note: Before Apple came up with the user-friendly term folder to represent an electronic holding tank for files, folders were called directories. In this chapter, you'll encounter the term directory almost exclusively. In any discussion of Unix, "directory" is simply the correct term.

Besides, using a term like "working folder" within earshot of Unix geeks is likely to get you lynched.

- **chris$** begins with your short user name. It reflects whoever's logged into the *shell* (see the box on the facing page), which is usually whoever's logged into the *Mac* at the moment. As for the $ sign, think of it as a colon. In fact, think of the whole prompt shown in Figure 16-2 as Unix's way of saying, "OK, Chris, I'm listening. What's your pleasure?"

Unless you've fiddled with Terminal's preferences, the insertion point looks like a tall rectangle at the end of the command line. It trots along to the right as you type.

Unix Programs

An enormous number of programs have been written for Unix. And thanks to thousands of open-source developers—programmers all over the world who collaborate and make their work available for the next round of modification—much of this software is freely available to all, including Mac OS X users.

Each Unix command generally calls up a single application (or *process*, as geeks call it) that launches, performs a task, and closes. Many of the best-known such applications come with Mac OS X.

Here's a fun one: Just type *uptime* and press Enter or Return. (That's how you run a Unix program: Type its name and press Return.) On the next line, Terminal shows you how long your Mac has been turned on continuously. It shows you something like: "13:09 up 8 days, 15:04, 1 user, load averages: 1.24, 1.37, 1.45"—meaning your Mac has been running for 8 days, 15 hours nonstop.

You're finished running the *uptime* program. The $ prompt returns, suggesting that Terminal is ready for whatever you throw at it next.

UP TO SPEED

bash, Terminal, and Shells

One Unix program runs automatically when you open a Terminal window: *bash*. It's Apple's chosen *shell* for Mac OS X 10.6.

A *shell* is a Unix program that interprets the commands you've typed, passes them to the *kernel* (the operating system's brain), and then shows you the kernel's response.

In other words, the shell is the Unix Finder. It's the program that lets you navigate the contents of your hard drive, see what's inside certain folders, launch programs and documents, and so on.

There are actually several different shells available in Unix, each with slightly different command syntax. All the popular ones—like *tcsh, ksh,* and *zsh*—come with Mac OS X. (You can choose among them as your default shell using, of all things, the Accounts pane of System Preferences. Click the 🔒, enter your Administrator password, and then Control-click

or right-click your account name in the list; choose Advanced Options. There, on the Advanced Options panel, you'll find the Login Shell box, where you can make the change.) But on a clean installation of Snow Leopard, Terminal comes set to use *bash*.

bash evolved from the original *sh* shell, which was named the Bourne shell after its inventor. *bash* got its name, then, as the Bourne Again Shell (get it?).

You can open additional Terminal windows (100 or more, depending on how many other programs are running) by choosing File→New ShellWindow. Even slicker, Terminal lets you open multiple sessions in *tabs* (just like with Safari) by choosing File→New Tab.

Each window and tab runs independently of any others. For proof, try opening several windows and then running the *cal* command in each.

Try this one: Type *cal* at the prompt, and then press Return. Unix promptly spits out a calendar of the current month.

```
OfficeMac:~ chris$ cal
    September 2009
Su Mo Tu We Th Fr Sa
       1  2  3  4  5
 6  7  8  9 10 11 12
13 14 15 16 17 18 19
20 21 22 23 24 25 26
27 28 29 30


OfficeMac:~ chris$
```

This time, try typing *cal 4 2010*, *cal -y*, or *cal -yj*. These three commands make Unix generate a calendar of April 2010, a calendar of the current year, and a calendar of *Julian* days of the current year, respectively.

Tip: The mouse isn't very useful at the command line. You generally move the cursor only with the ← and → keys. (The Delete key works as it always does.)

You *can* use the mouse, however, to select text from anywhere in the window (or other programs) and paste it in at the prompt. You can also use the mouse to drag an icon off your desktop into the Terminal window, as shown in Figure 16-3.

Navigating in Unix

If you can't see any icons for your files and folders, how are you supposed to work with them?

UP TO SPEED

Pathnames 101

In many ways, browsing the contents of your hard drive using Terminal is just like doing so with the Finder. You start with a folder, and move down into its subfolders, or up into its parent folders.

In this chapter, you'll be asked to specify a certain file or folder in this tree of folders. But you can't see their icons from the command line. So how are you supposed to identify the file or folder you want?

By typing its *pathname*. The pathname is a string of folder names, something like a map, that takes you from the *root level* to the next nested folder, then to the next one, and so on.

(The root level is, for learning-Unix purposes, the equivalent of your main hard drive window. It's represented in Unix by a single slash. The phrase */Users,* in other words, means "the Users folder in my hard drive window"—or, in Unix terms, "the Users directory at the root level.")

One way to refer to the Documents folder in your own Home folder, for example, would be */Users/chris/Documents* (if your name is Chris, that is).

You have no choice but to ask Unix to tell you what folder you're looking at (using the *pwd* command), what's in it (using the *ls* command), and what folder you want to switch to (using the *cd* command), as described in the following pages.

pwd (Print Working Directory, or "Where am I?")

Here's one of the most basic navigation commands: *pwd*, which stands for *print working directory*. The *pwd* command doesn't actually print anything on your printer. Instead, the *pwd* command types out, on the screen, the *path* Unix thinks you're in (the working directory).

Try typing *pwd* and pressing Return. On the next line, Terminal may show you something like this:

```
/Users/chris/Movies
```

Terminal is revealing the working directory's *path*—a list of folders-in-folders, separated by slashes, that specifies a folder's location on your hard drive. */Users/chris/Movies* pinpoints the Movies folder in Chris's Home folder (which, like all Home folders, is in the Users directory).

Tip: Remember that capitalization counts in Unix. Command names are almost always all lowercase (like *cal* and *pwd*). But when you type the names of *folders,* be sure to capitalize correctly.

---

ls (List, or "What's in here?")

The *ls* command, short for *list,* makes Terminal type out the names of all the files and folders in the folder you're in (that is, your working directory). You can try it right now: Just type *ls* and then press Return. Terminal responds by showing you the names of the files and folders inside in a list, like this:

```
Desktop    Downloads Movies    Pictures  Sites
Documents Library    Music     Public
```

In other words, you see a list of the icons that, in the Finder, you'd see in your Home folder.

Note: Terminal respects the limits of the various Mac OS X accounts (Chapter 12). In other words, a Standard or Administrator account holder isn't generally allowed to peek further into someone else's Home folder. If you try, you'll be told, "Permission denied."

You can also make Terminal list what's in any other directory (one that's *not* the working directory) just by adding its pathname as an *argument*. Arguments are extra pieces of information after the command that refine how the command should run. (Remember the calendar example? When you wanted the April 2010 calendar, you typed *cal 4 2010*. The "4" and "2010" parts were the arguments—that is, everything you typed after the command itself.)

To see a list of the files in your Documents directory, then, you could just type *ls /Users/chris/Documents.* Better yet, because the ~ symbol is short for "my home directory," you could save time by typing *ls ~/Documents*. The pathname "~/Documents" is an argument that you've fed the *ls* command.

About flags

As part of a command's arguments, you can sometimes insert *option flags* (also called *switches*)—modifying characters (or short phrases) that affect how the command works, just like option settings do in GUI applications. In the calendar example, you can type *cal -y* to see a full-year calendar; the *-y* part is an option flag.

Option flags are almost always preceded by a hyphen (-), although you can usually run several flags together following just one hyphen. If you type *ls -al*, both the *-a* and *-l* flags are in effect.

Here are some useful options for the *ls* command:

- *-a.* The unadorned *ls* command even displays the names of *invisible* files and folders—at least by the Finder's definition. The Unix shell uses its own system of denoting invisible files and folders, and ignores the Finder's. That doesn't mean you're seeing everything; files that are invisible by the Unix definition still don't show up.

  You can use one of the *ls* command's flags, however, to force even Unix-invisible files to appear. Just add the *-a* flag. In other words, type this: *ls -a*. Now when you press Return, you might see something like this:

  ```
  .                        Desktop          Music
  ..                       Documents        Pictures
  .CFUserTextEncoding      Downloads        Public
  .DS_Store                Library          Sites
  .Trash                   Movies
  ```

- *-F.* As you see, the names of invisible Unix files all begin with a period (Unix folk call them *dot files*). But are these files or folders? To find out, use *ls* with the *-F* option (capitalization counts), like this: *ls -aF*. You're shown something like this:

  ```
  ./                       Desktop/         Music/
  ../                      Documents/       Pictures/
  .CFUserTextEncoding      Downloads/       Public/
  .DS_Store                Library/         Sites/
  .Trash/                  Movies/
  ```

  The names of the items themselves haven't changed, but the *-F* flag makes slashes appear on directory (folder) names. This example shows that in your home directory, there are 12 other directories and two files.

- *-G.* Here's a fascinating flag that makes *ls* display color-coded results: blue for directories, red for programs, normal black-on-white type for documents, and so on.

- *-R.* The -R flag produces a *recursive* listing—one that shows you the directories *within* the directories in the list. Listing all of the home directory could take several pages, but if you type *ls -R Movies*, for example, you might get something like this:

```
Bad Reviews.doc  Old Tahoe Footage 2 Picnic Movie 2  Reviews.doc
./Old Tahoe Footage 2:
Tahoe 1.mov    Tahoe 3.mov    Tahoe Project File
Tahoe 2.mov    Tahoe 4.mov
./Picnic Movie 2:
Icon?      Media      Picnic Movie 2 Project
./Picnic Movie 2/Media:
Picnic Movie 1 Picnic Movie 3 Picnic Movie 5
Picnic Movie 2 Picnic Movie 4 Picnic Movie 6
```

In other words, you've got two subdirectories here, called Old Tahoe Footage 2 and Picnic Movie 2—which itself contains a Media directory.

Tip: As you can tell by the *cal* and *ls* examples, Unix commands are very short. They're often just two-letter commands, and an impressive number of those use *alternate hands* (*ls, cp, rm,* and so on).

The reason has partly to do with conserving the limited memory of early computers and partly to do with efficiency: Most programmers would just as soon type as little as possible to get things done. User-friendly it ain't, but as you type these commands repeatedly over the months, you'll eventually be grateful for the keystroke savings.

---

cd (Change Directory, or "Let Me See Another Folder")

Now you know how to find out what directory you're in, and how to see what's in it, all without double-clicking any icons. That's great information, but it's just information. How do you *do* something in your command line Finder—like switching to a different directory?

To change your working directory, use the *cd* command, followed by the path of the directory you want to switch to. Want to see what's in the Movies directory of your home directory? Type *cd /Users/chris/Movies* and press Return. The $ prompt shows you what it considers to be the directory you're in now (the new working directory). If you perform an *ls* command at this point, Terminal shows you the contents of your Movies directory.

That's a lot of typing, of course. Fortunately, instead of typing out that whole path (the *absolute* path, as it's called), you can simply specify which directory you want to see *relative* to the directory you're already in.

For example, if your Home folder is the working directory, the relative pathname of the Trailers directory inside the Movies directory would be *Movies/Trailers*. That's a lot shorter than typing out the full, absolute pathname (*/Users/chris/Movies/Trailers*).

If your brain isn't already leaking from the stress, here's a summary of the three different ways you could switch from *~/(your home directory)* to *~/Movies*:

- **cd /Users/chris/Movies.** That's the long way—the absolute pathname. It works no matter what your working directory is.

- **cd ~/Movies.** This, too, is an absolute pathname that you could type from anywhere. It relies on the ~ shorthand (which means "my home directory," unless you follow the ~ with another account name).

- **cd Movies.** This streamlined *relative* path exploits the fact that you're already in your home directory.

Tip: Actually, there's a fourth way to specify a directory that involves no typing at all: *dragging the icon* of the directory you want to specify directly into the Terminal window. Figure 16-3 should make this clear.

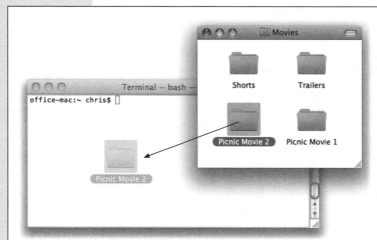

Figure 16-3:
This may be the quickest way of all to identify a directory or file you want to manipulate: Don't type anything. When you drag icons directly from the desktop into a Terminal window, the icon's pathname appears automatically at the insertion point. Terminal even adds backslashes to any special characters in these pathnames for you (a necessary step known as escaping *the special characters; see page 619).*

.. (Dot-Dot, or "Back Me Out")

So now you've burrowed into your Movies directory. How do you back out?

Sure, you could type out the full pathname of the directory that encloses Movies—if you had all afternoon. But there's a shortcut: You can type a double period (..) in any pathname. This shortcut represents the *current directory*'s *parent directory* (the directory that contains it).

To go from your home directory up to */Users*, for example, you could just type *cd ..* (that is, *cd* followed by a space and two periods).

You can also use the dot-dot shortcut *repeatedly* to climb multiple directories at once, like this: *cd ../..* (which would mean "switch the working directory to the directory two layers out.") If you were in your Movies directory, *../..* would change the working directory to the Users directory.

Another trick: You can mix the .. shortcut with actual directory names. For example, suppose your Movies directory contains two directories: Trailers and Shorts. Trailers is the current directory, but you want to switch to the Shorts directory. All you'd have to do is type *cd ../Shorts,* as illustrated in Figure 16-4.

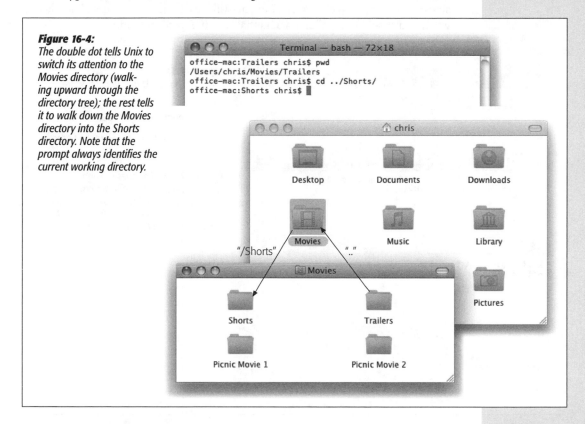

Figure 16-4:
The double dot tells Unix to switch its attention to the Movies directory (walking upward through the directory tree); the rest tells it to walk down the Movies directory into the Shorts directory. Note that the prompt always identifies the current working directory.

Keystroke-Saving Features

By now, you might be thinking that clicking icons would still be faster than doing all this typing. Here's where the typing shortcuts of the *bash* shell come in.

Tab completion

You know how you can highlight a file in a Finder window by typing the first few characters of its name? The tab-completion feature works much the same way. Over time, it can save you miles of finger movement.

It kicks in whenever you're about to type a pathname. Start by typing the first letter or two of the path you want, and then press Tab. Terminal instantly fleshes out the rest of the directory's name. As shown in Figure 16-5, you can repeat this process to specify the next directory-name chunk of the path.

Some tips for tab completion:

- Capitalization counts.

- Terminal adds backslashes automatically if your directory names include spaces, $ signs, or other special characters. But you still have to insert your own backslashes when you type the "hint" characters that tip off Tab completion.

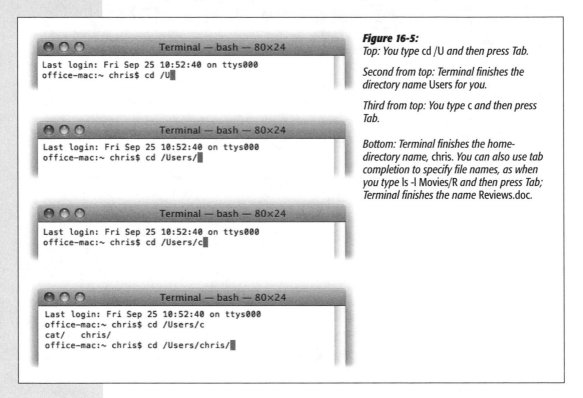

Figure 16-5:
Top: You type cd /U *and then press Tab.*

Second from top: Terminal finishes the directory name Users *for you.*

Third from top: You type c *and then press Tab.*

Bottom: Terminal finishes the home-directory name, chris. *You can also use tab completion to specify file names, as when you type* ls -l Movies/R *and then press Tab; Terminal finishes the name* Reviews.doc.

- If it can't find a match for what you typed, Terminal beeps.

If it finds *several* files or directories that match what you typed, Terminal beeps; when you press Tab again, terminal shows you a list of them. To specify the one you really wanted, type the next letter or two and then press Tab again.

Using the history

You may find yourself at some point needing to run a previously entered command, but dreading the prospect of re-entering the whole command. Retyping a command, however, is never necessary. Terminal (or, rather, the shell it's running) remembers the last 500 commands you entered. At any prompt, instead of typing, just press the ↑ or ↓ keys to walk through the various commands in the shell's memory. They flicker by, one at a time, at the $ prompt—right there on the same line.

Wildcards

Wildcards are special characters that represent other characters—and they're huge timesavers.

The most popular wildcard is the asterisk (*), which means "any text can go here." For example, to see a list of the files in the working directory that end with the letters *te,* you could type *ls *te.* Terminal would show you files named Yosemite, BudLite, Brigitte, and so on—and hide all other files in the list. If the wildcard matches any directories, you'll also see the *contents* of those directories as well, just as though you'd used *ls* with each of the full directory names.

Likewise, to see which files and directories begin with "Old," you could type *ls Old** and press Return. You'd be shown only the names of icons in the working directory called Old Yeller, Old Tahoe Footage, Olduvai Software, and so on.

If you add the asterisk before *and* after the search phrase, you find items with that phrase *anywhere* in their names. Typing *ls *jo** will show you the files named Mojo, johnson, Major Disaster, and so on.

Tip: Using * by itself means "show me everything." To see a list of what's in a directory *and* in the directories *inside it* (as though you'd highlighted all the folders in a Finder list view and then pressed ⌘-right arrow), just type *ls **.

WORKAROUND WORKSHOP

No Spaces Allowed

Terminal doesn't see a space as a space. It thinks that a space means, for example, "I've just typed a command, and what follows is an argument." If you want to see what's in your Short Films directory, therefore, don't bother typing *ls ~/Movies/Short Films*. You'll only get a "No such file or directory" error message, thanks to the space in the Short Films directory name.

Similarly, % signs have a special meaning in Unix. If you try to type one in a pathname (because a directory name contains %, for example), you'll have nothing but trouble.

Fortunately, you can work around this quirk by using a third reserved, or special, character: the backslash (\). It says, "Ignore the special meaning of the next character—a space, for example. I'm not using it for some special Unix meaning. I'm using the following space as, well, a space." (At a Unix user-group meeting, you might hear someone say, "Use the backslash character to *escape* the space character.")

The correct way to see what's in your Short Films directory,

then, would be *ls ~/Movies /Short\ Films*. (Note how the backslash just before the space means, "This is just a space—keep it moving, folks.")

Of course, if you have to enter a lot of text with spaces, it'd be a real pain to type the backslash before every single one. Fortunately, instead of using backslashes, you can enclose the whole mess with single quotation marks. That is, instead of typing this:

cd /Users/chris/My\ Documents/Letters\ to\ finish/Letter\ to\ Craig.doc

…you could just type this:

cd '/Users/chris/My Documents/Letters to finish/Letter to Craig.doc'

It can get even more complicated. For example, what if there's a single quote *in* the path? (Answer: Protect *it* with double quotes.) Ah, but you have years of study ahead of you, grasshoppa.

Directory Switching

A hyphen (-) after the *cd* command means "Take me back to the previous working directory." For example, if you changed your working directory from *~/Movies/Movie 1* to *~/Documents/Letters*, simply enter *cd -* to change back to *~/Movies/Movie 1*. Use *cd -* a second time to return to *~/Documents/Letters*. (Note the space between *cd* and the hyphen.)

Tip: If you're doing a lot of switching between directories, you'll probably find it quicker to open and switch between two Terminal windows or tabs, each with a different working directory.

The ~ Shortcut

You already know that the tilde (~) character is a shortcut to your home directory. But you can also use it as a shortcut to somebody else's home directory simply by tacking on that person's account name. For example, to change to Miho's home directory, use *cd ~miho*.

Special keys

The *bash* shell offers dozens of special keystroke shortcuts for navigation. You may recognize many of them as useful undocumented shortcuts that work in any Cocoa application, but even more are available (and useful) in Terminal:

Keystroke	Effect
Control-U	Erases the entire command line you're working on (to the insertion point's left).
Control-A	Moves the insertion point to the beginning of the line.
Control-E	Moves the insertion point to the end of the line.
Control-T	Transposes the previous two characters.
Esc-F	Moves the insertion point to the beginning of the next word.
Esc-B	Moves the insertion point to the beginning of the current word.
Esc-Delete	Erases the previous word (defined as "anything that ends with a space, slash, or most other punctuation marks; periods and asterisks not included"). You have to hold down Esc as you press Delete; repeat for each word.
Esc-D	Erases the word, or section of a word, following the insertion point.
Esc-C	Capitalizes the letter following the insertion point.
Esc-U	Changes the next word or word section to all uppercase letters.
Esc-L	Changes the next word or word section to all lowercase letters.

Working with Files and Directories

The previous pages show you how to navigate your directories using Unix commands. Just perusing your directories isn't particularly productive, however. This section shows you how to *do* something with the files you see listed—copy, move, create, and delete directories and files.

Tip: You're entering Serious Power territory, where it's theoretically possible to delete a whole directory with a single typo. As a precaution, consider working through this section with administrator privileges turned off for your account, so that you won't be able to change anything outside your home directory–or to be really safe, create a new, test account just for this exercise so even your personal files won't be at risk.

---

cp (Copy)

Using the Unix command *cp*, you can copy and rename a file in one move. (Try *that* in the Finder!)

The basic command goes like this: *cp path1 path2*, where the *path* placeholders represent the original file and the copy, respectively.

Copying in place

To duplicate a file called Thesis.doc, you would type *cp Thesis.doc Thesis2.doc*. (That's just one space between the names.) You don't have to call the copy *Thesis2*—you could call it anything you like. The point is that you wind up with two identical files in the same directory with different names. Just remember to add a backslash before a space if you want to name the copy with two words (*Thesis\ Backup*, for example).

Tip: If this command doesn't seem to work, remember that you must type the *full* names of the files you're moving–including their file name suffixes like .doc or .gif, which Mac OS X usually hides. Using the *ls* command before a copy may help you find out what the correct, full file names should be. Or you may just want to use the Tab-completion feature, making Terminal type the whole name for you.

Copying and renaming

To copy the same file into, say, your Documents folder instead, just change the last phrase so that it specifies the path, like this: *cp Reviews.doc ~/Documents/Reviews2.doc*.

FREQUENTLY ASKED QUESTION

The Slash and the Colon

OK, I'm really confused. You say that slashes denote nested directories. But I also know that traditionally, colons (:) denote the Mac's internal folder notation, and that's why I can't use colons in the names of my icons. What's the story?

At the desktop, the Mac still uses colons as path separators instead of the slash. Therefore, you *are* allowed to use slashes in file names in the Finder, but not a colon.

Conversely, in Terminal, you can use colons in file names but not slashes!

Behind the scenes, Mac OS X automatically converts one form of punctuation to the other, as necessary. For example, a file named *Letter 6/21/2010* in the Finder shows up as *Letter 6:21:2010* in Terminal. Likewise, a directory named *Attn: Jon* in Terminal appears with the name *Attn/ Jon* in the Finder. Weird–and fun!

Tip: Note that *cp* replaces identically named files without warning. Use the *-i* flag (that is, *cp -i*) if you want to be warned before *cp* replaces a file like this.

Copying without renaming

To copy something into another directory without changing its name, just use a pathname (without a file name) as the final phrase. So to copy Reviews.doc into your Documents folder, for example, you would type *cp Reviews.doc ~/Documents*.

Tip: You can use the "." directory shortcut (which stands for the current working directory) to copy files from another directory *into* the working directory, like this: *$ cp ~/Documents/Reviews.doc* . (Notice the space and the period after *Reviews.doc*.)

Multiple files

You can even copy several files or directories at once. Where you'd normally specify the source file, just list their pathnames separated by spaces, as shown in Figure 16-6.

```
cp Tahoe1.mov Tahoe2.mov ../FinishedMovies
```
The files you want to copy   Where you want to put them

Figure 16-6:
The first argument of this command lists two different files. The final clause indicates where they go.

POWER USERS' CLINIC

Your Metadata's Safe with Us

Metadata means "data about data." For example, the handwritten note on a shoebox of photos is metadata for the image data inside, reminding you of the photos' date, location, camera information, or even which CDs hold the digital versions. This metadata lets you locate and access the actual data quickly (and also helps you decide if you should go to the trouble in the first place).

Computer files have metadata too, and the more the computer can scribble down, the easier it can operate with the bazillions of files living on your hard drive. The Mac has always stored some file metadata in one way or another, but these days, it really goes whole hog. It now recognizes a Unix feature called *extended attributes* to store all kinds of file metadata.

In fact, many of the features described in this book, like Time Machine and Downloaded Application Tagging, depend on extended attributes to perform their magic. Apple also uses

extended attributes now to keep track of traditional Mac metadata like *resource forks* (features carried over from OS 9 that Mac OS X still has to recognize).

When you create, modify, or move files in the Finder, you don't have to worry about extended attributes; the Mac always keeps them together with their associated files.

When you're working with files on the command line, however, you have to be more cautious. Ever since Tiger (Mac OS X 10.4), the most common Unix file tools, like *cp, mv, tar,* and *rsync* (with the *-E* flag), manage extended attributes correctly. However, as you explore with other tools, it's wise to use them to duplicate rather than move files, until you're sure all the bits stay together.

The command line tool for peeking in on your extended attributes is *xattr*, which you'll learn about later on in this chapter.

You can also use the * wildcard to copy several files at once. For example, suppose you've got these files in your iMovie Projects directory: Tahoe1.mov, Tahoe2.mov, Tahoe3.mov, Tahoe4.mov, Script.doc, and Tahoe Project File. Now suppose you want to copy *only* the QuickTime movies into a directory called FinishedMovies. All you'd have to do is type *cp *mov ../FinishedMovies* and press Return; Mac OS X instantly performs the copy.

If you wanted to copy *all* those files (not just the movies) to another directory, you'd use the * by itself, like this: *cp * ../Finished Movies*.

Unfortunately, if the iMovie Projects directory contains other *directories* and not just files, that command produces an error message. The Unix *cp* command doesn't copy directories within directories unless you explicitly tell it to, using the -R option flag. Here's the finished command that copies everything in the current directory—both files and directories—into FinishedMovies: *cp -R * ../FinishedMovies*.

Here's one more example: a command that copies everything (files and directories) with *Tahoe* in its name into someone else's Drop Box directory: *cp -R *Tahoe* ~miho/ Public/Drop\ Box*.

mv (Moving and Renaming Files and Directories)

Now that you know how to copy files, you may want to move or rename them. To do so, you use the Unix command *mv* almost exactly the same way you'd use *cp* (except that it always moves directories inside of directories you're moving, so you don't have to type -R).

The syntax looks like this: *mv oldname newname*. For example, to change your Movies directory's name to Films, you'd type *mv Movies Films*. You can rename both files and directories this way.

Moving files and directories

To rename a file and move it to a different directory simultaneously, just replace the last portion of the command with a pathname. To move the Tahoe1 movie file into your Documents directory—and rename it LakeTahoe at the same time—type this: *mv Tahoe1.mov ~/Documents/LakeTahoe.mov*.

All the usual shortcuts apply, including the wildcard. Here's how you'd move everything containing the word Tahoe in your working directory (files and directories) into your Documents directory: *mv *Tahoe* ~/Documents*.

Option flags

You can follow the *mv* command with any of these options:

- *-i.* Makes Terminal ask your permission before replacing a file with one of the same name.

- *-f.* Overwrites like-named files without asking you first. (Actually, this is how *mv* works if you don't specify otherwise.)

- *-n.* Doesn't overwrite like-named files; just skips them without prompting.

[handwritten note: OR use "BURN TO DISK" in OS X.]

• -v. Displays *verbose* (fully explained) explanations on the screen, letting you know exactly what got moved.

Tip: If you use a combination of options that appear to contradict one another—like the *-f, -i,* and *-n* options—the last option (farthest to the right) wins.

By the way, the *mv* command never replaces a *directory* with an identically named *file*. It copies everything else you've asked for, but it skips files that would otherwise wipe out folders.

mkdir (Create New Directories)

In the Finder, you make a new folder by choosing File→New Folder. In Terminal, you create one using the *mkdir* command (for *make directory*).

Follow the command with the name you want to give the new directory, like this: *mkdir 'Early iMovie Attempts'* (the single quotes in this example let you avoid having to precede each space with a backslash).

The *mkdir* command creates the new directory in the current working directory, although you can just as easily create it anywhere else. Just add the pathname to your argument. To make a new directory in your Documents→Finished directory, for example, type *mkdir ~'/Documents/Finished/Early iMovie Attempts'*. (The first quote comes after the ~, so that it preserves that character's special meaning by not escaping it.) Thanks to Spotlight's constant eye on file activity, the new directory appears *immediately* in the Finder.

Tip: If there *is* no directory called Finished in your Documents directory, you just get an error message—unless you use the *-p* option, which creates as many new directories as necessary to match your command. For example, *mkdir -p '~/Documents/Finished/Early iMovie Attempts'* would create both a Finished directory and an Early iMovie Attempts directory inside of it.

---

touch (Create Empty Files)

To create a new, empty file, type *touch filename*. For example, to create the file practice. txt in your working directory, use *touch practice.txt*.

And why would you bother? For the moment, you'd use such new, empty files primarily as targets for practicing the next command.

*rm (*Remove Files and Directories)

Unix provides an extremely efficient way to trash files and directories. With a single command, *rm*, you can delete any file or directory—or *all those* that you're allowed to access with your account type.

The dangers of this setup should be obvious, especially in light of the fact that *deletions are immediate* in Unix. There is no Undo, no Empty Trash command, no "Are you sure?" dialog box. In Unix, all sales are final.

The command *rm* stands for "remove," but it could also stand for "respect me." Pause for a moment whenever you're about to invoke it. For the purpose of this introduction to *rm*, double-check that administration privileges are indeed turned off for your account.

To use this command, just type *rm*, a space, and the exact name of the file you want to delete from the working directory. To remove the file *practice.txt* you created with the *touch* command, for example, you'd just type *rm practice.txt.*

To remove a directory and everything in it, add the *-r* flag, like this: *rm -r Practice-Folder.*

If you're feeling particularly powerful (and you like taking risks), you can even use wildcards with the *rm* command. Now, many experienced Unix users make it a rule to *never* use *rm* with wildcards while logged in as an administrator, because one false keystroke can wipe out everything in a directory. But here, for study purposes only, is the atomic bomb of command lines, the one that deletes *everything* in the working directory: *rm -rf *.*

Tip: Be doubly cautious when using wildcards in *rm* command lines, and triply cautious when using them while logged in as an administrator.

If you're using Time Machine, you have a safety net, of course. But why tempt fate?

Just after the letters *rm*, you can insert options like these:

- *-d* deletes any empty directories it finds, in addition to files. (Otherwise, empty directories trigger an error message.)

- *-f* squelches any attempts to get your attention, even if there's a problem, like a permission error or nonexistent file. The command proceeds, full speed ahead.

- *-i* (for *interactive*) makes the Mac ask for confirmation before each deletion.

- *-P* securely overwrites the file three times. (It's an alternative to the *srm* command described next.)

srm (Secure Removal)

srm is a command line version of the Finder's Secure Empty Trash function (page 86). It lets you choose just *how* thoroughly Mac OS X scrubs the hard drive spot where the deleted file once sat.

The *srm* utility lets you specify three general levels of deletion:

- **Simple.** The -s flag tells *srm* to perform a *simple* secure removal, overwriting the deleted material with random data just once. It's faster than the Finder's Secure Empty Trash, but not as thorough.

- **Medium.** The -m flag designates *medium* level, which overwrites the unwanted data seven times with various types of random and not-so-random data. This is similar to what you get when you use the Finder's Secure Empty Trash command, and it's thorough enough to meet U.S. Department of Defense security requirements.

- **Strong.** If you don't specify either -s or -m, *srm* will perform a *strong* secure removal. That entails recording over the spot where the deleted file sat *35 times,* each time using a different string of data as specified by the Gutmann algorithm. (And what is the Gutmann algorithm? A series of data patterns that make recovery of an erased file almost impossible. More than you ever wanted to know is at *www.cs.auckland.ac.nz/~pgut001/pubs/secure_del.html.*)

The bottom line: To make sure no one ever, ever reads that poem you typed out for your cat one lonely, bleary-eyed evening, type *srm "My Twinkie.doc".* That will be the end of it, and neither the CIA nor Norton Utilities will ever know what it was.

echo (A Final Check)

You can make *rm* or *srm* less risky by prefacing it with the *echo* command. It makes Terminal type out the command a second time, this time with a handy list of exactly what you're about to obliterate. If you've used wildcards, you see the names of the files that will be affected by the * character. If you type *echo rm -r *,* for example (which, without the *echo* part, would normally mean "delete everything in this directory"), you might see a list like this:

```
rm -r Reviews.doc  Tahoe Footage  Picnic Movie  Contract.doc
```

Once you've reviewed the list and approved what Terminal is about to do, *then* you can retype the command without the *echo* portion.

Note: The *rm* command doesn't work on file or directory names that begin with a hyphen (-). To delete these items from your working directory, preface their names with a dot slash (./), like this: *rm ./-Recipes.doc.*

Online Help

Mac OS X comes with nearly 1,400 Unix programs like the ones described in this chapter. How are you supposed to learn what they all do?

Fortunately, almost every Unix program comes with a help file. It may not appear within an elegant, gradient-gray Snow Leopard window—in fact, it's pretty darned plain—but it offers much more material than the regular Mac Help Center.

These user-manual pages, or *manpages,* hold descriptions of virtually every command and program available. Mac OS X, in fact, comes with manpages on almost 7,500 topics—over 40,000 printed pages' worth.

Alas, manpages rarely have the clarity of writing or the learner-focused approach of the Mac Help Center. They're generally terse, just-the-facts descriptions. In fact, you'll probably find yourself needing to reread certain sections again and again. The information they contain, however, is invaluable to new and experienced Unix fans alike, and the effort spent mining them is usually worthwhile.

Using *man*

To access the manpage for a given command, type *man* followed by the name of the command you're researching. For example, to view the manpage for the *ls* command, enter: *man ls.*

Tip: The *-k* option flag lets you search by keyword. For example, *man -k applescript* produces a list of all manpages that refer to AppleScript, whereupon you can pick one of the names in the list and *man* that page name.

Now the manual appears, one screen at a time, as shown in Figure 16-7.

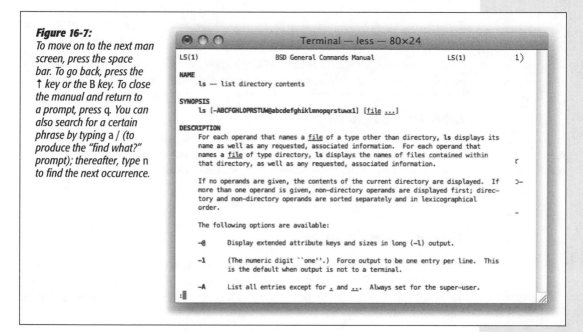

Figure 16-7:
To move on to the next man screen, press the space bar. To go back, press the ↑ key or the B key. To close the manual and return to a prompt, press q. You can also search for a certain phrase by typing a / (to produce the "find what?" prompt); thereafter, type n to find the next occurrence.

A typical manpage begins with these sections:

• **Name.** The name and a brief definition of the command.

• **Synopsis.** Presents the syntax of the command, including all possible options and arguments, in a concise formula. For example, the synopsis for *du* (disk usage) is as follows: *du [-H | -L | -P] [-a | -s | -d depth] [-c] [-h | -k | -m | -g] [-x] [-I mask] [file ...].*

That line shows all the flags available for the *du* command and how to use them.

Brackets ([ ]) surround the *optional* arguments. (*All* the arguments for *du* are optional.)

Vertical bars called *pipes* (|) indicate that you can use only one item (of the group separated by pipes) at a time. For example, when choosing options to use with *du*, you can use *either* -H, -L, or -P—not two or all three at once.

The word *file* in the synopsis means "type a pathname here." The ellipsis (…) following it indicates that you're allowed to type more than one pathname.

- **Description.** Explains in more detail what the command does and how it works. Often, the description includes the complete list of that command's option flags.

For more information on using *man,* view its *own* manpage by entering—what else?—*man man.*

Tip: The free program ManOpen, available for download at *www.missingmanuals.com,* is a Cocoa manual-pages reader that provides a nice looking, easier-to-control window for reading manpages.

Or why not just use Dashboard? Download the *NIX Manual widget (from this book's "Missing CD" page at *www.missingmanuals.com,* for example). It provides an equally attractive interface to the manpages.

Other Online Help

Sometimes Terminal shoves a little bit of user manual right under your nose—when it thinks you're having trouble. For example, if you use the *mkdir* command without specifying a pathname, *mkdir* interrupts the proceedings by displaying its own synopsis as a friendly reminder (subtext: "Um, this is how you're *supposed* to use me"), like this: *usage: mkdir [-pv] [-m mode] directory...*

Terminal Preferences

If you spend endless hours staring at the Terminal screen, as most Unix junkies do, you'll eventually be grateful for the preference settings that let you control how Terminal looks and acts. In fact, Terminal lets you manage your preferences in an ingenious way.

Instead of having a single set of options saved (as with other applications), Terminal manages your options as named settings groups, allowing you to quickly apply different settings to different windows at any time using the Inspector window (Shell→Show Inspector).

You can also save the layout of entire groups of windows, each with their own settings in effect, into a single configuration, allowing you to recreate those layouts in an instant.

Snow Leopard Spots: If you choose Window→Split Pane (⌘-D), you wind up splitting your Terminal window into an upper pane and a lower pane. That can be handy when you keep certain scripts running all the time. The two panes mirror the same command, but now you can scroll to different positions within each pane, keeping tabs on different parts of the same output at the same time. (The other Snow Leopard enhancement in Terminal is a new standard font, which is definitely prettier than the old one.)

Configure your settings using Terminal's Preferences panel (Figure 16-8), which you get to by choosing Terminal→Preferences (of all places).

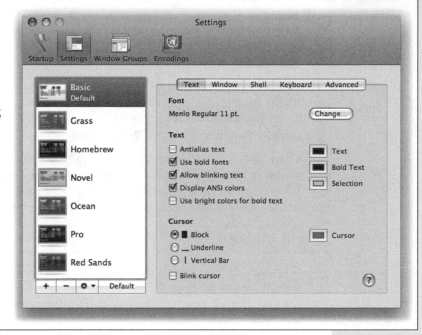

Figure 16-8:
To access the Terminal Inspector, choose Terminal→Show Inspector (or press ⌘-I). This window shows all your Terminal saved settings. To apply any to an existing window, just select the window and then a setting.

Startup

The Startup tab lets you configure what Settings or Window group Terminal should use to open (in case you want something other than the default). This tab also gives you another way to switch from *bash* to a different default shell. (Where it says "Shells open with," choose "command (complete path)" and then type */bin/bash* for *bash,* or */bin/tcsh* for *tcsh.* New Terminal windows will then open with that shell.)

Settings

This tab is the heart of Terminal's preferences management. On the left: a list of settings categories. On the right: the options for the currently selected category. Terminal comes with several preconfigured settings, and you can add and remove these and your own using the **+** and **−** buttons below the list. (To restore all the options for the prepackaged settings to their original state, select Restore Defaults from the ✿ menu.)

To see your changes reflected instantly in a Terminal window, make sure the window you're watching is using the same setting you're modifying.

Text

Here's where you control what the insertion point looks like, along with choices of fonts and colors.

Note: No matter what font you choose, typed characters align vertically. Terminal spaces them out that way, even if they're not monospaced fonts like Courier, Monaco, or Menlo (Terminal's new standard font).

Window

- **Title.** Turn on the elements you'd like the current Terminal window to display in the title bar. Remember, your preferences can be different for each setting group; you might therefore want the windows' title bars to identify the differences.

- **Window Size.** The Dimensions boxes affect the width in characters (columns) and height in lines (rows) of new Terminal windows. (Of course, you can always resize an existing window by dragging its lower-right corner. As you drag, the title bar displays the window's current dimensions.)

- **Color.** Not only can you set the background color, but you also can set its *opacity* as well, making your Terminal windows translucent—a sure way to make novices fall to their knees in awe. Just drag the slider to the right and watch the background of the active window nearly disappear, like the Cheshire Cat, leaving only text.

Tip: This effect looks especially cool if you make the Terminal window black with white or yellow writing.

- **Scrollback.** As your command line activity fills the Terminal window with text, older lines at the top disappear from view. So that you can get back to these previous lines for viewing, copying, or printing, Terminal offers a *scrollback buffer,* which sets aside a certain amount of memory—and adds a scroll bar—so that you can do so. Terminal stores the data in this buffer very efficiently, so you should have no problem keeping this at its default unlimited setting. However, if you do get the crazy urge to display all 1.6 million lines from the manpages, you just might run out of memory if you don't set a limit.

Note: And how would you do that? By running this command, of course: *find /usr/share/man/man* -type f -exec man -P cat {} \;*

Shell

- **Startup.** Enter a command here (for example, *cal -y*), and each time you open a new window, you'll see its output and then get a new prompt. (If you just want the output without a new prompt, check "Run inside shell.")

- **When the shell exits.** When you're finished fooling around in Terminal, you end your session either by closing the window, or more properly, by typing *exit* (or pressing Control-D) at the prompt. The "When the Shell Exits" setting determines what happens when you do that.

- **Prompt before closing.** Shell commands can take some time to complete. In some cases, when you attempt to close a Terminal window before its work is finished, Terminal asks you if you're sure you want to cancel the process and lose your work. The options here let you configure when you want to be prompted, if ever, and even which processes you *don't* want Terminal to warn you about.

Keyboard

These controls let you choose keyboard shortcuts that help you navigate your Terminal window, or that send strings of canned text to the shell. As your Unix prowess grows, these shortcuts become more useful.

Tip: For some Unix geeks, the non-Unixy location of the Control key has been frustrating enough to keep them from using Macs. They use that key constantly and would rather not have to rewire their brains to handle the changed location.

But this problem is easily remedied. In System Preferences, in Keyboard & Mouse, the Modifier Keys button lets you swap the Control and Caps Lock keys' functions, allowing the confused pinkies of Unix-heads to once again find their way.

Window Groups

Once you've gone to town with Terminal settings, you might end up with a mosaic of windows spread across your display (or displays)—your main Terminal window, a couple of *man* (user-manual) windows, a *top* window showing all the running programs, and so on. You gotta love it: Each window has its own color scheme and title to reflect what it's doing, and all the windows are sized perfectly to contain their text output.

It would be a shame to lose all of that when you quit Terminal. Fortunately, you won't have to, thanks to Window Groups.

Choose Window→Save Windows as Group and name the group. You'll be able to recreate your masterpiece when you return to Terminal by selecting that group name from Window→Open Window Group. (Of course, your original output won't be there, but any commands you've configured to run at startup will display their new output.)

The Window Groups Preferences tab is just a place to view these groups and delete any you no longer need. Using the ✿ pop-up menu, you can also export these groups as files to import into other machines (or other accounts).

Connect to Server

When you use Terminal to connect to other computers across a network—a common Terminal task—you use commands like *ssh* and *ftp* in conjunction with the other computers' names or IP addresses. For example, you might type *ssh bertha.acmeco. com* or *ssh 192.168.43.76*.

The trouble is, these IP names and addresses are hard to remember—and the numbers may change. To make connecting easier, Terminal can use the magic of Bonjour—a networking feature in which Macs announce their presence to the network, using their plain-English names. Bonjour lets you browse other Macs on your network just as you'd browse them in the Finder (Chapter 13).

To get started, choose File→New Remote Connection. Continue as shown in Figure 16-9.

Tip: Even if the remote machine isn't running Bonjour, you can still add its address to the Server list manually by clicking the **+** button below it. Likewise, all command lines entered in the bottom field get added to the pop-up menu beside it, allowing you to quickly reconnect without having to browse at all.

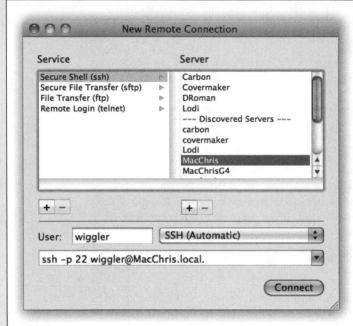

Figure 16-9:
From the left side, choose the service you want; from the right, choose from a list of machines whose Remote Login and FTP checkboxes are turned on in the Sharing panel of System Preferences. Type your account name into the User box. As you adjust the connection options, the box at the bottom shows the Unix command you're building. Click Connect to open a new Terminal window and send that command inside it.

Terminal Tips and Tricks

After you've used Terminal awhile, you may feel ready for a few of these power tips:

Switching Windows

You can switch among your various Terminal windows by pressing ⌘-1, ⌘-2, and so on (up to ⌘-9). You'll be able to identify the windows easily if you choose to include the Command key in the title bars. (Use the Window section of the Settings Preference pane.)

Non-Contiguous Selection

You can select blobs of text, just as in Microsoft Word or TextEdit. To select a single rectangle of text anywhere in the window, Option-drag through it. To select multiple rectangles, Option-⌘-drag. You can then copy and paste just those selected blobs.

Double-Clickable Unix Tools

Most people are used to thinking of Unix applications as programs you run from within Terminal. Many, though, appear in the Finder as regular old icons—and you can open them by double-clicking, just as you would a traditional Mac OS X program. This trick isn't very useful for commands that require flags. But for some, like *cal,* clicking provides a quick way to run the program, especially if you keep it in your Dock.

To double-click a Unix program, though, you first have to *find* it—and that may not be easy. Mac OS X's Unix directory structure is labyrinthine indeed.

But why not ask Terminal where the program is? You can do exactly that using the *which* command: *which cal,* for example. Terminal responds with */usr/bin/cal,* telling you that *cal* resides in the */usr/bin* directory.

To get there, use the *open* command in Terminal, like this: *open /usr/bin.* A window opens in the Finder; inside, you'll find the *cal* icon. Drag the icon to the right side of the Dock.

From now on, when you click that Dock icon, a new Terminal window opens, automatically displaying this month's calendar. You've shaved several precious seconds off the time it would have taken you to open iCal.

Changing Permissions with Terminal

Permissions is a largely invisible, but hugely important, Mac OS X and Unix feature. The behind-the-scenes permissions setting for a file or folder determines whether or not you're allowed to open it, change it, or delete it. Permissions are the cornerstone of several important Mac OS X features, including the separation of user accounts and the relative invulnerability of the operating system itself.

POWER USERS' CLINIC

The Termination of .term Files?

The ability to save different sets of windows settings is actually nothing new to Terminal. In earlier versions, you could export a *.term* file that stored a window's (or window group's) settings. Opening the .term file opened a new window (or window group) with those settings.

In today's Terminal, you get easier management for these settings and a different way of storing them. Instead of using a separate file for each setting, Terminal now saves them all in the single com.apple.Terminal.plist file (in ~/Library/Preferences).

If you had any .term files in the standard location (~/Library/Application Support/Terminal) when you first opened Snow Leopard's Terminal, they still appeared in the Inspector—but Terminal no longer reads them.

Instead, upon Terminal's very first launch, those files' settings are copied into the new com.apple.Terminal.plist file. That's why, after the first time you open Terminal, adding additional .term files to ~/Library/Application Support/Terminal doesn't make them appear in the Inspector. To do that, double-click the .term files in the Finder; Terminal imports them.

Double-clicking a .term file still opens a Terminal window using those settings. But if that's what you want, why be so passé? Instead, double-click the newer *.terminal* files you get by exporting either your window or window groups settings.

You'll find the Export command on the ✿ menu of both the Settings and Window Groups tabs of the Preferences panel.

As you know from Chapter 13, you can get a good look at the permissions settings for any file, folder, or disk by highlighting it and choosing File→Get Info in the Finder. But even there, you're not seeing *all* the permission settings Unix provides, and every now and then, you might want to. Suppose, for example, that you're a teacher in charge of a computer lab containing 25 Macs. On each computer, you've created Standard accounts (see Chapter 12) for five students, for a total of 125 student accounts.

Soon after the students start using the lab, you notice a bit more giggling and frantic typing than you'd expect from students researching Depression-era economics. You nonchalantly stroll to the end of the room and do a quick about-face at one of the desks. Aha—iChat! Horribly depressed by the comments you read there regarding your fashion sense, you vow to keep students from using that application ever again.

You have several options:

- **Delete iChat from the Applications folder.** Unfortunately, the Computer Club meets in your classroom after school, and its members routinely use iChat to communicate. (Talking out loud, after all, is *so* 20th century.)

- **Use Parental Controls.** You can open System Preferences, click Accounts, and click Parental Controls. You'd then click to configure Finder & System, select Some Limits, and turn off the iChat checkbox from the list of allowable applications. Repeat 124 times. (Though it is nice that Screen Sharing lets you do this remotely.)

- **Buy, install, and configure Mac OS X Server.** Then you can create and configure workgroups with any permission settings you want. (Apple offers a four-day training course if you get stuck.)

- **Use Terminal.** Go to a Mac, fire up Terminal, and type a quick command to turn off iChat's *execute permissions* for Standard account holders. (This process won't affect the Computer Club, because its members all have Administrator accounts.) Repeat only 24 times.

  In fact, if walking to each machine is too much work, you can even use the *ssh* technique described in Chapter 22 to run the command *remotely* from a single machine, while seated in the comfort of your own teacher's chair.

  This, of course, is by far the best solution. It'll take several pages to work through this example. But in the process, you'll learn an amazing amount about Terminal and the Unix underpinnings of Mac OS X.

Note: The original Unix permission system has been around longer than disco, and still serves well in Mac OS X. But Leopard introduced a secondary permission system to help make some of its new features work. These *Access Control Lists* (ACLs) provide much finer control of permissions, allowing you, for example, to assign multiple owners and groups to a single file. ACLs are also behind the file-sharing permissions described on page 95.

Not all files, or even most files, on your Mac use ACLs. But when they're present, the ACL permissions override the file's Unix permissions. For details on ACLs, download this chapter's free appendix, "Access Control Lists," from the "Missing CD" page at *www.missingmanuals.com*.

Looking at Permissions

In general, when you double-click a file icon in the Finder, it opens either *as* a program or opens *into* a program (if it's a document).

But most Mac OS X application icons in the Finder are really folders *posing* as single files. Inside the folder, or *package,* are all the files that application depends on to run, including the actual application file itself, the one that opens when you double-click the package icon. If you turn off the *execute permission* for that inner nugget, you prevent it from running—and, as in this classroom example, you can turn it off for certain kinds of account holders and not others.

To inspect the permissions for iChat, open the Applications folder. Control-click the iChat icon. From the shortcut menu, choose Show Package Contents. A new Finder window opens, revealing the contents of the iChat application package.

Open the Contents→MacOS folder; inside you find the individual iChat program file. (Nobody would ever bother opening iChat by double-clicking *this* icon, but it's possible.) You *could* inspect its permissions by highlighting the inner iChat icon, choosing File→Get Info, and then expanding the Sharing and Permissions section.

The Unix way is faster. In Terminal, just use the *ls* command like this:

```
ls -l /Applications/iChat.app/Contents/MacOS
```

The *-l* flag produces a *long list*—an expanded display showing extra information about each item in the directory, in this case its single iChat file. Terminal's response is something like this:

```
total 10616
-total 4424
-rwxr-xr-x  1 root  wheel  5844848 Jul 28 22:28 iChat
```

Thanks to the *-l* option, the first line displays the grand total size on disk of all the loose files in the directory: 4424. (It's measured in 512-byte blocks. If you also included the *-k* flag, you would see this measurement in kilobytes. Remember that part of the reason Snow Leopard occupies so much less disk space is that many of its system files are compressed on the disk. That's why the "on disk" size and actual size of a folder's contents don't always add up.)

Next you see the name of the one inhabitant of the MacOS directory: *iChat.* (If there were more, you would see each item on its own line.) But what is *-rwxr-xr-x?* Is Terminal having a meltdown?

Not at all; you're just seeing more Unix shorthand, listed in what are supposed to be helpful columns. Figure 16-10 breaks down the meaning of each clump of text.

- **Type.** The first character of the line indicates the *file type*—usually **d** (a directory), **l** (a *symbolic link*—the Unix version of an alias), or, as in this case, a **hyphen** (a file).

- **File mode.** Rammed together with the type (like this: *rwxr-xr-x*) is a string of nine characters. It indicates, in a coded format, the actual access permissions for that item, as described in the next section.

- **Owner.** Terminal's response also identifies the account name of whoever owns this file or directory, which is usually whoever created it. Remember, *root* means that Mac OS X itself owns it. That's why even administrators generally aren't allowed to delete directories that bear "root" ownership.

Note: In the Finder's Get Info windows, you may see ownership listed as *System.* That's Apple's kinder, gentler term for *root.*

- **Group.** After the owner comes the name of the *group* that owns this file or directory. "Wheel," as in "big wheel," indicates the group with the highest powers (administrators are not part of this group); the "admin" group contains all administrators.

- **Pathname.** At the end of the line (following the file's size and date) comes the path of this file or directory, relative to the listed directory.

File-Mode Code

To understand the coded nine-character file-mode section, you need a good grasp of the topics covered in Chapter 13. There you'll find out that as you create new files and directories, you can specify who else is allowed to see or make changes to them. In fact, you can specify these permissions for three different categories of people: the owner (usually yourself), your group, and everyone else.

The file-mode column is made of three subcolumns (Figure 16-10), which correspond to those same three categories of people: *owner*, *group*, and *everybody else.*

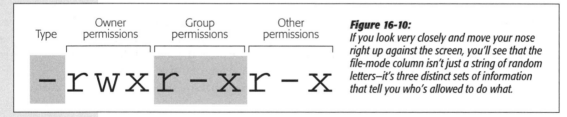

Figure 16-10:
If you look very closely and move your nose right up against the screen, you'll see that the file-mode column isn't just a string of random letters—it's three distinct sets of information that tell you who's allowed to do what.

Within each sequence, three characters describe the *read (r), write (w),* and *execute (x)* permissions that this person or group has to this file or directory (more on these concepts in a moment). A hyphen (-) means, "Nope, this person isn't allowed this kind of access." In Figure 16-10, you can see that, if you were the owner of this file, you could do anything you want to it—because there are no hyphens.

There's an *x* in the other columns, too, meaning that *anyone* can execute (launch) this file. Since there's also a *w* in the owner column, that user (root) could, in theory, even make changes to the file (although there would never be a reason to do so).

The three forms of access—read, write, and execute—have slightly different meanings when applied to files and directories:

- **Read access** to a *file* means someone can open and read it. (In the case of a program like iChat, the system needs to "read" the file on your behalf in order to run it.) Read access to a *directory* (folder), on the other hand, just means someone using Terminal can see a list of its contents using a command like *ls*.

- **Write access** to a *file* means someone can modify and save changes to it. Write access to a *directory* means someone can add, remove, and rename any item the folder contains (but not necessarily the items within its subdirectories).

Note: Turning off write access to a certain file doesn't protect it from deletion. As long as write access is turned on for the *folder it's in,* the file is still trashable.

To protect a certain file from deletion, in other words, you must also worry about the access settings of the *folder* that encloses it.

- **Execute access,** when applied to an application, means people can run that particular program. (In fact, Unix distinguishes applications from ordinary files by checking the status of this setting.)

  Of course, you can't very well "run" a directory. If this *x* bit is turned on for a directory, it's called the *searchable* bit (as opposed to the *execute access* bit), and it means you can make it the working directory, using the *cd* command. You still can't see what's in the folder if you don't also have read permissions, but you're welcome to read or copy a file in it as long as you know its full pathname.

Group Detective Work

Back to the task of keeping iChat from launching. The *x* in every user category tells you that anyone can run this program. Your mission, should you choose to accept it, is to change these settings so that one class of account holder can run iChat (Admin), but not another (Standard).

As you've seen, every file's set of permissions identifies both an owner and a group. The group that owns the iChat file is *wheel*, but as you would expect, the Admin class of users is part of the admin group (though not part of wheel). If you want to allow only administrators and anyone else in the *admin* group to run the program, then you need to also change its group to *admin*.

You just have to make sure that no other account holders—Standard ones—are also part of the *admin* group. That's easy enough to find out.

To find out what Unix groups *you* belong to, type *id* in Terminal and press Return. On the next line, Terminal types out a list of items beginning with your account name—that's your user ID (your *uid*)—followed by the name of your primary group (your *gid*). Next are the names of all the groups that include your account. (The Mac refers to accounts and groups by number, which are listed here.) If you have an Administrator account, it's probably something like *uid=506(chris) gid=20(staff)*

*groups=20(staff),401(com.apple.sharepoint.group.1),204(_developer),100(_lpopera-
tor),98(_lpadmin),81(_appserveradm),80(admin),79(_appserverusr),61(localaccoun
ts),12(everyone).*

But you want to find what groups incorporate *Standard* account holders. To determine
what groups someone else's account belongs to, type *id casey* (or whatever the account
name is). You'll probably see that Casey doesn't belong to the admin group. And, in
fact, that's true for all Standard account holders. (If you prefer a little less output, the
groups command used similarly will show you only the group names.)

All right then: The *admin* group contains only Admin users. As far as permissions are
concerned, then, Standard account holders fall into the *everyone else* category.

You just need to turn off iChat's execute permissions for *everyone else* and change
iChat's group to *admin* to complete your task. Doing so allows only the file's owner
(root) and members of its group (admin) to execute the file (that is, to open the
program). All other account holders, meaning Standard account holders, are out of
luck. They'll actually have to pay attention in class.

chmod (Change Mode)

The Unix command for changing file modes (permissions) is *chmod* (for change
mode). Here's the command you use on the iChat file:

```
chmod o-x /Applications/iChat.app/Contents/MacOS/iChat
```

And here's how to understand it.

The command line begins, naturally, with the *chmod* command itself, and ends with
the pathname of the iChat file.

In between are three characters that make up the three parts of a mode-change
clause: *o-x.*

The first character, *o*, represents the class of user that the change affects. In this spot,
you can type *u* to symbolize the file's owner, *g* for its group, *o* for other (everyone
else), and *a* to indicate all three classes at once.

The second character represents the operation to perform, which in most cases is
either to add a permission (use the **+** symbol) or remove one (use the **−** sign).

The final character specifies which permission to change: *r* for read, *w* for write, or
x for execute.

The complete *chmod* command provided above, then, says, "Remove the execute
permissions for others," which is precisely what you want to do.

Permission to Change Permissions

If you actually try the *chmod* command described above, however, you get only an
error message ("Operation not permitted").

Only the *owner* of an item can change its permissions. And you're not iChat's owner;
root is (that is, Mac OS X itself).

So how do you solve the problem? One solution would be to turn on the root account as described on page 655, and then log on as *root*. But that's a hassle, and turning on the root account always entails a security risk.

Instead, you could open the Get Info window for the iChat application file, make yourself the owner, and then type in your name and password to prove you're an administrator. Then open Terminal, use the *chmod* command now that you're the file's owner, return to the Finder, open Get Info again, and change the file's permissions back to *root*.

For a Unix guru, that's an *awful* lot of steps for something that should take only a few keystrokes. As it turns out, the final possibility is quick and easy, which explains its popularity in Unix circles. It's the *sudo* command.

sudo

sudo is a cool command name. Technically, it's short for *superuser do,* which means you're allowed to execute any command as though you'd logged in with the root (superuser) account—but without actually having to turn on the root account, log out, log back in again, and so on.

It's also a great command name because it looks as though it would be pronounced "pseudo," as in, "I'm just *pretending* to be the root user for a moment. I'm here under a pseudonym." (In fact, you pronounce it "SOO-doo," because it comes from *superuser do*. In the privacy of your own brain, though, you can pronounce it however you like.)

Note: Only Administrator account holders can use the *sudo* command.

If you have the root account—or can simulate one using *sudo*—you can override any permissions settings, including the ones that prevent you from changing things in the Applications directory (like iChat).

Now you're ready to change the permissions of that infernal iChat application file. To use *sudo*, you must preface an entire command line with *sudo* and a space. Type this:

```
sudo chmod o-x /Applications/iChat.app/Contents/MacOS/iChat
```

Taken slowly, this command breaks down as follows:

- *sudo.* "Give me the power to do whatever I want."

- *chmod.* "Change the file mode…"

- *o-x.* "…in this way: remove execute permission for others…"

- */Applications/iChat.app/Contents/MacOS/iChat.* "…from the file called iChat, which is inside the Applications→iChat.app→Contents→MacOS folder."

The first time you run *sudo,* you're treated to a stern talking-to that means business: "WARNING: Improper use of the sudo command could lead to data loss or the deletion of important system files. Please double-check your typing when using sudo. Type 'man sudo' for more information.

"To proceed, enter your password, or type Ctrl-C to abort."

In other words, *sudo* is a powerful tool that lets you tromp unfettered across delicate parts of Mac OS X, so you should proceed with caution. At the outset, at least, you should use it only when you've been given specific steps to follow, as in this chapter.

Now *sudo* asks for your usual login password, just to confirm that you're not some seventh-grader up to no good. If you are indeed an administrator, and your password checks out, *sudo* gives you a 5-minute window in which, by prefacing each command with *sudo,* you can move around as though you're the all-high, master root account holder. (If you don't use *sudo* again within a 5-minute span, you have to input your password again.)

The last step, then, is to change the iChat's group to *admin*.

chgrp (Change Group)

The Unix command for changing a file's group ownership is *chgrp* (for change group), and it will do the deed:

```
sudo chgrp admin /Applications/iChat.app/Contents/MacOS/iChat
```

By this point, you should be able to guess that this command allows you (with *sudo*) to change the group ownership to admin of the file /Applications/iChat.app/Contents/MacOS/iChat.

UP TO SPEED

Beware the Dread Typo

Use *sudo* with caution, especially with the *rm* command. Even a single typing error in a *sudo rm* command can be disastrous.

Suppose, for example, that you intended to type this:

sudo rm -ri /Users/Jim/Pictures

…but you accidentally inserted a space after the first slash, like this:

sudo rm -ri / Users/Jim/Pictures

You've just told Terminal to delete *all data on all drives!*

Because of the extra space, the *rm* command sees its first pathname argument as being only /, the root directory. The -r flag means "and all directories inside it."

Good thing you added the *-i* flag, which instructs Mac OS X to ask you for confirmation before deleting each directory. It's almost always a good idea to include *-i* whenever you use *sudo* with *rm.*

History buffs (and Unix fans) may remember that Apple's first iTunes 2 installer, released in October 2001, contained a tiny bug: the tendency to erase people's hard drives. (Oops!) Apple hastily withdrew the installer and replaced it with a fixed one. Behind the scenes, an improperly formed *rm* command was the culprit.

Now whenever anyone who isn't an administrator tries to open iChat, its icon bounces just once in the Dock before dying painlessly.

To restore its original permissions, use the same commands, but in the *chmod* command, replace the **−** with a **+**, like this:

```
sudo chmod o+x /Applications/iChat.app/Contents/MacOS/iChat
```

Then rerun the *chgrp* command, but replace *admin* with *wheel*:

```
sudo chgrp wheel /Applications/iChat.app/Contents/MacOS/iChat
```

Note: Apple has these default permissions set for a reason: utmost security. While your changes won't immediately let the bad guys in, it's best not to leave these permissions in place unless you really need them. In any case, whenever you run the Mac's Repair Permissions function (either automatically, which happens each time you install a Mac OS X update, or manually, using Disk Utility), iChat returns to its original permissions settings. You have to rerun the command if you want its protections in place.

Protecting Files En Masse

It could happen to you. You've got yourself a folder filled with hundreds of files—downloaded photos from your digital camera, for example. Most are pretty crummy, but the ones you took in Tahoe (which therefore have *Tahoe* in their file names) are spectacular. You want to protect those files from deletion without having to turn on the Locked checkbox (page 88) of every file individually.

Here again, you *could* operate in the Finder, just like ordinary mortals. You could use Spotlight to round up all files with *Tahoe* in their names, highlight them in the search results window, choose File→Get Info, and then turn on Locked for all of them at once. But doing it the Unix way builds character.

When you turn on a file's Locked checkbox, Mac OS X turns on an invisible switch known to Unix veterans as the *user immutable flag.* Not even the superuser is allowed to change, move, or delete a file whose user immutable flag is turned on.

The command you need to change such flags is *chflags*—short for *change flags,* of course. You can follow the *chflags* command with three arguments: its own option flags, the file flags, and the pathname of the file whose flags are being changed. In this case, the flag you care about is called *uchg* (short for *user changeable;* in other words, this is the immutable flag).

To protect all the Tahoe shots in one fell swoop, then, here's what you'd type at the prompt:

```
chflags uchg ~/Pictures/*Tahoe*
```

The asterisks are wildcards that mean "all files containing the word Tahoe in their names." So in English, you've just said, "Change the immutable flag (the Locked checkbox setting) for all the Tahoe files in my Pictures folder to 'locked.' "

Tip: To *unlock* a file, thus turning off its *uchg* flag, just add the prefix "no," like this: *chflags nouchg ~/Pictures/*Tahoe*.*

To view the results of your handiwork right in Terminal, issue this command: *ls -lO ~/Pictures* (or any other path to a folder containing locked items). That's the familiar *ls* (list) command that shows you what's in a certain directory, followed by an *-l* flag for a more complete listing, and an *-O* flag that produces a "flags" column in the resulting table.

In any case, Terminal might spit out something like this:

```
total 830064
-rw-r—r—1 chris   chris   —     158280000  Jun 16 20:05 Sunset.jpg
-rw-r—r—1 chris   chris   uchg   58560000  Jun 16 20:05 NewMoon.jpg
-rw-r—r—1 chris   chris   uchg  107520000  Jun 16 20:05 Tahoe.jpg
-rw-r—r—1 chris   chris   uchg  100560000  Jun 16 20:05 Buddy.jpg
```

The fourth column, the product of the *-O* flag, lists any file flags that have been set for each file. In this case, three of the files are listed with uchg, which represents the user immutable (locked) flag. (The hyphen for the first listed file means "no flags"—that is, not locked.)

Making Files Hide

Back at the school computer lab, you're still grumpy. The students leave piles of file and folder icons splattered across all the Macs' desktops, and you've had enough. Not only is it a sign of laziness and disorganization, but the icons cover the desktop picture of the hallowed school mascot: the southern hairy-nosed wombat.

You've warned them enough, and now it's time for action: No World of Warcraft at lunchtime unless the desktops are clean in 15 minutes!

As you finish writing the new rule on the whiteboard, you turn to face the students' Mac screens—and you're stunned. The full, uncluttered image of your beloved marsupial gazes back from the Macs' displays; the offending icons are gone. How could that be? There hasn't even been time for the students to select all the icons and drag them to the Trash!

Apparently the students weren't as lazy as you thought: They've been learning the Way of the Terminal. What they actually did was sweep all those icons under the rug, Unix style, with this command:

```
chflags hidden ~/Desktop/*
```

They manipulated another file flag, called the hidden flag. The command turns on the hidden flag for all files (indicated by the asterisk) in the Desktop folder—and so their icons disappear. The actual file is still there; but you just can't see it in the Finder anymore.

Of course, you're not about to let some punk kids pull one over on you. In your copy of Terminal, you deftly type *chflags nohidden ~/Desktop/** to bring the icons back.

The students have 13 minutes left to really clean their desktops.

20 Useful Unix Utilities

So far, you've read about only a handful of the hundreds of Unix programs that are built into Mac OS X and ready to run. Yes, *ls* and *sudo* are very useful tools, but they're only the beginning. As you peruse beginner-level Unix books and Web sites (see Appendix E), for example, you'll gradually become familiar with a few more important terms and tools.

Here's a rundown of some more cool (and very safe) programs that await your experimentation.

Tip: If you don't return to the $ prompt after using one of these commands, type *q* or, in some cases, *quit*, and then hit Return.

---

bc

Mac OS X and Windows aren't the only operating systems that come with a basic calculator accessory; Unix is well equipped in this regard, too.

When you type *bc* and hit Enter, you get a copyright notice and then...nothing. Just type the equation you want to solve, such as *2+2*, or *95+97+456+2-65*, or *(2*3)+165-95*(2.5*2.5)*, and then press Return. On the next line, *bc* instantly displays the result of your calculation.

(In computer land, * designates multiplication and / represents division. Note, too, that *bc* solves equations correctly; it calculates multiplication and division before addition and subtraction, and inner parentheses before the outer ones. For more *bc* tricks and tips, type *man bc* at the prompt.)

kill

Mac OS X offers no shortage of ways to cut the cord on a program that seems to be locked up or runnning amok. You can force quit it, use Activity Monitor, or use *kill*.

The *kill* program in Terminal simply force quits a program, as though by remote control. (It even works when you SSH into your Mac from a remote location, as described in Chapter 22.) All you have to do is follow the *kill* command with the ID number of the program you want to terminate.

And how do you know its ID number? You start by running *top*—described in a moment—whose first column shows the PID (process ID) of every running program.

Tip: Unless you also use *sudo,* you can *kill* only programs you "own"–those running under your account. (The operating system itself–*root*–is always running programs of its own, and it's technically possible that other people, dialing in from the road, are running programs of their own even while you're using the Mac!)

When you hear Unix fans talk about *kill* online, they often indicate a number flag after the command, like this: *kill -9*. This flag is a "noncatchable, non-ignorable kill." In other words, it's an industrial-strength assassin that accepts no pleas for mercy from the program you're killing.

If you check *top* and find out that BeeKeeper Pro's process ID is 753, you'd abort it by typing *kill 753* and then pressing Return. If it still appears to be breathing, add the -9 flag like this: *kill -9 753*, which should deliver the fatal blow. You might even need to rerun the command until you receive output similar to *kill: 753: no such pid*, telling you that indeed, that process is no more; please hold your fire.

open

What operating system would be complete without a way to launch programs? In Mac OS X's version of Unix, the command is easy enough: *open -a*, as in *open -a Chess*. The -a flag allows you to specify an application by name, regardless of where it is on your hard drive, exactly the way Spotlight does it. You can even specify which document you want to open into that program like this: *open -a Preview FunnyPhotoOfCasey.tif*.

Tip: The -e flag opens any text document in TextEdit (or whatever your default text editor may be), like this: *open -e Diary.txt*. This shortcut saves you from having to specify TextEdit itself.

The real utility of this command might not be apparent at first, but imagine doing something like this in the Finder: Select from a folder of hundreds of HTML files those that contain the word "Sequoia" in their file names and preview them all with the OmniWeb browser, regardless of what application they're actually associated with. You could do it with the help of the Spotlight command, but that would take quite a few steps. In Terminal, though, you just switch to that directory (using the *cd* command) and type *open -a OmniWeb *Sequoia**. Done!

Of course, you may not often bother simply *launching* programs and documents this way. Nevertheless you can see how useful *open* can be when you're writing automated scripts for your Mac, like those used by the *launchd* command scheduler program (page 408).

ps

The *ps* (process status) command is another way to get a quick look at all the programs running on your Mac, even the usually invisible ones, complete with their ID numbers. (For the most helpful results, use the -e and -f flags like this: *ps -ef*. For a complete description of these and other flags, type *man ps* and hit Return.)

shutdown

It's perfectly easy to shut down your Mac from the menu. But using *shutdown* with its -h flag (for *halt*) in Terminal has its advantages. For one thing, you can control *when* the shutdown occurs, using one of these three options:

- **Now.** You can safely shut down by typing *shutdown -h now*. (Actually, only the root user is allowed to use *shutdown,* so you'd really type *sudo shutdown -h now* and then type in your administrator's password when asked.)

- **Later today.** Specify a time instead of *now*. Typing *sudo shutdown -h 2330,* for example, shuts down your machine at 11:30 p.m. today (*2330* is military time notation for 11:30 p.m.).

- **Any time in the next 100 years.** To make the machine shut down at 5:00 p.m. on December 9, 2010, for example, you could type *sudo shutdown -h 1012091700.* (That number code is in year [last two digits]:month:date:hour:minute format.)

Tip: Once you set the auto-shutdown robot in motion, you can't stop it easily. You must use the *kill* command described earlier to terminate the *shutdown* process itself. To find out *shutdown*'s ID number in order to terminate it, look for the *pid* number in the output of the shutdown command, or use the *top* or *ps* command.

There are still more useful flags. For example:

- Using the *-r* flag instead of *-h* means "restart instead of just shutting down," as in *sudo shutdown -r now.*

- You can use shutdown to knock all connected network users off your machine without actually shutting down. Use the *-k* flag, like this: *sudo shutdown -k now.*

One of the most powerful uses of *shutdown* is turning off Macs by remote control, either from across the network or across the world via Internet. That is, you can use *SSH* (described in Chapter 22) to issue this command.

tar, gzip, zip

You know how Mac OS X can create compressed .zip archive files?

Terminal lets you stuff and combine files in these formats with the greatest of ease. To compress a file, just type *gzip,* a space, and then the pathname of the file you want to compress (or drag the file directly from the desktop into the Terminal window). When you press Enter or Return, Mac OS X compresses the file.

"Tarring" a folder (combining its contents into a single file—a *tarball,* as Unix hepcats call it) is only slightly more complicated. You have to specify the resulting file's name, followed by the actual directory pathname, like this: *tar -cf Memos.tar /Users/chris/ Memos.* Add the *-z* flag if you want to tar *and* compress the folder: *tar -czf Memos. tar.gz /Users/chris/Memos.*

To combine and compress files using *zip,* just specify a name for the zip file and the names of the items to zip, like this: *zip StaffordLake.zip Stafford** (which would cram all files in the working directory whose name begins with *Stafford* into a single archive).

To zip a *folder,* include the *-r* flag as well: *zip -r Memos /Users/chris/Memos.*

In any case, if you switch to the Finder, you see that the file or folder you specified is now compressed (with the suffix *.gz*), combined (with the suffix *.tar*), or both (with the suffix *tar.gz* or *.zip*).

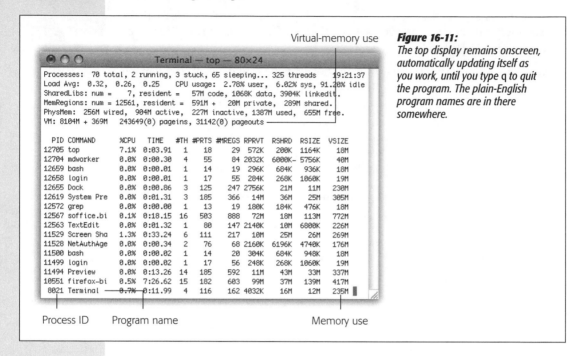

Virtual-memory use

Process ID   Program name   Memory use

Figure 16-11:
The top display remains onscreen, automatically updating itself as you work, until you type q to quit the program. The plain-English program names are in there somewhere.

Unfortunately, the command line *zip* utility doesn't handle extended attributes properly (see the next page), so stick with *tar* and *gzip* if you want to create guaranteed Mac-friendly archives. The best format is a gzipped tarball, which the Finder will properly open with a double-click. (If you only *gzip* a file without tarring, the Finder won't preserve any extended attributes when opening it.) You can also use these utilities to open combined and compressed files, but they can easily overwrite existing items of the same name if you're not careful. Use the Finder or StuffIt Expander to eliminate that worry.

Note: The *gzip* command deletes the original file after gzipping it. The *tar* and *zip* commands, on the other hand, "stuff" things but leave the originals alone.

top (table of processes)

When you type *top* and press Return, you get a handy table that lists every program currently running on your Mac, including the obscure background ones you probably never even knew existed (Figure 16-11).

You also get statistics that tell you how much memory and speed (CPU power) they're sucking down. In Snow Leopard, you get a new line that shows the amount of data moved to and from the network as well as the amount read or written to disk (since you last started your Mac). In this regard, *top* is similar to Activity Monitor, described on page 408.

Tip: If you type *top -u,* you get a list sorted by CPU usage, meaning the power-hungry programs are listed first. If your Mac ever seems to act sluggish, checking *top -u* to see what's tying things up is a good instinct.

xattr (extended attributes)

The *xattr* command lets you see and manage the extended attributes (EAs) of your files—the invisible metadata that describes all kinds of characteristics of every file, from the exposure of a digital camera shot to the tempo of a song in iTunes. (Chapter 3 has much more on metadata and searching for it.)

Running *xattr* * lists any EAs in your working directory. If you ran it in your ~/ Downloads folder, the command might look like this:

```
MacChris:Downloads chris$ xattr  *
GoogleEarthMac.dmg: com.apple.diskimages.fsck
GoogleEarthMac.dmg: com.apple.diskimages.recentcksum
GoogleEarthMac.dmg: com.apple.metadata:kMDItemWhereFroms
GoogleEarthMac.dmg: com.apple.quarantine
MacPorts-1.8.0-10.6-SnowLeopard.dmg: com.apple.diskimages.fsck
MacPorts-1.8.0-10.6-SnowLeopard.dmg: com.apple.diskimages.re-
centcksum
MacPorts-1.8.0-10.6-SnowLeopard.dmg: com.apple.
metadata:kMDItemWhereFroms
MacPorts-1.8.0-10.6-SnowLeopard.dmg: com.apple.quarantine
NeoOffice-3.0-Intel.dmg: com.apple.metadata:kMDItemWhereFroms
NeoOffice-3.0-Intel.dmg: com.apple.quarantine
```

Only three files are listed, but each of their EAs gets its own line. What you'll find in common to all of these files is that they hold a "com.apple.quarantine" EA.

You know how, the first time you open a program on your Mac, you get the dialog box shown in Figure 12-15 (page 493)? Now you know how the Mac knows that this is the first time you ran it: That detail was stored as one of its extended attributes.

If you really can't stand those messages, you could use another Unix command to prevent the nag box from appearing. For example, before installing NeoOffice, you could simply remove the quarantine EA from its downloaded disk image file using the *xattr* command's *-d* flag, like this:

```
xattr -d com.apple.quarantine NeoOffice-3.0-Intel.dmg
```

You can also use the *ls* command to see EAs. When you use just the *-l* flag with *ls*, files with EAs show an @ sign at the end of the permission codes:

```
MacChris: Downloads ls -l NeoOffice-3.0-Intel.dmg
-rw-r--r--@ 1 chris  staff  167536744 Mar 28 11:58 NeoOffice-3.0-Intel.dmg
```

To see what those EAs are, add the @ flag:

```
MacChris:Downloads chris$ ls -l@ NeoOffice-3.0-Intel.dmg
-rw-r--r--@ 1 chris  staff  167536744 Mar 28 11:58 NeoOffice-3.0-Intel.dmg
com.apple.metadata:kMDItemWhereFroms                196
com.apple.quarantine            74
```

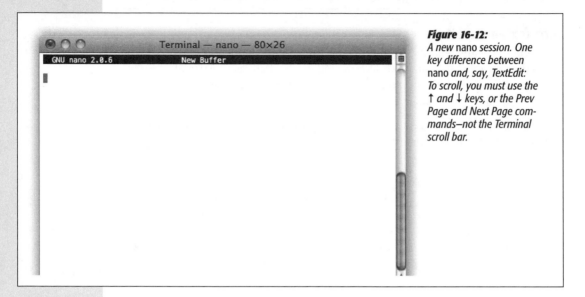

Figure 16-12:
A new nano *session. One key difference between* nano *and, say, TextEdit: To scroll, you must use the ↑ and ↓ keys, or the Prev Page and Next Page commands—not the Terminal scroll bar.*

Aliases

Aliases in Unix have nothing to do with traditional Macintosh icon aliases. Instead, Unix aliases are more like text macros, in that they're longish commands you can trigger by typing a much shorter abbreviation.

For example, remember the command for unlocking all the files in a folder? (It was *sudo chflags -R nouchg [pathname]*. To unlock everything in your account's Trash, for example, you'd type *sudo chflags -R nouchg ~/.trash*.)

Using the *alias* command, however, you can create a much shorter command (*unlock,* for example) that has the same effect. (The *alias* command takes two arguments: the alias name you want, and the command it's supposed to type out, like this: *alias unlock='sudo chflags -R nouchg ~/.trash'*.)

The downside is that aliases you create this way linger in Terminal's memory only while you're still in the original Terminal window. As soon as you close it, you lose your aliases. When you get better at Unix, therefore, you can learn to create a .bash_profile file that permanently stores all your command aliases. (Hint: Open or create a file called .bash_profile in your home directory, and add to it one alias command per line.)

nano, emacs, vim

One way to create and edit text files containing aliases (and to perform other command-related tasks) is to use *nano*, a popular text editor that's an improved version of the *pico* editor (see Figure 16-12). In fact, if you try to run *pico*, *nano* opens instead.

As you'll discover just by typing *nano* and pressing Return, *nano* is a full-screen Unix application. You enter text in *nano* much as you do in TextEdit, yet *nano* is filled with features that are especially tailored to working with Unix tasks and commands.

Nor is *nano* the only text editor that's built into the Unix under Mac OS X. Some Unix fans prefer the more powerful and complex *vim* or *emacs*, in the same way that some people prefer Microsoft Word to TextEdit.

date

Used all by itself, the *date* command simply displays the current date and time. However, you can use its long list of date "conversion specifications" (enter *man date* to see all of them) to format the date string in any conceivable way. Begin the string with a **+** and then enter the formatting you like, mixing in any regular text as well, like this:

```
office-mac:~ chris$ date +"I can't believe it's already week %V
of %Y, here in the %Z time zone. But what do you expect on a %A
at %l:%M %p?"
I can't believe it's already week 23 of 2010, here in the PST
time zone. But what do you expect on a Wednesday at 8:21 PM?
```

GEM IN THE ROUGH

Eliza, I Have Issues with My Mother

Therapy, whether it's about your frustrations with your Mac or any other subject, is expensive. Still, it feels good to talk to someone about whatever's bothering you—and Mac OS X is ready to listen.

Hidden in the *emacs* text-editing program is a fully unlicensed automated psychoanalyst named Eliza. To enter her office, open Terminal, type *emacs* and press Return. After the introductory screen has appeared, press Shift-Esc, type *xdoctor*, and then press Return.

```
● ● ●              Terminal — emacs-i386 — 80×24
I am the psychotherapist.  Please, describe your problems.  Each time
you are finished talking, type RET twice.

I have issues with my mother.

Tell me something about your family.

It's extremely dysfunctional. We basically try to kill each other.

This is not a healthy way of thinking.

You're telling me!

Why do you say I am telling you?

I'm sorry, I'm sorry.

Is it because of your plans that you say you are sorry you are sorry?

█
-uuu:**-F1  *doctor*        All L20    (Doctor Fill)----------------------
```

"I am the psychotherapist," Eliza begins. "Please, describe your problems. Each time you are finished talking, type RET twice." (She means, "Press the Return key twice.")

As you can see from this illustration, she isn't exactly Sigmund Freud. But she's very entertaining, and surprisingly responsive.

When your session is finished, press Control-X and then Control-C to exit *Eliza* and *emacs*.

Note: Be careful about using *date* with *sudo*. If you do, and accidentally forget the leading **+**, you reset your Mac's built-in clock.

grep

The *grep* program is a *filter*, a powerful program designed to search data for text that matches a specified pattern. It can pass on the processed result to another program, file, or the command line itself.

You specify the text pattern you want *grep* to search using a notation called *regular expressions*. For example, the regular expression *dis[ck]* searches for either *disk* or *disc*. Another example: To search for lines in a file containing the addresses from 200 to 299 Redwood Way, you could tell grep that you're looking for "\<2[0-9][0-9] *Redwood Way*".

One terrific thing about *grep* is that its search material can be part of any file, especially plain text files. The text files on your Mac include HTML files, log files, and—possibly juiciest of all—your email mailbox files. Using *grep*, for example, you could search all your Mail files for messages matching certain criteria, with great efficiency and even finer control than with Spotlight.

find

Now that Spotlight's on the scene, you might wonder why you would need to use the Unix *find* command. Well, for one, *find* takes file searching to a whole new level. For example, you can find files based on their permissions, owner name, flag settings, and of course any kind of name pattern you can think of using regular expressions.

Also, like with most other Unix commands, you can "pipe" the *find* command's list of found files straight into another program for further processing. You might do this to change their names, convert them to other formats, or even upload them to a network server.

Perhaps best of all, since you can run *find* with *sudo*, you can look for files existing *anywhere* on your hard disk, regardless of directory permission settings.

To find all the files in your home directory with "Bolinas" in their names, for example, you would use this command:

```
find ~/ -name '*Bolinas*'
```

Or, to ignore capitalization:

```
find ~/ -iname '*Bolinas*'
```

And this command searches for all the *locked* files in your home directory:

```
find ~/ -flags uchg
```

mdfind

If you have a soft spot in your heart for Spotlight, you'll be happy to see the *mdfind* command in Terminal. It performs the same kinds of searches, finding by metadata like music genre or exposure data for photos.

To find all reggae songs, for example, try:

```
mdfind 'kMDItemMusicalGenre == "Reggae"'
```

To find all photos you shot with the flash on:

```
mdfind 'kMDItemFlashOnOff == "1"'
```

The *mdls* command reveals all the metadata for a particular file, like the IMG_3033.jpg picture in this example:

```
ongaku:Photos$ mdls IMG_3033.JPG
kMDItemAcquisitionMake       = "Canon"
kMDItemAcquisitionModel      = "Canon PowerShot S3 IS"
kMDItemAperture              = 4.65625
kMDItemBitsPerSample         = 32
kMDItemColorSpace            = "RGB"
kMDItemContentCreationDate   = 2007-06-30 14:51:07 -0700
kMDItemContentModificationDate = 2007-06-30 14:51:07 -0700
kMDItemContentType           = "public.jpeg"
```

You can find more about constructing your queries here: *http://developer.apple.com/mac/library/documentation/Carbon/Conceptual/SpotlightQuery/Concepts/QueryFormat.html.*

POWER USERS' CLINIC

Secrets of Virtual Memory

The *top* command's table offers a fascinating look at the way Mac OS X manages memory. In the "VM" section, for example, you'll see current statistics for *pageins* and *pageouts*—that is, how many times the virtual-memory system has had to "set down" software code for a moment as it juggles your open programs in actual memory. (These numbers are pointed out in Figure 16-11.)

The pageins and pageouts statistics are composed of two different numbers, like this: *45451(0) pageins, 42946(0) pageouts*. The bigger number tells you how many times your Mac has had to shuffle data in and out of memory since the Mac started up. The number in parentheses indicates how much of this shuffling it's done within the *past second*.

The pageouts value is the number to worry about. If it stays above zero for a while, your Mac is gasping for RAM (as the hard drive thrashing sounds and program-switching delays are probably also telling you).

In the listing of individual programs, the last four columns provide details about the memory usage of each listed program. The one you care about is the RPRVT (Resident Private) column, which shows how much memory each program is actually using at the moment. This number goes up and down as you work, illustrating the miracle of Mac OS X: Programs don't just grab a chunk of memory and sit there with it. They put that RAM back in the pot when they don't need it.

---

launchd

launchd is a multitalented Unix program responsible for launching system programs, during startup or anytime thereafter. Part of its job is triggering certain commands according to a specified schedule, even when you're not logged in. People can use *launchd* to trigger daily backups or monthly maintenance, for example. You can program your unattended software robot by editing simple property list files.

Mac OS X comes set up to run *launchd* automatically; it's the very first process that starts up when the Mac does. It launches all your other startup items, in fact. (If you open the Activity Monitor program in your Applications→Utilities folder, you'll see it listed among the administrator processes that your Mac is running all the time.)

In fact, *launchd* comes with three under-the-hood Unix maintenance tasks already scheduled: a daily job, a weekly job, and a monthly job. They come set to run at 3:15 a.m. (the first two), and 5:30 a.m. If your Mac isn't generally turned on in the middle of the night, these healthy jobs may never run.

You can either leave your Mac on overnight every now and then or, if you're feeling ambitious, change the time for them to be run. A glance at *man launchd.plist* shows you how. (Hint: It involves using *sudo nano* and editing the three com.apple.periodic property list files in /System/Library/LaunchDaemons—but be careful not to mess with anything else in there!)

Note: Some other Unix systems (and versions of Mac OS X) use the *cron* utility to run these jobs. *cron* also exists on Snow Leopard and will start working as it does elsewhere—the minute you add a new *cron* job. See the *cron* and *crontab* manpages for details.

---

ftp

FTP (and its relative, telnet) aren't exclusively Unix programs, of course. Techies from all walks of operating-system life have used telnet for years whenever they want to tap into another computer from afar, and FTP to deliver and download software files. Details on FTP are in Chapter 22.

Putting It Together

The Unix syntax and vocabulary presented in this chapter is all well and good, and it'll give you the rosy glow of having mastered something new. But it still doesn't *entirely* explain why Unix gives programmers sweaty palms and dilated pupils.

The real power of Unix comes down the road—when you start stringing these commands together.

Suppose, for example, you want to round up all the TIFF image files related to your Yosemite project, scale them to a common size, convert them to JPEG files, and copy them to an FTP site. How would you go about it?

You could, of course, use Spotlight to search for all TIFF files that have "Yosemite" in their names. But what if your images were named otherwise but kept in folders with Yosemite in their names? You would have to find those folders first, and then the TIFF files within them.

You could perform the next step (scaling and converting the image) either manually or by a preprogrammed script or Automator workflow, using a program like Photoshop or even iPhoto. Once the images were all done, you'd need to collect them and then use your favorite FTP program to upload them to the server.

If you've mastered Unix, though, you could shave 12 minutes off of your workday just by changing to an empty working directory (in this example, ~/Stage) and typing this as one long line:

```
find ~ -type f -ipath '*yosemite*tif' -print0 | xargs -0 sips
-Z 250 -s format jpeg --out ~/Stage && ftp -u ftp://ftp.coast-
photo.com/Incoming *
```

Even after almost 50 pages of Unix basics, that mass of commands probably looks a tad intimidating. And, indeed, if you've never programmed before, even the following breakdown may make your eyes glaze over. Nevertheless, pieces of it should now look familiar:

- **find ~ -type f -ipath '*yosemite*tif' -print0 |**. This segment searches your home directory (*~*) for files (*-type f*) whose pathnames (*-ipath*, meaning "capitalization doesn't matter") contain the word *Yosemite* and end in *tif*. Remember, the asterisks

---

The Famous Animated-Desktop Trick

It was one of the first great Mac OS X hacks to be passed around the Internet: the classic "screen-saver-on-the-desktop" trick. In this scheme, your desktop shows more than some wussy, motionless desktop picture. It actually displays one of the Screen Effects animation modules.

Start by choosing the screen saver module you prefer, using the Screen Effects panel of System Preferences. (The one called "flurry" makes a good choice.)

Then, in Terminal, type: */System/Library/Frameworks/Screen Saver.framework/Resources/ScreenSaverEngine.app/ Contents/MacOS/ScreenSaverEngine -background &*

Finally, press Return. (Note that there are no spaces or Returns in the command, even though it appears broken onto more than one line here.)

Presto: The active screen saver becomes your desktop picture! Fall back into your chair in astonishment.

Once you've regained your composure, look in the Terminal window again. The number that follows the [1] in the following line is the *process ID* of your background desktop program.

You'll need that number when it comes time to turn *off* the effect, which is a good idea, since the desktop/screen saver business drains a massive amount of your Mac's processing power. The whole thing is a gimmicky showoff stunt you'll generally want to turn off before conducting any meaningful work.

To turn off this effect, type *kill 496* (or whatever the process ID is), and then press Return.

And if you get tired of typing out that long command, download xBack from *www.gideonsoftworks.com/xback. html*. It's a simple piece of shareware that lets you turn this effect, plus many additional options, on and off with the click of a mouse.

---

here are wildcard characters. The command so far makes a list of all matching files, which it keeps in its little head.

The *-print0* command formats this list of found files' pathnames, separating them with the *null character* (a special character programmers use to indicate where one string of text ends and another begins) instead of the usual spaces. It lets the command work with pathnames that contain spaces, a common occurrence on Macs (but a rarity in Unix). You'll see how it does this shortly.

Then comes the *pipe* (the vertical bar), which you can use to direct the results (output) of one command into the input of another. In this case, it sends the list of found pathnames on to the next command.

- **xargs -0 sips -z 250 -s format jpeg --out ~/Stage &&.** *xargs* is an argument builder. In this case, it builds an argument from the list of files it received from the *find* command and provides it to *sips* for processing. In other words, *xargs* hands a list of files to *sips*, and *sips* runs the same command on each one.

POWER USERS' CLINIC

X11

If you've ever poked around in your /Applications/Utilities folder, you might have spotted the program called X11.

No, it's not the code name of a top-secret project Apple forgot to remove before shipping Snow Leopard. X11 is another name for the X Window System, a GUI that came to being on Unix systems at about the same time the Macintosh was introduced. ("GUI" stands for *graphic user interface,* and it means "icons, windows, and menus like you're used to—not typing commands at a prompt.")

More importantly, X11 lets your Mac run many of the Unix GUI applications, both free and commercial, that have become available over the years.

Getting X11 to work right with Mac OS X used to require some fiddling. But in Snow Leopard, you can run it without fuss. X11 comes with several "X" programs, which are found in */usr/X11/bin.* Your shell knows about this directory, and Terminal knows about X11, so you can run these applications like any other command.

To launch the X11 clock, for example, start in Terminal. Type *xclock* and press Return. After a moment, the X11 icon appears in your Dock—and a small clock window appears beside your other windows, just like any normal program.

(As you'll discover, X11 programs are more visually pleasing than Unix code. But they have not, ahem, been designed by Steve Jobs.)

To stop the X application, you can close its window, or press Control-C in Terminal. (No new prompt appears while the X application is running.)

Many other X applications come with Snow Leopard; in Terminal, type *ls /usr/X11/bin* to list them. Some interesting ones to try are xterm, xcalc, glxgears, and xman. You can even add more X applications by downloading and compiling source code (a daunting task for anyone new to Unix), or through a "ports" system like MacPorts (*www.macports.org*), which provides software packages "ported" to Mac OS X for easier installation.

The *-0* flag tells *xargs* that the pathnames are separated by the null character. (Otherwise, *xargs* would separate pathnames at each space character, which would choke *sips*.)

For each file it gets, *sips* first scales the image's largest dimension to 250 pixels, and its other dimension proportionally. (That way, any image will fit into a 250 × 250-pixel box on a Web page, for example.)

sips then sets the format (*-s format*) of the image to JPEG and saves it, with the correct .jpg extension, in the ~/Stage directory.

The double ampersands (&&) at the end of this fragment tell the shell to run the next command only when it's *successfully* finished with the previous one. (If it fails, the whole thing stops here.) So, once *sips* is done with each file it gets from *xargs*, the shell moves on to this:

- **ftp -u ftp://ftp.coast-photo.com/Incoming ***. The *ftp* utility included with Snow Leopard can upload and download files with a single command. In this case, the command uploads (*-u*) every file from the working directory (as specified by the

---

POWER USERS' CLINIC

The Root Account

Standard, Administrator, Managed, Sharing Only, and Guest aren't the only kinds of accounts. There's one more, one that wields ultimate power, one person who can do anything to any file anywhere. This person is called the *superuser*.

Unix fans speak of the superuser account—also called the *root* account—in hushed tones, because it offers absolutely unrestricted power. The root account holder can move, delete, rename, or otherwise mangle any file on the machine, no matter what folder it's in. One wrong move—or one malicious hacker who manages to seize the root account—and you've got yourself a $2,000 doorstop. That's why Mac OS X's root account is completely hidden.

Truth is, you can enjoy most rootlike powers without actually turning on the root account. Here are some of the things the root account holder can do—and the ways you can do them without ducking into a phone booth to become the superuser:

See crucial system files that are ordinarily invisible. Of course, you can also see them easily by using the freeware program TinkerTool (page 657). You can also use the Terminal program described in this chapter.

Peek into other account holders' folders (or even trash them). You don't have to be the superuser to do this—you just have to be an administrator who's smart enough to use the Get Info command, as described on page 88.

Use powerful Unix system commands. Some of the Unix commands you can issue in Mac OS X require superuser powers. As noted in this chapter, however, there's a simple command—the *sudo* command—that grants you root powers without you actually having to *log into* the root account. Details are on page 639.

Using the *sudo* command is faster, easier, and more secure than using the root account. It doesn't present the risk that you'll walk away from your Mac while logged in as the root user, thereby opening yourself up to complete annihilation from a passing evildoer (in person or over the Internet).

But if you're a Unix geek, and you want to poke around the lowest levels of the operating system, or you're in a time of crisis, and you really, really need to log in with the root account, see the free downloadable appendix to this chapter ("Enabling the Root Account"). It's available on this book's "Missing CD" page at *www.missingmanuals.com*.

---

asterisk—that is, all of the *sips*-processed files) to the Incoming directory of the *coast-photo.com* FTP site.

Note: As written, this command works only if you don't need a password to get into the FTP site. Otherwise, build your FTP account name and password into its address like this: *ftp://chris:password@ftp.coast-photo. com/Incoming*.

When you press Return or Enter after this gigantic command, Mac OS X scans all the directories inside your home directory, rounds up all the Yosemite-related images, scales them, converts and renames them, and then uploads each to the FTP directory.

Once you've gained some experience with Unix commands and programs like these, you'll find it fairly easy to adapt them to your own tasks. For example, here's a more versatile command that searches a directory called Projects for all TIFF files modified after 6:00 that morning, converts them to thumbnail-sized JPEGs, plops them into the images directory of your FTP-accessible Web server, and then moves them all to your Backup directory:

```
cd ~/Stage && find ~/Projects -type f -iname *tif -newermt 6:00
-print0 | xargs -0 sips -Z 128 -s format jpeg --out ~/Stage &&
ftp -u ftp://carlos:birdie@ftp.coast-photo.com/htdocs/images *
&& mv * ~/Backup/
```

Tip: You don't have to type out that entire command line every time you need it; you can save the whole thing as a *.command* file on your desktop that runs when double-clicked.

First, create a new plain text document; you can use TextEdit. Type in the entire command you want to memorialize. Save the document with a name ending with *.command*—for example, ProcessImages.command. (Documents with this extension appear with a spiffy icon in the Finder.)

Next, make that file itself executable by using the *chmod* command. If, for example, you want only the owner of the ProcessImages.command file, you would type: *chmod u+x ProcessImages.command*.

With just a few more keystrokes, you could modify that command to collect some files, lock them, and place copies of each in every account holder's home directory, as well as several different servers at the same time. What's more, it emails you a report when it's done. Using *launchd*, you could even configure this routine to trigger itself automatically every day at 11:00 p.m. Considering the hundreds of Unix programs included with Mac OS X and the thousands of others available on the Internet, the possibilities are limitless.

For some guidance in picking up your Unix career from here, see Appendix E.

Hacking Mac OS X

Chapter 9 shows you how to customize your desktop picture, error beep, and screen saver. But if you're sneaky, creative, or just different, you can perform more dramatic visual and behavioral surgery on your copy of Mac OS X—from changing the startup screen image to replacing the "poof" that appears when you drag something off the Dock with a new animation of your own. All you need is a few of Mac OS X's less obvious tools, or some free downloadable customizing software, and a few recipes like the ones in this chapter.

Some of these tricks are frivolous. Some are functional and useful. And although Apple sanctions not a one, all are perfectly safe.

TinkerTool: Customization 101

If you poke around the Mac OS X Web sites and newsgroups long enough, you'll find little bits of Unix code being passed around. One of them purports to let you change the genie animation you see when you minimize a window to the Dock. Another eliminates the drop shadow behind icon names on your desktop. Yet another lets you change the transparency of the Terminal window (Chapter 16)—a cool, although not especially practical, effect.

If you really want to fool around with these bits of Unix code, go for it. You can find most of these tidbits at Web sites like *www.macosxhints.com*.

But the truth is, there's no good reason for you to subject yourself to the painstaking effort of typing out Unix commands when easy-to-use, push-button programs are available to do the same thing.

TinkerTool, for example, is a free utility that offers an amazing degree of control over the fonts, desktop, Dock, scroll bar arrows, and other aspects of the Mac OS X environment.

Here are some of the highlights:

- **Kill the animations.** When you open any icon, expand a Get Info panel, and so on, you see little animated expansion effects. It's nice, but it takes time. TinkerTool can turn them off (see Figure 17-1).

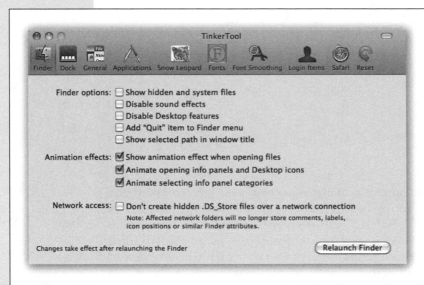

Figure 17-1:
TinkerTool is a double-clickable program that makes changes only to your account settings. (Mercifully, it's free. You can get it from this book's "Missing CD" page at www.missingmanuals.com.)

- **Dock.** TinkerTool lets you give hidden programs transparent icons on the Dock and specify the Dock's position on the screen—left, right, bottom, or *top*—and even whether it's centered or flush against one corner. TinkerTool also unlocks a third option for the animation of windows collapsing onto the Dock. In addition to the standard Mac OS X choices (Genie and Scale), you also get something called Suck In (no comment).

Tip: TinkerTool can even turn off the glassy, 3-D look of the Dock, which isn't universally adored.

- **Scroll bars.** TinkerTool gives you greater control over the placement of Mac OS X's scroll bar arrows—together at one end of the scroll bar, duplicated at both ends of the scroll bar, and so on.

- **Visibility.** TinkerTool can make the thousands of invisible Unix files appear as full-blooded icons. (Power users, you know who you are.)

- **Fonts.** TinkerTool lets you change the fonts for dialog boxes, menus, title bars, help balloons, and so on.

What's terrific about TinkerTool is that it's completely safe. It's nothing more than a front end for a number of perfectly legitimate Unix settings that Apple simply opted to make unavailable in the regular Finder. Furthermore, the changes you make using TinkerTool are stored in your own Home→Library folder—that is, they affect only your account. Whatever changes you make don't affect the Mac experience for anyone else using your machine. And TinkerTool's Reset pane makes it easy to restore *everything* back to the way it was before you started fooling around.

Redoing Mac OS X's Graphics

The professional interface artists at Apple use Adobe Photoshop, just like professional artists everywhere else. But in Mac OS X, they've made very little effort to cover their tracks. In Cocoa programs and even a few Carbonized ones, every element of the famous Aqua interface is nothing more than a Photoshop-generated graphics file.

The beauty of graphics files, of course, is that you can edit them. Maybe you just want to adjust the colors. Maybe you found a replacement graphic online. Or maybe you actually want to draw a new graphic from scratch. In each of these cases, by using a program like Adobe Photoshop or Photoshop Elements, you can dress up your own desktop in your own way.

In addition to a little artistic talent, all you need to know is how to open the graphics that constitute the interface of each program. The routine generally goes like this:

1. **In the Finder, open the Applications folder. Control-click (or right-click) the icon of the program you want to edit; choose Show Package Contents from the shortcut menu.**

   You may remember from Chapter 5 that most Mac OS X programs may *look* like single icons, but they're actually disguised folders containing all their own support files.

   You can choose almost any Cocoa program to edit in this way: Address Book, Chess, iChat, Mail, iPhoto, Safari, iDVD, iMovie, TextEdit, whatever.

2. **Open the Contents→Resources folder.**

   Inside are the objects of your search: the graphics files (often in TIFF or PDF format) that constitute the "face" of the program you're editing. (Sometimes they're one more folder down, in a folder representing your language—English.lproj, for example.)

   When you're editing in iPhoto, for example, the Resources folder contains the graphics that create slideshow playback buttons, the toolbar buttons, and so on. There's nothing to stop you from swapping in photos of your friends' heads in their places. Figure 17-2 shows another example.

   While you're at it, you may also want to open up Mac OS X's Mail program and redesign its toolbar icons. The sky's the limit!

Tip: If you think you may want to return to the program's original look after your experiment, make a safety copy of these files before proceeding.

3. **Open the TIFF files in Photoshop.**

   Edit them brilliantly.

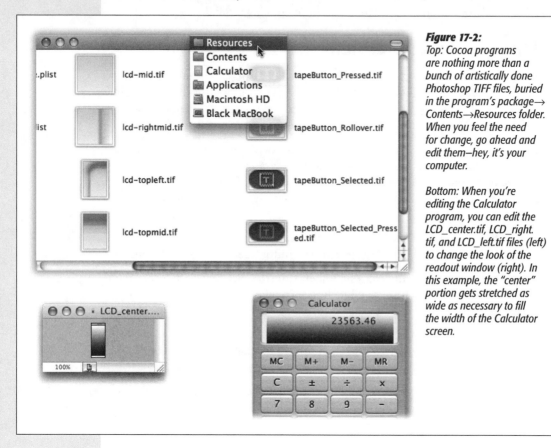

Figure 17-2:
Top: Cocoa programs are nothing more than a bunch of artistically done Photoshop TIFF files, buried in the program's package→ Contents→Resources folder. When you feel the need for change, go ahead and edit them—hey, it's your computer.

Bottom: When you're editing the Calculator program, you can edit the LCD_center.tif, LCD_right. tif, and LCD_left.tif files (left) to change the look of the readout window (right). In this example, the "center" portion gets stretched as wide as necessary to fill the width of the Calculator screen.

4. **Save your changes.**

   The deed is done. You now have a program you can definitely call your own.

Editing the Trash, Dashboard, and Finder Icons

You can edit the Finder, Dashboard, and Trash (empty and full) Dock icons exactly as described above—but you have to peek into a different corner to find them. The Dock program isn't in your Applications folder; it's in your System folder. And in Mac OS X, the System folder is sacred territory, forbidden to humans. An error message lets you know that you're not allowed to edit the graphics files that make up Mac OS X itself (rather than its applications).

In this Mac OS X hack and in several others in this chapter, you have to find a way around this kind of OS self-protection. You can go about it in either of two ways:

- Log into Mac OS X as the *root user,* as described on page 655.

- Simpler yet: ⌘-drag the icon you want out of the System folder, edit a copy of it (preserve the original, just in case), and then ⌘-drag it back into place.

  As soon as you begin to ⌘-drag one of these sacred files, Mac OS X asks you to prove your hackworthiness by entering an administrator's name and password— and then it lets you proceed with your surgery.

In any case, to edit the Finder or Trash icons, start by opening the System→ Library→CoreServices folder. Control-click Dock and choose Show Package Contents from the shortcut menu. The Dock window opens. Open the Contents→Resources folder. These are the graphics you want to edit (as PNG graphics instead of TIFF): *finder.png, trashempty.png, trashfull.png,* and *dashboard.png.*

Replacing the Poof

When you drag an icon off the Dock or toolbar, it disappears with a puff of virtual smoke—a cute, cartoon-like animation that Apple's been trying to work into its operating systems ever since the days of the Newton palmtop. Most people find this tiny, 1-second display of interface magic charming and witty, but others argue that it demeans the dignity of the otherwise professional-looking Mac OS X.

Figure 17-3:
The "poof" animation is nothing more than five individual frames of cartoon smoke, 128 pixels square. You'll find its file sitting inside the Dock package, as described in the previous section, along with the finder.png and Trash files. As shown here in Photoshop Elements, you can substitute any graphics you want, as long as you fit them evenly on this 640-pixel-tall "film strip" (that is, 128 pixels times five). Save, quit, and then restart.

If you follow that latter camp, you can replace the animation just by editing Apple's own five-frame "poof" animation. Figure 17-3 shows the procedure.

Editing Your Menulets

You can colorize the little menu bar symbols fondly called menulets, or even completely redesign their graphics. Like many other Mac OS X screen elements, these are nothing more than little tiny graphics saved in PDF format.

Here again, you can't save changes to them unless you (a) log in as the root user, or (b) ⌘-drag the original files to the desktop, edit them, and then ⌘-drag them back in. Open the System→Library→CoreServices→Menu Extras folder.

Here, you can find individual files (actually packages) for almost every menulet: Battery, Clock, Displays, and so on. Open whichever one you want to customize (AirPort menu, for example) by Control-clicking it and choosing Show Package Contents. As usual, open the Contents→Resources folder.

Inside are a number of TIFF files that represent the various forms your menulet might take; the Volume icon, for example, seems to emit different numbers of sound waves depending on your volume setting. Edit each of the graphics as you see fit. (The ones whose names are tagged with an *s* or *w* represent the inverted *highlighted* graphic, which you see when you actually click the menulet.)

Replacing the Finder Icons

This one's easy: Just download CandyBar, a simple drag-and-drop program. With no technical skill whatsoever, you can use this program to replace the icon pictures

Figure 17-4:
To use CandyBar, just drag your new icons into the appropriate slots. When you restart the Mac, you'll find your new icons in place. Restoring the original icons is equally simple.

featured on your folders, your disks, and the Finder toolbar. It even comes with several collections of perky (but nonphotorealistic) replacement icons (Figure 17-4).

Rewriting the Words

Mac OS X stores the text and settings of its menus, dialog boxes, and other elements in special text files called *plist* (for Property List) files. They sit in one of the three Library folders (in your Home folder, the System folder, or the hard drive window).

The easiest way to edit them is to use Apple's Property List Editor, a program that came on your Mac OS X Developer CD. Once you've installed your developer tools as described on page 428, you can find Property List Editor in Developer→ Applications→Utilities.

There are hundreds of plist files, so some experimentation and patience is required. Most of the cool changes you can make to your plists can be made much more easily using TinkerTool, described at the beginning of this chapter. Here, however, is an example of a smaller change you can make this way.

Renaming the Trash

It's called Trash, but in Mac OS X, it looks more like an office wastebasket. When inspiration on the work you're *supposed* to be doing runs dry, consider remedying this discrepancy by changing the name of the Trash icon to something more appropriate.

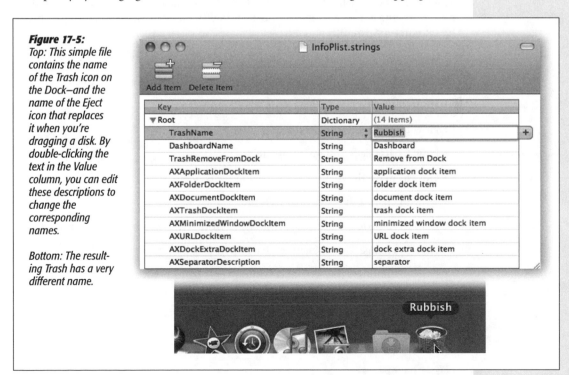

Figure 17-5:
Top: This simple file contains the name of the Trash icon on the Dock—and the name of the Eject icon that replaces it when you're dragging a disk. By double-clicking the text in the Value column, you can edit these descriptions to change the corresponding names.

Bottom: The resulting Trash has a very different name.

In PropertyList Editor, choose File→Open. Navigate to System→Library→Core Services→Dock→Contents→Resources→English.lproj→InfoPlist.strings.

Click the Root triangle to view and edit the settings, as directed in Figure 17-5.

Once you're finished making the change, choose File→Save As, and save your edited plist document to the desktop. Now replace the original document (after making a safety copy, if you like) with your edited version, using either of the techniques described on page 661.

In any case, the next time you log in, you see your new name on the Trash.

Rewording the Dock

Using the same routine just described, you can edit all the commands that pertain to the Dock—both its commands in the menu (Dock Preferences, Turn Magnification On, and so on) and the shortcut menus that pop out of the Dock icons themselves. These wordings are in System→Library→Core Services→Dock.app→Contents→Resources→English.lproj→DockMenus.plist. Click the flippy triangles to see the various commands you can rewrite.

Your Bright Hacking Future

Someone could write a whole book on hacking Snow Leopard, and somebody probably will (or has). Plenty more little recipes are floating around the Web. Lots of them involve typing a few commands into Terminal (Chapter 16), but that's really not so bad if you type carefully.

Here, for example, is a sample of the hacks you can find at *www.macosxhints.com:*

- How to turn a group of images in Preview into a multipage PDF file.
- How to change the Dock's colors with Automator.
- How to remove Spotlight from the menu bar.
- How to disable Spotlight completely.
- How to make the menu bar stop being translucent.
- How to change the Dictionary's font.
- How to remove the outer-space imagery from Time Machine's background.
- How to change Time Machine's backup interval.
- How to eliminate the blue-and-white stripes from Finder list views.
- How to bring back rounded window corners.
- How to disable certain Front Row menu items.
- How to modify the gray startup Apple logo.

Happy hacking!

Part Five:
Mac OS Online

5

Internet Setup & MobileMe

A s Apple's programmers slogged away for months on the massive Mac OS X project, there were areas where they must have felt like they were happily gliding on ice: networking and the Internet. For the most part, the Internet already runs on Unix, and hundreds of extremely polished tools and software chunks were already available.

There are all kinds of ways to get your Mac onto the Internet these days:

- **WiFi.** Wireless hot spots, known as WiFi (or, as Apple calls it, AirPort), are glorious conveniences, especially if you have a laptop. Without stirring from your hotel bed, you're online at high speed. Sometimes for free.

- **Cable modems, DSL.** Over half of the U.S. Internet population connects over higher-speed wires, using *broadband* connections that are always on: cable modems, DSL, or corporate networks. (These, of course, are often what's at the other end of an Internet hot spot.)

- **Cellular modems.** A few well-heeled individuals enjoy the go-anywhere bliss of *USB cellular modems,* which get them online just about anywhere they can make a phone call. These modems are offered by Verizon, Sprint, AT&T, and so on, and usually cost $60 a month.

- **Tethering.** *Tethering* is letting your cellphone act as a glorified Internet antenna for your Mac, whether connected by a cable or a Bluetooth wireless link. In general, the phone company charges you a hefty fee for this convenience.

- **Dial-up modems.** It's true: Plenty of people still connect to the Internet using a modem that dials out over ordinary phone lines. The service is cheap, but the connection is slow, and their numbers are shrinking.

This chapter explains how to set up each one of these. It also describes some of Mac OS X's offbeat Internet featurettes. It tackles MobileMe, Apple's $100-a-year suite of essential and nonessential Internet features; Internet Connection Sharing, which lets several computers in the same household share a single broadband connection; and the system-wide Internet bookmarks known as *Internet location files*.

The Best News You've Heard All Day

If you upgraded to Snow Leopard from an earlier version of the Mac OS, breathe easy; you're already online, since the installer picked up your networking and Internet settings from that earlier installation. The moment you see the Mac OS X desktop, you're ready to use the Internet (and skip the next two pages).

Read on, however, if you need to plug in the Internet settings manually. If you're setting up a new Mac, or if you've just used Mac OS X's "clean install" option (Appendix A), or if you simply want to create a new Internet account, you definitely have some typing to look forward to.

Tip: If you haven't yet set up an Internet connection, reading the next few pages will guide you through plugging the proper settings into System Preferences.

If you're more of a doer than a reader, however, you may prefer the "Assist me" button at the bottom of the Network pane of System Preferences. It asks how you want to connect to the Internet (by dial-up modem, DSL, cable modem, and so on) and then walks you through the process of typing in the settings, if necessary.

Network Central—and Multihoming

In this chapter, you'll be spending a lot of time in the Network pane of System Preferences (Figure 18-1). (Choose →System Preferences; click Network.) This list summarizes the ways your Mac can connect to the Internet or an office network—Ethernet, AirPort wireless, Bluetooth, FireWire, cellular modem card, VPN (Chapter 22), and so on.

Multihoming

The *order* of the network connections listed in the Network pane is important. That's the sequence the Mac uses as it tries to get online. If one of your programs needs Internet access and the first method isn't hooked up, then the Mac switches to the next available connection automatically.

In fact, Mac OS X can maintain multiple simultaneous network connections—Ethernet, AirPort, dial-up, even FireWire—a feature known as *multihoming*.

This feature is especially relevant for laptops. When you open your Web browser, your laptop might first check to see if it's at the office, plugged into an Ethernet cable, which is the fastest, most secure type of connection. If there's no Ethernet, it looks for an AirPort network. Finally, if it draws a blank there, the laptop reluctantly dials the modem. It may not be the fastest Internet connection, but it's all you've got at the moment.

Here's how to go about setting up the connection attempt sequence you want:

1. **Open System Preferences. Click the Network icon.**

   The Network Status screen (Figure 18-1) brings home the point of multihoming: You can have more than one network connection operating at once.

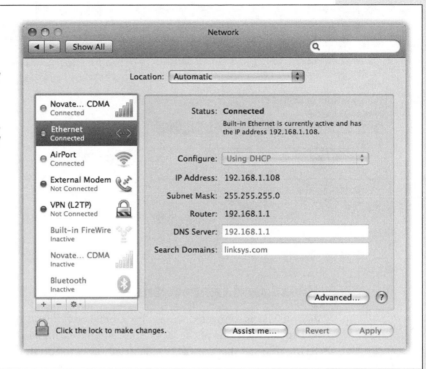

Figure 18-1:
You set up all your network connections here, and you can connect and disconnect to all your networks here. The listed network connections are tagged with color-coded dots. A green dot means turned on and connected to a network; yellow means working, but not connected at the moment; red means you haven't yet set up a connection method.

2. **From the ✿ pop-up menu, choose Set Service Order.**

   Now you see the display shown in Figure 18-2. It lists all the ways your Mac knows how to get online, or onto an office network.

3. **Drag the items up and down the list into priority order.**

   If you have a wired broadband connection, for example, you might want to drag Built-in Ethernet to the top of the list, since that's almost always the fastest way to get online.

4. **Click OK.**

   You return to the Network pane of System Preferences, where the master list of connections magically re-sorts itself to match your efforts.

Your Mac will now be able to switch connections even in real time, during a single Internet session. If lightning takes out your Ethernet hub in the middle of your Web surfing, your Mac will seamlessly switch to your AirPort network, for example, to keep your session alive.

All right then: Your paperwork is complete. The following pages guide you through the process of setting up these various connections.

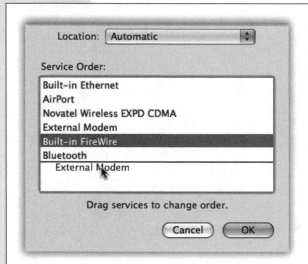

Figure 18-2:
The key to multihoming is sliding the network connection methods' names up or down. Note that you can choose a different connection sequence for each location. (Locations are described later in this chapter.)

Broadband Connections

If your Mac is connected wirelessly or, um, *wirefully* to a cable modem, DSL, or office network, you're one of the lucky ones. You have a high-speed broadband connection to the Internet that's always available, always on. You never have to wait to dial.

Automatic Configuration

Most broadband connections require *no setup whatsoever.* Take a new Mac out of the box, plug in the Ethernet cable to your cable modem—or choose a wireless network from the 🛜 menulet—and you can begin surfing the Web instantly.

That's because most cable modems, DSL boxes, and wireless base stations use *DCHP.* It stands for *dynamic host configuration protocol,* but what it means is: "We'll fill in your Network pane of System Preferences automatically." (Including techie specs like IP address and DNS Server addresses.)

Manual Configuration

If, for some reason, you're not able to surf the Web or check email the first time you try, it's remotely possible that your broadband modem or your office network *doesn't* offer DHCP. In that case, you may have to fiddle with the Network pane of System

Preferences, preferably with a customer-support rep from your broadband company on the phone.

On the Network pane, click your Internet connection (AirPort, Built-in Ethernet, cellular modem, whatever). Click Advanced; click TCP/IP. Now you see something like Figure 18-3.

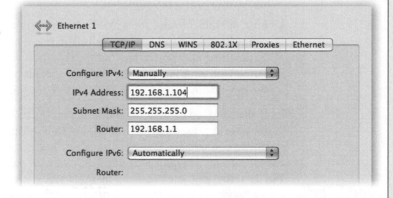

Figure 18-3:
Don't be alarmed by the morass of numbers and periods—it's all in good fun. (If you find TCP/IP fun, that is.)

In this illustration, you see the setup for a cable-modem account with a static IP address, which means you have to type in all these numbers yourself, as guided by the cable company. The alternative is a DHCP server account, which fills most of it in automatically.

Note: There's a bright side to having a static IP address, an Internet address that's all your own and won't change. Because your Mac has this one reliable address, several cool Mac OS X features are available to you. For example, it's easier to access your files from anywhere in the world, as described in Chapter 22.

Ethernet Connections

The beauty of Ethernet connections is that they're super-fast and super-secure. No bad guys sitting across the coffee shop, armed with shareware "sniffing" software, can intercept your email and chat messages, as they theoretically can when you're on wireless.

And 99 percent of the time, connecting to an Ethernet network is as simple as connecting the cable to the Mac. That's it. You're online, fast and securely, and you never have to worry about connecting or disconnecting.

AirPort (WiFi) Connections

AirPort is Apple's term for the 802.11 (WiFi) wireless networking technology. If you have it, your Mac can communicate with a wireless base station up to 300 feet away, much like a cordless phone. Doing so lets you surf the Web from your laptop in a hotel room, for example, or share files with someone across the building from you.

Chapter 13 has much more information about *setting up* an AirPort network. The real fun begins, however, when it comes time to *join* one.

Sometimes you just want to join a friend's WiFi network. Sometimes you've got time to kill in an airport, and it's worth a $7 splurge for half an hour. And sometimes, at some street corners in big cities, WiFi signals bleeding out of apartment buildings might give you a choice of several free hot spots to join.

Your Mac joins WiFi hot spots like this:

- First, it sniffs around for a WiFi network you've used before. If it finds one, it connects quietly and automatically. You're not asked for permission, a password, or anything else; you're just online. (It's that way, for example, when you come home with your laptop every day.) For details on this memorization feature, see the box below.

- If the Mac can't find a known hot spot, but it detects a new hot spot or two, a message appears on the screen (Figure 18-4), displaying their names. Double-click one to connect.

Tip: If you don't want your Mac to keep interrupting you with its discoveries of new hot spots—it can get pretty annoying when you're in a taxi driving through a city—you can shut them off. In System Preferences, click Network, click AirPort, and then turn off "Ask to join new networks."

The Super-Secret, New, Hot-Spot Management Box

If you open System Preferences→Network, click AirPort in the left-side list, and then click Advanced, you see the dialog box shown here. It lets you manage the list of WiFi hot spots that Mac OS X has memorized on your travels.

For example, you can delete the old ones. You can also double-click a WiFi net's name to type in and store its password. Finally, you can drag the hot spots' names up and down the list to establish a priority for making connections when more than one is available.

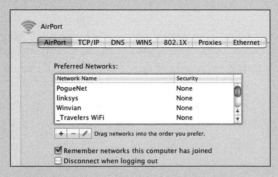

Ordinarily, Mac OS X memorizes the names of the various hot spots you join on your travels. It's kind of nice, actually, because it means you're interrupted less often by the "Do you want to join?" box.

But if you're alarmed at the massive list of hot spots Mac OS X has memorized—for privacy reasons, say—here's where you turn off "Remember any network this computer has joined."

- If you missed the opportunity to join a hot spot when the message appeared, or if you joined the wrong one or a non-working one, then you have another chance. You can always choose a hot spot's name from the 🛜 menulet, as shown in Figure 18-4 at right. A 🔒 icon indicates a hot spot that requires a password, so you don't waste your time trying to join those (unless, of course, you *have* the password).

Snow Leopard Spots: It always takes a computer a few seconds—maybe 5 or 10—to connect to the Internet over WiFi. In Snow Leopard, the 🛜 menulet itself pulses, or rather ripples, with a black-and-gray animation to let you know you're still in the connection process. It's an anti-frustration aid. (Oh, and also, each hot spot's signal strength now appears right in the menulet.)

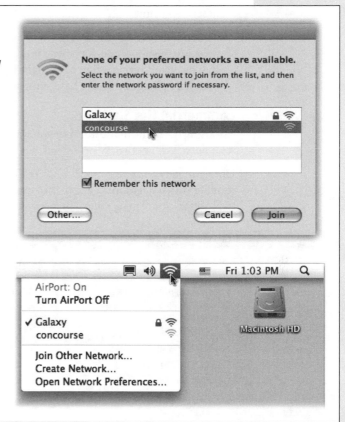

Figure 18-4:
Top: Congratulations—your Mac has discovered new WiFi hot spots all around you! In Snow Leopard, you even get to see the signal strength right in the menu. Double-click one to join it. But if you see a 🔒 icon next to the hot spot's name, beware: It's been protected by a password. If you don't know it, then you won't be able to connect.

Bottom: Later, you can always switch networks using the AirPort menulet.

Before you get too excited, though, some lowering of expectations is in order. There are a bunch of reasons why your 🛜 menulet might indicate that you're in a hot spot, but you can't actually get online:

- **It's locked.** If there's a 🔒 next to the hot spot's name in your 🛜 menulet, then the hot spot has been password protected. That's partly to prevent hackers from "sniffing" the transmissions and intercepting messages, and partly to keep random passersby like you off the network.

- **The signal's not strong enough.** Sometimes the WiFi signal is strong enough to make the hot spot's name show up in your 🛜 menu, but not strong enough for an actual connection.

- **You're not on the list.** Sometimes, for security, hot spots are rigged to permit only *specific* computers to join (see the box below), and yours isn't one of them.

- **You haven't logged in yet.** Commercial hot spots (the ones you have to pay for) don't connect you to the Internet until you've supplied your payment details on a special Web page that appears automatically when you open your browser, as described below.

- **The router's on, but the Internet's not connected.** Sometimes wireless routers are broadcasting, but their Internet connection is down. It'd be like a cordless phone that has a good connection back to the base station in the kitchen—but the phone cord isn't plugged into the base station.

Commercial Hot Spots

Choosing the name of the hot spot you want to join is generally all you have to do—if it's a *home* WiFi network.

Unfortunately, joining a *commercial* WiFi hot spot—one that requires a credit card number (in a hotel room or airport, for example)—requires more than just connecting to it. You also have to *sign into* it before you can send so much as a single email message.

POWER USERS' CLINIC

The Secret Life of the AirPort Menulet

Here's something not one Mac fan in a thousand knows about: a secret diagnostic mode in the 🛜 menulet.

Turns out that if you press the Option key as you open the 🛜 menulet, you get a special treat: a faint gray *interior* menu that identifies some diagnostic details of your current wireless network. You get to see the hot spot's channel, your current data rate, and the MAC address of your AirPort card.

A MAC address has nothing to do with Macs; Windows PCs have MAC addresses, too. It stands for Media

Access Control, although the equivalent term, Ethernet Hardware Address, is much more descriptive. It's a unique identifier for your networking card, whether it's your Ethernet card or your AirPort circuitry.

Every now and then, somebody will ask for your MAC address—usually when helping you troubleshoot network problems or get onto a *really* exclusive WiFi hot spot. (Some hot spots are so restrictive, the network administrator has to register *each MAC address* that's allowed to use it.)

> 🛜 ◀) 📶 (2:30) Fri Sep 25 3:32 PM
>
> AirPort: On
> **Turn AirPort Off**
>
> ✓PogueNet   🛜
>   PHY Mode: 802.11g
>   BSSID: 0:3:93:ea:d2:25
>   Channel: 10 (2.4 GHz)
>   Security: None
>   RSSI: −56
>   Transmit Rate: 54
>
> Join Other Network...
> Create Network...
> Open Network Preferences...

To do that, open your Web browser. You'll see the "Enter your payment information" screen either immediately or as soon as you try to open a Web page of your choice. (Even at free hot spots, you might have to click OK on a welcome page to initiate the connection.)

Supply your credit card information or (if you have a membership to this WiFi chain, like Boingo or T-Mobile) your name and password. Click Submit or Proceed, try *not* to contemplate how this $8 per hour is pure profit for somebody, and enjoy your surfing.

Broadband Connections

Cellular Modems

WiFi hot spots are fast and usually cheap—but they're hot *spots*. Beyond 150 feet away, you're offline.

No wonder laptop luggers across America are getting into *cellular* Internet services. All the big cellphone companies offer ExpressCards or USB sticks that let your laptop get online at high speed *anywhere* in major cities.

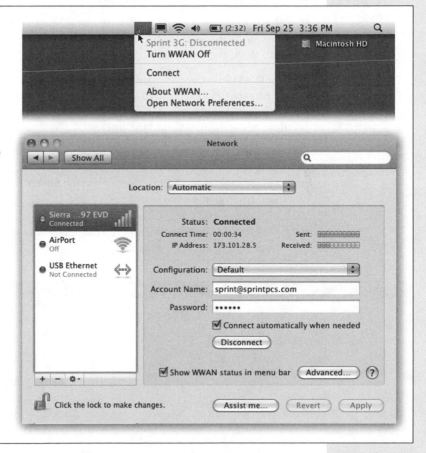

Figure 18-5:
In System Preferences→ Network, click your cellular modem's icon. Click Connect to get online—or, better yet, turn on "Show WWAN status in menu bar." (It stands for Wireless Wide-Area Network, if that helps.) Next time, you'll be able to connect by choosing Connect from this menulet instead of lumbering off to System Preferences.

No hunting for a coffee shop; with a cellular Internet service, you can check your email while zooming down the road in a taxi. (Outside the metropolitan areas, you can still get online wirelessly, though much more slowly.)

Verizon, Sprint, and AT&T all offer cellular Internet networks with speeds approaching a cable modem. So why isn't the world beating a path to this delicious technology's door? Because it's expensive—at this writing, $60 a month on top of your phone bill.

To get online, insert the card or USB stick; it may take about 15 seconds for the thing to latch on to the cellular signal.

Now you're supposed to make the Internet connection using the special "dialing" software provided by the cellphone company. Technically, though, you may not need it; Snow Leopard comes set to autorecognize most cellular modems. You can start and stop the Internet connection using the menulet—no phone-company software required (see Figure 18-5).

Dial-up Modem Connections

If you ask Apple, dial-up modems are dead. Macs don't even come with built-in modems anymore. You can get an external USB modem for $50, but clearly, Apple is trying to shove the trusty dial-up technology into the recycling bin.

Still, millions of people never got the memo. If you're among them, you need to sign up for Internet service. Hundreds of companies, large and small, would love to become your *Internet service provider* (ISP), generally charging $20 or so per month for the privilege of connecting you to the Internet.

Once you've selected a service provider, you plug its settings into the Network pane of System Preferences. You get the necessary information directly from your ISP by consulting either its Web page, the instruction sheets that came with your account, or a help-desk agent on the phone.

Note: The following instructions don't pertain to America Online. It comes with its own setup program and doesn't involve any settings in System Preferences.

PPPoE and DSL

If you have DSL service, you may be directed to create a *PPPoE service.* (You do that on the Network pane of System Preferences; click your Ethernet connection, and then choose Configuration→Create PPPoE Service.)

It stands for PPP over Ethernet, meaning that although your DSL "modem" is connected to your Ethernet port, you still have to make and break your Internet connections manually, as though you had a dial-up modem.

Fill in the PPPoE dialog box as directed by your ISP (usually just your account name and password). From here on in, you start and end your Internet connections exactly as though you had a dial-up modem.

Setting Up the Modem

Open System Preferences and click Network. If your modem isn't already listed, click the **+** button at lower left; from the Interface pop-up menu that appears, choose External Modem, and then click Create.

Your modem connection now appears in the list at the left side of the pane. Click it. Now fill in the blanks like this:

- **Configuration.** It's called Default at first, which is fine. If you like, you can choose Add Configuration from this pop-up menu and then name it after your ISP (*EarthLink*, for example).

- **Telephone Number.** This is the local access number your modem is supposed to dial to connect to your ISP.

Tip: If you need your Mac to dial a 9 or an 8 for an outside line (as you would from within a hotel), or *70 to turn off Call Waiting, add it to the beginning of the phone number followed by a comma. The comma means "Pause for 2 seconds." You can also put the comma to good use when typing in the dialing sequence for a calling-card number.

- **Account Name.** This is your account name with your ISP. If you're BillG@earthlink. net, for example, type *BillG* here.

- **Password.** Specify your ISP account password here. Turn on "Save password" if you'd rather not retype it every time you connect.

The Advanced Button

Click the Advanced button to bring up a special dialog box filled with tweaky, soon-to-be-obsolete modem settings (Figure 18-6). Most of the action is on two tabs.

The Modem tab

On the Modem tab, you specify which kind of modem you have. Roughly 99.99999 percent of Macs with modems have *Apple* modems, which is why the pop-up menu already says "Apple." If you, the heretic, have some other kind of modem, choose its name from the pop-up menu.

Some other handy settings:

- **Wait for dial tone before dialing.** This setting is for you, North American laptop owners. Because the dial tones in certain foreign countries sound weird to the Mac, it therefore won't dial; it's still listening for that good old North American dial tone. In that case, turning off this checkbox makes the Mac dial bravely even though it hasn't heard the sound it's listening for.

- **Dialing.** Specify what kind of phone service you have—Tone, or in a few rural locations, Pulse.

• **Sound.** By clicking Off, you make your Mac dial the Internet silently, sparing sleeping family members or dorm roommates from having to listen to your modem shriek as it connects.

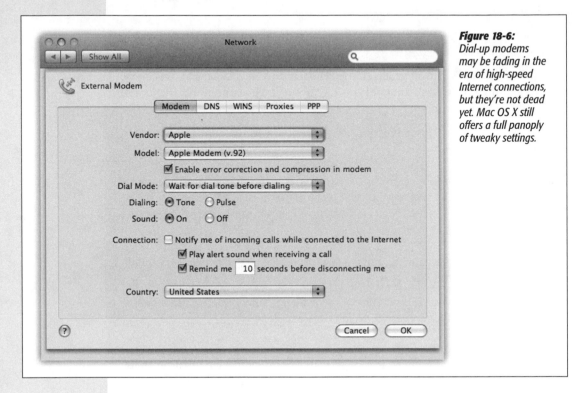

Figure 18-6:
Dial-up modems may be fading in the era of high-speed Internet connections, but they're not dead yet. Mac OS X still offers a full panoply of tweaky settings.

The PPP tab

On the PPP tab, you can specify how long the Mac waits before hanging up the phone line after your last online activity, and how many times the Mac should redial if the ISP phone number is busy.

And you'll almost certainly want to turn on "Connect automatically when needed." It makes your Mac dial the Internet automatically whenever you check your email or open your Web browser.

Going Online

If you didn't turn on "Connect automatically when needed," then you can make your Mac dial the Internet manually, in one of two ways:

• **Use the Network pane.** Right here in System Preferences, you can click Connect to make the connection.

- **Use the menulet.** If you were smart, however, you turned on "Show modem status on menu bar" in System Preferences→Network. It adds the ☎ menulet to the upper-right corner of your screen, which lets you get online with one quick menu choice (Figure 18-7).

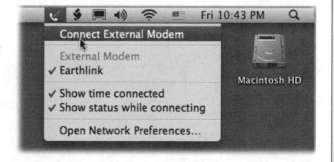

Figure 18-7:
Life is simplest when you've told your Mac to dial automatically when it needs to get online. But you can also go online on command, using this menulet.

Disconnecting

The Mac automatically drops the phone line 15 minutes after your last activity online. In fact, if other people have accounts on your Mac (Chapter 12), the Mac doesn't even hang up when you log out. It maintains the connection so the next person can surf the Net without redialing.

Of course, if other people in your household are screaming for you to get off the line so they can make a call, you can also disconnect manually. Choose Disconnect from the ☎ menulet.

Tip: If you have more than one ISP, or if you travel between locations with your laptop, don't miss the Location feature. It lets you switch sets of dial-up modem settings—including the local phone number—with a simple menu selection. It's described next.

Switching Locations

If you travel with a laptop, you know the drill. You're constantly opening up System Preferences→Network so you can switch between Internet settings: Ethernet at the office, WiFi at home. Or maybe you simply visit the branch office from time to time, and you're getting tired of having to change the local access number for your ISP each time you leave home (and return home again).

The simple solution is the →Location submenu, which appears once you've set up more than one Location. As Figure 18-8 illustrates, all you have to do is tell it where you are. Mac OS X handles the details of switching Internet connections.

Creating a New Location

To create a *Location,* which is nothing more than a set of memorized settings, open System Preferences, click Network, and then choose Edit Locations from the Location pop-up menu. Continue as shown in Figure 18-9.

Tip: You can use the commands in the ✿ menu to rename or duplicate a Location.

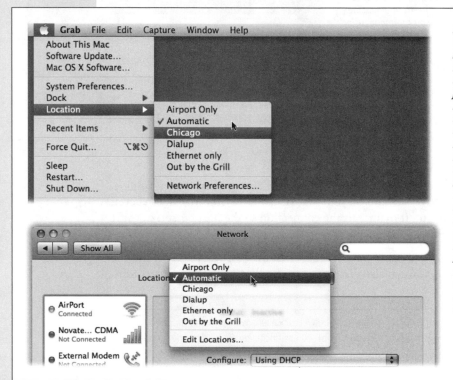

Figure 18-8:
The Location feature lets you switch from one "location" to another just by choosing its name—either from the ❖ menu (top) or from this pop-up menu in System Preferences (bottom). The Automatic location just means "the standard, default one you originally set up." (Don't be fooled: Despite its name, Automatic isn't the only location that offers multihoming, described earlier in this chapter.)

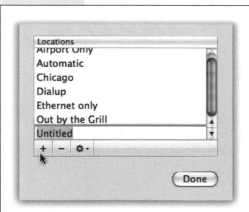

Figure 18-9:
When you choose Edit Locations, this list of existing Locations appears; click the + button. A new entry appears at the bottom of the list. Type a name for your new location, such as Chicago Office or Dining Room Floor.

When you click Done, you return to the Network panel. Take this opportunity to set up the kind of Internet connection you use at the corresponding location, just as described on the first pages of this chapter.

If you travel regularly, you can build a *list* of Locations, each of which "knows" the way you like to get online in each city you visit.

A key part of making a new Location is putting the various Internet connection types (Ethernet, AirPort, Modem, Bluetooth) into the correct order. Your connections will be slightly quicker if you give the modem priority in your Hotel setup, the AirPort connection priority in your Starbucks setup, and so on.

You can even turn off some connections entirely. For example, if you use nothing but a cable modem when you're at home, you might want to create a location in which *only* the Ethernet connection is active. Use the Make Service Inactive command in the ✿ menu.

Conversely, if your laptop uses nothing but WiFi when you're on the road, your Location could include *nothing* but the AirPort connection. You'll save a few seconds each time you try to go online, because your Mac won't bother hunting for an Internet connection that doesn't exist.

Making the Switch

Once you've set up your various locations, you can switch among them using the ✿→Location submenu, as shown in Figure 18-8. As soon as you do so, your Mac is automatically set to get online the way you like.

Tip: If you have a laptop, create a connection called Offline. From the Show pop-up menu, choose Network Port Configurations; make all the connection methods in the list inactive. When you're finished, you've got yourself a laptop that will never attempt to go online. It's the laptop equivalent of Airplane Mode on a cellphone.

Internet Sharing

If you have cable modem or DSL service, you're a very lucky individual. You get terrific Internet speed and an always-on connection. Too bad only one computer in your household or office can enjoy these luxuries.

It doesn't have to be that way. You can spread the joy of high-speed Internet to every Mac (and PC) on your network in either of two ways:

- **Buy a router.** A *router* is a little box, costing about $50, that connects directly to the cable modem or DSL box. In most cases, it has multiple Internet jacks so you can plug in several Macs, PCs, and/or wireless base stations. As a bonus, a router provides excellent security, serving as a firewall to keep out unsolicited visits from hackers on the Internet.

• **Use Internet Sharing.** Mac OS X's Internet Sharing feature is the software version of a router: It distributes a single Internet signal to every computer on the network. But unlike a router, it's free. You just fire it up on the one Mac that's connected directly to the Internet—the *gateway* computer.

But there's a downside: If the gateway Mac is turned off or asleep, the other machines can't get online.

Most people use Internet Sharing to share a broadband connection like a cable modem or DSL. But there are other times when it comes in handy. If you have a cellular modem, for example, you might want to share its signal via WiFi so the kids in the back seat can get online with their iPod Touches. You could even share a tethered Bluetooth cellphone's Internet connection with a traveling companion who needs a quick email check.

The only requirement: The Internet-connected Mac must have some *other* kind of connection (Ethernet, AirPort, Bluetooth, FireWire) to the Macs that will share the connection.

Turning On Internet Sharing

To turn on Internet Sharing on the gateway Mac, open the Sharing panel of System Preferences. Click Internet Sharing, as shown in Figure 18-10, but don't turn on the checkbox yet.

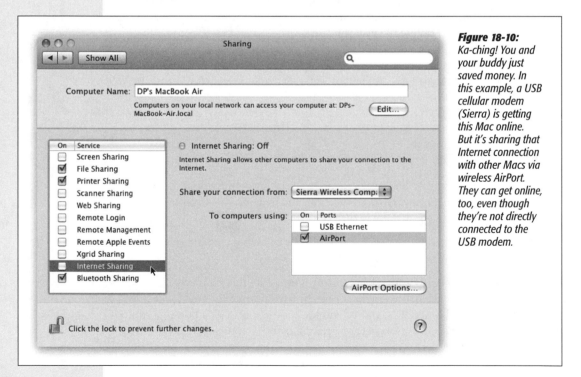

Figure 18-10:
Ka-ching! You and your buddy just saved money. In this example, a USB cellular modem (Sierra) is getting this Mac online. But it's sharing that Internet connection with other Macs via wireless AirPort. They can get online, too, even though they're not directly connected to the USB modem.

Before you do that, you have to specify (a) how the gateway Mac is connected to the Internet, and (b) how it's connected to the other Macs on your office network:

- **Share your connection from.** Using this pop-up menu, identify how *this Mac* (the gateway machine) connects to the Internet—via Built-in Ethernet, AirPort, cellular modem, or Bluetooth DUN (dial-up networking—that is, tethering to your cellphone).

- **To computers using.** Using these checkboxes, specify how you want your Mac to rebroadcast the Internet signal to the others. (It has to be a *different* network channel. You can't get your signal via AirPort and then pass it on via AirPort.)

Note: Which checkboxes appear here depends on which kinds of Internet connections are turned on in the Network pane of System Preferences. If the gateway Mac doesn't have AirPort circuitry, for example, or if AirPort is turned off in the current configuration, the AirPort option doesn't appear.

Now visit each of the other Macs on the same network. Open the Network pane of System Preferences. Select the network method you chose in the second step above: AirPort, Built-in Ethernet, or FireWire. Click Apply.

If the gateway Mac is rebroadcasting using AirPort—by far the most common use of this feature—you have one more step. In your ⚡ menulet, you'll see a strange new "hot spot" that wasn't there before, bearing the name of the gateway Mac. (It might

---

POWER USERS' CLINIC

Internet Sharing as a Bridge

Ordinarily, only one Mac has Internet Sharing turned on: the one that's connected directly to the Internet.

But sometimes, you might want another Mac "downstream" to have it on, too. That's when you want to *bridge* two networks.

Consider the setup shown here: There are really two networks: one that uses AirPort, and another connected to an Ethernet hub.

If you play your cards right, all these Macs can get online simultaneously, using a single Internet connection.

Set up the gateway Mac so that it's an AirPort base station, exactly as described on these pages.

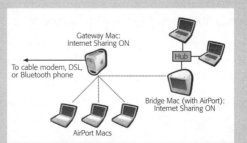

Gateway Mac:
Internet Sharing ON

To cable modem, DSL,
or Bluetooth phone

Hub

Bridge Mac (with AirPort):
Internet Sharing ON

AirPort Macs

Start setting up the *bridge* Mac the way you'd set up the other AirPort Macs—with AirPort selected as the primary connection method, and "Using DHCP" turned on in the Network panel.

Then visit the bridge Mac's Sharing panel. Turn on Internet Sharing here, too, but this time select "To computers using: Built-in Ethernet."

The bridge Mac is now on both networks. It uses the AirPort connection as a bridge to the gateway Mac and the Internet—and its Ethernet connection to share that happiness with the wired Macs in its own neighborhood.

---

say, for example, "Casey's MacBook Air.") Choose its name to begin your borrowed Internet connection.

As long as the gateway Mac remains on and online, both it and your other computers can get onto the Internet simultaneously, all at high speed, even Windows PCs. You've created a *software* base station. The Mac itself is now the transmitter for Internet signals to and from any other WiFi computers within range.

Tip: Now that you know how to let a wireless Mac piggyback on a wired Mac's connection, you can let a wired Mac share a wireless connection, too. Suppose, for example, that you and a buddy both have laptops in a hotel lobby. You're online, having paid $13 to use the hotel's WiFi network. If you set up Internet Sharing appropriately, your buddy can connect to yours via an Ethernet cable or even a FireWire cable and surf along with you—no extra charge.

MobileMe

In January 2000, Apple CEO Steve Jobs explained to the Macworld Expo crowds that he and his team had had a mighty brainstorm: Apple controls *both ends* of the connection between a Mac and the Apple Web site. As a result, Apple should be able to create some pretty clever Internet-based features as a reward to loyal Mac fans. Later that same day, the Apple Web site offered a suite of *free* services called iTools.

Then the technology bubble burst.

These days, those Internet services, later renamed .Mac and now called MobileMe, cost $100 per year. Much of it is based on the central Web site *www.me.com* (Figure 18-11).

Signing Up for MobileMe

Open System Preferences and click the MobileMe icon. Click Learn More. You now go online, where your Web browser has opened up to the MobileMe sign-up screen. Fill in your name and address, make up an account name and password, turn off the checkbox that invites you to get junk mail, and so on.

Finally, back at System Preferences→MobileMe, fill in the account name and password you just composed, if necessary. Now the preference pane has magically sprouted four tabs, which you'll meet in the following pages.

Let your grand tour of MobileMe's motley features begin.

MobileMe Sync

For many people, this may be the killer app for MobileMe right here: The *me.com* Web site, acting as the master control center, can keep multiple Macs, Windows PCs, and iPhones/iPod Touches synchronized.

It works by storing the master copies of your stuff—email, calendars, address books, Web bookmarks, Dock items, passwords, notes, email account details, and Dashboard widgets—on the Web. (Or "in the cloud," as the pretentious product managers would say.)

Figure 18-11:
The MobileMe features appear as buttons on the me.com Web site. Here's all your email, your address book, and your calendar, which get auto-synchronized among your Macs, PCs, and iPhones. Here, too, are any photos or videos you've published from Snow Leopard, and any files you've stashed on your iDisk.

Whenever your Macs, PCs, or iPhones/Touches are online, they connect to the mother ship and update themselves. Edit an address on your iPhone and shortly thereafter, you'll find the same change in Address Book (on your Mac) and Outlook (on your PC). Send an email reply from your PC at the office and you'll find it in your Sent Mail folder on the Mac at home. Add a Web bookmark anywhere and find it everywhere else.

Actually, there's a fourth place where you can work with your data: on the Web. At *www.me.com*, you can log in to find Web-based clones of iCal, Address Book, and Mail; there's even a mini-iPhoto.

To set up syncing, open System Preferences→MobileMe→Sync. Turn on the checkboxes of the stuff you want to be synchronized all the way around:

- **Bookmarks.** If a Web site is important enough to merit bookmarking while you're using your laptop, why shouldn't it also show up in the Bookmarks menu on your desktop Mac at home, your iPhone, or your PC at work?

- **Calendars, Contacts.** This is a big one. There's nothing as exasperating as realizing that the Address Book you're consulting on your home Mac is missing somebody you're *sure* you entered—on your computer at work. This option keeps all your Macs' Address Books and iCal calendars synchronized. Delete a phone number at work, and you'll find it deleted on your Mac at home, too.

- **Dashboard Widgets.** Now the configuration and setup of your widgets on Mac A are synced to Macs B, C, and D, so they all match.

- **Dock Items.** Not the biggest deal in the world, but if you've put some time into setting up your Dock on one Mac, it's nice to find it set up identically on your other Macs.

- **Keychains.** All your Macs can have the same passwords memorized. Worth its weight in gold.

- **Mail Accounts, Rules, Signatures, and Smart Mailboxes.** These refer to your account settings and preferences from Mac OS X's Mail program, not the email messages themselves.

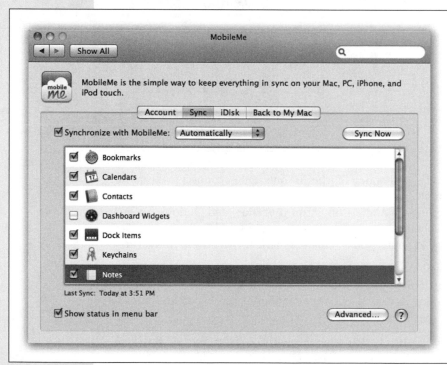

Figure 18-12:
To set up MobileMe sync, open System Preferences. Click MobileMe, and then click the Sync tab. Turn on the checkboxes for the information you want synchronized. Use the pop-up menu at the top to set up an automatic sync schedule. While you're at it, turn on "Show status in menu bar" so you'll be able to start or stop the syncing manually, too.

- **Notes.** This option refers to the notes you enter in Mail's Notes feature (Chapter 19). How great to make a reminder for yourself on one Mac and have it reminding you later on another one. (If you have Microsoft Office, you'll see an Entourage Notes option here, too.)

- **Preferences.** All your System Preferences settings.

- **Other apps.** Non-Apple programs can install their own Sync options at the bottom of this list. Microsoft Entourage offers to sync your notes, for example, and TextExpander (typing-substitution shareware) keeps your list of typing abbreviations in sync among Macs.

To set up MobileMe syncing, turn on the checkboxes for the items you want synced, as shown in Figure 18-12.

After the first sync, you can turn on the checkboxes on the other Macs, too, in effect telling them to participate in the great data-sharing experiment.

The first time they try, they may get confused. "Hold on. *My* address book is empty, but the one I'm downloading from the Internet (from the other Mac) is loaded. Who wins?" You get the dialog box shown in Figure 18-13, which lets you decide how to proceed.

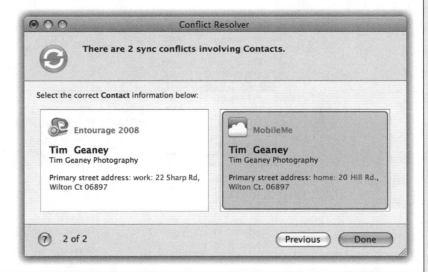

Figure 18-13:
This message lets you decide how to proceed when data on one of the synced Macs is wildly different from what's been "published" by another Mac. You can merge the information from the two (a great way to combine address books or calendars), make this Mac's data wipe out the other's ("Replace data on MobileMe"), or make the Internet-based data replace this computer's ("Replace data on computer").

The iDisk

The iDisk is an Internet-based hard-drive icon on your desktop that makes a perfect intermediate parking place for files you want to shuttle from one computer to another. Or you can just use it for offsite backup of your most important files. (Your MobileMe account comes with 20 gigabytes of storage. In your account settings at *www.me.com*, you can decide how to divide up that storage between your iDisk and the other MobileMe stuff, like Mail and your Web sites. And, of course, you can pay more money for more storage.)

Furthermore, you can pull the iDisk onto *any* computer's screen—Mac or Windows—at your office, at your home, at your friend's house, so you don't need to carry around a physical disk to transport important files.

Pulling it onto your screen

Apple must really love the iDisk concept, because it has devised about 300 different ways to pull the iDisk icon onto your screen (Figure 18-14):

- **Choose Go→iDisk→My iDisk** (or press Shift-⌘-I).

- **Click the iDisk icon in the Sidebar** (of a Finder window or a Save or Open dialog box).

- **Choose Go→Connect to Server.** At the bottom of the resulting dialog box, type *http://idisk.me.com/casey* (substitute your actual account name for *casey*). Press Return. Type your MobileMe name and password if necessary, and then click Connect. (This is the quickest approach if you're using somebody else's Mac.)

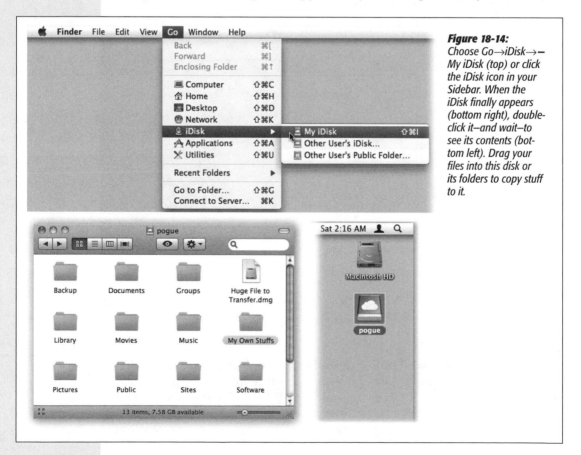

Figure 18-14:
Choose Go→iDisk→—My iDisk (top) or click the iDisk icon in your Sidebar. When the iDisk finally appears (bottom right), double-click it—and wait—to see its contents (bottom left). Drag your files into this disk or its folders to copy stuff to it.

- **Visit *www.me.com* and click the iDisk icon.** Type in your name and password, and then click Return. Finally, click Open Your iDisk. (Clearly, this is a lot more work than the one-click methods already described. Use this technique when you're using a public machine far from home, for example.)

At this point, the iDisk behaves like an external hard drive. You can drag files or folders from your hard drive into one of the folders on the iDisk.

Thereafter, you can retrieve or open whatever you copied to the iDisk. Open one of the folders on it; you can now open, rename, trash, or copy (to your hard drive) whatever you find inside.

Making the iDisk fast and synchronized

As you can imagine, copying files to and from a disk on the Internet is slower than copying them between hard drives on the same Mac. The iDisk has a reputation, therefore, of being very slow.

But the iDisk doesn't have to run at the speed of an anesthetized slug. Behind the scenes, Mac OS X can keep a full, invisible *copy* of the iDisk's contents on your hard drive. When you add something to the iDisk, therefore, it *seems* to appear there instantly—even when you're not online—because all you've done is copy something onto a secret stash of your own drive. The Mac will begin the process of transmitting the copy to the *online* iDisk at the next opportunity. In short, you can leave the iDisk's icon onscreen for as long as you like, even when you're offline.

To turn on this feature, see Figure 18-15.

GEM IN THE ROUGH

The 20-Gigabyte Email Attachment

People use the iDisk for all kinds of things: as backup, as a bucket to carry files between computers, and so on. But here's one of the coolest features of all: You can *email* anything on your iDisk to anyone.

Ordinarily, you can't attach anything bigger than 5 or 10 megabytes to an email message. But iDisk email "attachments" can be enormous—many gigabytes. That's because they're not really attached to the email at all; you're simply sending your colleague a *link* to download something from your iDisk.

To use this feature, go to *www.me.com*. Log in. Click the iDisk button on the toolbar. In the list of your iDisk contents, click the file you want to send, and then click Share File. Fill in the email address of the recipient; a short message; and, if you like, a password to protect the download.

Once your colleagues receive your email from the me.com Web site, they have but to click the link in the message to download your huge file immediately.

Tip: If you have Macs in different locations (home and office, for example), you can keep your key files synchronized among all of them by turning on this automatic iDisk syncing on all the machines. (The new Snow Leopard option, "Always keep the most recent version of a file," makes this arrangement especially worry-free because you no longer have to worry about version conflicts.) You've burned your last "Take Home" CD!

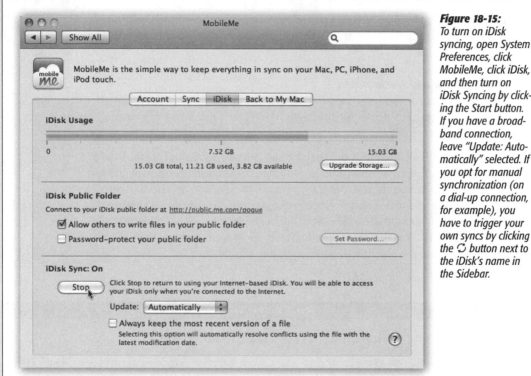

Figure 18-15:
To turn on iDisk syncing, open System Preferences, click MobileMe, click iDisk, and then turn on iDisk Syncing by clicking the Start button. If you have a broadband connection, leave "Update: Automatically" selected. If you opt for manual synchronization (on a dial-up connection, for example), you have to trigger your own syncs by clicking the ↻ button next to the iDisk's name in the Sidebar.

The Public folder

In general, whatever you put onto your iDisk is private and password-protected. There's one exception, however: Whatever you put into the *Public* folder on any iDisk can be seen, opened, and copied by other MobileMe members. All they need is your member name—not your password (although you *can* password-protect it, if you like). Think of the iDisk Public folder as the long-lost twin of the Public folder in your own Home folder.

The Public folder is terrific for storing family photos where anyone who's interested can look at them. It's also handy when you're collaborating; just post the latest drafts of your work in the Public folder for your coworkers to review.

To view someone *else's* Public folder (suppose the person's MobileMe name is Ski-Bunny23), use one of these techniques:

- **From Mac OS X 10.3 or later.** Choose Go→iDisk→Other User's Public Folder. Type in *SkiBunny23*, and hit Return.

- **Mac OS X 10.1 or 10.2.** Choose Go→Connect to Server. At the bottom of the dialog box, type *http://idiskMobileMe.com/skibunny23/Public*. Click Connect or press Return. If a password is required, use *public* as the user name and, well, the password as the password.

Tip: Actually, there's a simpler way: Use iDisk Utility, described below.

- **From Mac OS 9.** Choose ⌘→Chooser, click AppleShare, click the Server IP Address button, type *idiskMobileMe.com* in the Server Address box, and then click Connect. Enter *SkiBunny23* and the password (if any), and then click Connect. Select the iDisk, and then click OK.

- **From Windows.** See the box below.

After a minute or so, a new iDisk icon appears on your desktop bearing that member's name. Double-click it to view its contents. You can copy these files to your hard drive or double-click them to open them directly.

Tip: If you have an iPhone or iPod Touch, don't miss the free iDisk App (which you can download from the App Store). It lets you view, open, and forward anything on your iDisk—right from your phone or iPod. (You can't put anything new onto the iDisk this way, but still—in a pinch, how great it would be to pass on the McGillicuddy proposal to a client when you're on a beach somewhere, far from a computer!)

---

iDisk options

In System Preferences→MobileMe→iDisk, you're offered these Public-folder options:

POWER USERS' CLINIC

The iDisk from Windows

Once, you could get to your iDisk only from a Macintosh. These days, you can bring your iDisk onto the screen of any computer, even one running Windows or Linux.

Now you can *access* your iDisk files from any computer on earth—just go to *www.me.com* and log in. Doesn't matter if you're on Mac, Windows, or Joe-Bob's Discount OS.

But if you want that iDisk icon *on your desktop* so you can easily drag and drop files, then the procedure is slightly more complex. You're going to create a new "hard drive" in your PC's Computer window, whose icon represents the iDisk.

Choose Start→Computer. In the Computer window, click "Map network drive" in the toolbar. When you're asked for the disk's address, type *http://idisk.me.com/casey* (or whatever your MobileMe name is). Click "Connect using a different user name." Enter your MobileMe member name and password, and then click OK. Your iDisk appears on the desktop; you can work with it as you would any other hard disk.

- **Allow others to write files in your public folder.** Ordinarily, other people can deposit stuff into your Public folder as well as copy things out. If you'd rather set it up so that only *you* can drop things in there, then turn off this checkbox.

- **Password-protect your Public folder.** Probably a good idea if you decide to make your Public folder available for deposits.

Email

Apple offers an email address to each MobileMe member.

Probably anyone who can *get* to the Apple Web site already *has* an email account. So why bother? The first advantage is the simple address: *YourName@me.com.* (You can also use *YourName@mac.com* interchangeably.)

Second, MobileMe addresses are integrated into Mac OS X's Mail program, as you'll see in the next chapter. And finally, you can read your MobileMe email from any computer anywhere in the world, via the me.com Web site, or on your iPhone/iPod Touch.

Galleries

Within iPhoto, iMovie, Final Cut, and even QuickTime Player, you'll find handy, one-click MobileMe Gallery buttons. They let you post the selected photos or movies on your private corner of the me.com Web site. (You're always shown the Web address of the resulting gallery, so you can tell your friends how to find it.)

This is not the same as posting to, say, Flickr or YouTube, where a cacophony of ads and blinking and ugly text distracts from the presentation. MobileMe galleries are handsome and classy, with black backgrounds and subtle animations. You get all kinds of interesting options, too—for example, you can offer your fans the chance to download full-quality versions of your photos and movies (so family members can print their own copies, for example). And you can permit other people to post their own photos on your galleries, for a better one-stop nostalgia shopping experience about that wedding or reunion.

Web Sites

If you use Apple's iWeb program to design your own Web sites, then MobileMe provides another one-click publishing opportunity. Your Web pages have a happy, hassle-free home on the Web, without your having to know HTML or work an FTP program to post them online.

Once you've posted Web pages, you'll find the source files at *me.com* by clicking the iDisk icon on the toolbar. The Sites heading at left contains the iWeb folder that houses your actual Web-site files.

Note: That's also where you'll find the HomePage folder, containing the Web-site files that the old .Mac Web site let you create online. That was before Apple got more interested in selling copies of iWeb, and let HomePage quietly die.

Internet Location Files

An Internet location file (Figure 18-16) is like a system-wide bookmark: When you double-click one, your Web browser opens to that page, or your email program generates an outgoing message to a predetermined addressee. You could put a folder full of location files for favorite Web sites into the Dock. Do the same with addresses to which you frequently send email. Thereafter, you save a step every time you want to jump to a particular Web page or send email to a particular person—just choose the appropriate name from the Dock folder's Stack. (It's fine to rename them, by the way.)

Figure 18-16:
To create an Internet location file, drag a highlighted address from a program like TextEdit to your desktop. Although Web and email addresses are the most popular types, you can also create location files for the addresses of newsgroups (news://news.apple. com), FTP sites (ftp://ftp.apple. com), AppleShare servers (afp:// at/Engineering:IL5 3rd Floor), AppleTalk zones (at://IL5 2nd Floor), and even Web pages stored on your Mac (file://Macintosh HD/ Website Stuff/home.html).

Mail & Address Book

E mail is a fast, cheap, convenient communication medium. In fact, these days, anyone who *doesn't* have an email address is considered some kind of freak.

If you do have an email address or two, you'll be happy to discover that Mac OS X includes Mail, a program that lets you get and send email messages without having to wade through a lot of spam (junk mail). Mail is a surprisingly complete program, substantially speeded up for Mac OS 10.6, and it's filled with shortcuts and surprises around every turn.

And this desktop post office offers more than just mail—among other things, you can also use the program as a personal notepad and a newsreader for your favorite Web sites.

Not bad for a freebie, eh?

Setting Up Mail

What you see the first time you open Mail may vary. If you've signed up for a MobileMe account (and typed its name into the MobileMe pane of System Preferences), then you're all ready to go; you see the main Mail window full of messages. If you don't get the offer to set up an account, choose File→Add Account to jump-start the process. (That's also how you add other accounts later.)

If you get your mail from some other service provider, like Verizon, Comcast, Gmail, Yahoo, or whatever, Mail setup is almost as easy. Apple has rounded up the acronym-laden server settings for 30 popular mail services and built them right in.

All you have to do is type your email name and password into the box (Figure 19-1). If Mail recognizes the suffix (for example, *@gmail.com*), and if "Automatically set up account" is turned on, then Mail does the heavy lifting for you.

Snow Leopard Spots: If you work in a company that uses Microsoft's Exchange networked mail/calendar system, the good news rolls on. Just entering your email address and password is usually enough to connect to the corporate email system. For details and caveats, see page 305.

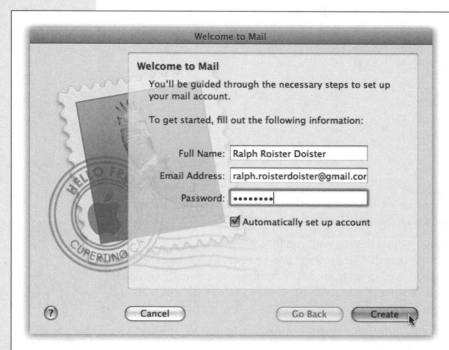

Figure 19-1:
Mail takes the pain, agony, and acronyms out of setting up an email account on your Mac. Forget about remembering your SMTP server address (or even what SMTP stands for), and just type your email address and password into the box. If you use a mainstream mail service like Gmail, Hotmail, Yahoo, Comcast, or Verizon, Mail configures your account settings automatically after you click the Create button.

Now, if you use a service provider that Mail *doesn't* recognize when you type in your email name and password—you weirdo—then you have to set up your mail account the long way. Mail prompts you along, and you confront the dialog boxes shown in Figure 19-2, where you're supposed to type in various settings to specify your email account. Some of this information may require a call to your Internet service provider (ISP).

Here's the rundown:

- **Account Type** is where you specify what flavor of email account you have. See the box on page 699 for details; check with your ISP if you're not sure which type you have.

- **Account Description** is for your reference only. If you want an affectionate nickname for your email account, type it here.

- **Full Name** (shown in Figure 19-1) will appear in the "From:" field of any email you send. Type it just the way you'd like it to appear.

Figure 19-2:
These dialog boxes let you plug in the email settings provided by your Internet service. If you want to add another email account later, choose File→Add Account, and then enter your information in the resulting dialog box. (Or, if you like doing things the hard way, choose Mail→Preferences→Accounts tab, click the + in the lower-left corner of the window, and then enter your account information in the fields on the right.)

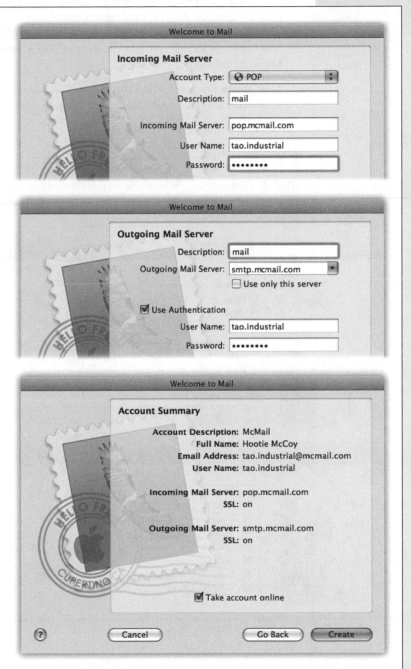

- **Email Address** is the address you were assigned when you signed up for Internet services, such as *billg@microsoft.com*.

- **Incoming Mail Server, Outgoing Mail Server** are where you enter the information your ISP gave you about its mail servers. Usually, the incoming server is a *POP3 server,* and its name is related to the name of your ISP, such as *popmail.mindspring.com*. The outgoing mail server (also called the *SMTP server*) usually looks something like *mail.mindspring.com*.

- **User Name, Password.** Enter the name and password provided by your ISP. (Often, they're the same for both incoming and outgoing servers.)

Click Continue when you're finished.

Mail can also import your email collection from an email program you've used before—Entourage, Thunderbird, Netscape/Mozilla, Eudora, or even a version of Mac OS X Mail that's stored somewhere else (say, on an old Mac's hard drive). Importing is a big help in making a smooth transition between your old email world and your new one.

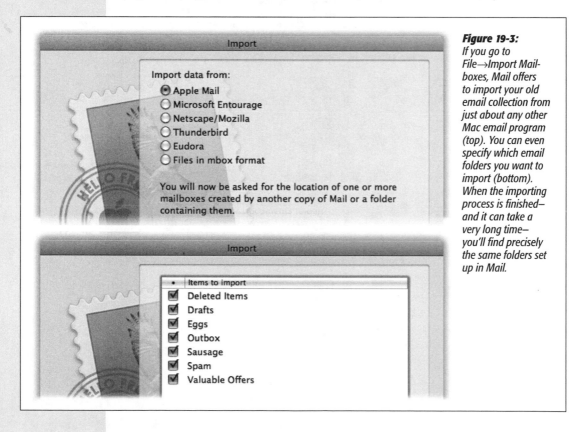

Figure 19-3:
If you go to File→Import Mailboxes, Mail offers to import your old email collection from just about any other Mac email program (top). You can even specify which email folders you want to import (bottom). When the importing process is finished—and it can take a very long time—you'll find precisely the same folders set up in Mail.

To bring over your old mail and mailboxes, choose File→Import Mailboxes. Figure 19-3 has the details.

POP, IMAP, Exchange, and Web-based Mail

When it comes to email, there are four primary flavors of *servers* (Internet computers that process email): *POP* (also known as POP3), *IMAP* (also known as IMAP4), *Exchange*, and *Web-based*. Each has its own distinct taste, with different strengths and weaknesses. (AOL mail could be considered a fifth kind, but if you Google *AOL mail as IMAP account*, you'll find instructions on reading your AOL mail as if it came from a regular IMAP account.)

POP accounts (Post Office Protocol) are the most common kind on the Internet. A POP server transfers your incoming mail to your hard drive before you read it, which works fine as long as you're using only one computer for email.

If you want to take your email along on the road, you have to copy the Mail folder from your Home→Library folder into the corresponding location on your laptop's hard drive. That way, when you run Mail on the laptop, you'll find your messages and attachments already in place.

IMAP servers (Internet Message Access Protocol) are newer and have more features than POP servers, but they aren't as common. IMAP servers keep all of your mail online, rather than making you store it on your hard drive; as a result, you can access the same mail regardless of the computer you use. IMAP servers remember which messages you've read and sent, to boot. It's a great setup if, for example, you check your email on an iPhone, because the deletions and replies you process on the phone will be there on your Mac when you get home.

(A MobileMe account is an IMAP account, which is why you can access the mail in your Inbox repeatedly from any Mac in the world, anywhere you go. You can opt for a Gmail account to be an IMAP account, too.)

One downside to this approach, of course, is that you can't delete your email—or read it for the first time—unless you're online, because all your mail is on an Internet server. Another disadvantage is that if you don't conscientiously manually delete mail after you've read it, your online mailbox eventu-

ally overflows. Sooner or later, the system starts bouncing new messages back to their senders, annoying your friends.

Exchange servers are popular in corporations and some schools. Most of the time, employees tap into these servers using a Windows program like Outlook. Corporate geeks like Exchange servers because they're easy to set up and maintain, and because they offer many of the same features as IMAP servers. Luckily, Mail can now read and send email through Exchange servers as though your Mac were just another beige PC.

Free, Web-based services like Hotmail, Yahoo, and Gmail also store your mail on the Internet, but you can use a Web browser on any computer to read and send messages. They're slower and more cumbersome to use than "regular" email accounts, but they're usually free. Unfortunately, Mail can't check accounts that are entirely Web-based.

Fortunately, the big-name Web-based email services also offer POP or IMAP servers. If you have a MobileMe account, for example, you'll find that you can read your email using either a Web browser or Mail (which, in the background, taps into the MobileMe IMAP server). Same goes for Google's Gmail service, which lets you check your email either on the Web—or using either a POP or IMAP server (see Gmail's help pages for details on making that work).

Conversely, more and more POP and IMAP accounts are also offering a *Web-based* component. For example, whoever provides your Internet service—EarthLink, Verizon, or Speakeasy, for instance—probably provides both POP service and a Web-based way of accessing your email, so you can access your mail either from home or from an Internet café in Bangladesh.

All Mail cares about, though, is whether your email account allows POP, IMAP, or Exchange access; what you do on the Web is, as far as Mail is concerned, your own business.

Checking Your Mail

You get new mail and send mail you've already written using the Get Mail command. You can trigger it in any of several ways:

- Click Get Mail on the toolbar.

- Choose Mailbox→Get All New Mail (or press Shift-⌘-N).

Note: If you have multiple email accounts, you can also use the Mailbox→Get New Mail submenu to pick just *one* account to check for new mail.

- Control-click (or right-click) Mail's Dock icon, and choose Get New Mail from the shortcut menu. (You can use this method from within any program, as long as Mail is already open.)

- Wait. Mail comes set to check your email automatically every few minutes. To adjust its timing or to turn this feature off, choose Mail→Preferences, click General, and then choose a time interval from the "Check for new messages" pop-up menu.

Now Mail contacts the mail servers listed in the Accounts pane of Mail's preferences, retrieving new messages and downloading any files attached to those messages. It also *sends* any outgoing messages that couldn't be sent when you wrote them.

Tip: The far-left column of the Mail window has a tiny Mail Activity monitor tucked away; click the second tiny button at the lower-left corner of the Mail window to reveal Mail Activity. If you don't want to give up Mailboxes-list real estate, or if you prefer to monitor your mail in a separate window, you can do that, too. The Activity Viewer window gives you a Stop button, progress bars, and other useful information. Summon it by choosing Window→Activity, or by pressing ⌘-0.

Also, if you're having trouble connecting to some (or all) of your email accounts, choose Window→Connection Doctor. There, you can see detailed information about which of your accounts aren't responding. If your computer's Internet connection is at fault, you can click Network Diagnostics to try to get back online.

The Mailboxes List

If you used early versions of Mail, the first thing you may notice is that the Mailbox panel isn't just for mailboxes anymore. Categories like Reminders and RSS Feeds can appear there, too, as shown in Figure 19-4. But the top half of this gray-blue column on the left side lists all your email accounts' folders (and subfolders, and sub-subfolders) for easy access. Mail looks quite a bit like iTunes (and iPhoto, and the Finder)—except here you have mailboxes where your iTunes Library and connected iPods would be.

In the Mailboxes panel, sometimes hidden by flippy triangles, you may find these folders:

- **Inbox** holds mail you've received. If you have more than one email account, you can expand the triangles to see separate folders for your individual accounts. You'll see this pattern repeated with the Sent, Junk, and other mailboxes, too—separate accounts have separate subheadings.

Tip: If Mail has something to tell you about your Inbox (like, for instance, that Mail can't connect to it), a tiny warning triangle appears on the right side of the Mailboxes column. Click it to see what Mail is griping about.

If you see a lightning-bolt icon, that's Mail's way of announcing that you're offline. Click the icon to try to connect to the Internet.

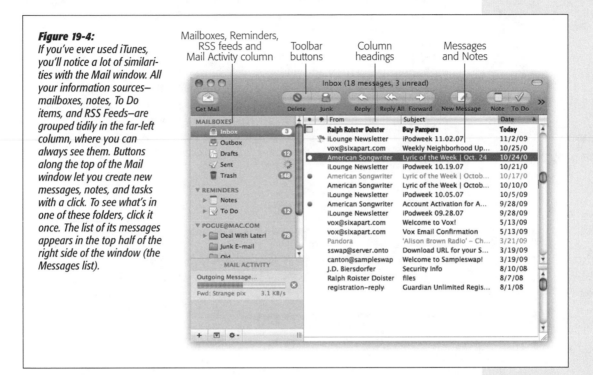

Figure 19-4:
If you've ever used iTunes, you'll notice a lot of similarities with the Mail window. All your information sources—mailboxes, notes, To Do items, and RSS Feeds—are grouped tidily in the far-left column, where you can always see them. Buttons along the top of the Mail window let you create new messages, notes, and tasks with a click. To see what's in one of these folders, click it once. The list of its messages appears in the top half of the right side of the window (the Messages list).

Mailboxes, Reminders, RSS feeds and Mail Activity column

Toolbar buttons

Column headings

Messages and Notes

- **Outbox** holds mail you've written but haven't yet sent (because you were on an airplane when you wrote it, for example). If you have no mail waiting to be sent, the Outbox itself disappears.

- **Drafts** holds messages you've started but haven't yet finished and don't want to send just yet.

- **Sent,** unsurprisingly, holds copies of messages you've sent.

- **Trash** works a lot like the Trash on your desktop, in that messages you put there don't actually disappear. They remain in the Trash folder until you permanently delete them or move them somewhere else—or until Mail's automatic trash-cleaning service deletes them for you.

- **Junk** appears automatically when you use Mail's spam filter, as described later in this chapter.

• **Reminders.** Any Notes you've jotted down while working in Mail are here. To Do items hang out here as well. (Both are described later in this chapter.)

• **RSS Feeds.** Who needs to bop into a Web browser to keep up with the news? Mail brings it right to you while you're corresponding, as described in a moment.

• **Mail Activity.** You don't need to summon a separate window to see how much more of that message with the giant attachment the program still has to send. To reveal the Mail activity panel, shown in Figure 19-4, click the second tiny icon in the bottom left side of the Mail window.

• **Preview pane.** The difference between Figure 19-4 and 19-5 is the Preview pane—the bottom half of the main window, which shows the contents of whatever message you've selected in the list. If you're not already seeing this pane, drag the bottom edge of the window, marked with a dot, upward (as shown in the box on the facing page); that's the movable border between window halves.

Snow Leopard Spots: For the first time, you can now drag the mailboxes up and down in the list. Sweet.

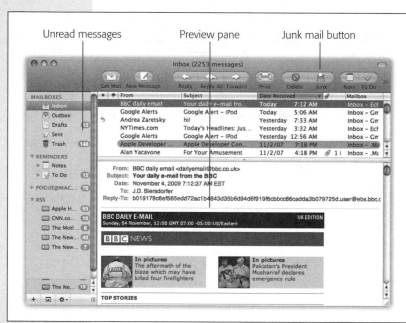

Unread messages   Preview pane   Junk mail button

Figure 19-5:
The many panes of Mail. Click an icon in the Mailboxes column to see its contents in the Messages list. When you click the name of a message in the Messages list (or press the ↑ and ↓ keys to highlight successive messages in that list), you see the message itself, along with any attachments, in the Preview pane.

Click one of the column headings (From, Subject, and so on) to sort your mail collection by that criterion.

Writing Messages

To send an email, click New Message in the toolbar or press ⌘-N. The New Message form, shown in Figure 19-6, opens. Here's how you go about writing a message:

1. **In the "To:" field, type the recipient's email address.**

If somebody is in your Address Book, type the first couple of letters of the name or email address; Mail automatically completes the address. (If the first guess is wrong, type another letter or two until Mail revises its guess.)

Tip: If you find Mail constantly tries to autofill the address of someone you don't really communicate with, you can zap that address from its memory by choosing Window→Previous Recipients. Click the undesired address, and then click Remove From List.

As in most dialog boxes, you can jump from blank to blank (from "To:" to "Cc:," for example) by pressing Tab. To send this message to more than one person, separate the addresses with commas: *bob@earthlink.net, billg@microsoft.com,* and so on.

Tip: If you send most of your email to addresses within the same organization (like *reddelicious@apple.com, grannysmith@apple.com,* and *winesap@apple.com*), Mail can automatically turn all *other* email addresses red. It's a feature designed to avoid sending confidential messages to outside addresses.

To turn this feature on, choose Mail→Preferences, click Composing, turn on "Mark addresses not ending with," and then type the "safe" domain (like *apple.com*) into the blank.

GEM IN THE ROUGH

The Mighty Morphing Interface

You don't have to be content with the factory-installed design of the Mail screen. You can control almost every aspect of its look and layout.

For example, you can control the main window's information columns exactly as you would in a Finder list view window—make a column narrower or wider by dragging the right edge of its column heading, rearrange the columns by dragging their titles, and so on.

You can also control *which* columns appear using the commands in the View→Columns menu. Similarly, you can *sort* your email by clicking these column headings, exactly as in the Finder. Click a second time to reverse the sorting order.

The various panes of the main window are also under your control. For example, you can drag the divider bar between the Messages list and the Preview pane up or down to adjust the relative proportions, as shown here. In fact, you can get rid of the Preview pane altogether by double-clicking the divider line, double-clicking just above the vertical scroll

bar, or dragging the divider line's handle all the way to the bottom of the screen. Bring it back by dragging the divider line up from the bottom.

You can also control the Mailboxes pane. Drag the thin vertical line that separates this tinted column from the white messages area to make the column wider or narrower. You can even drag it so tightly that you see only the mailboxes' icons. You can make the column disappear or reappear by choosing View→Hide Mailboxes (or View→Show Mailboxes), or by pressing Shift-⌘-M.

Finally, you have full control over the toolbar, which works much like the Finder toolbar. You can rearrange or remove icon buttons (by ⌘-dragging them); add interesting new buttons to the toolbar (by choosing View→Customize Toolbar); change its display to show *just* text labels or *just* icons—either large or small (by repeatedly ⌘-clicking the white, oval, upper-right toolbar button); or hide the toolbar entirely (by clicking that white button or using the View→Hide Toolbar command).

---

2. To send a copy to other recipients, enter their addresses in the "Cc:" field.

Cc stands for *carbon copy*. Getting an email message where your name is in the "Cc:" line implies: "I sent you a copy because I thought you'd want to know about this correspondence, but I'm not expecting you to reply."

Tip: If Mail recognizes the address you type into the "To:" or "Cc:" box (because it's someone in your Address Book, for instance), the name turns into a shaded, round-ended box button. Besides looking cool, these buttons have a small triangle on their right; when you click one, you get a list of useful commands (including Open in Address Book).

These buttons are also drag-and-droppable. For example, you can drag one from the "To:" box to the "Cc:" field, or from Address Book to Mail.

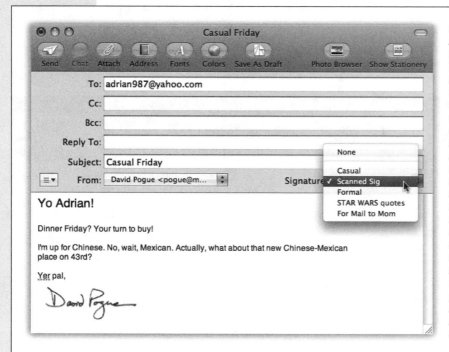

Figure 19-6:
A message has two sections: the header, *which holds information about the message; and the* body, *the big empty area that contains the message itself. In addition, the Mail window has a* toolbar, *which offers features for composing and sending messages. The Signature pop-up menu doesn't exist until you create a signature; the Account pop-up menu lets you pick which email address you'd like to send the message from (if you have more than one email address).*

3. Type the topic of the message in the Subject field.

It's courteous to put some thought into the Subject line. (Use "Change in plans for next week," for instance, instead of "Yo.") And leaving it blank only annoys your recipient. On the other hand, don't put the *entire* message into the Subject line, either.

4. **Specify an email format.**

There are two kinds of email: *plain text* and *formatted* (which Apple calls Rich Text). Plain text messages are faster to send and open, are universally compatible with the world's email programs, and are greatly preferred by many veteran computer fans. And even though the message itself is plain, you can still attach pictures and other files. (If you want to get really graphic with your mail, you can also use the *Stationery* option, which gives you preformatted message templates to drop in pictures, graphics, and text. Flip to page 710 for more on using stationery.)

Resourceful geeks have even learned how to fake some formatting in plain messages: They use capitals or asterisks instead of bold formatting (**man* is he a GEEK!*), "smileys" like this— :-) —instead of pictures, and pseudo-underlines for emphasis (*I _love_ Swiss cheese!*).

By contrast, formatted messages sometimes open slowly, and in some email programs the formatting doesn't come through at all.

To control which kind of mail you send on a message-by-message basis, choose from the Format menu either Make Plain Text or Make Rich Text. To change the factory setting for new outgoing messages, choose Mail→Preferences; click the Composing icon; and choose from the Message Format pop-up menu.

Tip: If you plan to send formatted mail, remember that your recipients won't see the fonts you use unless their machines have the same ones installed. Bottom line: For email to Mac and Windows owners alike, stick to universal choices like Arial, Times, and Courier.

---

5. **Type your message in the message box.**

You can use all standard editing techniques, including copy and paste, drag and drop, and so on. If you selected the Rich Text style of email, you can use word processor–like formatting (Figure 19-7).

As you type, Mail checks your spelling, using a dotted underline to mark questionable words (also shown in Figure 19-7). To check for alternative spellings for a suspect word, Control-click it. From the list of suggestions in the shortcut menu, click the word you really intended, or choose Learn Spelling to add the word to the Mac OS X dictionary. You can read much more about Mac OS X's built-in spelling/grammar checker (and typing expander) in Chapter 6.

If you're composing a long email message, or if it's one you don't want to send until later, click the Save as Draft button, press ⌘-S, or choose File→Save As Draft. You've just saved the message in your Drafts folder. It'll still be there the next time you open Mail. To reopen a saved draft later, click the Drafts icon in the Mailboxes column and then double-click the message you want to work on.

6. **Click Send (or press Shift-⌘-D).**

Mail sends the message.

Tip: To resend a message you've already sent, Option-double-click the message in your Sent mailbox. Mail dutifully opens up a brand-new duplicate, ready for you to edit, readdress if you like, and then send again.

(The prescribed Apple route is to highlight the message and then choose Message→Send Again, but that's not nearly as much fun.)

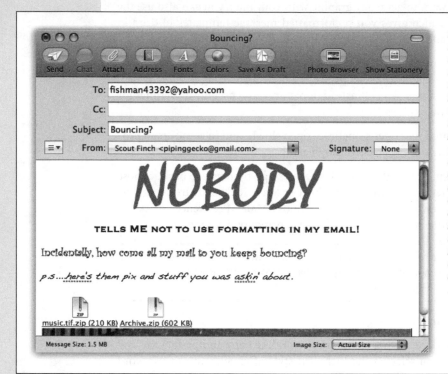

Figure 19-7:
If you really want to use formatting, click the Fonts icon on the toolbar to open the Font panel, or the Colors icon to open the Color Picker dialog box. The Format menu (in the menu bar) contains even more controls: paragraph alignment (left, right, center, or justify), and even Copy and Paste Style commands that let you transfer formatting from one block of text to another.

If you'd rather have Mail place each message you write in the Outbox folder instead of connecting to the Net when you click Send, choose Mailbox→Take All Accounts Offline. While you're offline, Mail refrains from trying to connect, which is a great feature when you're working on a laptop at 39,000 feet. (Choose Mailbox→Take All Accounts Online to reverse the procedure.)

Attaching Files to Messages

Sending little text messages is fine, but it's not much help when you want to send somebody a photograph, a sound, or a Word document. To attach a file to a message you've written, use one of these methods:

- Drag the icons you want to attach directly off the desktop (or out of a folder) into the New Message window. There your attachments appear with their own hyperlinked icons (shown in Figure 19-7), meaning that your recipient can simply click to open them.

Tip: Exposé was *born* for this moment. Hit ⌘-F3 to make all open windows flee to the edges of the screen, revealing the desktop. Root around until you find the file you want to send. Begin dragging it; without releasing the mouse, press ⌘-F3 again to bring your message window back into view. Complete your drag into the message window. (On old plastic keyboards, press F11 instead.)

Mail makes it look as though you can park the attached file's icon (or the full image of a graphics file) *inside* the text of the message, mingled with your typing. Don't be fooled, however; on the receiving end, all the attachments will be clumped together at the end of the message (unless your recipient also uses Mail or you've sent pictures with Stationery).

- Drag the icons you want to attach from the desktop onto Mail's Dock icon. Mail dutifully creates a new, outgoing message, with the files already attached.

- Click the Attach icon on the New Message toolbar, choose File→Attach File, or press Shift-⌘-A. The standard Open File sheet now appears so you can navigate to

---

UP TO SPEED

Bcc:, Reply-To, and Priority

A *blind carbon copy* is a secret copy. This feature lets you send a copy of a message to somebody secretly, without any of the other recipients knowing that you did so. To view this field when composing a message, choose View→Bcc Address Field.

You can use the "Bcc:" field to quietly signal a third party that a message has been sent. For example, if you send your co-worker a message that says, "Chris, it bothers me that you've been cheating the customers," you could Bcc your supervisor to clue her in without getting into trouble with Chris.

The "Bcc:" box is useful in other ways, too. Many people send email messages (corny jokes, for example) to a long list of recipients. You, the recipient, have to scroll through the long list of names the sender placed in the "To:" or "Cc:" field.

But if the sender used the "Bcc:" field to hold all the recipients' email addresses, you, the recipient, won't see anybody else's names at the top of the email. In the "To:" box, you might see the sender's name, or "undisclosed recipients," or nothing at all. (Spammers have also learned this trick, which is why it usually looks like you're the only recipient of a junk message when there are actually millions of other people who received the same message.)

Another hidden field you can add to your messages is *Reply-To.* (Choose View→Reply-To Address Field.) That field has one simple purpose: to make the recipient's email program reply to a different email address than the one you sent the message from. For example, if your business email address isn't working but you absolutely *have* to send a field report to your boss, you can send the message from your personal email account but put your business address in the Reply-To field. That way, when your boss emails you back to congratulate you, the email goes to your business account.

Finally, if you click the three-line pop-up button on the left side of an email message and choose Customize, you can enable one more hidden header option: *Priority.* (It's the pop-up menu with an exclamation mark in it.) If you turn on the checkbox next to that pop-up menu and click OK, all your email messages let you set how important they are on a three-tiered scale.

The good part about this system is that it lets your recipient see that an email you've sent is, for example, urgent. The bad part is that not every email program displays the priority of email—and even if your recipient's email program *does* display your message's priority, there's no guarantee that it'll make him respond any faster.

---

and select the files you want to include. (You can choose multiple files simultaneously in this dialog box. Just ⌘-click or Shift-click the individual files you want as though you were selecting them in a Finder window.)

Once you've selected them, click Choose File (or press Return). You return to the New Message window, where the attachments' icons appear, ready to ride along when you send the message.

To remove an attachment, drag across its icon to highlight it, and then press the Delete key. (You can also drag an attachment icon clear out of the window into your Dock's Trash, or choose Message→Remove Attachments.)

Signatures

Signatures are bits of text that get stamped at the bottom of your outgoing email messages. A signature might contain a name, a postal address, a pithy quote, or even a scan of your *real* signature, as shown in Figure 19-6.

You can customize your signatures by choosing Mail→Preferences and then clicking the Signatures icon. Here's what you should know:

POWER USERS' CLINIC

Attachment Tricks

Nowadays, what's *attached* to an email message is often more important than the message itself. You might send a PowerPoint file to a co-worker or send your aunt a picture of your new dog, for example, without bothering to write anything more than "See attached" in the body of the message.

That's why it's such a pain when email attachments don't go through properly—or when they're too big to send at all. Luckily, Mac OS X now provides three tools for making attachments smaller and more compatible with Windows, so you'll never get another angry "I *can't* see attached!" reply again.

If you're sending images along with your message, you can shrink them down right in Mail. Use the Image Size pop-up menu in the lower-right corner of the window to pick a smaller size for the images (like Medium or Small).

You can keep tabs on the total size of your attachments in the lower-left corner of the window, too. Ideally, you should keep the total under 2 MB, so dial-up sufferers don't get annoyed—and so your message doesn't get rejected by your recipient's ISP for being too big.

Use the Finder to compress big files before you send them. As described on page 91, the Finder creates zip-compressed files, which generally take up much less space than the originals.

You can pick from two different formats for your attachments: normal or Windows-friendly. Normal attachments open correctly on both Macs and PCs. Trouble is, a normal attachment may show up on a PC accompanied by a useless second attachment whose name starts with "._" (which your recipients should just ignore).

Windows-friendly attachments, on the other hand, always work correctly on PCs—but may not open at all on Macs. Unless you work in an all-Windows company, then, stick with the normal setting.

To use the Windows-friendly setting for an open message, choose Edit→Attachments→Send Windows Friendly Attachments. (If no message is open, the command says "*Always Send Windows Friendly Attachments*" instead). You can also adjust the setting on a per-email basis using the Send Windows Friendly Attachments checkbox at the bottom of the attachment dialog box.

- **To build up a library of signatures that you can use in any of your accounts:** Select All Signatures in the leftmost pane, and then click the **+** button to add each new signature (Figure 19-8). Give each new signature a name in the middle pane, and then customize the signatures' text in the rightmost pane.

Tip: If you ever get tired of a signature, you can delete it forever by selecting All Signatures→[your signature's name], clicking the **−** button, and then clicking OK.

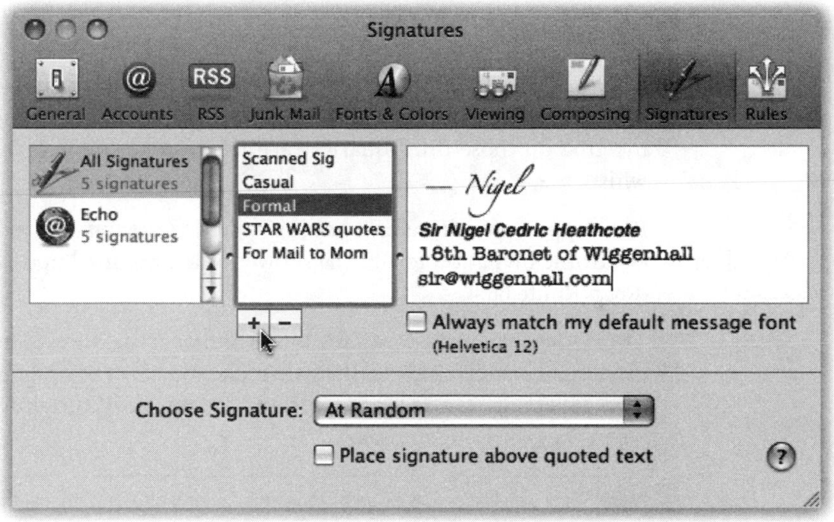

Figure 19-8:
After naming your signature in the middle pane and typing the text on the right, don't miss the Format menu, which you can use to dress up your signature with colors and formatting. You can even paste a picture into the signature box. Click OK when you're finished. (You can use formatted signatures only when sending Rich Text messages.)

- **To make a signature available in one of your email accounts:** Drag the signature's name from the middle pane onto the name of the account in the leftmost pane. In other words, you can make certain signatures available to only your work (or personal) account, so you never accidentally end up appending your secret FBI contact signature to the bottom of a birthday invitation you send out.

- **To assign a particular signature to one account:** In the left pane, click an account; choose from the Choose Signature pop-up menu. Each time you compose a message from that account, Mail inserts the signature you selected.

Tip: To make things more interesting for your recipients, pick At Random; Mail selects a different signature each time you send a message. Or, if you're not that much of a risk-taker, choose In Sequential Order; Mail picks the next signature in order for each new message you write.

Remember that you can always change your signature on a message-by-message basis, using the Signature pop-up menu in any new email message.

- **To use the signature feature as a prefix in replies:** Turn on "Place signature above quoted text." If you turn on this setting, your signature gets inserted *above* any text that you're replying to, rather than below. You'd use this setting if your "signature" said something like, "Hi there! You wrote this to me!"

Tip: If you're into consistent typographical styling, also turn on "Always match my default font." That setting makes sure that any messages you send contain the signature in the same font as the rest of the message, lending it an air of professionalism.

Stationery

Rich text—and even plain text—messages are fine for your everyday personal and business correspondence. After all, you really won't help messages like, "Let's have a meeting on those third-quarter earnings results" much by adding visual bells and whistles.

But suppose you have an occasion where you *want* to jazz up your mail, like an electronic invitation to a bridal shower or a mass-mail update as you get your kicks down Route 66.

These messages just cry out for Mail's *Stationery* feature. Stationery means colorful, predesigned mail templates that you make your own by dragging in photos from your own collection. Those fancy fonts and graphics will certainly get people's attention when they open the message.

Note: They will, that is, if their email programs understand HTML formatting. That's the formatting Mail uses for its stationery. (If *HTML* rings a bell, it's because this HyperText Markup Language is the same used to make Web pages so lively and colorful.)

It might be a good idea to make sure everyone on your recipient list has a mail program that can handle HTML; otherwise, your message may look like a jumble of code and letters in the middle of the screen.

To make a stylized message with Mail Stationery:

1. **Create a new message.**

   Click File→New Message, press ⌘-N, or click the New Message button on the Mail window toolbar. The choice is up to you.

2. **On the right side of the toolbar on the New Message window, click Show Stationery.**

   A panel opens up, showing you all the available templates, in categories like "Birthday" and "Announcements."

3. **Click a category, and then click a stationery thumbnail image to apply it to your message.**

   The body of your message changes to take on the look of the template.

4. **If you like what you see, click the Hide Stationery button on the toolbar to fold up the stationery-picker panel.**

Tip: If you don't like the background color, try clicking the thumbnail; some templates offer a few different color choices.

Now, without question, Apple's canned stationery looks fantastic. The only problem is, the photos that adorn most of the templates are pictures of *somebody else's* family and friends. Unless you work for Apple's modeling agency, you probably have no clue who they are.

Fortunately, it's easy enough to replace those placeholder photos with your *own* snaps.

5. **Add and adjust pictures.**

Click the Photo Browser icon on the message toolbar to open up a palette that lists all the photos you've stored in iPhoto, Aperture, and Photo Booth (Figure 19-9).

Tip: If you don't keep your pictures in any of those programs, you can drag any folder of pictures onto the Photo Browser window to add them.

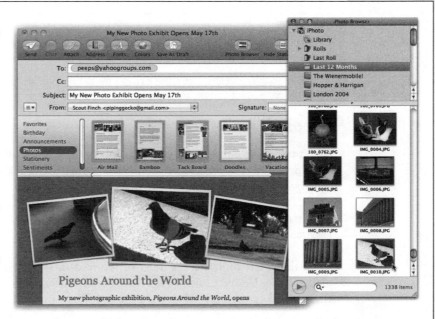

Figure 19-9:
To use Stationery, start by clicking a template, then add your own text in place of the generic copy that comes with the template.

Click the Photo Browser button at the top of the message window to open your Mac's photo collections (shown at right), and then drag the images you want into the picture boxes on the stationery template. You don't have to know a lick of HTML to use the templates—it's all drag, drop, and type, baby.

Now you can drag your own pictures directly *onto* Apple's dummy photos on the stationery template. They replace the sunny models.

To resize a photo in the template, double-click it. A slider appears that lets you adjust the photo's size within the message. Drag the mouse around the photo window to reposition the picture relative to its frame.

6. **Select the fake text and type in what you really want to say.**

Unless you're writing to your Latin students, of course, in which case "Duis nonsequ ismodol oreetuer iril dolore facidunt" might be perfectly appropriate.

In any case, as you type over the dummy text, your words are autoformatted to match the template design.

Once you've got that message looking the way you want it, address it just as you would any other piece of mail, and then click the Send button to get it on its way.

Tip: You're not stuck with Apple's designs for your Stationery templates; you can make your own. Just make a new message, style the fonts and photos the way you want them, and then choose File→Save as Stationery. You can now select your masterwork in the Custom category, which appears down at the end of the list in the stationery-picker panel.

If you decide that the message would be better off as plain old text, click Show Stationery on the message window. In the list of template categories, click Stationery and then Original to strip the color and formats out of the message.

Tip: If you find you're using one or two templates a lot (if, for example, all your friends are having babies these days), drag your frequently used templates into the Favorites category so you don't have to go wading around for them.

To remove one from Favorites, click it, and then click the ⊗ in the top-left corner of the thumbnail.

Reading Email

Mail puts all incoming email into your Inbox; the statistic after the word *Inbox* lets you know how many messages you haven't yet read. New messages are also marked with light-blue dots in the main list.

Tip: The Mail icon in the Dock also shows you how many new messages you have waiting; it's the number in the red circle.

Click the Inbox folder to see a list of received messages. If it's a long list, press Control-Page Up and Control-Page Down to scroll. (Page Up and Page Down without the Control key scrolls the Preview pane instead.)

Click the name of a message once to read it in the Preview pane, or double-click a message to open it into a separate window. (If a message is already selected, pressing Return or Enter also opens its separate window.)

Tip: Instead of reading your mail, you might prefer to have Mac OS X read it *to* you, as you sit back in your chair and sip a strawberry daiquiri. Highlight the text you want to hear (or choose Edit→Select All), and then choose Edit→Speech→Start Speaking. You'll hear the message read aloud, in the voice you've selected on the Speech pane of System Preferences (Chapter 9).

To stop the insanity, choose Edit→Speech→Stop Speaking.

Once you've viewed a message, you can respond to it, delete it, print it, file it, and so on. The following pages should get you started.

Threading

Threading is one of the most useful mail-sorting methods to come along in a long time. When threading is turned on, Mail groups emails with the same subject (like "Raccoons" and "Re: Raccoons") *as a single item* in the main mail list.

To turn on threading, choose View→Organize by Thread. If several messages have the same subject, they all turn light blue to indicate their membership in a thread (Figure 19-10).

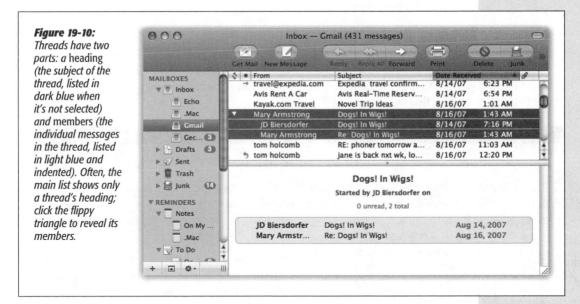

Figure 19-10:
Threads have two parts: a heading *(the subject of the thread, listed in dark blue when it's not selected) and* members *(the individual messages in the thread, listed in light blue and indented). Often, the main list shows only a thread's heading; click the flippy triangle to reveal its members.*

Here are some powerful ways to use threading:

- **View a list of all the messages in a thread** by clicking its heading. In the Preview pane, you see a comprehensive inventory of the thread (Figure 19-10). You can click a message's name in this list to jump right to it.

- **Move all the members of a thread to a new mailbox** simply by moving its heading. You might find this useful, for example, when you've just finished a project and want to file away all the email related to it quickly. (As a bonus, a circled number tells you how many messages you're moving as you drag the heading.) You can even delete all the messages in a thread at once by deleting its heading.

- **Examine thread members from multiple mailboxes.** Normally, threads display only messages held in the *same* mailbox, but that's not especially convenient when you want to see both messages (from your Inbox) and your replies (in your Sent box). To work around that problem, click Inbox, and then ⌘-click the Sent mailbox (or any other mailboxes you want to include). Your threads seamlessly combine related messages from all the selected mailboxes.

- **Quickly collapse all threads** by choosing View→Collapse All Threads. If your main list gets cluttered with too many expanded threads, this is a quick way to force it into order. (If, on the other hand, your main list isn't cluttered *enough*, choose View→Expand All Threads.)

- **Send someone all the messages in a thread** by selecting the thread's heading and clicking Forward. Mail automatically copies all the messages of the thread into a new message, putting the oldest at the top. You might find this useful, for instance, when you want to send your boss all the correspondence you've had with someone about a certain project.

Adding the Sender to Your Address Book

When you choose the Message→Add Sender to Address Book command, Mail memorizes the email address of the person whose message is on the screen. In fact, you can highlight a huge number of messages and add *all* the senders simultaneously using this technique.

UP TO SPEED

All the Little Symbols

The first column of the main email list shows little symbols that let you know at a glance how you've processed certain messages. The most common one is, of course, the light-blue dot (●), which means "new message." (After reading a message, you can mark it once again as an *unread* message by choosing Message→Mark→As Unread [Shift-⌘-U]—or by Control-clicking the message's name and then choosing Mark→As Unread from the shortcut menu.)

You might also see these symbols, which represent messages you've replied to (↩), forwarded (➡), redirected (⤳), or flagged (⚑).

A well-guarded secret, however, is that the "replied to" and "forwarded" symbols aren't just indicators—they're also *buttons*.

When you see one of these symbols next to your original message, click it to jump straight to your reply (or forwarded message). You're spared the trouble of having to search through all your mailboxes.

Incidentally, you may have noticed that Mail marks a message as having been read the moment you click it. You can change it back to unread by using its shortcut menu—but there's also a more permanent workaround.

If you hide the Preview pane by double-clicking the divider bar just above it, Mail no longer marks messages "read" just because you clicked them in the list. (You can bring back the Preview pane by double-clicking just above the vertical scroll bar, or by dragging the divider bar back up from the bottom.)

Thereafter, you'll be able to write new messages to somebody just by typing the first few letters of her name or email address.

Data Detectors

Data detectors are described on page 235. They're what you see when Mac OS X recognizes commonly used bits of written information: a physical address, a phone number, a date and time, a flight number, and so on. With one quick click, you can send that information into the appropriate Mac OS X program, like iCal, Address Book, the Flights widget in Dashboard, or your Web browser (for looking an address up on a map).

This is just a public-service reminder that data detctors are especially useful—*primarily* useful, in fact—in Mail. Watch for the dotted rectangle that appears when you point to a name, address, date, time, or flight number.

Snow Leopard Spots: When someone sends you what looks like a date and time—"Hey, we're getting together for a luau at my apartment on 6/12/2010 at 8:30 pm! Hope you can come!"—the data detector goes one better. Now the pop-up menu that opens when you click the ▼ button actually proposes, "Create New iCal Event." (It even works for less specific wording, like, "Can you come over Thursday afternoon at 3:30?")

You look over the proposed appointment (you'll probably want to edit the title), and that's it—Mail actually creates an appointment on your iCal automatically!

Opening Attachments

Just as you can attach files to a message, so people often send files to you. Sometimes they don't even bother to type a message; you wind up receiving an empty email message with a file or two attached. Only the presence of the file's icon in the message body tells you there's something attached.

Tip: Mail doesn't ordinarily indicate the presence of attachments in the Messages list. It can do so, however. Just choose View→Columns→Attachments. A new column appears in the email list—at the far right—where you see a paper-clip icon and the number of file attachments listed for each message.

Mail doesn't store downloaded files as normal file icons on your hard drive. They're actually encoded right into the *.mbox* mailbox databases described on page 724. To extract an attached file from this mass of software, you must proceed in one of these ways:

- Click the Quick Look button in the message header. Instantly, you're treated to a nearly full-size preview of the file's contents. Yes, Quick Look has come to email. Its strengths and weaknesses here are exactly as described in Chapter 1.

Tip: If the attachments are pictures, clicking Quick Look gives you a full-screen slideshow of every attached image.

If you jiggle the mouse a little during the slideshow, you get a useful row of slideshow-control buttons along the bottom of the screen, too.

- Click the Save button in the message header to save it to the Mac's Downloads folder, nestled within easy reach in the Dock.

Tip: If you don't want to use the Downloads folder, you can choose a new autosave location for attachments by choosing Mail→Preferences→General→Downloads Folder.

- Control-click (or right-click) the attachment's icon, and choose Save Attachment from the shortcut menu. You'll be asked to specify where you want to put it. Or save time by choosing Save to Downloads Folder, meaning the Downloads folder in the Dock.

- Drag the attachment icon out of the message window and onto any visible portion of your desktop (or any visible folder).

- Click the Save button at the top of the email, or choose File→Save Attachments. (If the message has more than one attachment, this maneuver saves all of them.)

Tip: The Save button at the top of the Preview pane doubles as a pop-up menu; if you click it and keep the mouse button pressed, you can select from several other options for saving the attachments—like importing them into iPhoto or downloading only one of them.

- Double-click the attachment's icon, or single-click the blue link underneath the icon. If you were sent a document (a photo, Word file, or Excel file, for example), it now opens in the corresponding program.

Note: After the attachment is open, use the File→Save As command to save the file into a folder of your choice. Otherwise, any changes you make to the document won't be visible except when you open it from within Mail.

- Control-click the attachment's icon. From the shortcut menu, you can specify which program you want to use for opening it, using the Open With submenu.

Replying to a Message

To answer a message, click the Reply button on the message toolbar (or choose Message→Reply, or press ⌘-R). If the message was originally addressed to multiple recipients, you can send your reply to everyone simultaneously by clicking Reply All instead.

A new message window opens, already addressed. As a courtesy to your correspondent, Mail places the original message at the bottom of the window, set off by a vertical bar, as shown in Figure 19-11.

Tip: If you highlight some text before clicking Reply, Mail pastes *only that portion* of the original message into your reply. That's a great convenience to your correspondent, who now knows exactly which part of the message you're responding to.

At this point, you can add or delete recipients, edit the Subject line or the original message, attach a file, and so on.

Tip: Use the Return key to create blank lines in the original message. Using this method, you can splice your own comments into the paragraphs of the original message, replying point by point. The brackets preceding each line of the original message help your correspondent keep straight what's yours and what's hers.

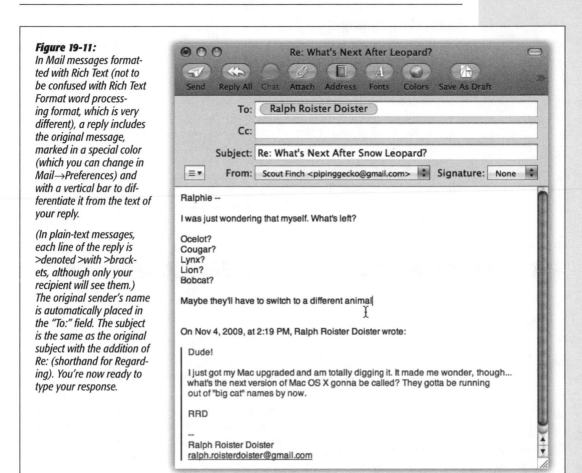

Figure 19-11:
In Mail messages format-ted with Rich Text (not to be confused with Rich Text Format word process-ing format, which is very different), a reply includes the original message, marked in a special color (which you can change in Mail→Preferences) and with a vertical bar to dif-ferentiate it from the text of your reply.

(In plain-text messages, each line of the reply is >denoted >with >brack-ets, although only your recipient will see them.) The original sender's name is automatically placed in the "To:" field. The subject is the same as the original subject with the addition of Re: (shorthand for Regard-ing). You're now ready to type your response.

When you're finished, click Send. (If you click Reply All in the message window now, your message goes to everyone who received the original note, *even* if you began the reply process by clicking Reply. Mac OS X, in other words, gives you a second chance to address your reply to everyone.)

Forwarding Messages

Instead of replying to the person who sent you a message, you may sometimes want to pass the note on to a third person.

To do so, click the Forward toolbar button (or choose Message→Forward, or press Shift-⌘-F). A new message opens, looking a lot like the one that appears when you reply. You may wish to precede the original message with a comment of your own, along the lines of: "Frank: I thought you'd be interested in this joke about your mom."

Finally, address it as you would any outgoing piece of mail.

Redirecting Messages

A redirected message is similar to a forwarded message, with one useful difference: When you forward a message, your recipient sees that it came from you. When you redirect it, your recipient sees the *original* writer's name as the sender. In other words, a redirected message uses you as a low-profile relay station between two other people.

Treasure this feature. Plenty of email programs, including Outlook and Outlook Express for Windows, don't offer a Redirect command at all. You can use it to transfer messages from one of your own accounts to another, or to pass along a message that came to you by mistake.

To redirect a message, choose Message→Redirect, or press Shift-⌘-E. You get an outgoing copy of the message—this time without any quoting marks. (You can edit redirected messages before you send them, too, which is perfect for April Fools' Day pranks.)

WORKAROUND WORKSHOP

Dial-up Blues

If you're among the few, the proud, who still connect to the Internet with a dial-up modem, you may find that Mail is painfully slow at opening and reading email—and that it slows down other Internet programs, like your Web browser, whenever it checks for new mail.

Fortunately, you can take a few steps to speed up Mail (and, indirectly, your other Internet programs):

Cut back on mail checks. Choose Mail→Preferences, click General, and change the "Check for new mail" pop-up to "Every hour," or even "Manually." That way, Mail won't tie up your phone line by trying to connect every 5 minutes.

Whenever you have a choice, don't sign up for HTML email. HTML mail takes far longer to arrive than plain email. Therefore, if you ever sign up for companies' email updates (like Apple's eNews bulletin or *The New York Times's* Personal Tech newsletter), choose to receive the messages as text, not HTML.

Turn off graphics in formatted mail. If you have no choice but to receive HTML messages, the least you can do is block the pictures, which are the biggest and slowest elements of a formatted message.

To do that, choose Mail→Preferences, click Viewing, and then turn off "Display remote images in HTML messages." From now on, you'll see a special Load Images button at the top of the Preview pane whenever you select an HTML message. If you feel that the empty boxes (where the graphics would have appeared) really deprive the message of its oomph, then click that button to make Mail download all the images in the current message—this time only, because you've asked for them.

Don't auto-download attachments. If you use an IMAP, MobileMe, or Exchange account, you can set up Mail so it won't download attachments until you tell it to.

Open the Accounts pane of Mail's preferences, select your account, click Advanced, and choose "All messages, but omit attachments" from the pop-up menu in the middle. From now on, Mail won't download attachments unless you command it to do so.

Printing Messages

Sometimes there's no substitute for a printout. Choose File→Print, or press ⌘-P to summon the Print dialog box.

Filing Messages

Mail lets you create new mailboxes in the Mailboxes pane. You might create one for important messages, another for order confirmations from Web shopping, still another for friends and family, and so on. You can even create mailboxes *inside* these mailboxes, a feature beloved by the hopelessly organized.

Mail even offers *smart mailboxes*—self-updating folders that show you all your mail from your boss, for example, or every message with "mortgage" in its subject. It's the same idea as smart folders in the Finder or smart playlists in iTunes: folders whose contents are based around criteria you specify (Figure 19-12).

Figure 19-12:
Mail lets you create self-populating folders. In this example, the "New Mail from Mom" smart mailbox will automatically display all messages from her that you've received in the past week.

The commands you need are all in the Mailbox menu. For example, to create a new mailbox folder, choose Mailbox→New Mailbox, or click the **+** button at the bottom of the Mailboxes column. To create a smart mailbox, choose Mailbox→New Smart Mailbox.

Mail asks you to name the new mailbox. If you have more than one email account, you can specify which one will contain the new folder. (Smart mailboxes, however, always sit outside your other mailboxes.)

Tip: If you want to create a folder-inside-a-folder, use slashes in the name of your new mailbox. (If you use the name *Cephalopods/Squid*, for example, then Mail creates a folder called Cephalopods, with a subfolder called Squid.) You can also drag the mailbox icons up and down in the drawer to place one inside another.

None of those tricks work for smart mailboxes, however. The only way to organize smart mailboxes is to put them inside a smart mailbox *folder*, which you create using Mailbox→New Smart Mailbox. You might do that if you have several smart mailboxes for mail from your coworkers ("From Jim," "From Anne," and so on) and want to put them together in one collapsible group to save screen space.

When you click OK, a new icon appears in the mailbox column, ready for use.

You can move a message (or group of messages) into a mailbox folder in any of three ways:

- Drag it out of the main list onto a mailbox icon.

- In the list pane, highlight one or more messages, and then choose from the Message→Move To submenu, which lists all your mailboxes.

- Control-click (or right-click) a message, or one of several that you've highlighted. From the resulting shortcut menu, choose Move To, and then, from the submenu, choose the mailbox you want.

Of course, the only way to change the contents of a *smart* mailbox is to change the criteria it uses to populate itself. To do so, double-click the smart mailbox icon and use the dialog box that appears.

Flagging Messages

Sometimes you'll receive email that prompts you to some sort of action, but you may not have the time (or the fortitude) to face the task at the moment. ("Hi there… it's me, your accountant. Would you mind rounding up your expenses for 1999 through 2009 and sending me a list by email?")

That's why Mail lets you *flag* a message, summoning a little flag icon in a new column next to a message's name. These indicators can mean anything you like—they simply call attention to certain messages. You can sort your mail list so that all your flagged messages are listed first; click the flag at the top of the column heading.

To flag a message in this way, select the message (or several messages) and then choose Message→Mark→As Flagged, or press Option-⌘-L, or Control-click (right-click) the

---

TROUBLESHOOTING MOMENT

Rebuilding Your Mail Databases

Mail keeps your messages in a series of mailbox database files in your Home→Library→Mail folder.

Over time, as you add and delete hundreds of messages from these database files, some digital sawdust gets left behind, resulting in peculiarities when addressing messages or general Mail sluggishness. You also wind up with *massive* message files hidden on your hard drive, which can consume hundreds of megabytes of disk space. That's a particular bummer if you like to copy your message databases to your laptop when you go on a trip.

Fortunately, it's easy enough to *rebuild the message databases*. Doing so cleanses, repairs, and purges your message files. As a result, you wind up with a much more compact and healthy database.

To rebuild a mailbox, highlight it in the Mailboxes column in Mail. (Highlight several by ⌘-clicking, if you like.) Then choose Mailbox→Rebuild. Mac OS X takes several minutes (or hours, depending on the size of your mailboxes) to repair and compact your database—but if you're experiencing Mail weirdness or slowness, it's well worth the sacrifice.

---

message's name in the list and, from the shortcut menu, choose Mark→As Flagged. (To clear the flags, repeat the procedure, but use the Mark→As Unflagged command instead.)

***

Tip: This whole flagging business has another useful side effect. When Mail finds messages it thinks are spam, it marks them with little trash-bag icons in the flag column. If you sort your mail by flag, then all your spam gets grouped together—which is great if you want to do one big spam-cleaning by dragging it all to the Trash.

Finding Messages

When you deal with masses of email, you may come to rely on Mail's *dedicated* searching tools. They're fast and convenient, and when you're done with them, you can go right back to browsing your Message list as it was.

Finding messages within a mailbox

The box in the upper-right corner of the main mail window is Mail's own private Spotlight. You can use it to hide all but certain messages, as shown in Figure 19-13.

***

Tip: You can also set up Mail to show you only certain messages that you've *manually* selected, hiding all others in the list. To do so, highlight the messages you want, using the usual selection techniques (page 71). Then choose View→Display Selected Messages Only. (To see all of them again, choose View→Display All Messages.)

***

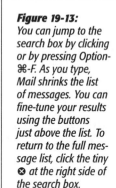

Figure 19-13:
You can jump to the search box by clicking or by pressing Option-⌘-F. As you type, Mail shrinks the list of messages. You can fine-tune your results using the buttons just above the list. To return to the full message list, click the tiny ⊗ at the right side of the search box.

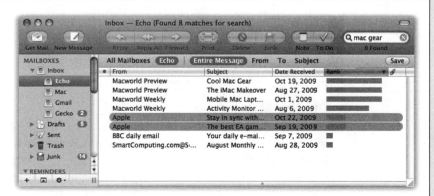

In Snow Leopard, this search box is powerful indeed. For example:

- You have the power of Spotlight charging up your search rankings; the most relevant messages for your search appear high on the list. And Notes and To Do items show up in the search results now, too.

- When you're searching, a thin row of buttons appears underneath the toolbar. You can use these buttons to narrow your results to only messages with your search term

***

in their *subject*, for example, or to only those messages in the currently selected mailbox.

- When you select a message in the search view, the Preview pane pops up from the bottom of the window. If you click Show in Mailbox, on the other hand, you exit the search view and jump straight to the message in whatever mailbox it came from. That's perfect if the message is part of a thread, since jumping to the message also displays all the other messages from its thread.

- If you think you'll want to perform the current search again sometime, click Save in the upper-right corner of the window. Mail displays a dialog box with your search term and criteria filled in; all you have to do is give it a name and click OK to transform your search into a smart mailbox that you can open anytime.

Finding text within an open message

You can also search for certain text *within* an open message. Choose Edit→Find→Find (or press ⌘-F) to bring up the Find dialog box (Figure 19-14).

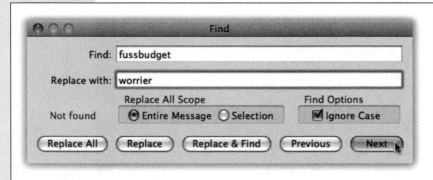

Figure 19-14:
The Find box works just as it does in a word processor, except that the Replace function works only on messages you've written yourself— Mail doesn't let you change the words of mail you've received. (Lawyers would have a field day with that one.)

Deleting Messages

Sometimes it's junk mail. Sometimes you're just done with it. Either way, it's a snap to delete a selected message, several selected messages, or a message that's currently before you on the screen. You can press the Delete key, click the Delete button on the toolbar, choose Edit→Delete, or drag messages out of the list window and into your Trash mailbox—or even onto the Dock's Trash icon.

Tip: If you delete a message by accident, the Undo command (Edit→Undo or ⌘-Z) restores it.

All these commands move the messages to the Trash folder. If you like, you can then click its icon to view a list of the messages you've deleted. You can even rescue messages by dragging them back into another mailbox (back to the Inbox, for example).

Method 1: Emptying the Trash folder

Mail doesn't vaporize messages in the Trash folder until you "empty the trash," just like in the Finder. You can empty the Trash folder in any of several ways:

- Click a message (or several) within the Trash folder list, and then click the Delete icon on the toolbar (or press the Delete key). Now those messages are *really* gone.

- Choose Mailbox→Erase Deleted Messages (⌘-K). (If you have multiple accounts, choose Erase Deleted Messages→In All Accounts.)

- Control-click (or right-click) the Trash mailbox icon, and then choose Erase Deleted Messages from the shortcut menu. Or choose the same command from the ✿ pop-up menu at the bottom of the window.

- Wait. Mail will permanently delete these messages automatically after a week.

  If a week is too long (or not long enough), you can change this interval. Choose Mail→Preferences, click Accounts, and select the account name from the list at left. Then click Mailbox Behaviors, and change the "Erase deleted messages when" pop-up menu. If you choose Quitting Mail from the pop-up menu, Mail will take out the trash every time you quit the program.

Method 2: Deleted mail turns invisible

Mail offers a second—and very unusual—method of deleting messages that doesn't involve the Trash folder at all. Using this method, pressing the Delete key (or clicking the Delete toolbar button) simply hides the selected message in the list. Hidden messages remain hidden, but don't go away for good until you use the Rebuild Mailbox command described in the box on page 720.

If this arrangement sounds useful, choose Mail→Preferences; click Accounts and select the account from the list on the left; click Mailbox Behaviors; and then turn off the checkbox called "Move deleted messages to a separate folder" or "Move deleted messages to the Trash mailbox." (The checkbox's wording depends on what kind of account you have.) From now on, messages you delete vanish from the list.

They're not really gone, however. You can bring them back, at least in ghostly form, by choosing View→Show Deleted Messages (or pressing ⌘-L). Figure 19-15 shows the idea.

Using this system, in other words, you never truly delete messages; you just hide them.

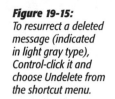
Figure 19-15:
To resurrect a deleted message (indicated in light gray type), Control-click it and choose Undelete from the shortcut menu.

At first, you might be concerned about the disk space and database size involved in keeping your old messages around forever like this. Truth is that Mac OS X is perfectly capable of maintaining many thousands of messages in its mailbox databases—and with the sizes of hard drives nowadays, a few thousand messages aren't likely to make much of a dent.

Meanwhile, there's a huge benefit to this arrangement. At some point, almost everyone wishes they could resurrect a deleted message—maybe months later, maybe years later. Using the hidden-deleted-message system, your old messages are always around for reference. (The downside to this system, of course, is that SEC investigators can use it to find incriminating mail that you thought you'd deleted.)

When you do want to purge these messages for good, you can always return to the Special Mailboxes dialog box and turn the "Move deleted mail to a separate folder" checkbox back on.

Archiving Mailboxes

Time Machine (Chapter 6) keeps a watchful eye on your Mac and backs up its data regularly—including your email. If you ever delete a message by accident or otherwise make a mess of your email stash, you can duck into Time Machine right from within Mail.

But not everybody wants to use Time Machine, for personal reasons—lack of a second hard drive, aversion to software named after H. G. Wells novels, whatever.

Yet having a backup of your email is critically important. Think of all the precious mail you'd hate to lose: business correspondence, electronic receipts, baby's first message. Fortunately, there's a second good way to back up your email—*archive it*, like this:

1. **In the Mailboxes column, choose which mailbox or mailboxes you want to archive.**

   If you have multiple mailboxes in mind, Control-click (or right-click) each one until you've selected all the ones you want.

2. **At the bottom of the Mail window, open the ✿ pop-up menu and choose Archive Mailbox(es).**

POWER USERS' CLINIC

Secrets of the Mbox Files

Mail keeps your messages in a series of mailbox database files in your Home→Library→Mail folder, inside folders named for your accounts (Outbox, Deleted Messages, and so on).

Knowing this permits you to perform a number of interesting tricks. First of all, now you know what files to back up for safekeeping.

Second, now you know which files to copy to your laptop to maintain email continuity when you travel.

And finally, if you have messages on an old Mac that you'd like to copy to your new one, you know where they're stored.

You can also get to this command by choosing Mailbox→Archive.

3. **In the box that appears, navigate to the place you want to stash this archive of valuable mail, like a server, flash drive, or folder. Click Choose.**

Your archived mailboxes are saved to the location you've chosen. You can now go back to work writing new messages.

Later, if you need to pull one of those archives back into duty, choose File→Import Mailboxes. Choose the "Mail for Mac OS X" option and navigate back to the place you stored your archived mailboxes.

Note: If you archive mailboxes on a regular basis, don't worry about changing the name of the .mbox file to prevent it from overwriting a previous archive. Mail is smart enough to stick a number at the end of the new file name for you.

Message Rules

Once you know how to create folders, the next step in managing your email is to set up a series of *message rules* (filters) that file, answer, or delete incoming messages automatically based on their contents (such as their subject, address, and/or size). Message rules require you to think like the distant relative of a programmer, but the mental effort can reward you many times over. Message rules turn Mail into a surprisingly smart and efficient secretary.

Setting up message rules

Here's how to set up a message rule:

1. **Choose Mail→Preferences. Click the Rules icon.**

The Rules pane appears, as shown at top in Figure 19-16.

GEM IN THE ROUGH

The Email Answering Machine

If you're going on vacation, you can turn Mail into an email answering machine that sends a canned "I'm away until the 15th" message to everyone who writes you.

To do so, set the first set of pop-up menus in the Rules dialog box so that they say Account and the name of your account. In the bottom half of the dialog box, select Reply to Message from the pop-up menu. Click "Reply message text," and then type your boilerplate reply in the resulting box.

Keep in mind, though, that mail rules work only when Mail is open and connected to the Internet. If your computer is set to turn off after a certain period of time, therefore, make sure to disable that feature before you go on vacation.

Also: If you subscribe to mailing lists, set up another mail rule that intercepts and files them *before* your answering-machine rule kicks in. Otherwise, you'll incur the wrath of other Internet citizens by littering their email discussion groups with copies of your auto-reply message.

---

2. Click Add Rule.

Now the dialog box shown at bottom in Figure 19-16 appears.

3. Use the criteria options (at the top) to specify how Mail should select messages to process.

For example, if you'd like the program to watch out for messages from a particular person, you would set up the first two pop-up menus to say "From" and "Contains," respectively.

To flag messages containing *loan, $$$$, XXXX, !!!!*, and so on, set the pop-up menus to say "Subject" and "Contains."

You can set up *multiple* criteria here to flag messages whose subjects contain any one of those common spam triggers. (If you change the "any" pop-up menu to say "all," then *all* the criteria must be true for the rule to kick in.)

Figure 19-16:
Top: Mail rules can screen out junk mail, serve as an email answering machine, or call important messages to your attention. All mail message rules you've created appear in this list. (The color shading for each rule is a reflection of the colorizing options you've set up, if any.)

Bottom: Double-click a rule to open the Edit Rule dialog box, where you can specify what should set off the rule and what it should do in response.

4. **Specify which words or people you want the message rule to watch for.**

   In the text box to the right of the two pop-up menus, type the word, address, name, or phrase you want Mail to watch for—a person's name, or *$$$$*, in the previous examples.

5. **In the lower half of the box, specify what you want to happen to messages that match the criteria.**

   If, in steps 1 and 2, you've told your rule to watch for junk mail containing *$$$$* in the Subject line, here's where you can tell Mail to delete it or move it into, say, a Junk folder.

   With a little imagination, you'll see how the options in this pop-up menu can do absolutely amazing things with your incoming email. Mail can colorize, delete, move, redirect, or forward messages—or even play a sound when you get a certain message.

   By setting up the controls as shown in Figure 19-16, for example, you'll have specified that whenever your mother *(mom@mcmail.com)* sends something to your Gmail account, you'll hear a specific alert noise as the email is redirected to a different email account, *chickadee745@hotmail.com.*

6. **In the very top box, name your mail rule. Click OK.**

   Now you're back to the Rules pane (Figure 19-16, top). Here you can choose a sequence for the rules you've created by dragging them up and down. Here, too, you can turn off the ones you won't be needing at the moment, but may use again one day.

Tip: Mail applies rules as they appear, from top to bottom, in the list. If a rule doesn't seem to be working properly, it may be that an earlier rule is intercepting and processing some messages before the "broken" rule even sees them. To fix this, try dragging the rule (or the interfering rule) up or down in the list.

The Anti-Spam Toolkit

Spam, the junk that now makes up more than 80 percent of email, is a problem that's only getting worse. Luckily, you, along with Mail's advanced spam filters, can make it better—at least for *your* email accounts.

Using the Junk Mail Filter

You'll see the effects of Mail's spam filter the first time you check your mail: A certain swath of message titles appears in color. These are the messages that Mail considers junk.

Note: Out of the box, Mail doesn't apply its spam-targeting features to people whose addresses are in your Address Book, to people you've emailed recently, or to messages sent to you *by name* rather than just by email address. You can adjust these settings in Mail→Preferences→Junk Mail tab.

During your first couple of weeks with Mail, your job is to supervise Mail's work. That is, if you get spam that Mail misses, click the message, and then click the Junk button at the top of its window, or the Junk icon on the toolbar. On the other hand, if Mail flags legitimate mail as spam, slap it gently on the wrist by clicking the Not Junk button. Over time, Mail gets better and better at filtering your mail; it even does surprisingly well against the new breed of image-only spam.

The trouble with this so-called Training mode is that you're still left with the task of trashing the spam yourself, saving you no time whatsoever.

Once Mail has perfected its filtering skills to your satisfaction, though, open Mail's preferences, click Junk Mail, and click "Move it to the Junk mailbox." From now on, Mail automatically files what it deems junk into a Junk mailbox, where it's much easier to scan and delete the messages en masse.

Tip: Don't miss the "Trust Junk Mail headers set by your Internet Service Provider" option in the Junk Mail pane of the preference window. If you turn on that checkbox, Mail takes your ISP's word that certain messages are spam, giving you a *double* layer of spam protection.

More Anti-Spam Tips

The Junk filter goes a long way toward cleaning out the spam from your mail collection—but it doesn't catch everything. If you're overrun by spam, here are some other steps you can take:

- **Don't let the spammers know you're there.** Choose Mail→Preferences, click Viewing, and turn off "Display remote images in HTML messages." This option thwarts a common spammer tactic by blocking graphics that appear to be embedded into a message but are actually retrieved from a Web site somewhere. Spammers use that embedded-graphics trick to know that their message has fallen on fertile ground—a live sucker who actually looks at these messages—but with that single preference switch, you can fake them out.

- **Rules.** Set up some message rules, as described on the preceding pages, that autoflag messages as spam that have subject lines containing trigger words like "Viagra," "Herbal," "Mortgage," "Refinance," "Enlarge," "Your"—you get the idea.

- **Create a private account.** Above all, if you're overrun by spam, consider sacrificing your address to the public areas of the Internet, like chat rooms, online shopping, Web site and software registration, and newsgroup posting. Spammers use automated software robots that scour every public Internet message and Web page, recording email addresses they find. (In fact, that's probably how they got your address in the first place.)

  Using this technique, at least you're now restricting the junk mail to a secondary mail account. Reserve a separate email account for person-to-person email.

Here are some suggestions for avoiding spammers' lists in the first place:

- **Don't ask for it.** When filling out forms online, turn off the checkboxes that say, "Yes, send me exciting offers and news from our partners."

- **Fake out the robots.** When posting messages in a newsgroup or message board, insert the letters NOSPAM somewhere into your email address. Anyone replying to you via email must delete the NOSPAM from your email address, which is a slight hassle. Meanwhile, though, the spammers' software robots will lift a bogus email address from your online postings.

- **Never reply to spam.** Doing so identifies your email address as an active one and can lead to even more unwanted mail. Along the same lines, never click the "Please remove me from your list" link at the bottom of an email unless you know who sent the message.

And for goodness' sake, don't *order* anything sold by the spammers. If only one person in 500,000 does so, the spammer makes money.

RSS Feeds

Mail gets more than *mail*. It also helps you keep yourself up to date with the world outside—and within your own little corner of it.

For example, the ability to subscribe to those constantly updating news summaries known as *RSS feeds* has saved a lot of people a lot of time over the years. After all, why waste precious minutes looking for the news when you can make the news find you?

With Mail, you don't even have to waste the seconds switching from your Inbox to your browser or dedicated RSS program to get a fresh dose of headlines. They can appear right in the main Mail window. You don't even have to switch programs to find out which political candidate shot his foot off while it was still in his mouth.

In fact, if you find it too exhausting to click the RSS icon in the Mailboxes list, you can choose instead to have all your RSS updates land right in your Inbox along with all your other messages.

Adding RSS Feeds

With just a few clicks, you can bring the news of the world right in with the rest of your mail. Choose File→Add RSS Feeds, and then proceed as shown in Figure 19-17.

Tip: As you turn on the feeds you want to see in Mail, ⌘-click to select a bunch of feeds at once.

If you want the RSS headlines to appear in your Inbox like regular email messages, turn on "Show in Inbox." Finally, once you've chosen the feeds you want to see, click Add. Your feeds now appear wherever you told them to go: either the Inbox or the Mailboxes column.

Now, in the RSS category of your Mailboxes list, the names of your RSS feeds show up; the number in the small gray circle tells you how many unread headlines are in the list. If a feed headline intrigues you enough to want more information, click "Read More…" to do just that. Safari pops up and whisks you away to the Web site that sent out the feed in the first place.

Tip: Click the up arrow button next to a feed's name to move all its updates into your Inbox; there, they appear with the same blue RSS label, but they behave as though they're an Inbox category to spare you having to flip back and forth between two distant areas of the Mailboxes list.

If you *accidentally* click that arrow, and you don't really want 57 headlines from RollingStone.com peppering your daily dose of mail, click the feed's name and then click the down-pointing arrow next to it; it returns to the RSS section of the list. Alternatively, you can Control-click (or right-click) the feed name under Mailboxes and turn off "Show in Inbox" from the shortcut menu.

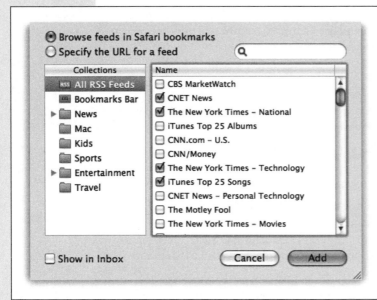

Figure 19-17:
In the Add RSS Feeds box, you can click to add sites you've already subscribed to in Safari. If you don't already have the feed bookmarked in Safari, click "Specify a custom feed URL" and paste the feed's address into the resulting box. If you've got a ton of feeds and don't want to wade through them all, use the search box to seek out the specific feed you need.

Managing Feeds

Now that you've got your feeds in Mail, you may want to fiddle around with them.

- **Updating.** You can change the frequency of your news updates by choosing Mail→Preferences→RSS→Check for Updates. You can automatically update them every half hour, every hour, or every day. You can also command Mail to update a certain feed *right now;* Control-click the feed's name in the Mailboxes list and, from the shortcut menu, choose "Update BBC News" (or whatever its name is).

- **Archiving.** You can save and store a whole batch of feeds in an archive file, just as you can do with regular mailboxes; choose Mailbox→Archive Feed. A dialog box walks you through saving a copy of all the messages to a backup drive or other location for safekeeping.

- **Sharing.** If you want to share the news with a friend, Control-click a headline; from the shortcut menu, choose Forward (or Forward as Attachment) to pop the info into a new Mail message that you can send off to your pal.

- **Renaming.** You don't have to use the site's full name in your Mail window—after all, "WaPo" fits much better in the Mailboxes column than "Washington Post." To rename a feed, select it and then choose Mailbox→Rename Feed. Type in the new name and press Return. (You can also Control-click or right-click the name to bring up the Rename Feed option.)

- **Deleting.** After you've read a news item and are done with it, click the Delete button at the top of the window. You can tell Mail to dump all the old articles after a certain amount of time (a day, a week, a month) in Mail→Preferences→RSS→Remove Articles.

  Or, to get rid of an RSS feed altogether, select it and then choose Maibox→Delete Feed. (Control- or right-clicking the name gives you the same option.)

Notes

Let's face it: No operating system is complete without Notes. You *have* to have a place for little reminders, phone numbers, phone messages, Web addresses, brainstorms, shopping-list hints—anything that's worth writing down, but too tiny to justify heaving a whole word processor onto its feet.

The silly thing is how many people create reminders for themselves by *sending themselves an email message.*

That system works, but it's a bit inelegant. Fortunately, Mac OS X has a dedicated Notes feature. As a bonus, it syncs automatically to the Notes folder of your iPhone's mail program, or to other computers, as long as you have an IMAP-style email account (see the box on page 699).

Notes look like actual yellow notepaper with ruled lines, but you can style 'em, save 'em, and even send 'em to your friends. You can type into them, paste into them, and attach pictures to them. And unlike loose scraps of paper or email messages to yourself that may get lost in your mailbox, Notes stay obediently tucked in the Reminders section of the Mailboxes list so you can always find them when you need them.

Tip: Ordinarily, Notes also appear in your Inbox, at the top. If you prefer to keep your Inbox strictly for messages, though, you can remove the Notes. Choose Mail→Preferences→Accounts→Mailbox Behaviors, and then turn off "Store notes in Inbox." The Notes will still be waiting for you in the side column, down in the Reminders area.

To create a Note, click the Note button on the Mail toolbar. You can also choose File→New Note or press Control-⌘-N to pop up a fresh piece of onscreen paper.

Once you have your Note, type your text and click the Fonts and Colors buttons at the top of the window to style it. To insert a picture, click the Attach button, and then find the photo or graphic on your Mac you want to use. Figure 19-18 shows an example.

Note: You can also attach other kinds of files to a Note—ordinary documents, for example. But you can't send such Notes to other people—only Notes with pictures.

Figure 19-18:
They may look like little pads of scratch paper, but Mail Notes let you paste in Web addresses and photos alongside your typed and formatted text. If you want to share, click the Send button to have the entire Note plop into a new Mail message, ready to be addressed.

When you're finished with your Note, click Done to save it. When you look for it in the Reminders category of the Mailboxes list, you'll see that Mail used the first line of the Note as its subject.

To delete a Note for good, select it and press the Delete key.

If you've worked hard on this little Note and want to share it, double-click it to open the Note into a new window. Click the Send button on its toolbar. Mail puts the whole thing into a new Mail message—complete with yellow-paper background—so your pal can see how seriously (and stylishly) you take the whole concept of "Note to self."

To Dos

You've got all this mail piling up with all sorts of things to remember: dinner dates, meeting times, project deadlines, car-service appointments. Wouldn't it be great if you didn't have to remember to look through your mailbox to find out what you're supposed to be doing that day?

It would, and it is, thanks to Mail's To Do feature. And the best part is that Mail accesses the *same* To Do list as iCal. The same task list shows up in both programs.

Figure 19-19:
Top: If a message brings a task that you need to complete, you can give yourself an extra little reminder, right in Mail. Highlight the pertinent text and click the To Do button to add a large, colorful reminder to the top of the message.

Bottom: Click the arrow next to the first line of the To Do for a quick and easy way to set a due date/time and alarm, and also to choose which calendar you want to use for this particular chore.

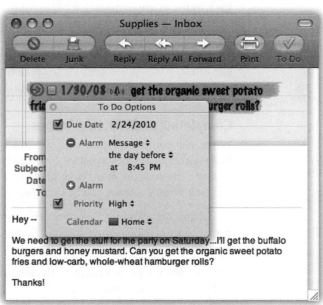

Creating To Dos

You can use To Dos in several different ways. For example, when you get an email message that requires further action ("I need the photos for the condo association newsletter by Friday"), highlight the important part of the text. Then do any of these things:

- Click To Do in the message window's toolbar.

- Choose File→New To Do.

- Press Option-⌘-Y.

- Control-click (or right-click) the highlighted text, and then choose New To Do from the shortcut menu.

In each case, Mail pops a copy of the selected text into a yellow strip of note-style paper at the top of the message, as shown in Figure 19-19.

That task is also listed in the Reminders area of the Mailboxes list. If you need to see *all* the tasks that await you from all your mail accounts, click the flippy triangle to have it spin open and reveal your chores. The number in the gray circle indicates how many To Do items you still need to do.

Tip: Control-click (or right-click) any item in this To Do list to open a shortcut menu that offers useful controls for setting its due date, priority, and *calendar* (that is, iCal category).

When you click the To Do area of the Mailboxes list, all your tasks are listed in the center of the Mail window. Click the gray arrow after each To Do subject line to jump back to the original message it came from.

Tip: Not all of your life's urgent tasks spring from email messages. Fortunately, you can create standalone To Dos, too. Just click the To Do button at the top of the Mail window when no message is selected. A blank item appears in your To Do list with the generic name "New To Do." Select the name to overwrite it with what this reminder is really about: *Buy kitty litter TODAY* (or whatever).

Completing and Deleting To Dos

When you complete a task, click the small checkbox in front of the To Do subject line—either in the message itself or in the Reminders list. Once you've marked a task as Done this way, the number of total tasks in the Reminders list goes down by one, and that's one less thing you have to deal with.

To delete a big yellow To Do banner from a message, point to the left side of the banner until a red handwritten-looking X appears. Click the X to zap the To Do banner from the message.

You can delete a To Do item from the Reminders list by selecting it and then pressing Delete, among other methods.

To Do List: Mail/iCal Joint Custody

Seeing your To Do items in Mail is great—when you're working in Mail. Getting them into iCal is even better, though, because you can see the big picture of an entire day, week, or month. Mail and iCal share the exact same To Do list. Create a To Do in one program, and it shows up *instantly* in the other one.

Tip: You can even set the due date and priority of a task from within Mail. Those controls are in the To Do Options balloon (Figure 19-19). Open this balloon by Control-clicking the task and choosing Edit To Do, or just click the large arrow button that appears to the left of a To Do banner in an email message window. Later, in iCal, if you double-click a To Do item and then click "Show in Mail," you get whisked back to the original message, sitting right there in Mail.

Address Book

Address Book is Mac OS X's little-black-book program—an electronic Rolodex where you can stash the names, job titles, addresses, phone numbers, email addresses, and Internet chat screen names of all the people in your life (Figure 19-20). Address Book can also hold related information, like birthdays, anniversaries, and any other tidbits of personal data you'd like to keep at your fingertips.

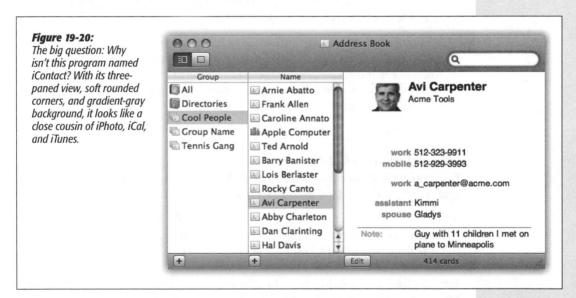

Figure 19-20:
The big question: Why isn't this program named iContact? With its three-paned view, soft rounded corners, and gradient-gray background, it looks like a close cousin of iPhoto, iCal, and iTunes.

Once you make Address Book the central repository of all your personal contact information, you can call up this information in a number of convenient ways:

- You can launch Address Book and search for a contact by typing just a few letters in the Search box.

- Regardless of what program you're in, you can use a single keystroke (F12 is the factory setting, or the ⏏ key on aluminum keyboards) to summon the Address

Book Dashboard widget. There, you can search for any contact you want. When you're done, hide the widget with the same quick keystroke.

- When you're composing messages in Mail, Address Book automatically fills in email addresses for you when you type the first few letters.

Tip: If you choose Window→Address Panel (Option-⌘-A) from within Mail, you can browse all your addresses without even launching the Address Book program. Once you've selected the people you want to contact, just click the "To:" button to address an email to them—or, if you already have a new email message open, to add them to the recipients.

- When you use iChat to exchange instant messages with people in your Address Book, the pictures you've stored of them automatically appear in chat windows.

- If you've bought a subscription to the MobileMe service (Chapter 18), you can synchronize your contacts to the Web so you can see them while you're away from your Mac. You can also share Address Books with fellow MobileMe members: Choose Address Book→Preferences→Sharing, click the box for "Share your address book," and then click the + button to add the MobileMe pals you want to share with. You can even send them an invitation to come share your contact list. If you get an invitation yourself, open your own Address Book program and choose Edit→Subscribe to Address Book.

- Address Book can send its information to an iPod or an iPhone, giving you a "little black book" that fits in your shirt pocket, can be operated one-handed, and comes with built-in musical accompaniment. (To set this up, open iTunes while your iPod or iPhone is connected. Click the iPod/iPhone's icon; on the Contacts or Info tab, turn on "Synchronize Address Book Contacts.")

You can find Address Book in your Applications folder or in the Dock.

Creating Address Cards

Each entry in Address Book is called a *card*—like a paper Rolodex card, with predefined spaces to hold all the standard contact information.

To add a new person, choose File→New Card, press ⌘-N, or click the + button beneath the Name column. Then type in the contact information, pressing the Tab key to move from field to field, as shown in Figure 19-21.

Tip: If you find yourself constantly adding the same fields to new cards, check out the Template pane of Address Book's Preferences (Address Book→Preferences). There, you can customize exactly which fields appear for new cards.

Each card also contains a free-form Notes field at the bottom, where you can type any other random crumbs of information you'd like to store about the person (pet's name, embarrassing nicknames, favorite Chinese restaurant, and so on).

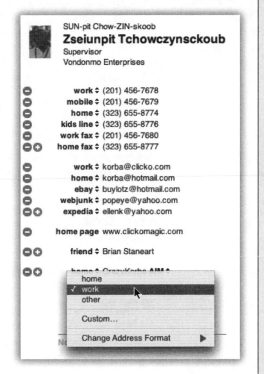

Figure 19-21:
If one of your contacts happens to have three office phone extensions, a pager number, two home phone lines, a cellphone, and a couple of fax machines, no problem—you can add as many fields as you need. Click the little green + buttons when editing a card to add more phone, email, chat name, and address fields. (The buttons appear only when the existing fields are filled.) Click a field's name to change its label; you can select one of the standard labels from the pop-up menu (Home, Work, and so on) or make up your own labels by choosing Custom, as seen in the lower portion of this figure.

This example shows some unusual fields that you can plug into your address cards. The phonetic first/last name fields (shown at top) let you store phonetic spellings of hard-to-pronounce names. The other fields store screen names for instant messaging networks like Jabber and Yahoo. To add fields like these, choose from the Card→Add Field menu.

Editing an address

When you create a new address card, you're automatically in Edit mode, which means you can add and remove fields and change the information on the card. To switch into Browse Mode (where you can view and copy contact information but not change it), click the Edit button or choose Edit→Edit Card (⌘-L). You can also switch *out* of Browse Mode in the same ways.

Tip: Regardless of which mode you're in—Edit or Browse—you can *always* type, drag, or paste text into the Notes field of an address card.

Adding addresses from Mail

You can also make new contacts in the Address Book right in Mail, saving you the trouble of having to type names and email addresses manually. Select a message in Mail, then choose Message→Add Sender to Address Book (or press ⌘-Y). Presto: Mac OS X adds a new card to the Address Book, with the name and email address fields already filled in. Later, you can edit the card in Address Book to add phone numbers, street addresses, and so on.

Importing Addresses

The easiest way to add people to Address Book is to import them from another program like Entourage, Outlook Express, or Palm Desktop.

Address Book isn't smart enough to read an Entourage or Outlook Express database—it can only import files in vCard format, the less common LDIF format, or tab-separated or comma-separated database files (described next).

It's a fine art, this importing business; all kinds of things can go wrong. The fields (like Name, Street, Phone) may not be in the right order. Tab-separated export files may not have the right number of empty fields. And so on.

For best results, choose Address Book→Help, and search for "Importing contacts from other applications." The resulting page gives special tips for each kind of export/import file format.

About vCards

Address Book exchanges contact information with other programs primarily through *vCards.* vCard is short for *virtual business card.* More and more email programs send and receive these electronic business cards, which you can identify by their .vcf file name extensions (if, that is, you've set your Mac to display these extensions).

If you ever receive an email with a vCard file attached, drag the .vcf file into your Address Book window to create an instant entry with a complete set of information. You can create vCards of your own, too. Just drag a name out of your Address Book and onto the desktop (or into a piece of outgoing mail).

Tip: In addition to letting you create vCards of individual entries, Address Book makes it easy to create vCards that contain several entries. To do so, ⌘-click the entries in the Name column that you want included, and drag them to the desktop. There, they'll appear all together as a single vCard. You can even drag an item from the Group column to the desktop to make a vCard that contains all the group's entries.

Keep this trick in mind if you ever want to copy all your contacts from an old PC to a new Mac. By creating a single vCard containing all your contacts, you've made it trivial to import them into the copy of Address Book running on your new Mac.

Syncing with Google, Yahoo, MobileMe, or Exchange

Yeah, it's a big deal, baby: Address Book can synchronize its contacts with any of four external Rolodexes that may be very important to you: Your Gmail (Google) contacts, Yahoo contacts, MobileMe address book, or your company's Microsoft Exchange master address book.

For details on Exchange, see the end of Chapter 8; for MobileMe, see Chapter 18.

If you keep an address book in Yahoo or Gmail, choose Address Book→Preferences→Accounts. Click "On My Mac." Turn on the checkbox you want, and proceed as shown in Figure 19-21.

Tip: Once you've set up this online syncing, the two-way updating takes place hourly. If you can't wait that long, here's how to force a sync on command: Open the iSync program in your Applications folder, choose iSync→Preferences, and then select "Show status in menu bar." From now on, you can choose Sync Now from that menulet whenever you want Address Book to check in with its online twin.

Figure 19-21:
When you turn on one of these checkboxes, you first get a legal disclaimer; ignore it and click Agree.

Now you're asked to enter your Yahoo or Gmail name and password. Once that's done, presto!—your Mac's Address Book and online contacts are kept in sync. Even their photos, if your online address book has them, show up in Address Book!

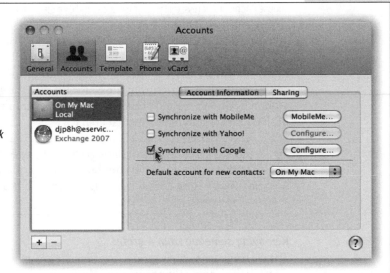

Groups

A *group* is a collection of related address cards, saved under a single descriptive name (visible in Figure 19-20).

Organizing your contacts into groups can make them much easier to find and use—especially when your database of addresses climbs into the hundreds. For example, if you regularly send out a family newsletter to 35 relatives, you might gather the address

---

POWER USERS' CLINIC

The Windows-to-Address-Book Journey

Getting names and addresses out of one Mac program and into another is one thing. But what if your contacts are stored on a Windows PC running Microsoft Outlook, the most-used contact manager in the world?

Easy: Use Outlook's Export command to create a tab-delimited text file containing all your contacts. Then copy the text file to your Mac.

In Address Book, choose File→Import→Text File, locate the file you exported from Outlook, and click Open. After a short delay, your new contacts appear, ready to go in Address Book.

---

cards of all your assorted siblings, cousins, nieces, nephews, uncles, and aunts into a single group called Family. When addressing an outgoing message using Mail, you can type this group name to reach all your kin at once. A person can be a member of as many different groups as you want.

Tip: When you send an email message to a group en masse, how does Mail know which email address to use for each person?

Because you've *told* it. Choose Edit→Edit Distribution List. A special dialog box appears, listing everyone in each group, along with each person's complete list of email addresses. (Use the tiny pop-up menu above the list to choose Phone or Address; that way, you can also indicate the preferred phone number and mailing address.)

To create a group, click the **+** button at the bottom of the Group column in the Address Book window, or choose File→New Group (Shift-⌘-N.) Type a name for the newly spawned group icon in the Group column, and then populate it with address cards by dragging entries from the Name list into the group. Clicking a group name automatically locates and displays (in the Names column) all the names that are part of that group—and hides any that aren't.

Tip: To turn a set of address cards into a group very quickly, select multiple entries from the Names column—by either Shift-clicking the names (to make contiguous selections) or by ⌘-clicking (for non-contiguous selections)—and then choose File→New Group From Selection. You end up with a new group containing all the selected names.

Removing someone from a group

To take someone out of a group, first click the group name, and then click the person's name in the Name column and press the Delete key. If you want to remove the person from Address Book *itself*, click Delete in the resulting dialog box. Otherwise, just click "Remove from Group" or press Return. Address Book keeps the card but removes it from the currently selected group.

POWER USERS' CLINIC

Automatic Notifications

In Address Book, notifying friends and family that your email address has changed is a piece of cake.

Choose Address Book→Preferences→General and turn on "Notify people when my card changes." From now on, whenever you change the information in your own address card (like home address, email address, or phone number), Address Book asks whether you want to send a notification email–a virtual change-of-address card. If you do, click Notify.

In the resulting dialog box, choose which groups of people you want to notify, and then personalize the outgoing message. When you click Send, Address Book delivers an email to all the people in the groups you chose, attaching your new vCard (page 738). When your recipients get the email, they can simply drag the vCard into their own Address Books to update their information about you.

(If you ever want to send updates to your contacts *manually*, just choose File→Send Updates.)

Note: If you selected All in the Group column, rather than a specific group, you don't get a "Remove from Group" option. Instead, the Mac just asks you to confirm that you do, in fact, want to permanently remove the card.

Adding Pictures

You can dress up each Address Book entry with a photo. Whenever you're editing somebody's address book card, drag a digital photo—preferably 64 pixels square, or a multiple of it—onto the empty headshot square; the image shows up. Or double-click the picture well; now you can either browse to a picture on your hard drive by clicking Choose, or, if this person is *with* you, take a new photo by clicking the camera icon. (Don't miss the swirly button next to it, which lets you apply nutty Photo Boothish effects.) At that point, you can enlarge, reposition, and crop the new photo.)

You don't necessarily have to use a photo, of course. You could add any graphic that you want to represent someone, even if it's a Bart Simpson face or a skull and cross-bones. You can use any standard image file in an address card—a JPEG, GIF, PNG, TIFF, or even a PDF.

From now on, if you receive an email from that person, the photo shows up right in the email message.

GEM IN THE ROUGH

Cool Group Tricks

Dragging cards into and out of groups can be a great way to spend an afternoon, but groups can actually be powerful timesavers. For example, if a card is selected in the Name column, you can quickly highlight *all* the groups it belongs to by pressing the Option key.

If you've created a lot of groups, it can be very difficult to find a specific one—especially because Address Book's Search box looks only for individual cards. To get around this limitation, click in the Group list and then type the first few letters of a group's name. Address Book jumps right to the first matching group.

You can even add groups to *other* groups. You might find it useful to keep a Nieces group and a Nephews group, for example, but to keep both groups inside a master Family group. To do this, create the two groups. Then ⌘-click them in the Group list and Option-drag them onto the Family group. Now, whenever you select Family, you'll see both

Nieces and Nephews listed among the rest of the cards; double-click either group to see its members.

Also, don't miss the Smart Groups feature of the Address Book. Smart address groups, like smart folders in the Finder, automatically populate themselves with items that match criteria you specify. For example, you might create a smart group called Apple Employees that lists all your contacts with "apple.com" in their email addresses.

To create a smart group, choose File→New Smart Group (Option-⌘-N). Then use the resulting dialog box (which looks a lot like Mail's smart mailbox dialog box) to specify how you'd like the smart group to fill itself.

Once you're done, you can use your new smart group much like you'd use a regular group. You can't add contacts to a smart group yourself, of course, but you can still send an email to all the members of a smart group, for example, or drag one to the Finder to create a composite vCard.

Tip: If you've got snapshots in iPhoto, it's particularly easy to add a picture to any address card. Just drag a picture directly from the main iPhoto window to the picture frame on the address card to insert it.

Replacing and removing a picture

To replace a photo on an address card, just drag a new image on top of the old one. If you want to get rid of an existing picture without replacing it, select the card, then choose Card→Clear Custom Image (or, in Edit mode, press Delete).

Finding an Address

You can search for an Address Book entry inside the currently selected group by typing a few letters of a name (or address, or any other snippet of contact information) in the Search box (Figure 19-22). To search *all* your contacts instead of just the current group, click All in the Group list.

Tip: You can press ⌘-F to jump directly to the search field and start typing. Your savings: one mouse click.

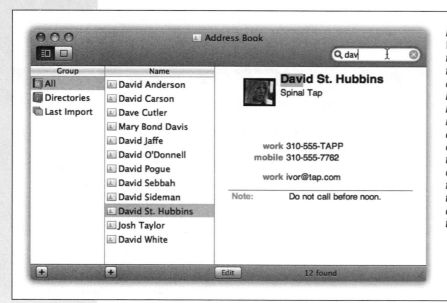

Figure 19-22:
With each letter you type, Address Book filters your social circle and displays the number of matches at the bottom. The matching records themselves appear in the Name column, the first of the matching card entries appears in the far-right pane, and the matching text itself appears highlighted in the matching card.

If Address Book finds more than one matching card, use the ↓ and ↑ keys, or Return and Shift-Return, to navigate through them.

Once you've found the card you're looking for, you can perform some interesting stunts. If you click the label of a phone number ("home" or "office," for example), you see the Large Type option: Address Book displays the number in an absurdly gigantic font that fills the entire width of your screen, making it possible to read the number as you dial from across the room. You can also click the label of an email address to create a preaddressed email message, or click a home page to launch your Web browser and go to somebody's site.

You can also copy and paste (or drag) address card info into another program or convert it into a Sticky Note.

Tip: *Once you find a street address in your Address Book, you can find those coordinates on a map by Control-clicking (or right-clicking) the address part of the card and choosing "Map Of" from the shortcut menu, as shown in Figure 19-23. Your Web browser obediently leaps up to display the address on a Google map.*

Figure 19-23:
The options that become available when you click the field labels on an address card vary according to field type. Pop-up menus let you send email, open a Web page, or view a map, depending on the type of field you've clicked.

Changing the Address Book Display

You can't do much to customize Address Book's appearance, but the Preferences pane (Address Book→Preferences) gives you at least a couple of options in the General pane that are worth checking out:

- **Display Order**. Choose to have names displayed with the first name followed by the last name, or vice versa.

- **Sort By**. Sort the entries in Address Book by either first or last name.

- **Font Size**. Choose from Regular, Large, or Extra Large. Unfortunately, you can't change anything else about the font used in the Address Book; the color, face, and style are all locked down.

Printing Options

When you choose File→Print and click the ▼ to expand the Print box, the Style pop-up menu offers four ways to print whatever addresses are selected at the moment:

- **Mailing Labels.** This option prints addresses on standard sheets of sticky mailing labels—Avery, for example—that you buy at office-supply stores.

Tip: As you manipulate settings, you can see your changes in the preview pane on the left. If the preview is too small for you to see, use the Zoom slider. (It doesn't affect your printout.)

- **Envelopes.** This feature is great if you have bad handwriting; rather than hand-addressing your envelopes, you can have Address Book print them out for you. Use the Layout pop-up menu to pick the size of your envelopes—it's usually listed on the outside of the envelope box.

Note: Both the Mailing Labels and Envelopes options print only the contacts for which you have, in fact, entered physical mailing addresses.

- **Lists.** If all you want is a paper backup of your Address Book entries, use this setting. In the Attributes list, turn on the checkboxes of the fields you want printed—just name and phone number, for example.

- **Pocket Address Book.** This feature prints out a convenient *paper* address book from your virtual one. If you pick Indexed from the Flip Style pop-up menu, each page's edge will even list the first letters of the last names listed on the page, making it a cinch to find the page with the address you want. (Here again, you can pick which fields you'd like to include—phone numbers, addresses, and so on.)

As you fiddle with the options presented here, you get to see a miniature preview, right in the dialog box, that shows what you're going to get.

No matter which mode you choose, the only cards that print are the ones that were selected when you chose File→Print. If you want to print *all* your cards, therefore, click All in the Group column before you print.

Tip: You can combine the smart-groups feature with the printing features in one clever way: to print yourself a portable phone book when you're heading off for a visit to a different city. That is, set up a smart group that rounds up everyone you know who lives in Chicago, and then print that as a pocket address book.

Address-Book Backups

Your Address Book may represent *years* of typing and compiling effort. Losing all that information to a corrupted database or a hard drive crash could be devastating. Here are three ways to protect your Address Book data:

- **Turn on MobileMe syncing.** A MobileMe account has its privileges—and one of them is automatic synchronizing with the MobileMe mothership online.

- **Back up your entire Address Book database.** Open your Home→Library→Application Support folder. Copy the entire Address Book folder to another disk—burn it to a CD, download it to your iPod, or upload it to a file server, for example.

- **Back up your whole Mac with Time Machine.** Chapter 6 tells you how.

Safari

The Internet has come a long way since its early days in the 1960s, when it was a communications network for universities and the military. Today, that little network has morphed into an international information hub, an entertainment provider, and the world's biggest mall. For that, we can thank the development of the World Wide Web—the visual, point-and-click face of the Internet.

Apple is obviously intrigued by the possibilities of the Internet. With each new release of Mac OS X, more clever tendrils reach out from the Mac to the world's biggest network: Dashboard, the Wikipedia link in the Dictionary program, Web clippings, Back to My Mac, and so on.

But Apple's most obvious Internet-friendly creation is Safari, a smartly designed window to the Web (available for Mac OS X and, believe it or not, Windows). This chapter is all about Safari; its compass icon in the Dock points the way to your Internet adventure.

FREQUENTLY ASKED QUESTION

Where to Specify Your Preferred Mail and Browser Programs

Hey! Where the heck do I specify what browser I want to open when, say, I click a link in an email message? It used to be in the Internet panel of System Preferences, but that panel doesn't exist anymore!

This is going to sound a little odd. But to indicate that you want some other browser to be your favorite, you start

by opening Safari. Choose Safari→Preferences, click the General tab, and choose from the Default Web Browser pop-up menu.

You change email programs using the same twisted logic: You open Mail and then open its Preferences.

Safari

If you want something done right, you have to do it yourself.

That must be what Apple was thinking when it wrote its own Web browser a few years ago, which so annoyed Microsoft that it promptly ceased all further work on the Mac version of its own Internet Explorer.

Safari is beautiful, fast, and filled with delicious features. In Snow Leopard, it's faster than before, and badly behaving plug-ins no longer crash the whole browser; instead, the faulty plug-in just closes itself. You see an empty space on the page where that plug-in's video or animation would have appeared, and you can reload the page if you want to try again.

Safari is not, however, Internet Explorer, and so some Web sites—a few banking sites, for example—refuse to acknowledge its existence. For these situations, you might try the Mac version of Firefox, a free browser available at *www.getfirefox.com*.

Browsing Basics and Toolbars

You probably know the drill when it comes to Web browsers. When you click an un-derlined *link (hyperlink)* or a picture button, you're transported from one Web page

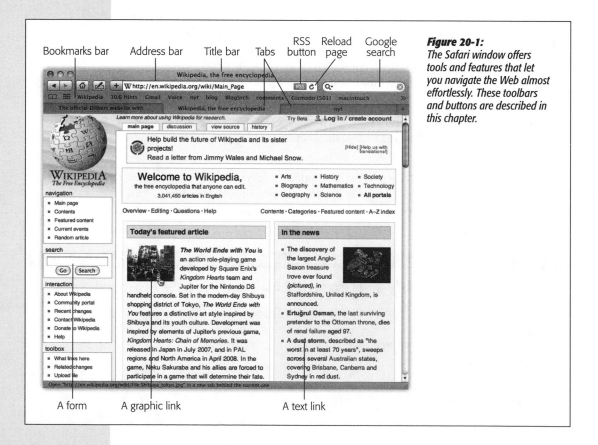

Bookmarks bar   Address bar   Title bar   Tabs   RSS button   Reload page   Google search

A form   A graphic link   A text link

Figure 20-1:
The Safari window offers tools and features that let you navigate the Web almost effortlessly. These toolbars and buttons are described in this chapter.

to another. One page might be the home page of General Motors; another might contain critical information about a bill in Congress; another might have baby pictures posted by a parent in Omaha.

Tip: Text links aren't always blue and underlined. In fact, trendy Web designers sometimes make it very difficult to tell which text is clickable and which is just text. When in doubt, move your cursor over some text; if the arrow changes to a pointing-finger cursor, you've found yourself a link.

Some of the other Safari tips may not be obvious:

- **Graphics worth saving.** When you see a picture you'd like to keep, Control-click (or right-click) it and choose Save Image to Desktop (or Save Image to iPhoto, or just Save Image) from the shortcut menu. Safari stores it as a new graphics file, freed from its birthplace on the Web. (You can specify where Safari saves downloaded pictures on the Safari→Preferences→General tab. In that case, the shortcut menu's wording changes to say, for example, "Save Image to 'Pictures.'")

Tip: You can also save a graphic to the desktop just by dragging it there, right out of the Safari window.

- **Scroll bars.** Instead of using the scroll bar to move up and down the page, it's often easier to press the space bar each time you want to see more. Press Shift-space to scroll *up*. (The space bar serves its traditional, space-making function only when the insertion point is blinking in a text box or the address bar.)

  You can also press your ↑ and ↓ keys to scroll one line at a time. Page Up and Page Down scroll in full-screen increments, while Home and End whisk you to the top or bottom of the current Web page. And if your mouse has a scroll wheel, it works, too. (Hold Shift while you're rolling the wheel to scroll *horizontally*.)

  On a laptop, drag with two fingers to scroll, as usual.

Safari Toolbars

Many of Safari's most useful controls come parked on toolbars and buttons that you can summon or hide by choosing their names from the View menu. Here's what they do:

Address bar

When you type a new Web page address (URL) into this strip and press Return, the corresponding Web site appears.

Note: If only an error message results, then you may have mistyped the address, or the Web page may have been moved or dismantled—a relatively frequent occurrence in today's rapidly-changing Web.

Similarly, you'll see an error message if Safari can't connect to the Internet at all. (This error message is a masterpiece of clarity: "You are not connected to the Internet.")

In that case, click Network Diagnostics to see if Mac OS X can track down the source of your connection trouble. Once you get back online, Safari automatically loads any pages you've been waiting to read.

Because typing out Internet addresses is so central to the Internet experience and such a typo-prone hassle, the address bar is rich with features that minimize keystrokes. For example:

- You don't have to click the address bar before typing; just press ⌘-L.

- You can highlight the entire address (so it's ready to be typed over with a new one) by clicking the very upper or lower edge of the address bar text box. Alternatively, you can click the small icon just to the left of the current address, or triple-click the address bar, or press ⌘-L.

- You don't have to type out the whole Internet address. You can omit the *http://*, *www*, and *.com* portions; Safari fills in those standard address bits for you. To visit NYTimes.com, for example, a speed freak might press ⌘-L to highlight the address bar, type *nytimes*, and then press Return.

Tip: You're Web surfing, and you suddenly need to look up an appointment in iCal. What do you do?

The power user opens other programs right from within Safari by typing ical:// in the address bar—or ichat://, addressbook://, or sherlock://—and then pressing Return. (Unfortunately, Apple programs are generally the only ones that work with this URL-launching trick.)

You can also type mailto: to open a new outgoing email message in your default email program, or mailto:steve@apple.com to pre-address that outgoing message to Steve Jobs. (Of course, remember to replace that email address with that of someone you'd actually like to contact.)

GEM IN THE ROUGH

Let AutoFill Do the Typing

Safari can also remember user names, passwords, and other information you type into the text boxes you encounter in your Web travels.

To turn on this great feature, visit the Safari→Preferences→AutoFill tab. If you turn on "Using info from my Address Book card," then whenever you're supposed to fill in your shipping address on a Web form, you can click the AutoFill button in the address bar to have Safari fill in the blanks for you automatically. (If you don't see the AutoFill button—see Figure 20-2—choose its name from the View menu, or use Edit→AutoFill Form to do the deed instead.)

Alternatively, just click a text box—Name, for example—and start typing. As soon as Safari recognizes a familiar scrap of your contact information, it fills out the rest of the word automatically. (If it guessed wrong, just keep typing.)

If, in Preferences, you turn on "User names and passwords," then each time you type a password into a Web page, Safari offers to memorize it for you. It's a great time- and brain-saver, even though it doesn't work on all Web sites. (Of course, use it with caution if you share an account on your Mac with other people.)

When you want Safari to "forget" your passwords—for security reasons, for example—revisit that Safari→Preferences→AutoFill tab. Click one of the Edit buttons, and then delete the Web site names for which your information has been stored.

Turn on Other Forms if you'd like Safari to remember the terms you've typed into search engines, shopping sites, online gaming sites, and so on.

- When you begin to type into the address bar, the AutoComplete feature compares what you're typing against a list of Web sites that you've recently visited or that you've saved as bookmarks. Safari displays a drop-down list of Web addresses that seem to match what you're typing. To spare yourself the tedium of typing out the whole thing, click the correct complete address with your mouse, or use the ↓ key to reach the desired listing and then press Return. The complete address you select pops into the address bar.

Tip: You might wonder why the View menu even offers you the chance to hide the address bar. If it were hidden, how could you use the Web?

Simple: Even with this bar hidden, you can briefly summon it by pressing ⌘-L. Type the address you want and then press Return to make the bar disappear again. That's good news for people with small screens—and for Mac trivia collectors.

Address-bar buttons

You can summon or dismiss a number of individual buttons on the address bar, in effect customizing it (Figure 20-2). It's worth putting some thought into this tailoring, because some of these buttons' functions are really handy. So here's a catalog of your options:

- **Back/Forward.** Click the Back button (◄) to revisit the page you were just on. *Keyboard shortcut:* Delete, or ⌘-←.

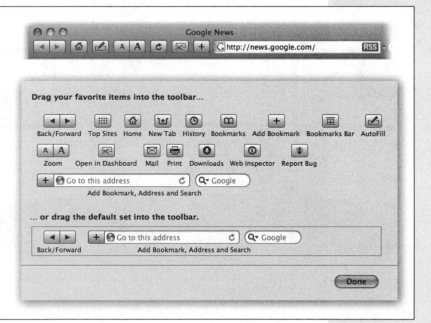

Figure 20-2:
To summon this toolbar-tailoring screen, choose View→Customize Address Bar. Then drag the buttons you want directly onto the address bar. Some of them lack text labels once installed, but all offer tooltip labels you can read by pointing to the button without clicking.

Once you've clicked ◄, you can then click the ► button (or press ⌘-→ to return to the page you were on before you clicked the Back button. Click and hold the ◄ button for a drop-down list of *all* the Web pages you've visited during this online session.

That pop-up menu lists the sites by name, as in "The New York Times—Breaking News, World News & Multimedia." To view the actual *addresses* instead, Option-click (and hold the mouse down on) the Back or Forward button.

Tip: Instead of clicking and holding the ◄ or ► button for these tricks, you can save half a second of waiting by just Control-clicking.

- **Top Sites.** This new Safari 4 feature opens up the highly visual dashboard shown in Figure 20-3. These thumbnails represent what Safari has determined are your favorite Web sites, as calculated by how often and how recently you've visited them.

Figure 20-3:
You can open the Top Sites display either by clicking the Top Sites button on the toolbar or by choosing History→ Top Sites. Click a page to revisit it; a star in the corner means "This page has changed since your last visit."

- **Home.** Click to bring up the Web page you've designated as your home page (in Safari→Preferences→General tab).

- **New Tab.** Creates a new tab (embedded window), described later in this chapter.

- **History.** Click to open the list of Web sites you've visited recently in a window—a much easier-to-navigate display than the History *menu*.

- **Bookmarks, Add Bookmark.** When you find a Web page you might like to visit again, click Add Bookmark. You can also press ⌘-D, choose Bookmarks→Add Bookmark, or drag the tiny icon from the address bar directly onto your Bookmarks bar.

As shown in Figure 20-4, Safari offers to add this Web page's name (or a shorter name that you specify for it) either to the Bookmarks menu or to the Bookmarks bar (described below). The next time you want to visit that page, just select its name in whichever location you chose.

Tip: Press Shift-⌘-D to add the bookmark to the menu instantly—no questions asked, no dialog box presented.

The ⌗ (Bookmarks) button opens the Bookmarks editing window (Figure 20-4). Here you can rearrange the names in your Bookmarks menu easily, or peruse them by scrolling through their giant Cover Flow thumbnails—a great feature in a Web browser, because a visual representation of a page is a lot more helpful than some Web address.

(Even without the ⌗ button, you can get there by choosing Bookmarks→Show All Bookmarks or by pressing Option-⌘-B.)

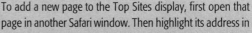

POWER USERS' CLINIC

Customizing Top Sites

Ordinarily, the Top Sites display changes over time, as your tastes and your activity change. But you can override Safari's attempt to curate this page in various ways. For example, you can pin a certain site so that it never leaves the Top Sites screen, or you can manually add a page.

It all happens when you click the Edit button in the lower left. Each thumbnail sprouts two buttons in the corner: the X button (this page will never again appear on Top Sites) and the thumbtack button (this page will always appear in Top Sites, even if you don't visit it much).

To add a new page to the Top Sites display, first open that page in another Safari window. Then highlight its address in the address bar and drag it right onto the Top Sites page. You can also drag a Web link from an email message, text document, Web page, or any other source to the Top Sites page.

You can reorder the thumbnails, too, just by dragging them around on this screen.

Finally, you can change the thumbnail size on this Edit screen, too. Use the Small/Medium/Large control in the lower right; smaller thumbnails means more of them fit (24, 12, or six, respectively).

In the resulting organization window, drag the bookmarks up and down. Figure 20-4 also shows you how to perform more dramatic management tasks, like editing, renaming, or deleting bookmarks.

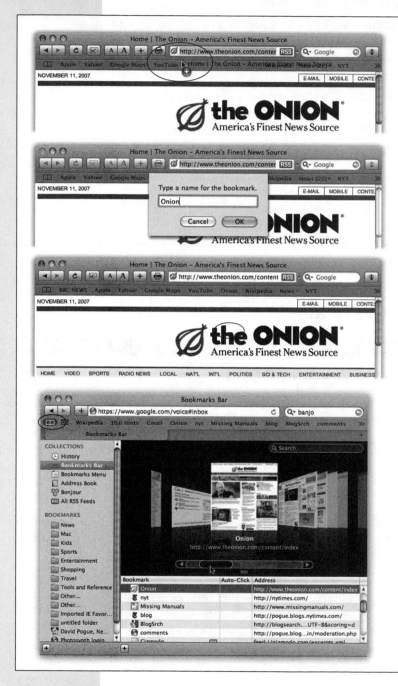

Figure 20-4:

Top: Once you've got a juicy Web page on the screen, you can drag its tiny page-logo icon (as circled) from the address bar directly onto the Bookmarks bar or menu.

Second from top: Safari realizes that you may prefer a shorter name to appear on the space-limited bar, so it offers you the chance to type in a label you prefer.

Third from top: When you click OK, the new button appears on the bar, as shown here. (You can also drag any link to the bar, such as a blue underlined phrase from a Web page, or even an icon from your desktop!) To remove a button, drag it off the bar; to rearrange the icons, just drag them.

Bottom: Click the ⌨ icon (circled) to open the Organize Bookmarks window. Here, you can drag names up or down to rearrange the list, or drag them into a "folder" that becomes a submenu in the Bookmarks menu. (Create a submenu by clicking the + button below the list.) You can edit a bookmark by clicking once on its name or URL, or delete one by pressing Delete.

- **Bookmarks Bar.** Hides or shows the horizontal toolbar that lists your favorite bookmarks. (The equivalent of choosing View→Bookmarks Bar).

- **AutoFill.** Click this button to make Safari fill in Web order forms with your name, address, and other information. See the box on page 748.

- **Text Size.** You can adjust the point size of a Web page's text using these buttons. When you visit a Web site designed for Windows computers—whose text often looks too small on Mac screens—you can use these buttons to bump up the size. The keyboard shortcuts are ⌘-plus or ⌘-minus.

- **Open in Dashboard.** This icon is the key to creating Dashboard *Web clips,* as described on page 215. Click this button, and then select the part of the page you want to widgetize. It's the equivalent of the File→Open in Dashboard command.

- **Mail.** Opens a new, outgoing email message in your email program. The Subject line contains the *name* of the site you were visiting; the body contains a link to it. You can address the message, add a comment ("Re: your comment that 'no expert' recommends trampolines for children"), and send it.

- **Stop/Reload.** Click the Stop button (or Esc, or ⌘-period) to interrupt the downloading of a Web page you've just requested (if you've made a mistake, for instance).

  Once a page has finished loading, the Stop button turns into a Refresh button. Click this circular arrow (or press ⌘-R) if a page doesn't look or work quite right, or if you want to see the updated version of a Web page (such as a breaking-news site) that changes constantly. Safari redownloads the Web page and reinterprets its text and graphics.

- **Google Search.** Here's one of Safari's most profoundly useful features—a Search box that automatically sends your search request to Google.com, the world's most popular Web search page. Press Option-⌘-F to deposit your insertion point inside this rounded text box, type something you're looking for—*phony baloney,* say—and then press Return. Safari takes you directly to the Google results page.

Tip: The tiny ▾ at the left end of the Google bar is a pop-up menu. It offers two categories of listings, in hopes of saving you time and typing. First, there are Suggested Searches (you may notice that these pop up automatically as you type into the Search box, too). These suggestions come from Google's own Suggest feature. The second category: your most recent searches.

Bonus Tip: If you Control-click (or right-click) a highlighted word or phrase on a Web page, you can choose Google Search from the shortcut menu to search for that text. And, even cooler, this trick works in all Cocoa programs—not just Safari.

- **Print.** You can add a printer icon to Safari for point-and-click paper action if you don't want to bother with ⌘-P.

Tip: Safari automatically shrinks your printouts, if necessary, by up to 10 percent, if doing so will avoid printing a second page with just one or two lines of text on it. Nice.

- **Downloads.** This button opens your Downloads window, which shows the progress of whatever file you're downloading, shows your history of recent downloads, and contains double-clickable icons of the downloads that let you jump right to them on the hard drive.

Tip: In Safari→Preferences→General, you can opt to have your download listings removed from the Downloads window as soon as they've been successfully downloaded. You might want to do that for privacy reasons, or just because there's no reason to keep looking at them in the list once they're done.

- **Report Bug.** Ladies and gentlemen, this is Apple at its most humble. This insect-shaped button opens a tiny "Dear Apple" box, where you can tell Apple about a Safari feature or Web page that doesn't work. If you click Options, you can even send Apple a screen illustration of, for example, a screwy Web-page layout that Safari delivered.

Bookmarks bar

The Bookmarks menu is one way to maintain a list of Web sites you visit frequently. But opening a Web page from that menu requires *two mouse clicks*—an exorbitant expenditure of energy. The Bookmarks bar (View→Bookmarks Bar), on the other hand, lets you summon a few *very* favorite Web pages with only one click.

Tip: If you have a bunch of bookmarks stored in another Web browser, use that browser's export feature to save them to a file, and then use Safari's File→Import Bookmarks command to save you the time of re-entering the bookmarks by hand.

Figure 20-4 illustrates how to add buttons to, and remove them from, this toolbar.

Tip: As shown in Figure 20-4, you can drag a link from a Web page onto your Bookmarks bar. But you can also drag a link directly to the desktop, where it turns into an Internet location file. Thereafter, to launch your browser and visit the associated Web page whenever you like, just double-click this icon.

Better yet, stash a few of these icons in your Dock or Sidebar for even easier access.

Status Bar

The Status bar at the bottom of the window tells you what Safari is doing (such as "Opening page…" or "Done"). When you point to a link without clicking, the Status bar also tells you which URL will open if you click it. For those two reasons, it's a very useful strip, but it doesn't appear when you first run Safari. You have to summon it by choosing View→Show Status Bar.

Tips for Better Surfing

Safari is filled with shortcuts and tricks for better speed and more pleasant surfing. For example:

SnapBack

The little orange SnapBack button (◂), which sometimes appears at the right end of the address bar or Google search bar, takes you instantly back to the Web page whose address you last typed (or whose bookmark you last clicked), or to your first Google results page.

The point here is that, after burrowing from one link to another in pursuit of some Google result or Amazon listing, you can return to your starting point without having to mash the Back button over and over again. (The SnapBack button doesn't appear until you've actually clicked away from the first page you visited.)

Snow Leopard Spots: What happened? Apple was so excited when it invented SnapBack—but in Safari 4, SnapBack has been snapped back a bit. There's no longer a keyboard shortcut to snap back, no longer a way to mark any random page as your "SnapBack" page.

Still, you can always hit the Delete key (or ⌘-◂) to go back a page, or Shift-Delete (⌘-▸) to go forward. Those should ease the sting a bit.

Stifle Pop-Ups and Pop-Unders

The world's smarmiest advertisers inundate us with *pop-up* and *pop-under* ads—nasty little windows that appear in front of the browser window or, worse, behind it, waiting to jump out the moment you close your current window. They're often deceptive, masquerading as error messages or dialog boxes, and they'll do absolutely anything to get you to click inside them.

If this kind of thing is driving you crazy, choose Safari→Block Pop-Up Windows, so that a checkmark appears next to the command. It's a war out there—but at least you now have some ammunition.

Note: This feature doesn't squelch small windows that pop up when you click a link—only windows that appear unbidden.

Even unbidden windows, however, are sometimes legitimate (and not ads)—notices of new banking features, warnings that the instructions to use a site have changed, and so on. Safari can't tell these from ads and stifles them, too. So if a site you trust says, "Please turn off pop-up blockers and reload this page," then you know you're probably missing out on a useful pop-up message.

And one more thing: These days, the evildoers of the Internet have begun to create pop-up windows using nonstandard programming code that Safari and other browsers can't do anything about. Fortunately, they're still fairly rare.

Three Ways to Magnify Web Text

If it seems as though a lot of Web sites are designed with type that's too small to read; it's not just you and your aging eyes. Macs and Windows come with different screen resolutions, so a site designed for one kind of computer may look too small on another.

CHAPTER 20: SAFARI

755

Fortunately, Safari is extremely well equipped to help you with this problem. In fact, it offers three different solutions:

- **Enlarge the screen.** Press ⌘-plus or ⌘-minus to enlarge or reduce the entire Web page. Or use the two-finger "spread" gesture on your laptop trackpad. Or use the Zoom button, if you've added it to your toolbar. The advantage of this method is that the whole Web page's layout remains proportional.

- **Blow up just the text.** If you turn on View→Zoom Text Only, then all those short-cuts serve to magnify or shrink *only the text* on your page. Graphics remain at their original size. You're now distorting the original layout, but you're maximizing the amount of reading you can do before you have to scroll.

- **Specify a minimum type size.** This may be the best option of all, because it saves you all that zooming. Open Safari→Preferences→Advanced, and set the "Never use font sizes smaller than" option to, for example, 14 points. Now *every* Web page shows up with legible text. (Except a few oddballs that use weird coding to prevent text-size changing.)

Keyboard Control

Efficiency freaks generally prefer keyboard shortcuts to using the mouse, so Safari is filled with them.

Press Tab to jump from one text box or pop-up menu to the next on your Web page. Add the Option key to jump from one *link* to another (and when you highlight a link, press Return to "click" it).

Tip: For a shockingly complete list of Safari's keyboard shortcuts, open the Help menu. In the search box at the top of the menu, type *Safari shortcuts*. Wait a moment. Click "Safari shortcuts" in the list of Help topics.

Impersonating Internet Explorer

Sooner or later, you'll run into a Web site that doesn't work in Safari. Why? When you arrive at a Web site, your browser identifies itself. That's because many commercial Web sites display a different version of the page depending on the browser you're us-ing, thanks to differences in the way various browsers interpret Web layouts.

But because you're one of the minority oddballs using Safari, your otherwise beloved Web site tells you: "Sorry, browser not supported." (Will this problem change now that Apple has released a Windows version of Safari? We can only hope.)

In such times of trouble, you can make Safari *impersonate* any other browser, which is often good enough to fool the picky Web site into letting you in.

The key to this trick is Safari's Develop menu, which is generally hidden. You can make it appear by choosing Safari→Preferences→Advanced tab. Turn on "Show Develop menu in menu bar."

The new Develop menu appears right next to Bookmarks. Most of its commands are designed to appeal to programmers, but the submenu you want—User Agent—is useful to everyone. It lets Safari masquerade as a different browser. Choose User Agent→Internet Explorer 7.0, for example, to assume the identity of a popular Windows browser.

Tip: If you're into Web-page coding or design, you should know that Safari's Develop menu also houses the Web Inspector. Control-click (or right-click) any part of a Web page—image, text, link—and choose Inspect Element from the shortcut menu.

The Web Inspector highlights the element you clicked and opens a window so you can see every little bit of HTML coding that went into putting that item on the page. You also see the style sheets, images, and other files displayed in the Inspector's window—making it really easy to see (and learn) how the page was made.

Faster Browsing Without Graphics

Graphics are part of what makes the Web so compelling. But they're also responsible for making Web pages take so long to arrive on the screen. Without them, Web pages appear almost instantaneously—and you still get fully laid-out Web pages with all their text and headlines.

To turn off graphics, choose Safari→Preferences→Appearance tab. Turn off "Display images when the page opens," and close the Preferences window. Now try visiting a few Web pages and enjoy the substantial speed boost. (If you wind up on a Web page that's nothing without its pictures, then return to Safari→Preferences, turn the same checkbox on, and then reload the page.)

Where am I?

As you dig your way down into a Web site, you may wish you had left a trail of bread crumbs to mark your path. Ah, but Safari has already thought of that. See Figure 20-5.

Figure 20-5:
If you ⌘-click the title bar (centered just above the address bar), Safari displays the "ladder" of pages you descended to arrive at the current one.

Viewing Web Pages Offline

You don't have to be connected to the Net to read a favorite Web page. You can save it on your hard drive so you can peruse it later—on your laptop during your commute, for example—just by choosing File→Save As.

To save the *entire* page, along with all its images, movies, and so on, choose Web Archive from the Format pop-up menu. (Choose Page Source only if you intend to *edit* the raw HTML Web documents and then repost them, or if you just want to study the underlying code.)

As a handy bonus, in Snow Leopard, Quick Look now recognizes Safari sites you save in this way.

Tip: When you buy something online, don't waste paper by printing out the final "This is your receipt" page. Instead, choose File→Print and, from the PDF pop-up button, choose Save PDF to Web Receipts folder. Safari saves it as a PDF file into a tidy folder (in your Home→Documents folder) called Web Receipts. Nice touch!

Expanding Web Forms

If the customer-service comment form on that corporate Web site doesn't give you enough room to rant properly, you can resize the text box right on the page—a *very* welcome feature in Snow Leopard. Figure 20-6 tells all.

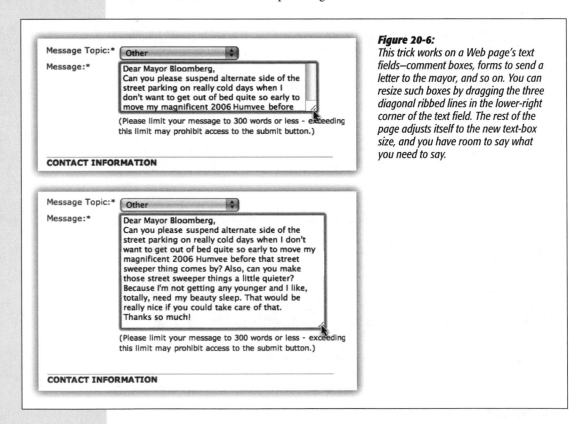

Figure 20-6:
This trick works on a Web page's text fields–comment boxes, forms to send a letter to the mayor, and so on. You can resize such boxes by dragging the three diagonal ribbed lines in the lower-right corner of the text field. The rest of the page adjusts itself to the new text-box size, and you have room to say what you need to say.

Sending a Page to a Friend

Safari provides two ways of telling a friend about the page you're looking at. You might find that useful when you come across a particularly interesting news story, op-ed piece, or burrito recipe.

- **The send-the-whole-page method.** While looking at a page, choose File→Mail Contents of This Page (⌘-I) to open a new Mail message with a copy of the *actual* Web page in the body. Address the message and click Send.

- **The send-a-link method.** To send just a *link* to the page you're looking at, choose File→Mail Link to This Page (Shift-⌘-I). Then proceed as usual, addressing the message and clicking Send.

  Links take only a split second for your recipient to download, and they're guaranteed to display properly in all email programs. All your recipients have to do is click the link to open it in their Web browsers.

Designate Your Start Page

What's the first thing you see when you open Safari? Is it the Apple news Web site? Is it the Top Sites display (Figure 20-3)?

Actually, that's up to you.

Choose Safari→Preferences→General tab. Here, the "New windows open with" pop-up menu offers choices like these:

- **Top Sites.** The thumbnail view of your favorites sites makes a great starting point.

- **Home Page.** If you choose this option, then Safari will open up with whatever page you've specified in the "Home page" box. Google—or its news page, *http://news.google.com*—is a good starting place. So is your favorite newspaper home page, or *www.macsurfer.com,* a summary of the day's Mac news coverage around the world, or maybe *www.dilbert.com* for today's Dilbert cartoon.

  If you're already *on* the page you like, just click Set to Current Page.

- **Empty Page.** Some people prefer this setup, which makes Safari load very quickly when you first open it. Once this empty window opens, *then* you can tell the browser where you want to go today.

- **Bookmarks.** Whenever you open a new window or launch Safari, you see your full list of bookmarks. You can then choose exactly which page you want to open.

- **Tabs for Bookmarks Bar.** This intriguing new option creates a row of tabs in a single window—one for *every* icon on your Bookmarks bar. The idea, of course, is to have not just one favorite Web page waiting for you in the morning, but *all* the ones you visit frequently, pre-loaded and ready to go.

- **Choose Bookmarks folder.** This option is similar to "Tabs for Bookmarks Bar," except that it starts you off with tabs for *any* random bunch of Web sites—not just the ones on your Bookmarks bar. The trick is to build a *folder* full of bookmarks (Figure 20-4), and choose *that* as the basis for your auto-opening tabs.

Note: An identical pop-up menu is available for "New tabs open window." That is, you can specify one starter-page preference for new tabs and another for new windows.

Finding Text on Web Pages

The Google search bar can help you find Web sites that match your keywords. But some pages are so long, dense, or poorly designed that finding the words *on* the page needs a whole 'nother search engine. Fortunately, Safari's search-within-the-page function shines a light on the words or phrase you're seeking.

To use it, press ⌘-F and then type your search word into the Find box (Figure 20-7). As Safari locates the word or words, it displays them within a bright yellow box and dims the background of the rest of the page. The Find bar also tells you how many times the word or phrase occurs on the page; you can jump to each instance. Click the ⊗ to start over with new search terms, or click Done to close the Find bar and return to your normal browsing activity.

Figure 20-7:
Once you enter your keywords (Eagles, in this case), the browser dims the page and highlights every instance of that word— making it much easier to find what you're looking for across a crowded Web page.

The History Menu

The History menu lists the Web sites you've visited in the past week or so, neatly organized into subfolders like "Earlier Today" and "Yesterday." (A similar menu appears when you click *and hold* on the Back or Forward button.) These are great features if you can't recall the URL for a Web site you remember having visited recently.

Tip: See Safari's Help menu? It features a Search box that lets you search all the menu commands in Safari—including Safari's History menu. That's just a crazy powerful feature. It means you can re-find a site without having to hunt through all the History submenus manually; just search for a word you remember in the title.

You can also view your History in a more expansive view—in Cover Flow view, in fact—by clicking the ⌘ at the left end of your toolbar. You enter the Bookmarks-management view, described in Figure 20-4.

Tip: Having History available in the Bookmarks window is very handy, because you can drag a Web page from your History into your Bookmarks menu, folder, or bar. That is, you can bookmark a Web site long after your initial visit.

Zoom in on PDF Pages

PDF files are all over the Web as, among other things, forms to download, online brochures, and scanned book pages. But they aren't always especially readable in a browser window.

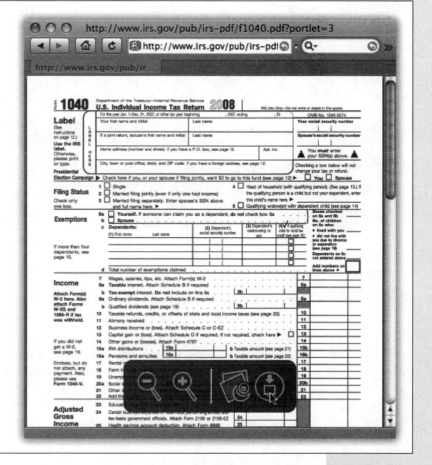

Figure 20-8:
If you're having trouble reading the tiny type in a PDF, hover your mouse at the bottom of it to invoke Safari's PDF toolbar. You can zoom out, zoom in, open the file in the Mac's Preview program, or even download it from the Web site with a well-placed click.

Unless, that is, you're using Safari. The next time you're squinting at a PDF in the window, point to the bottom edge of the document; you'll see a toolbar appear like the one in Figure 20-8. With these four icons, you can zoom out, zoom in, open the file in Preview, or save the PDF file itself to your Downloads folder.

Tabbed Browsing

Beloved by hardcore surfers the world over, *tabbed browsing* is a way to keep a bunch of Web pages open simultaneously—in a single, neat window. Figure 20-9 illustrates.

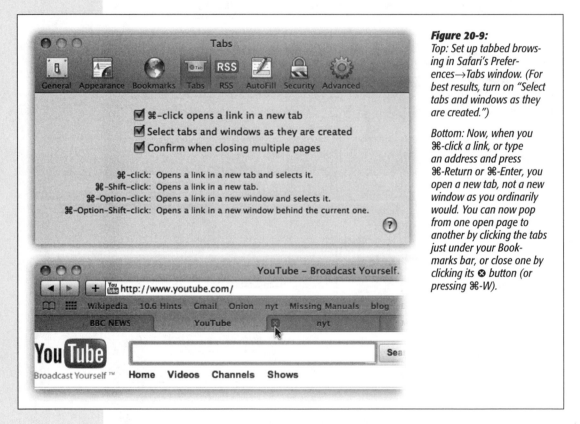

Figure 20-9:
Top: Set up tabbed browsing in Safari's Preferences→Tabs window. (For best results, turn on "Select tabs and windows as they are created.")

Bottom: Now, when you ⌘-click a link, or type an address and press ⌘-Return or ⌘-Enter, you open a new tab, not a new window as you ordinarily would. You can now pop from one open page to another by clicking the tabs just under your Bookmarks bar, or close one by clicking its ⊗ button (or pressing ⌘-W).

Turning on tabbed browsing unlocks a whole raft of Safari shortcuts and tricks, which are just the sort of thing power surfers gulp down like Gatorade:

- If there's a certain set of Web sites you like to visit daily, put the bookmarks into one folder, using Bookmarks→Add Bookmark Folder and the Bookmarks organizer window (Figure 20-4). You can then load all of them into a single tabbed window, simply by selecting the resulting "folder" in the Bookmarks menu—or the Bookmarks bar—and choosing Open in Tabs from the submenu.

The beauty of this arrangement is that you can start reading the first Web page while all the others load into their own tabs in the background.

Tip: Click the ⌘ icon at the left end of the Bookmarks bar. In the Bookmarks organizer, click the Bookmarks Bar item in the left-side list. Now you can see an Auto-Click checkbox for each listed folder.

If you turn on this checkbox, then you'll be able to open all the bookmarks in that folder into tabs, all at once, merely by clicking the folder's name in the Bookmarks bar. (If you want to summon the normal menu from the folder, just hold the mouse button down.)

- A variation on a theme: When you have a bunch of pages open in tabs, you can drag the tabs across the window to rearrange the order. When you have them the way you want them, Control-click (or right-click) a tab, and then choose Add Bookmark for These [*Number*] Tabs from the shortcut menu. You can save your saved tabs to the Bookmarks bar and load all those pages with one click.

FREQUENTLY ASKED QUESTION

Erasing Your Tracks—and Private Browsing

So, about this History menu: I'd just as soon my wife/husband/boss/parent/kid not know what Web sites I've been visiting. Must that History menu display my movements quite so proudly?

Some people find it creepy that Safari maintains a complete list of every Web site they've seen recently, right there in plain view of any family member or coworker who wanders by.

To delete just one particularly incriminating History listing, click the ⌘ icon at the left end of the Bookmarks bar; in the resulting Bookmarks organizer window, click History. Expand the relevant date triangle, highlight the offending address, and then press your Delete key. Click ⌘ again to return to normal browsing. You've just rewritten History!

Or, to erase the entire History menu, choose History→Clear History.

Of course, the History menu isn't the only place where you've left footprints. If you choose Safari→Reset Safari instead, you also erase all other shreds of your activities: any cookies (Web-page preference files) you've accumulated, your list of past downloads, the cache files (tiny Web graphics on your hard drive that a browser stores to save time when you return to the page they came from), and so on. This is good information to know; after all, you might be nominated to the Supreme Court someday.

That's a lot of work just to cover my tracks; it also erases a lot of valuable cookies, passwords, and History entries I'd like to keep. Is all that really necessary just so I can duck in for an occasional look at the Hot Bods of the Midwestern Tax Preparers' Association Web site?

No, it's not. A feature called private browsing lets you surf without adding any pages to your History list, searches to your Google search box, passwords to Safari's saved password list, or autofill entries to Safari's memory. (Apple says this feature is intended for use at public Macs, where you don't want to reveal anything personal to subsequent visitors. Ha!)

The trick is to choose Safari→Private Browsing before you start browsing. Once you OK the explanation box, Safari records nothing while you surf. (Nothing, that is, except cookies. Your tracks, in other words, are not completely hidden. You can erase cookies, if need be, in Safari→Preferences→Security.)

When you're ready to browse "publicly" again, choose Safari→Private Browsing once more so the checkmark goes away. Safari again begins taking note of the pages you visit—but it never remembers the earlier ones.

In other words, what happens in Private Browsing stays in Private Browsing.

- If you Option-click a tab's ⊗ button, you close all the tabs *except* the one you clicked. The same thing happens if you hold down Option and choose File→Close Other Tabs, or if you press Option-⌘-W.

- If you Option-⌘-click a link, it opens in a separate window, rather than a new tab. (When tabbed browsing is turned *off*, you just ⌘-click a link to open a new window.)

- If you find yourself with a bunch of separate browser windows all over your screen, you can neatly consolidate them all into one nicely tabbed Safari window by choosing Window→Merge All Windows.

- If you Shift-⌘-click a link, Safari opens that page in a tab *behind* the one you're reading. That's a fantastic trick when you're reading a Web page and see a reference you want to set aside for reading next, but you don't want to interrupt whatever you're reading.

FREQUENTLY ASKED QUESTION

Cookie Control

Help! I'm afraid of cookies! The cookies are trying to watch me!

Cookies are something like Web page preference files. Certain Web sites—particularly commercial ones like Amazon.com—deposit them on your hard drive like little bookmarks so that they'll remember you the next time you visit. Most cookies are perfectly innocuous— and, in fact, are extremely helpful, because they help Web sites remember your tastes. Cookies also spare you the effort of having to type in your name, address, credit card number, and so on, every time you visit these Web sites.

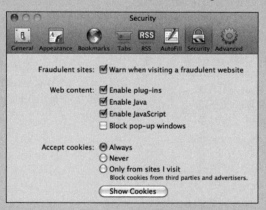

But fear is widespread, and the media fans the flames with tales of sinister cookies that track your movements on the Web. If you're worried about invasions of privacy, Safari is ready to protect you.

Once the browser is open, choose Safari→Preferences→ Security tab. The buttons in this dialog box are like a paranoia gauge. If you click Never, you create an acrylic shield around your Mac. No cookies can come in, and no cookie information can go out. You'll probably find the Web a very inconvenient place; you'll have to re-enter your information upon every visit, and some Web sites may not work properly at all.

A less-drastic choice is "Only from sites I visit," which accepts cookies from sites you want to visit but blocks cookies deposited on your hard drive by sites you're not actually visiting—cookies an especially evil banner ad gives you, for example.

Note, too, the Show Cookies button, which reveals the shockingly complete list of every cookie you've accumulated so far—and offers you the chance to delete the ones that don't look so savory.

RSS: The Missing Manual

In the beginning, the Internet was an informational Garden of Eden. There were no banner ads, pop-ups, flashy animations, or spam messages. Back then, people thought the Internet was the greatest idea ever.

Those days, unfortunately, are long gone. Web browsing now entails a constant battle against intrusive advertising and annoying animations. And with the proliferation of Web sites of every kind—from news sites to personal Web logs (*blogs*)—just reading your favorite sites can become a full-time job.

Enter RSS, a technology that lets you subscribe to *feeds*—summary blurbs provided by thousands of sources around the world, from Reuters to Apple to your nerdy next-door neighbor. You can use a program like Safari to "subscribe" to updates from such feeds and then read any new articles or postings at your leisure (Figure 20-10).

The result: You spare yourself the tedium of checking for updates manually, plus you get to read short summaries of new articles without ads and blinking animations. And if you want to read a full article, you can click its link in the RSS feed to jump straight to the main Web site.

Figure 20-10:
The Length slider controls how much text appears for each RSS blurb; if you drag it all the way to the left, you're left with nothing but headlines. To change the number and order of the articles being displayed, use the sort options on the right. And if you feel a sudden desire to tell your friends about an amazing RSS feed you've just discovered, use the "Mail Link to This Page" link in the lower-right section of the window.

Note: RSS stands for either Rich Site Summary or Really Simple Syndication. Each abbreviation explains one aspect of RSS—either its summarizing talent or its simplicity.

Viewing an RSS Feed

So how do you sign up for these free, automatic RSS "broadcasts"? Watch your address bar as you're surfing the Web. When you see a blue RSS button appear (identified back in Figure 20-1), Safari is telling you, "This site has an RSS feed available."

To see what the fuss is all about, click that button. Safari switches into RSS-viewing mode. At this point, you have two choices:

- **Add the RSS feed as a bookmark.** Use the Bookmarks→Add Bookmark command, and add the feed to your Bookmarks menu, Bookmarks bar, or Mail as you would any Web page. From now on, you'll be able to see whether the RSS feed has had any new articles posted—without actually having to visit the site. Figure 20-11 (top) has the details.

- **Close the RSS feed altogether.** To do so, just click the RSS button again. You're left back where you started, at whatever Web page you were visiting.

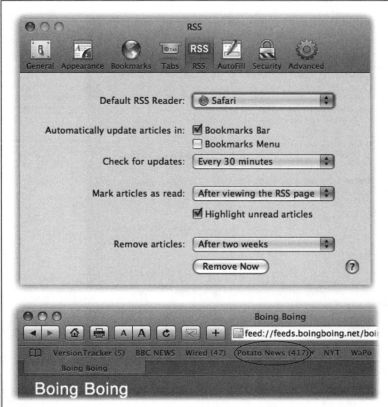

Figure 20-11:
Top: Want to specify when Safari should check for updates to your RSS bookmarks? In Safari→Preferences, click RSS. Turn on Bookmarks Bar and Bookmarks Menu. (If you're an especially impatient person, select "Every 30 minutes" from the "Check for updates" pop-up menu.)

Bottom: Next to your RSS feeds' names (in this screenshot, VersionTracker and Wired), a number tells you how many new articles are waiting for you. If you have a bookmark folder containing several RSS feeds in it (here, Potato News), the number reflects the total number of new articles in that folder's feeds. Never again will you have to check a Web site for updates the old-fashioned way.

RSS Tricks

RSS is a tremendously flexible and powerful technology, especially in Safari. The fun never ends, as these tricks illustrate.

Creating RSS summaries

If you create a new bookmark folder and fill it with RSS feeds, you can see the *total* number of new articles right next to the folder's name (Figure 20-11, bottom). You might create a folder of Mac news feeds, for instance, so you know whenever there's a important event in the Mac world.

From then on, by clicking the folder's name (and opening its pop-up menu), you can see which feeds have new articles; they're the ones with numbers next to their names. If you ⌘-click a bookmark folder's name—in either the Bookmarks bar or the Bookmarks menu—Safari shows you *all* the feeds, neatly collated into one big, easily digestible list for your perusing pleasure. (If you're billing by the hour, you can also choose View All RSS Articles from the folder's pop-up menu to achieve the same effect.)

Tip: To make the merged list more useful, click New under the Sort By heading. Now Safari displays any new articles at the top of the list, regardless of what site they came from, so you don't have to hunt through the list for new articles yourself.

The personal clipping service

The search box at the right of any RSS-viewing window works pretty much as you'd expect: It narrows down the list of articles to only those that contain your search terms.

But that's barely scratching the surface of the search field's power. If you've adopted the feed-merging trick described above, the Search box can search *several* feeds at once—perfect, for example, if you want to see all the news from Mac sites that has to do with iTunes.

Now how much would you pay? But get this—you can then save the search itself as a bookmark. Use the Bookmark This Search link at the lower-right corner of the window. Give the bookmark a name, choose where it should appear in Safari, and then click Add.

You've just turned Safari into a high-tech personal clipping service. With one click on your new bookmark, you can search all your news sources simultaneously—the feeds you've selected—for the terms you want. You've just saved yourself *hours* of daily searching—not to mention the expense of a real clipping service.

Tip: Mail can display your RSS feeds, too. Flip back to page 729 if you skipped that chapter.

The RSS screen saver

In System Preferences→Desktop & Screen Saver→Screen Saver tab, you'll find the RSS Visualizer screen saver, an impressive display indeed. When you click Options and select an RSS feed, you set up Mac OS X to get news from that feed whenever you're away from your Mac. When the screen saver comes on, you're treated to a 3-D animation of the news from that site—and astonished gazes from coworkers.

If a news story grabs your interest, press the number key mentioned at the bottom of the screen. The screen saver fades out, and Safari displays the associated article.

Tip: But what if the feed you want isn't part of Safari's repertoire? No problem. Add the feed to your Safari bookmarks and relaunch System Preferences.

Make feeds open automatically

It's easy enough to set up any favorite Web site as your start page. But you can also make an RSS feed—or a list of feeds—your home page. Open the feeds you want, choose Safari→Preferences→General tab, click Set to Current Page, and choose "Home Page" from the "New windows open with" pop-up menu.

In other words, suppose you start by opening a list of local, national, international, business, and sports news feeds. In that case, you've just made yourself a fantastic imitation of newspaper headlines, but tailored to *your* interests with spectacular precision: The Francis J. McQuaid Times (or whatever your name is).

Tip: If you've turned on tabbed browsing, you can Shift-⌘-click headlines. That makes the full articles open in background tabs while you continue to read the headlines.

Articles in this arrangement are timelier than anything you could read in print—and they're free. If you miss a day of reading the headlines, no problem; they stick around for days and disappear only once you've read them. Finally, when you're done reading, you don't have to worry about recycling your "newspaper." No trees were harmed in the making of this publication. Welcome to the future of news: customized, free, up-to-date, and paperless.

Tip: To find more RSS feeds, visit a site like *www.syndic8.com*, or just watch for the appearance of the blue RSS button in the address bar. And if you want more power in an RSS reader, try out a program like NetNewsWire (*http://ranchero.com/netnewswire/*), which offers many more power-user features.

iChat

Somewhere between email and the telephone lies a unique communication tool called *instant messaging*. Plenty of instant messenger programs run on the Mac, but guess what? You don't really need any of them. Mac OS X comes with its very own instant messenger program called iChat, built right into the system and ready to connect to your friends on the AIM, Jabber, or GoogleTalk networks.

In Snow Leopard, iChat was the focus of a lot of refinement and polish. Video conversations now require much lower bandwidth, meaning that slower Internet connections may now be eligible to try out video chats. The window for iChat Theater (when you show a movie or slideshow presentation to someone on the other end) can now be four times as big as before (640 × 480 pixels, for example). And so on.

To start up iChat, go to Applications→iChat, or just click iChat's Dock icon. This chapter covers how to use iChat to communicate by video, audio, and text with your online pals.

Welcome to iChat

iChat does five things very well:

- **Instant messaging.** If you don't know what instant messaging is, there's a teenager near you who does.

  It's like live email. You type messages in a chat window, and your friends type replies back to you in real time. Instant messaging combines the privacy of email and the immediacy of the phone.

In this regard, iChat is a lot like the popular AOL Instant Messenger (AIM) and Buddy Chats. In fact, iChat lets you type back and forth with any of AIM's 150 million members, which is a huge advantage. (It speaks the same "chat" language as AIM.) But iChat's visual design is pure Apple.

- **Free long distance.** If your Mac has a microphone, and your buddy's does, too, the two of you can also chat *out loud,* using the Internet as a free long-distance phone. Wait, not just the two of you—the *10* of you, thanks to iChat's party-line feature.

- **Free videoconferencing.** If you and your buddies all have broadband Internet connections and a camera—like the one built into many Mac models—or even a digital camcorder, up to four participants can join in *video* chats, all onscreen at once, no matter where they happen to be in the world. This arrangement is a jaw-dropping visual stunt that can bring distant collaborators face to face without plane tickets— and it costs about $99,900 less than professional videoconferencing gear.

- **File transfers.** Got an album of high-quality photos or a giant presentation file that's too big to send by email? Forget about using some online file-transfer service or networked server; you can drag that monster file directly to your buddy's Mac, through iChat, for a direct machine-to-machine transfer. (It lands in the other Mac's Downloads folder.)

- **Presentations.** You can open up most kinds of documents, at nearly full size, to show your video buddy, right there in the iChat window, without actually having to transfer it. That's iChat Theater.

Three Chat Networks

iChat lets you reach out to chat partners on three networks:

- **The AIM network.** If you've signed up for a MobileMe address (the paid kind or the free kind described below) or a free AOL Instant Messenger (AIM) account, you can chat with anyone in the 150 million-member AOL Instant Messenger network.

- **The Jabber network.** Jabber is a chat network whose key virtue is its *open-source* origins. In other words, it wasn't masterminded by some corporate media behemoth; it's an all-volunteer effort, joined by thousands of programmers all over the world. There's no one Jabber chat program (like AOL Instant Messenger). There are dozens, available for Mac OS X, Windows, Linux, Unix, iPhone, Palm organizers, and so on. They can all chat with one another across the Internet in one glorious frenzy of typing.

  And now there's one more program that can join the party: iChat.

- **Google Talk.** Evidently, Google felt that there just weren't enough different chat programs, because it released its own in 2005.

Behind the scenes, it uses the Jabber network, so Google Talk doesn't really count as a different *network*. (Hence the headline.) But it does mean you can use iChat to converse with all those Google Talkers, too.

- **Your own local network.** Thanks to the Bonjour network-recognition technology, you can communicate with other Macs on your own office network without signing up for anything at all—and without being online. This is a terrific feature when you're sitting around a conference table, idly chatting with colleagues using your wireless laptop (and the boss thinks you're taking notes). It's also handy when you want to type little messages throughout the day to a family member downstairs, or a roommate 15 feet away.

Each network generally has its own separate Buddy List window and its own chat window, but you *can* consolidate all your chats into a single window (page 778).

You log into each network separately using the iChat→Accounts submenu, but you can be logged into all of them at once. This is a great option if your friends are spread out among different chat networks.

Note: If you're on AOL's AIM service, why would you want to use iChat instead? Easy: Because iChat is a nice, cleanly designed program that's free of advertisements, chatbots, and clunky interface elements.

Otherwise, however, chatting and videoconferencing works identically on all three networks. Keep that in mind as you read the following pages.

Signing Up

When you open iChat for the first time, you see the "Welcome To iChat" window (Figure 21-1). This is the first of several screens in the iChat setup sequence, during which you're supposed to tell it which kinds of chat accounts you have and set up your camera, if any.

An *account* is a name and password. Fortunately, these accounts are free, and there are several ways to acquire one.

Tip: The easiest procedure is to set up your accounts before you open iChat for the first time, because then you can just plug in your names and passwords in the setup screens.

You can input your account information later, though. Choose iChat→Preferences, click the Accounts button, click the **+** button, and choose the right account type (Jabber, MobileMe, Google Talk, or AIM) from the Account Type pop-up menu.

How to Get a Free MobileMe Account

If you're already a member of Apple's MobileMe service (Chapter 18), iChat fills in your member name and password automatically.

If not, you can get an iChat-only MobileMe account for free. To get started, do one of these two things:

- Click the "Get an iChat Account" button that appears on the second Setup Assistant screen.

- Choose iChat→Preferences, click the Accounts button, click the **+** button, and click Create New MobileMe Account.

Either way, you go to an Apple Web page, where you can sign up for a free iChat account name. You also get 60 days of the more complete MobileMe treatment (usually $100 a year) described in Chapter 18. When your trial period ends, you lose all the other stuff MobileMe provides, but you do get to keep your iChat name.

Note: If your MobileMe name is missingmanualguy, you'll appear to everyone else as missingmanualguy@mac.com. The software tacks on the "@me.com" suffix automatically.

Figure 21-1:
The iChat setup assistant gives you the chance to input your account names and passwords if you already have them. Only one of these screens ("Set up iChat Instant messaging") offers you the chance to create a chat account, in this case a free MobileMe account. Otherwise, you're expected to have a name and password (for AIM, Google Talk, or Jabber, for example) already.

How to Get a Free Jabber (or Gmail) Account

You can't create a Jabber account using iChat. Apple expects that, if you're that interested in Jabber, you already have an account that's been set up by the company you work for (Jabber is popular in corporations) or by you, using one of the free Jabber programs.

Alternatively, you can just sign up for a free Google Talk account, which is the same as having a free Gmail account. (Go to Gmail.com to sign up for one.)

Once you've got a Gmail address, choose iChat→Preferences→Accounts, and click the **+** button. Under Account Type, choose Google Talk and type in your complete Gmail address (like *gwashington@gmail.com)* and password. Your Gmail name pops up on iChat's Jabber list—along with any of your Gmail contacts who are already online and yapping.

How to Get a Free AIM Account

If you're an America Online member, your existing screen name and password work; if you've used AIM before, you can use your existing name and password.

If you've never had an AIM account, then choose AIM from the Account Type pop-up menu, and then click Get an iChat Account. You're taken to the Web, where you can make up an AIM screen name.

The Buddy Lists

Once you've entered your account information, you're technically ready to start chatting. All you need now is a chatting companion, or what's called a *buddy* in instant-messaging circles. iChat comes complete with a Buddy List window where you can house the chat "addresses" for all your friends, relatives, and colleagues out there on the Internet.

Actually, to be precise, iChat comes with *three* Buddy Lists (Figure 21-2):

- **AIM Buddy List.** This window lists all your chat pals who have *either* MobileMe or AIM accounts; they all share the same Buddy List. You see the same list whether you log into MobileMe or your AIM account.

Snow Leopard Spots: You can now conduct audio and video chats with other AIM members, Mac or PC. They just need the latest version of the AIM program—and, of course, a Webcam.

- **Jabber List.** Same idea, except that all your contacts in this window must have Jabber or Google Talk accounts.

- **Bonjour.** This list is limited to your local network buddies—the ones in the same building, most likely, and on the same network. You can't add names to your Bonjour list; anyone who's on the network and running iChat appears automatically in the Bonjour list.

Making a List

When you start iChat, your Buddy Lists automatically appear (Figure 21-2). If you don't see them, choose the list you want from the Window menu: [Your MobileMe/AIM account], Bonjour List, or Jabber List. (Or press their keyboard shortcuts: ⌘-1, ⌘-2, or ⌘-3.)

Adding a buddy to this list entails knowing that person's account name, whether it's on AIM, MobileMe, or Jabber. Once you have it, you can either choose Buddies→Add Buddy (Shift-⌘-A) or click the **+** button at the bottom-left corner of the window.

Down slides a sheet attached to the Buddy List window, offering a window into the Address Book program (Chapter 19).

Tip: As you accumulate buddies, your Buddy List may become crowded. If you choose View→Show Offline Buddies (so that the checkmark disappears), only your currently online buddies show up in the Buddy List—a much more meaningful list for the temporarily lonely.

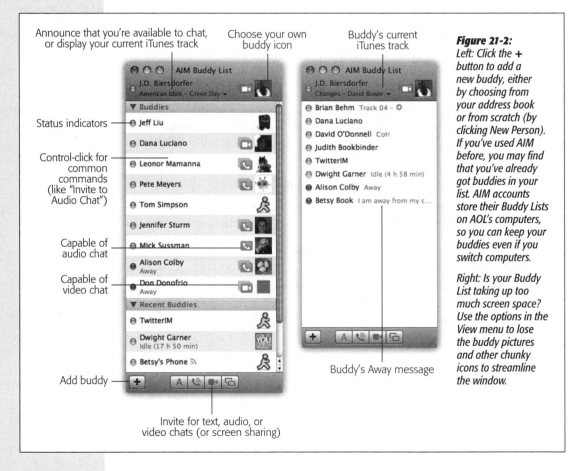

Announce that you're available to chat, or display your current iTunes track

Choose your own buddy icon

Buddy's current iTunes track

Status indicators

Control-click for common commands (like "Invite to Audio Chat")

Capable of audio chat

Capable of video chat

Add buddy

Invite for text, audio, or video chats (or screen sharing)

Buddy's Away message

Figure 21-2:
*Left: Click the **+** button to add a new buddy, either by choosing from your address book or from scratch (by clicking New Person). If you've used AIM before, you may find that you've already got buddies in your list. AIM accounts store their Buddy Lists on AOL's computers, so you can keep your buddies even if you switch computers.*

Right: Is your Buddy List taking up too much screen space? Use the options in the View menu to lose the buddy pictures and other chunky icons to streamline the window.

If your chat companion is already in Address Book, scroll through the list until you find the name you want (or enter the first few letters into the Search box), click the name, and then click Select Buddy.

If not, click New Person and enter the buddy's AIM address, MobileMe address, or (if you're in the Jabber list) Jabber address. You're adding this person to both your Buddy List and to your Address Book.

Broadcasting Your Status

Using the pop-up menu just below your name (Figure 21-3, right), you can display your current mental status to *other* people's Buddy Lists. You can announce that you're Available, Away, or Drunk. (You have to choose Edit Status Menu for that last one; see Figure 21-3, left.)

Better yet, if you have music playing in iTunes, you can tell the world what you're listening to at the moment by choosing Current iTunes Song. (Your buddy can even click that song's name to open its screen on the iTunes Store, all for Instant Purchase Gratification.)

For some people, by far the juiciest status option is Invisible (available for MobileMe and AIM accounts only). It's like a *Star Trek* cloaking device for your onscreen presence (Figure 21-3). Great for stalkers!

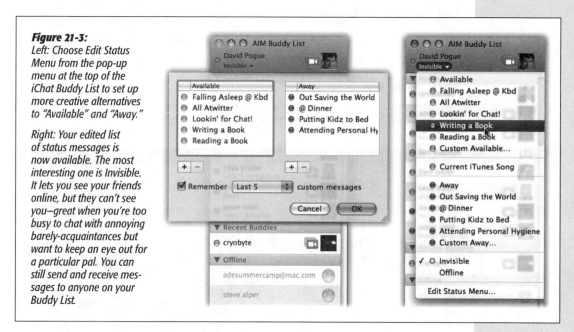

Figure 21-3:
Left: Choose Edit Status Menu from the pop-up menu at the top of the iChat Buddy List to set up more creative alternatives to "Available" and "Away."

Right: Your edited list of status messages is now available. The most interesting one is Invisible. It lets you see your friends online, but they can't see you—great when you're too busy to chat with annoying barely-acquaintances but want to keep an eye out for a particular pal. You can still send and receive messages to anyone on your Buddy List.

Sorting and Sizing your Friends

In View→Sort Buddies, you can rearrange your buddies as they're listed in the Buddy Lists:

- **By Availability.** Your available pals move to the top of the list, sorted alphabetically by last name. Unavailable buddies (marked by red dots and visible Away messages) get shoved to the bottom.

- **By First Name, By Last Name.** Just what you'd think.

- **Manually.** This option lets you drag your friends up and down your Buddy List in order of your purely personal preferences, regardless of the alphabet.

Tip: In View→Buddy Names, you can chose to see your friends listed by Full Names, Short Names (usually the first name), or by Handle (IM screen name). If your Buddy List is showing screen names ("jdeaux444") mixed in with proper names ("Johann Deux"), it's because you haven't recorded the real-nameless people's real names. Click a buddy's name, choose Buddies→Show Info, then click Address Card to fill in the person's first and last names.

Once you get a lot of people piled on your list, all with their buddy pictures and audio/video chat icons, you may feel like iChat is taking up way too much screen real estate. If you want a more space-efficient view of your Buddy List (like the one shown on the right in Figure 21-2), go to the View menu and turn off Show Buddy Pictures, Show Audio Status, or Show Video Status. You can turn off Buddy Groups here as well, if you'd prefer to see your buddies in one undivided list.

Let the Chat Begin

As with any conversation, somebody has to talk first. In chat circles, that's called *inviting* someone to a chat.

They Invite You

To "turn on your pager" so you'll be notified when someone wants to chat with you, run iChat. Hide its windows, if you like, by pressing ⌘-H.

GEM IN THE ROUGH

Making iChat Auto-Answer

When you invite another Mac to a video chat, someone has to be sitting in front of it to accept your invitation. That's an important privacy feature, of course, because it prevents total strangers from peeking in on you when you're walking around in your underwear.

But having to have a live human at the other end is kind of a bummer if you just want to peek in on your house, your kids, or your spouse while you're away, using your iSight camera or camcorder as a sort of security cam or nannycam. In the pre-Leopard days, you

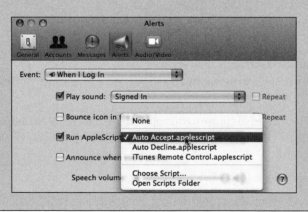

could set up iChat to auto-answer your video-chat invitations only by using add-on software or geekster Terminal commands.

Since Leopard, though, that option has been available right out of the box.

Choose iChat→Preferences→Alerts and then turn on Run AppleScript script. From the adjoining pop-up menu, choose Auto Accept.

From now on, iChat will love all your buddies and accept their invites immediately.

When someone tries to "page" you for a chat, iChat comes forward automatically and shows you an invitation message like the one in Figure 21-4. If the person initiating a chat isn't already in your Buddy List, you'll simply see a note that says "Message from *[name of the person]*."

Tip: If you're getting hassled by someone on your AIM/MobileMe Buddy List, click his screen name and choose Buddies→Block Person. If the person isn't online at the time, go to iChat→Preferences→Accounts→Security and click the button for "Block specific people." Click the Edit List button, and then type in the screen name of the person you want out of your IM life.

Figure 21-4:
You're being invited to a chat! Your buddy wants to have a typed chat (top left) or a spoken one (top right). To begin chatting, click the invitation window, type a response in the bottom text box if you like (for text chats), and click Accept (or press Return). Or click Decline to lock out the person sending you messages—a good trick if someone's harassing you.

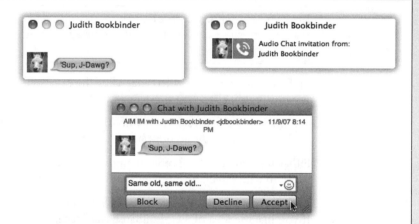

iTunes by Remote Control

Thanks to some sneaky AppleScripting (Chapter 7), you can use iChat as a glorified music-system remote control for another Mac. Specifically, you can sit at Mac #1, controlling the iTunes playback of Mac #2 elsewhere in the house. That's handy when Mac #2 is connected to your sound system, and you really don't feel like getting up off the couch.

To set it all up, start on Mac #1, the one you'll be using in person. In iChat, choose iChat→Preferences→Accounts. Click Bonjour, and turn on Use Bonjour Instant Messaging. Close the window.

On Mac #2, the one with iTunes, open iChat. Choose iChat→Preferences→Alerts. From the Event pop-up menu,

choose Message Received. Turn on Run AppleScript Script on this Mac, and then select iTunes Remote Control from the pop-up menu.

Now, while seated at Mac #1, you can control Mac #2's music playback by typing one-word commands into iChat. You can type any of these commands: play, pause, status, next, previous, mute, unmute, or help. After you type your command (like mute when the phone rings and you're blasting Green Day), hit the Return key to make iTunes on the other Mac obey your orders.

You'll get responses in the iChat window, too. For example, if you send "next," iChat types back, "Playing next track. Now playing 'In This Diary' by The Ataris.")

You Invite Them

To invite somebody in your Buddy List to a chat:

- For a text chat, double-click the person's *name*, type a quick invite ("You there?"), and press Return.

  You can invite more than one person to the chat. Each time you click the **+** button at the bottom of the Participants list, you choose another person to invite. (Or ⌘-click each name in the Buddy List to select several people at once and then click the A button at the bottom of the list to start the text chat.) Everyone sees all the messages anyone sends.

Snow Leopard Spots: If you have more than one account (and they're turned on), then you can specify which account you want to use for this chat by clicking the ▼ next to your pal's name at the top of the invitation screen. Handy!

- To start an audio or video chat, click the microphone or movie-camera icon in your Buddy List (shown in Figure 21-2).

To initiate a chat with someone who *isn't* in the Buddy List, choose File→New Chat With Person. Type the account name, and then click OK to send the invitation.

Either way, you can have more than one chat going at once. Real iChat nerds often wind up with screens overflowing with individual chat windows.

But in modern times, you can now contain all your conversations in a single window. If you like the idea of a consolidated chatspace, choose iChat→Preferences→Messages and slap a checkmark in the "Collect chats in a single window" box. Figure 21-5 shows the result.

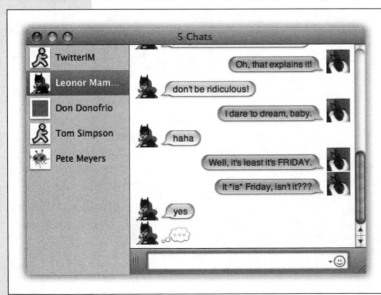

Figure 21-5:
Now, when you're conversing with several buddies, you can bounce between conversations by clicking the buddy names on the side of the window. It's not as adventurous as keeping all your chats going in separate windows, but it's a lot easier to hide when the boss comes your way.

Text Chatting

A typed chat works like this: Each time you or your chat partner types something and then presses Return, the text appears on both of your screens (Figure 21-6). iChat displays each typed comment next to an icon, which can be any of these three things:

- **A picture they added.** If the buddy added her *own* picture—to her own copy of iChat, a Jabber program, or AOL Instant Messenger—it will be transmitted to you, appearing automatically in the chat window. Cool!

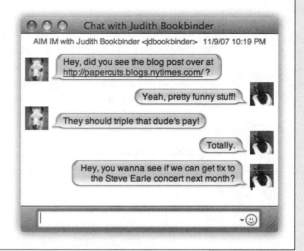

Figure 21-6:
As you chat, your comments always appear on the right. If you haven't yet created a custom icon, you'll look like a blue globe or an AOL running man. You can choose a picture for yourself either in your own Address Book card or right in iChat. And Web links your pals paste into messages are perfectly clickable–your Web browser leaps right up to take you to the site your friend has shared.

Getting Animated in iChat

Most people find the text that scrolls by quite dynamic enough. But if you need more activity in the iChat window, you can also add moving icons to liven up your Buddy List. Such an icon, an animated GIF file, is actually built of several individual frames that are played in succession, creating a crude sort of animation.

To find an animated GIF file worthy of representing you or your buddies, look online, where thousands are available. Search for them with Google, or visit sites like *www.gifanimations.com* or *www.gifs.net*.

Once you've secured a good animated GIF, add it to your iChat profile (as described on the previous page), choose iChat→Preferences→General, and then turn on "Animate buddy pictures."

You can even make your own animated GIF icons in Photo Booth (Chapter 10). Take a four-frame picture using the 4-up photo option, taking care to make four different crazy faces as the camera snaps four times.

When the four shots show up in the Photo Booth photo tray, click the Buddy Picture button to make that shot your new iChat photo.

You can assign a Photo Booth animated GIF to another buddy, too; choose File→Export from the Photo Booth menu. Save the file to your Mac and add it to your Address Book card for that pal. (Whether or not you tell your friend what image you've associated with his screen name is up to you.)

- **A picture you added.** If you've added a picture of that person to the Buddy List or Address Book, you see it here instead. (After all, your vision of what somebody looks like may not match his own self-image.)

- **Generic.** If nobody's done icon-dragging of any sort, you get a generic icon—either a blue globe (for MobileMe people), a light bulb (for Google Talkers), or the AOL Instant Messenger running man (for AIM people).

To choose a graphic to use as your own icon, click the square picture to the right of your own name at the top of the Buddy, Jabber, or Bonjour list. From the pop-up palette of recently selected pictures, choose Edit Picture to open a pop-up image-selection palette, where you can take a snapshot with your Mac's camera or choose a photo file from your hard drive. Feel free to build an array of graphics to represent yourself—and to change them in midchat, using this pop-up palette, to the delight or confusion of your conversation partner.

Tip: When you minimize the iChat message window, its Dock icon displays the icon of the person you're chatting with—a handy reminder that she's still there.

In-chat Fun

Typing isn't the only thing you can do during a chat. You can also perform any of these stunts:

- **Open the drawer.** Choose View→Show Chat Participants to hide or show the "drawer" that lists every person in your current group chat. To invite somebody new to the chat, click the **+** button at the bottom of the drawer, or drag the person's icon out of the Buddy List window and into this drawer.

- **Format your text.** You can press ⌘-B or ⌘-I to make your next typed utterance bold or italic. Or change your color or font by choosing Format→Show Colors or Format→Show Fonts, which summons the standard Mac OS X color or font palettes. (If you use some weird font that your chat partners don't have installed, they won't see the same typeface.)

- **Insert a smiley.** When you choose a face (like Undecided, Angry, or Frown) from this quick-access menu of smiley options (at the right end of the text-reply box), iChat inserts it as a graphic into your response.

  On the other hand, if you know the correct symbols to produce smileys—that :) means a smiling face, for example—you can save time by typing them instead of using the pop-up menu. iChat converts them into smiley icons on the fly, as soon as you send your reply.

- **Send a file.** Choosing Buddies→Send File lets you send a file to *all* the participants in your chat.

  Better yet, just drag the file's icon from the Finder into the box where you normally type. (This trick works well with pictures, because your conversation partner sees the graphic right in his iChat window.)

This is a fantastic way to transfer a file that would be too big to send by email. A chat window never gets "full," and no attachment is too large to send.

Snow Leopard Spots: You can now use Quick Look on a file someone's sending you in iChat, to have a full-size look at it before downloading. Just choose File→Quick Look after someone's sent you something (or click its thumbnail and press the space bar).

This method halves the time of transfer, too, since your recipients get the file *as* you upload it. They don't have to wait 20 minutes for you to send the file, and then another 20 minutes to download it, as they would with email or FTP.

Note, though, that this option isn't available in old versions of the AOL Instant Messenger program—only new versions and iChat.

If you have multiple conversations taking place—and are flinging files around to a bunch of people—you can keep an eye on each file's progress with the File Transfer Manager. Choose Window→File Transfers (or press Option-⌘-L) to pop open an all-in-one document delivery monitor.

Tip: If you've opened the Participants drawer (View→Show Chat Participants), you can drag files from the Finder onto individual participants' names in this drawer to send files directly to them.

- **Get Info on someone.** If you click a name in your Buddy list, and then choose Buddies→Show Info (or Control-click someone's name and choose Show Info from the shortcut menu), you get a little Info window about your buddy, where you can edit her name, email address, and picture. (If you change the picture here, you'll see it instead of the graphic your buddy chose for herself.)

    If you click the Alerts tab at this point, you can make iChat react when this particular buddy logs in, logs out, or changes status—for example, by playing a sound or saying, "She's here! She's here!"

GEM IN THE ROUGH

The Chat Transcript

Every now and then, you wish you could preserve a chat for all time—a particularly meaningful conversation with a friend, lover, or customer-service agent.

On the iChat→Preferences→Messages panel, you can turn on "Save chat transcripts to" (and choose a folder on your hard drive). From now on, the text of your conversations is automatically saved in that folder. To view a chat later, double-click its icon. It opens within iChat, compete with all its colors and formatting.

While you're at it, you might also want to turn on a new Snow Leopard feature: "In new chapter window, show." What that means is, the next time you chat with someone, your last chat message with that buddy (or your last five, 25, 100, or 250) pop up automatically in a new window, for your reference. (Bonus tip: Edit→Mark Transcripts stamps the current date and time on each transcript.)

Even if you don't turn on this checkbox, you can save individual chats in progress by choosing File→Save a Copy As.

- **Send an Instant Message.** Not everything in a chat session has to be "heard" by all participants. If you choose Buddies→Send Instant Message, you get a *private* chat window, where you can "whisper" something directly to a special someone behind the other chatters' backs.

- **Send a Secure Message.** Fellow MobileMe members can engage in encrypted chats that keep the conversation strictly between participants. If you didn't turn on encrypted chats when you set up your MobileMe account in iChat, choose iChat→Preferences→Accounts→Security, and then click Enable.

- **Send Email.** If someone messages you, "Hey, will you email me directions?" you can do so on the spot by choosing Buddies→Send Email. Your email program opens up automatically so you can send the note along; if your buddy's email address is part of his Address Book info, the message is even preaddressed.

- **Send an SMS message to a cellphone.** If you're using an AIM screen name or MobileMe account, you can send text messages directly to your friends' cellphones (in the United States, anyway). Choose File→Send SMS. In the box that pops up, type the full cellphone number, without punctuation, like this: *2125551212*.

  Press Return to return to the chat window. Type a very short message (a couple of sentences, tops), and then press Return.

Tip: If iChat rudely informs you that your own privacy settings prevent you from contacting "this person," choose iChat→Preferences, click Accounts, click your chat account, and turn on "Allow anyone."

Obviously, you can't carry on much of an interactive conversation this way. The only response you get is from AOL's computers, letting you know that your message has been sent. But what a great way to shoot a "Call me!" or "Running late—see you tonight!" or "Turn on Channel 4 right now!!!" message to someone's phone.

On the other hand, if you're going to be away from your Mac for a few hours, you can have iChat forward incoming chat messages to *your* cellphone. Choose iChat→Preferences→Accounts and click Configure AIM Mobile Forwarding. In the resulting window, fill in your own cellphone number, so the incoming messages know where to go.

Popping the Balloons

The words you might have for iChat's word-balloon design might be "cute" and "distinctive." But it's equally likely that your choice of adjectives includes "juvenile" and "annoying."

Fortunately, behind iChat's candy coating are enough options tucked away in the View menu that you'll certainly find one that works for you (see Figure 21-7).

You can even change iChat's white background to any image using View→Set Chat Background. Better yet, find a picture you like and drag it into your chat window; iChat immediately makes it the background of your chat. To get rid of the background and revert to soothing white, choose View→Clear Chat Background.

Audio Chats

iChat becomes much more exciting when you exploit its AV Club capabilities. Even over a dial-up modem connection, you can conduct audio chats, speaking into your microphone and listening to the responses from your speaker.

Figure 21-7:
iChat can look like almost anything. Here, for example, is what a chat looks like with the balloon effect turned off (giving you colored rectangles instead). You can even turn off balloons and pictures if they bother you that much. You can also hide the names. You make these changes for a chat in progress using the View menu. You can also change the color and typeface settings in the iChat→Preferences→Messages panel.

If you have a broadband connection, though, you get a much more satisfying experience—and, if you have a pretty fast Mac, up to 10 of you can join in one massive, free conference call from across the Internet.

A telephone icon next to a name in your Buddy List tells you that the buddy has a microphone and is ready for a free Internet "phone call." If you see what appear to be stacked phone icons, then your pal's Mac has enough horsepower to handle a *multiple-person* conference call. (You can see these icons back in Figure 21-2.)

To begin an audio chat, you have three choices:

- Click the telephone icon next to the buddy's name.

- Highlight someone in the Buddy List, and then click the telephone icon at the bottom of the list.

- If you're already in a text chat, choose Buddies→Invite to Audio Chat.

Once your invitation is accepted, you can begin speaking to each other. The bars of the sound-level meter let you know that the microphone—which you've specified in the iChat→Preferences→Audio/Video tab—is working.

Tip: Although the audio is full-duplex (you can hear and speak simultaneously, like a phone but unlike a walkie-talkie), there may be a delay, like you're calling overseas on a bad connection. If you can't hear anything at all, check out iChat's Help system, which contains a long list of suggestions.

Video Chats

If you and your partner both have broadband Internet connections, even more impressive feats await. You can conduct a free video chat with up to four people, who show up on three vertical panels, gorgeously reflected on a shiny black table surface. This isn't the jerky, out-of-audio-sync, Triscuit-sized video of days gone by. If you've got the Mac muscle and bandwidth, your partners are as crisp, clear, bright, and smooth as television—and as big as your screen, if you like.

People can come and go; as they enter and leave the "videosphere," iChat slides their glistening screens aside, enlarging or shrinking them as necessary to fit on your screen.

Apple offers this luxurious experience, however, only if you have luxurious gear:

- **A video camera.** It can be the tiny iSight camera that's embedded above the screens of iMacs and laptops; an external FireWire iSight camera; an ordinary digital camcorder; or a golf-ball Webcam that connects via FireWire instead of USB.

Tip: You and your buddy don't both need the gear. If only you have a camera, for example, you can choose Buddies→Invite to One-Way Video Chat (or Audio Chat). Your less-equipped buddy can see you, but has to speak (audio only) or type in response.

- **Bandwidth.** You need Internet upload/download speeds of at least 100 kilobits per second for basic, tiny video chats with one other person, and a minimum of 384 Kbps for four-way video chats. And those are for the *smallest* video windows. Starting a video chat at the highest video quality requires 300 Kbps uploading bandwidth. That requirement is a heck of a lot lower than in the pre–Snow Leopard iChat, but it may still be too rich for residential DSL packages.

POWER USERS' CLINIC

Bluetooth Headset Voice Chats

If hollering at your computer isn't your preferred method of civilized conversation, you can conduct your audio (and video) chats while wearing a Bluetooth headset instead.

If you haven't paired your headset with your Mac yet, go to iChat→Preferences→Audio/Video and click the button for Set Up Bluetooth Headset. This fires up the Mac's Bluetooth Setup Assistant program to guide you through the process.

After you get your Bluetooth headset married to your Mac, go to →System Preferences→Output and select your headset in the list.

Click the Input tab in the box to fiddle with the volume levels so you're not too loud and distorted when you speak into the mike—and not deafened when sound comes into your head.

Tip: As you're beginning to appreciate, iChat's system requirements are all over the map. Some features require very little horsepower; others require tons.

To find out exactly which features your Mac can handle, choose Video→Connection Doctor; from the Show pop-up menu, choose Capabilities. There's a little chart of all iChat features, showing checkmarks for the ones your Mac can manage.

If you see a camcorder icon next to a buddy's name, you can have a full-screen, high-quality video chat with that person, because they, like you, have a suitable camera and a high-speed Internet connection. If you see a *stacked* camcorder icon, then that person has a Mac that's capable of joining a four-way video chat.

To begin a video chat, click the camera icon next to a buddy's name, or highlight someone in the Buddy List and then click the camcorder icon at the bottom of the list. Or, if you're already in a text chat, choose Buddies→Invite to Video Chat.

A window opens, showing *you*. This Preview mode is intended to show what your buddy will see. (You'll probably discover that you need some kind of light in front of you to avoid being too shadowy.) As your buddies join you, they appear in their own windows (Figure 21-8).

Figure 21-8:
That's you in the smaller window. To move your own mini-window, click a different corner, or drag yourself to a different corner. If you need to blow your nose or do something else unseemly, Option-click the microphone button to freeze the video and mute the audio. Click again to resume.

And now, some video-chat notes:

- If your conversation partners seem unwilling to make eye contact, it's not because they're shifty. They're just looking at *you*, on the screen, rather than at the camera—and chances are you aren't looking into your camera, either.

- Don't miss the Video→Full Screen command! Wild.

- You can have video chats with Windows computers, too, as long as they're using a recent version of AOL Instant Messenger. Be prepared for disappointment, though; the video is generally jerky, small, and slightly out of sync. That's partly due to the cheap USB Webcams most PCs have, and partly due to the poor video *codec* (compression scheme) built into AIM.

- If you use iChat with a camcorder, then you can set the camera to VTR (playback) mode and play a tape right over the Internet to a buddy on the other end! (The video appears flipped horizontally on your screen but looks right to the other person.)

- You can capture a still "photo" of a video chat by ⌘-dragging the image to your desktop, or by choosing Video→Take Snapshot (Option-⌘-S).

- Don't want to see yourself in the picture-in-picture window during your video chat? Choose Video→Hide Local Video.

- This cutting-edge technology can occasionally present cutting-edge glitches. The video quality deteriorates, the transmission aborts suddenly, the audio has an annoying echo, and so on. When problems strike, iChat Help offers a number of tips; the Video→Connection Doctor can identify your network speed. (iChat video likes *lots* of network speed.)

- Just as you can save your typed transcripts of instant message conversations, you can record your audio and video chats. Once you start a chat, choose Video→Record Chat. Your buddy is asked if it's OK for you to proceed with the recording (to ward off any question of those pesky wiretapping laws); if permission is granted, then iChat begins recording the call.

  When you've got what you want, click Stop. Your recordings are automatically saved into Home→Documents→iChats (AAC files for audio conversations, MPEG-4 files for video chats). From there, you can drag them into iTunes to play or sync them up with an iPod or iPhone. Yes, you can now relive those glorious iChat moments when you're standing in line at the grocery store.

Bluescreen Backdrops and Video FX

If your video chats look like a bunch of cubicle-dwellers sitting around chatting at their desks, you can liven things up with one of iChat's most glamorous and jaw-dropping features: photo or video *backgrounds* for your talking head. Yes, now you can make your video chat partners think you're in Paris, on the moon, or even impersonating a four-panel Andy Warhol silkscreen.

Note: The iChat and Photo Booth backdrop effects are serious, serious processor hogs; they require bandwidth, man, serious bandwidth—at least 128 Kbps for both upload and download speeds.

Here's how to prepare your backdrop for a video chat:

1. **Go to iChat→Preferences→Audio/Video.**

   A video window opens so you can see yourself.

2. **Press Shift-⌘-E (or go to Video→Show Video Effects).**

   The Effects box appears, looking a lot like the one in Photo Booth (Chapter 10); a lot of the visual backdrops are quite similar. Click the various squares of the tic-tac-toe grid to see how each effect will transform you in real time: making your face bulbous, for example, or rendering you in delicate colored pencil shadings.

   The first two pages of effects all do video magic on *you* and everything else in the picture. If you want one of those, click it; you're done. There's no step 3. Your video-chat buddies now see you in your distorted or artistic new getup.

   The second two pages of effects, however, don't do anything to your image. Instead, they replace the *background*.

   This is the really amazing part. In TV and movies, replacing the background is an extremely common special effect. All you have to do is set up a perfectly smooth, evenly lit, shadowless blue or bright green backdrop behind the subject. Later, the computer replaces that solid color with a new picture or video of the director's choice.

   iChat, however, creates exactly the same special effect (Figure 21-9) without requiring the bluescreen or the greenscreen. Read on.

3. **Click the background effect you want.**

   Suppose, for example, that you've clicked the video loop showing the Eiffel Tower with people walking around. At this point, a message appears on the screen that says, "Please step out of the frame."

4. **Duck out of camera range (or move off to one side).**

   See, iChat intends to memorize a picture of the *real* background—without you in it. When you return to the scene, your high-horsepower Mac then compares each pixel of its memorized image with what it's seeing now. Any differences, it concludes, must be *you*. And *that* is how it can create a bluescreen effect without a bluescreen.

Note: To make this work, both the camera and the background must be perfectly still. If the lighting or the visuals shift or change in any way, you may get some weird, glitchy effects where your real background bleeds through.

---

5. **When the screen says, "Background detected," step back into the frame.**

   Zut alors! You are now in virtual Paris. Go ahead and start the video chat with your friends, and don't forget your beret.

If you want to clear out the background or change it, click the Original square in the middle of the Effects palette and then choose a different backdrop. (You can also change backdrops in midchat by choosing Video→Show Video Effects to open the Effects palette.)

If things get too weird and choppy onscreen, you can restore the normal background by choosing Video→Reset Background. (That's also handy if you suddenly have to have a video talk with your boss about your excessive use of iChat while he's away on his business trip.)

Tip: You can use one of your own photos or video clips as iChat backdrops, too. In the Video Effects box, click the arrows on the bottom until you get to the screen with several blank User Backdrop screens. Next, drag a photo or video from the desktop directly onto one of the blank screens. Click it just like you would any of Apple's stock shots.

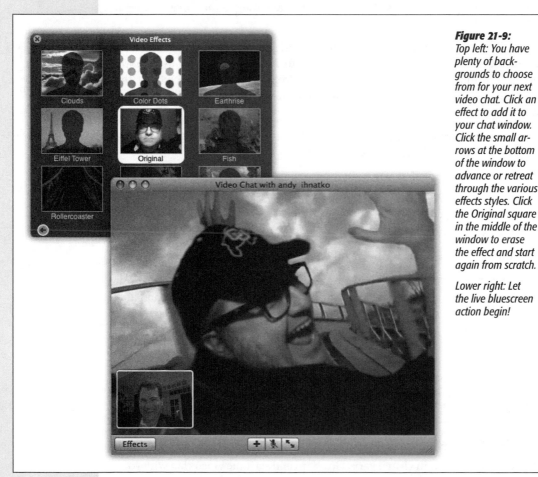

Figure 21-9:
Top left: You have plenty of backgrounds to choose from for your next video chat. Click an effect to add it to your chat window. Click the small arrows at the bottom of the window to advance or retreat through the various effects styles. Click the Original square in the middle of the window to erase the effect and start again from scratch.

Lower right: Let the live bluescreen action begin!

Sharing Your Screen

As you've seen already in this chapter, iChat lets you share your thoughts, your voice, and your image with the people on your Buddy Lists. And now, for its next trick, it lets you share…*your computer*.

iChat's screen sharing feature is a close relative of the *network* screen-sharing feature described in Chapter 13. It lets you see not only what's on a faraway buddy's screen, but *control* it, taking command of the distant mouse and keyboard. (Of course, screen sharing can work the other way, too.)

You can open folders, create and edit documents, and copy files on the shared Mac screen. Sharing a screen makes collaborating as easy as working side by side around the same Mac, except now you can be sitting in San Francisco while your buddy is banging it out in Boston.

And if you're the family tech-support specialist—but the family lives all over the country—screen sharing makes troubleshooting a heckuva lot easier. You can now jump on your Mom's shared Mac and figure out why the formatting went wacky in her Word document, without her having to attempt to *explain* it to you over the phone. ("And then the little thingie disappeared and the doohickey got scrambled…")

Snow Leopard Spots: Once you're controlling someone else's screen remotely, your keyboard shortcuts now operate their Mac instead of yours. Press ⌘-Tab to bring up the application switcher, hit ⌘-Q to quit a program, use all the Exposé and Spotlight shortcuts, and so on.

To make iChat screen sharing work, you and your buddy must both be running Macs with Leopard or Snow Leopard. On the other hand, you can share over any account type: AIM, MobileMe, Google Talk, Bonjour, or Jabber.

To begin, click the sharee's name in your Buddy List.

- If you want to share *your* screen with this person, choose Buddies→Share My Screen.

- If you want to see *her* screen (because she has all the working files on her Mac), choose Buddies→Ask to Share.

Note: Similar commands are available in the Screen Sharing pop-up button—the one that looks like two overlapping squares at the bottom of the Buddy List window. The commands say "Share My Screen with casey234" and "Ask to Share casey234's screen."

Once the invitation is accepted, the sharing begins, as shown in Figure 21-10. To help you communicate further, iChat politely opens up an audio chat with your buddy so you can have a hands-free discussion about what you're doing on the shared machine.

If you're seeing someone else's screen, you see his Mac desktop in full-screen view, right on your own machine. You also see a small window showing your own Mac; click it to switch back to your own desktop.

Tip: To copy files from Mac to Mac, drag them between the two windows. Files dragged to your Mac wind up in your Downloads folder.

If something's not right, or you need to bail out of a shared connection immediately, press Control-Escape on the Mac's keyboard.

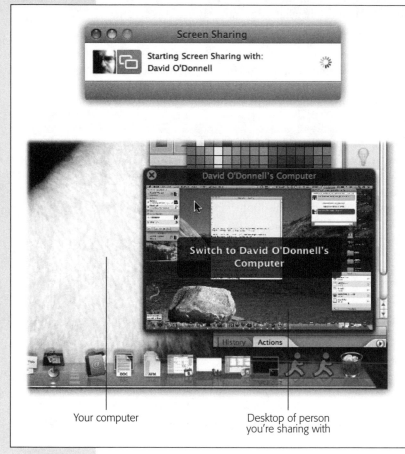

Figure 21-10:
Top: You either send or receive an invitation to start sharing your screen, but make sure you know with whom you're dealing before accepting the offer and starting the sharing process.

Bottom: When you're sharing someone else's screen, you have the option to click back and forth between the two Mac screens.

Your computer

Desktop of person you're sharing with

iChat Theater

Talk about the next best thing to being there. The iChat Theater feature lets you make pitches and presentations to people and committees in faraway cities—without standing in a single airport-security line.

That's because iChat Theater turns the chat window into a presentation screen for displaying and narrating your own iPhoto or Keynote slideshows, QuickTime movie files, and even text documents. Your buddy, on the other end of the iChat line, sees these documents at nearly full size—with you in a little picture-in-picture screen in the corner.

All you need is:

- **Some stuff to show off.** iChat Theater can display exactly the same kinds of files that Quick Look (Chapter 1) can display: Word, Excel, and PowerPoint documents, photos, text and HTML files, PDF files, audio and movie files, fonts, vCards, Pages, Numbers, Keynote, and TextEdit documents, and so on.

- **A zippy broadband Internet connection.** iChat Theater likes 384 kilobits per second or faster; check with your Internet provider if you aren't sure of your connection speed.

To get the show running, you can take one of two approaches.

Figure 21-11:
Top: You can start an iChat Theater session by choosing File→Share a File with iChat Theater, or as shown here, by simply dropping the file on an open video chat window and going for the iChat Theater option.

Bottom: Once you've started a Theater show in Chat, the shared file takes center stage so you both can look at it and discuss amongst yourselves.

- **If a video chat is under way,** you can just drag the file(s) you want to share into the video window. iChat asks if you want to *send* the file to the person or *share* it with iChat Theater (Figure 21-11, top). Click iChat Theater, of course.

- **If no video chat is in progress,** choose File→Share a File in iChat Theater. Locate the file you want to present on your hard drive. When iChat asks you to start a video chat with the buddy who's going to be your audience, click the video-camera icon next to that person's name (or choose Video→Invite to Video Chat).

When your friend accepts, the curtain goes up, as shown the bottom of Figure 21-11. The file you're sharing takes center stage (er, window) and your buddy appears in a little video window off to the side. Click the ■ button to expand the view to full screen.

If you have iPhoto '08 or later, sharing picture albums is one menu command away: Choose File→Share iPhoto with iChat Theater. When the Media Browser pops up, pick the album you want to present. The first picture in the selected album appears in the iChat window before iPhoto itself opens, so you can use iPhoto's nice controls for cruising forward (or backward) through your album.

The same thing happens if you're running a Keynote presentation in iChat Theater: The first slide shows up in the chat window while the Keynote program launches to provide you with the proper controls to click through the rest of the slides in the presentation.

When the show is over, close the window to end the iChat Theater session.

Snow Leopard Spots: If you have multiple chats open—any kind of chats—you can close all of them at once except the active one, if you like. Control-click inside the active chat window; from the shortcut menu, choose Close Other Chats.

---

iChat Tweaks

If you've done nothing but chat in iChat, you haven't even scratched the surface. The iChat→Preferences dialog box gives you plenty of additional control. A few examples:

- **General pane.** If you turn on **Show status in menu bar,** you bring the iChat *menulet* to your menu bar. It lets you change your iChat status (Available, Away, and so on), whether you're in iChat or not.

  And if you turn off "When I quit iChat, set my status to Offline," then quitting iChat doesn't actually log you out. When someone wants a chat with you, iChat opens automatically.

  The General pane is also where you tell iChat what to do when you're temporarily away from the Mac. You can have it automatically reply to chat invitations with your personalized "I'm not here" message. When you come back to the Mac or wake it up from sleep, you can have iChat flip your status from Away to Available all by itself.

- **Accounts pane.** If you have more than one AIM, Jabber, or MobileMe account, you can switch among them here. Your passwords are conveniently saved in your Mac OS X Keychain.

- **Messages pane.** The Messages preference panel lets you design your chat windows—the background color, word balloon color, and typeface and size of text you type.

  If you want to set a special background image for your chats, you can do that as well—just drag a graphics file into the chat preview box on this pane. You can revert to a white background by choosing View→Clear Background.

Tip: Here's a little tweak, right on the Messages pane, that nobody ever mentions: the preference setting called "Watch for my name in incoming messages." It alerts you anytime anyone, in any of the open chats, types your name, even if you're doing something else on the Mac. (As in, "Casey, are you there? Casey!? CASEY!!")

- **Alerts pane.** Here, you can choose how iChat responds to various events. For example, it can play a sound, bounce its Dock icon, or say something out loud whenever you log in, log out, receive new messages, or run an AppleScript, as described earlier in this chapter.

- **Audio/Video pane.** This is where you get a preview of your own camera's output, limit the amount of *bandwidth* (signal-hogging data) the camera uses (a troubleshooting step), and specify that you want iChat to fire up automatically whenever you switch on the camera.

GEM IN THE ROUGH

iChat on Autopilot

If you've read this chapter all the way through, then you know that iChat can respond to chat invitations by running an AppleScript. And if you've read Chapter 7, you know that AppleScript is capable of…almost anything.

As a proof of concept, Apple's AppleScript product manager has created a truly evil script that you can choose in the iChat→Preferences→Alerts→Run AppleScript pop-up menu. It's called iChat Autopilot; you can download it from this book's "Missing CD" page at *www.missingmanuals.com*.

In short, this very special script simulates your end of the chat. It carries on a fairly generic conversation, periodically typing perfectly plausible all-purpose utterances, occasionally excusing yourself while you answer the doorbell, and otherwise doing an excellent impersonation of a distracted, preoccupied, but still well-meaning you.

Let it run. Give your buddies the satisfaction of knowing you're there for them. Even though you're really watching TV downstairs.

SSH, FTP, VPN, & Web Sharing

E mail and Web surfing may be the most popular Internet activities, but the world's most gigantic network has many other uses. The general idea is always the same, though: letting one computer reach out and touch another.

Mac OS X offers a few features that embrace the more literal aspects of that notion. For example, you can turn your Mac into a *Web server*—an actual living Web site that anyone on the Internet can visit. This chapter also explores various advanced methods of manipulating your own Mac from the road, including *remote access* technologies like long-distance file sharing, FTP, SSH, and virtual private networking (VPN).

Note: Most of these technologies are designed for full-time Internet connections (cable modem or DSL, for example). If you have a dial-up modem, these features work only when you're actually online. Still, they may occasionally be useful anyway. You could always get online, call up a friend and say, "Check out my Web site right now—here's the current IP address" or call someone back home to say, "I have to grab a file off my hard drive. Could you make the Mac on my desk go online?"

Web Sharing

Using the Sharing pane of System Preferences, you can turn your Mac into a Web site (or *server*), accessible from the Web browsers of people on your office network, the Internet at large, or both.

This feature assumes, of course, that you've already created some Web pages. For this purpose, you can use Web design programs (Apple's Pages, for example) or save documents out of TextEdit or Word as Web pages. Or you could let Mac OS X build Web pages for you using iPhoto or Image Capture.

After you provide your friends and coworkers with your Mac's Web site address, they can view your Web pages, graphics, and documents in their own Web browsers. And whenever you're online, your Web site is also available to anyone on the Internet—but you don't have to pay a penny to a Web-hosting company.

UP TO SPEED

The IP Address Mess: Port Forwarding

There are so many ways to connect to your Mac from another computer. You can use Web sharing, SSH, file sharing, screen sharing, and so on. They're easy to use—when you want to connect across your home or office network.

When you want to connect from across the *Internet*, though, things get complicated fast.

In that case, you need to know your home Mac's IP address. (It stands for Internet Protocol.) An IP address is always made up of four numbers separated by periods, like 192.168.1.104. Every computer on earth that's directly connected to the Internet has its own unique IP address.

Now, if you have only one Mac, and it's connected directly to your broadband modem, no big deal. You can find out its IP address by opening System Preferences, clicking Sharing, and clicking File Sharing.

Unfortunately, your Mac at home probably *isn't* connected directly to the Internet. If you're like most people, it's connected to a router, or maybe an AirPort base station, so that several computers in your house can share the same Internet connection. In this setup, the *router* (or base station) has a unique IP address—not the Macs connected to it.

(The router doles out private IP addresses to each computer in your house or office, usually beginning with 192 or 10. If you check your Mac's IP address in System Preferences, you'll find out only its *private* address—not the public one that's accessible from the Internet. To find out that information, you have to check your router or base station's configuration screen; check the router's manual for instructions.)

All right: How are you supposed to connect to one particular Mac if it's connected to a router and doesn't have a true, "public" IP address?

One solution is Back to My Mac, the remote-access feature described on page 543. It solves the behind-the-router problem for you, but it requires a MobileMe account.

Otherwise, your only hope is to turn on a router feature called *port forwarding*. It makes the router pass signals intended for a specific port to one particular computer on the network. For example, you could direct all port-80 communications to the Mac doing Web serving, for example, and all 548 traffic to a Mac doing file sharing.

The point is that, even with port forwarding, you still can't access two different machines using the same port. (For some services, including *ssh* and Timbuktu, you can work around this limitation by logging into the machine specified for port forwarding, and then from that machine, log into the others on the rest of the network.)

Turning on port forwarding doesn't require a programming degree, but it's not simple by any means. For starters, the steps are different for every router model.

Fortunately, you can find guided tutorials on the Web. You can use Google to search for your particular router model, or check *www.portforward.com*, which offers free step-by-steps for hundreds of router models, including Apple's AirPort base stations. Even so, try to arrange the assistance of someone who knows networking.

In this chapter, the term "your IP address" means your *public* IP address. If you have only one Mac, that's its IP address. If you have a router or wireless network, use *that* device's IP address—as passed along by port forwarding.

Mac OS X's Web Sharing feature isn't some feeble junior version, either. Inside Mac OS X is *Apache,* one of the strongest and most popular Unix Web server programs—precisely the same one that drives 60 percent of the Internet's commercial Web sites.

The bottom line: If you build it, they won't necessarily come. But you'll have the capacity to handle them if they do.

Firing Up Web Sharing

Here's how you turn your Mac into a low-budget Web site:

1. **Put the HTML documents, graphics, and files you want to publish into your Home→Sites folder.**

   Every account's Home folder has a Sites folder, and therefore the Mac can actually serve up lots of Web sites at once.

   Your Web site's home page, by the way, won't appear unless it's named *index.html.* (Apple has already put an *index.html* document into your Sites folder, just to give you the idea; feel free to replace it.) And the other files you put in Sites aren't accessible unless they're *linked* from your index.html page.

2. **Open System Preferences; click Sharing. Turn on the Web Sharing checkbox (Figure 22-1).**

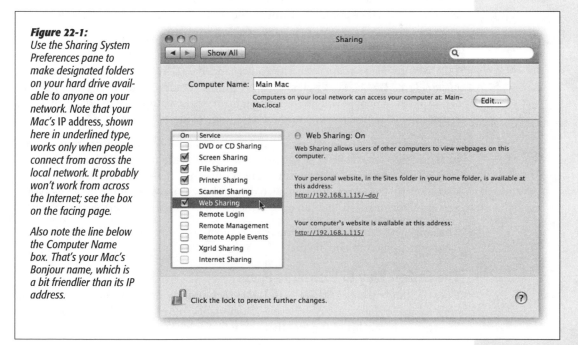

Figure 22-1:
Use the Sharing System Preferences pane to make designated folders on your hard drive available to anyone on your network. Note that your Mac's IP address, shown here in underlined type, works only when people connect from across the local network. It probably won't work from across the Internet; see the box on the facing page.

Also note the line below the Computer Name box. That's your Mac's Bonjour name, which is a bit friendlier than its IP address.

You've just made the contents of your Sites folder available to anyone who connects to your Mac.

3. **Send your network address to your friends and coworkers.**

   People on your local office network can use your Mac's Bonjour name to connect. It appears at the top of the Sharing pane, as shown in Figure 22-1. For example, your colleagues can type *http://office-mac.local/~chris* into their Web browsers, where *office-mac.local* is your Mac's Bonjour name.

   If other people will be connecting from the Internet, you need to figure out your public IP address; as noted in the box on page 796, that might be your *router's* IP address, not your Mac's.

   Your Mac Web site's address might be, for example, *http://111.222.3.44/~chris/* (the number is your public IP address, and the name should be your short user name). Don't forget the final slash. Tell your friends to bookmark it so they won't have to remember all that.

You've just put your Mac-based Web page on the Internet for all to see—that is, all who know your secret Web address. Maybe you'll want to distribute the address only to other people on your office network, using your tiny Web site as a distribution source for documents. Or maybe you'll want to go whole-hog, hosting an e-commerce Web site (read on).

The Mac's Own Web Site

The instructions above show you how to create a Web site in your Home→Sites folder. In other words, they guide you through the process of creating a *personal* Web site.

But if you have an Administrator account (Chapter 12), you can also put your Web pages into the main hard drive window's Library→WebServer→Documents folder. This is your Mac's *main* Web site folder, and its address is simply, for example, *http://111.222.3.44/*. That is, it's just your public IP address, no user name needed. (Here again, if people will be connecting from across your office network, they can replace the IP number with your Mac's Bonjour name.)

Working with this primary Web site folder is only slightly different from the personal ones described above. Because you're now working inside an official Mac OS X system folder, you must mind your permissions. Using the File→Get Info command, you should set up the permissions of any folders and documents *inside* the Library→Web-Server→Documents folder (an Images folder, for example) as described on page 517.

That way, you can ensure that you're in control of which visitors are allowed to do what with your Web documents.

The Easiest Way to Distribute Files

Here's a handy secret: If there isn't a document whose name is *index.html* in your Sites folder (or Library→WebServer→Documents folder), then visitors see, in their browsers, a handy list of the files that *are* in that folder (see Figure 22-2).

This is a terrific convenience: It offers a quick, simple way for you to make a bunch of documents available for downloading. All your visitors have to do is click one of these file names. It downloads immediately, no matter what kind of computer your Web visitor is using.

Tip: This has nothing to do with Web sharing, but it's kind of cool: You can see the contents of *any* folder on your Mac, just by typing its folder pathname into a Web browser's address bar. For example, to see what's in your Documents folder, type *file:///Users/chris/Documents/* into Safari's address bar. You get a tidy list like the one shown in Figure 22-2, revealing what's in that folder. Click a link to open it. (If you're using Safari, you open a Finder window revealing the folder's contents instead.).

Figure 22-2:
Here's a great way to make files available to other people on your network or collaborators across the Internet. Just put your files into the Sites or Library→WebServer→ Documents folder and make sure nothing is named index.html. *The Parent Directory link takes you to the folder that contains this one—in this case, the Library→WebServer→ Documents folder.*

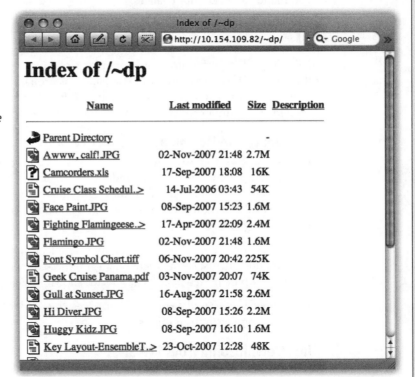

More on Apache

As noted above, Apache is the most popular Web-serving software in the world. As you can well imagine, it's powerful, reliable—and very technical. It is, after all, a Unix program.

You can read more at any of these sources:

- **The Apache manual.** To open it up, type *http://localhost/manual/* into your browser's address bar. You won't get far reading this thing if you haven't spent some time at a technical college, but at least you'll know what you're up against.

- *Apache: The Definitive Guide.* A book from O'Reilly.

- **MacOSXHints.com.** Dozens of Mac OS X fans have posted specific Apache-tweaking tips and tricks at *www.macosxhints.com*.

Note, too, that you can get yourself an attractive graphic front end for the various Apache settings, either in the form of Tenon's iTools program ($350) or the free Webmin (*www.webmin.com/osx.html*). They still require an understanding of the technical aspects of Web hosting, but at least you're spared having to type out Unix commands to make your changes.

FTP

FTP sites (file transfer protocol) store pieces of software that can be accessed from the Internet. If you've heard of FTP at all, it was probably under one of two circumstances—either you've downloaded software from an Internet FTP site, or you've created and maintained your own Web site.

Uploading and Downloading from FTP Sites

Hooking into an FTP site generally requires an FTP *client program* that runs on the kind of computer you use (Mac, Windows, or whatever). On Mac OS X, popular FTP client programs include the shareware programs Transmit, Fetch, Interarchy, and Captain FTP, and the free RBrowser (which is available from the "Missing CD" page at *www.missingmanuals.com*).

Using these programs, Web designers, for example, can view a list of all the text and graphics documents, sitting there on an Internet-connected computer somewhere, that make up their Web pages. The effect is shown in Figure 22-3.

When they want to update one of those pages, they add it to this list; to delete a Web page, they remove it from this list.

Just Downloading from FTP Sites

If you're just going to *look at* and *download* files (but not upload or delete any), you don't even need a special FTP program. You can get to the files much more directly using one of these two methods:

- Any old Web browser will work. Open Safari, for example, and type *ftp://ftp.apple.com* (or whatever the address is) into the address bar. A dialog box asks for an account name and password, if they're required. Once you're in, you switch to the Finder and see the contents of the FTP site as a window full of standard file icons. (In other browsers, you may see the list of the FTP site right in the browser window.)

- Using the Finder's Go→Connect to Server command, you can mount read-only FTP volumes right on your desktop, much like a public iDisk.

In the Connect to Server dialog box, just enter the address of the file server you would like to mount—*ftp://ftp.apple.com,* for example. You'll soon see the ftp.apple.com icon appear on your desktop, looking just like your other disks. Open it up and drag out whatever you want to download.

Becoming an FTP Server

Thanks to Mac OS X and its Wonder Unix, you can also turn your own Mac *into* an FTP site. Once again, the key is the Sharing pane of System Preferences; this time, turn on the File Sharing checkbox, click Options, and click "Share files and folders using FTP." Click OK.

Tip: It's best not to share your files over the *Internet* using FTP. Your name and password wind up being sent unencrypted, meaning that a snooper could intercept them.

FTP is fine for sharing files over your home or office network. But for Internet use, turn on Remote Login in System Preferences→Sharing. Then other people can connect to your Mac, and browse its files, either using *ssh* (if they're tech-savvy) or a program like the free CyberDuck. Just change the program's protocol from FTP to either SFTP or SCP.

Figure 22-3:
Top: To access your Mac OS X machine from across the Internet, fire up a program like RBrowser and use the address ftp://111.222.33.4 *(or whatever your public IP address is).*

Bottom: Once you're looking at an FTP server's contents, you can drag files from your desktop into the list. Copy them to your Mac by dragging them out of the list onto your desktop, or open them by double-clicking.

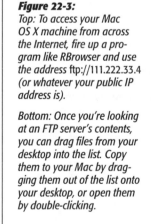

At this point, you, or other people you trust, can connect to your FTP server by running an FTP program like RBrowser (see Figure 22-3) or just typing *ftp://111.222.33.4* (or whatever your IP address is) into their Web browsers.

Connecting from the Road

You can also connect to your Mac's regular File Sharing feature (Chapter 13) from over the Internet. This feature is a blessing to anyone who travels, whether with a laptop or to a branch office, because you'll never be up the creek without a paddle if you discover that you left an important file at home.

The easiest way to go about it is to use Back to My Mac, which is one of Apple's MobileMe services.

If you'd rather spend time than money, though, you can set up a remote file-sharing system on your own. Start by setting up the home-base Mac for file sharing, as directed in Chapter 13; then figure out your Mac's public IP address, as described in the box on page 796.

Finally, once you're on the road, go online and proceed like this:

1. **Choose Go→Connect to Server.**

   The Connect to Server dialog box appears, as shown in Figure 22-4.

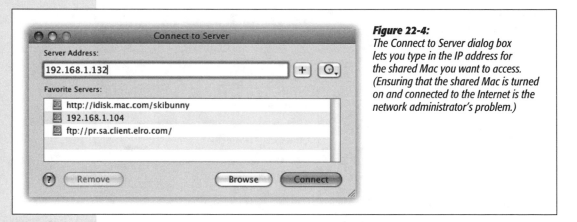

Figure 22-4:
The Connect to Server dialog box lets you type in the IP address for the shared Mac you want to access. (Ensuring that the shared Mac is turned on and connected to the Internet is the network administrator's problem.)

2. **Type in the public IP address of the Mac to which you want to connect, and then click Connect (or press Return).**

   See the box on page 796 for a discussion of public vs. private IP addresses.

3. **Enter your name and password, and then click Connect.**

   From here, it's just as though you were connecting to another computer on your office network (Chapter 13), although it's a good bit slower. But when you're in Hong Kong and need a document from your Mac in Minneapolis, you may not care.

Remote Access with SSH

Are you a geek? Take this simple test at home. Do you get excited about Mac OS X's ability to permit SSH access?

If you answered "What's SSH?" or "I'm *already* being quiet," then the following discussion of Unix remote control may not interest you. To be sure, SSH is not a program with a graphic user interface (icons and menus). You operate it from within a program like Terminal by typing commands, exactly as described in Chapter 16.

If you're willing to overlook that little peccadillo, though, SSH (Secure Shell) is an extremely powerful tool. It lets you connect to your Mac from anywhere—from across the network or across the Internet. And once you're connected, you can take complete control of it, copying files, running commands, rearranging folders, or even shutting it down, all by remote control.

Getting In

Here's how you go about using SSH:

1. **Set up your Mac by opening the Sharing panel of System Preferences, and then turning on the Remote Login checkbox.**

   You've just told the Mac it's OK for you (or other people with accounts on your machine) to connect from the road. Quit System Preferences.

2. **Go away.**

   You can move to another machine on the network, or another computer on the Internet (if you've dealt with the port-forwarding issue described on page 796). Once you're online with that other machine, you can contact your home-base machine from within a program like Terminal.

Tip: It doesn't have to be Terminal, and it doesn't have to be a Mac. You can get *SSH client* programs for almost any kind of computer.

For pre–OS X Macs, for example, you can try MacSSH or NiftyTelnet SSH, both of which you can download from this book's "Missing CD" page at *www.missingmanuals.com.* For Windows, try Putty (*www.puttyssh.org*).

---

3. **At the prompt, type *ssh -l chris 111.222.3.44.* Press Return.**

   Instead of *chris,* substitute your short account name (as you're known on the Mac you're tapping into), and replace the phony IP address shown here with your real public address. (If your Mac back home has a domain name unto itself, such as *macmania.com,* you can type that instead of the IP address. And if you've turned on port forwarding, use your cable modem/DSL box's IP address.)

If all goes well, the *ssh* command acknowledges your first successful connection by displaying a message like this: "The authenticity of host '111.222.3.44 (111.222.3.44)' can't be established. RSA key fingerprint is d9:f4:11:b0:27:1a:f1: 14:c3:cd:25:85:2b:78:4d:e7. Are you sure you want to continue connecting (yes/no)?" (This message won't appear on subsequent connections.) You're seeing SSH's security features at work.

4. **Type** *yes* **and press Return.**

   Now you see one more note: "Warning: Permanently added '111.222.3.44' (RSA) to the list of known hosts." You're then asked for your account password.

5. **Type your account password and press Enter.**

   You're in. Issue whatever commands you want. You can now conduct a full Unix Terminal session as described in Chapter 16—but by remote control.

Tip: For a more thorough description of SSH and its options, type *man ssh* at the prompt.

Remote Control Program Killing

One of the most common uses of SSH is quitting a stuck program. Maybe it's a program that doesn't respond to the usual Force Quit commands—maybe even the Finder or Terminal. Or maybe, having just arrived in Accounting on the fifth floor, you realize that you accidentally left your Web browser, open to Dilbert.com, up on your screen in clear view of passersby.

In any case, you'd fire up Terminal and proceed like this (what you type is shown in bold; the Mac's responses are in normal type):

```
home-mac:~ chris$ ssh 172.24.30.182
The authenticity of host '111.222.3.44 (111.222.3.44)' can't be
established. RSA key fingerprint is d9:f4:11:b0:27:1a:f1:14:c3:c
d:25:85:2b:78:4d:e7.
Are you sure you want to continue connecting (yes/no)? yes
Warning: Permanently added '172.24.30.182' (RSA) to the list of
known hosts.
chris@111.222.3.44's password: fisheggs
Last login: Thu Apr 22 17:23:38 2010
Welcome to Darwin!
office-mac:~ chris$ top -u
```

The *top -u* command, as described in Chapter 16, displays a list of running programs. After a block of memory statistics, you might see a list like this:

```
294 top          6.5%  0:01.10  1   16   26   276K   416K   652K 27.1M
293 bash         0.0%  0:00.03  1   12   15   168K   856K   768K 18.2M
292 login        0.0%  0:00.01  1   13   37   140K   408K   492K 26.9M
291 Terminal     0.0%  0:05.50  3   60  115  2.99M  5.41M  6.59M  149M
```

```
287 HotKey       0.0%  0:00.34  4  151   78   760K  2.24M  2.67M 96.5M
283 Finder       0.0%  0:02.04  2   89  162  3.95M  17.1M  15.5M  165M
282 SystemUISe   0.9%  0:01.51  2  241  327  3.03M  7.85M  8.54M  158M
281 Dock         0.0%  0:00.24  2   77  132   780K  10.7M  2.80M  139M
```

As you can see, the Finder is process number 283. If that's the stuck program, then, you could quit it like so:

```
office-mac:~ chris$ kill 283
```

Or if you're sure of the program's exact name, just use the *killall* command with the program's name instead of its process ID. To handle a stuck Finder, you would type this:

```
office-mac:~ chris$ killall Finder
```

Either way, the Finder promptly quits (and relaunches in a healthier incarnation, you hope). You could also, at this point, type *sudo shutdown -h now* to make your Mac, elsewhere on the network, shut down. (Terminal doesn't type any kind of response.)

If you ended your SSH session by shutting down the other Mac, you can just close the Terminal window now. Otherwise, type *exit* to complete your SSH session.

Tip: Want a quicker, dirtier method of doing ssh that doesn't even require knowing the other machine's IP address? OK: Open Terminal. Choose Shell→New Remote Connection. In the list of connection types, choose ssh/ftp/telnet. Every Bonjour-enabled Mac on your network shows up; click one and then click Connect to connect!

Virtual Private Networking

After reading the previous pages, you might assume it's a piece of cake for businesspeople to connect to their corporate networks across the Internet from wherever they happen to be: their homes, hotel rooms, or their local Starbucks. But even though the steps on the preceding pages work fine if you're dialing into your *home* machine, they'll probably fail miserably when you want to connect to a corporate network. There's one enormous obstacle in your way: Internet security.

The typical corporate network is guarded by a team of steely-eyed administrators for whom Job Number One is preventing access by unauthorized visitors. They perform this job primarily with the aid of a super-secure firewall that seals off the company's network from the Internet.

So how can you tap into the network from the road? One solution is to create a hole in the firewall for each authorized user—software that permits incoming Internet traffic only from specified IP addresses like your Mac's. Unfortunately, this setup isn't bulletproof, security-wise. It's also a pain for administrators to manage.

Back in the dial-up modem days, you could dial directly into the corporate network, modem-to-modem. That was plenty secure, but it bypassed the Internet, and therefore wound up being expensive. (Want proof? Try this simple test: Make a call from

---

the Tokyo Hilton to the Poughkeepsie Sheet Metal home office. Have a look at your hotel bill when you check out.)

Fortunately, there's a third solution that's both secure and cheap: the *Virtual Private Network,* or *VPN.* Running a VPN allows you to create a super-secure "tunnel" from your Mac, across the Internet, and straight into your corporate network. All data passing through this tunnel is heavily encrypted; to the Internet eavesdropper, it looks like so much undecipherable gobbledygook.

And it's free—whether you're accessing the Internet via your home DSL, a local ISP number from a hotel, or wirelessly from your stool at Starbucks.

Remember, though, that VPN is a corporate tool, run by corporate nerds. You can't use this feature without these pieces in place:

- **A VPN server.** This is a big deal. If your tech department tells you they don't have one, then that's that—no tunneling for you.

  If they do have one, then you'll need to know the type of server it is. Mac OS X's VPN software can connect to VPN servers that speak *PPTP* (Point to Point Tunneling Protocol), *L2TP/IPsec* (Layer 2 Tunneling Protocol over IP Security), or Cisco IPSec. Most corporate VPN servers work with at least one of these protocols.

  You'll also need to know the Internet address of your VPN server (for example, *vpn.ferrets-r-us.com*).

- **An account on the remote network that allows VPN access.** Your remote network can be set up in many different ways, but in every case, you'll still need to confirm with your network administrator that your account on it allows VPN access.

- **All necessary account information.** Make sure you have all the scraps of connection information you'll need to dial in. That would include your **user (account) name,** at the very least. You may also need an **Windows Domain name;** VPN servers are often part of Microsoft Windows Server networks, which won't let you in until you know this domain name.

  Some networks also may require that you type in the currently displayed password on an **RSA SecurID card,** which your administrator will provide. This James Bond-ish, credit card–like thing displays a password that changes every few seconds, making it rather difficult for hackers to learn "the" password. (If your network doesn't require a SecurID card, you'll need a **standard password** instead.)

  Finally, if your office offers L2TP connections, you'll need yet another password called a **Shared Secret** to ensure that the server you're connecting to is really the server you intend to connect to.

Setting Up the VPN Connection

If you're lucky, your company's network geek has provided you with a VPN settings file, a little double-clickable icon that automatically opens the Network pane of System Preferences and fills in the blanks for you. If not, you can do all that manually:

1. **Open System Preferences. Click Network. Click the + button below the list of connections at the left side.**

   The "Select the interface" sheet appears.

2. **From the pop-up menu, choose VPN.**

   Now a new pop-up menu appears, called VPN Type; you're supposed to choose either L2TP (Layer 2 Tunneling Protocol), PPTP (Point to Point Tunneling Protocol), or Cisco IPsec (IP Security). Find out which system your company's network uses.

Snow Leopard Spots: The Cisco type is new in Snow Leopard, which is great news for everyone whose companies use Cisco gear. Even so, Snow Leopard can't connect to all Cisco setups; in some cases, you'll still have to use Cisco's own connection software to dial in.

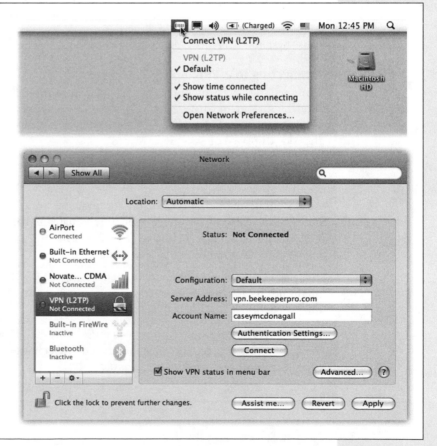

Figure 22-5:
You're on your way to joining the corporate network—from thousands of miles away. Virtual private networking is ideal for the paranoid (because it's very secure) and the cheap (because you're using the Internet as a giant wire connecting you to your office).

3. **Choose the type of VPN from the VPN Type pop-up menu. Type a name for this connection (it can be anything you want). Click Create.**

   You return to the main Network pane, where the settings boxes for your VPN are waiting (Figure 22-5).

4. **Fill in the server address and account name. Click Authentication Settings to specify your password and other security settings.**

   Here, for example, is where you indicate that you have one of those SecurID cards.

5. **Click OK. Turn on "Show VPN Status in menu bar."**

   That checkbox makes the VPN menulet appear; it's your ticket to getting connected (Figure 22-5, top).

Tip: If you always connect to the same VPN, you can turn on VPN on Demand. It autoconnects you to your corporate VPN every time you direct your Web browser to a Web site, file server, or resource that requires the VPN connection, saving you some steps.

To set this up, click Advanced. (You can see this button in Figure 22-5.) Click VPN on Demand; click **+**. Enter the corporate VPN domain. You're good to go—as long as you've got your network geek's permission. (Some of them get antsy about VPN on Demand, since it could be a security risk if your laptop is stolen.)

Close System Preferences. You're ready to connect.

Connecting to a VPN

Connect the way you normally do—via cable modem, DSL, office network, modem, AirPort, or whatever. Once you're online, choose your VPN's name from the VPN menulet. You'll be asked for your credentials: your password, for example, or the code displayed on your SecurID card.

If all goes well, several status messages go by. The last one says, "Connected To" and gives the IP address of the network equipment you've reached out and touched.

At this point, you're connected to the corporate network. You can perform the same network-related tasks you could if you were actually in that office: Check your email, view internal corporate Web pages, access internal FTP servers, make printouts on laser printers thousands of miles away, and so on.

You generally can't *browse* things, though. That is, depending on your network, you might not be able to use your Sidebar to view a list of the other computers on the office network, or see a list of networked printers.

In this case, to access these services, you must know their IP addresses. For example, to connect to a shared folder on another computer, choose Go→Connect to Server, type its network address, and press Return.

Tip: To connect to a shared folder on a Windows machine, the address looks like this: *smb://111.222.33.4/sales-docs*. Of course, you'd substitute the correct IP address for the dummy one shown here, and insert the actual name of the shared folder. (You can also use its *DNS name* instead of the IP address, if you know it, like this: *smb://big-blue-server.ferret-lan.com/sales-docs.*)

When you're finished accessing the remote network, choose Disconnect from the VPN menulet. (Accessing other Web sites can be slow while you're on a VPN.)

The Fine Points of VPN

For all the wonders of VPN, here are some possible complications:

- If you're using a *router* at home (a little box that shares one cable modem or DSL box with several computers), it might not be able to handle the tunneling protocols, or it might not have that feature turned on. Check the router's manual, or ask its manufacturer for more information. For example, the first-generation (silver) AirPort base stations can't handle VPNs at all.

- If the corporate network doesn't seem to like your name and password, you might need to add your NT domain name and a *backwards* slash to the beginning of your account name (like this: *dom01\msmith*) before trying again.

    If you're able to make the connection but experiencing trouble reaching services by their DNS names (for example, *big-blue-server.com*), your Mac could be having difficulty finding the right DNS server. Working with your network administrator, open the Network pane of System Preferences. Click VPN, then click Advanced, and then DNS; enter the desired DNS server addresses in the DNS Servers box. Click OK, then Apply, and then try the VPN connection again.

- If you're still having problems using the VPN, look at the *logs* (automatically kept technical records) for clues to share with your network administrator. To view these records, open the Console program (in Applications→Utilities). Click Show Log List, expand the /var/log section, and click ppp.log.

Part Six:
Appendixes

6

Installing Mac OS X 10.6

I f your computer came with Snow Leopard already installed on it, you can skip
this appendix—for now. But if you're running an earlier version of the Mac OS
and want to savor the Snow Leopard experience, this appendix describes how to
install the new operating system on your Mac.

As you'll soon discover, the installation process was the recipient of much love from
Apple this time around. The whole thing is simpler, faster—and smaller; Snow Leopard
requires half the disk space of the previous Mac OS X, saving you at least 6 gigabytes.
(The savings comes from removing hundreds of printer drivers you'll never use; removing some code that made Mac OS X compatible with pre-Intel processors; and
using clever compression tricks to keep the system software small.)

The new installer is much smarter, too. There's no longer any need for the classic "clean
install" described later in this appendix; every installation is, in effect, a clean install. A
built-in compatibility checker warns you if you have startup software (drivers or kernel
extensions) known to be incompatible with Snow Leopard, and quarantines them
by putting them into an Incompatible Software folder until you can deal with them.

You don't have to restart the Mac when running the installer, either.

The new installer is even power-failure friendly. If something goes wrong during
the installation, you can just run the installer from the DVD again; it picks up right
from where it left off.

Getting Ready to Install

For starters, you need to make sure you and your Mac have what it takes to handle Mac OS X—specifically:

- **A Macintosh with an Intel processor.** Those old PowerPC Macs (PowerBooks, iBooks, PowerMacs, eMacs, and pre-2006 iMacs and Mac minis) have finally fallen off the Mac OS X upgrade path. Basically, most Macs manufactured since 2006 are eligible.

- **Free hard disk space.** You need 5 GB free to install Mac OS X 10.6. (Believe it or not, that's *half* the space requirements of the last version. Doesn't Apple know how the world works?!) You need a little more space if you install the Developer Tools, less if you decline to install all the optional languages.

- **A lot of memory.** Apple recommends at least 1 GB of memory, but Mac OS X absolutely *loves* memory. For the greatest speed, install 2 gigabytes—more if you can afford it. (And these days, you probably can.)

- **The latest firmware.** *Firmware* describes the low-level, underlying software instructions that control the actual circuitry of your Mac. Every now and then, Apple updates it for certain Mac models, and it's very important that your Mac have the absolute latest. If yours doesn't, a message will appear to let you know during the installation. Some Macs might just spit the DVD right out. Quit the installer and grab the latest updater from *http://support.apple.com/kb/HT1237*.

- **A copy of Snow Leopard to install.** Apple sells Mac OS X Snow Leopard in two ways. There's the regular Snow Leopard DVD ($30), for example, and there's the Family Pack ($50), which authorizes you to install Mac OS X on up to five Macs in the same household. (Neither version is copy-protected; only the honor system stops you from installing it on a sixth Mac.)

Technically, the $30 price of Snow Leopard is available only if you already have Mac OS X 10.5 (Leopard) installed. If you have Tiger (10.4), for example, you're supposed to buy the Mac Box Set, which costs $170 and includes Snow Leopard,

---

POWER USERS' CLINIC

The Partitioning Question

Before you install Snow Leopard, you might want to confront the issue of *partitioning* your Mac's hard drive—dividing its space so that it shows up on your desktop with two different icons and two different names. You can keep Snow Leopard on one and Tiger on the other, for example. Now you can live like a king, enjoying all the advantages of people who have two separate hard drives.

As a bonus, the Mac even comes with a partitioning program: Disk Utility. And it no longer requires first erasing the drive completely; you can repartition on the fly, without disturbing whatever is already on the drive.

For details, see page 295.

---

iLife '09 (iPhoto, iMovie, GarageBand, iWeb, and iDVD), and iWork '09 (Pages, Numbers, and Keynote).

But—don't tell anyone—it turns out that the $30 version also installs just fine if you have an earlier Mac OS X version. It's against Apple's rules, but it works.

- **A full backup.** It's a really, *really* good idea to back up your entire Mac before you begin this, or any, upgrade. Even if things go wrong for only, say, 0.01 percent of Mac owners, that's still thousands of people. If you don't have a second hard drive, this is your excuse to buy one; they're dirt cheap these days. If you have Mac OS X Leopard already, you can use it to make a complete, automatic backup of your Mac as it is now.

Two Kinds of Installation

The Mac OS X installer can perform two kinds of installations; it's much simpler than previous installers. Here they are:

- **Automatic.** Double-click it and forget it. This kind of installation preserves everything on your Mac. Every program, setting, and file will be exactly as you had it. In essence, this kind of installation just works through your System folder, updating each component and disturbing nothing else.

- **Erase & Install.** There aren't many reasons to opt for this power-user technique, but it's here if you want it. This version erases your entire hard drive. When it's finished installing Snow Leopard, it then offers you the chance to reinstall all your programs and files from a backup (which you did make, right?).

POWER USERS' CLINIC

The Compatibility Sidebar

The Snow Leopard installer checks to make sure you don't have any incompatible startup software that might give you grief. If it finds any of these software bits (drivers and kernel extensions, for example), it moves them into a Quarantine folder so they won't give you grief.

Snow Leopard doesn't do anything about *programs* that are incompatible, though–regular apps in your Applications folder–and there are a few. It's your job to check to make sure they've all been updated to 10.6-compatible versions.

There are a few other software categories that don't work with Snow Leopard. They won't cause you any problems–

they just won't work. That includes input managers (software add-ons that modify programs like Safari); shortcut menu plug-ins (which add new commands to the shortcut menu that appears when you Control-click something); and old Mail plug-ins. None of these work in Snow Leopard.

Finally, Snow Leopard "breaks" a few non-Apple menulets, the little menu-bar status icons. (Some of the methods available to software companies to create menulets have been shut down.) At this point, most software companies have already updated their menulets to work properly, but you may have to do some Google scavenging to find out.

The Automatic Installation

The installation process takes about 45 minutes, but for the sake of your own psyche, set aside a whole afternoon. Once the installation is over, you'll want to play around, organize your files, and learn the lay of the land.

1. **Insert the Mac OS X DVD.**

   If you're installing Snow Leopard on a MacBook Air, you'll have to use the Remote Disc trick described on page 425.

2. **Double-click the Install Mac OS X icon in the disc's main window (Figure A-1).**

   The Mac takes you directly to the first Installer screen, featuring two buttons: Utilities and Continue.

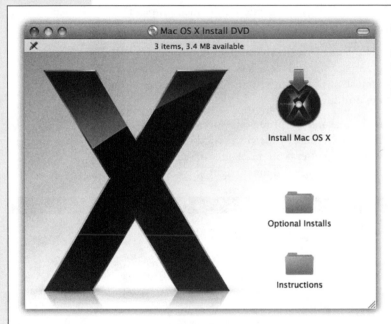

Figure A-1:
Your installation adventure is about to begin. The very first step, though, is restarting the Mac, which the installer invites you to do.

The Utilities, if you were to click that button, include programs like Disk Utility (to erase or partition your hard drive), Terminal (to do some Unixy preparatory steps), System Profiler (to see how much memory this machine has), Reset Password (if you've forgotten yours), and more.

If you do decide to take that detour to another program, then when you quit it, you'll return to the Installer program, right where you left off

As you're seeing already, the installer follows a pattern: Read the instructions, make a couple of choices, and click Continue to advance to the next screen. As you go, the list on the left side of the screen reveals where you are in the overall procedure.

Tip: You can back out of the installation at any time before step 6, just by choosing Installer→Quit Installer. When the Restart button appears, click it. Then eject the Mac OS X disc, either by holding down the mouse button while the computer restarts or, if you have a tray-loading CD drive, by pushing its Eject button during the moment of darkness during the restart.

3. **Click Agree to pass the Software License Agreement screen.**

   The Software License Agreement requires you to agree with whatever Apple's lawyers say.

4. **Choose the disk or partition where you want to install Mac OS X.**

   The installer proposes the screamingly obvious hard drive: the main one inside your Mac.

   If you have other drives, you can click Show All Disks to see their icons and choose one. (Yellow exclamation-mark icons mean, "You can't install here," for one technical reason or another.)

   The easiest way to proceed from here is to click Install. But don't.

   Instead, take the time to click Customize.

5. **Click Customize.**

   The Installer shows you a list of the various chunks that constitute Mac OS X. A few of them are easily dispensable. For example, if you turn off Additional Fonts, Language Translations (for Japanese, German, French, and so on), and the X11 Unix kit, you save a staggering *400 megabytes*. It's like getting a whole mini-hard drive for free (ka-ching!). Click Done when you're finished gloating.

Snow Leopard Spots: In the olden days, you'd also be advised at this point to turn off the drivers for the printers you'll never own or use (under Printer Support). In Snow Leopard, you don't have to worry; the installer already proposes installing only the drivers for printers you've used recently, or that are connect to the Mac right now. If you ever get a new printer, Mac OS X will download the software for it automatically.

   On the other hand, do turn on Rosetta and, if you like, QuickTime 7 (page 583)—although if you ever need these, the Mac will download and install them for you automatically from the Internet. And you can always install them later from the Optional Installs folder on your Mac OS X DVD.

6. **Click OK, then Install.**

   Now you're in for a 30- to 45-minute wait as the Installer copies software onto your hard drive. (That's why, if you're using a laptop and it's not plugged in, you'll be encouraged to plug it in.) At one point, it restarts the Mac from the DVD and carries right on.

   When the installer's finished, you see a message indicating that your Mac will restart in 30 seconds. If you haven't wandered off to watch TV, click the Restart button to end the countdown and get on with it.

Snow Leopard Spots: If the installer found a bit of startup software that's incompatible with Snow Leopard, a message on the screen lets you know at this point. It informs you that the offending software has been moved into a folder on your desktop called Incompatible Software, just so you know what's going on.

Mac OS X 10.6 is now installed on your Mac—but you're not quite ready to use it yet. See "The Setup Assistant" on the facing page.

The Erase & Install Option

If Mac OS X version 10.0 through 10.5-point-anything is on your hard drive, the Snow Leopard installer can neatly nip and tuck its software code, turning it *into* version 10.6. Everything remains just as you had it: your accounts, folders, files, email, network settings, everything-else settings, and so on.

In the olden days, this sophisticated surgery *very occasionally* left behind a minor gremlin here and there: peculiar cosmetic glitches, a checkbox that didn't seem to work, and so on. In the popular lore of Mac, therefore, gurus suggested that a clean install—a "nuke 'n' pave," where you *erase the hard drive completely* and then install Mac OS X afresh—was a safer way to go.

TROUBLESHOOTING MOMENT

Journaling

If you decide to erase your hard drive before installing Snow Leopard, you're offered a choice of several formats for your hard drive, like "Mac OS Extended (Journaled)" and "Unix File System." If you choose the first option, you turn on a special background feature of OS X known as *file journaling.*

When file journaling is turned on, your Mac keeps a personal diary of everything you do on your hard drive–opening, saving, deleting files, and so on. Journaling offers two benefits: a shorter startup time and safety in the event of a crash.

Here's how it works: When you press the power button, Mac OS X checks to see whether your computer was shut down properly (by choosing →Shut Down, for example, instead of just pulling out the plug).

If you didn't shut down properly, Mac OS X examines your hard drive the next time you start up to see if it needs repair. It has to scan the whole drive–which can take anywhere from a couple of minutes (if your hard drive is less than 10 GB) to a couple of hours (if your hard drive is more than 200 GB). Thanks to file journaling, however, Snow Leopard can tell

what was happening when your computer shut down–and therefore spend a lot less time checking your hard drive.

There are some downsides to the journaled format, however. First, this procedure doesn't actually recover what you were working on when your Mac shut down; it can only try to keep files you already saved from getting corrupted. Second, file journaling can make it take slightly longer for your programs to save files.

Mac OS X doesn't prevent you from having different hard drives with different formats. You can use the journaled format on your main hard drive, but not on your external FireWire drive–or vice versa. (If you ever want to change the format of one of your disks, use Disk Utility, although you'll have to erase all the information on the disk first.)

If you leave your Mac on all the time (if you run it as a Web server, for example), it's a good idea to use the journaled hard drive format. Keep in mind, too, that blackouts affect your hard drive just as much as pulling the plug. So if you live in Iraq, a solar-powered house, or anywhere else where power is inconsistent, journaling can be a lifesaver.

That option is still available in Snow Leopard. You might use it when you're about to sell your Mac and want to ensure that no trace of your former stuff is still there. Otherwise, there's little good reason to opt for this more dramatic purging.

The Erase & Install Option

If you're absolutely certain that you won't regret *completely erasing the computer*, follow the previously outlined steps 1 and 2. On the first screen, though, click Utilities, then Restart. Enter your administrator's name and password; click OK to restart from the DVD.

Select your language (a screen that now appears only when you start up from the Snow Leopard DVD) and click the right-arrow button. This time, click on the Install screen, and choose Utilities→Disk Utility. Click your hard drive's name, click Erase, confirm that the format is Mac OS Extended (Journaled), click Erase, and click Erase again. (By the way, you're about to *erase your entire hard drive*.)

When the erasing is complete, choose Disk Utility→Quit Disk Utility. You return to the installer screen, and you can resume from step 3 above.

Of course, you'll wind up with a factory-fresh, nearly empty Mac. You'll have to restore all your files and programs from your backup.

The Setup Assistant

When the Mac restarts after the installation, the first thing you experience is one of the most visually stunning post-installation OS startup movies in history: a fly-through of deep space, accompanied by scooby-dooby music and a fancy parade of 3-D, computer-generated translations of the word "Welcome." Once Apple has quite finished showing off its multimedia prowess, you arrive at a Welcome screen.

Note: You also hear a man's voice letting you know that if you're blind, you can press Esc to hear audio guidance for setting up the Mac and learning VoiceOver.

If you do so, you're treated to a crash course in VoiceOver, the Mac's screen-control/screen-reading software. This, by the way, is the only time you'll be offered this tutorial, so pay attention. (Hint: Here are the basics. Hold down the Control and Option keys and press the arrow keys to highlight different elements of the screen, hearing them pronounced. When a new window opens, press Control-Option-Shift-W to read the contents of the window. Press Control-Option-space bar to "click.")

Once again, you're in for a click-through-the-screens experience, this time with the aim of setting up your Mac's various options. After answering the questions on each screen, click Continue.

The number and sequence of information screens you encounter depend on whether you've upgraded an existing Mac or started fresh, but here are some of the possibilities:

• **Welcome.** Click the name of the country you're in.

- **Select Your Keyboard.** Different countries require different keyboard layouts. For example, if you choose the Canadian layout, pressing the] key on a U.S. keyboard produces the ç symbol. Click Continue.

- **Do you already own a Mac?** If you choose "Transfer my information from another Mac," the installer will assist you in sucking all your old programs, files, folders, and settings from the old Mac to the new one.

You can connect your Mac to the other one over a network—even a wireless one—or using FireWire Disk Mode (page 242).

You're using the Mac OS X Migration Assistant, shown in Figure A-2. The bottom of the screen lets you know how much stuff you've tagged for transferring, and how much disk space remains on the new Mac.

When you click Transfer, the data-copying process begins.

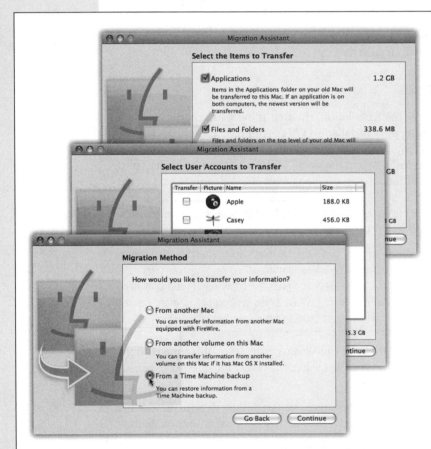

Figure A-2:
The Migration Assistant is actually pretty amazing. It brings over to your new Mac (or new Mac OS X installation) all the files, settings, folders, and even installed programs from an older Mac—or, in times of tragedy, from a Time Machine backup (see Chapter 6).

Along the way, you'll be asked whose account folder(s) you want brought over, which other stuff (like applications, files, and folders) to copy, and which sorts of settings you want.

When it's all over, you might have to reactivate a couple of Adobe programs, but otherwise, you should be ready to roll on your new (or new-feeling) Mac.

- **Select a Wireless Service.** This is your chance to introduce the Mac to any wireless networks in the vicinity. Click the network name you want to join, if you see it. If you don't see it, click Rescan to make the Mac sniff again in an attempt to locate the network. Or if there's no wireless hot spot at all—hey, it could happen—click Different Network Setup.

  In that event, you're offered choices like AirPort wireless, Cable modem/DSL modem, Local network (Ethernet), and "My computer does not connect to the Internet" (bummer!). When you click Continue, you may be asked for specific information—the local access number, account name, and password, and so on—regarding your Internet account. See Chapter 18 for advice on filling in these settings.

- **Enter Your Apple ID.** Here, you're offered the chance to type in, or create, an Apple ID—which is your email address. An Apple ID doesn't cost anything, but it makes life easier if you want to buy songs from the iTunes Store, order gift books or prints from iPhoto, and so on. (If you have a MobileMe account—see Chapter 18—put that account info here.)

- **Registration Information.** This is your chance to become a grain of sand on the great beach of the Apple database (and to set up your own "card" in Mac OS X's Address Book program).

Tip: If you're not interested in providing your personal information to Apple, or if you've already done so during a previous installation, press ⌘-Q. A message offers you Skip, Shut Down, and Cancel buttons. If you click Skip, you jump straight ahead to "Create Your Account," below.

- **A Few More Questions.** Where will you primarily use this computer? What best describes what you do? Do you want to get junk mail from Apple?

- **Create Your Account.** Most of the steps up to this point have been pretty inconsequential, but this is a big moment. You're about to create your *account*—your Administrator account, in fact, as described in Chapter 12.

FREQUENTLY ASKED QUESTION

Selective Installs

Whoops! I accidentally trashed my copy of the Calculator. How can I get it back? Do I have to reinstall the whole, seething mass of Mac OS X?

Fortunately, no. If you know the secret, you can install only specific components of Mac OS X without having to install the whole darned thing.

What you need is Pacifist, a shareware program that lets you install individual files and folders from the archipelago that is the collection of Mac OS X installation discs.

Technically, the Mac OS X installer is composed of dozens of subinstallers known as .pkg package files, which the installer opens one after another. That's the point of Pacifist—it lets you open an individual .pkg file.

Pacifist can also check existing installations and find missing or altered files. You can download it from this book's "Missing CD" page at *www.missingmanuals.com.*

All you have to do is make up a name, usually a short variation of your name, and a password. Choose carefully, because you can't easily change your account name later.

What you come up with here is extremely important, especially if several people use this Mac at different times, or if other people connect to it on a network. See page 469 for details on creating a password and a hint that will help you remember it.

If you're the only one who uses your Mac, it's perfectly OK to leave the password blank empty.

- **Select a Picture For This Account.** If your Mac has a built-in camera (laptops and iMacs do), you can take a photo of yourself to use as your account icon. Just click "Take a video snapshot." You get a 3-second countdown, and then the Mac snaps your photo. (You can always reshoot it.) Adjust the cropping by dragging inside the photo, and adjust the size by dragging the slider beneath it.

  If you're camera-shy, of course, you can choose "Choose from the picture library" and find an Apple-provided icon instead.

- **Your MobileMe Information.** If you have a MobileMe membership, Apple cheerfully lets you know when it will expire.

- **Thanks for being a MobileMe member.** Aw, shucks.

- **Thank You.** When you click Go, you wind up at the Mac OS X desktop, just as described in Chapter 1.

Uninstalling Mac OS X 10.6

There isn't any easy way to remove Mac OS X 10.6 if you decide you don't like it.

The chief problem is that thousands of its pieces are invisible. Even if you start up the Mac from another disk and then drag all the visible Mac OS X folders to the Trash, you'll leave behind many megabytes of software crumbs that you can't see.

So if you want to retreat to something earlier, back up the data that's worth preserving—mainly, your Home folder and Applications folder—and then erase the hard drive or partition and reinstall the operating system that you prefer.

Troubleshooting

Whether it's a car engine or an operating system, anything with several thousand parts can develop the occasional technical hiccup. Mac OS X is far more resilient than its predecessors, but it's still a complex system with the potential for occasional glitches.

Most freaky little glitches go away if you just try these two steps, one at a time:

- Quit and restart the wayward program.

- Log out and log back in again.

It's the *other* problems that'll drive you batty.

Minor Eccentric Behavior

All kinds of glitches may befall you, occasionally, in Mac OS X. Your desktop picture doesn't change when you change it in System Preferences. A menulet doesn't open when you click it. A program won't open—it just bounces in the Dock a couple of times and then stops.

When a single program is acting up like this, but quitting and restarting it does no good, try the following steps, in the following sequence.

First Resort: Repair Permissions
An amazing number of mysterious glitches arise because the *permissions* of either that item or something in your System folder—that is, the complex mesh of interconnected Unix permissions described in Chapter 12—have become muddled.

When something doesn't seem to be working right, therefore, open your Applications→ Utilities folder and open Disk Utility. Proceed as shown in Figure B-1.

This is a really, *really* great trick to know.

Snow Leopard Spots: The Repair Permissions routine is a lot faster and more solid-feeling than before. For starters, the "Estimated time" remaining readout is much more accurate than it used to be.

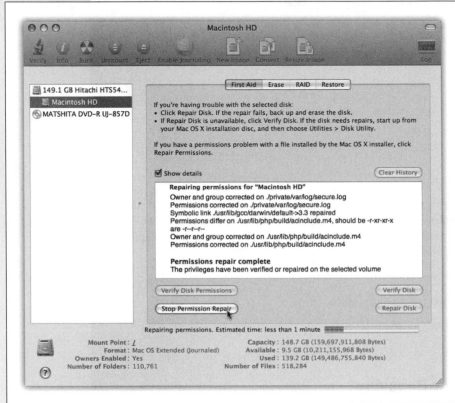

Figure B-1:
Click your hard drive's name in the left-side list; click the First Aid tab; click Repair Disk Permissions; and then read an article while the Mac checks out your disk. If the program finds anything amiss, you'll see messages like these. Among the text, you may recognize some Unix shorthand for read, write, and execute privileges (Chapter 16).

Second Resort: Look for an Update

If a program starts acting up immediately after you've installed Mac OS X 10.6, chances are good that it has some minor incompatibility. Chances are also good that you'll find an updated version on the company's Web site.

Third Resort: Toss the Prefs File

A corrupted preference file can bewilder the program that depends on it.

Before you go on a dumpfest, however, take this simple test. Log in using a *different account* (perhaps a dummy account that you create just for testing purposes). Run the problem program. Is the problem gone? If so, then the glitch exists only when *you* are logged in—which means it's a problem with *your* copy of the program's preferences.

Return to your own account. Open your Home folder→Library→Preferences folder, where you'll find neatly labeled preference files for all the programs you use. Each ends with the file name suffix *.plist*. For example, com.apple.finder.plist is the Finder's preference file, com.apple.dock.plist is the Dock's, and so on.

Put the suspect preference file into the Trash, but don't empty it. The next time you run the recalcitrant program, it will build itself a brand-new preference file that, if you're lucky, lacks whatever corruption was causing your problems.

If not, quit the program. You can reinstate its original .plist file from the Trash, if you'd find that helpful as you pursue your troubleshooting agenda.

Remember, however, that you actually have *three* Preferences folders. In addition to your own Home folder's stash, there's a second one in the Library folder in the main hard drive window (which administrators are allowed to trash), and a third in the System→Library folder in the main hard drive window (which nobody is allowed to trash—at least not without one of the security-bypass methods described in the box on the next page).

In any case, the next time you log in, the Mac creates fresh, virginal preference files.

Fourth Resort: Restart

Sometimes you can give Mac OS X or its programs a swift kick by restarting the Mac. It's an inconvenient step, but not nearly as time-consuming as what comes next. And it can fix problems that cropped up when you started up the computer.

Last Resort: Trash and Reinstall the Program

Sometimes reinstalling the problem program clears up whatever the glitch was.

First, however, throw away all traces of it. Open the Applications folder and drag the program's icon (or its folder) to the Trash. In most cases, the only remaining pieces to discard are its .plist file (or files) in your Home→Library→Preferences folder, and any scraps bearing the program's name in your Library→Application Support folder. (You can do a quick Spotlight search to round up any other pieces.)

Then reinstall the program from its original disc or installer—after first checking the company's Web site to see if there's an updated version, of course.

Frozen Programs (Force Quitting)

The occasional unresponsive application has become such a part of Mac OS X life that, among the Mac cognoscenti online, the dreaded, endless "please wait" cursor has been given its own acronym: SBOD (Spinning Beachball of Death). When the SBOD strikes, no amount of mouse clicking and keyboard pounding will get you out of the recalcitrant program.

Here are the different ways you can go about *force quitting* a stuck program (the equivalent of pressing Ctrl-Alt-Delete in Windows), in increasing order of desperation:

- **Force quit the usual way.** Choose →Force Quit to terminate the stuck program, or use one of the other force-quit methods described on page 153.

- **Force quit the sneaky way.** Some programs, including the Dock, don't show up at all in the usual Force Quit dialog box. Your next attempt, therefore, should be to open the Activity Monitor program (in Applications→Utilities), which shows *everything* that's running. Double-click a program and then, in the resulting dialog box, click Quit to force quit it. (Unix hounds: You can also use the *kill* command in Terminal, as described on page 643.)

Tip: If you find yourself having to quit the Dock more than once, here's an easier way: Make yourself a little AppleScript (Chapter 7) consisting of a single line: *tell application "Dock" to quit.* Save it as an application. Whenever you feel that the Dock (or Spaces or Exposé, which technically belong to the Dock) needs a good kick in the rear, double-click your little AppleScript.

- **Force quit remotely.** If the Finder itself has locked up, you can't very well get to Activity Monitor (unless it occurred to you *beforehand* to stash its icon in your Dock—not a bad idea). At this point, you may have to abort the locked program from another computer across the network, if you're on one, by using the *SSH* (secure shell) command. The end of Chapter 22 offers a blow-by-blow description of how you might terminate a program by remote control in this way, either from elsewhere on the office network or even from across the Internet.

Tip: If all of this seems like a lot to remember, you can always force restart the Mac. On most Macs, you do that by holding down the power button for 5 seconds. If that doesn't work, press Control-⌘-power button.

WORKAROUND WORKSHOP

Fixing Permissions Problems the Manly Way

Sooner or later, when you try to move, rename, or delete a certain file or folder, you may get an error message like "The folder 'Junk' could not be opened because you do not have sufficient access privileges"—or "The operation could not be completed because this item is owned by Chris" (or by *root,* which means by Mac OS X itself).

What they're trying to say is, you've run into a permissions problem.

As noted in Chapter 12, Mac OS X is designed to accommodate a number of different people who share the same Mac over time. Nobody is allowed to meddle with other people's files or folders. But even if you're the solo operator of your

Mac, you still share it with Mac OS X itself (which the error messages may refer to as *root* or *system*).

In any case, if you're confident that whatever you're trying to do isn't some kind of nihilistic, self-destructive act like trashing the Applications folder, it's easy enough to get past these limitations. Just highlight the recalcitrant file or folder and then choose File→Get Info. In its window, you'll find a Sharing & Permissions panel that lets you give yourself read and write privileges—if you have an Administrator account, that is. (Just don't perform this surgery on files in the System folder.)

Now you can do whatever you like with this folder.

Can't Move or Rename an Icon

If you're not allowed to drag an icon somewhere, the error message that appears almost always hits the nail on the head: You're trying to move a file or folder that *isn't yours*. The box on the facing page explains the solutions to this problem.

Application Won't Open

If a program won't open (if its icon bounces merrily in the Dock for a few seconds, for instance, but then nothing happens), begin by trashing its preference file, as described on page 824. If that doesn't solve it, reinstalling the program, or installing the Snow Leopard-compatible update for it, usually does.

Startup Problems

Not every problem you encounter is related to running applications. Sometimes trouble strikes before you even get that far. The following are examples.

Kernel Panic

When you see the cheerful, multilingual dialog box shown in Figure B-2, you've got yourself a *kernel panic*—a Unix nervous breakdown.

(In such situations, *user panic* might be the more applicable term, but that's programmers for you.)

If you experience a kernel panic, it's almost always the result of a *hardware* glitch—most often a bad memory (RAM) board, but possibly an accelerator card, graphics card, SCSI gadget, or USB hub that Mac OS X doesn't like. A poorly seated AirPort card can bring on a kernel panic, too, and so can a bad USB or FireWire cable.

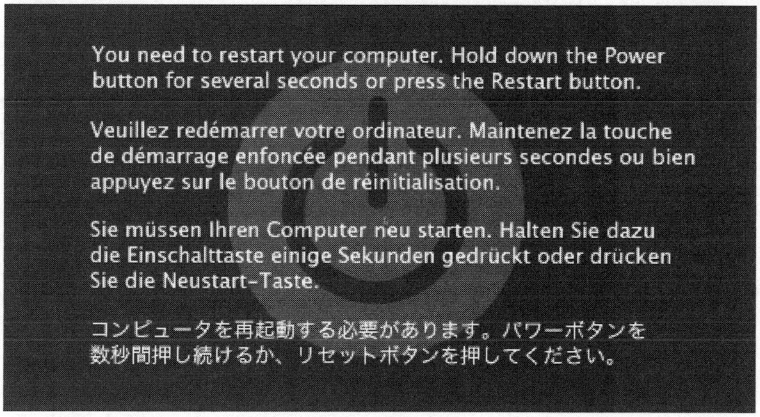

Figure B-2:
A kernel panic is almost always related to some piece of add-on hardware. And look at the bright side: At least you get this handsome dialog box in Snow Leopard. That's a lot better than the Mac OS X 10.0 and 10.1 effect—random text gibberish superimposing itself on your screen.

> You need to restart your computer. Hold down the Power button for several seconds or press the Restart button.
>
> Veuillez redémarrer votre ordinateur. Maintenez la touche de démarrage enfoncée pendant plusieurs secondes ou bien appuyez sur le bouton de réinitialisation.
>
> Sie müssen Ihren Computer neu starten. Halten Sie dazu die Einschalttaste einige Sekunden gedrückt oder drücken Sie die Neustart-Taste.
>
> コンピュータを再起動する必要があります。パワーボタンを数秒間押し続けるか、リセットボタンを押してください。

If simply restarting the machine doesn't help, detach every shred of gear that didn't come from Apple. Restore these components to the Mac one at a time until you find out which one was causing Mac OS X's bad hair day. If you're able to pinpoint the culprit, seek its manufacturer (or its Web site) on a quest for updated drivers, or at least try to find out for sure whether the add-on is compatible with Mac OS X.

Tip: This advice goes for your Macintosh itself. Apple periodically updates the Mac's *own* "drivers" in the form of a *firmware update.* You download these updates from the Support area of Apple's Web site (if indeed Mac OS X's own Software Update mechanism doesn't alert you to their existence).

There's one other cause for kernel panics, by the way, and that's moving, renaming, or changing the access permissions for Mac OS X's essential system files and folders—the Applications or System folder, for example. (See Chapter 12 for more on permissions.) This cause isn't even worth mentioning, of course, because nobody would be that foolish.

Safe Mode (Safe Boot)

In times of troubleshooting, Windows fans press an F-key to start up in Safe Mode. That's how you turn off all nonessential system-software nubbins in an effort to get a sick machine at least powered up.

Although not one person in a hundred knows it, Mac OS X offers the same kind of emergency keystroke. It can come in handy when you've just installed some new piece of software and find that you can't even start up the machine, or when one of your fonts is corrupted, or when something you've designated as a Login Item turns out to be gumming up the works. With this trick, you can at least turn on the computer so that you can uninstall the cranky program.

The trick is to *press the Shift key* as the machine is starting up. Hold it down from the startup chime until you see the words "Safe Boot," in red lettering, on the login screen.

Welcome to Safe Mode.

What have you accomplished?

- **Checked your hard drive.** The Shift-key business makes the startup process seem to take a very long time; behind that implacable Apple logo, Mac OS X is actually scanning your entire hard drive for problems.

- **Brought up the login screen.** When you do a safe boot, you must click your name and enter your password, even if you normally have Automatic Login turned on.

- **Turned off your kernel extensions.** All kinds of software nuggets load during the startup process. Some of them, you choose yourself: icons you add to the Login Items list in the System Preferences→Accounts pane. Others are normally hidden: a large mass of *kernel extensions,* which are chunks of software that add various features to the basic operating system. (Apple's kernel extensions live in your System→Library→Extensions folder; others may be in your Library→StartupItems folder.)

If you're experiencing startup crashes, some non-Apple installer may have given you a kernel extension that doesn't care for Mac OS X 10.6—so in Safe Mode, they're all turned off.

- **Turned off your fonts.** Corrupted fonts are a chronic source of trouble—and because you can't tell by looking, they're darned difficult to diagnose. So just to make sure you can at least get into your computer, Safe Mode turns them all off (except the authorized, Apple-sanctioned ones that it actually needs to run, which are in your System→Library→Fonts folder).

- **Trashed your font cache.** The font cache is a speed trick. Mac OS X stores the visual information for each of your fonts on the hard drive so the system won't have to read every single typeface off your hard drive when you open your Font menus or the Font panel.

  When these files get scrambled, startup crashes can result. That's why a Safe Boot moves all these files into the Trash. (You'll even see them sitting there in the Trash after the startup process is complete, although there's not much you can do with them except walk around holding your nose and pointing.)

- **Turned off your login items.** Safe Mode also prevents any Finder windows from opening *and* prevents your own handpicked startup items from opening—that is, whatever you've asked Snow Leopard to auto-open by adding them to the System Preferences→Accounts→Login Items list.

  This, too, is a troubleshooting tactic. If some login item crashes your Mac every time it opens, you can squelch it just long enough to remove it from your Login Items list.

Tip: If you don't hold down the Shift key until you click the Log In button (after entering your name and password at the login screen), you squelch *only* your login items but *not* the fonts and extensions.

Once you reach the desktop, you'll find a long list of standard features inoperable. You can't use DVD Player, capture video in iMovie, use a wireless network, use certain microphones and speakers, or use your modem. (The next time you restart, all this goodness will be restored, assuming you're no longer clutching the Shift key in a sweaty panic.)

In any case, the beauty of Safe Mode is that it lets you get your Mac going. You have access to your files, so at least the emergency of crashing-on-startup is over. And you can start picking through your fonts and login items to see if you can spot the problem.

Gray Screen During Startup

Confirm that your Mac has the latest firmware, as described earlier. Detach and test all your non-Apple add-ons. Finally, perform a disk check (see page 414).

Blue Screen During Startup

Most of the troubleshooting steps for this problem (which is usually accompanied by the Spinning Beachball of Death cursor) are the same as those described under "Kernel Panic" on page 827.

Forgotten Password

If you or one of the other people who use your Mac have forgotten the corresponding account password, no worries: Just read the box on page 487.

Fixing the Disk

The beauty of Mac OS X's design is that the operating system itself is frozen in its perfect, pristine state, impervious to conflicting system extensions, clueless Mac users, and other sources of disaster.

That's the theory, anyway. But what happens if something goes wrong with the complex software that operates the hard drive itself?

Fortunately, Mac OS X comes with its own disk-repair program. In the familiar Mac universe of icons and menus, it takes the form of a program in Applications→Utilities called Disk Utility. In the barren world of Terminal and the command line interface, there's a utility that works just as well but bears a different name: *fsck* (for file system check).

In any case, running Disk Utility or its alter ego *fsck* is a powerful and useful troubleshooting tool that can cure all kinds of strange ills, including these problems, among others:

- Your Mac freezes during startup, either before or after the Login screen.

- The startup process interrupts itself with the appearance of the text-only command line.

- You get the "applications showing up as folders" problem.

Method 1: Disk Utility

The easiest way to check your disk is to use the Disk Utility program. Use this method if your Mac can, indeed, start up. (See Method 2 if you can't even get that far.)

Disk Utility can't fix the disk it's *on* (except for permissions repairs, described at the beginning of this appendix). That's why you have to restart the computer from the Snow Leopard installation disc (or another startup disk), and run Disk Utility from there. The process goes like this:

1. **Start up the Mac from the Mac OS X DVD.**

    The best way to do that is to insert the disc and then restart the Mac while holding down the C key.

You wind up, after some time, at the Mac OS X Installer screen. Don't be fooled— installing Mac OS X is *not* what you want to do here. Don't click Continue!

2. **Click Utilities. Then choose Utilities→Disk Utility.**

That's the unexpected step. After a moment, the Disk Utility screen appears.

Tip: You could also skip steps 1 and 2 by starting up from an external hard drive. Just run its own copy of Disk Utility to check your Mac's hard drive.

---

3. **Click the disk or disk partition you want to fix, click the First Aid tab, and then click Repair Disk.**

The Mac whirls into action, checking a list of very technical disk-formatting parameters.

If you see the message, "The volume 'Macintosh HD' appears to be OK," that's meant to be *good* news. Believe it or not, that cautious statement is as definitive an affirmation as Disk Utility is capable of making about the health of your disk.

Disk Utility may also tell you that the disk is damaged but that it can't help you. In that case, you need a more heavy-duty disk-repair program like DiskWarrior (*www. alsoft.com*).

Method 2: *fsck* at the Console

Disk Utility isn't of much use when you can't find the Snow Leopard DVD, when your DVD drive isn't working, or when you're in a hurry to get past the startup problems that are plaguing your machine. In those cases, you'll be glad you can boot into the Mac's raw Unix underlayer to perform some diagnostic (and healing) commands.

Specifically, you'll be glad that you can run the Unix program *fsck,* for which Disk Utility is little more than a pretty faceplate.

Like any Unix program, *fsck* runs at the command line. You launch it from the all-text, black Unix screen by typing *fsck* and pressing Return. (You can also use *fsck -f.*)

You can't, however, just run *fsck* in Terminal. You have to run it when the usual arsenal of graphic-interface programs—like the Finder and its invisible suite of accessory programs—isn't running.

Single-user mode (⌘-S at startup)

The Terminal program is the best known form of Mac OS X's command line, but it's not the only one. In fact, there are several other ways to get there.

In general, you don't hear them mentioned except in the context of troubleshooting, because the Terminal program offers many more convenient features for doing the same thing. And because it's contained in a Mac OS X–style window, Terminal is not as disorienting as the three methods you're about to read.

All these techniques take you into *console mode,* shown in Figure B-3. In console mode, Unix takes over your screen completely, showing white type against black, no windows or icons in sight. Abandon the mouse, all ye who enter here; in console mode, you can't do anything but type commands.

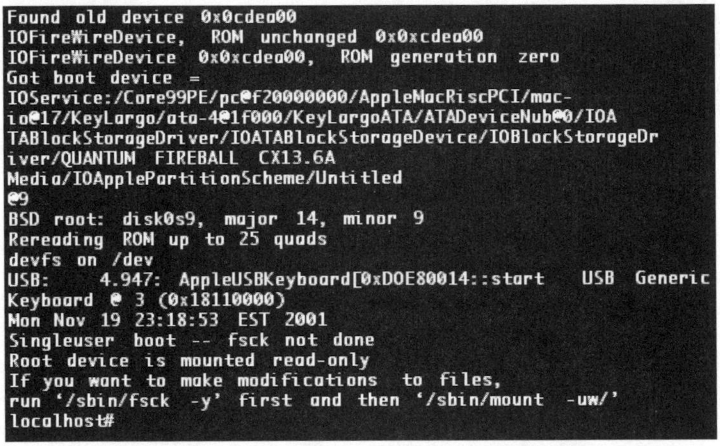

```
Found old device 0x0cdea00
IOFireWireDevice,   ROM unchanged 0x0xcdea00
IOFireWireDevice  0x0xcdea00,   ROM generation  zero
Got boot device =
IOService:/Core99PE/pc@f20000000/AppleMacRiscPCI/mac-
io@17/KeyLargo/ata-4@1f000/KeyLargoATA/ATADeviceNub@0/IOA
TABlockStorageDriver/IOATABlockStorageDevice/IOBlockStorageDr
iver/QUANTUM  FIREBALL  CX13.6A
Media/IOApplePartitionScheme/Untitled
@9
BSD root: disk0s9, major 14, minor 9
Rereading  ROM up to 25 quads
devfs on /dev
USB:    4.947: AppleUSBKeyboard[0xDOE80014::start    USB  Generic
Keyboard @ 3 (0x18110000)
Mon Nov 19 23:18:53  EST 2001
Singleuser  boot  -- fsck not done
Root device is mounted read-only
If you want to make modifications  to files,
run '/sbin/fsck -y' first and then '/sbin/mount  -uw/'
localhost#
```

Figure B-3:
In console mode, your entire screen is a command line interface. Unix jockeys can go to town here. Everyone else can timidly type fsck -y after the localhost:/ root # prompt—see this prompt on the very last line?—and hope for the best.

POWER USERS' CLINIC

Journaling vs. *fsck*

Mac OS X 10.6 comes with *journaling* turned on. Journaling means that the Mac keeps a diary about every tiny bit of hard drive activity. In event of a crash or freeze, the Mac knows precisely what was going on at the time, and precisely which files might have been damaged.

In theory, then, you'll never need *fsck* at all. After all, there's nothing to check. The Mac's journaling software is always on top of things—and, if the journal indicates that there was trouble saving a file, Mac OS X can finish or undo the change.

Even Apple concedes, however, that in the real world, things can still go wrong, even with journaling turned on.

That's why, when you attempt to use *fsck* as described on these pages, a message will inform you that, hey, you don't *need* to repair your disk. Thanks to journaling, there's no damage to repair.

If you decide to proceed on the off chance that something's gone wrong behind your journal's back, just use the *-f* flag to force the disk check, like this: *fsck -f.*

Note, however, that you may see a series of *phony* error messages when you do this. If you see any of these messages, you should ignore them:

- "Volume bitmap needs minor repair"

- "Invalid volume free block count" or "block count changed from XX to YY"

- "Volume header needs minor repair"

- "Incorrect block count for file"

If you see any *other* error messages, though, let *fsck* go ahead and repair them.

To get there in times of startup troubleshooting, press ⌘-S while the Mac is starting up. (If you're stuck at the frozen remnants of a previous startup attempt, you may first have to force restart your Mac; hold down the ⏻ button for five seconds.)

Instead of arriving at the usual desktop, you see technical-looking text scrolling up a black screen as the Mac runs its various startup routines. When it finally stops at the *localhost #* prompt, you're ready to type commands. You're now in what's called *single-user mode,* meaning that the Unix multiple-accounts software has yet to load. You won't be asked to log in.

At the *localhost #* prompt, type *fsck -y* (note the space before the hyphen) and press Return. (The *y* means "yes," as in "yes, I want you to fix any problems automatically.") If the Mac refuses because journaling is turned on (page 818), you can also type *fsck -fy* to force the disk check.

Tip: Even though you've gone to all this trouble for the sake of running *fsck,* you can also use *ls, cd, rm,* or any of the other Unix commands described in Chapter 16 while you're here.

Now the file system check program takes over, running through five sets of tests. When it's complete, you'll see one of two messages:

- **The volume Macintosh HD appears to be OK.** All is well. Type *exit* and press Return to proceed to the usual Login screen and desktop.

- **File system was modified.** A good sign, but just a beginning. You need to run the program again. One *fsck* pass often repairs only one layer of problems, leaving another to be patched in the next pass. Type *fsck -y* a second time, a third time, and so on, until you finally arrive at a "disk appears to be OK" message.

Type *exit* at the prompt and press Return to get back to the familiar world of icons and windows.

FREQUENTLY ASKED QUESTION

Viruses? What Viruses?

One great thing about the old Mac OS was that there were hardly any viruses to worry about—all the nasties seemed to be written for Windows. But now that we're using Unix, which has been around for 30 years and has a huge user base, is it time to worry again?

Nope. There are even fewer viruses for Unix than for the Mac OS.

You still need to be careful with Word and Excel macro viruses, of course. If you open a Word or Excel attachment sent by email from someone else, and a big fat dialog box warns you that it contains macros, simply click Disable Macros and get on with your life. And you still need an antivirus program for Windows if you run it on your Mac (Chapter 8).

Otherwise, you have little to worry about. After eight years, there hasn't been one single Mac OS X virus outbreak—partly because virus writers have a smaller "audience" in Mac fans, and partly because Mac OS X is more difficult to hack.

Sleep well.

Where to Get Troubleshooting Help

If the basic steps described in this chapter haven't helped, the universe is crawling with additional help sources. In general, this is the part in any Mac book where you're directed to Apple's Support Web site, to various discussion forums, and so on—and, indeed, those help sources are listed below.

But the truth is, the mother of all troubleshooting resources is not any of those—it's Google. You'll find more answers faster using Google than you ever will using individual help sites. That's because Google includes all those help sites in its search!

Suppose, for example, that you've just installed the 10.6.1 software update for Snow Leopard, and it's mysteriously turned all your accounts (including your own) into Standard accounts. And without any Administrator account, you can't install new programs, change network settings, add or edit other accounts, and so on.

You could go to one Web site after another, hunting for a fix, repeating your search—or you could just type *Leopard 10.6.1 standard accounts* into Google and hit Enter. You'll get your answers after just a few more seconds of clicking and exploring the results.

Help Online

These Web sites contain nothing but troubleshooting discussions, tools, and help:

- **Apple Discussion Groups** (*http://discussions.apple.com*). The volume and quality of question-and-answer activity here dwarfs any other free source. If you're polite and concise, you can post questions to the multitudes here and get more replies from them than you'll know what to do with.

- **Apple's help site** (*www.apple.com/support*). Apple's help site includes downloadable manuals, software updates, frequently asked questions, and many other resources.

  It also has a Search box. It's your ticket to the Knowledge Base, a collection of 100,000 individual technical articles, organized in a searchable database, that the Apple technicians themselves consult when you call for help. You can search it either by typing in keywords or by using pop-up menus of question categories.

- **MacFixIt** (*www.macfixit.com*). The world's one-stop resource for Mac troubleshooting advice; alas, you have to pay to access the good stuff.

Help by Telephone

Finally, consider contacting whoever sold you the component that's making your life miserable: the printer company, scanner company, software company, or whatever.

If it's a Mac OS problem, you can call Apple at 800-275-2273 (that's 800-APL-CARE). For the first 90 days after your purchase of Mac OS X, the technicians will answer your questions for free.

After that, unless you've paid for AppleCare for your Mac (a 3-year extended warranty program), Apple will charge you to answer your questions. Fortunately, if the problem turns out to be Apple's fault, they won't charge you.

The Windows-to-Mac Dictionary

Maybe you were persuaded by the Apple "Switch" ad campaign. Maybe you like the looks of today's Macs. Or maybe you've just endured one virus, spyware download, or service pack too many. In any case, if you're switching to Mac OS X from Windows, this appendix is for you. It's an alphabetical listing of every common Windows function and where to find it in Mac OS X. After all, an operating system is an operating system. The actual functions are pretty much the same—they're just in different places.

Tip: If this listing only whets your appetite for information about making the switch, read *Switching to the Mac: The Missing Manual,* Snow Leopard Edition. In addition to an expanded version of this appendix, it also contains useful information on moving your files from the PC to the Mac, copying over your email, transferring your contacts to Address Book, and so on.

About [this program]

To find out the version number of the program you're using, don't look in the Help menu. Instead, look in the *application* menu next to the menu—the one that bears the name of the program you're in. That's where you find the About command for Macintosh programs.

Accessibility Options control panel

The special features that let you operate the computer even with impaired vision, hearing, or motor control are called Universal Access in Mac OS X. They're in System Preferences (see Chapter 9).

Active Desktop

The Mac never displays Web pages directly on the desktop—and knowing Apple, that's probably a point of pride. But Dashboard (Chapter 5) keeps Internet data only a keystroke away.

Add Hardware control panel

The Mac requires no program for installing the driver for a new external gadget. The drivers for most printers, mice, keyboards, cameras, camcorders, and other accessories are preinstalled. If you plug something into the Mac and find that it doesn't work immediately, just install the driver from the included CD (or the manufacturer's Web site).

Add or Remove Programs control panel

Here's another one you just don't need on the Macintosh. Installing a program onto the Mac is described on page 195. Removing a program simply involves dragging its icon to the Trash. (For a clean sweep, inspect your Home→Library→Preferences and Library→Application Support folders to see if any preference files got left behind.)

All Programs

There's no Programs menu built into Mac OS X, like the one on the Windows Start menu. If you'd like one, drag your Applications folder into the end of the Dock. Now its icon is a tidy pop-up menu of every program on your machine.

Alt key

On the Mac, it's the Option key, although the key usually says "Alt" on it too. (In some countries, it says *only* Alt.) You can substitute Option for Alt in any keystroke in most popular programs. The Option key has a number of secondary features on the Mac, too: It hides the windows of one program when you click into another, and so on.

Automatic Update

The →Software Update command does exactly the same thing.

Backspace key

It's in the same place on the Macintosh keyboard, but it's called the Delete key.

Battery Level

The battery-level graph (⬜) for your Mac laptop now appears in the menu bar, rather than in the system tray. (If you don't see it, open System Preferences→Energy Saver and turn it on.)

BIOS

You'll never have to update or even think about the ROM of your Macintosh (the approximate equivalent of the BIOS on the PC). It's permanent and unchanging. The very similar *firmware* of your Macintosh does occasionally have to be updated in order to work with a new version of the Mac operating system or some dramatic new feature—once every four years, perhaps. You'll be notified on the screen when the time comes.

Briefcase

The Briefcase is a Windows invention designed to help you keep your files in sync between a laptop and a desktop computer. The iDisk, available to members of Apple's $100-a-year MobileMe service, is like a 20-gigabyte version. It's always available to any computer, since it lives on the Internet, and it offers a feature that automatically keeps the most recent versions of your documents synced among your Macs. Chapter 18 has the details.

Calculator

The Calculator program in Mac OS X is almost identical to the one in Windows, except that it can also perform conversions (temperature, distance, currency, and so on) and features an editable "paper tape." It sits in your Applications folder and is described in Chapter 10. (There's a simpler Calculator in Dashboard, too; see the end of Chapter 5. And don't forget that you can type quick math equations into the Spotlight menu.)

Camera and Scanner Wizard

When you connect a digital camera or scanner to your Mac, iPhoto or Image Capture opens automatically and prepares to download the pictures automatically. Details are in Chapter 10.

CDs

To open the CD/DVD drawer, or, if you have a slot-loading drive, to spit out the disc that's in it, hold down the ⏏ key on your Mac keyboard. If it's an older Mac keyboard without a ⏏ key, you can eject a CD (or any other disc) by Control-clicking (or right-clicking) its desktop icon and then choosing Eject from the shortcut menu. There are various other ways to eject a disc, but the point is that you never do so by pushing the Eject button on the disc drive itself.

Character Map

This Windows program helps you find out what keys you need to press to trigger trademark symbols, copyright symbols, and other special characters. The equivalent on the Mac is called the Keyboard Viewer (page 235)—but the Character Palette (page 233) is even easier to use.

Clean Install

The Mac OS X 10.6 installer can give you a fresh copy of the operating system, just as the Windows installer can. Instructions are in Appendix A.

Clipboard

The Mac's Clipboard works much like the one in Windows. In the Finder, you can choose Edit→Show Clipboard to see whatever you most recently copied or cut.

Command line

In Mac OS X, the command line is alive and well—but it speaks Unix, not DOS. You get to it by opening Terminal, which is described in Chapter 16.

Control Panel

The Control Panel in Mac OS X is called System Preferences, and you open it from your menu. As in Windows XP or Vista, you can view these icons either by category or in a simple alphabetical list: Just choose either Organize by Categories or Organize Alphabetically from the View menu.

Copy, Cut, Paste

When you're editing in a word processor or graphics program, the Mac OS X Cut, Copy, and Paste commands work exactly as they do in Windows.

At the desktop, however, there are a few differences. You can indeed copy icons and paste them into a new window using the Copy and Paste commands—but you just can't *cut* them out of a window, as you can in Windows. On the other hand, Mac OS X offers a handy secondary feature: If you paste into a word or text processor instead of into another desktop window, you get a list of the names of the icons you copied.

Ctrl key

On the Macintosh, you generally substitute the ⌘ key in keystrokes that would involve the Control key in Windows. In other words, the Save command is now ⌘-S instead of Ctrl-S, Open is ⌘-O instead of Ctrl-O, and so on.

Date and Time

To set your Mac's calendar and clock, open Date & Time in System Preferences.

Delete Key (Forward Delete)

Most desktop Mac keyboards have a forward-delete key (labeled ⌦ or *Del*) exactly like the ones on PCs. On Mac laptops, and on Apple's aluminum keyboards, you trigger the forward-delete function by pressing the Delete key while simultaneously pressing the Fn key.

Desktop

The Macintosh desktop is pretty much the same idea as the Windows desktop, with a few key differences:

- Disk icons show up on the Mac desktop as soon as they are inserted or connected. You don't have to open a window to see their icons.

- You change the desktop picture using the Desktop & Screen Saver panel of System Preferences.

- The Trash is an icon in the Dock, not on the desktop.

Directories

Most people call them *folders* on the Mac.

Disk Defragmenter

There's no such utility included with Mac OS X; the system auto-defragments in the background. (A *defragmenting* program moves around the pieces of files on your hard drive in an effort to optimize their placement and speed of opening.)

Disks

Working with disks is very different on the Mac. Every disk inside, or attached to, a Macintosh is represented on the screen by an icon. Mac OS X does have something like the Computer or My Computer window (choose Go→Computer), but both the icons on the desktop and the icons in the Computer window reflect only the disks currently inserted in your Mac. You'll never see an icon for an empty drive, as you do on Windows, and there's no such thing as drive letters (because the Mac refers to *disks,* not to *drives*—and refers to them by name).

Display control panel

The functions of the Windows Display control panel lurk in the Mac OS X System Preferences program—just not all in one place. You set up your desktop picture and screen saver using the Desktop & Screen Saver pane and adjust your monitor settings using the Displays pane. (Mac OS X offers no equivalent to the Appearance tab in Windows, for changing the system-wide look of your computer.)

DLL files

The Macintosh equivalent of DLL files—shared libraries of programming code—are invisible and off-limits. As a result, no Macintosh user ever experiences DLL conflicts or out-of-date DLL files.

DOS prompt

There's a command line in Mac OS X, but it's Unix, not DOS. For details, see Chapter 16.

Drivers

See "Add or Remove Programs."

End Task dialog box

If some Macintosh program is hung or frozen, you escape it pretty much the same way you would in Windows: by forcing it to quit. To bring up the Force Quit dialog box, you press Option-⌘-Esc or choose ￼→Force Quit.

Exiting programs

You can quit a program either by choosing Quit from the menu bearing its name (next to the ￼ menu), or by right-clicking (or Control-clicking) its Dock icon and then choosing Quit from the pop-up menu.

Explorer

The Mac has its own "tree" view of the files and folders on your hard drive: list view. By expanding the "flippy triangles" of your folders, you build a hierarchy that shows you as much or as little detail as you like.

If you prefer the Explorer effect of clicking a folder in *one* pane to see its contents in the next, try Column view instead. Both views are described in Chapter 1.

Favorites

In Mac OS X, there isn't one single Favorites menu that lists both favorite Web sites and favorite icons. The Bookmarks menu of Safari, the Web browser, lists only Web sites, and the Favorites folder at the desktop (page 81f) lists only favorite files, folders, disks, and other icons.

Faxing

Faxing is built into Snow Leopard; it's described in Chapter 14. (Hint: Choose File→ Print; from the PDF button at the bottom of the Print dialog box, choose Fax PDF.)

File Sharing

See Chapter 13 for an in-depth look at the Macintosh networking and file-sharing system.

Floppy disks

Floppy drives on Macs disappeared in about 1998. It's much more efficient to transfer files between machines using an Ethernet cable or improvised wireless network (Chapter 13), a CD or DVD that you burned (Chapter 11), your Internet-based iDisk (Chapter 18), or email (Chapter 19).

Folder Options

The Folder Options control panel in Windows is a collection of unrelated settings that boil down to this:

- **General tab.** Exactly as in Windows, it's up to you whether or not double-clicking a folder opens up a second window—or just changes what's in the first one. On the Mac, you make these changes using the Finder→Preferences command. There you'll find the option called "Always open folders in a new window."

- **View tab.** Most of the options here don't exist on the Mac. For example, system files are *always* hidden on the Mac; you can't opt to make them visible (at least not with the built-in controls). You can, however, choose whether you want to see the file name extensions in your desktop windows (like .doc and .html). Choose Finder→Preferences→Advanced, and turn "Show all file extensions" on or off.

- **File Types tab.** Just as in Windows, you can reassign certain document types so that double-clicking opens them up in the program of your choice. But on the Mac, you can reassign either a whole class of files at once, as in Windows, *or* one file at a time. To do it, you use the Get Info window as described on page 175.

- **Offline Files.** There's no equivalent feature on the Mac.

Fonts

The Mac and Windows both use TrueType, PostScript, and Open Type fonts. (In fact, your Mac can even use the exact font files you had in Windows.) On the Mac, however, there are actually three different folders that can contain them. A complete discussion is in Chapter 14.

Help and Support

At the desktop, choose Help→Mac Help. In other programs, the Help command is generally at the right end of your menus, exactly as in Windows.

Hibernation

The Mac can't hibernate at all, as modern PCs do, cutting all power but remembering what programs and documents you had open for a faster restart later. Sleep mode is the closest it gets; see "Standby Mode."

Internet Explorer

Microsoft has abandoned the Mac version of Internet Explorer. Apple would prefer, of course, that you try Safari, its own Web browser, but many a power user prefers Firefox, which is nearly identical to the Windows version.

Internet Options

On the Mac, you find the options for your Web browser by choosing Safari→ Preferences.

IRQs

They don't exist on the Mac.

Java

This interpreter of tiny Web-page programs is alive and well in Mac OS X. Java programs run fine in all Mac Web browsers.

Keyboard control panel

You can make exactly the same kinds of settings—and more—on the Keyboard & Mouse pane of System Preferences.

Logging in

The multiple-accounts feature of Mac OS X is extremely similar to that of Windows 2000, XP, Vista, and 7. In each case, you can, if you wish, create a requirement to log in with a name and password before using the computer. This arrangement keeps separate the documents, email, and settings of each person who uses the computer. (Chapter 12 tells all.)

Mail control panel

Mac OS X comes with its own email program (described in Chapter 19); all of its settings are contained within the program.

Maximize button

On the Mac, clicking the Zoom button (the green button in the upper-left corner of a window) does something like the Maximize button in Windows: It makes your window larger. On the Mac, however, clicking the zoom button never makes the window expand to fill the entire screen. Instead, the window grows—or *shrinks*—precisely enough to enclose its contents.

Menus

On the Macintosh, there's only one menu bar, always at the very top of the screen. The menus change depending on the program and the window you're using, but the point is that the menu bar is no longer inside each window you open.

Tip: Just because you don't see the little underlines in the menus doesn't mean you can't operate all the menus from the keyboard, as in Windows. See page 178 for details.

Minimize button

You can minimize a Mac OS X window to the Dock, just the way you would minimize a Windows window to the taskbar. You do so by double-clicking its title bar, pressing ⌘-M, choosing Window→Minimize Window, or clicking the yellow Minimize button at the top left of a window. (Restore the window by clicking its icon in the Dock.)

Mouse control panel

The equivalent settings can be found in the Mouse panel of System Preferences.

(My) Computer

The Mac's Computer window is very similar (choose Go→Computer), in that it shows the icons of all disks (hard drive, CD, and so on). On the other hand, it shows *only* the disks that are actually inserted or connected. (See "Disks.")

(My) Documents, (My) Pictures, (My) Music

The equivalent buckets for your everyday documents, music files, and pictures are the Documents, Pictures, and Music folders in your Home folder.

(My) Network Places

On the Mac, the "network neighborhood" is almost always on the screen: It's the Sidebar, the panel at the left side of every Finder window. All the Macs and PCs on your network are always listed here, in the Shared category (unless you turned this feature off in Finder→Preferences, of course).

Network Neighborhood

See the previous entry.

Notepad

There's no Mac OS X Notepad program. But give Stickies a try (page 396), or use the system-wide Notes feature (page 731).

Personal Web Server

To find out how to turn your Mac into a state-of-the-art Web server, see Chapter 22.

Phone and Modem Options control panel

To find the modem settings for your Mac, see page 676.

Power Options

To control when your Mac goes to sleep and (if it's a laptop) how much power it uses, use the Energy Saver pane of System Preferences (Chapter 9).

Printer Sharing

To share a USB inkjet printer with other Macs on the network, open the Sharing pane of System Preferences on the Mac with the printer. Turn on Printer Sharing.

To use the shared printer from across the network, open the document you want to print, choose File→Print, and choose the name of the shared printer from the first pop-up menu.

Printers and Faxes

For a list of your printers, open the Print & Fax pane of System Preferences (Chapter 14). For details on faxing, see "Faxing."

PrntScrn key

You capture pictures of your Mac screen by pressing Shift-⌘-3 (for a full-screen grab) or Shift-⌘-4 (to grab a selected portion of the screen). There are many options available; see the end of Chapter 14.

Program Files folder

The Applications folder (Go→Applications) is like the Program Files folder in Windows—except that you're not discouraged from opening it and double-clicking things. On the Macintosh, every program bears its true name; Microsoft Word, for example, is called Microsoft Word, not WINWORD.EXE.

Properties dialog box

You can call up something very similar for any *icon* (file, folder, program, disk, printer) by highlighting its icon and then choosing File→Get Info. But objects in Macintosh *programs* generally don't contain Properties dialog boxes.

Recycle Bin

Mac OS X has a Trash icon at the end of the Dock. In general, it works exactly like the Windows Recycle Bin—and why not, since the Macintosh Trash was Microsoft's inspiration?—but there are a couple of differences. The Macintosh never automatically empties it, for example. That job is up to you; the simplest way is to Control-click it, or right-click it, and choose Empty Trash from the shortcut menu.

The Mac never bothers you with an "Are you sure?" message when you throw something into the Trash, either. The Mac interrupts you for permission only when you choose File→Empty Trash. And you can even turn that confirmation off, if you like (in Finder→Preferences).

To put icons into the Trash, drag them there, or highlight them and then press ⌘-Delete.

Regional and Language Options control panel

The close equivalent is the International panel of System Preferences.

Registry

There is no registry. Let the celebration begin!

Run command

The Mac's command line is Terminal (Chapter 16).

Safe Mode

You can press the Shift key during startup to suppress the loading of certain software libraries, but Mac OS X's "safe mode" isn't quite as massively stripped down as Windows's Safe Mode.

ScanDisk

Just like Windows, the Mac automatically scans and, if necessary, repairs its hard drive every time your machine starts up. To run such a check on command, open Disk Utility (located in the Applications→Utilities folder), click the name of your hard drive, and then click the First Aid tab.

Scheduled Tasks

To schedule a task to take place unattended, use the *launchd* Unix command in Terminal (Chapter 16), or one of the scheduling programs listed at *www.versiontracker.com*.

Scrap files

On the Mac, they're called *clipping files,* and they're even more widely compatible. You create them the same way: Drag some highlighted text, or a graphic, out of a program's window and onto the desktop. There it becomes an independent clipping file that you can drag back in—to the same window or a different one.

Screen saver

The Mac's screen savers are impressive. Open System Preferences and click the Desktop & Screen Saver icon.

Search

In Mac OS X, you have the ultimate file-searching tool: Spotlight (Chapter 3). Get psyched!

To find Web sites, use the Google Search box at the top of the Safari browser.

Shortcut menus

They work exactly the same as they do in Windows. You produce a shortcut menu by Control-clicking things like icons, list items, and so on. (If you have a two-button mouse, feel free to right-click instead of using the Control key.)

Shortcuts

On the Mac, they're known as *aliases*. See page 80.

Sounds and Audio Devices

Open System Preferences; click the Sound icon. You may also want to explore the Audio MIDI Setup program in Applications→Utilities.

Speech control panel

The Mac's center for speech recognition and text-to-speech is the Speech panel of System Preferences. As Chapter 15 makes clear, the Mac can read aloud any text in any program, and it lets you operate all menus, buttons, and dialog boxes by voice alone.

Standby mode

On the Mac, it's called Sleep, but it's the same idea. You make a Mac laptop sleep by closing the lid. You make a Mac desktop sleep by choosing →Sleep, or just walking away; the Mac goes to sleep on its own, according to the settings in the Energy Saver pane of System Preferences.

Start menu

There's no Start menu in Mac OS X. Instead, you stash the icons of the programs, documents, and folders you use frequently onto the Dock at the edge of the screen, or into the Places section of the Sidebar at the left edge of every Finder window.

Exactly as with the Start menu, you can rearrange these icons (drag them horizontally) or remove the ones you don't use often (drag them away from the Dock and then release). To add new icons of your own, just drag them into place (applications go to the left of the Dock's divider line, documents and folders to the right).

StartUp folder

To make programs launch automatically at startup, include them in the list of Login Items in the System Preferences→Accounts pane.

System control panel

The Mac has no central equivalent of the System window on a Windows PC. But its functions have analogs here:

- **General tab.** To find out your Mac OS X version number and the amount of memory on your Mac, choose →About This Mac.

- **Computer Name tab.** Open System Preferences, click Sharing, and edit your computer's network name here.

- **Hardware tab.** The closest thing the Mac has to the Device Manager is System Profiler (in your Applications→Utilities folder).

- **Advanced tab.** In Mac OS X, you can't easily adjust your virtual memory, processor scheduling, or user profile information.

- **System Restore tab.** Mac OS X's Time Machine feature is like System Restore on steroids; see Chapter 6.

- **Automatic Updates tab.** Choose →Software Updates.

- **Remote tab.** Mac OS X Snow Leopard offers remote control in the form of Screen Sharing, described in Chapter 13.

System Tray

The Mac OS X equivalent of the system tray (also called the notification area) is the row of *menulets* at the upper-right corner of your screen.

Taskbar

Mac OS X doesn't have a taskbar, but it does have something very close: the Dock (Chapter 4). Open programs are indicated by a small, shiny dot beneath their icons in the Dock. If you hold down your cursor on one of these icons (or Control-click it, or right-click it), you get a pop-up list of the open windows in that program, exactly as in Windows XP, Vista, and 7.

On the other hand, some conventions never die. Much as in Windows, you cycle through the various open Mac programs by holding down the ⌘ key and pressing Tab repeatedly.

Taskbar and Start Menu control panel

To configure your Dock (the equivalent of the Taskbar and Start menu), choose →Dock→Dock Preferences, or click the Dock icon in System Preferences.

"Three-fingered salute"

Instead of pressing Ctrl-Alt-Delete to jettison a stuck program on the Mac, you press Option-⌘-Esc. A Force Quit dialog box appears. Click the program you want to toss, click Force Quit, confirm your choice, and then relaunch the program to get on with your day.

ToolTips

Small, yellow identifying balloons pop up on the Mac almost as often as they do in Windows. Just point to a toolbar icon or truncated file name without clicking. (There's no way to turn these labels off.)

TweakUI

The closest equivalent for this free, downloadable, but unsupported Microsoft utility for tweaking the look of your PC is TinkerTool for Mac OS X. It's described in Chapter 17.

User Accounts control panel

Like Windows 2000, XP, Vista, and 7, Mac OS X was designed from Square One to be a multiuser operating system, keeping each person's files, mail, and settings separate. You set up and manage these accounts in System Preferences→ Accounts (Chapter 12).

Window edges

You can enlarge or shrink a Mac OS X window only by dragging its lower-right corner—not its edges.

Windows (or WINNT) folder

Mac OS X's operating system resides in a folder simply called System, which sits in your main hard drive window. Exactly as in recent Windows versions, you're forbidden to add, remove, or change anything inside. Also as in Windows, most of it is invisible anyway.

Windows logo key

The Mac has no equivalent for the ⊞ key on most PC keyboards.

Windows Media Player

The Mac comes with individual programs for playing multimedia files:

- **QuickTime Player** (Chapter 15) to play back movies and sounds.

- **iTunes** (Chapter 11) to play CDs, Internet radio, MP3 files, and other audio files. (As a bonus, unlike Windows XP, iTunes can even *create* MP3 files.)

- **DVD Player** (Chapter 11) for playing DVDs. This program is in the Applications folder.

Windows Media Player *is,* however, available in an aging Macintosh version, paradoxical though that may sound. You can download it from *www.microsoft.com/mac.*

Windows Messenger

Mac OS X's instant-messaging, audio- and videoconferencing software is called iChat, and it's described in Chapter 21.

WordPad

The TextEdit program (in the Applications folder) is a word processor along the lines of WordPad. It can even open and save Word files, as WordPad can.

Zip files

Zip files exist on the Mac, too, and you create them almost the same way: Control-click (or right-click) a file or folder and choose Compress from the shortcut menu.

Where to Go from Here

I f read in a comfortable chair with good lighting, this book can be the foundation of a sturdy Mac OS X education. But particularly when it comes to mastering the Unix side of this operating system, years of study may await you still.

Web Sites

The Web is the salvation of the Mac OS X fan, especially considering the information vacuum that marked Mac OS X's early days. The Internet was the only place where people could find out what the heck was going on with their beloved Macs. Here are the most notable Web sites for learning the finer points of Mac OS X.

Mac OS X

- *www.macosxhints.com*. A gold mine of tips, tricks, and hints—many very nerdy, but many very handy, too.

- *www.macintouch.com*. An excellent daily dose of reporting about Mac questions, problems, and news.

- *www.osxfaq.com*. Unix tips and techniques, frequently asked questions, and links to useful sites.

- *www.versiontracker.com* and *www.macupdate.com*. Massive databases that track, and provide links to, all the latest software for Mac OS X.

- *www.apple.com/developer*. Even if you aren't a developer, joining the Developer Connection (Apple's programmers' club) gets you an email newsletter and access to the discussion boards, which are a great place for hearing Mac news first—all for free. (Pay $500 a year to become a Select member, and you get CDs mailed to you containing upcoming versions of Mac OS X.)

- *www.macobserver.com.* A good source for news and commentary about the Mac and related products.

- *www.macworld.com.* The discussion boards are an ideal place to find solutions for problems. When a bug pops up, the posts here are a great place to look for fixes.

- *www.macfixit.com.* The ultimate Mac troubleshooting Web site, complete with a hotbed of Mac OS X discussion.

- *www.macdevcenter.com.* O'Reilly's own Mac site. Full of tutorials, news, and interesting *weblogs* (techie diaries).

- *www.geekculture.com.* A hilarious satire site, dedicated to lampooning our tech addiction—especially Apple tech. Perhaps best known for the David Pogue's Head icon for Mac OS X (*http://geekculture.com/download/davidpogue.html*).

Or perhaps not.

Mac OS X–Style Unix Lessons and Reference

- *http://osxdaily.com/category/command-line/.* A good command reference with a lot of Mac-specific tips you can use in Terminal or the console.

- *www.ee.surrey.ac.uk/Teaching/Unix.* A convenient, free Web-based course in Unix for beginners.

Tip: Typing *unix for beginners* into a search engine like Google nets dozens of superb help, tutorial, and reference Web sites. If possible, stick to those that feature the *bash* shell; that way, everything you learn online should be perfectly applicable to navigating Mac OS X via Terminal.

Free Email Newsletters

- **The OS X list.** Once you've signed up (at *www.themacintoshguy.com/lists/index.html*), your email inbox will overflow with Mac OS X discussion, chatter, and discoveries. A great place to ask questions, both simple and difficult.

- **TidBITS.com.** A free, weekly Mac newsletter with lots of useful tricks, reviews, and news.

- **Apple's own newsletters.** At *www.apple.com/enews/subscribe,* you can sign up for free weekly newsletters on a variety of topics: music, QuickTime, programming, and so on.

Advanced Books, Programming Books

By a happy coincidence, this book is published by O'Reilly Media, the industry's leading source of technical books for Mac users, programmers, and system administrators. If this book has whetted your appetite for more advanced topics, these current and upcoming books on Unix, programming Mac OS X, and administering large networks could come in handy.

Mac Essentials

- *AppleScript: The Missing Manual* by Adam Goldstein. This book is a patient, witty guide to the basics of scripting your Mac with AppleScript. Step-by-step examples include batch-renaming files in the Finder, altering and applying text styles in TextEdit, tweaking QuickTime movie files, and much more.

- *Mac OS X for Unix Geeks* by Ernest E. Rothman, Brian Jepson, and Rich Rosen. This book is a bridge between Apple's OS and the more traditional Unix systems. Offers a complete tour of Mac OS X's Unix shell and helps you find the facilities that replace or correspond to standard Unix utilities.

- *Mac OS X Snow Leopard Pocket Guide* by Chris Seibold. Need a handy guide to Mac OS X that you can carry around in your laptop bag? This small book fits in your pocket just as easily as it does your computer bag and includes hundreds of tips for using and configuring Mac OS X 10.6.

- *Big Book of Apple Hacks* by Chris Seibold. Hacky, techy projects for tweaking the Mac, the iPod, iPhone, and AppleTV.

Unix Essentials

- *Learning the bash Shell*, 3rd Edition, by Cameron Newham. If you plan on using the Terminal application to do Unixy stuff on your Mac, this book shows you your way around Snow Leopard's default shell, *bash*.

- *Learning GNU Emacs*, 3rd Edition, by Debra Cameron, James Elliott, Marc Loy, Eric S. Raymond, and Bill Rosenblatt. A guide to the GNU *emacs* editor, one of the most widely used and powerful Unix text editors.

- *Learning the vi and vim Editors*, 7th Edition, by Linda Lamb, Elbert Hannah, and Arnold Robbins. A complete guide to editing with *vi* and *vim*, the text editors available on nearly every Unix system.

- *Unix Power Tools*, 3rd Edition, by Shelley Powers, Jerry Peek, Tim O'Reilly, and Mike Loukides. Practical advice about most every aspect of advanced Unix: POSIX utilities, GNU versions, detailed *bash, tcsh*, and *ksh* shell coverage, and a strong emphasis on Perl.

Mac OS X Administration

- *Postfix: The Definitive Guide* by Kyle D. Dent. If you're planning to run your own email server, this book shows you how to configure and run Mac OS X's built-in mail server, Postfix.

- *Apache: The Definitive Guide*, 3rd Edition, by Ben Laurie and Peter Laurie. Describes how to set up and secure the Apache Web server software.

- *Apache Cookbook, 2nd Edition,* by Ken Coar and Rich Bowen. A collection of configuration examples for all Apache users, from novices to advanced practitioners.

The Master Mac OS X Secret Keystroke List

Here it is, by popular, frustrated demand: The master list of every secret (or not-so-secret) keystroke in Mac OS X Snow Leopard, including all the keys you can press during startup. Clip and post to your monitor (unless, of course, you got this book from the library).

Note: For the most part, the following list doesn't include the keystrokes already listed in your menus, like ⌘-P for Print, ⌘-S for Save, and so on.

Startup Keystrokes

Keys to Hold Down	Effect
C	Starts up from a CD
D	Starts up from the first partition
N	Starts up from network server
R	Resets the laptop screen
T	Puts the Mac into FireWire Target Disk mode
Option	Shows icons of all startup disks and partitions, so you can choose one for starting up.
Shift-Option-⌘-Delete	Starts up from external drive (or CD)
Option-⌘-P-R	Zaps the parameter RAM (PRAM). (Hold down until you hear the second chime.)
Option-⌘-O-F	Brings up Open Firmware screen (pre-Intel Macs).

⌘-V	Shows Unix console messages during startup, logout, and shutdown
⌘-S	Starts up in single-user (Unix command-line) mode
Mouse down	Ejects a stuck CD or DVD
6 and 4 keys	Starts up in 64-bit mode
Shift	Just after powering up: Turns off *kernel extensions*
Shift	Just after logging in: Prevents Finder windows and startup items from opening. (They'll return the next time you start up.)

In the Finder

⌘-space	Highlights Spotlight box
Option-⌘-space	Opens Spotlight window
→, ←	Expands or collapses a selected folder in list view
Option-→	Expands a folder in a list view *and* all folders inside it
Option-←	Collapses folder *and* all folders inside it
⌘-↑	Opens parent folder
Shift-Option-⌘-↑	Selects the Desktop
⌘-↓ (or ⌘-O)	Opens the selected icon
Option-click the flippy triangle	Expands or collapses all folders within that window
Tab	Selects next icon alphabetically
Shift-Tab	Selects previous icon alphabetically
space bar	Opens Quick Look preview of highlighted icon(s)
space bar	During a spring-loaded folder drag, opens the disk or folder under mouse immediately
Option-click Zoom button	Enlarges the window to full screen
Option-click Close button	Closes all Finder windows
Option-click Minimize button	Minimizes all windows (works in most apps)
⌘-drag an icon	Moves it into, or out of, the System folder (administrator password required)
Option	Changes Quick Look button to Slideshow button
⌘-drag	Rearranges or removes menulets or toolbar icons

⌘-click window title — Opens a pop-up menu showing the folder path

Menu

Option — Changes "About This Mac" to "System Profiler"

Option — Eliminates confirmation box from Restart, Shut Down, and Log Out

Finder Menu

Option — Eliminates confirmation box from Empty Trash and Secure Empty Trash

Shift-⌘-Q — Logs out

Shift-Option-⌘-Q — Logs out without confirmation box

Shift-⌘-Delete — Empties the Trash

Shift-⌘-Delete — Puts back a highlighted icon in the Trash

Shift-Option-⌘-Delete — Empties the Trash without confirmation box

Option-"Empty Trash" — Empties the Trash without confirmation box

⌘-comma — Opens Preferences

⌘-H — Hide this program

Shift-⌘-H — Hide other programs

File Menu

⌘-N — New Finder window

Shift-⌘-N — New folder

Option-⌘-N — New smart folder

⌘-O or ⌘-↓ — Open

Control-⌘-O — Open in new window

Option-click File menu — Changes "Open With" to "Always Open With"

⌘-W — Close window

Option-⌘-W — Close All

⌘-I — Get Info

Option-⌘-I — Show Inspector

Control-⌘-I — Summary Info (of selected icons)

⌘-D — Duplicate

⌘-L — Make Alias

⌘-Y — Quick Look

Option-⌘-Y — Slideshow (of selected icons)

⌘-R	Show Original (of alias)
⌘-T	Add to Sidebar
Shift-⌘-T	Add to Favorites
⌘-Delete	Move to Trash
⌘-E	Eject
⌘-F	Find
Shift-⌘-F	Find by Name

Edit Menu

⌘-Z	Undo
⌘-C, ⌘-X, ⌘-V	Copy, Cut, Paste
⌘-A	Select All
Option-⌘-A	Deselect All

View Menu

⌘-1, -2, -3, -4	Icon, list, column, Cover Flow views
Control-⌘-1, -2, -3, -4, -5, -6	Arrange by Name, Date Modified, Date Created, Size, Kind, Label
Option	Changes "Clean Up Selection" to "Clean Up"
Option	Changes "Keep Arranged By" to "Arrange By"
Option-⌘-T	Show/Hide Toolbar
⌘-J	Show/Hide View Options palette

Go Menu

⌘-[, ⌘-]	Back, Forward
⌘-↑	Enclosing folder
Control-⌘-↑	Enclosing folder in new window
Shift-⌘-C	Computer window
Shift-⌘-H	Home window
Shift-⌘-D	Desktop window
Shift-⌘-K	Network window
Shift-⌘-I	Open iDisk
Shift-⌘-A	Applications window
Shift-⌘-G	Go to Folder
⌘-K	Connect to Server

Window Menu

⌘-M	Minimize
Option-⌘-M	Minimize All
Option	Changes "Bring All to Front" to "Arrange in

Front"

Help Menu

Shift-⌘-?   Opens help search box

Power Keys

Control-⏏   Brings up dialog box for shutdown, sleep, or
                                      restart

Option-⌘-⏏   Sleep
Control-Option-⌘-⏏   Shut Down
Control-⌘-power   Restart

The Dock

Option-click a Dock icon   Switches to new program and hides previous
                                      one

Option-⌘-D   Hides/shows the Dock
⌘-click a Dock or Stacks icon   Reveals its actual Finder icon
Option-⌘-click a Dock icon   Switches to this program and hides all others
Control-click a Dock icon   Opens a shortcut menu
Hold mouse down on Dock app icon   Triggers Exposé (shows all windows of that app
                                      in miniature)

⌘-drag an icon onto a Dock icon   Prevents Dock icons from moving, so you can
                                      drop your icon onto one of them

⌘-drag a Dock icon   Drags the actual item
Option-⌘-drag an icon onto the Dock Forces Dock program icon to open the icon
                                      you're dropping

Managing Programs

Option-click a Dock icon   Switches to new program and hides previous
                                      one

Option-click in a window   Switches to new program and hides previous
                                      one

⌘-H   Hide this program's windows (works in most
                                      apps)

Option-⌘-H   Hide all *other* programs' windows (most apps)
F8   Spaces: Enters "big picture" view of your virtual
                                      screens (if you've turned on Spaces)

Shift-F8   Spaces: Enters "big picture" view in slow motion
Control-1, 2, 3, 4...   Jump to a specific Spaces screen
Control-↑, ↓, ←, →   Next Spaces screen in this direction

F9	Exposé: Shrinks and tiles all windows in all programs
Shift-F9	Exposé: Shrinks and tiles all windows in slow motion
F10	Exposé: Shrinks and tiles all windows in frontmost program
F11	Exposé: Flings all windows in all programs to edges of screen, revealing desktop
F12	Dashboard widgets
⌘-Tab	Press and release: Switches back and forth between current and previous open program
⌘-Tab	Hold down ⌘: Displays floating icons of open programs. Press Tab repeatedly to cycle through them. (Add Shift to cycle *backward* through open programs on the Dock.)
⌘-~	Switches to next open window in this program. (Add Shift to cycle in the opposite direction.)
Option-⌘-Esc	Opens the Force Quit dialog box (to close a stuck program)
Shift-⌘-3	Captures the screen image as a PDF file on your desktop
Shift-⌘-4	Produces a crosshairs; drag to capture a selected portion of the screen as a PDF graphics file. (Press space to get the "camera" cursor that snips out just a menu, icon, or window.)
⌘-space	Switches keyboard layout (if more than one is installed). (If you use Spotlight, you must choose a different keystroke for this function.)

Dialog Boxes

⌘-comma	Opens Preferences dialog box (any Apple program)
Esc	"Clicks" the Cancel button in a dialog box
Enter or Return	"Clicks" the OK button (or other blue, highlighted button) in a dialog box
Option-⌘-F	Moves insertion point to the Search box in most Apple programs
⌘-D, ⌘-R	"Clicks" the Don't Save or Replace button

Index

Index

Z

Colophon

This book was written on MacBook Air that remained attached to David Pogue like an appendage. It was tytped in Microsoft Word, with substantial assistance from the typing-shortcut program TextExpander (*www.smileonmymac.com*).

The book's screen illustrations were captured with Ambrosia Software's Snapz Pro X (*www.ambrosiasw.com*), edited in Adobe Photoshop CS4 (*www.adobe.com*), and overlaid with labels, lines, and circles in Macromedia Freehand MX.

The author composed the index, entry by entry, using a highly tweaked FileMaker database and a clever Perl script that converted FileMaker's output into a fully formatted index.

The book was designed and laid out in Adobe InDesign CS4 on a MacBook Pro G5 and Mac Pro Intel G5. The fonts include Formata (as the sans-serif family) and Minion (as the serif body face). To provide the symbols (, ⌘, ⏏, and so on), Phil Simpson designed two custom fonts using Macromedia Fontographer.

The book was then exported as Adobe Acrobat PDF files for final transmission to the printing plant in Michigan.